"NEED A RIDE?"

Tom Luther gave the pretty, dark-haired hitchhiker his most winning smile. Mary Brown tossed her duffel bag into the back of the truck, telling him where she was headed as she climbed in beside him. But as they drove through the dark, unlit, snow-covered streets, she lost her bearings. Luther went down a dead-end street and turned the truck around.

"This is as good a place as any," he said. "Take your clothes off."

Mary lunged for the door handle. Her head exploded with light and pain as Luther punched her in the left side of the face. He grabbed her hair and slammed her head into the door, then shoved her onto the floor of the truck.

"Take off your clothes, bitch." His winning smile was gone now.

Whimpering, Mary made another desperate grab for the door, but he hit her again. She started to cry.

"Shut up, bitch!" The curses rained out of his mouth as he hit her again and again. Wanting only to survive, she took off her clothes.

Luther grabbed a wooden-handled carpenter's hammer. She screamed as he raped her with it.

The torment seemed to last forever. She waited for the death blow to come. But Luther had suddenly gone motionless, looking down at his bloody hands.

"Can I get out?" she asked tentatively.

"No. I want to take you somewhere."

From his tone, Mary knew it was somewhere he could kill her and dump her body like trash.

BOOK YOUR PLACE ON OUR WEBSITE AND MAKE THE READING CONNECTION!

We've created a customized website just for our very special readers, where you can get the inside scoop on everything that's going on with Zebra, Pinnacle and Kensington books.

When you come online, you'll have the exciting opportunity to:

- View covers of upcoming books
- Read sample chapters
- Learn about our future publishing schedule (listed by publication month *and author*)
- Find out when your favorite authors will be visiting a city near you
- Search for and order backlist books from our online catalog
- Check out author bios and background information
- Send e-mail to your favorite authors
- Meet the Kensington staff online
- Join us in weekly chats with authors, readers and other guests
- Get writing guidelines
- AND MUCH MORE!

**Visit our website at
http://www.pinnaclebooks.com**

MONSTER

Steve Jackson

Pinnacle Books
Kensington Publishing Corp.

http://www.pinnaclebooks.com

This book is dedicated to my parents, who were always there to turn on the lights and chase away the monsters when I was a child. What I know of love, honor, truth and sacrifice, I learned first from those two good people.

PINNACLE BOOKS are published by

Kensington Publishing Corp.
850 Third Avenue
New York, NY 10022

First Printing: November, 1998
10 9 8 7 6 5 4 3 2 1

Printed in the United States of America

Chapter One

March 28, 1993—Somewhere in the mountains west of Denver, Colorado

It was sometime after 2 A.M. when the small car pulled into the gravel turnoff from the highway and rolled to a stop with its lights out. A dark figure emerged from the driver's door, pausing a moment to make sure he was alone on the mountainside.

The night was bitterly cold, and the wind howled like wolves, rattling the tall dry grasses that poked through the snow. A stream rushed noisily over rock in the valley below, invigorated by the spring thaw.

Rock, bush, and tree cast black shadows in the moonlight, but no headlights appeared on the highway. Satisfied, the man opened the rear door and, leaning over, reached inside. Straining against the dead weight, he hauled the body of a young woman out and onto the ground.

Cher Elder lay unconscious and naked in the moonlight. He had beat her, punching her repeatedly in the face, and strangled her to the point of nearly passing out before he raped her. Then he fractured her skull with a blow from behind.

It had been a mistake to go anywhere with this man. But Cher, a pretty 20-year-old whose schoolbooks were laid out neatly at home for a future she would never see, was a friendly young woman, always laughing, trusting. She'd had no reason to fear him, until it was too late—when he changed into a monster.

The man reached back into the car and removed something small and dark from under the front seat and put it in his pocket. Then he half-dragged, half-carried Cher to a place out of sight from the road. As she lay helpless, he pulled the gun from his pocket and pressed it against her head, just above and behind her left ear. Three quick shots echoed briefly off the surrounding hills, then were swallowed by the wind.

The man thought for a moment, looking down at the body as dark blood seeped into the ground beneath her head. Crouching, he picked up Cher's hand and tugged a ring from her lifeless finger.

Scott Richardson reluctantly climbed off his Harley-Davidson. It was days like this when all he wanted was to head the bike up one of the mountain passes west of Denver and ride. Forget the crimes and the tragedies, and clear his mind in the fresh air and sunshine as he leaned into each curve and opened up the throttle on the straightaways.

But duty called, so he turned and walked into the Lakewood city building, down the stairs and, after punching in a code number, through the police department's security doors. He had just poured a cup of the bitter black brew that passed for coffee in the squad room when the detective division secretary, Donna, handed him a slip of paper. "Some guy named Tom Luther called, said he's the one you're looking for. Here's his number."

"Thanks, Donna," Richardson said, taking the note. He was expecting the call—*has to be the mystery man in the videotape*, he thought—but he hadn't known the man's name, nor had he anticipated the call coming so soon.

Donna stood watching but was disappointed when Richardson turned away without further comment. Lean and handsome, despite the thinning of his coal black hair, the soft-spoken Texan wasn't an imposing man physically, even though his fellow detectives kidded that his thick, Fu Manchu mustache made him look more like an outlaw biker than a cop. But it was his coffee-brown eyes that suspects found intimidating, especially when he was angry and they turned as dark as his mood.

His eyes were dark now. There was a girl missing, more than likely dead, from his adopted home of Lakewood, a bedroom community washed up against the Rocky Mountains due west of Denver. And this Tom Luther character had something to do with it, he thought. There had been too many false leads in his career, let alone this case, to get too excited, but Luther smelled like the real thing.

Richardson took a deep breath and let it go slowly to take the edge off as he walked back to his cubicle in the crowded office. He sat back in his chair and put his worn cowboy boots up on the desk to collect his thoughts before he called Mr. Luther.

As he did, he glanced up at the photograph of the dark-haired young woman he'd tacked to the wall. Cher Elder. The picture hung purposely near the photos of the five things he loved most in the world: his wife, Sabrina; his three-year-old twin sons, Brent and Brandon; hunting; and his Harley-Davidson softtail motorcycle. ("Not necessarily in that order," Sabrina teased when she was in a good mood, a little more pointedly when ticked at him.)

Richardson's gaze shifted to the photograph of Sabrina. A pretty woman. Blond, hazel eyes set in an oval face, and an east Texas drawl soft as a spring breeze off the prairie. They'd been together since she was a 13-year-old Texas rose and he a 17-year-old rebel just out of high school. They married five years later, in 1984, shortly after he'd been made a detective on the tiny Gladewater, Texas, police force—at 22, one of the youngest detectives in that state. She'd put up with a lot of crap ever since, including the long hours and fears that came with being a cop's wife.

Working in the rough-and-ready oiltown of Gladewater in Gregg County, a swamp-covered hotbed for car thieves and drug dealers, he'd had his head busted open by a pool cue and come within millimeters of being shot a couple of times. But when he'd tried to quit police work for her sake, it was Sabrina who'd said, "You know you're a cop, now get your butt back where you belong."

They moved to Denver in 1985, and he joined the Lakewood

Police Department. The twins were born in 1990. It was hard to believe that they'd been married now for nearly ten years.

Richardson looked back at the photograph of Cher Elder. It was a portrait shot taken shortly before she disappeared. She was smiling, and a hint of the mischievousness he'd been told about played at the corners of her mouth and in her green eyes. It was a nice picture of a nice girl. Twenty years old.

Cher, 5'3" and 120 pounds, had been reported missing by her father, Earl Elder, on March 31, 1993. Richardson got the case on April 1.

According to the dispatch report, Mr. Elder had contacted other family members and friends, including the girl's boyfriend, one Byron Eerebout, after no one had seen her for several days. There was a possible siting at a local bingo hall the preceding Sunday, March 28, but nothing since. Earl was "very concerned as his daughter has never failed to return home, or be in contact with family," the dispatch officer had written.

Richardson's first impulse had been to let it slide. Chances were the so-called "missing person" was pissed off at her folks or her boyfriend and was getting even by sunning herself on a beach in Acapulco. Wait a week and, often as not, those cases resolved themselves with the subject turning up back at home.

Call it case management, but he had a whole stack of assaults and robberies that demanded his attention before he was going to leap too far into a missing person case. He had dropped the file back in the basket when his partner, Detective Mike Heylin, poked his face into his cubicle with an offer to go work out at a local gym. *It can wait,* Richardson told himself, grabbing his coat.

As he lifted weights at the gym, he'd tried to push the Cher Elder case out his mind, but something nagged at him. Nothing he could explain, but he had learned to trust his instincts. So much so that he mentioned the case to Heylin as they drove back to the department, something he normally wouldn't have bothered with on such a trivial matter.

"To hell with it," he muttered. "I oughta just let it sit. But as soon as I say that, sure as hell, it'll turn into a homicide. Guess I'll place a couple of calls." Heylin just nodded. He knew that once a case started eating at his partner, there was no stopping him.

It was now April 20. Cher had been missing for three weeks, a long time to be sunning in Mexico.

Richardson customarily tacked the photographs of victims in his cases on the walls near those of his family. It was hard to think of someone as just another case if that person was smiling at him from the wall every morning when he came to work and every evening when he left. Particularly the homicides or, he corrected himself, the suspected homicides.

The photograph reminded him that Case No. 93-31067 was a girl whose family loved her every bit as much as he loved his boys. Cher's family was suffering now, wondering what had become of her, blaming themselves, as families do, for something they had no control over. He suspected he couldn't do anything for Cher, but it was his responsibility to bring her family some peace and, if she was indeed dead, her killer to justice.

It was a mission he took personally, even if it hadn't started that way. And it was a damn good thing he'd listened to his instincts and picked up a telephone or he might have missed the one piece of evidence that would allow him to someday, soon he hoped, take Cher Elder's picture off the wall.

· Just that morning Heylin reminded him, "You said if you didn't call on it, sure enough, it'd turn into a homicide. You called, but it looks like that's what we got anyway."

Richardson had nodded. There was no use denying the obvious. In his heart, he'd known almost from the beginning . . . when the Eerebout boys started lying. He'd known for sure three days ago when an officer found Cher's car abandoned in a grocery store parking lot.

While some homicide cops made a big show of not getting emotionally involved in their cases, he approached his work from the opposite direction. He wanted to know everything he could about the victim. In the past three weeks, he had learned as much as he could about Cher Elder, and what he learned had convinced him that she wasn't the sort of girl who dumped her car and ran away without contacting her family and friends.

"Slow down," he told himself periodically. "She may be on that beach in Mexico." It became almost a mantra and it was a good practice in theory: avoid putting on blinders, consider everything. But he knew better.

This case just plain bothered him more than most. He'd seen

his share of victims walk to their fates with their eyes open. It wasn't uncommon for one of them to be portrayed as some kind of choir girl by her family and friends only for him to find out that she'd been running dope, or prostitutin', or a hundred other dangerous and illegal things. But this case was different. Cher was different. Her mistake, he believed, was that she had fallen in love with Byron Eerebout, a petty thief and small-time drug dealer.

Now nobody would admit to having seen Cher since the early morning hours of March 28 when, according to Byron, he peeked out his apartment window and watched her drive away. Of course that all depended on which version of the story Byron, or his younger brothers, J.D. and Tristan, were telling on any given day.

Richardson didn't mind the changing stories. The Eerebouts were a convict's kids. They weren't going to fall down on their knees and confess just 'cause he looked at 'em cross-eyed. But let them run off at the mouth and, sooner or later, they'd slip. "Get their lips movin'," was his motto, and sure enough, he'd caught Byron in several lies and that told him a lot. After all, why lie about a missing persons case?

If he hadn't missed his guess, this Tom Luther fellow was the grey-haired mystery man caught on a videotape with Cher by a casino security camera on the night of March 27, a Saturday. It was a piece of the puzzle, one he'd almost missed.

The grey-haired man, according to witnesses, was a friend of Byron's. But that morning, Byron denied knowing him.

Richardson hadn't called him on the lie. "Guess I'll have to give this to the news media," he shrugged instead, pulling the tape from the VCR, "and get this guy's face plastered all over the television and newspapers. See if anybody knows who he is."

The ploy worked faster than he dared hope. Byron walked out of the interrogation room, promising to contact him if "anything else comes to me." An hour later, while he was out for a spin on the motorcycle, Donna took the call from Tom Luther. "I'm the one he's lookin' for," Luther had told her.

"You're right, bud," Richardson muttered as he lifted his boots off the desk, picked up the telephone, and punched in the number left by Tom Luther. "You're the one I'm lookin' for—but for what?"

The telephone rang. "Hello?" a male voice answered. *Just get his lips movin'*, Richardson told himself, *and this will be over in nothin' flat.*

"Hello, Mr. Luther, please," Richardson said.

"Yeah. This is he." The voice from the other end of the line was cautious.

"Hi. How you doin'? I gotta message here that you called." Richardson tried to sound friendly and confused, as if he couldn't figure out why he'd been contacted.

"Okay. And you?" Luther responded. "The Eerebout boys called and told me you guys had a picture of me, uh, you know, and were going to plaster it all over the news and stuff. So I figured I better give you a call."

Richardson listened carefully. Luther had no regional accent that he could discern, maybe a little country, but there was something he couldn't quite put his finger on. *Keep him talking*, he thought, *and see what shakes.* He started by asking innocent questions—like Luther's address, which was in Fort Collins, a college town 60 miles straight north of Denver, and the correct spelling of his name.

After a couple minutes of this, it was Luther who cut to the chase. "The reason the boys were playing stupid, all right, is 'cause I just was recently released from the joint."

There we go, Richardson thought, *somethin' right off the bat. The guy's an ex-con. That's what I was picking up in his voice—that ol' prison tough guy bullshit.* He wondered what the charges had been but let Luther keep talking.

"They were playin' stupid, hopin' that maybe this girl would just pop up somewheres or somethin', or . . . call her people, you know what I mean, to let everybody know that she's okay, see? I-I-now, I don't trust, uh, the cops. I mean, I'm gonna tell you that straight up. You know I've had some bad experiences with 'em. You know, prison guards. The detectives that originally arrested me on my case, you know what I mean, said that I made a statement which I never made . . ."

Richardson scowled, his dark eyebrows knitting a solid line

above his eyes. Another innocent "victim" of the system. *How many times have I heard that one?* he thought. Ain't no criminals in prison, just a bunch of innocent guys who got railroaded by crooked cops, grandstanding DAs, bad judges, and ignorant juries.

Next, he'll start talking about his poor, abused childhood, Richardson thought. *Well, mine wasn't so all-fired happy either, buddy.*

Richardson's father, an alcoholic who had abused his wife and two sons, shot and killed himself shortly before Scott's 13th birthday. Doyle Richardson had drilled a heightened sense of moral duty into his boys ("There's right and there's wrong, and you gotta choose where you stand"), but along the way forgot to tell them that he loved them.

Richardson's teenaged years had been spent hell-bent for leather, and those who knew him, including his mother, had wondered which side of the law he would wind up on. He'd been on his own at 16 with a fast car and not much else to his name except a reputation for wildness. But then he had gone to Gladewater to visit his father's grave, and met Sabrina.

So he'd stayed and, working two jobs, put himself through community college as a criminal justice major. He was a cop by 19, so young that his partners had to buy his bullets for him, the same year Sabrina's parents finally let them go out on a date.

Everything he had, everything he was, he got by working hard and patience; nobody had handed him anything. So Richardson didn't put much stock in the stories of criminals who whined that they'd had a rough childhood. *I somehow managed to stay out of prison,* he thought when Luther began complaining about the police hounding him, *and no one's lookin' at me now 'cause some girl's missin'.*

Out loud, he sympathized, which seemed to encourage Luther. The ex-con repeated himself. "You know, they said I made a confession, which I never made."

Now, Richardson thought, get him while he's on the defensive. "Let's break the ice right off the bat," he interrupted. "I'm not gonna jack with you, I'm not gonna jack with anybody. All we're concerned about is findin' Cher and makin' sure Cher's okay."

Luther relented a little. "Now I can understand that, you know what I mean, but like I say, now the boys, you know, see I just—I just did ten years, ten months, twenty-three days. All on an assault." Luther paused. "On a sexual assault case," he finally added. "That's why they were bein' protective of my identification."

Bells and sirens began going off in Richardson's head. A sexual assault? *No sense getting caught hiding that skeleton in the closet, eh Luther?* The questions were popping up in his mind so quick, he could hardly keep up with the other man's explanation of how he'd met the Eerebout boys through their father, Jerald "Skip" Eerebout. Skip had been his cellmate and best friend in prison, he said.

"All I wanted to know," Richardson interjected, "was more about what Cher was doing the night of March 27."

Luther was prepared for the question. "What happened was, you know, she was at Byron's house. Okay? And Byron came over with this other girl named Gina. Well Cher, she thought she and him, Byron and her, had a little more of a thing goin', you know what I mean?"

Richardson grunted affirmatively. He'd already heard that Byron and Cher had been fighting over Gina Jones. That much he figured was true. Now, where was the truth going to make a U-turn into fiction?

"So what I tried to do, is I tried to calm the situation. I tried talkin' to her, tellin' her, you know, 'Just hold off,' you know, 'Let him spin his oats. He'll come back to you.' I wanted to get her away from the apartment. I made several suggestions. 'Well, let's go to a bar.' "

But Cher, he said, who he'd met at Byron's on a couple other occasions, wanted to go see a friend who worked in a Central City casino in the mountains northwest of Denver. So he had offered to go along for company.

In fact, he let her drive his new car, a sporty blue Geo Metro, he said, while he sat back in the passenger seat and downed a few beers. They got to the casinos, met up with Cher's friend, drank a couple more beers, played the slot machines.

"We closed the place down. Then she drove us back to Byron's. She went in to talk to him, but he was in bed with Gina. So, you know, she leaves very upset. So I follow her out of the apartment. I'm tryin' to talk to her, you know, she's cryin' and stuff.''

Cher told him she was going to call an old high school buddy named Gary. ''That was the only guy that she ever could trust. You know what I mean?'' She left, and he went back into the apartment. ''I slept for three hours on the floor then got up and drove home to Fort Collins.''

When Luther ran out of steam, Richardson asked if he could meet with him. Experience taught him that it was harder to lie face-to-face and man-to-man, and easier for him to judge a suspect's reactions. But the ex-con danced away from the question by saying he'd be happy to answer any questions—over the telephone.

To give himself more time to find a way to set up a meeting, Richardson asked Luther for the registration number on his car. He heard Luther speak to someone else in the room before responding.

''Who you talkin' to there?'' Richardson asked. He wanted to know as many of Luther's associates as possible; no telling who would be the key to this thing.

''My lady friend, Debrah,'' Luther replied.

Richardson made a quick note. ''So when was the last time you saw Cher?'' he asked. He didn't want Luther guessing at which things he might think were important—like girlfriends.

''When she left that morning . . .''

''Did you stop anywhere on the way back?''

Luther hesitated before replying. ''Yeah. We did.''

''Where'd you stop?''

''Um, in Golden,'' Luther replied nervously.

Golden. Richardson pictured the little town to the north of Lakewood and just off the highway that ran up into the mountains to Central City. He noticed the reluctance in Luther's voice. *Got to be the girlfriend,* he thought. *Ol' Tom doesn't want to talk in front of her about stopping to park with Cher Elder.*

It was the opening he was looking for. ''Is your lady friend sittin' right there?'' he asked.

''Yeah,'' Luther laughed. He sounded relieved that the detective had finally caught on.

Richardson laughed, too, just like they were best friends pulling one over on their wives. "Let's stop that conversation. That's gonna get you in a tight spot, isn't it?"

"I think so," was the good-humored reply.

The moment was ripe. Richardson again pressed for a meeting. Just one good ol' boy who knew how to keep a secret from the women to another. This time Luther was agreeable. But with a caveat. "Like I say, I don't trust cops . . ."

"I'm not gonna jack with ya, Tom," Richardson interrupted as he felt his fish trying to wriggle off the hook.

Quick as a bullet, Luther was angry. "That's what everybody says. 'I'm not gonna jack with ya, I'm not gonna give you the runaround.' But as soon as you run my, you know, my credentials . . . I'm gonna be like a suspect on your missing person."

Richardson was surprised by the suddenness of the change. Cool one moment, hot the next. He noticed that as Luther's temper rose, so did his prison-speak. He had to head this off quick before Luther remembered that convicts aren't supposed to talk to cops.

"I don't care what the background is," the detective interjected. It was a white lie; he actually cared a lot, but he said, "I care about today."

Luther turned his anger off as quickly as he had turned it on. He said that Richardson could come meet him in Fort Collins if he could get there before he had to go to work that evening.

But maybe it wasn't even necessary? he ventured. After all, he'd told the detective everything he could think of. But had Richardson checked out a former boyfriend of Cher's, went by a funny name, a guy named Garfus? "She had quite a lot of trouble with him. He wanted to be physical with her." He suggested turning up the heat on Garfus.

Richardson recognized the deflection attempt. This had to be another part of the story they'd rehearsed, he thought. He'd already heard about Garfus from Byron, but Garfus had an airtight alibi—he'd been out of the state when Cher disappeared. He turned the conversation back to Luther's girlfriend. "How'd you meet Debbie?"

"I've been with *Debrah,*" Luther corrected him on the name, "for about two and a half years. I met her while I was locked up at the state hospital in Pueblo, Colorado. She was a nurse there on their surgical unit."

"Okay. What's her last name, Tom?"

"Snider. S-N-I-D-E-R."

"Okay," Richardson said, satisfied that he would soon be meeting the mysterious grey-haired stranger from the videotape. "We wanna make sure that Cher's okay and everything, um, because Byron pretty much created this unpleasant situation for you, by coverin' up and lyin' and everything to us."

Richardson wanted to sound as if Byron was the focus of his investigation to put Luther at ease. He had no idea if the Eerebouts were lying to protect Luther, if Luther was lying to protect the Eerebouts, or they were all lying to protect each other. But someone was lying, and it was his job to find out who.

The ex-con took the bait and jumped to the defense of his friend's son. "Well, like I said, you know, in fact, this is the first time he's said anything to me about it. He just says, 'Hey, you know, I figured I wouldn't say nothin' to you, 'cause I didn't want you to be upset about it.' I am very, you know, paranoid of the cops."

Richardson ignored the comment. "All right, well, we'll be out there in a little bit. Thanks a lot, bud."

He hung up the telephone. The clock was ticking. He had to get to Fort Collins before Luther changed his mind or decided he wanted an attorney. And the longer Luther had to rehearse his story, the harder it'd be to catch him. But Richardson also wanted to know as much as he could about Luther before they met. He alerted his partner to get ready to move. Then he searched for Luther's records on the Colorado Criminal Information Computer.

There wasn't a lot of detail, but what there was was interesting as hell. According to the printout, Luther had been arrested in Summit County, Colorado, on February 13, 1982, and charged with attempted murder, kidnapping, and sexual assault. He'd pleaded guilty to assault and second degree sexual assault more than a year later, in July 1983, and served almost eleven years before being released in January.

Out three months and already connected to a missing girl. *Fast work, bud,* Richardson thought shaking his head. He took the printout back to his desk. He looked again at the photograph of Cher then he placed another call, this time to the Summit

County Sheriff's Office in the ski-resort town of Breckenridge. The receptionist passed him to Sheriff Joe Morales.

"What can I do for ya?" Morales asked after the introductions were dispensed with.

"Well, what can you tell me about Thomas Edward Luther?" Richardson asked. There was a long silence, and he wondered if the line had gone dead. He had expected a little confusion, or at least some sort of delay while Morales went to pull an eleven-year-old file. He didn't expect the reply he got a moment later.

Morales sighed, then asked, "Who'd he kill?"

Chapter Two

January 6, 1982—Breckenridge, Colorado

As Richardson listened, Morales explained how he had been a young deputy sheriff in Summit County eleven years earlier when he first met Thomas Edward Luther. "And what I know about him and what I suspect are two different animals."

There wasn't time to tell Richardson the whole story, just the basics. But after they hung up, Morales sat in his office lost in thought, remembering when it all began—January 6, 1982.

It had been a bitterly cold day in Breckenridge, the county seat, but better known for its skiing. The temperature had been hovering around twenty degrees below zero for several days, the sort of cold that made it hurt to breathe and the snow complain underfoot like pieces of styrofoam rubbed together.

About 4:30 that afternoon, Annette Kay Schnee came stomping into the town pharmacy accompanied by an unkempt, but otherwise pretty, woman with dark, shoulder-length hair. The pharmacy clerk recognized Annette, a petite young woman—all of 5'1" and 110 pounds, who also had shoulder-length brown hair— but not her companion.

"They didn't quite seem to belong together," the clerk later told police detectives. Still, they acted like good friends. While the pharmacist filled Annette's prescription they strolled through the store, laughing and commenting about various items.

Annette was only ten weeks shy of her twenty-second birthday. A popular high school cheerleader back in her home town of Sioux City, Iowa, she hadn't quite figured out what she wanted to do with her life after graduation. So she had shelved plans to go to college and worked in a beauty salon before moving to Breckenridge to ski and have a little fun.

Her mom had fretted about her oldest child moving so far away. "What if you get sick? What if you need me and I'm not there?" But Annette had promised to be careful and called often.

Annette had only lived in the Breckenridge area for eighteen months but was already considered a "townie" by the tight-knit locals. That was in part because the pretty young woman was willing to try almost any crazy stunt, including participating in the annual Outhouse Race, in which contestants mount outhouses on skis and barrel down a ski slope, hopefully, but not always, getting to the bottom in one piece. She supported herself by working part-time as a bartender in Breckenridge at night and full-time as a maid at the Holiday Inn in Frisco, fifteen miles to the north, during the day.

Unlike jet-set Vail and Aspen, Breckenridge was off the beaten track in those days—a small, relatively quiet ski town with a main street of quaint Victorian storefronts, a variety of restaurants for the aprés ski crowd, and a few rowdy bars. The locals were mostly two kinds: young ski buffs, who worked at the resort or in the restaurants, bars, and hotels, and old-timers who loved the surrounding mountains of the Gore Range enough to put up with the tourists and the long winters at 10,000 feet above sea level. Except for the occasional bar brawl or burglary, there wasn't much in the way of crime—hadn't been a murder in years—and even young, pretty women like Annette felt safe hitchhiking.

Annette was supposed to work that night at the bar. Her uniform was already laid out neatly on her bed in the cabin she rented in Blue River, a collection of ski chalets and cabins a few miles south of Breckenridge on Highway 9. But she hadn't been feeling well and went to see a doctor in Frisco.

Later that afternoon, friends saw her hitchhiking along Highway 9 outside of Frisco and gave her a ride to their turnoff a couple miles shy of Breckenridge. She waved goodbye as they drove off and stuck her thumb out again. She was on her way home but wanted to stop first to fill a new prescription. Her friends weren't worried about her; she was dressed for the weather, including two pairs of wool socks, one long pair that covered her calves and an ankle-high pair over them.

A half hour after her friends dropped her off, Annette walked into the pharmacy with the other woman. At the cash register, she turned to her companion and asked, "Didn't you want cigarettes?" The other woman smiled and grabbed a pack of Marlboros.

Annette paid for the cigarettes and prescription, which she placed in the daypack she carried. The clerk watched as the two women then walked out of the store and into the fast-approaching winter night.

A few hours later, Bobby Jo Oberholtzer was waiting on the south end of Breckenridge for a ride to her home in Alma, twenty miles to the south on the other side of Hoosier Pass. A dozen Alma residents made the daily commute, preferring the solitude and lower housing costs of their tiny village on the highway between the ski resort and Colorado Springs and Denver.

Bobby Jo was well-known and popular in Alma, to which she and her husband, Jeff, had moved from Racine, Wisconsin, several years earlier. On most workdays, Bobby Jo caught rides with friends to and from Breckenridge where she worked as a secretary for a realty office. When she missed a ride, she stuck out her thumb.

Bobby Jo's hitchhiking made Jeff nervous, but they only had an old truck and he needed it for his appliance repair business. She wasn't the sort of woman who could be told what she could and couldn't do anyway. Although she was only 5'3" and 110 pounds, she'd fight like a cornered wildcat if pushed. So Jeff fashioned a heavy brass key ring for her with which to wallop any attacker. She kept the key ring clipped to the outside top of the daypack she always carried and promised to be careful.

Bobby Jo had just turned 29 that past Christmas, a beautiful woman with blond, shoulder-length hair and merry blue eyes. On January 6, she got up at about 5:30 to get an early start on what began as a great day. She arrived at work to learn that she was getting a substantial pay raise.

A little after 6 P.M., Jeff Oberholtzer was outside shoveling snow from the walk in front of their house and watching the traffic on Highway 9 for his wife when the telephone rang. Running inside, he answered. It was Bobby Jo. She told him the good news and said she was going to a Breckenridge bar to celebrate with two friends. The friends, another young couple, lived near Alma and would be giving her a ride home afterwards.

"They're good people," Jeff said, relieved that his wife wouldn't be trying to hitchhike over 11,000-foot Hoosier Pass on such a miserably cold night. They discussed dinner plans and hung up. He went back outside to finish shoveling.

In Breckenridge, Bobby Jo and her friends went to the bar where she had a couple of drinks. By 7:30, it was apparent that her friends had decided to make a night of it, but Bobby Jo wanted to go home.

"No problem," she said, "I'll hitchhike. There should still be some late traffic heading over the pass." So she bundled up and headed for the convenience store at the end of town; its parking lot was used by locals as a pickup spot for hitchhikers headed south.

Shortly before 8 P.M., a friend driving a truck spotted Bobby Jo standing in the cold and pulled over. Bobby Jo opened the passenger door and leaned in to warm up.

"I'm going as far as Blue River," the driver said. But Bobby Jo shook her head. Blue River was only a few miles down the road. Thanks but no thanks, she didn't want to get stranded on that lonely stretch of the highway on such a night. At least here, she could run into the store to warm up until she got a ride to take her all the way to Alma.

"I'll see you later," she said and closed the door. The driver pulled away. He'd later tell detectives that he made it home in time for the start of an 8 o'clock movie on the television, unaware that when he looked into his rearview mirror at Bobby Jo stamping her feet in the snow, it would be the last time anyone saw her alive.

Except for whoever killed her.

* * *

An hour earlier in Alma, Joe Urban stopped to see his friend Jeff Oberholtzer, who was just finishing shoveling snow. Times were tough for Urban. He said he was thinking about heading to Denver to hock his watch for gas and oil.

Jeff suggested they go instead to the local gas station and make a trade. "But we'll have to hurry 'cause they close at seven," he said. The station owner wasn't interested in Joe's watch, so Jeff charged gas and oil for his friend and bought a six-pack of beer from the liquor store next to the gas station. The pair went back to Jeff's where they drank the beer and watched television.

Urban left about 8 o'clock. Jeff continued watching a movie, although he was getting increasingly upset at his wife for not calling to say she was going to be later than expected. He fell asleep with the television on.

A little after midnight, he was startled out of his slumber by an ambulance siren. His first thought was that something had happened to his wife—maybe she had been struck crossing the dark highway trying to get home. The ambulance continued down the highway. He lay back down to wait but fell asleep again. He woke about 2 A.M.; Bobby Jo was still not home.

Oberholtzer decided to look for her. About 2:45 that morning, he banged on the door of the couple who were supposed to have given his wife a ride home. Yeah, she had been with them at the bar, said the sleepy man, but she left sometime between seven-thirty and eight.

"She should have been back long before we got home, Jeff," he said. "But she had three rum and Cokes . . . maybe she stayed in Breckenridge?"

Jeff nodded. Yeah, maybe that was it . . . if so, he was going to give her a piece of his mind for not calling. Climbing into his truck, he drove over Hoosier Pass, the old engine chugging and gasping for air as it crawled past the parking lot at the top.

In Breckenridge he went to the realty office to see if maybe she had decided at the last minute to spend the cold night on the couch. But the office was dark and nobody answered his knock. About 3:30, torn between fear and anger, he contacted the Breckenridge police. The dispatcher took a missing person report and promised he'd get the word out to the patrol officers.

Jeff Oberholtzer spent the rest of the night driving, trying to think of where his wife might have gone. At last he went home, hoping Bobby Jo would be there with a tale about some misadventure she'd had. They'd have a good laugh after he let her know what he thought of her hitchhiking home at night. But the house was cold and empty. He sat down to think about his options.

The telephone startled him out of his stupor; he rushed to pick it up, sure that someone was calling to say his Bobby Jo was in the hospital, but alive. The call was from Donald Hamilton, a rancher who lived near the town of Como, more than ten miles north of Fairplay, an old mining community where the highway now forked—one way to Como and then beyond to Denver, the other towards Colorado Springs. It was another six miles from Fairplay to Alma.

"I found a license belonging to Barbara Jo Oberholtzer this morning," the rancher said, "and looked up your number in the phone book. It was in my yard and [I] thought she might be lookin' for it." The rancher fell silent when Jeff explained that his wife was missing.

"I . . . I'll be by to pick it up," Jeff said, thanking the rancher and hanging up. What the hell was Bobby Jo's license doing in Como? It meant whoever flung it into Hamilton's yard had come right past their house the night before. "I knew right then that she was dead," he later told police.

Still, he was going to need help to find her, dead or alive. He called his brother, James, and asked him to go get Bobby Jo's license and see if there was anything else at the ranch that might indicate what had happened to her.

After hanging up with James, he called his friends. He asked them to accompany him along the lonely stretch of highway between Alma and the Hamilton property looking for clues. About four miles from the ranch, they found Bobby Jo's red backpack twenty feet beyond a fence that paralleled the highway. Oberholtzer noticed that the heavy brass key ring was missing from its clip.

Walking along the roadside, the searchers found one of Bobby Jo's wool mittens—it had blood on it—and then a facial tissue with more blood. Someone picked up a Marlboro cigarette butt lying on top of the snow near the tissue. With tears in his eyes, Jeff looked at the bloody items and hoped his tough little wife had hurt her attacker.

As Jeff and his friends were making their discoveries, James Oberholtzer arrived at the Hamilton ranch and picked up the license. Walking along the roadside, he and the old rancher found papers that had come from Bobby Jo's wallet, but not the wallet itself.

Unknown to all the searchers, earlier that morning a snowplow driver had discovered a leather pouch belonging to the missing woman on top of a snowbank between Alma and the Hoosier Pass summit. Hoosier is the dividing line between Summit County to the north and Park County to the south. Whatever had happened to Bobby Jo, her possessions had been strewn along the road on the south side of the pass. Jeff decided to report his wife missing to the Park County Sheriff's Office, just in case word didn't make it over from the Breckenridge police.

Oberholtzer demanded that a search party be organized. But despite the bloody items, he was told to sit tight. "She'll probably turn up," the deputy on duty said.

Angry, Jeff and his companions went out on their own. Some drove slowly along the highway, others took side roads.

Two of the Oberholtzers' friends on cross-country skis made their way up the pass, parallel to the highway. About 3 P.M., they emerged from the tree line, a couple hundred yards from the summit. They saw something lying at the bottom of a snow embankment. It was Bobby Jo.

When Highway 9 reaches the Hoosier Pass summit, most pine trees in the surrounding forest have given up the climb. Those that do struggle in the thin air and through the harsh winters are stunted and twisted into grotesque shapes by the wind. In January, it is a barren and lonely place, snow-shrouded and viciously cold.

So it was the night Barbara "Bobby Jo" Oberholtzer died, her blue eyes open and staring up at the sky, her face frozen in a look of despair that would forever haunt those who found her and those appointed to find her killer.

Rushing to the scene, investigators from both counties began piecing together the events of the night before by following tracks in the snow. Evidently, there had been a struggle in the small parking area at the summit of the pass where a vehicle with Bobby Jo in it had pulled over. Her attacker, or attackers, were apparently trying to subdue her—a pair of plastic handcuffs of a sort often used by law enforcement agencies and known as "flex cuffs" was attached to one of the dead woman's wrists but not the other. Bobby Jo escaped, perhaps in the fight that left blood on her mitten, and fled by running along the shoulder of the highway in the direction of the tree line 200 yards away.

Maybe if she had reached the trees, she would have been able to hide and been safe, although she would have been alone on top of a desolate mountain pass in sub-zero temperatures. She only made it 100 yards.

There were no footprints in the snow tracking hers, so investigators theorized that her assailant had followed in the vehicle. As the assailant pulled alongside, Bobby Jo turned to flee away from the road. She twisted when her attacker fired a shot at his escaping prey, the bullet grazing the right side of her chest, and she stumbled down the embankment. The gunman fired again, this time hitting her in the back. The wound was fatal, but she continued floundering forward into the hip-deep snow.

The sound of gunfire must have carried in the cold, clear night and echoed off the granite faces of nearby peaks, but there was no one to hear. Still, the killer didn't take a chance of being discovered and drove off with his victim still alive.

Mortally wounded, Bobby Jo did not give up. Realizing that the gunman had left, she backtracked toward the highway, knowing that her only chance was to flag down a motorist. She struggled to crawl up the steep embankment, leaving a trail of blood.

It was impossible. Her body temperature dropping, her movements growing sluggish, she turned over onto her back and slid to the bottom of the embankment. There, looking up into the Colorado skies, a billion brilliant stars wheeling above her, she died.

* * *

In the parking lot, investigators found Bobby Jo's gray knit cap and the mate of the mitten found earlier that day nearly twenty miles away. It wasn't until the next day, when the investigators returned, that Bobby Jo's brass key ring was discovered in the snow of the parking lot.

Making a final sweep of the lot, a police officer also found an orange, ankle-high wool sock. Picking it up was almost an afterthought because it didn't match anything worn by Bobby Jo; chances were it had been lost by some skier, but it was placed with the other items—just in case.

An autopsy revealed that Bobby Jo Oberholtzer died from hypothermia and blood loss. A large caliber, hollow-point bullet jacket was found in her body. There was no evidence that she had been raped or otherwise assaulted, perhaps because she escaped before her attacker could bind her wrists. True to her scrappy nature, she had not died without a fight—the blood on the mitten and the tissue was not Bobby Jo's.

In a way, those who loved Bobby Jo were fortunate. There was sadness and anger and fear, but they had a body to bury back in Racine. There was no mystery to what had happened to Bobby Jo, only questions about who and why.

On the other hand, Annette Schnee's family and friends had nothing. Reported missing by her boyfriend after she failed to come home or report to either of her two jobs, police could find no trace of her. She was simply gone.

Investigators discovered her bartender's outfit neatly laid out at her home, ready for work. Friends who had given her a ride hitchhiking and a pharmacy clerk came forward with what little information they had. But there were no other clues.

In fact, the only connection police could make between the murder of Bobby Jo and the disappearance of Annette was that both had been hitchhiking in the same direction on the same evening, neither made it home, and they were petite, pretty, and wore their hair to their shoulders.

The incident threw Summit County, and particularly Breckenridge, into a panic. Two women had been attacked for no discernible reason: neither had been carrying much money, nor were they believed to be involved in anything illegal like drug dealing. One of them had been gunned down and left to die a miserable death in the snow, the other was missing and presumed dead. It was beyond understanding. A monster was loose, but who?

Publicly, the police played their cards close to the vest, including how Bobby Jo was murdered. She had not been raped, they said, but they weren't discounting that as a possible motive. Meanwhile, they cautioned, they had no reason to suspect foul play in the case of Annette Schnee; she had last been seen in the company of another woman with whom she appeared to be friends. And that was about as much as they would say about either case during the first week.

Lacking much real information, rumors began to fly among the citizens of Breckenridge. Calls poured into the local weekly newspaper, *The Summit County Journal.* Another woman had been found murdered on a different pass. Raped. Stabbed. Shot. A body had been discovered in a local housing development. Welding rods had something to do with it.

The police, officially and unofficially, tried to squelch the rumors of other deaths. Nope, they said, one girl dead, one missing. It did little good. In the bars, men talked loudly about forming vigilante groups to find the killer, though no one knew quite where to start. Women discussed buying guns, and some went out and did so.

Neighbors reported the "suspicious" behavior of neighbors with whom they'd been otherwise friendly for years. Strangers were regarded silently. Suspicion fell on Jeff Oberholtzer; maybe he had come to pick up his wife that night and also somehow met up with Annette . . . after which he'd killed them both, then launched an elaborate cover-up.

"Anger. Fear. Frustration. Those three words describe the emotions spinning in the minds of Summit County residents as a result of the recent kidnapping/murder of Bobby Jo Oberholtzer of Alma," wrote a *Summit County Journal* editor a week after the killing.

"Adding to the initial report that a woman was found dead on Hoosier Pass in Park County is the report that a female resident of Breckenridge has been missing for more than a week, and could also be a victim. Reports of similar circumstances have added additional fuel to the already frenzied and muddy situation.

"As for the rumors, and we're sure there are a multitude of those we've not even heard about yet, they all have someone [being] dead."

Two weeks passed, and it was clear the police were at a loss. The killer could have been anyone: the husband, a boyfriend, some local nut case or, Breckenridge being famous for its slopes, a skier from one of the big cities east of the mountains, or even a visitor from some city thousands of miles away.

The Colorado Bureau of Investigation said the two cases, as well as a recent murder of a former Breckenridge resident in Denver, were unrelated. "Authorities continue to report there is no evidence connecting the two incidents, although both women fit similar descriptions and disappeared on the same day," the newspaper reported.

A man and a woman hitchhiking along the same highway reported seeing a woman resembling Oberholtzer in a dark GMC or Chevrolet pickup truck with what they thought were two men. The couple said they refused a ride because they would have had to ride in the back of the truck.

Breckenridge Police Chief Ralph Schultz told the newspaper that a hypnotist was being used to try to get more information out of the couple. "We can't be sure it was her," he cautioned.

Meanwhile, the Summit County Sheriff's Office had been following a more nebulous lead provided by a Denver psychic. She called to say that she believed that Schnee was alive and living in a cabin three miles from Breckenridge. But deputies checked at least ten cabins in the area the psychic described, known as French Gulch, and turned up "zilch," according to a detective.

In the same newspaper, Police Chief Schultz made an unusual plea. "It's possible some person in the county may at some earlier time have been sexually assaulted by the Oberholtzer murderer, and, because of the stigma attached to that crime, has failed to report the facts to the police," he said. "It's also possible such an assault, if reported, could give law enforcement officers the lead they need to eventually find the murderer."

The editorial writer added, "Schultz is hopeful a victim of

sexual assault who, for personal reasons, has not come forth previously, will do so now and that her story will give his investigation a direction.''

As the rumors flew, a young deputy named Joe Morales found himself as frustrated as his neighbors. A patrol officer, he wasn't privy to details of the ongoing investigation. He just hated what it was doing to his adopted home.

Joe's father had emigrated from Mexico to Colorado in search of a better life for himself and his young wife, with whom he hoped to start a family. Through hard work and frugality, he was eventually able to buy an auto-body shop in Denver and proudly became a U.S. citizen. He was an honest man whose success hinged on his customers and friends knowing that they could take him at his word. "There is right, Joseph, and there is wrong," he would tell his son. "There are no areas in between."

Although not a skier, the senior Morales had loved the mountains and often brought his family to Breckenridge for vacations during the summer. Young Joe shared his father's love and dreamed of a day he would move to the high country permanently.

Broad-shouldered and clean-cut, Joe joined the U.S. Marines out of high school. He left the service after several years and decided he wanted to be a cop, especially when he saw a job opening with the Summit County Sheriff's Office in 1981.

It was everything he hoped it would be. Breckenridge was still the sort of town where people didn't bother to lock their doors. Anybody who had lived there more than a couple of months knew everybody else, and they watched out for each other. Even strangers were greeted warmly, so long as they didn't act too much like the monied snobs in Vail or Aspen.

The only violent crime was apt to be the heat of passion sort of thing—friends who got in an argument after having a little too much to drink and took a few swings. A night in the pokey and they were friends again by morning. There was the occasional robbery of a gas station or convenience store, usually by some stranger passing through. But people in these parts couldn't remember the last time there'd been a murder so near Breckenridge until Bobby Jo Oberholtzer.

The disappearance of the two women changed the town. Forever, Morales thought. It would never again be as innocent, as trusting. He noted the rifles and shotguns appearing in the formerly empty gun racks of pickup trucks. He heard the whispered accusations between neighbors.

The general feeling among most of the other officers, both on and off the case, was that the killer was long gone. After all, Bobby Jo's things had been found scattered for twenty miles along the highway in the direction of Denver. In a way, they sounded relieved.

Privately, Morales hoped that the killer was still around. "He might have tossed her things along the highway to make investigators think that he was headed toward Denver," he argued over more than one cup of coffee.

Whoever had done this to Bobby Jo, and probably Annette, was a women-hater, an animal who wanted to see them hurt and afraid before they died. What's more, this guy wasn't going to stop—this was how he got his kicks. *Unless someone stops him,* Morales thought, hoping that he'd get the opportunity. He wanted to see the face of this monster, the antithesis of everything he believed in. Maybe the killer would make a play for the gun he'd used to kill Bobby Jo—then he'd give the coward the justice he deserved.

Probably wouldn't have the cajones *to take on a man,* Morales thought as he was wrapping up a late-night shift on the morning of February 13. The deputy's fantasy of grim justice came abruptly to a halt when a call came over the radio. The police in Silverthorne, a town a few miles north of Frisco, were asking area police agencies for help.

"Be on the lookout for a white male, early twenties, brown hair, blue eyes, driving a dark-green or dark-colored pickup truck with wood in the bed," said the dispatcher. "Suspect wanted for sexual assault/attempted homicide, Silverthorne-Frisco area, approximately zero, three hundred hours."

Chapter Three

February 13, 1982—Frisco, Colorado

Three hours before Joe Morales heard the call over his radio, at 2:15 A.M., a Trailways bus pulled into the parking lot of the laundromat that served as the bus depot in Frisco. The bus driver was in a hurry as he unloaded the five passengers—a family of four and a 21-year-old woman—who were getting off before he continued on to California. He was already running thirty-five minutes behind schedule.

The driver handed the young woman, Mary Brown, the duffel bag that held her clothes and other necessities for the ski vacation that had brought her to the mountains. A small woman, her bag was nearly as big as she was.

Mary looked around for her friends who were supposed to meet her. They had come up earlier from Denver, but she had remained behind to finish her second job and caught the last bus out of town. She thought about driving but was afraid her old clunker of a car couldn't take the seventy-five-mile drive into the mountains, climbing more than 4,000 feet in altitude in the process, and she didn't want to be stranded alone on the highway at night.

Now, however, Brown's friends were nowhere in sight. She worried that they had already come and gone due to the bus's tardiness.

"There's a police station two blocks that way," the bus driver said, pointing down the main street. "Or you can stay in the laundromat." He then climbed back on board and the bus pulled away as Mary searched her purse for the telephone number of the condominium where her friends were staying in Silverthorne. She had written the number on a piece of paper but now couldn't find it. Then she remembered leaving it on her bureau in her haste to pack.

The air was so cold Mary Brown could already feel her ears

burning with the first warnings of frostbite. She shivered. The laundromat was locked despite the "Open" sign in the window. She was trying to decide whether to walk to the police station or call a taxi when a pickup truck swung into the parking lot. The driver rolled down his window.

"Anybody need a ride?" he asked, quickly explaining that he was a driver for Summit County Taxi Service. He was off-duty, he said, but considering the weather, he would be happy to help out.

"No thanks, we only live a couple blocks from here," said the man as his family trudged off through the squeaking snow.

Mary frowned. If this had been Denver, there was no way she would have accepted a ride from a stranger. She had been raised in a conservative, strait-laced family—hitchhiking was something good girls didn't do. *But this is the mountains,* she thought, laid-back, friendly, a place where people helped one another.

She looked her would-be benefactor over. He didn't appear dangerous. In fact, he was kind of cute, about her age, with curly brown hair, bright blue eyes, and a nice smile. He was smiling now as he said, "My name's Tom. Come on, hop in, I'll take you where you want to go."

Thomas Edward Luther gave the young woman what he considered one of his most winning smiles. He'd been born twenty-five years earlier on June 23, 1957, in the tiny burg of Hardwick, Vermont, the eldest of three boys and two girls.

It was far from a perfect childhood, and he still carried some dangerous emotional baggage from it, though you'd never know it to look at him. His father, Woodrow Luther, worked for the local gas company; his mother, Betty, a pretty, petite woman with dark shoulder-length hair, worked as a nurse's aide and kept the house. Betty was prone to screaming rages, generally directed at her children, especially Tom. When she "got out of hand," Woodrow would put her back in her place with his fists. And there were darker secrets in Tom's childhood, but he kept those to himself.

Luther left home soon after his father died with his mom telling him that he was no good and would never amount to anything. There was a period of living with bums under a bridge in New York City and another hanging out on the beaches of

Southern California. But he bought his truck in California and eventually made his way to the Colorado high country in 1978 at the invitation of a friend from his old home town.

In 1981, Luther met his girlfriend, Sue Potter, at a bar in Frisco. She was pretty and dark-haired, six years older than Tom, and had recently taken a job as a police officer trainee for the town. However, she quit that job shortly after meeting him. It seemed that her career choice didn't mesh well with Luther's part-time activities of small-time drug dealing and burglaries, which he used to supplement his income as a woodcutter and construction worker. Police work had been a good job, but she was, as she later confided to a detective, "very, very much in love."

At first everything had gone well between them. They rode her horses, exploring the thousands of acres of surrounding U.S. National Forest lands, checking out long-abandoned mine sites and little-known trails. The sex was good ("Nothing kinky," she told the same detective). She complained sometimes when she thought that he might be prowling around looking for other women, but he had a way of convincing her that she was the one who was being unreasonable.

Only once had he gotten physical with her, flinging the car keys so hard at her head that, even though he missed, they stuck in the wall. But now, a year after they met, they were arguing a lot. He thought she was clinging and dependent, that she wanted to control him. He wanted to break it off, but was torn by not wanting to hurt her, which only made him feel trapped and resentful.

Lately, he had been entertaining a fantasy. In it he stalked a woman, waited for just the right moment, and then, looking into his victim's frightened eyes, announced that he was going to rape her. However, in the fantasy, the woman willingly acceded to his demands, and they both enjoyed the sex.

It was a pleasant little diversion whenever he got into it with Sue, as he had that night. He stomped out of the trailer home they shared with another woman on the outskirts of Frisco, feeling like he was owed a night on the town. He went to the Moose Jaw bar, a locals' hangout, where he downed a half-dozen beers and chased them with shots of peppermint Schnapps.

Luther wasn't especially large, just 5'11" and 180 pounds, but his work kept him muscular with big, rough workman's hands. He could hold a lot of liquor and appear reasonably sober. After all, he'd been drinking since childhood, combining it with marijuana, amphetamines, and LSD in his teenaged years. When he was 15, his parents had checked him into the Waterberry State Hospital in Vermont for a thirty-day observation period because of his frequent use of hallucinogens. But that was the extent of any efforts to get him off drugs or alcohol, and he'd been at it ever since—mostly cocaine, pot, and booze by this time.

He had a pretty good buzz going as he sat in his truck across from the laundromat that night and watched the "sweet young thing" get off the bus. Cruising bus depots and picking up hitchhikers were good ways to meet women, he often told his friends.

"Come on, hop in," he now coaxed the girl. She reminded him of his mother . . . her size and the way she wore her hair.

Shrugging, Mary Brown went around to the passenger side. Tossing her duffel bag into the back of the truck on top of some firewood, she opened the door and got in. She explained that she was trying to find her friends who were staying at a condominium in Silverthorne. It was owned by one of the girl's parents. She told him what she believed to be the name of the owner.

"I'm pretty sure I know someone over in Silverthorne by that name," he responded. Reassured, Brown tried to recall the directions she had been given as Luther drove from the parking lot and headed out of town, taking the turn toward Silverthorne.

They arrived in Silverthorne and began searching, turning this way and that as she thought she recognized landmarks. But it was dark and every snow-covered street with its dark, unlit homes looked the same. It was soon clear that she was lost. "Why don't you take me to a police station, and I'll try to find them from there," she said.

Luther just kept driving through the quiet neighborhood, saying he had just one more place to check. One more street. He was pissed off that the bitch couldn't remember simple directions and had him driving around for an hour. He turned onto a street of widely spaced homes surrounded by deep snow. The street dead-ended in a confusion of drifts.

Mary, now nervous as her benefactor grew quiet, his smile

tight and hard, asked again to be taken to a police station. "I don't think the house is down there," she said indicating the winter wasteland beyond the drifts.

Luther nodded and swung the truck around. But then he pulled over. "I don't think we're going to find your friends," he said matter-of-factly. "But this is as good a place as any. Take off your clothes."

Brown lunged for the door handle. Suddenly, her head exploded with light and pain as Luther punched her in the left side of her face. He grabbed her hair and slammed her head into the door, then shoved her onto the floor of the truck.

"Take off your clothes, bitch!" he snarled. The smile was gone.

"Please," Mary begged. "Just take my money and let me go."

"Shut up!" he yelled, punching her again. "And take off your clothes."

"I can't move . . ."

"Shut up or I'll kill you!" he warned. Reaching down he ripped her ski vest off. Shaking and whimpering, Mary made another desperate grab for the door, but he hit her again, knocking her back. She started to cry. "I'm going to die."

"Shut up, bitch!" Luther demanded as he pulled up her shirt and grabbed a breast, asking if her boyfriend did the same and whether she liked it. When she didn't answer, his rage boiled over again. "Bitches. Whores." The curses rained out of his mouth as he hit her again and again. He shoved her against the door and demanded that she remove her pants. Wanting only to survive, she complied.

A moment later, she screamed and grabbed his arm as he shoved his hand inside her. "Let go," he ordered and hit her in her already bloody face again. Unzipping his pants, he tried unsuccessfully to masturbate. Frustrated, he ordered her to help, but he still could not get an erection, which only made him angrier.

Mary Brown would later write in her police statement: "I asked if he had done this before. He said yes, several times. That's when he picked up the hammer. I thought he was going to hit me with it."

Luther had grabbed a wooden-handled carpenter's hammer.

Brown saw it and cried out, "I'm going to die. I know I'm going to die." He punched her again and pushed her back. He ordered her to insert it into her vagina. She began to do as told, but when her attempts were apparently too tentative for him, he grabbed the handle and rammed it into her body, raping her with the tool.

Mary braced herself—her blood-smeared head against the passenger window, her bloody left hand pressed to the back window. She tried not to scream, aware that her screaming only seemed to incite him to further violence. But he shoved the hammer harder, and she cried out in pain despite her fears. He struck her in the eye with his fist.

"My eye," she cried. "My eye is gone."

"No, it isn't, bitch. Shut up!"

Luther continued raping her with his hammer. Every time he pushed, she screamed and grabbed at his arm, only to be punched. And every time he punched, her blood sprayed onto the windows, the dashboard, the seats.

The torment seemed to last forever, during which she urged herself not to pass out—God only knew what would happen if she did. Then Luther stopped and removed his hammer. "Turn around," he said. Believing that he was about to kill her, Brown fought back.

"I didn't want to die," she later recalled. "I wanted to get out. I remembered reading something about defending yourself and poked my thumbs into his eyes."

It didn't work. Instead, it enraged Luther more, and he began beating her over and over with his fists. He grabbed her by the back of her hair and slammed her head into the windshield of his truck hard enough to crack the glass. All the while, Mary, repeated to herself, *Don't pass out. Don't pass out.*

Finally, Luther grabbed her by the throat and began choking her. She could hear her neck bones crunching, but beyond the pain and terror, she suddenly found herself thinking of her family and friends, how much she loved them. She didn't want to be some nameless, faceless body left to rot somewhere in the Colorado mountains, her loved ones never knowing what had become of her. It wasn't fair. It wasn't right. She hadn't done anything to deserve this.

Angry, Brown reached up and ripped at her attacker's face

with her fingernails. He screamed with pain and rage and stopped choking her, but began hitting her again until she slumped against the door. He picked up the hammer he had dropped and ordered her to turn around.

Resigned to death, Mary complied, turning her beaten and naked body, preferring not to see the hammer as it made its deadly arc toward her head. But he had a final act of terror to perform first; he shoved the handle into her again, this time raping her anally.

Brown found new strength to scream. After what seemed like hours, he finally stopped. She waited for the death blow. But there was nothing.

Hesitantly, fearfully, she looked around. Luther sat motionless, looking down at his bloody hands.

"Can I put my clothes on?" she asked, hoping that, his rage spent, he might let her live.

"Go ahead," he mumbled.

"Can I get out?"

"No," he said, "I want to take you somewhere."

Something in his tone told her that wherever "somewhere" was, she didn't want to go. Crying as she pulled on her clothes, she blurted out, "I'm not old enough to die. I deserve a chance to live as long as you have."

His answer was chilling. "I ain't that much older than you." But his anger seemed exhausted.

"Can I open a window?" she asked and began to reach for the door. His answer was a fist to her face.

Racked with pain, hardly able to see, she could picture in her mind being taken somewhere to be killed and her body dumped like trash. She knew then that he wasn't going to let her go . . . he'd told her his name, even pointed out the street where he lived as they were driving out of Frisco.

He started the truck as her tears mixed with the blood on her face. But he drove only a few feet before stopping again. His hands came up to grip his head as he started to mumble. She knew he wasn't speaking to her. He seemed engaged in some internal struggle. Mumbling. Muttering. Rubbing his head with blood-covered hands.

"Can I go?" she asked flinching from the blow she expected.

"Yes, go," he yelled instead. "Take everything . . ." But

Mary was already out the door, reaching into the truck's bed to remove her duffel bag. Then she ran before he could change his mind.

Her left eye was swollen shut and blood poured over her right. Slipping. Falling. Rising only to fall again. Each time she fell she felt she wouldn't be able to get up again and the thought crossed her mind to just lie down and give in. The cold was numbing and she could feel it sapping her energy.

But something within wouldn't let her give up; she struggled again to her feet, leaving a bright red trail as she staggered through hip-deep snow that lay between her and the nearest dark house. Any moment she expected to feel the hand of her attacker dragging her back . . . back to a lonely grave "somewhere."

She reached the house, knocked on the door, and screamed for help. The world was a nightmare. Monsters lurked in the black shadows beneath the trees. No one was home.

Abandoning her duffel bag, she set off through the snow to a house across the road, only to pull up in terror when she noticed a truck in the driveway. Cautiously, she approached and looked in the back; there was no wood, it wasn't his truck.

Staggering, she reached the front door but couldn't raise her hand to knock. Growing dizzy and afraid that she would pass out and freeze to death, she willed herself to try the door handle. It wasn't locked and gave to the pressure.

"Help me!" she screamed, entering the house. "Please, someone help me!" She walked a few steps into the living room and fell to the floor.

Frightened voices called out in the dark. Lights came on. People were around her. She heard voices but it was all a confused jumble. Then very distinctly she heard a woman's voice cry out, ". . . third one in a month."

It was 3:30 in the morning when Silverthorne police officer Pam Smith arrived at the scene of a 911 emergency call. She found what appeared to be a young woman—it was difficult to assess the victim's age because of the blood and disfigurement— lying on the living room floor, sobbing hysterically.

Smith tried to assure Mary (she was able to get the girl's

name) and gently asked what had happened. "He used a hammer," the girl cried. "I hurt—I hurt so bad."

The ambulance arrived simultaneously with Silverthorne Detective Tom Snyder who assumed the lead in the case. He told Smith to accompany the young woman to the Summit County Medical Center to see if she would say anything about her assailant. On the way to the clinic, a female paramedic began to remove Mary's shirt but she clutched at the attendant's hands and, through broken lips, said, "Not with him here." She indicated the male paramedic. He nodded and moved to the front of the ambulance; the way this girl looked, he didn't blame her for not wanting any men nearby.

It was a ten-mile drive to the medical center, during which Mary did her best to answer the police woman's questions. The pain seemed to start at her head and go down to those areas the monster, as she thought of him, had violated. She wondered if she was going to die and tried to concentrate on the questions, hoping that by helping the police she would remain conscious and therefore alive. "He drove a pickup," she said. The pain shot through her, and she cried out again, "And he used a hammer."

The ambulance was met at the medical center by Dr. James Bachman. Mary resisted his attempts to examine her. Smith had to calm the hysterical woman, saying, "He has to look at you to find out about your injuries." Finally, Mary relented although she continued to sob and whimper from the pain.

Bachman couldn't believe one human had done this to another; the girl looked like she had been in a head-on car accident. Her head was swollen to the size of a basketball; her left eye was a slit and she was bleeding out of her ears. He feared skull fractures and a concussion, possibly brain hemorrhaging. Just how bad, he couldn't tell—that sort of equipment was in Denver. But X-rays revealed that the young woman's assailant had broken the C-7 vertebra at the base of her neck, either from a blow or perhaps when he choked her—the purple bruises from his fingers were already evident around her neck. Another blow might have killed her or left her paralyzed. One of her fingers was broken, as if he had tried to tear it off. And she had been severely lacerated vaginally and anally in a manner that made it clear what she meant when she cried about her assailant using a hammer.

Worried that her injuries might be life-threatening, Bachman left to contact a life-flight helicopter from one of the big Denver trauma hospitals. In the meantime, the police contacted Linda Batura, the county's rape victim counselor. She arrived at the clinic and hurried into the examination room as the doctor was wrapping up his initial evaluation.

A half hour later, Batura, obviously shaken, emerged from the room to talk to Detective Snyder. Mary Brown had begun to calm down, with the help of a sedative, and was able, though brokenly, to relate the events after she got off the bus. The offer of a ride. The sudden, unprovoked blitz attack. The rage. The hammer.

The girl, Batura told the detective, had been assaulted in a dark, possibly green, pickup truck with firewood in the back. The suspect had light brown hair, blue eyes, and would have scratches on his face because the girl had used her nails to fend him off. "She said the front windshield will be cracked where he pushed her head into it," Batura said.

In the past two years, much of it at a similar job in Denver, Batura had worked with more than 200 rape victims. "The only other person I had seen that looked so bad and seemed so injured was a female sexual assault victim in the Denver city morgue," she wrote in her report that morning.

"I am amazed that she is alive. I have seldom seen such injuries sustained by a live victim. She literally 'fought for her life!' "

High winds prevented any life-flight helicopters from flying to Summit County that morning. Brown was loaded into an ambulance for the ride back down from the mountains less than six hours after she arrived.

After Mary Brown was taken away, police officers spread out in the neighborhood to locate any evidence. One found the duffel bag at the empty home across the street; others followed a trail of blood that led to snow-tire tracks in the snow. As a detective left the housing area about 4 A.M., he saw a car driving slowly down a street two blocks away. He pulled the car over. Inside were three young women.

"We're trying to find a friend of ours. We were supposed to pick her up at the bus station, but she wasn't there," one explained. The detective nodded. "There's been an accident. You better follow me."

A bulletin went out to all Summit County law enforcement agencies: white male, early twenties, brown hair, blue eyes, driving a dark-green, or dark-colored, pickup truck with wood in the bed. Suspect wanted for sexual assault/attempted homicide, Silverthorne-Frisco area, approximately zero, three hundred hours.

About 5 A.M., Frisco police officer Larry Woetjen was patrolling the town looking for the suspect's vehicle. He was just passing a trailer home when he noticed a dark blue pickup parked in the driveway.

Trucks in the mountains are about as common as trees, but this one had Woetjen doing a double-take. As clear as if it had been stenciled there, he could see a rusty-red handprint on the vehicle's back window. The truck wasn't green, but he could see firewood stacked in the back. He radioed for backup.

The first officer to arrive was Deputy Joe Morales. He and Woetjen met down the block from the trailer park and crept back to the truck. As they grew close, they could see that the passenger-side window was covered with the same rusty-red blood. Shining his flashlight through the driver's window, Morales noticed that blood had run down the passenger door in a sheet. The seat looked as if someone had spilled a can of red paint; red smears and drops of blood were everywhere, as if someone had dipped a rag in that paint can and whipped it around.

"Jesus," he whispered, feeling sick to his stomach, "the girl survived this?"

The two young officers went back to their vehicles to wait for more backup. Whoever had done this was obviously one vicious son of a bitch, and no one knew if he was armed. The time also gave them a chance to run the truck's license plate. It came back as a 1977 GMC truck registered to Thomas Edward Luther.

Detective Snyder arrived and the three went back to the trailer.

Go around to the back door, the detective signaled Woetjen. With their guns drawn, he and Morales went up to the door and knocked. A woman answered.

"Do you know whose truck that is?" Snyder asked, pointing.

"It's my boyfriend's," the woman replied. Morales looked hard at the woman, surprised to see it was Sue Potter, whom he'd met when she was a police trainee.

"Could we talk to him?"

"Yeah," she replied. "Come in."

If Potter didn't act surprised about the sudden appearance of two police officers, one in uniform and one in plainclothes, it was because she had already been forewarned.

When Luther got home two hours earlier, he found her awake in the dark. "I got in a fight with a couple of guys at the bar," he said as he undressed and crawled into bed. "They were trying to rip me off for some coke."

Then his voice cracked. "I . . . I think I might have killed one of them. The police will probably be here in the morning."

Before Potter could ask a question, he added, "All I want to do now is sleep." But apparently he had some energy left, because they made love before he passed out.

Morales and Snyder followed Potter to a back bedroom, passing another sleepy woman who sat on a couch in the living room. Flicking on a hallway light, Morales could see a man sitting on a bed in the dark and ordered him out. As he walked past the young deputy, the man whispered, "Please don't say anything to her," indicating Potter, who had returned to the living room.

As Luther came into the light, Morales and Snyder were stunned. But it wasn't the glassy blood-shot eyes or the jittery movements of a man coming off some kind of high that shocked them. It was the long bloody scratches that ran down his face and the smeared blood stains on his face and hands. He looked like he had been in a fight with a mountain lion.

Potter stared at her boyfriend as the detective read him his rights. "Do you understand?" Snyder asked when finished.

"Yeah," Luther muttered. "I know why you're here."

Luther was dressed in a bathrobe. Snyder asked Potter if she would get her boyfriend his clothes. She came out of the dark bedroom with a jean jacket, a shirt, and a pair of jeans; they were covered with dried blood.

"Can we take these?" Snyder asked Luther, who responded with a nod.

"Would you be willing to come with me to the Summit County Medical Center?"

"Yes, I want to cooperate."

"You realize that we have probable cause to arrest you for an incident in Silverthorne this morning."

"I understand."

As Snyder handcuffed Luther and led him away to his car, Morales had a hard time believing this meek fellow was the same monster who had caused the bloodbath he had seen in the truck. *Maybe he's just that way around women,* the deputy thought. If that was the case, he was even more thankful that the arrest had gone off without an incident when Potter, sobbing as she retold her boyfriend's admission that he might have killed someone, indicated that she had a loaded .38-caliber police revolver under her pillow.

Morales left the trailer for the medical center to pick up and transport the prisoner to the jail in Breckenridge. As he waited at the center, he tried to locate Undersheriff Joe Antonio because, as he would later write in his report, "of other pending assault and homicide cases under investigation." He was thinking of Oberholtzer and Schnee.

There seemed to him to be a lot of similarities, starting with the fact that Oberholtzer, Schnee, and this new girl were all about the same size and either hitchhiking or looking for a ride. From what he understood, the latest victim was lucky to be alive.

True, this girl had been beaten, raped, and choked, of which there was no evidence in the Oberholtzer case. Then again, Bobby Jo had escaped before she was tracked down and killed, and no one knew what had happened to Annette. And while it was also true that Mary Brown hadn't been shot like Bobby Jo, Morales knew from his studies at the police academy that serial killers didn't always use the same method from victim to victim. Some were opportunistic—whatever was handy—and clever. This girl had been attacked in a neighborhood where a shot might have attracted attention, not on some lonely mountain pass.

Morales couldn't reach Antonio. So he left his concerns on the answering machine for the detective handling the Oberholtzer case.

About 7 A.M., Snyder turned Luther over to Morales, who placed the prisoner in his patrol car. "He's a strange one. I asked him again if he'd submit voluntarily to tests," the detective said with Luther out of earshot. "He said, 'Yes, I want to. I'm really sorry about all this. How's the girl?' "

Snyder shook his head. The suspect had also asked Dr. Bachman to kill him when the doctor was taking a blood sample by putting an air bubble in his vein.

A few minutes later, as Morales was heading to Breckenridge, he noticed his prisoner was suddenly growing restive and breathing hard. He looked into his rearview mirror, just as Luther blurted out, "Why don't you just kill me? Just pull over and shoot me!" The young deputy kept driving, not knowing that many years later he would wish that he had obliged his prisoner's request.

Luther was booked into the Summit County Jail on charges of first degree assault and first degree sexual assault—other charges, including attempted murder, would be added later. Soon Snyder showed up at the jail to see if Luther would talk. By now, the young man had calmed down and was smoking a cigarette. He agreed to cooperate but said he would only give an oral statement, nothing in writing.

"Mind if I take notes?" Snyder asked.

"No, go right ahead."

Luther related how he saw Mary and the family outside the bus station and had asked if they needed a ride. Only the girl had accepted. As they drove to Silverthorne, he said, "She started flirting with me."

"How do you mean?" the detective asked.

"Oh, I don't know. You know, looks and little suggestive things she said. "They drove around for about an hour before he pulled over, him having "picked up on the flirting." Suddenly, and for no reason, the girl went nuts, shouting "No," scratching at his eyes and kicking the windshield of his truck, breaking it.

"I lost it," he said, "and hit her a couple of times to shut her up." Then he'd ordered her to take off her clothes, after which he'd raped her vaginally and anally with the hammer "to humiliate her."

"When she wouldn't stop screaming, I hit her a couple more times . . . but that just seemed to make it worse. All of a sudden my head cleared and I realized what was happening. . . . I told her to get her clothes on. . . . Then I said I was goin' to take her somewhere so that I'd have a longer time to get away."

Luther stamped out his cigarette and sighed. "I told Sue that I thought I had killed someone and that you guys would be comin' for me." He started to say something more but stopped and shook his head. "I'm . . . I'm too, you know, upset and I don't want to talk anymore."

Snyder walked out of the interrogation room and saw Morales talking with another deputy, Derek Wooden, who was working the desk that morning. Morales motioned him over.

"When I brought him in, he said right in front of me and Derek here, 'Why do I keep doing these things?' " Morales said. "Then he looked at us kinda funny and changed it real quick to, 'Why did I do this thing?' "

Chapter Four

Spring 1982—Breckenridge, Colorado

A month after Tom Luther was arrested for rape and attempted murder, a detective walked into the Breckenridge pharmacy and asked for the clerk who had been the last to see Annette Schnee.

"Can I help you?" the young woman asked approaching the detective.

"Yeah. Does this look like the woman you saw with Annette?" the detective asked. He placed a photocopy of Sue Potter's driver's license photo on the counter and stood back.

The detective was following up on suggestions that Luther might be involved in the Oberholtzer and Schnee cases. Potter matched the clerk's general description of the mystery woman—right height, right weight, pretty with dark, shoulder-length hair parted in the middle. But apparently the detective didn't think much of the theory: the photocopy he brought was badly overexposed; the figure in the photograph was hardly more than a silhouette, except for the smile that stood out from the blackness like the Cheshire Cat's.

The clerk bent over to look. She frowned. "Could be," she said, "but it's too dark to say for sure."

The detective shrugged; maybe he'd come back with a better copy. It would have been easy, he even could have ordered the original photograph from the Department of Motor Vehicles. But he never returned.

It was typical of the detective work early on in the Oberholtzer and Schnee cases. The investigation was cursory, communication among investigators and between departments poor, and some vital information was ignored or misplaced. Would it have made a difference to future tragedies? No one can say for sure, but it couldn't have made anything worse.

Sue Potter's police revolver was confiscated and sent to the Colorado Bureau of Investigation for ballistics testing to determine if the bullet found in Bobby Jo's body could have been fired from that gun. The results were negative, but the report was lost, a fact that would hinder later attempts to investigate the case.

Luther was himself interviewed briefly by a detective and denied any involvement in the murder of Bobby Jo or the disappearance of Annette. The detective left the jail with no useful information, but wrote in his report, "I got the distinct impression that he had a strong dislike for women."

Another detective who contacted Summit County Taxi was told that Luther had been one of the company's best drivers—prompt, reliable, and willing to work a lot of hours, rarely taking two days off in a row. If he sometimes acted like a know-it-all, the company president said, he was still well-liked by the other employees, including the women, who were "shocked" at the accusations against their former colleague. However, the man conceded after checking his records that Luther had not worked on January 6, the evening that Oberholtzer and Schnee disappeared, or on January 7.

However, the investigation centered on Bobby Jo's husband, Jeff Oberholtzer. Police know that most murders are not committed by strangers, and there was information that pointed in Jeff's direction.

Jeff had initially denied knowing Annette Schnee, but a witness had seen her in his truck in Breckenridge several months before her disappearance. After being shown a photograph of Annette, but without being told of the witness's statement, Jeff Oberholtzer said that he hadn't recognized the name but knew the face: he'd picked her up hitchhiking one day in Blue River and given her a ride to Frisco.

The witness's information had drawn the police's attention to Bobby Jo's husband like crows to roadkill. Oberholtzer remained the prime suspect, but even there the police failed to thoroughly check out his story.

The mistakes went beyond the haphazard work of the detectives assigned to the cases. During Luther's incarceration in the Summit County Jail, as well as several other jails to which he transferred as he awaited trial, he proved to be a talkative prisoner. In the coming months, a half-dozen inmates in different jails would come forward with information that Luther had implicated himself in a number of rapes and murders, including the Oberholtzer and Schnee cases.

On the afternoon of April 22, 1982, Dillon John Curtis, a 36-year-old small-time drug dealer, walked into the Summit County Sheriff's Office. He had been Luther's cellmate for about six weeks, he said, and had gained his trust. Now a free man, he was troubled.

"I got something to tell you about Luther and that girl what's been missin.' What's her name? Schnee?" he said to a deputy.

Luther had told him that he'd been abused by his mother during childhood and had blamed the assault on Mary Brown on her. Curtis said he'd had a cousin who reminded him of Luther, a cousin who had started by raping and beating women, escalating the violence until he killed one.

"I don't want that on my conscience, if he did these other girls," Curtis explained. "And what he did to that girl with the hammer makes me sick."

Luther had talked about an old, abandoned mine shaft near Frisco where a body could be hidden, Curtis said. The location was known only to Luther and his girlfriend, Sue Potter, who had discovered it while riding their horses.

Curtis said he knew more. If the police were interested, he would write them out a "ten-page" statement. But Curtis wasn't asked to give that statement for more than ten years.

In May, an inmate named John Martin approached a deputy at the Summit County Jail and said he had information about Tom Luther. He would later claim his information regarded the murder of two women, one of whom Luther had left lying face down in a stream.

On the day before the Fourth of July 1982, an eleven-year-old boy was walking along a dead-end road that borders Sacramento Creek between the towns of Alma and Fairplay searching for a good place to fish. He was about two miles from where the creek intersects Highway 9.

Looking through a break in the brush that lined the creek, the boy saw the body of a woman ten feet below. She lay face down in the water. Annette Schnee had been found.

An autopsy revealed that Schnee had been shot once in the back with a hollowpoint bullet fired from a large caliber handgun—a .38 or .357. The bullet, which wasn't recovered, passed through her body at an angle, suggesting she had escaped, or had been let go to run, and reached the creek just as the killer fired from the road above.

On the night she disappeared, the snow on the lonely Park County road would not have been plowed much past the point where her body was discovered. The chance of any other traffic coming on the scene during the murder, or for the rest of the winter for that matter, would have been very small; the killer had chosen the place well. But was it because he was familiar with the area or just lucky? investigators wondered.

Cold weather and cold water had helped preserve the body. Still, Annette Schnee had been in the creek for a long time and decomposition had progressed to the point that it was impossible to determine if she had been raped. However, it was apparent that Annette's clothes had been removed and that she'd dressed again in a hurry. Her shirt was on inside out. One foot was wearing a long, blue wool sock; its mate was stuffed in the pocket of Annette's hooded sweatshirt.

On the other foot was an orange, ankle-high wool sock. Its

mate was back in the evidence locker of the Summit County Sheriff's Office along with the other items gathered on top of Hoosier Pass, where Bobby Jo's body had been found in January.

The suspected connection between the murders of the two women was futher strengthened in September when Schnee's daypack was discovered by a hiker in the woods on the Breckenridge side of Hoosier Pass, a few hundred yards from the parking lot. But it was the orange socks that had confirmed what everyone familiar with the case had believed from the beginning: Bobby Jo and Annette had met the same monster on that cold January night.

For a first-time offender, Luther adapted to the role of hardened convict rather easily. In early April, an informant told Deputy Wooden that Luther was planning an escape.

Luther planned to start a fire or beat up another inmate, the informant said, to get moved to a segregation cell away from the prying eyes of guards and inmates. Then he was going to saw his way out through the wire mesh covering the window of his cell with a jeweler's saw, or maybe pick the door lock with a large paper clip he had secreted. "Or he's talkin' about attacking one of the guards at lock down and running out of the building, where his girlfriend will have a car waiting."

If that failed and he was later convicted of raping Mary Brown, Luther bragged that he had friends who would ambush his transport on the way to prison. "I don't give a fuck if anybody gets killed because I will get out of here," the informant quoted Luther.

Two days later, jail clerk Debbie Moe and sheriff's office secretary Arlene Sharp overheard him talking to his girlfriend. Potter was saying that she couldn't picture herself living in Mexico. "But if that's where you think you'll have to go, I'll live there with you.

Moe wrote the conversation up in a report because of the escape rumor. Based on the report and the informant's allegations, guards shook down Luther's cell and frisked him. A paper clip "key" was discovered in his shoe, which to their surprise actually worked the lock. A decision was made to move Luther to a more secure jail in Arapahoe County just south of Denver.

For his trial, Luther was appointed a young public defender, James Nearen, Jr. The lawyer notified the court that he intended to present an insanity defense, contending that his client was mentally unable to form intent to rape Mary Brown or distinguish between right and wrong at the time of the offense. It would mean a jury trial just to determine the sanity issue.

On June 10, psychologist Marvin H. Firestone met with Luther at the Arapahoe County Jail at the request of Nearen. They started with Luther's childhood.

"My mother had problems," Luther told him. "She was real jealous of my dad because we kids wanted to be with him. She never could say, 'I love you.' We never got along."

Luther related one incident as a boy when he came home with a jackknife he had purchased at a store. "She thought I stole it and started beating my head against the stove trying to get me to admit it." She had finally taken him, bruised and bleeding, to the store where the owner backed Tom's story. "She just shrugged and said I could have stole it."

Luther said he left home at 12 to get away from his mother but returned two years later, having fared no better in the outside world. The death of his father at age 47, when Tom was 17, was a significant loss in his life and there had been no reason to remain in Vermont.

The morning of the attack on Mary Brown, Luther told the psychologist, he made love to his girlfriend, but they had later argued and he left to cool off by dealing drugs and drinking at a local bar. He described himself as drunk and "spacy from the cocaine" when the bar closed.

The offer of a ride to Brown was an attempt to do a good deed, Luther told Firestone. It went bad after it was apparent that she was lost and asked him to take her to a police station. He only wanted to talk about her options when, "I turned off my truck and asked, 'What now?' But she panicked and started kicking. She broke my windshield."

Luther said he was trying to calm her by holding her down on the floor of the truck when she found the hammer and struck him in the head. "She was raving mad . . . screaming rape. I punched her in the head three or four times.

"I was angry so I made her take her clothes off." Luther said he wanted to teach Brown a lesson because she had unjustly accused him of rape. "Everything happened so quick," he said. "I have a bad temper, especially when I've been drinking.

"I went home real upset and began to cry."

Luther said he wasn't thinking clearly after he let Brown go. "I was trying to figure out why I did those things. I was confused."

"Her hair, the girl's," Luther had stammered, "her hair looked like my mother's when she was younger, the way they both wore it."

In his subsequent report, Firestone wrote that Luther had the capacity to know what he was doing when he made his comments to the police and allowed them to seize evidence without a warrant on the morning of February 13, 1982. However, even though blood tests taken within minutes after his arrest revealed no traces of cocaine, Firestone apparently accepted Luther's claim that he was under the drug's effects.

"There is a good possibility that, under the influence of cocaine and alcohol, the subject disassociated and acted out many repressed angers which were primarily attached to his relationship with his mother."

On June 18, 1982, Mary Brown was standing in the hallway of the Summit County courthouse waiting for a pre-trial hearing when she noticed a pretty, dark-haired woman approaching.

Physically, most of the apparent injuries from the attack had healed. She no longer had to wear the neck brace for her broken vertebra, the grotesque swelling and bruising of her face was gone, and time had eased the pain where she had been raped with the hammer handle. However, she'd been left with partial hearing loss in one ear, nerve damage to the muscles around her neck, migraine headaches, and nerve damage to the finger that had been broken.

However, the major hurdle she faced was psychological, which was every bit, if not more, debilitating. For months after the attack, Brown had tried to blot it out of her mind. She was strong; she told herself that she could get through it. But instead of getting better, she got worse as repressed memories ate at her subconscious.

The formerly outgoing young woman was terrorized by the

mere presence of men. She had been unable to go back to her
boyfriend. Even as the weeks turned into months, she was cautious and timid when introduced by friends to a man. She rarely
went out, except to work. Any strange man who approached her,
no matter how innocently and even in the midst of a crowd in
broad daylight, sent her into quaking hysterics.

Then there had been telephone calls from ''friends'' of Thomas
Luther who told her that she must have been mistaken. That
she had identified the wrong man in the police line-up. Some
anonymously told her that pursuing the conviction of Luther
could be hazardous: they had her telephone number and obviously knew where she worked in Denver. She lived in constant
fear of monsters who hid in the shadows.

At last, she sought help from Carolyn Agosta, a Denver psychologist who had formed a group for women such as Mary
called Ending Violence Effectively. Within five days of her first
counseling sessions, Brown began experiencing nightmares and
flashbacks of the attack. In one flashback, she recalled looking
over her shoulder and seeing a gun pointed at her.

Agosta consoled Mary, telling her that the nightmares and
flashbacks were all part of the healing process. She would have
to deal with the attack, not blot it out, if she ever wanted to
regain her life.

To the court, Agosta testified at a preliminary hearing that
the attack could prevent Mary Brown from ever again wanting
an intimate relationship with a man. The violence had also
impacted her family who, fearing that Luther and his friends
might come after them to silence Mary, had moved from their
residences. ''It is all part of the continuing victimization of [Mary
Brown],'' Agosta wrote. ''It will affect the rest of her life.''

Brown would never be the same naive young woman she had
been before that terrible ordeal, but she was determined to go
on. She knew that real peace would come only when she had
faced Thomas Luther in court and sent him to prison for as long
as the law would allow. She promised herself that she wouldn't
let him skate by on the insanity defense; she would testify, and
he would stand trial and be found guilty of attempted murder,
which carried the possibility of 45 years in prison.

So she went to every hearing, even when the district attorney
assured her it was not necessary at that juncture in the proceed-

ings. That's why she was standing in the hallway when the dark-haired young woman approached.

Sue Potter had remained faithful to Thomas Luther despite the evidence against him. In later years, investigators would wonder why.

Potter walked up to Mary Brown and said, "You got the wrong man. He's glad you're doing all right."

Mary stood stunned, realizing who the woman was from the police reports. How could she still believe in that monster? But she was too frightened to speak. She turned and fled into the courtroom.

In September 1982, Luther was back in the Summit County Jail waiting for another court hearing when he spotted John Martin, who was also back at the jail from the penitentiary for a hearing.

Word was out that Martin was a snitch, the lowest form of life in the convict world—below even child molesters and rapists. When Luther saw him, Martin told jail officials, he walked over and said, "I'm going to kill you just like those girls."

The younger man then grabbed him, but Martin screamed for help and was rescued by a deputy. Martin told an undersheriff at the jail that Luther wanted to kill him because of something Luther had said the previous spring.

The undersheriff made notes of the conversation. "Luther stated he killed two up here and dumped their bodies in the woods. Luther said he would have killed the third one but something clicked and he didn't. Luther stated also if he gets out of this deal, he is going to kill this girl."

Martin said he would testify and was willing to try to remember more details. In exchange, he wanted his current prison term reduced six months.

The undersheriff contacted the Summit County district attorney and was told to make a deal if the information was solid. But as the undersheriff told an investigator many years later, following his retirement, "there wasn't time" to pursue the matter and the notes ended up in the Oberholtzer/Schnee file. Disregarded.

When Martin returned to the penitentiary in Canon City, he

was locked up in segregation away from the general prison population for his own protection. The Corrections Department had received information that Luther was trying to get him killed by another inmate.

In the meantime, rumors were circulating that Luther had bragged to still others about shooting two girls near Breckenridge. In October, a detective was sent to interview a convicted sex offender named Ronald Montoya, who had approached officials at the Adams County Jail, one of many where Luther was held for a period of time as he awaited trial.

Luther had told him that he was being investigated for murdering two girls. Now, according to Montoya, he wanted three more people killed: Mary Brown, Sue Potter, and John Martin.

Luther told him he'd pay Montoya an ounce of cocaine—worth about $2,000—to arrange the death of Brown to prevent her from testifying against him. He knew from his friends that she was working at a restaurant in Denver; he had the restaurant address and her home address—both of which checked out.

"He said he picked her up and tried to rape her, but he couldn't get it up, so he used the hammer," Montoya said. "He said he was going to kill her by shooting her when she got out of the truck, but there were houses nearby, and he was afraid the shot would be heard."

Montoya said that Luther had laughed about the cops "screwing up" when they arrested him because they hadn't located two other pistols, a .45 and a .38-caliber, two sawed-off shotguns, 25 pounds of pot, and four ounces of cocaine. His girlfriend, whom Luther called "Lips," had gotten rid of everything. But now Luther wanted "Lips" dead, too.

According to Montoya, Potter had dumped Luther for another man and removed $500 from his bank account. "He said he would like to be the one to kill her himself, if he could get out. He wanted her face blown off.

"Lips is scared to death of Luther because she knows something. . . . Every time he talks about her, he gets real wild and crazy-acting."

As for Martin, Montoya said, Luther told him that the older convict "knows too much and talked too much. . . . Martin could be a witness against him because of what he told him about the rape and death of a girl." Luther wanted Montoya to contact the Mexican Mafia at the penitentiary to have Martin killed. He was willing to pay $500.

Montoya said he also had his own, firsthand information incriminating Luther. Three months earlier, he said, he was watching television with Luther when there was a newscast about a missing girl. "He said, 'They'll never find the bitch,' " Montoya recalled. "After that he got real quiet and wouldn't talk for three days."

But Luther had approached him again. He said he'd met a girl at a bar in Breckenridge. They'd left to snort cocaine; afterwards he'd asked her to perform an apparently indecent sexual act. "But she said 'No,' and called him a pervert. He flipped out and started choking her."

Montoya said that Luther had killed the girl—he had only guessed that it was by strangulation because Luther hadn't mentioned anything else. "He dumped her body up in the mountains, under some brush."

From what police could ascertain, Martin and Montoya had never met. Yet their stories were amazingly similar. Luther had supposedly told both of them that he had killed other women and dumped their bodies in the woods, which was also close to what Dillon John Curtis had said in his interview. Martin and Montoya also claimed that Luther admitted raping Mary Brown with the hammer handle and said he had considered shooting her before deciding against it.

If Montoya was telling the truth, Luther now wanted Mary Brown, Sue Potter, and John Martin dead. Killing Mary made a certain amount of twisted sense; without her testimony, he couldn't be convicted. Maybe he wanted Potter murdered out of jealousy or a feeling of betrayal for dumping him and taking his money—or was it because she knew something that might incriminate him?

But why try to pay to have Martin killed? Unless he had told the old snitch something that could hurt him someday.

A week later, the detective who interviewed Montoya met with Sue Potter. She was now living with another man but refused to disclose his name or where she was working. It was evident she didn't trust anybody involved with the Luther case and now wanted nothing to do with her old boyfriend.

The detective told her that he had information that Luther was trying to have her killed and that she had gotten rid of several guns for him. "That's bullshit," she responded. "The only guns we had were my service revolver and a .22 rifle."

"Luther's claiming that he killed two girls," the detective continued.

"I have no information about that," Potter said. "I don't know what he did when he went out by himself . . . that was one of the problems we were having—he wouldn't take me with him."

The detective asked again about the guns and threatened that if Luther was tied to murder and she had disposed of the guns, she could be charged with being an accessory. Potter was incensed. "There were no other guns!" she yelled.

What about the threats to kill her? the detective asked.

Potter shrugged. "He's crazy. He's probably capable of it," she said. Then she thought again. "I don't think he'd do it." Her lips were tight, angry, but the detective thought that her eyes looked frightened.

Potter soon moved from Colorado. She told the young woman friend who had been sleeping in the trailer the morning Tom Luther was arrested that if he got out of prison and came looking for her to say that she had left with no forwarding address.

During the last part of 1982, Luther was examined by two more forensic psychologists—one for the defense and one for the prosecution. With each interview, his story changed subtly. His intentions had been misunderstood. The girl attacked him. He was just trying to calm her down. Each psychologist had a different prognosis on Luther's rehabilitation, but they all agreed that without it, he would remain violently explosive around women.

In October, Luther spoke with Robert E. Pelc, who had been retained by Nearen, in the Adams County Jail. Much of the information discussed earlier with Firestone was repeated during this evaluation, including more about his mother's "highly unpredictable and violent'' mood swings, "the source of much of his childhood distress.''

In his report, Pelc noted that Luther had begun drinking at 9 years old and by the time he dropped out of school after the ninth grade, the boy had a serious drinking problem. "He is now a regular consumer of alcohol . . . describing drinking binges that last from 90 to 100 days.''

Drug use had begun at the age of 12. He claimed to have used hallucinogens such as LSD and mescaline more than 100 times. But he had stopped using them because, he told Pelc, "They are just too hard on me. I would be burned out for days after doing them. My mind couldn't take it. It was no fun anymore. I was getting paranoid and schizophrenic worrying about the cops.'' He had since taken to cocaine, using as much as seven grams a week by the time of his arrest.

Living with Potter was causing a lot of stress, "as she was unemployed and used his money to support her horses.'' Luther described his former girlfriend as clinging, "with considerable financial, social, and emotional dependence on him which was quite frustrating to Mr. Luther.''

"I wanted out of that relationship but felt stuck. I didn't want to hurt her,'' Luther told him.

Luther denied striking Mary Brown with the hammer or that he actually pushed the handle into her or masturbated during the attack. "He further denied any loss of consciousness, although he remembered noting blood, 'and then came to my senses. I must be sick.' ''

During the interview, Pelc noted that Luther's behavior ranged from calm, quiet responses to "more vocal expressions of anger.''

"His emotional state was capable of rapid change. He accepted some responsibility for his actions . . . although he feels that the exact details have been exaggerated and that others are attempting to persecute him.''

Pelc found that Luther's cognitive functioning—that is, his perception, memory, and judgment—was normal and that he had above average intelligence. "Clinically, he presents signs of some psychological dysfunction . . . although nothing to suggest the presence of psychotic behavior.

"Instead, it is more likely that Mr. Luther at times feels

isolated, alienated and misunderstood by others. He may harbor strong feelings of inferiority and insecurity. These feelings could become manifest in various long-standing physical complaints. However, they could also become evident in impulsive acts of resentment and hostility."

At one point during the examination, Pelc gave Luther a test in which he was supposed to fill in the blanks. One's temper is ... "UNPREDICTABLE," Luther wrote. Aggression is ... "AN ACT OF BEING TENCE (sic)." Pelc surmised that Luther's addiction to drugs and alcohol was a means of "self-medicating" the tension he felt.

"Under certain conditions—high distress and some provocation—" Pelc reported, "he might be expected to respond with an inappropriate, intense anger which lacks control.

"The frustration of searching for the victim's destination could have served as a trigger for explosive and violent behavior."

Pelc determined that there was "an absence of a planned, specific intent to commit these acts." However, it was also his opinion that Luther was aware of his activities and that he acted knowingly.

Luther, the psychologist reported, was in need of long-term intensive psychotherapy. "From this process, he might be able to reconcile earlier events of his life, establish a firmer sense of personal identity, and make a better adjustment in the future."

Pelc's evaluation was followed in December by an examination by Dr. Jeffrey Metzner, a psychiatrist with the Colorado State Hospital in Pueblo on behalf of the prosecution. Again, the examination began with Luther's recounting of his troubled childhood before moving on to the assault for which he was arrested.

"Mr. Luther states that his mother," Metzner wrote in his report, "is now putting on a show for everybody 'that she cares ... but she's not capable of loving or caring about anybody else.' "

This time, Luther's account of the attack was more heated, especially after he described getting hit in the head with the hammer and pummeling Mary Brown with his fists. "I was hollering 'bitch,' 'slut' ... I dared her to hit me again with the hammer. I said I would make her drive the hammer up her ass.

"I remember saying something about her wanting to get raped.

I can't remember clearly ... it was like a blackout state for a few minutes."

Luther said he began to "snap out of it" while straddling Brown with his hands around her throat. "She was crying and there was blood on the window. She was begging me not to kill her. I remember thinking that I was getting sick and demented.

"I don't remember telling her to take her clothes off, but I do remember telling her to put her pants on.

"She wanted to know where I was going to take her and whether I was going to kill her. I kept reassuring her. I wondered what I should do. I hoped that maybe I would not get into trouble, but I had given her my name and address. I just told her to get out and drove back home."

Luther told Metzner that when he got back to the trailer, he thought about committing suicide. Then he considered cleaning the blood off the windows of his truck. "But I was real tired and just went to bed."

Metzner noted that Luther said he was willing to take the blame for the assault, but only "if I did it." He knew he had punched Brown, but was "unclear about his participation in the other allegations." He now said he didn't remember whether he beat or raped his victim with the hammer.

Luther denied raping other women in the past or physically abusing former girlfriends. Sex with Potter, he said, was satisfactory, although he also masturbated daily.

Metzner noted that Luther apparently had no history of fire-setting behavior, cruelty to animals, or enuresis—"involuntary bed-wetting"—during childhood. (While that might seem a strange combination of factors to the layman, a large branch of forensic psychiatry believes that such behavior, known as "the triad," taken in total is a redflag of a potential serial killer. Any one factor alone, especially bed-wetting, is no cause for alarm, but statistics have indicated a strong correlation when all three are present.)

"I am not very optimistic regarding his long-term prognosis due to the nature and chronicity of his problems," Metzner wrote in his report. "But he is not suffering from mental disease or defect which renders him incapable of understanding the nature and course of the proceedings against him or assisting his defense. He is legally competent to proceed.

"It is also my professional opinion that Mr. Luther was capable of distinguishing right from wrong with respect to these acts and had not suffered such an impairment of mind to destroy the willpower and render him incapable of choosing the right and refraining from doing the wrong."

At the conclusion of their reports, both Pelc and Metzner concluded that Luther suffered from mixed personality disorders. "With," Metzner added, "explosive and antisocial features."

It was an important distinction. Insane people don't know the difference between right and wrong. But a serial killer with an antisocial personality disorder knows the difference. He simply doesn't care.

As 1983 arrived and then moved toward Luther's oft-postponed trial date in April, he increasingly played the part of the "crazy" inmate. He got into fights with smaller inmates with little provocation; he threw food, set trash can fires, and constantly challenged the authority of his jailers, although always when there was little physical risk to himself. At one point, he demanded to be allowed to make an obscene telephone call to First Lady Nancy Reagan.

The jailers' reports indicated that they saw his tantrums as attempts to bolster his insanity defense. They took pains to note that despite his offbeat antics, he always seemed coherent and the incidents well-planned.

Still, there was no doubt that he was suffering from depression and anxiety attacks. His jailers believed that Luther had himself been raped by three prisoners in the Arapahoe County Jail. His jail records included a lengthy list of sometimes daily ingestion of prescription drugs such as Valium for his nerves and lithium, a powerful anti-depressant.

Luther was back in the Summit County Jail at 1:30 A.M. on February 1 when he started yelling for guards to bring him a new mattress blanket and, curiously, Band-aids™. The guard arrived to discover that Luther had cut his wrists and then, using his own blood, neatly written in big block letters: "FUCK YOU!", "COCKSUCKER" and "THE DA KNOWS I DID NOT RAPE HER." The cuts weren't life-threatening, and the act was seen as a stunt geared at his insanity defense rather than a legitimate suicide attempt.

Luther often complained of various ailments from migraine headaches to indigestion. In early March, he demanded to be taken to a doctor. But when he arrived and saw that the physician was Dr. Bachman, who had testified against him at pre-trial hearings ("The worst beating I had ever seen."), Luther refused treatment.

Instead he began ranting as the deputy accompanying him took hold of his arm. "I wouldn't let him diagnose a hemorrhoid."

He spat at Bachman. "I can't stand your fuckin' guts. I would rather punch your fuckin' face in than look at you. You are just lucky that I have these fuckin' cuffs on."

If found insane, Luther would have been committed to the state psychiatric hospital until such time, possibly a very short time if he was clever, as the doctors there deemed he was no longer a threat. But the tantrums and the changing stories he told the psychiatrists did him little good.

On April 5, 1983, his insanity trial began, more than a year after the attack on Mary Brown. Three days later, after only a few hours of deliberation, the jury found him to be sane at the time of the offense and competent to assist in his defense at a criminal trial.

Luther, who by attempting to use the insanity defense had admitted the crime to the psychologists, now was allowed to change his plea to "not guilty". A new trial date was set for July 11.

As disappointed as Luther was at the result of his first trial, Mary Brown was ecstatic. The defense attorney had managed to keep her from testifying about the most gruesome and violent aspects of the attack, contending that such emotional information would unfairly inflame the jury against his client. And the deputy district attorney, of which there had been several handling the case at different times in the past year, had done little to battle Nearen's arguments.

But in July, thanks to the jury, she would get her day in court. She would take back her life from Thomas Edward Luther. Or so she believed.

* * *

On May 18, 1983, Summit County inmate Troy Browning, a tall, skinny 22-year-old accused of having sexually assaulted a 16-year-old girl he picked up at a bus station, sidled up to a guard. In a low voice, he asked if a meeting could be arranged with a representative of the district attorney's office. Tom Luther, he said, had asked him to arrange for the murder of Mary Brown.

A deputy district attorney came to the jail the next day and, after Browning was taken from his cell using a fabricated excuse so as not to identify him as a snitch, they met secretly. Browning related how ten days earlier, Luther had asked to speak with him away from the other inmates.

Browning was due to have a bond hearing near the end of May and had let other inmates know that he expected to be released before his trial. Luther saw it as an opportunity. Apparently because Browning was charged with a similar crime, Luther thought "a deal" could be worked out.

"He wants me to kill the witness in his case," Browning to the prosecutor. Luther had suggested that he shoot Mary Brown from a distance with a hunting rifle. "Then he says he'll sit back and laugh at the cops because they won't be able to convict him and will have to let him go.

"In exchange, he said that when he's released, he'll kill the victim in my case."

Browning said Luther had resented Mary Brown's "snob" attitude towards him and raped her to humiliate her. "He said he drove on her with the hammer and was guilty of the charges against him. . . . He also said he had a gun in a holster behind the seat and had pulled it out and drawn a bead on her spine when she had her back to him. He didn't shoot because there were too many people living in that area."

"It seemed worth talkin' about," Browning said, but he put Luther off. Then he decided against it, but Luther had approached him several more times. "And he said if I took this to the DA, he'd see to it that I was killed, too."

The deputy district attorney asked if Browning would be willing to wear a hidden microphone and try to get Luther to talk again. Browning replied that he was "shaky" about the idea. If he got caught, Luther's reaction would be swift and violent, and

Browning would have a "snitch jacket" following him to prison, which could be deadly. But at last he agreed.

The next day, Browning was summoned to the Summit County Courthouse as if to attend a hearing on his case. In the men's room, he was stripped to his shorts and a microphone was taped to him by a detective. With the tape machine turned on, Browning affirmed that he had not been coerced or promised anything in return for his cooperation.

Fifteen minutes later, Browning was back in the jail trying to wake Tom Luther, who was napping in his cell. "Hey Tom. Tom. Tom. I hate to bother you right now, man," he said as the deputy in another part of the jail recorded the conversation. "I hate to bother you right now. Okay?"

There was the sound of rustling as Luther woke up. "I gotta get the details," Browning said. "I'll be going to court here pretty quick, and then they'll be taking me out of the county as soon as court's over with."

"Okay," Luther replied. "She's five foot, four inches in height. Dark hair, dark eyes, weighs a hundred and ten pounds. Acts real skittish and scared when she's around strangers—a little weird—like a crazy woman."

"Okay," Browning responded. "Now what is it you're gonna want done?"

At that point, Luther said nothing. He just pointed his finger to his head like it was the barrel of a gun and his thumb the hammer. Browning knew he needed to get Luther to say more so he asked, "Yeah, but how? If she's skittish around strangers, how?"

Luther, sounding exasperated, said, "Just sit back in a fuckin' hole somewhere and blow her fuckin' head off. Then get the hell out of there. That'd do just fine."

"Okay," Browning said. "If I do this then we still got our deal?"

"For your arrest?" Luther asked. "Oh yeah. Guaranteed. Definitely. That was the deal that was made."

Browning wondered if he had enough and decided to press further. "What do you think would be the easiest way?"

Luther pulled out a piece of paper and wrote the address of a mortgage company where Brown worked during the day near downtown Denver. Or, he said, Browning could get her new home address. He knew through his spies that Mary had recently moved out of the home of a friend.

"The best thing to do is call up the Department of Motor Vehicles when you get out of here, you know, and say that you found an abandoned car," Luther explained. "Say that it ain't got no license plates on it but you found a couple names on some papers and want to check them out.

"One is Frank Brown, that's her father, and check Mary Brown. Since she moved out, she's probably got a brand new license with her new home address right on it."

"Just go there?" Browning asked. "Should I go to her house?"

Luther said Browning could follow Mary from her home to work and decide where the best opportunity to kill her would be. "All right," Browning agreed. "I'll take care of it."

Luther smiled and nodded. "Then I'll call you up as soon as I get on that black top."

A few minutes later, Browning was back with the detective. "I think I got more than enough for what you need," the inmate said. And he did indeed. The next day, a charge of conspiracy to commit murder was added to the other charges Luther faced: two counts of attempted murder, two counts of first degree assault, second degree sexual assault, and kidnapping.

The prosecution now had an airtight case. Luther's confessions to the psychiatrists for the insanity trial couldn't be used, but the state had a living witness who could point to her attacker in court and describe the horrific nature of the assault to a jury. The prosecutor also had Luther's own statements to the arresting officers, and his statements made to other inmates, including Browning, that he had committed the rape and that he had considered killing her that night with a gun. There wasn't a jury in the land who wouldn't have convicted him as charged.

But on June 23, 1983, the deputy district attorney, who had only assumed the case a few weeks earlier, announced a plea agreement to the press. Luther had agreed to first degree assault and second degree sexual assault in exchange for the other charges from February 13 being dropped.

It was a done deal before Mary Brown even heard about it. She was outraged when told. It was bad enough that Luther had only been charged with second degree sexual assault, rather than first degree (because, according to Colorado law, he had used a "foreign instrument" rather than his body). Now she felt betrayed.

"You didn't even ask me," she complained.

"The defense attorney and I thought it would save you the trauma of a trial," the prosecutor offered lamely.

"You had no right," she cried. But there was nothing she could do; the attorneys, Judge Richard Hart, and Luther had already signed off on it.

On September 1, Luther was sentenced to fifteen years in the state penitentiary for second degree sexual assault and twelve years for first degree assault. He was allowed to serve the sentences concurrently and was given credit for the 563 days he had already spent in jail. With good time, Nearen told him, he'd be out in seven years.

A short time later, after his attorney vainly attempted to suppress the tape made by Troy Browning, Luther pleaded guilty to conspiracy to commit murder and was sentenced to another three years in exchange for that sentence also running concurrently with the others. Browning may as well not have even gone through the effort of taping Luther; other than many years later, it was more proof to Luther's hunters that he would rather kill innocent women than pay for his crimes.

In Denver, Mary Brown was left with her nightmares. For the sake of expediency, she had been denied her chance to face her attacker and describe to a jury the sort of monster they had before them. Now, she would have to pick up the pieces of her life without the catharsis of a trial.

In Breckenridge, Deputy Morales, who in ten years would win election as the sheriff of Summit County, was angry at the prosecution for not insisting that Luther plead guilty to attempted murder or go to trial. Never would have been too early to let that monster out of prison as far as he was concerned.

The words "why do I do these things" echoed in his mind. And in his heart he knew that someday he would hear the name Thomas Edward Luther again—and it would be in connection with another young woman in trouble.

Chapter Five

June 15, 1984—Buena Vista, Colorado

When Dr. John Macdonald, a native of New Zealand, arrived at the University of Colorado Health Sciences Hospital in 1950, all faculty members were required to spend some time on the "security ward," evaluating prisoners sent to them by the courts. It was their responsibility to determine sanity questions before the trial and then afterward, a convicted felon's potential "dangerousness" for the pre-sentence report given to the judge.

At the time, Macdonald had not specialized in forensic psychiatry, but he soon found that the world of sex offenders, killers, and robbers was infinitely more interesting work from a psychiatric point of view than the routine complaints of the mostly middle-aged good citizens who constituted the majority of his colleagues' practices.

Whatever else they might be, criminals were men of action—if they were poor, they got a gun and robbed a store—and compelling fodder for study. He was soon in charge of the ward and by 1960 was the director of psychiatry for the teaching hospital, responsible for the training of young psychiatric residents in the delicate arts of interviewing and diagnosing criminals.

Sometimes it was easy. Under the stress of facing heavy prison sentences, even the death penalty, the psychological defenses of many criminals were impinged. They often said more than they intended or made offhand remarks without realizing what the words revealed. Invariably, criminals believed that they were smarter than the rest of society, particularly the police; being apprehended was always a matter of bad luck, carelessness, "snitches," or unfair police tactics. Many had over-inflated egos and/or insecurities that made it almost necessary for them to brag about their exploits.

Others however, especially the sociopaths, were clever and

manipulative, always trying to read their evaluators' minds and adapt their answers accordingly. "Bear in mind," Macdonald would tell the residents who accompanied him on his rounds, "while you're making your psychiatric evaluations that they're making a psychiatric evaluation of you and probably much quicker."

Most criminals could be counted on to lie, exaggerate, and misinform—especially if they thought that by doing so, they might get something for themselves. But over the years, Macdonald had refined his interview techniques to sift through the chaff and get to the kernels of truth. He believed that his work helped society in general, and the police in particular, understand why criminals acted as they did, how their thought processes worked and, particularly in the case of serial rapists and serial killers, how best to catch and convict them.

Yet Macdonald was not content to just talk to inmates and review official records of their crimes. Criminals altered their stories about as often as most people changed socks. And much of what he was interested in might never make it into the official records or have anything to do with a suspect's guilt or innocence.

So to gather his information, Macdonald began "hanging out" in 1970 with various units of the Denver Police Department. Robbery. Homicide. Sex offenses. Many officers were at first suspicious of what the eccentric little man with the funny accent who looked like some village librarian might be up to, but they gradually came to trust him to the point that he was given his own desk at police headquarters.

Every Friday evening, he rode with police officers and detectives until dawn. He interviewed perpetrators, victims (if they lived), witnesses, even the officers at the scene while the body was—figuratively and sometimes literally—still warm, in his quest to understand the nature of crime.

As one of the top forensic psychiatrists in the country, he had written a half-dozen books on topics from rape to robbery to murder. He lectured at police academies around the country and the world. He had appeared more than 200 times in court as an expert witness, sometimes for the defense, but mostly for the prosecution.

Since 1951, he had interviewed more than 290 murderers, several of them serial killers. Serial rapists and serial killers, he found, tended to have a number of common factors in their backgrounds. Other than "the triad"—a concept he had helped define and then championed—high percentages had also been sexually abused as children and had witnessed violence in the home between genders or abnormal sexual behavior, such as incest. The most dangerous of all had sadistic qualities to their crimes.

Macdonald was careful to make distinctions, such as the man who got too drunk at an office party and assaulted an unwilling female. Chances were such a man, if caught and punished, wouldn't be a repeat offender. But serial rapists and killers were not likely to stop until caught and put away. Forever.

Macdonald also believed that almost all serial murders of women were sexual in nature, even if the victim wasn't actually raped or her clothing removed. For many of the killers (nearly always men because there are few recorded cases of female serial killers), he knew that sexual release or pleasure often occurred when hurting or killing the victim, not necessarily during the act of rape itself.

In June 1984, he wasn't actually working on a study. But when two police detectives with the Denver sex offenders unit asked if he wanted to accompany them to interview convicted rapists for a training tape, he quickly agreed. He was constantly testing his theories and profiles of criminal archetypes to see how they held up.

The detectives and Macdonald drove the 150 miles from Denver to the Buena Vista Correctional Facility, a medium-security Colorado prison located a few miles south of the town of Buena Vista in the Arkansas Valley. The plan was to spend two days interviewing a half-dozen or so sex offenders to create a training tape to teach police officers what to watch for in these men, as well as interview techniques. The first day, the interviews were short and sweet, as the detectives and Macdonald sifted for the most interesting candidates to talk to at length the next day.

They had little time to review the records of the inmates they interviewed and therefore knew little more about them than that the men had been convicted for sex crimes. The detectives and psychiatrist were looking for those who seemed bright and willing to talk about their experiences. One of those selected was Thomas Edward Luther.

*   *   *

Every prisoner who goes into the Colorado correctional system is first evaluated to determine such things as their tendency for violence, likelihood of escape attempts, and their potential as victims in the general population. At the Colorado Correctional Diagnostic Center, a team of psychologists, social workers, and corrections personnel also develops a personality profile of the incoming prisoners, noting quirks (including psychoses and personality disorders) and watching for signs—like genuine remorse and interest in prison mental health programs—that the prisoner is a good candidate for rehabilitation.

When Luther arrived at the center in September 1983, he complained that while what he did to Mary Brown was "terrible," he considered himself to be a victim of the criminal justice system. "The police and press made me out to be some kind of ogre and heinous person. The facts were not truly portrayed."

The evaluators noted that Luther "tends to display an excessive amount of tact and skill at manipulation." They agreed with the earlier psychological profiles that labeled him antisocial with other "borderline" personality disorders. "He is a neurotic person whose defense mechanisms interfere with his adjustment," noted one report. "He has difficulty being himself. He's a bullshitter, a brown-noser, and a braggart.

"He has a strong drive to avoid discomfort . . . He feels the need to assert himself but behaves meekly and self-effacing around men. . . . Elements of bizarre thinking are also shown."

Luther, they said, had above-average intelligence. They reported that he experienced intermittent crying spells and needed medicine to stabilize his moods. "His behavior undergoes rapid swings from passivity to loud threats of violence."

Discrepancies in Luther's various accounts of his drug use, particularly on the night of the assault, "suggests a tendency to overemphasize the effects of substance abuse on his behavior," one report stated. "The lack of consistencies in stories given by Thomas suggest a poor prognosis at dealing honestly with substance abuse."

The reports noted that Luther had said that the victim looked like his mother and that he had first established a position of trust—the Good Samaritan—with his victim before his sudden blitz attack. And that later he had attempted to have his victim killed so that she couldn't testify against him in exchange for his murdering another woman. Not exactly the sort of thing to get him high points for remorse.

When Macdonald and the two detectives arrived to talk to him, Luther had been in the Department of Corrections system for nearly twenty months. He had put on twenty pounds of muscle since he'd raped Mary Brown, working out with other inmates on the prison weight room equipment. He was getting bigger, stronger, and if possible, more bitter and dangerous.

There was nothing physically intimidating about the young man who entered the interview room. He wasn't huge, though he was muscular. He didn't look dangerous.

In fact, Macdonald thought, *he is a rather a nice-looking, if unremarkable, chap.* Clean shaven. Blue eyes. A mane of curly brown hair.

Then again, Macdonald knew that the worst of these men, the serial killers, often didn't stand out in a crowd and went out of their way to appear normal. It was often this ability to be chameleons, changing to blend into the environment and appear non-threatening, that made them so dangerous. They were usually above average in intelligence, and generally described as good-looking and good-natured—the sort of guy whose friends, family, and neighbors were always quoted in newspapers as saying they had no idea he was capable of such heinous crimes or flatly denying the possibility.

Charming, intelligent Ted Bundy had been such a man. John Gacey, who dressed up like a clown for children's parties and murdered boys, was another. Monsters in sheep's clothing. A ladies' man and a funny fat guy. But Macdonald and the detectives knew little about Luther, only that he had raped a young woman in Summit County two years earlier.

The room where the interviews took place was essentially empty except for the chairs they sat on. Luther perched on the edge of his seat across from his questioners with his back toward a wall of beige bricks. He was in a good mood. Joking with the cops, he nodded at Macdonald. "Hey, how you doing today, doc? He's the one wants me to draw pictures of women."

The detectives and Macdonald laughed; it was a good opening. "How long you in for?" a detective asked.

For some reason, Luther laughed again before answering. "Fourteen years on second degree sexual assault and fifteen years on first degree assault. I gotta serve half of the biggest number. I'll be out in 1989."

They began by talking about his childhood, his troubles with his mother and the loss of his father. As Luther spoke, he tended to cup his chin in one hand with a finger across his mouth or he clasped his hands in front on his lap as if he didn't trust them not to betray him.

He said he'd been born and raised in Vermont, which is where he hoped to go when released from prison. Although he'd only been through the ninth grade, he proudly announced that he'd received his high school equivalency diploma in prison and had recently completed an accounting class.

One of the detectives asked, "What do you want to do when you get out besides go to Vermont?"

"I'd like to be a social worker. Work with abused children with noplace to go to vent their anger," Luther said, looking at his questioners as if he expected them to laugh. "If that's possible."

The answer seemed to take the detectives by surprise. "This isn't a sex thing with kids is it?" one asked suspiciously.

Luther smiled. Of course they'd ask that question. He shook his head and said, "I have no sexual preferences for children."

Did he have any other convictions? "No," Luther began, then changed his mind. "Well, when I was young, me and a friend stole pumpkins and smashed them on the road. We were arrested for criminal mischief and fined $50—which was a lot back then. My dad took it out on my rear end."

What did he think of his father and mother?

His father was a fair man, sensible, Luther replied. His mom was another story. "She had a lot of ups and downs, a lot of problems growing up with us kids.

"She was real young when she got married and to be honest, I believe she was quite bitter about having to be a mother at such a young age and not be able to go out in the world and do what she wanted to do."

Luther paused and looked down at his hands, his fingers interlaced, before continuing. "She took her frustrations out on her children."

Macdonald noted the young man's demeanor when talking about his mother. While trying to determine the root causes behind why a man rapes a woman, it was always important to find out who they were really attacking. Who was he truly mad at? It usually wasn't the victim, but a former girlfriend, a mother, even a certain type of woman for a perceived slight years ago.

The detectives wanted to know if anybody else in Luther's family 'had ever been in trouble with the law. "Well, my brother—there was an incident that happened to him," Luther said. "He shot a girl. He was in a drunken stupor.

"I don't really know what it was about, but obviously he was embittered about something and stepped out of a car and shot a girl pumpin' gas into her car—" here Luther chuckled "—with a shotgun."

The girl had survived and even gone to the judge to testify on behalf of his brother. "Me and a cousin went and talked to the girl, and she found it in her heart to have pity on him."

"You threaten her?" a detective asked.

Luther was ready for that one, too. "No," he said and smiled.

The conversation moved to the rape of Mary Brown. Luther said he didn't want to talk about it but agreed to answer specific questions.

He remembered the night as being so cold that even with the heater running full blast in his pickup, he couldn't get the windows to defrost. He saw the people at the bus depot and went over to ask if he could call a cab for them. "I wasn't on duty, but I got commissions for finding customers."

The family didn't need help. The girl said she didn't have the money and would just wait for her friends. "She had limited cash for her ski weekend," he said. "I been there myself, hitch-hiked across the country a half-dozen times. I offered to help if I could."

Luther described how they drove around for forty-five minutes without being able to locate the residence. "She had no idea where she was going. I could feel myself getting aggressive and perturbed."

"What kind of person was she?" a detective asked.

The question seemed to stump Luther. He had to think about

it before he answered. "She was very friendly, saying how nice I was for driving her." He laughed bitterly. "At least until I started getting perturbed and she backed off on the ego strokes."

He grew angrier, his voice harder. "She was a little stuffy, acted like a princess type, a little rich girl pullin' a game or somethin'."

"She remind you of your mother?" a detective asked.

Luther laughed. "Yeah. She did remind me of my mom . . . when she started screamin'."

He began to mention a similarity in hair styles when it was time to switch videotapes. After the conversation picked up again, one of the detectives asked if Luther had any trouble getting along in prison. They all knew what he meant. The men in a penitentiary all had mothers or wives or sisters or girlfriends on the outside; rapists were often dealt with harshly.

"Other inmates mess with you," Luther shrugged. "Oh, I might take a guy into the shower and punch him in the nose. Them's the breaks. You have to do it every once in awhile."

The detectives let Luther have his macho moment before turning the conversation back to the connection between his mother and the assault on Brown. "You were saying something about hairdos?"

"Yeah," Luther nodded. "Mom had a streak of white or gray that she'd had since she was young, so she dyed her hair coal black. It was a lot like that girl's. That and the way she parted her hair like my mom."

Was he thinking about his mother when he attacked the girl? "No," he said slowly, "but certain things do trigger me off. Things I'm tryin' to get in touch with."

For the first time, Luther grew more animated. He turned his hands loose to act out his descriptions. "For instance, a female that hollers or—" here he raised his fist and made a throwing motion "—slams something or throws something at me, my gut reaction is violent. I want to get hostile and violent."

"What if it's a man?"

Luther shook his head. "No, I deal with it."

"And if it's a woman?"

"For some reason, it pisses me off," Luther responded. "Like the nurses here are not as patient with some people as they should be. They got some real good screamers here." Suddenly, his voice grew high like a woman's, pinched with anger, as he imitated the prison nurses. " 'Come out of there. What you doin' in here?'

"I react to that . . . I want . . ." Luther, his face screwed into a mask of anger, stabbed at the air with a finger, "I want to turn around and say, 'Hey, shut up you such and such.' "

Luther caught himself. His hands found each other again and he pulled them to his lap.

"Your dad ever hit your mom?" a detective asked.

"Yes."

"Ever see him do it?"

"Yes."

"He ever beat her up?"

Luther paused. "Noooo," he said slowly, "but one slap from a man of his size was as much as beating her up, yeah."

"You ever beat up a girlfriend?"

"No," he said, this time quickly. Then he looked at his questioners; there was no telling how much they actually knew about him. "I, well, had a girlfriend who one time tried gettin' physical with me and tried to hit me with something."

The hands came loose again as he acted out how he grabbed the former girlfriend and threw her down.

"I tried to walk away, but she attacked me again." He slapped at the air with the back of his hand, imitating how he had struck her. "Jeez," he said, chuckling and shaking his head, "the amount of damage was amazing." He looked up as if he suddenly realized that laughing had been inappropriate. "It made me feel like a real asshole."

Macdonald wasn't particularly concerned about Luther's tendency to laugh when he talked about the violence in his or his family's past. It could be just nerves or embarrassment. It would have taken much longer than he had to uncover whether the laughter was tied to enjoying the pain of others.

In the meantime, Luther had continued on, talking about the sexual assault that had landed him in prison.

"I didn't get real violent with the young lady until she started screaming," Luther said. "Mostly that was out of fear, I believe. Just my paranoia of the cops: 'Oh my God, they're gonna catch me with coke in my pocket and pot under my seat.' "

"She make you real mad?" a detective asked.

Luther laughed. "Oh yeah." As if he could hardly believe his own rage, he shook his head and chuckled again.

"What triggered that?"

Luther shrugged. "I don't know what triggered it. I guess it got to a point where I just didn't want to have control or didn't feel I should have control or . . ." he nodded emphatically, as if he had just made a great breakthrough, "I guess that's it. I felt like I shouldn't have control. I felt it must be all right to go ahead and light her up. Or punch her out, ya know? 'Cause she was askin' for it."

Luther went on, "This was accepted behavior in my family with my mom and dad." He spread his hands and shrugged as if there had been no other options. "My mom would get out of hand and Pops would do what he had to do to take care of it.

"If it meant slappin' her," he said, slapping the back of his own hand, "she got slapped. . . . Like one time, she walked up and hit him right in the forehead with a brass bookend, and he just punched her, *pang!*"

Luther giggled. "It knocked her right out. And that was that."

It was evident that Luther knew he shouldn't be laughing, but he was having a hard time controlling himself. "I mean it's not a funny thing to think about, but, jeez, you just have to laugh."

A detective asked if he was aware of at what point he decided to rape his victim.

"I was completely in a rage," Luther said growing somber again. His eyes flashed as he relived the night. "I was in no frame of mind to be dealin' with any situation. I should have left.

"But I needed to overpower the area. It was my domain. I'm the lion." As he spoke, Luther held his hands in front of his body and half rose from his seat as if he was a big cat pouncing on its prey. "This is my kingdom that you're in right now. And you're going to play by my rules."

Luther's voice grew hard and cruel as he described his effort to gain power and control over his victim. Two years had passed, but it was as if he could still see his frightened quarry cowering beneath him. The thrill of the hunt was in his eyes.

Perhaps realizing that he was revealing more about himself than he intended, Luther made an effort to calm himself, sitting back down in his seat as he knit his fingers together and placed his hands on his lap. He smiled and shrugged as he added, ''And, uh, it just got totally out of hand.''

Poor girl, Macdonald thought. The allusion to predator and prey was an apt one. It must have been terrifying. Rape was about anger and power, not just sex, although it was the mistake of the politically correct to try to remove sex from the equation.

The girl was fortunate to survive. He had run into plenty of cases in which the original intention had been to rape but the woman ended up beaten or stabbed to death before her clothing was even removed. Sometimes orgasm occurred while killing. Then, like any normal man who had just had sex, the killer's drive to perform the actual act was greatly diminished and he would leave. In Macdonald's experience, many detectives had made the mistake of ruling out sex as a motive just because the victim had not been raped or disrobed.

Luther said he was angry when he pulled his truck to the side of the road, but he wasn't thinking about sex. ''She assumed I was going to tell her to take her clothes off. . . . This is what she says I said, but it's not what happened.''

The girl thought she had to defend herself, he said, and tried to scratch out his eyes. ''I punched her. Mostly it was a slap, to try to calm her down. She kicked the windshield and broke it . . . that really made me angry and I started to hit her harder.

''She's really neurotic at this time, and I'm gettin' madder. I pinned her on the floor and told her, 'I don't want to do nothin', and I don't want to hurt you. Calm down and I'll take you where you want to go.' ''

The girl had agreed, Luther said, but she found the hammer on the floor of the truck and struck him in the head.

''It just made me mad. . . . She had every opportunity in the world, I felt, to calm down. I pinned her and rained punches that cut her above her eye and the side of her face puffed up.''

As Luther spoke, his eyes narrowed into slits. His voice was tight and mean. ''I backed off and said, 'Go ahead, go ahead and hit me again with that hammer.' I was daring her to hit me. 'Hit me and when you do I'm gonna shove it right up your ass.'

''I guess she figured it was her only shot because she tried. I punched her and tried to shove it up her anus.''

As he recounted his version of the events of the night, Luther made no mention of how the attack had somehow gone from a slap and immediate scuffle to a now nude woman he was trying to rape anally. He claimed that he was unable to rape his victim with the hammer handle. "Thank God," he added for the detectives' benefit.

"You see, the thing got more demented. At this point, there was a lot of blood on her head and blood all over the side window," he continued. "I had gotten that rush out of me. But what really brought me to was this girl beggin' me to let her suck on my penis."

Luther looked up. "I was trying to reason with it. 'Is this really happening? I must be sick, really sick.'

"I was thinking about committing suicide at that point. I was going to drive her to a police station and give myself up. She thought I was going to kill her. I stopped. They were going to catch me anyway, so I just let her go."

Suddenly changing subjects, Luther angrily denounced the prosecution witnesses, such as Dr. Bachman, for "exaggerating" his victim's injuries. "Essentially, she had a torn ligament in her neck and a broken finger."

The detectives asked about his arrest by Detective Snyder. "Well, he acted like he wanted to be friends," Luther replied. "The other guys . . . they were doing a good cop, bad cop routine on me. . . . The guy who took me to the jail told me, 'I should take those fuckin' handcuffs off and kick you out on the road and watch you run so I can shoot you.'

"He said, 'When you asked that doctor to put a bubble in your arm, I'd have done it.'

"I was in no shape to hear all this. I was devastated by the whole thing." He denied confessing; Detective Snyder took notes "that only he could read" and got the story wrong.

"When did you know you were in trouble?" a detective asked.

"About a week after I got locked up," Luther responded. "I was in a deep depression. I was wandering around that place like a lost puppy who'd been hit by a car and was barely conscious. The cops would talk in front of inmates and lie about what I done.

"The press got into it big-time. They shish-kebabed me. I was front page news for a month every time I went to court. It was all totally inaccurate. The way the police and the press went about it made me bitter. The press sensationalized as much as they could; they called me the 'hammer handle rapist.' ''

Luther felt greatly wronged about other accusations as well. ''There was these two young ladies who were murdered. They'd been beaten and shot and, I guess, sexually assaulted.'

''Instead of checking it out and keeping it quiet, the police told the newspapers I was a damn suspect in those crimes. There was a lynch mob outside the jail; they had to move me to Arapahoe County Jail.''

Luther was lying. Although there was a lot of newspaper coverage of his crime against Mary Brown and, separately, of the Oberholtzer and Schnee cases, the police never connected the two for the newspapers. And there was no lynch mob outside the jail; he was moved because he was an escape risk. But the detectives and Macdonald knew nothing of this.

The detectives let him whine for several minutes about all the injustices that had been done him. Then they had enough. What, one detective asked, should be done with someone who did what he had done?

''Well, the first thing would be to get them extensively evaluated psychologically, so he could learn about his problem and there would be some way to pursue help for him,'' Luther answered.

''Do you think fifteen years was fair for what you did?''

Luther thought about the question. ''It was fair,'' he said, but then amended his answer. ''It was fair for someone who did not want to get help and would remain a high risk.''

''Are you a risk?'' a detective asked. ''If you could get out of here today, would you go or stay for help?''

Luther quickly answered, ''Go. I've learned to handle my anger. If I was in the same situation and saw the same things happening, I'd go seek help.''

Why didn't he like the police? another detective asked.

''They lied,'' he said, his lips again tight. ''They ridiculed me to no end and haunted and heckled me damn near every day.''

In the months following his arrest, he confessed, he got so bitter that he came up with an extravagant plan for revenge. He fantasized about going to Peru when he got out of prison to bring back "scads" of cocaine to sell in order to raise "a small army."

"Then I'd go devastate that entire area and everybody in it. I was gonna blow up Dillon Dam and wipe the place out." He had gone so far as to draw up little maps noting gas lines and power plants that he had seen as he was driven back and forth from the Summit County Courthouse to other jails.

"You still want to?" a detective asked.

Luther laughed, "Nah. I can't trip like that no more. What the police did wasn't right. But two wrongs don't make a right. I still have little 'stinges' [sic] of anger, but I can't grow personally if I keep trippin' on how to blow up Summit County."

"Anything you want to add, Tom? For policemen?"

"Yeah, go find the real criminals," he said, "and do what you have to do to them instead of some guy who's a first-time offender and has got a whole bunch of problems. Everybody arrested for a violent crime doesn't need to go to jail—that's what the public wants, but you have to look and see what the 'outcast' [sic] of that is going to be."

Macdonald and the detectives left the prison with their video-tape not knowing what role it would play in a future investigation.

There wasn't enough time to do a psychological evaluation of the young "lion" man and that wasn't why they had come. However, Luther's comments about wanting to bomb Summit County had interested Macdonald. Bombs and fire-setting, even if they were just fantasies, he placed in the same category. He wondered if there was any childhood history of bed-wetting, cruelty to animals, or sexual abuse.

Thomas Luther fit many of the other qualifications for a potential serial sex offender, maybe a killer. The violence between his mother and father. The physical abuse and lack of affection he had suffered at the hands of his mother. Luther had continued the cycle of violence, at the very least toward the former girlfriend he hit and the girl he raped.

There were certainly elements of sadism in his attack on the Summit County victim. The hammer, the choking, the taunting, and the savagery of the beating, even in what was Luther's own obviously toned-down version. That part about the girl screaming like his mother . . . he must have enjoyed that. After all, he was the lion and weren't cats famous for tormenting their prey before the kill?

Luther intimated that he had "blacked out," only "coming to" with his hands around the girl's throat. Many serial killers reported periods of having lost conscious will during their attacks.

Even the thoughts of suicide afterward weren't uncommon; these men didn't totally lack consciences, theirs simply didn't work very well. Most serial killers he had interviewed said they had felt remorse immediately after their attacks. They often hoped that the latest killing would satiate whatever drove them, only to have the bloodlust return.

Many even left clues or made stupid mistakes, consciously or unconsciously, like throwing their bloody clothes out a car window, as if trying to get caught. They lied to protect themselves, but often they didn't bother to keep their stories straight and would be caught in traps of their own making. It was as if they wanted someone to stop them from doing what they were powerless to stop themselves.

Luther said he had pointed out the street he lived on as he drove the girl to look for her friends. He said it was to put her at ease. But was he also aware—perhaps in the dark recesses of his mind where he didn't want to look—of what he might do and laying the groundwork to get caught? Only a lengthy evaluation could determine that, if it was even possible.

If Luther was a serial rapist, or a serial killer, seven years or a hundred years in prison wasn't going to change him. Young women are safe from lions only so long as the lions are kept in cages. But what would happen when this lion was free to hunt again?

Chapter Six

The jackrabbit broke from cover and bolted across the alkali flats of the desert outside of Belen, New Mexico, with two mongrel dogs yipping in hot pursuit. Ten-year-old Debrah Snider, her curly brown hair gathered in two pigtails, ran after the mutts, across the sand, and down into an arroyo where the rabbit gave them all the slip. It didn't matter; there would soon be a lizard, or maybe a muskrat over by the pond, to occupy a lonely little girl and her dogs.

Someday Belen would be absorbed by the city of Albuquerque, but in 1962, it was still an autonomous village—not much more than a feed store, a greasy spoon, and two service stations, surrounded by ranch lands and patches of desert that nobody wanted. Barren mountains rose to the east and dust devils whirled across the dry land like the restless spirits of the Indians who once lived there.

Debrah was a skinny tomboy in patched jeans who spoke with that peculiar New Mexico accent that was part Old Mexico and part Texas. She didn't have many friends, preferring the company of her dogs and the family horses, as well as the local wildlife, to that of humans. Animals could be trusted. Their behavior was predictable—even the scorpion was just following its own nature when it stung.

Following the jackrabbit chase, the mutts waited to move on again with their tongues lolling out of their mouths. But Debrah sat down with her back against the side of the arroyo, a Spanish word for the eroded gullies that criss-crossed the land, created by the sudden thunderstorms and flash floods of summer.

Debrah watched the clouds float across the pale blue sky and tried to imagine different figures in them. Knights. Dragons. The sorts of things little girls dream of, especially little girls for whom real life is less than a fairy tale.

The dogs began to fret, but on this day she was in no hurry to go anywhere. She was "running away from home" . . . again, hoping that this time someone would actually miss her and come looking. It hadn't worked yet.

Although born into a large family, her parents weren't affectionate with their children. They didn't believe in it. Her father, an alcoholic, sneeringly referred to young boys who clung to their mothers as "mama's boys." Public displays of affection between parents and their children he labeled "phony." And it never seemed to occur to him that Debrah might need the occasional hug or pat on the back.

The fact of the matter was that her dad didn't think much of females. Those who wore short skirts or showed a little too much cleavage were whores; the rest he placed in a category with Mexicans, who, he said, "are only slightly higher on the ladder than niggers." Her dad's critiques ringing in her ears, Debrah was uncomfortable wearing dresses and refused anything except jeans.

Her father was a big man, bigger still in his cowboy boots and the Stetson hat he always wore as the manager of the Belen feed store. If he'd had any hair left, it would have been blond and his eyes were blue. He could be a real charmer in a rough, cowboy way, if he wanted to, usually when he was trying to put some less-than-square business deal over on a customer.

When the customer left, so did the charm, and Debrah often heard him brag to his sons or the few friends that could abide him about how he'd "put one over" on some unsuspecting fool. She wondered how those friends would feel if they knew that he also laughed at them behind their backs.

"It's survival of the fittest out there," he'd tell his kids. "Don't never think you can't be replaced."

Debrah often wondered if that meant he was thinking about replacing her or her mother, whom he treated as little more than household help. After all, he'd sometimes point out, his wife was half Mexican.

Debrah skipped school a lot. And she didn't go to church very often, mostly because her parents rarely took her. Actually, she liked Catholic services and fervently prayed when she did attend that someday she would meet someone who would love her and pay attention to her. She was always on the lookout for some sign from God that her prayers were about to be answered. And so she was constantly disappointed.

Just like she was on that day when she waited in the arroyo for the sun to go down and still no one came to find her. Chilled and hungry, she had at last given up and gone home. When she walked through the door, her mother and father were yelling at each other and at the other kids. They didn't notice her come in or head to her room.

I could die and no one would even know it, she thought as she laid down on her bed and cried herself to sleep.

I could die and no one would even know it. Debrah Snider awakened from the dream. It was 1990. Her husband, Dennis, snored next to her. She had two sons sleeping in another room. And yet, she thought as she quietly got out of bed, there was still a lot of truth to that final thought before she woke.

No knight in shining armor had ever arrived, although she had plenty of dragons to slay, including dealing with bouts of severe depression since her teenaged years. Her parents had finally divorced when Debrah was 13. Her father had remarried, to a woman who didn't bother to disguise her dislike for her new stepdaughter.

When she was sixteen, Debrah made her first suicide attempt after an argument with her stepmother. She had walked out of her father's store and up the embankment to stand in the middle of Route 66 as semi's roared over the top of the hill and bore down on her.

The first few swerved only just in time as the drivers spotted the girl who stood facing them with her arms at her sides. Hearing the horns and the squeal of air brakes, her younger brother had run out of the store to drag Debrah back to safety. Her father's response was to say that the effort was only "a stupid way of trying to get attention."

Soon after, she moved to Fort Collins, Colorado, to work as a horse trainer for a couple who had befriended her. Her second suicide attempt, at age 19, followed the birth of her first son and the subsequent discovery that the baby's father was already married. He had said that he wanted a son, and she thought that by giving him what he wanted she would at last have someone to love and care for her. But he pushed her and his son away to remain with his wife.

So Debrah Snider swallowed a bottle of painkillers. But they not only didn't kill her, she ended up having to pay the hospital $100 for getting her stomach pumped.

What followed was a series of affairs with married men. It somehow felt safer to go into a relationship where she knew there would be no future. She didn't enjoy sex; it made her feel used and cheap. As a teenager she had walked in on her father and stepmother having intercourse, and the hated other woman's obvious enjoyment of the act had increased Debrah's distaste for such intimacy. But she desperately wanted to be loved, even if it was for only a few hours. Some of her lovers in the heat of the moment would whisper what she wanted to hear and promised to leave their wives for her, but they always lied. She figured that's just the way men were.

Nice single guys frightened her. Those were the ones she might accidently fall in love with, only to have her heart broken. Besides, nice guys didn't fit her image of a dragon-slayer: strong, protective, a little wild, and even a bit dangerous—like the wolf-dog hybrids she liked to raise—someone who would miss her and come looking if she was ever lost. That's why when she first met Dennis Syznski, a nice guy, at a country-western bar, she passed him off on a girlfriend despite his obvious attraction to her.

Debrah had a job working in a feed lot when she got the idea of buying calves that had been separated from their mothers to raise for a little extra money. One day, she approached the lot foreman, who had let it be known that there was a calf for sale. "How much you want?" she asked.

The foreman, a big, pot-bellied man whose breath smelled of beer even in the middle of the day, fixed his eyes on her chest and said, "Well, now, maybe we could just work something out in trade."

There was no mistaking what he meant by "in trade," and Debrah wasn't interested. "Fuck off," she told him. A week later, she was out of a job. The cattle market was down, the foreman explained, and the operation had to cut back.

"But I'm better at my job and have more seniority than some of the men you're keeping on," she protested. But, he shrugged, "they're family men, with mouths to feed." It was no good arguing that she had a young son, Chance, to support as well.

Angry and faced with making payments on a truck she had recently purchased, Debrah decided to get even. One night she crept back to the feed lot and filled the truck with bovine medication. Enough, she figured, to pay off the loan. But she wasn't much of a criminal. She tried to sell the pharmaceuticals back to the company that had sold them to the feed lot. They recognized the lot numbers, and she was arrested shortly afterward.

Debrah Snider pleaded guilty and was sentenced to "up to 10 years" at the women's prison in Canon City, Colorado. She left her son in the care of her mother and resigned herself to what she thought might as well be life behind bars.

She was surprised to discover that the Colorado Women's Correctional Facility wasn't so bad . . . sort of a dormitory with bars on the windows and doors that were locked at night. The matrons, as the female guards were called, and the counselors treated her well and encouraged her to get her high school equivalency diploma and begin working on college courses.

One Catholic matron got her interested in the church again. Debrah was still looking for signs from God and came to believe that her arrest and conviction might have been such a sign to set her on the right road. She was baptized in prison.

Debrah was also starting to soften toward Dennis Syznski. He had been disappointed when she indicated no interest but had been there for her when she went to court and wrote to her often in prison. He loved her, he said, and understood that while she might not love him now, perhaps she could learn to in the future. He was no dragon-slayer, but she knew that if she asked him to fetch her the moon, he'd spend the rest of his days trying to find a way. He wasn't a liar, nor a braggart either, just a good man.

Debrah said she'd give it some thought. She knew that when she got out of prison she wanted two things: land on which to raise animals and stability. Dennis certainly was the stable sort. So she relented. "Buy me some land where I can keep my animals," she said when he next came to visit. "And when I get out, we'll get married."

It seemed like no time at all when he wrote to tell her that he'd purchased forty-three acres outside the town of LaPorte just north of Fort Collins. And that's where he brought her after her release from prison in 1976.

The land was everything she wanted it to be. Away from people, where she could raise a menagerie along with her horses and cattle. There were buffalo and exotic deer, but her favorites were the wolves. She understood their natures—born killers, yet she felt she was safe around them so long as she respected that they were wild animals and needed to be watched carefully.

She soon discovered, however, that other things never change. Sex was still a miserable experience. Her husband didn't know how to be romantic or patient. She avoided contact with him. He was soon frustrated and accused her of marrying him when she had no intention of trying to be a good wife. Still, she managed to conceive and bore a second son, John, in 1978.

Trapped in a loveless marriage, Debrah Snider turned her attention to getting her nursing degree, followed in 1988 by a master's in psychology. She'd developed her interest in mental health while working as a nurse on psychiatric wards at various hospitals in northern Colorado. Most of the patients she encountered were simply lost souls who had been overwhelmed by the world. *They just need a little love and understanding,* she thought, *and I know just how they feel.*

Recalling her own suicide attempts, Debrah recognized that most such efforts were calls for help from people who didn't know how else to ask. But not always. She also knew that there were people for whom death would be a welcome release from a life not worth living. She knew because, at times, she was one of those people.

Debrah was thinking about suicide a lot in the spring of 1990 when she took a job at the state hospital in Pueblo, a 150-mile drive south of Fort Collins. If she died, she knew that her husband would take good care of the boys and her animals.

No one would miss me, she thought that morning when she climbed out of bed after the dream of Belen. Her hair was still long, brown, and wavy. She was a plain woman, not homely nor a beauty, who did little to accent her better features and still never wore dresses.

No one would miss me. The words kept repeating themselves

in her head as she drove to work and even as she stood outside a hospital room that afternoon reading a patient's chart.

There was an "alert" notice attached to the chart: "No women admitted unless accompanied by a guard." The patient was a convict. The state hospital was where they took inmates from the penitentiary in need of special medical attention. She had met quite a few inmates on her rounds, and usually didn't like them much.

Still, this chart intrigued her. *So, they have some real psycho stashed here,* she thought. The chart said his name was Thomas Edward Luther. He'd apparently had a violent allergic reaction to some prunes he'd eaten at the penitentiary.

"What's he going to do, kill me?" she said quietly as she knocked on the door and opened it. "He'd be doing me a favor."

Tom Luther was propped up on the bed and looking out the window at the sunny April day. *He doesn't look so bad,* Debrah thought as he turned his head to face her. *In fact, he's kind of cute.*

"Nice day," she said, nodding toward the window.

The man's smile, a nice smile, disappeared. "I suppose it's fine if you're not locked up."

Debrah was disappointed. It was a typical response from one of these guys, she thought. She had yet to meet an inmate who didn't spend most of his time feeling sorry for himself. "Mr. Luther, we all live in prisons of one sort or another," she replied. "Yours is just the physical kind."

Instead of getting angry with her as she expected, he laughed and his eyes flashed with appreciation. "Yeah," he conceded. "You're right."

Those blue eyes followed her around the room as she busied herself with little odds and ends, picking up some papers that had fallen to the floor, checking to see if he had any water. Her face burning with embarassment, she hurried from the room as soon as she felt she could without appearing as if she had only visited out of curiosity.

When she drove back to Fort Collins that evening, Debrah thought about the prisoner. He didn't seem dangerous—at least, she didn't feel like she was in any danger from him. In fact, he was rather . . . charming. She wondered why he was in prison.

The next day, she found an excuse to go back to his room. He was obviously pleased that she had returned.

"You married?" he asked.

The question caught her off guard. She blushed but managed to stammer, "Yes. And I have two children."

He mimed his disappointment which made her blush an even deeper shade. "You have nice hands," he said. "Working hands. I like to work with my hands, too. I'm a carpenter."

Debrah looked down at her hands. She'd never thought of them as "nice." They were rough and calloused, and both had Band-Aids on them—you didn't work with horses and wolf pups without getting your hands nicked and bruised.

Before long, she was telling the inmate with the pretty blue eyes and nice smile all about her ranch. He said he liked animals and wished that he could see her place. Fifteen minutes later, they were agreeing that they had a lot in common.

Something else she noticed. Throughout their conversation, Tom had been polite, a real gentleman. He didn't come on to her with little sexual innuendoes, or cuss, or let his eyes wander over her body like the other convicts did.

Debrah was in her car and driving home before she realized that the subject of his crime had never come up. *But it doesn't really matter,* she decided. *Everyone deserves a second chance, just like I was given, and I turned out all right.*

After that second meeting, Debrah Snider had several days off during which she thought a lot about Tom Luther. When she returned to work, she was disappointed to learn that he had been sent back to prison.

At first she decided that it was for the best. She was married. He was in prison. Getting involved would do neither of them any good, and she wasn't sure what she might want out of such a star-crossed acquaintance anyway.

Then again, talking to him had been the brightest spot in her month. *What would be the harm in just writing to him?* she thought. He'd said that he was lonely, too.

She made up her mind to do it, but it was against hospital policy for nurses to fraternize with inmates from the prison. Claiming that she had forgotten to make an entry on "Mr.

Luther's record," she got his file from the records clerk and secretly copied down his prison identification number.

She had no plans to lead Tom Luther on about some possible future romance. Like her past affairs with married men, this felt safe; he was behind bars and couldn't expect anything from her. In her very first letter, she let him know that she was sexually inhibited just so that he'd understand and keep any such interests to himself. She said she'd understand if he didn't want to write back, as he probably had any number of girlfriends. "I can tell you're a real ladies' man."

So she was surprised when she received a letter back from him in May. "I surely don't recognize myself as being such a 'charming person that women are frequently enchanted by me.' I'm very flattered that you thought so."

Debrah had asked him to tell her about himself. He started with a lie, saying he had been born in Quebec, Canada, and raised on a farm in Vermont. Everything else was exactly what he must have known would appeal to her: he liked the outdoors and working with animals; he wanted a quiet, simple life and gardens. He also told her that he would be getting out at the end of June.

"I liked you also. I remembered your long hair. You're really kinda cute and well built. What do you want with a convict?" He signed the letter, "Best wishes, Tom."

In his next letter, Luther described himself as her "knight in shining smiles" who was writing to tell her she wasn't the only lonely soul in town. Both images struck emotional chords in Debrah.

It broke her heart when he wrote about how his father had died "without getting to see any of his children grow up." There was no mention of an abusive mother, only of a woman who had a really tough time when her husband passed away but had kept a chin-up attitude, telling her children crying was for sissies.

In mid-June he wrote to tell her that he'd been "dogged" by the parole board and his release pushed back to January 1991. It was also the first time he had ever mentioned the crime that got him sent to prison, although not the official version.

"You see, I was sent here in February of '82 for an assault," he wrote. "I hope you aren't disappointed that I seem to be this assultive person. I will tell you this, I have learned my lessons.

This standing your ground shit is for fools and muscle heads which I am not anymore."

Debrah took that to mean that he had gotten into a fight with some other man. Standing his ground. Well, she wasn't the sort who could like a man who wouldn't stick up for himself or, she thought, someone he loved, even if it meant prison. When she wrote him back, she said she thought he'd received an unfair sentence; she'd heard of people who had done less time for murder.

She liked him even more when he replied that he accepted his punishment. After all, he said, he'd assaulted somebody with a hammer—over a drug deal gone awry.

All he wanted when he got out of prison, he said, was to leave Colorado for the green hills of Vermont. He would buy a small home on a few acres of land so he could grow beef cattle, have a few horses, fish, and be able to eat out of the garden.

Of course, much of what he wrote wasn't true. He fed her lies about the horses he'd owned, including a colt he'd supposedly raised since birth but had to sell after his arrest.

Luther seemed just a lonely man who'd made a mistake and paid for it dearly. He was sensitive and open, sharing confidences about his own failed relationships and his yearning for that "one good woman" to spend the rest of his life with.

Debrah found herself telling him about her problems with Dennis, and men in general. She didn't trust them, she said. But nevertheless, she was also lonely and "looking for a knight in shining armor . . . a dragon-slayer . . . who will wrap his arms around me and keep me safe."

Luther sympathized. He didn't want to take sides, he wrote, but Dennis seemed overbearing and not very understanding. But he was careful not to squeeze too much as he wound himself closer to her heart.

"I too have been lonely and unloved for many years," he wrote. "I have been locked up for 8½ years and really miss being hugged and kissed and told sweet things." The last few years had been particularly tough, he said. "It would be nice to have a love affair going without it being based on the physical act of making love."

Each of his, at this point weekly, letters edged a little closer to her fragile psyche. She was a good-looking woman, he wrote after she sent him a photograph. Maybe he could visit her place someday and spend a little time with her? They could take moonlight walks down quiet, country roads ... just holding hands and talking.

Debrah found herself wondering what it would be like to be wrapped up in his arms and "just plain cuddling," as he'd called it. He was so romantic and careful not to mention desiring sex with her, although as he grew bolder, he dropped hints—such as how all his former girlfriends had found him to be a "fantastic lover."

Debrah worried, but not too much, that she might be falling in love. It was a nice feeling; she certainly no longer thought about suicide and her depression had lifted—jolted only occasionally when hoped-for letters from him didn't arrive when expected.

Luther was even good to his mother. He said he telephoned her every Sunday. "Boy, I don't know what I would do without Ma. I guess I've learned why men can turn into Ma-ma's boys."

He was worried that his mother, who had survived several bouts with cancer, wouldn't tell him if she was really sick. She thought he might try a prison break in order to see her, so she wouldn't tell him the worst. "I keep telling her I'm not doing 8 1/2 years to mess it up again. I can't do another stretch."

About the only thing that disturbed Debrah Snider about her pen pal was that he seemed to have a lot of anger toward authorities. He told her he hated cops and prison guards. He even asked her to stop using return address stickers that she had received from Mothers Against Drunk Driving on her letters. He felt they had pushed some irresponsible legislation that was ruining good people by sending them to prison.

Debrah responded that she didn't think his resentment toward the police and other authority figures was good for his rehabilitation. He quickly wrote back that he didn't hate all cops, just those who had misled him or lied about him. She thought that was understandable.

In August, she decided that maybe it wouldn't hurt to give into his requests that she actually visit him in the prison. She drove down only to have more misgivings as she approached "The Walls," as the inmates referred to the maximum security Colorado Territorial Prison in Canon City. The concertina wire and towers with rifle-toting guards in plain view reminded her of what the men behind those walls were like. But then, Tom was also inside.

"You must have been eating something," he said, walking up to her in the visiting room. Before she could react, he wiped a bit of mustard from the side of her mouth. He was so gentle about it, she didn't know how to respond.

They talked for the next four hours, mostly about her—everything from her troubled marriage to her animals. When it was time for Debrah to leave, they stood facing each other. Suddenly, Tom reached out and pulled her to him, briefly kissing her on the cheek.

Debrah flushed angrily. He'd had no right to do that. She left quickly without looking back. She swore she was never coming back. This had gone too far. But as the miles to Fort Collins passed, her anger dissipated.

After all, they were friends weren't they? In fact, in the few short months they had been writing, he knew more about her and had provided more thoughtful suggestions than any counselor ever had. In their correspondence, he'd never made her feel ashamed of her lack of sexuality or stated that he even thought of her that way.

Debrah reached up and touched the place on her cheek he had kissed. She smiled. Yes, she thought, Tom was one heck of a nice guy.

The letter she received from him a few days later read like it had been written by a nervous teenager, which she thought was cute. "When I kissed you on the cheek, your skin felt so soft it made me wonder if your lips were even softer. Don't get mad. It's just been so long for me."

As she read, Debrah imagined what kissing his lips would be like. He seemed so vulnerable when he wrote that he wasn't sure if he was ready to take on the world outside "The Walls" without someone at his side. The whole world seems to be getting very violent and complex.

After that she visited him nearly every week, driving the nearly 200 miles to Canon City from Fort Collins. Between visits, she wrote letters and spent hours on the telephone with him. He was always interested in what she was doing, counseling her about her troubles, making suggestions about animal husbandry.

Before meeting Tom, Debrah didn't even own a dress. Now she bought two at his request. He wanted other inmates to see that he had a woman friend "with a real cute figure."

One of the dresses she modeled for Dennis. He had been amazingly accepting of his wife's developing friendship with a convict. In a way, he was relieved. A "responsible guy," he could never conceive of running out on his wife and sons, leaving them to handle the ranch work as best they could. But he was disappointed with his marriage and lonely, too. If some other guy was to come along and take his place with Debrah, well, he wouldn't fight it.

Still, sometimes he felt pangs of jealousy. Maybe if Debrah had ever reached out to him the way she did this Tom Luther, it might have worked out. He felt one of those pangs when she modeled the dress she had purchased for her next visit.

It was a southwestern-style dress that hugged her figure, made out of a red-dyed buckskin material with fringes and a large silver belt buckle. "It looks like your bathrobe," Dennis said.

Hurt and suddenly self-conscious, she almost threw the dress away. But she summoned her courage and wore it to see Luther. He positively gushed over how beautiful she looked. "Sexy . . . if you don't mind me saying so," he said. "I have to say, you really turn me on." He allowed his eyes to wander over her body, stopping here and there. And for once in her life, Debrah didn't mind.

In September, for the first time, he wrote using the words, "I love you. . . . You are my only pal in the whole wide world." For Debrah it was a sign. Yes, she wrote back, she loved him, too.

His only flaw remained his temper, especially when it came to female authorities. There was one counselor of some sort at the prison named Gloria Greene who particularly got to him.

When Debrah next went to visit, she told him she didn't like him talking like that about women. It offended her, even if it was true. And she wanted him to stop referring to police officers with such hatred. No matter what "lies" they'd told about him, he had to learn to forgive and move on.

*   *   *

Sometimes Tom accepted her criticism. His anger, he said, had been his source of energy for so long he couldn't always control it. But other times, he didn't take it so well.

Now that he knew how dependent she was on his letters and visits, he sometimes withheld himself to "punish" her. He wouldn't write and asked her not to write to him; or, he might remove her name from his visiting list without telling her. She'd show up at the prison, only to leave in tears when told she couldn't see him.

He'd wait for a little time to pass and then "forgive" her, carefully explaining her transgressions. With each episode, he set the hook a little deeper. He was, as others had noted, skilled at manipulation.

There was a lot about Thomas Luther that Debrah Snider was unaware of besides the crime for which he had been convicted. He had turned into something of a jailhouse lawyer who kept prison and court officials busy answering, at taxpayer expense, frivolous writs and lawsuits, both on his own case and those of other inmates, as well complaints about conditions at the prison.

Luther's intelligence and willingness to use the law library on behalf of others earned him a certain amount of safety in prison. And he had continued to explain his crime to other inmates as an assault on a woman who had ripped him off in a drug deal. He didn't mention that it was a sexual assault, and sometimes he even left off the detail that the victim was a woman.

Luther adapted well to prison life. He made friends, including two young inmates, Charles "Mongo" Kreiner, who was in for assaulting a man, and Dennis "Southy" Healey, a petty thief and small-time drug dealer, as well as an older drug dealer named Richard "Mortho" Brazell. But his best friend was Jerald "Skip" Eerebout, who was doing time for attempted murder. They would all figure prominently in events still far in the future.

Like most inmates, Luther blamed the law and his victim for his imprisonment. It had been a mistake, he said, to let Brown go. "The next one will not live," he told Mongo. "I'll bury her in the mountains and they'll never find her body."

The thorn in Luther's side was Gloria Greene, the director of the Corrections Department's sex offenders programs. In 1985, he'd completed the first phase of the program, mostly an introductory course that hadn't required much participation. In 1986, however, he discovered that the second phase, under the direction of Greene, was much more difficult. Inmates were required to participate in discussion groups and were confronted about their crimes and their views about women.

At first, Luther simply refused to speak. Then he grew increasingly resentful and belligerent toward Greene and other women counselors who pushed him. He began making veiled threats.

Finally, Greene kicked him out of the program and wrote a damaging report that marked him as a poor candidate for rehabilitation. In the years that followed, as the parole board continued to turn down his efforts for an early release, he realized he'd made a mistake. But Greene wouldn't let him back into the program. He swore to other inmates that someday if he got the chance, he would rape and kill Greene.

Luther had few visitors. His family never visited. Instead, he "adopted" families and friends of other convicts. In particular, he got to know Skip Eerebout's boys—Byron, J.D., and Tristan—watching them grow up over the years as they visited their father, and Skip's wife, Babe.

Friends sent him the occasional card or letter. A couple of women who had been given his name by mutual acquaintances also wrote, but they all soon dropped out of his life for one reason or another.

One such woman was Bernadette Florea, who had been introduced to him by friends after his arrest in 1982. A born-again Christian, Bernadette had taken it upon herself to minister to Luther in an effort to bring faith into his life. She visited him in the various jails to which he was assigned as he awaited his trial. Then she kept up a telephone and letter correspondence with him after he was sent to Canon City until 1984, when she noticed something that frightened her greatly.

Luther hadn't wanted to talk a great deal about the rape of Mary Brown whenever Bernadette pushed him to confess his sins and purge his conscience. But he did tell her that he beat the girl because she physically resembled his mother.

"I hate my mom," he had shrugged. "And the girl reminded me of her."

The conversation had disturbed Bernadette for more than his apparent lack of remorse. Petite with dark, shoulder-length hair parted in the middle, Bernadette realized with a chill that she, too, looked like Luther's mother when she was young. Afraid to just cut off the relationship—he would, after all, get out someday—she began distancing herself from Luther and eventually stopped responding to his letters.

Time after time, Luther's requests to have his conviction overturned or his sentence shortened had been turned down. His complaints that "my rights were violated" fell on deaf ears. But the bitterest pill of all for Luther came in late 1988, when he approached his mandatory parole date in 1989.

Luther went to the parole board hearing fully expecting to be told a date in the not-too-distant future when he would be released. He was angry. He had been given a year off the fifteen-year sentence in 1985, but otherwise he'd been made to do every minute of seven years with no early parole. Every time he'd come before the board Mary Brown and the deputy from Summit County, Joe Morales, had been there to recount all the gory details. Gloria Greene's letter in his file followed him to each hearing, too. Together they slammed the door on his release.

Now, believing the parole board would have no choice but to let him out, he swaggered into the room with a smirk on his face. He'd get his date and tell these bastards what he really thought of them. "Remember my number," he told the parole board director. "When this is over, you're going to want to know it." But he was in for a shock.

The parole board knew that Luther and Robert Thiret, who had raped a 3-year-old girl and then dropped her down an outhouse toilet in the mountains and left her for dead in 1983, were both coming up for mandatory parole.

Many years before, overcrowding in the state's prisons had caused the Colorado legislature to pass a law giving mandatory parole to any felon who had completed half his sentence. Now, however, the parole board was determined to keep Luther and Thiret, locked up as long as possible.

A weak case due to bad police work had forced the district attorney in Thiret's case to settle for a ten-year sentence. Neither man had ever shown any real remorse about their crimes or made much of an attempt to get help. The board believed they would remain dangerous when released and asked its lawyers to find a way to keep them in prison.

The answer was found ten hours before Luther was due before

the board. There was a loophole in the statutes governing parole board decisions that allowed the board to keep sex offenders beyond their parole dates—if they were deemed to still be a risk. The board's attorneys felt their statutes took precedence over the mandatory parole legislation (an opinion later upheld by the state Supreme Court).

So when Luther swaggered into the board hearing room, his parole was denied and he was told that they could keep him for another six years. Luther "went off" on the board, swearing that he would someday get out and then he would rape and kill their wives and children.

Luther had another reason to hate. The loophole in the law was all the proof he needed that he was being singled out and persecuted.

Thomas Luther apologized to Debrah. It was time, he said, to explain why he hated the police. They'd killed his children.

He'd met their mother in 1969, when he was in the Army and stationed at Fort Carson, south of Colorado Springs. Soon she was pregnant. His son was born when he was in Vietnam on August 25, 1970. A daughter was born March 11, 1973. They never married because they couldn't get along. But being with his kids and spending time with them was what kept him coming back to Colorado.

Shortly before he was sent to prison, he bought his son a motorcycle. A few years later his children were both on it when it was struck by an officer who was chasing a 16-year-old boy through a residential area in a car.

"My ex let them buy her with $170,000," he wrote. "Plus they charged the boy that the cops were running after with two counts of vehicular homicide. They sure didn't take responsibility for their actions."

To make matters worse, he said, prison officials hadn't notified him of the deaths for ten days. Then they took him to "the hole," stripped him, and only then told him the awful news.

"They kept me like that for five days," he wrote. "I cried for days and needed to be held and wanted so much to be able to hold my babies just one more time."

Maybe she could now understand where his anger came from, he said.

It was all, of course, a pack of lies. He'd never had any children, been married, or in the military, much less Vietnam. But Debrah, who also believed that he was two years older than her rather than five years younger, bought it.

When she read about the supposed death of his children, Debrah had not yet learned to recognize what she would later think of as harmless "Tom Luther stories". In fact, she thought the tragic account explained a lot about the man she was falling in love with. His anger. His vulnerability. His toughness. Still, she said as her own tears fell for the "murdered" children on the letter she wrote back, he was going to have to learn to control his anger if they were ever going to have a future together.

Luther agreed. It had taken prison and losing everything he had worked for, especially the kids, but he'd learned his lesson. That's why he'd forgiven his mother, whom he hadn't talked to in ten years, and told her he loved her.

Throughout the rest of 1991, and indeed the years beyond, he continued to heap more lies onto their relationship. He said he was a peerless hunter and fisherman with kills and trophies still on the record books. He and his dad had hunted mountain lions for the bounty and raised world-champion hunting dogs. One time, during his buffalo-raising days, he had to jump into a pen to distract an enraged bull "that was goring and stomping a guy." Only through his daring was his old girlfriend "Sue" and the other man's wife able to carry the man to safety.

Luther was always the hero of his stories, even those taking place in the penitentiary, such as the time he stopped prison hitmen from killing a young inmate over a drug deal: "They'll have to come through me first." In another, he wouldn't allow older inmates to rape a newcomer. And in one letter, he announced that he had been thrown in the hole because he dared stand up to the guards who were hurting his young friend, "Southy" Healey. It was hard, he said, but a price he was willing to pay for justice.

The lies piled up until he couldn't remember what he had told her and when. Here and there, Debrah would note one of the little inconsistencies. But it took much longer to uncover the big fibs; it was beyond her comprehension that someone would lie about the death of "his" children.

As she began to catch on that Tom wasn't always truthful with her, it didn't change how she felt about him. Men lied. It's just the way they were. Neither of them realized at the time that "Tom Luther stories" would ultimately be his downfall.

The tall tales she could accept. But she continued to be troubled about his anger. Luther blamed television and the media.

"Violence is so common that some people fantasize what it would be like to just kill someone to take out all the frustration and anger on them like the movie stars do," he wrote.

Debrah called him on it. "I know that after nine years prison life has got to have affected you," she responded, "but I had hoped you would be wanting to start changing the way it has affected you and start thinking in ways that are more aligned with functioning in society rather than a prison population.

"I'm sorry for the lecture . . . but I don't like 'convict Tom.' I like and want to have a relationship with Tom who gets lonely and needs to be held and hugged, the Tom who likes hounds, horses, and hiking. . . . When I get letters from the other Tom, it just sounds like one of the many convicts bitching about an unjust system . . . they're all innocent men kept there by a corrupt justice system."

Luther waited two weeks to respond. In part to punish and part because he had been moved to Centennial Correctional Facility, a higher security prison. Then he laid a guilt trip on her.

"I'm sorry that's how you feel," he wrote on November 3, 1990. "I feel that you are a little unfair."

He reminded her that, unlike some inmates, he hadn't used her to bring in dope. He had never asked her for money. "I needed love and friendship from someone with whom I could share intimacy. My impulse was to write and tell you if that's how you feel to screw yourself."

In the six months he had known her, he'd written fifteen times; they'd talked by telephone and she'd visited him in the prison at least once a week. She was dependent on him for her happiness. But he decided they better cool the relationship, at least for a time.

Debrah was devastated.

* * *

Luther did not write to her again until February 1991. And only after he had learned that she had driven to Canon City, hoping that he hadn't taken her off his visitors list and she would get a chance to talk to him. She was disappointed and had returned home more depressed than any time since she first met him.

Dennis was estranged. Her eldest son, Chance, had left home to join the service. Her other son, John, hardly paid any attention to her and was getting into minor scrapes with the law. She continued to write to Luther. But as weeks went by with no response, she wondered once more if anyone would even notice if she died.

When at last he wrote, her hands trembled as she opened the envelope with the Department of Corrections return address. He had written "Happy Valentine's Day" on the envelope and drawn his trademark—a smiling cartoon face topped with a halo. She prayed that he had forgiven her again.

Not quite. He told her that she was a very difficult person to get along with, and not to write to him when she was tired and cranky. He professed to be very sensitive and his feelings got hurt easily.

Still, he was willing to give her another chance. Then he changed the subject. He was sorry to hear that Chance had joined the service and hoped he would not end up in the Gulf War, like his friend Skip's son, Byron Eerebout.

He wrote her lies about living in Saudi Arabia and wanting to move to Canada or Mexico when he got out.

Luther ended by telling Debrah he cared about her and she could resume writing, although he wasn't ready to see her again.

In fact, they did not see each other again until April. Then it was as if nothing had ever come between them. His letters were more romantic than ever.

"There is no such thing as a knight in shining armor," he wrote. "I would, however, love to be yours, even for a day. I want to take you in my arms and carry you to a nice, quite [sic] cabin in the mountains. There we can practice being close and touching . . . just for starters."

As the weeks passed, his letters, which he now signed "Love,

Tom,'' grew more sexually oriented. He wanted to take showers with her. He hoped he could turn her on enough for her to be the sexual aggressor. ''In fact, I hope you can become an animal in the threshold of the intense passion we are going to share one day,'' he wrote, ''with multiple emotional orgasms before we even make love.''

Whenever his letters stepped over the line, she would write and tell him that she was uncomfortable with his fantasies. He would then apologize, assure her that he was also interested in her as a friend and looked forward to quiet hours spent just cuddling. A few paragraphs later, he'd be right back on the sex track.

However, Luther wasn't limited to sexual fantasies. He also was going to make the state pay, he wrote, for the additional years they'd tacked onto his sentence as soon as he won a lawsuit he had just filed. He figured two and a half years' back wages would be enough to buy that ranch in Vermont.

''I have a destiny in this life. . . . I believe you are going to be part of my destiny,'' he wrote. It won't always be easy, ''never in your life will you meet another person close to me in goodness and badness.''

And Debrah replied, ''God, I love you. Sometimes I practice detachment, because so many of the things you say bother me; but as soon as I read one of your letters or as soon as you touch me, all my efforts become fruitless.

''I guarantee your relationship with me will not be the same as with any relationship with any other woman from your past.''

Neither of them could have known then just how prophetic their words would be.

That fall, Debrah Snider got a new job as a nurse at the Colorado Corrections Diagnostic Center in Denver. In the meantime, Luther was transferred to the Fremont Correctional Facility. He didn't tell her and she had no idea that Fremont was where the state sent its most recalcitrant sex offenders.

On Debrah's first visit, a female guard hinted that Tom ''has problems with women,'' but there wasn't time for her to go into detail. ''Why would she say something like that?'' Debrah asked a few minutes later when he joined her in the visiting room. "You're in for assault."

Tom shrugged. They all had it in for him because he demanded that prisoners be respected, he said. Then he changed the subject.

A few days later, Debrah asked a friend at the diagnostic center to punch Tom's prison identification number into the computer. Her mother was visiting from New Mexico—a reconciliation that Debrah had agreed to at Tom's urging—and Debrah planned to take her to the prison in two days to meet him. But the Fremont guard's comments nagged at her.

Debrah's friend typed the numbers and stood back. Debrah blinked when she looked at the computer screen, and then asked her friend to make sure she'd punched in the correct numbers. It came up the same. According to the information, Tom, her Tom, had been sentenced to prison for assault . . . and sexual assault.

A rapist? There had to be a mistake. The next day she drove to the courthouse in Breckenridge where, according to the computer printout, Tom had been tried. She asked to see his file.

It was worse than anything she could have imagined. Mary's statement was there, as were the police reports of Deputy Morales and Detective Snyder. There was no drug deal, he had picked the poor girl up at a bus stop. Then he had brutally raped her, vaginally *and* anally with the wooden handle of a hammer. He had beaten the woman so badly that the windows of his truck had been smeared opaque with her blood.

Debrah started crying as she read the statement of Tom's victim. "I asked if he had done this before," the woman had written. "He said yes, several times. That's when he picked up the hammer. . . . I thought he was going to hit me with it."

And there was more. After the assault, Tom had gone home to his girlfriend and told her he thought that he had killed someone. Then he had slipped out of his bloody clothes and made love to her. Despite Tom's confession, this girlfriend had stuck by him through it all. What kind of woman would do that? Debrah wondered as she paid for copies of his records.

Driving back from the mountains, her eyes brimming with tears, she thought about steering her car off the road to tumble down some precipice, never to be missed. Only the desire to confront him kept her going.

She showed the files to her mother when she got home. "Well, it's bad," her mother conceded after she read them. "But it's also in the past. From what you've told me, he's a changed man."

Debrah nodded. Yes, the man in the files and the man she had fallen in love with did not seem to be the same. But it wasn't just the brutality of the rape. He had lied to her. If there was anything she hated, it was a liar. Her father had been a liar, her first son's father had been a liar, all those men with their wives had been liars. She had been lied to all of her life.

What else had he lied about? His past? The love letters? Their plans? Was it all smoke? She almost didn't go to the prison.

Almost. He'd later tell her that he knew she'd found out the moment he walked into the visiting room and saw her face. But he only shrugged when she told him that she had discovered his lie.

"I told you I had assaulted someone," he said. "You're the one who figured it had to be a man and just an assault." He denied that he had raped Mary with the hammer; in fact, he said, sex had very little to do with it. The girl had ripped him off in a drug deal and had then attacked him because she thought he was going to rape her.

Debrah didn't believe him. The woman's account was too real, too horrifying to be a lie. She had made up her mind to leave when Tom leaned over and touched her hand. There were tears in his eyes. "I love you, Deb," he said. "I just didn't know how to tell you without you cutting me out of your life."

In that moment, she forgave him. She couldn't help it. Without him, she had nothing to live for—and he wasn't the same man he had been in 1982. That man had been some sort of uncaring animal. Her Tom was sensitive and loving. He was a little wild, yes. He had a problem controlling his anger. But he was like one of her wolves—don't push him too far, recognize the two sides of his nature, and encourage the gentle one.

And I'm just the woman, she thought, *who can tame Tom Luther.*

* * *

"I can't get over how well you took the news about me. I didn't know what your reaction would be and tried to tell you a little at a time."

Debrah read the letter from Tom with satisfaction. For once in their relationship, she had the upper hand. With her support, he said, he'd get treatment when he got out of prison.

"You can't imagine how disappointed I was in myself when I did this crime. I detest, loathe, hate the violence in our society . . . being violent isn't my cup of tea.

"I promise I will never physically or mentally abuse you. I will just shut down and go away first."

Luther told her that if she saw "the signals"—such as his constant coming and going, flirting with other women, and anger—she was free to call him on it. He confessed that he was "addicted to sex". But it wasn't this admission that should have sent a danger signal to that part of her that was a psychiatric nurse, a signal she ignored; it was his next statement.

"I think about sex more when I get mad and aggressive," he wrote. "When I get angry, I naturally think of sexually demeaning thoughts. That's part of what happened with Mary.

"I wasn't intimidating enough when I was kicking the shit out of her. But when I got the idea to sexually abuse her, I had the effect of intimidation that I was seeking."

In October 1991, Debrah Snider testified before Judge Hart, pleading for a sentence reduction for Luther. Hart noted that he had received a number of letters and telephone calls of support from Luther's friends and family. But, he said, he also had a statement from Mary Brown urging him not to release her assailant.

In the nearly ten years since the attack, Brown had regained control of her life. She had been the prime mover behind legislation passed by the Colorado legislature that removed the distinction between "foreign object" and a rapist's body for determining second or first degree sexual assault. Rape was rape.

She had taken self-defense courses that had the added benefit of building her self-esteem, eventually becoming an instructor. And she had fallen in love with an understanding and patient man who held on when she tried to push him away; they had married.

She had been denied her chance to face Luther in court. But she had kept track of him and done everything she could to see that he stayed in prison for as long as possible. She told the judge she was still haunted by him. He already had tried to kill her not once, but twice. She feared he might try again.

In view of Brown's objections, Hart said he didn't feel he had enough evidence that would allow him to make a conscientious decision to release Luther. He wanted a psychiatric evaluation, independent of the Department of Corrections, as to whether Luther still posed a risk. He said he would rule later in the month.

Luther held out little hope. "It's this hammer shit that always comes up," he wrote. "That just gets their goat so bad that they can't even act professional.

"They have taken me to a private part of the penitentiary for seven days in a row where nobody could see and kicked the shit out of me. They deny me phone calls to my attorney and throw away my mail."

But, as always, he saved his most vitriolic abuse for the prison sex offenders program and Gloria Greene. "She deserves to be raped and beaten," he growled to Debrah as he paced in a corner of the visiting room like a trapped animal. "That'd show her what it's really like."

When Luther got that angry, it was as if he didn't know where he was or who he was talking to. His eyes reminded Debrah of the bull in a bullfight poster on the wall of the office where she worked. Injured and in pain from the sharp, hooked sticks sunk into its shoulders, the bull's red eyes were mirrors of hate and a desire to kill his tormentors.

"No one deserves that, Tom," she scolded him. But he didn't seem to hear her. As a psychology professional who had read the court files regarding his attack on Mary Brown, she recognized that Thomas Luther could be dangerous. But as a woman, she remained convinced that with her love and support, he could make it on the outside without posing a risk to other women. She'd just have to keep him away from temptation so that they could live a quiet, simple life together.

Snider wrote again to Judge Hart. Please, she said, "he's a

changed man who has suffered enough, and we want a chance at building a life together.'' She was worried; Tom seemed to be slipping into such a dark depression she feared he wouldn't come out of it . . . at least not alive.

Tom wrote to tell her that if the judge didn't let him go in January, he was ending their relationship for two reasons. The first was he didn't want her to suffer with him. He wanted her to find a man that could love her and give her support.

The second reason, he said, was he planned to take a hostage and make the guards kill him. He wasn't going to let the bastards abuse him for the rest of his life. He intended to go into his hate and combat training so he would be able to hurt and kill those bastards when he got out.

''I'm walking the edge of being a good man or just saying 'fuck it' and being worse than they could ever imagine out of spite. I was man enough to take my punishment, but these bastards don't know when to stop.''

A few days later, he got more bad news. Hart had decided against a sentence reduction. Luther decided to go on a hunger strike and withdraw his visitors list. He wrote Debrah to get his message across, that their deprivation and punishment had gone too far.

Chapter Seven

January 6, 1992—Alma, Colorado

Detective Richard Eaton of the Summit County Sheriff's Office stood beside Sacramento Creek listening to the silver movement of the water running beneath the thin coating of ice. He was at the spot where the body of Annette Schnee had been found by a boy on a fishing excursion nearly a decade earlier.

It was a beautiful, if lonely, place for Annette to have died, Eaton thought. The creek wound like a snake from the snow-capped peaks to the west across South Park, a high plain that lay between two arms of the Rocky Mountains, dotted with lonely ranch houses and the occasional small town like Alma. The land lay locked in winter beneath a pale blue sky, much as it had back when Annette was killed. Looking west, he could see the V-shaped cleft in the dark wall of mountains that identified Hoosier Pass, where Bobby Jo Oberholtzer died.

Around him bustled the film crew of the television docu-drama *Unsolved Mysteries,* which he had contacted late in 1991 in the hopes that a re-enactment of the deaths of the two women might generate new information from viewers. Eight years earlier, he had promised their families that he wouldn't stop until he brought the killer, or killers, to justice. But now, though he would admit it to no one, he was running out of ideas.

Eaton looked at his watch and cleared his throat. "In a couple of hours, it will have been exactly ten years since Annette Schnee was last seen alive," he announced. The film crew, actors, and private investigator Charlie McCormick stopped what they were doing and stood quietly looking at the surrounding beauty.

Eaton had been working on the Oberholtzer/Schnee cases since 1984, a year after he joined the Summit County Sheriff's Department. A Navy veteran, he had more or less drifted into law enforcement, working for small-town police departments before moving to the mountains.

A few inches short of six feet, pot-bellied, and laid-back, he didn't look much like a Hollywood version of a homicide detective. But his looks and demeanor were deceiving. Over the years, Eaton had proved to have the tenacity of fox trying to find a way into the henhouse when on a case. Especially this case.

The files on the two unsolved murders had been passed around a lot before he literally pulled them from a trashcan. Both the Summit and Park County sheriff's departments had worked on the cases. But except for McCormick, an intense, wiry private investigator who worked part-time for the Park County sheriff, all other efforts had ground to a halt.

When Eaton began looking at the files, the first thing that struck him was how disorganized the investigation had been. The files themselves were a mess; bits and pieces of notes and reports had been tossed in haphazardly. Some items were not even dated. But gradually, as he sifted, he came across the names of not only potential witnesses but possible suspects.

One of the latter had been some guy named Tom Luther,

who'd pleaded guilty in another case and had been sent to prison the year Eaton arrived in the county. But from what the detective could tell from the files, Luther had been looked at in connection with the two murders and nothing had come of it. Believing that his predecessors had done their jobs, Eaton turned his attention elsewhere.

In particular, he was interested in Jeff Oberholtzer. It was a good thing that Jeff had admitted giving Annette a ride after he was shown her picture. When her backpack was found near the Hoosier Pass parking lot a few months later, Jeff's business card was in her wallet, which might have been difficult to explain if he had continued pleading ignorance.

Like his predecessors, Eaton had considered Oberholtzer the prime suspect. He wasn't sure he believed Jeff's explanation for why he had been seen with Annette and began trying to fit the pieces together to make a case against the young man. But unlike his predecessors, Eaton, with McCormick working the Park County side, was meticulous, leaving no stone unturned.

Eaton and McCormick started by trying to track down and reinterview every witness, concentrating initially on information leading to Jeff Oberholtzer. To their surprise, they discovered that the police in 1982 had never interviewed Joe Urban, the man who had stopped at Jeff's house a little before 7 P.M. Urban was able to vouch for Jeff's whereabouts up to 8 P.M.

Suddenly, the detectives realized, Jeff Oberholtzer wasn't such a good target. Annette was last seen a little after 4:30 P.M. by the pharmacy clerk in the company of the mysterious dark-haired woman. She never made it home to change into her work clothes, which meant she was more than likely abducted between the pharmacy and Blue River where she lived, fifteen minutes away.

On the other hand, Bobby Jo called home and spoke to Jeff before going to the bar with her friends shortly before 6 P.M., a time her friends had later confirmed. Then she had been seen hitching at approximately 7:50 P.M. in Breckenridge.

If Jeff was involved, he would have had to have abducted Annette in Breckenridge sometime after 4:30, driven back over Hoosier Pass to the area of Sacramento Creek and killed her. Somewhere during that time he would have had her undress, possibly raped her, and then let her dress again. All by six o'clock, when he was home to receive his wife's telephone call.

After that he would then have to have calmly shoveled snow until Joe Urban arrived a few minutes before 7 P.M., gone to the gas station, a liquor store, and then back to his house to drink beer and watch television until eight. Then, only after his friend had left, could he have driven to Breckenridge, located his wife, taken her to the Hoosier Pass summit and there murdered her.

Eaton didn't want to put on blinders. Maybe Jeff's wife had called when she couldn't get a ride, and he met her in Breckenridge sometime after eight o'clock with a plan to kill her, he speculated.

Was it all possible? Only with an incredible amount of luck, timing, and cold-blooded precision, the detectives concluded. And what would have been the motive? Breckenridge was a small town and Alma smaller still; there weren't many secrets. Yet, there was no report from family or friends that the Oberholtzers weren't getting along and no evidence of a love triangle; in fact, Annette had a live-in boyfriend.

A vital piece of evidence also pointed away from Jeff. The blood on Bobby Jo's mitten wasn't his. He would have had to have had an accomplice.

After Eaton and McCormick tried to make the pieces fit every which way, and couldn't without over-stretching the bounds of reason, they invited Jeff Oberholtzer to meet with them at a Breckenridge restaurant. Jeff arrived not knowing what to expect. For years he had lived under a cloud; frustrated by police efforts and suspicions, he had tried investigating his wife's murder himself to no avail.

Now Eaton told him the good news. "Technically, you're still a suspect until I have the guy who did it," the detective said. "But for all intents and purposes, you're in the clear."

Oberholtzer started crying. "Now," he asked as he wiped his eyes, "can you look for the real killer?"

The news came as a relief to Bobby Jo's husband, but Eaton was back at square one. Years passed, but he couldn't let it go, working hundreds of hours on his own time chasing rumors, tracking ten-year-old stories, trying to put the files in order.

As he investigated their murders, he came to know the two women like old friends. He knew what they liked and what they didn't. He heard from their families about their childhoods and their future aspirations. They were both young and fun-loving, but also good people who didn't associate with criminals and weren't involved in drug dealing or anything else that might have pushed them toward their fates.

It had been a mistake to hitchhike. But neither of the women were stupid; if their "benefactor" had seemed odd or dangerous they would have turned down the offer for a ride. He was either someone they knew, or someone who appeared much different than the monster he turned out to be. They were simply in the wrong place at the wrong time.

Eaton got particularly close to Annette's family. If possible, the death of their daughter had been the hardest to deal with.

Months had passed after her disappearance with no word about Annette. At first, there had been dwindling hope that she was being held somewhere alive, or maybe a blow to the head had given her amnesia. But in their hearts, Annette's parents told Eaton, they had known their daughter was dead. She wasn't the sort of girl to have run off without telling them and, of course, the other young woman had been murdered the same night she disappeared. But until the young fisherman found her body, the healing could not begin. They could only wait and imagine her body lying in some lonely spot in the mountains, far from her loved ones.

The Schnees knew that Eaton had gone above and beyond what duty called for. Over the years, Annette's mother telephoned him from time to time, to check in or talk about their families or tell him about a just-remembered anecdote concerning her eldest daughter. She sent him a Christmas card every year and invited him to visit.

Eaton had at last taken her up on the offer, if for no other reason than to lend a shoulder to cry on. He felt badly that he had so little else to give them.

One night during the trip, Annette's mother had asked to see the photographs of her daughter's body. The remains had arrived in a sealed coffin, she said, and not being able to see Annette to say goodbye had left her empty.

"It was hard to believe that it was her in there," she said. "I kept wondering if perhaps there had been a mistake, even though my mind knew better. Please, I have to see her."

Eaton hesitated. "They're pretty bad." But she insisted. "Tell you what," he offered. "I'll show you the photographs of the other girl, Bobby Jo. Then, if you still want, I'll show you Annette.''

Mrs. Schnee nodded. The detective opened one of the heavy black binders into which he had organized papers and photographs of the case. Annette's mother looked at the photographs of Bobby Jo—a dead woman whose face was frozen into a mask of despair. She swallowed hard. "I still want to see my daughter."

Sighing, Eaton turned the pages to the photographs taken at Sacramento Creek and later at the morgue. When Mrs. Schnee finished looking, she blinked back her tears. "Thank you," she said and quietly left the room.

In January 1992, Annette's family had come to Colorado for the filming of the *Unsolved Mysteries* segment. They stood quietly with the others when Eaton made his announcement at the place where Annette, the happy child in their family photo albums, had been found.

The next day, the Schnees and Eaton gathered with everyone else at the top of Hoosier Pass as the film crew prepared to shoot the scene re-enacting Bobby Jo's final moments. To get the camera angles and lighting right, the director had the actress playing Bobby Jo lie down in the snow where the body had been discovered ten years earlier, almost to the hour.

It took the crew forty-five minutes to get everything just right. By then, the actress was shivering and turning blue from the cold. She was not dressed for the weather; in particular, her boots had been designed for fashion not practicality, and her feet felt like frozen blocks of ice.

The director told her to go warm up and come back for the final take. As the girl stood and moved painfully toward a trailer in the parking lot that had been set up as a dressing room, Annette's mother rushed forward to cover her with a blanket.

As Eaton watched Mrs. Schnee half-carry the poor girl to warmth and safety, he felt his throat tighten. A mother who had been too far away on the night a monster took her daughter was trying to make up for it the only way she could. When the actress returned to film the scene, he noticed that she was wearing the warm winter boots of Mrs. Schnee.

* * *

Luther's hunger strike lasted all of two weeks. He had hoped to bring the American Civil Liberties Union running to his cause by claiming to be a political prisoner, but was disappointed when the only person who seemed to care was Debrah Snider. And there, she may have cared too much even for his ego.

Debrah, of course, panicked that he would really carry out his death wish. He had been placed into a segregation cell again and not allowed any visitors. Kept from seeing him, her letters were filled with hysterical threats to kill herself. Maybe, she wrote, she'd drive onto railroad tracks and wait until a train came along. She'd make sure she left a note placing the blame on the uncaring attitude of the Department of Corrections.

"What the fuck are you doing?" Luther wrote back. "Just because you can't see me for a couple of weeks, you're falling apart at the seams and ready to do something stupid. Get a grip!" He signed the letter, "Tom, the time bomb."

But Luther wasn't about to chase her off. Debrah was sending him money orders to pay for their telephone bills and for him to buy himself a few extras at the prison canteen. More significantly, she'd also put up a $10,000 retainer to hire an attorney to look into ways to get him out.

Debrah was hopelessly in love. She was even beginning to accept his ardor and increasingly descriptive accounts of their future love-making.

Yet, Luther wasn't completely self-assured. In late January, he wrote to tell her that the attorney she hired wasn't working out because he wouldn't take directions. Their only hope, he said, might be to hire an independent psychologist to evaluate him in order to put Judge Hart's mind at ease. Thiret had been released in December 1990, so there was hope. But, he warned, she should be aware that he might have to finish his full sentence.

In their letters and during their visits, Tom and Debrah fantasized about what their lives would be like when he got out. He'd stay for awhile at her mother's cabin in the mountains near the lake. But he wouldn't remain in Colorado long, he said. The authorities were sure to harass him and, besides, he had a plan, his "project," to grow marijuana plants in the mountains of New Mexico.

The money, he said over her objections, would let him buy a ranch somewhere, maybe he'd even buy out Dennis's share of her place. Then they could quietly live together, raising animals and keeping to themselves. He assured her that he would drop the idea of the project if it looked too risky; he said he wouldn't do anything if it would cost him more than a couple more years in prison if he got caught.

In March, Luther began talking to psychologist Robert Atwell, whom Debrah hired to perform an evaluation at a cost of $6,000. Luther wrote to her of the initial meeting, that he was trying to be honest, but in the past honesty had always gotten twisted into something negative.

On April 2, he wrote again telling her that he had finished the evaluation. "I don't know how I did or what he thinks. I just let it all hang out. I hope he don't think I'm some kinda animal and he can see it clear to let me go to a halfway house of some kind." He signed off with his usual, "Can I lick you?"

As a month passed and Atwell still had not finished his report, Luther began to grow increasingly pessimistic and paranoid. Even if he got out, he said, the cops would never leave him be.

"They think I'm such a risk, they'll arrest me for something I didn't do and convict me on false testimony. They believe they are doing society a favor by getting someone like me off the streets."

Each week, his outlook grew grimmer. If Atwell's report was negative and the judge ruled against a sentence reduction, he didn't want her to visit anymore. He seemed to recognize that a battle was going on within him for what philosophers would have called his soul and psychologists his psyche. A setback would push him farther towards the darker side of either, if it wasn't already too late.

"I can just get my attitude right for revenge and hate," he wrote. "I'm driving myself crazy trying to be something for you that I can't be right now and, to tell you the truth, I probably won't be for weeks after I get out.

"I'm borderline. I need to retreat and watch myself extra close for awhile. I have a heart half bad and half good."

* * *

In June, Atwell issued his report. It was not encouraging, but certainly shed light on some of the missing elements of Luther's childhood and subsequent development.

Tom's sexual experiences began in childhood when he was molested by an adult male. "He reports that his victimization involved mutual masturbation," Atwell wrote. "He experienced ongoing guilt, shame, and confusion related to his sexuality following that experience.

"He identified lingering feelings of sexual inadequacy associated with the physical differences in size between his own penis and that of the perpetrator."

Shortly afterward, Atwell reported, Luther began indulging in "sex play" with other children, "in which he described himself as 'the abuser.' " At age 12, Luther was involved in a sexual relationship with a woman, apparently an aunt, Atwell wrote, who treated him as "her little man."

As an adult, his relationships with women were sexual rather than for emotional intimacy. "He says he has a very strong sex drive and enjoys daily, often repeated, love-making with his girlfriends. He currently masturbates daily."

By February 1981, Luther's relationship with Sue Potter was breaking down; they argued frequently, centered around his drug use and the financial burden she presented. During this time, Luther told Atwell, he developed a fantasy about being in control of a relationship that had evolved into a rape fantasy. "His fantasy was of having his position of control validated by a strange woman who would acquiesce after being stalked and confronted, and with whom he would then enjoy consensual sex.

"He denies, however, that he had this fantasy in mind when he picked up his victim at the bus terminal. . . . He believes that the rape occurred because he was acting out his need to be in control. He is unclear how that need might relate to his childhood conflicts with his mother . . . but he denies any current or ongoing rape fantasies."

Luther told the psychologist that he hoped for a "viable, satisfying relationship" when he got out of prison with Debrah Snider. She was "the only one who had any expectations of him."

The psychologist had his doubts. "Tom appears to have only limited access to his emotional experiences . . . his judgment in highly emotional situations is likely to reflect idiosyncratic interpretations of others' behavior toward him.

"Thomas Luther's emotional life is characterized by acute episodes of ragefulness . . . emotional storms. While his rage episodes are intense, they are generally short-lived. He denies any ongoing destructive or homicidal ideation related to people he is angry with, but acknowledges being overwhelmed by such feelings in the past.

"He reacts strongly to experience of invalidation and/or confrontation by women with anger and brooding resentment."

While Luther would prefer to have others think of him as a "hyper-responsible, good person, his vulnerability to psychological injury and his limited capacity to tolerate emotional discomfort without responding with rage, impedes his efforts."

"Tom frequently protects himself from injury by adopting a tough guy posture," Atwell reported.

The psychologist diagnosed Luther as having a personality disorder with "features of Sexual Sadism." "He in many ways appears to be a man continuing to be tormented by his childhood abuse."

Atwell's prognosis for Luther dealing with his anger was not encouraging. Tom, he said, continued to express "strong, hostile feelings toward women rooted both in his relationship with his mother and his aunt."

Luther had significant needs to be addressed in a sex offender treatment program but wasn't likely to get it through the Department of Corrections because of his hatred of the program's director, Atwell reported.

On the other hand, Tom's "history of explosive, violent release of aggression toward women mitigates against treatment in the community without the most stringent of safeguards." And he would probably fail in any program that demanded the client be confronted with his behavior, the predominant psychotherapy used with sex offenders.

The frightening dilemma, according to Atwell, was that Luther was unlikely to receive adequate treatment but would still complete his sentence in a maximum of four years and be released "without being rehabilitated and without any supervision requirements."

In other words, the lion would be back in his domain, hungrier and angrier than ever. And God help the woman who crossed his path when he was on the prowl.

Luther, of course, reacted to the report with anger. He chastised Debrah for hiring Atwell without laying any ground rules. For $6,000, they could have had the psychologist make a positive evaluation. He knew Atwell wasn't going to help his cause because Atwell was a sucker and believed in the system. He was not going to put his reputation on the line.

But when he wrote to her again on June 20, he had changed his tune because Judge Hart had said he would still consider placing Luther in a community corrections facility, essentially a halfway house with mental health programs. The judge was concerned about what would happen when Luther was freed. He would remain a prisoner, but he would have more independence and less restrictive visiting privileges ... maybe even weekend passes.

Luther felt this was a good thing and now felt Atwell had done a "very good job." "Facts are facts, and he paints a very clear picture of what you're dealing with. I hope that 'reading' it don't scare you away. . . . We've finally been given a chance to show all these creeps that don't believe in us," he wrote.

In 1992, Luther wrote nearly 200 letters to Debrah Snider, many of them begun on one day and ending several days later. At his most prolific he was spending $2 a week on stamps and another $100 a month for telephone calls. She, of course, paid.

Much of what he had to say dealt with daily prison life—the lack of "yard time," living with "slobs" in a seven by ten-foot cell, the quality of the food and, of course, the inhumane behavior of the guards. In September he complained that he hadn't been allowed out in the yard one day because his nine-year-old prisoner identification card no longer accurately described him. The card said he had brown hair, though by now it had turned gray.

His hatred had remained constant and he hoped God would give the guards to the devil.

Other letters were full of inmate ''humor.'' Many expressed his feelings for Debrah in romantic language. However, as the months passed his letters also grew more pornographic as he described the various positions he wanted to experience as he ''penetrated'' her. Invariably, she would respond that such detail made her uncomfortable and she was not at all sure she that she could live up to his expectations . . . or sometimes even wanted to. He would apologize in the next letter, then revert back.

Still, while she was alternately protesting or gingerly accepting the excesses of his libido, she was obsessively jealous of his frequent references to other women. In one, he hoped that she wouldn't mind that he fantasized about ''bedding them all.'' He mentioned that since she was still married to Dennis, perhaps he should have ''an extra wife.''

When she responded to that with anger, he wrote that he was only teasing . . . sort of. ''I've never told anyone that the root of my problems is I'm always looking for the ultimate experience. I'm never quite happy with what's normal. . . . Your conservativeness really makes me question if I'm some kind of over-sexed human.''

Of course, he said, he wouldn't share her with another man, nor did he really want another woman. He only wanted to be for her, and prayed to ''the Great Spirit'' almost daily to keep him from temptation. The only reason he would want other women would be to prove his manhood to himself.

However, he said, if she could ever see herself joining him with another woman, well . . . Debrah almost blew a gasket over that one. He pointed out that she was the one who was married while in love with another man.

Throughout most of this correspondence and visiting room affair, Debrah's husband, Dennis, had remained remarkably restrained. He offered to sign the ranch over to Debrah even though he had originally purchased it and supported it by working the same job for twenty-five years.

Luther was suspicious of his motives. ''He fears a threat just around the corner,'' he wrote. ''I'm a little afraid of him for you, lover. Emotions are unpredictable and he has a lot of stuff in there he don't know about.''

Later that summer, Dennis, hurting despite himself because of his failing marriage, fought bitterly with Debrah. Tom was using her, he said; he would leave her as soon as he got out and on his feet.

Debrah told Luther about the argument. He replied that if Dennis got in their way, he'd introduce him to his friend Mongo, who was now free. "Mongo not like mean people," Luther laughed.

When the arguments between Dennis and Debrah continued, Luther grew threatening. "He better stop upsetting you, or I'll see to it that his righteous ass meets God. You're my girl now and he better understand that. He's no longer your husband, I am. . . . I am the alpha male here."

Whatever sensitivity he showed toward Debrah, Luther was never far from his anger. In hindsight, his letters offered a fascinating glimpse of a man who may have wanted to be "a good guy," or at least to be thought of as such, but who could not control his darker nature. A man with a heart half good, half bad. The alpha wolf—the pack's best killer. His letters proved prescient.

"If I have to hide in the mountains and sneak out at night to be able to be with you that's what I'd do. I feel like howling with the wolf that's warning me of my weakness and death," he wrote in one letter.

And in another, "You're water all clean and pure, and I'm oil all dirty and spoiled. It's a fact, Deb, that oil and water don't mix. . . . There's death here and pain for many. I love you, Tom."

At times, he seemed to hold onto Debrah as if he knew that she was the only one who might have been able to save him. "A few years ago, I was convinced that I could go out of here and hunt these bastards down and kill them one at a time and get my revenge. But you reconditioned me with your love and tenderness. . . . I get on these kicks that I could be the monster."

It was hopeless. Lion, wolf, or monster, he was a predator, and Debrah Snider of all people should have known she couldn't change his nature. She certainly had enough hints. "I can't shake this anger," he wrote. "I'm trying to understand why I push when I should pull, why I hate when I want to love."

Perhaps then Luther had a premonition when he wrote, "I want to love you forever and be with you longer. . . . The only thing that could change that is something really unthinkable happening or you calling the law on me.'' He wondered if he really was allergic to prunes. ''Or did God put us together for a purpose.''

If so, it was not the purpose Luther had in mind.

Luther learned in August that he would not be accepted into the community corrections program; with his record as a violent offender they didn't want to take the chance. There was also a concern from his probation officer that the woman he listed as his main outside support was married with a family.

For once, Luther took bad news well. To hell with the community corrections program, he now hoped that Judge Hart would simply reduce his sentence and let him out at the end of the year. Time and again, he had reminded the judge that he was a victim of an unjust justice system, that he had accepted a plea bargain under an ''implied contract'' that he would be out in seven years.

Luther wrote to Hart asking him to consider probation with the stipulation that he get treatment. ''I would do very well with intense supervised probation because I want to perform the duties of a good man. I need to get my life going after this long time I've been away in a time lock. I need to stop being dead emotionally and love this wonderful caring woman that has come into my life.

''Please don't punish me any more. I've done that all my life to myself. Open the gate and let me start walking the road to prove myself. I'll make you proud sir.''

With the letter sent, Luther's bigger concern was keeping Debrah from going off the deep end. On Labor Day, after hearing about the community corrections rejection, she wrote him a letter talking about suicide again. She said she would wait until December to see if what he said about the judge commuting his sentence would come true. ''But I'm afraid. I'm afraid of your going crazy again. I don't want to feel the way I felt last November and December [when he went on his hunger strike and was moved into the segregation cell].''

"You can use your anger to shut out your feelings. I can't. I'd rather die like I felt today—sad, but okay.

"I hate Judge Hart. He may help your life if he cuts your sentence, but if things don't work out the way you think they will, he won't have helped my life at all."

She said she had lost her faith in God. "People who hurt other people can be forgiven for their mistakes. If they get to go to heaven, then I want the opportunity to donate my part of forever to them because I don't want to be anywhere forever with them. My interest in sex just died again. I love you, Debrah."

Luther responded by chastising her. He reminded her she talked about suicide and swearing off sex whenever something bad happened. He'd prefer she wrote to Judge Hart to tell him her family understood the situation.

"We both are going to get out of our prisons someday. . . . I'll throw my life away for you. I'll kill for you. But you're going to have to tuff [sic] it out and wait for me."

Debrah settled down and followed up on his request to write to Hart, assuring him of her family's acceptance of Tom. Then she took it a step further; she also asked her husband, Dennis, and 14-year-old son, John, to write as well.

Dear Judge Hart,

My name is Dennis. My wife Debrah Snider has a relationship that she is very serious about with a Mr. Thomas E. Luther who is in the Colorado correctional facility.

Debrah asked me to write and tell you that I know about this relationship, because she told me that there was a concern about letting Mr. Luther go before his sentence is up because Debrah is married.

Debrah and I have had some very rough times with our marriage in the last five years. Debrah and I came to an understanding that we would try just being friends and stay together for economic advantages rather than for mutual affection. This agreement did not work out for either of us.

Debrah and I have a small acreage that we have built up over the last fifteen years that she is afraid of losing.

I told her to find someone else and I would leave. I believe this marriage will end, even if Debrah did not find somebody else to share her life with.

Sincerely, Dennis Syzinski.

Dear Judge presiding Tom's case,

I'm hearing that you aren't letting Tom out. Now why is that?

I'm Debrah Snider's son John. You know my mom's the one that Tom is seeing. I have talked to Tom over the phone and saw him in some pictures. I know what crime he committed and how bad it was. Wait before you say anything! You should know that people can change and he has had something like 15 years to change.

My mom and he are really close. If my mom is having a really bad day and Tom calls, it's like rain to sunshine in half a second.

My parents have never been real close and being separated I think would make us all happy.

Thank you, John.''

Dear Judge Hart,

''I wish I could write you with the honesty of my fourteen-year-old son—untainted by the knowledge of the price of honesty; unhumbled by the appreciation of the power of your position, your ability to give orders that can affect the happiness of so many people who are now involved in Tom's case.

My children have grown up in a war zone. I did my best to love my husband and attempted therapy numerous times with him, only to have him leave therapy with the interpretation that he was 'getting screwed.' Our relationship has been functional at best.

I am grateful to my husband for staying to help keep me from losing my place and all that I have. . . . My husband hates the place, my animals, all my hopes and dreams, and was grateful for the possibility of someone rescuing him from his burden. I think for a moment that he was more disappointed by the denial of Tom's release than I was.

Tom has a niece and nephew whose lives are out of control and who are already involved in the abuse of chemicals at a very young age. He has asked me if I would help with these kids because their mother (his sister) is not able to control them due to her own chemical abuse. I'd be glad to help with these kids, but I can not do it alone. If Tom and I are able to do anything to help these kids, we need to begin now.

I hope you will be able to give us all something more concrete than just the false hopes of this last year. Tom is a good man and our being able to begin a life together will have a positive effect on me and my family (including my husband whom I can then give the divorce he has wanted for years).

No one except those directly involved know what's best for their lives. . . . I hope you will allow Tom and me to make the decisions that will affect our lives and the lives of the people we love, and that you will make the one decision that will affect Tom's life and my life that only you can make—the decision to let him go.

Sincerely, Debrah Snider

Even though Debrah was cooperating, Luther soon had another worry. His mother wrote to say she wanted to come visit him and attend a hearing in October before Judge Hart.

It would be the first time he had seen her since the late 1970s, he wrote to Debrah, and he wasn't sure if he was ready yet. "I've always hated my mother and kept my whole life from her.

"She feels guilty in some way for me being in here for the crime I committed. . . . I'm not sure I could control my tears and pain for her not being able to mother me when I needed her when I was young and in adolescence."

Actually, Luther may have been more worried about what his mother might tell his girlfriend. But, despite her son's misgivings, Betty Luther flew to Colorado in October. Debrah Snider picked her up at the airport, and Betty stayed with her and her family in La Porte where they had plenty of opportunity to talk.

The result was an angry letter from Debrah to Luther. He had lied to her again! For one thing, he was five years younger than she was. And his mother had never even heard of a former wife or children. "What else have you lied about?" she demanded.

When Luther wrote back he noted that he was angry with his mother for "telling my secrets." "I would have done it myself if I thought you could have handled it. I love you, Debrah, more than I've ever loved any woman. I would wash dishes in a restaurant if I could just be with you and share your life."

The age difference was easily explainable. He'd never dated women his own age because they weren't mature enough for him. He claimed Debrah was the closest in age of any woman he'd ever loved.

As for his story about the children, he just hadn't told her the whole truth. He said he'd met a girl in New York when he was 14 years old and out on his own. "Bernadette" was a junkie with two children—Glen and Glenda—from Colorado Springs. She'd moved to Vermont with him, but he'd kept her and her children a secret from his family.

Bernadette, he said, prostituted herself for drugs and often left the children in his care. They had called him dad. The little girl was deaf and he'd hold her and they'd cry together because they were both so empty. Bernadette's mother had written to tell him they were killed on a motorcycle.

"I'm sorry Debrah that I haven't always been truthful—that I've been misleading and straight out lied to you. When I first started seeing you, I never expected that we would fall in love and that after you learned about what I was in here for you would still consider a relationship with me. . . . When I get out, you can ask anything, and I will tell you the truth."

However, he went on, why did she have to know *everything* he had lied about? He suggested that she had some deep-seated psychological problem. He reminded her that Chance's father had lied to her and that it was probably old scars from that relationship that drove her to dig things out that might hurt their relationship. He told her to quit dwelling on the past and enjoy the future. After a couple of years, he would share his "pain, denials, and secrets."

Any tears he shed for his lost children when he wrote the letter would have been crocodile tears. It was just another lie, and Debrah even saw it as such. It didn't matter. She knew that her lover was an obviously troubled man. That he would be a liar was no surprise; men had lied to her for her entire life. It's just the way they were.

Debrah believed that he did love her, his letters practically oozed romance and eternal togetherness. She knew that he needed her. He had even said he would kill for her—not that she wanted to encourage that kind of talk, but it was the sort of thing a dragon-slayer might say . . . even an imperfect one. She began to call his lies "Tom Luther stories"—tall tales to build up his ego.

Someday, she thought, *I'll hold him to his promise to tell me all of his secrets. Someday, I'll make him tell the truth.*

Someday would never come.

Fate is a tightrope walker. A slip one way and events tumble out in one pattern, a slip another way and an entirely different future unfolds. If Luther had served the remaining two years of his sentence, certain individuals may have been spared tragedy, but perhaps only to have it visited on others at a later date with altogether different consequences.

In November, Hart relented and set a release date for Thomas Edward Luther of January 14, 1993. "With good time," Luther wrote Debrah excitedly, "I should be out by December 25. . . . I want to spend the first few weeks doing nothing but cuddling with you in bed. . . . Now, I need to write Skip and Mongo and tell them the good news."

Home for Christmas. To Debrah, it had to be a sign from God.

Now that he was really getting out, Debrah Snider and Luther went through a period of trying to sort out their feelings. It was one thing to imagine a future, quite another to have the future staring them in the face.

Luther wrote that for some reason he was staying in his cell as much as possible. It was where he felt safest. When he left, his neck got sore from tension and he felt panicky. He claimed to be experiencing anxiety attacks.

He admitted "being afraid" of freedom. He wished there was

a way he could start with a few day passes and retreat at night to the safety of his cell.

Debrah cautioned him that she wouldn't start enjoying sex right off the bat. He'd have to be slow and patient with her. Psychologist Sigmund Freud would have had a field day interpreting what it meant when, during this time, Debrah tried to castrate an ornery bull she owned and ended up killing the beast.

The march of time toward Luther's impending release had the pair alternating between frequent spats and giddy highs—such as his suggestion that they send Judge Hart a Christmas card. They would be married by then. He thought the judge would get a kick out of getting a card from Mr. and Mrs. Tom Luther.

Luther wasn't happy that Dennis Syznski was still around. He was not going to live in some cage on a mountain at Debrah's beck and call until she decided if he could take Syznski's place.

She was still upset that he apparently intended to pursue a life of crime, despite his assurance to make Judge Hart "proud." He talked about robbing banks so that he could buy her a ranch in New Mexico while he pursued his marijuana project. She didn't want to stay around to see him mess up again. She wrote that she was considering moving to Alaska.

To which he responded by accusing her of trying to hold him back, "just because I don't want to be a financial burden to you. . . . I'd like to lay my hands on some real cash. But knowing you, you would throw a fit and try to put that stupid suicide trip on me, which pisses me off and makes me feel guilty."

Reality was getting to be too much, he wrote, he didn't want to talk about him getting a job or treatment for awhile. "Let's talk about our first litter of puppies. Or having our first horse foal. Let's talk about our first walk to your water hole. Hand in hand. Two kids in love. Full of passion. . . . I love you so much, Deb. I'm going to marry you some day."

In mid-December, just two weeks from his release date, Luther couldn't take the pressure anymore. Complaining about stale crackers in the prison cafeteria, he started throwing food, was taken to a segregation cell and charged with attempting to start a riot. He tried to explain the incident to Debrah as refusing to "kiss ass," and that he'd still "beat the paperwork" regarding the cafeteria incident and get out as scheduled, but she didn't believe it.

On December 17, she wrote him a letter complaining about his lack of self-control, which he immediately marked up with his own comments and sent back.

"I feel like our relationship has regressed about 730 days," she wrote. "Last year when you did this I thought it would kill me, this year it doesn't hurt nearly as much. In fact, it only hurts slightly more than it did in 1990.

"I know that you are not dumb. But there are people who choose not to be involved with criminal activity and I am one of those people. I don't know what makes you think you should be special and not have to struggle like the rest of us ordinary people. This one thing that you want to do is illegal. You are choosing to make everyone who ever questioned my involvement with you right."

Alarmed and angry that she was discussing his plan so openly, Luther wrote in the margin: "They read the mail, and I said I'll give it up!"

Debrah's letter continued, "I wish you luck and I know now that I can't ever make you happy. You want things that ordinary people can't have, and I'm an ordinary person. . . . Dennis is not going anywhere. He told me that you would take off, and he was right. He may cause me unhappiness from time to time, but he is reliable."

Luther responded, "Fuck Dennis. You want him, keep him. You'll wake up someday."

"Those wonderful endorphin filled moments that we spent together in the visiting room," she continued, "are just memories that will soon be painful memories because I can't have the dreams we talked about, that I gambled my life on.

"I don't believe you will ever come back. If you are successful, you'll have enough money to buy yourself any place you want and you won't need to come back to hated Colorado. You won't need sexually inhibited me who believes in the system you hate.

"I don't think I regret any involvement with you," she wrote. "You gave me a taste of life and love that I would never have known without knowing you."

Luther added, "Want the rest?"

"It's very painful to have to accept that my Christmas was

traded for a tantrum over some crackers and my future is going to be traded for a criminal fantasy involving an easy start. I don't suppose that you'll ever understand that there are some places where some behaviors are never okay."

Debrah concluded by saying her only choices were Alaska or hell. "And I think Hell's the better choice because it's warmer. I love you, Debrah."

Luther also enclosed his own letter. "I don't think you really love me, Deb. You won't even give me a chance. I'll be here Christmas Day waiting to be picked up. If you love me come get me."

But she was right and he was wrong. The prison paperwork got through, giving him a new discharge date of January 5. He was to remain in segregation with no visitors until January 1.

"I'm sorry that this happened," he wrote. "I should have been in prerelease or some place to ease back into the world. But no, not Tom Luther. They want to send me out in the dead of winter totally dependent on everybody. They need to fucking die."

Debrah wrote back that, "I'm always going to do what I think is right or best, not necessarily what you think I should."

Typical of his light-switch personality, Luther's next letter was written as if nothing had happened. He was back on the sex track, discussing how he wanted to "mount" her "stallion style . . . since you don't like the term 'doggie-style.' I can't wait to feel your soft pink skin against mine." She noticed that the "weeks" he had once mentioned wanting to cuddle her in her mother's cabin were now down to "48 to 72" hours in a motel.

On Christmas Eve, he wrote one last warning. "The stuff in my files is going to follow me and haunt me for the rest of my life and probably the lives of whoever I'm around. That's why I want a ranch so I can keep to myself."

He said he had been troubled by a dream in which he beat his brother William's head in with a rock "because he was going to kill you."

"There was a lot of rage in the dream," he wrote. "I hope I'm not turning into a mass murderer. . . . In the future baby, if I'm doing something wrong, and I'm getting carried away and you can stop me, I would appreciate it. Love ya, Tom."

Chapter Eight

There is an old children's fable in which a frog and a scorpion meet at a rain-swollen creek. As the frog prepares to cross, the scorpion begs for a ride on his back.

"I am afraid that you would sting me, and I would die," the frog says. But the scorpion promises that he has no such intentions, and at last the frog agrees.

However, halfway across the creek, the scorpion suddenly stings the frog. "But why?" asks the frog as he begins to slip beneath the surface of the water. "Now we will both drown!"

"I couldn't help it," the scorpion says with a shrug. "It's my nature."

January 4, 1993—Fort Collins, Colorado

The day before Tom Luther was to be released from prison, Debrah Snider received a telephone call from Skip Eerebout. He was in Colorado and wanted to pick Luther up.

Debrah hesitated. She and Tom had another argument the day after he got out of segregation. He was still talking about getting even with "the cops" and going ahead with his marijuana project.

"When you get out, go ahead and call your friend Mongo to come and get you, 'cause I'm not gonna be there," she said. But he'd been so contrite in the letter he wrote after she left that she had forgiven him. If she didn't want him to do the project, he said, all she had to do was hold him "and tell me we don't need that. . . . I love you the mostest. Kiss me you fox."

Tomorrow was the day. They'd be together forever. That's what he said and she wanted more than anything to believe. She'd laid out the "Indian princess" dress she was going to wear, one Tom always said got him "hot." She went over in her mind a hundred times that first kiss away from the prying eyes of guards.

"Oh no, you don't," she finally told Skip. "After all the work I did to get him out, I'll be the one picking him up. You can come if you want, but we're going to want a little time alone after that."

Debrah wasn't sure why she had volunteered to let Tom's former cellmate go along for the ride. She had nothing personal against Skip Eerebout; from what Tom told her, he had a successful construction business in Chicago and led a Christian ministry for ex-convicts. Tom often talked about the Eerebout boys— Byron, J.D. and Tristan—and their mother, Pam Rivinius, who he called "Babe," like they were family.

It was just nerves about being alone with Tom, she thought. Still, she was relieved when Skip laughed and said, "No, you're right. . . . I'll catch up to him after you two have had a chance to get acquainted."

So Debrah went by herself on January 5, 1993, to pick up Tom Luther when he walked out of the Colorado penitentiary, a free man for the first time in almost eleven years. On the drive north to Fort Collins, they sat in her car like teenagers on a first date. He kept telling her how great she looked and tentatively put his hand on her thigh while she giggled like a nervous schoolgirl.

They spent the night in a motel. Tom was gentle and patient, and for one of the few times in her life, sex lived up to its billing. As she lay against his chest with his muscular arms around her, he said it was only going to get better. She believed him and silently scolded herself for ever doubting him.

However, the honeymoon lasted only until the next morning. At 8 A.M. there was a knock at the motel room door. It was Skip Eerebout.

"I gotta go," Luther explained. "One of our old cellies committed suicide in Colorado Springs . . . the cops were after him and he wasn't going to go back to The Walls.

"We're going to go console his widow," he said, pointing to Skip, who smiled and shrugged apologetically. "I was sure you'd understand."

Debrah nodded as she struggled against the tears that had sprung to her eyes. Luther lifted her chin with his right hand and gently kissed her. "I'll be back tonight, okay?"

Again she nodded and managed a small smile. What was one

day when they had the rest of their lives together? "I have some chores to do at the ranch," she said bravely. "I'll see you later then?"

Luther smiled and looked at Eerebout. "You bet," he said. Then they were gone.

It was two days later when Luther returned. He explained to his angry girlfriend that "things" they needed to take care of for the widow had taken longer than expected.

She was just going to have to learn to lighten up, he said. Once before he had warned her that his former lovers had always had trouble adjusting to his "comings and goings." It was something, he said now, that she was going to have to get used to— it was just his nature.

In the weeks that followed, Debrah Snider learned a lot about Tom Luther's nature. For one thing, even though he got a job, he had no intention of going straight. So much for washing dishes just to be near her.

Skip Eerebout had gone back to Chicago, but Tom was spending a lot of time with his sons, who lived in the Denver area. It was quickly apparent that the boys were thieves and drug dealers.

Luther would borrow Snider's truck and disappear for the weekend. When he returned, there'd be tools in the back, obviously stolen. The boys would visit him in Fort Collins and right in front of her brag about shoplifting excursions and burglaries.

Before Tom even had his first paycheck, he was flashing several hundred dollars which he used to rent an apartment a few miles from her ranch. "Won it in a poker game," he explained.

She knew it was a lie—Tom lied like some men breathe. But he wasn't even a good liar because he couldn't remember what story he told her from one day to the next. She knew from talking to members of his family that the whole sad tale about his "children" was made up, as was his claim that he had been in the army. The poker game was just another Tom Luther story.

However, there was something troubling her a lot more than the lies or even the stolen tools. It was the way he acted around women, particularly young, pretty women. He constantly flirted, whether it was with the teenaged clerk at the grocery checkout or a woman on the sidewalk. He considered himself a real ladies' man, but if they didn't respond, they were "stuck-up bitches."

Tom continued being a patient, even romantic, lover as far as she was concerned. But he couldn't see an attractive female without commenting about her body or what it would be like to have sex with her. He'd tease her about bringing another woman into their relationship.

At first, Debrah thought he was making his comments to hurt her feelings; he was always at his cruelest after they'd had an argument. But it was soon apparent that it simply wasn't safe for Tom to be around other women. With him it was never just teasing, never just looking. There was something in his eyes when women rejected his advances. Behind the smile was an angry, predatory hunger that needed to be fed.

Snider continued to live at her ranch, but spent as much time as he would allow with Luther. He started bringing pornographic videos back to his place and encouraged her to watch them with him as a sort of "sex therapy." The movies he picked were violent, rape-oriented fantasies in which a woman would be abducted and then repeatedly raped, often anally and sadistically, until she "learned to like it."

"Tom, rape is not something women 'learn to like,' " Debrah told him. But he just got mad and said she was no longer "allowed" to watch the movies with him.

She grew increasingly disturbed about his weekend disappearances. He'd leave Friday and come home Monday, even Tuesday, scruffy-looking from not shaving and complaining of exhaustion and sore muscles. He explained that his condition was because he had been playing touch football with the Eerebout boys.

Debrah didn't believe him. She couldn't imagine Tom or the Eerebout boys playing football every weekend. He often looked like he had been in a fight and would sleep all day until he had to go to work in the evening, turning down her sexual advances. She put it together—his attitude toward women, the pornography, the Summit County incident, and his weekend disappearances—and worried that he was attacking women.

She didn't know what to do. She was in love and didn't want to believe that the dark side of Tom was taking over. He could be so gentle and loving. Picking wildflowers to bring her. Happily helping around the ranch, especially with the wolves. Volunteering to help an elderly neighbor cut down a dead tree and turn it into firewood. Even Dennis accepted him into the family's life, keeping his thoughts to himself when Luther would come over to eat dinner and watch television.

If something went wrong with Debrah's day, all he had to do was touch her and it was okay. But the times she loved best were when she and Tom just sat around his place reading books. She loaned him a pair of silver, square-rimmed glasses; they looked a little funny but were serviceable until he could get his own prescription.

As long as I can be near him, she thought, *I can protect him when he gets the urge to prowl.* She found herself getting angry at young women who encouraged his flirting by smiling good-naturedly. It was more than jealousy. *Can't you see how dangerous he is?* she'd think as she glared at Tom and the girls. *I'm the only woman who can tame him.*

However, she began to wonder if she really could control Tom Luther. He wouldn't let her go with him on his weekend forays. He said he was planning "something big" that would set them up for life, but he didn't want to put her at risk if something went wrong.

Luther persuaded officials at a halfway house to release into his custody his prison friend Dennis "Southy" Healey by posing as the younger man's uncle and pleading that another relative was dying out of state. He explained to Debrah that he needed Southy, a pock-marked junkie and burglar whose arms were covered with strange prison tattoos, for his plan because the Eerebout boys were too young and unreliable.

Debrah tried to talk him out of whatever he was doing. "You can't be Joe Citizen from Monday to Friday and then a petty thief on the weekends," she said without voicing her other concerns. "You're going to get in trouble again."

"There ain't nothing petty about me," Luther replied angrily. If she didn't like it, she could walk away. After all, he said, he was doing this for the both of them.

Snider should have taken his advice and walked away. Luther was being offered a comfortable life, including a ranch and a woman who loved him. But it wasn't enough, and she had to suffer for it.

If she pushed too hard about his attitudes or activities, he'd put her on "restriction" and not allow her to visit until he forgave her. In a rare moment of insight, he agreed with her that it was dangerous for him to be alone with other women. But when she tried to get him into therapy, and even paid for a series of sessions, he found a way to sabotage her efforts by not showing up or refusing to participate when he did.

Suddenly, Debrah realized that she was going to lose him. He once wrote to her that he was on the edge of having to spend the rest of his life in prison. "I'm driving myself crazy trying to be something for you that I can't be right now and, to tell you the truth, I probably won't be for weeks after I get out." The words haunted her. How could he see the path he was on so clearly and not stop himself?

Feeling helpless, Snider decided to kill herself. This time, she thought, she would be scientific about it. She took into account her height and weight, and then looked into her medical books to determine how much alcohol she would have to consume to die. Then she went to a liquor store and picked up a bottle of 180-proof grain alcohol.

Luther was at work so she went to his apartment, where she wrote a note. "You are a liar and a petty thief. It's been one lie after another, and you'll never change. My death won't be so bad, my husband will take care of the children, and you'll be free to pursue a life of crime. I don't want to be around when you're caught. Goodbye. I love you, Debrah."

Placing the note on the kitchen table, she sat down and poured herself a glass of the liquor. Only she hadn't counted on the stuff tasting quite so horrible. She had a hard time getting it down without gagging. She took a big drink. Then another. And passed out.

Debrah woke later with her stomach in full revolt. She stumbled to the bathroom and threw up. In a stupor, she crawled into Tom's bed and fell asleep.

A couple of hours later, she heard Luther unlock the front door. She heard him pause in the kitchen and hoped he would realize how desperate she had been to write the note and come in to comfort her. Instead, he walked back to the bedroom, made a disgusted sound when he saw her on the bed, grabbed a sleeping bag and left.

When it was obvious that he wasn't going to return, she got up. He was sleeping on the floor in the kitchen.

"I'm sorry, Tom," she said, crying as she sank to the floor.

"That's all right, Deb," he replied. "We'll talk about it in the morning."

Tom stood up and bent over to pick her up off the floor. She scolded herself for ever doubting him as she pressed her face against his chest. He wasn't perfect, but her fears about him attacking women . . . that was just silly. He was good and gentle and. . . .

She was brought out of her thoughts by a sudden bolt of pain. He had run her hip into a corner of the wall as he carried her toward the bedroom.

"Sorry," he said. He dropped her on the bed and returned to the kitchen to sleep.

Debrah's hip hurt bad enough in the morning that he had to drive her to the hospital to have it X-rayed. It was a deep bruise. However what hurt worse was being put on restriction again. She wasn't to come around his apartment anymore until he'd had time to think.

Luther never asked what was troubling her so much that she would try to kill herself. He was more concerned with what her death might have done to him. "I'd have been in real trouble if you died in my apartment," he lectured her. "The cops would have been all over me."

Several days went by before he forgave her. Only this time, the relationship had changed dramatically; from that moment on, he was totally in control. He no longer told her when he was leaving or when he was coming back. He no longer had any compunction about asking her for money. If she complained when the Eerebout boys were visiting and treated her poorly, she was the one he told to leave.

"That's how important the boys are to me," he shrugged when she cried. "Skip is the best friend I ever had, and he expects me to look after them."

Still, Snider was not ready to give up on him. Somewhere was the man who had written nearly 300 love letters over two and a half years. She had to try to save him.

When Debrah learned that Luther, Healey, and one of Healey's sisters were casing expensive homes in Fort Collins and planning a burglary, she tipped off the police. She thought that if he got caught for something small, something for which he would receive a light sentence, he might realize how close he was to ruining the rest of his life. She would rather have waited for him another couple of years than have him commit a crime that would take him from her forever.

The plan didn't work after the trio spotted police in the area and gave up for the night. Still, Debrah wanted to believe that would be enough to get him to think twice about his life of crime. But she couldn't shake a feeling of impending doom.

In mid-March, she gave Luther the down payment and co-signed the loan papers for a new blue Geo Metro, a sporty, two-door coupe. She hoped that he would drive her to Washington to see a friend. Maybe, if she could get him away from the Eerebout boys and Healey, she could straighten him out.

"Can't," he said. "Got something big going down."

Debrah nodded. "Please be done when I get back."

"Okay, lover," he said and smiled his old sweet smile. "It'll be over, and then you and I will have the rest of our lives together."

In the two weeks that she was gone, Luther gave her even more reason to hope. He called often and wrote her several letters. He missed her. He loved her. It was all going to work out.

The night before she was leaving to return to Colorado, Debrah and her friend rented a movie, *Executioner's Song,* based on the book by Norman Mailer about Utah killer Gary Gilmore, who had been executed by a firing squad. *Tom ought to see this,* she thought, *maybe it would scare him straight.*

Debrah decided that she would rent the movie again when she got back and ask Tom to watch it with her. It would be too late.

Cher Elder was in love. She'd met her boyfriend, Byron Eerebout, at a party in January when he intervened between her and a former boyfriend who was pushing her around. Byron was kind of wild in a sexy, outlaw sort of way, and she knew he occasionally did drugs, but he was nice, tall and handsome. She was, after all, only 20 years old—a short, pretty girl without a whole lot of experience with men.

Born in Glenwood Springs, Colorado, Cher's parents had divorced when she was a little girl. She spent a lot of her early years bouncing between the two homes. As a teenager, Cher had lived in California for a time with her mother, Rhonda. When her mother remarried and moved back to Colorado, she had gone with her boyfriend to live in his hometown of Purdy, Missouri. Cher had broken up with the boy soon after they arrived, but she had stayed on, supporting herself by working two jobs while attending Purdy High School.

Purdy was a small, Bible-belt town of less than a thousand people in southwest Missouri. It was home mostly to poultry farmers and factory workers. Nothing much ever happened in Purdy, yet it was there that Cher got what should have been, in a world free of monsters, her fifteen minutes of fame.

Purdy was making national, even international, headlines, for a constitutional battle being waged between town youths and the religious conservatives who ran the school board over its century-old school dance ban. In September 1989, Cher and several of her high school friends were gathered at Hamburger Heaven, a local hangout, when a reporter from the *St. Louis Post-Dispatch* asked them about the controversy.

"I don't know what the big deal is," said Cher, a 17-year-old senior at the time. "You can't get pregnant by dancing."

Six months later, *Newsday* ran its own story about the dance ban along with a photograph of Cher and her friends as they "discuss the upcoming senior prom—a private function to circumvent the rules." The motion picture *Footloose* was based on the teenagers' battle.

In another local matter, Cher reported a teacher for carrying on an affair with her best friend. The accusation forced the teacher's resignation, as well that of the school board chairman who had tried to sweep the scandal under the rug.

Otherwise, Cher was a well-liked, if somewhat boisterous for local sensibilities, teenager. The good, quiet folks of Purdy chalked up her aggressive nature to the unfortunate circumstance of her having lived in California. She graduated from Purdy High with honors before moving back to Colorado to be near her parents and half-siblings.

In March 1993, Cher was working as a waitress at the Holiday Inn in Golden, Colorado, where her father Earl, half-sister Beth, and half-brother Jacob also lived. But she had bigger plans.

Cher had enrolled at a Denver business college to study accounting and expected to start classes on Monday, March 29. "I'm finally doing something with my life," she told her best friend Karen Knott during one of their daily chats. Another symbol of the change, Cher had cut her dark, shoulder-length hair into a short, punk style.

She was so excited about school that on Saturday, March 27, she neatly stacked all of her schoolbooks and supplies on a nightstand, and laid out her clothes, like a kindergartner getting ready for that first day. The only thing that came close to matching the excitement of her new life was her relationship with Byron Eerebout.

There had been other boyfriends in Denver, but nothing serious. Byron, on the other hand, had given her his ring, a gold band with three diamonds set in a diagonal across the face. It was too big for her finger, so she wrapped the band with string so she could wear it. When he mentioned that his apartment was lacking nice furniture, she gave him $700 to buy a waterbed to share with her.

On Saturday afternoon, Cher drove her silver Honda Civic to Byron's. In the past few days, they'd been having difficulties over a woman named Gina Jones, who had been hanging around the apartment. Byron claimed that Gina was "just a friend," but Cher wasn't so sure.

Byron wasn't home when she arrived, but she was let in by his younger brother, J.D. The youngest brother, Tristan, came out of a back bedroom and joined an older guy who was sitting on the couch, drinking a beer. His name was Tom and had been introduced to her on a couple of other occasions as a friend of Byron's father.

Byron arrived a few minutes later with Gina and Adriel Borghesi. The girls gave each other dirty looks, and Byron scrambled to keep them apart. Gina left but returned a few hours later to find Cher sitting on Byron's bed while he took a shower. It sent her through the roof. "Me or her," Gina told Byron.

When Byron told Cher that he was going to a local bar with

Gina and Adriel all hell broke loose. "You bastard!" Cher shouted as he left. "You son of a bitch!"

When Byron was gone and couldn't hear her anymore, Cher burst into tears. She was left alone in the apartment with J.D., Tristan, and Tom Luther, who offered her a shoulder to cry on. "Let him spin his oats," he sympathized. "He'll come back to you, you're a lot better lookin' than that girl."

In the meantime, he suggested, she needed to get her mind off Byron. Maybe she'd like to go get a drink, he said.

No, she replied. She wanted to go to Central City to see her friend Karen, who worked as a bartender in one of the casinos.

"Hey, that'd be great," he said. "We can take my new car."

Sniffing back her tears, Cher nodded. Tom seemed like a nice guy. In fact, he looked a lot like her father with his curly gray hair, blue eyes, and pleasant smile. She felt that she could trust him.

Cher had no idea that she would soon be in the newspapers again. Innocently, she climbed into Thomas Luther's new blue Geo Metro. "And that," as J.D., who watched them drive off, would one day remark, "was a mistake right there."

Something pulled Rhonda Edwards out of a deep sleep. She sat upright in bed and looked at the clock: 3:05 A.M. It was Sunday morning, March 28.

She didn't know what woke her, but she knew that something was terribly wrong. She was suddenly afraid for her family. Her first thought was of her second husband, Van, a long-haul trucker who was out on the road. Had there been an accident?

Then she thought about her only child, Cher. She was so far away. What if she needed her? Rhonda lived in Grand Junction in the northwest corner of the state, a five-hour drive from Denver.

Rhonda thought about calling. *But this is silly,* she thought. *I had a bad dream, and now I want to wake everybody up in the middle of the night.*

Instead, she wrote the time down in her diary. She and Van liked to record their dreams when he was on the road and compare notes later to see if they had experienced any psychic connections. Rhonda believed that she had a special sensitivity to such things, especially when it came to her family. She lay back down to sleep but remained awake for the rest of the night, waiting for the telephone to ring.

The sun finally came up and the shadows of the night fled back to their hiding places. Rhonda decided the dream must have been a bit of indigestion or concern for Van.

The telephone call didn't come for two more days.

Debrah Snider arrived back in Fort Collins, Colorado, a little after noon on Monday, March 29. She stopped at her place only long enough to drop a few things off before heading to Tom's. She was surprised to find him still in bed with the shades drawn. Sitting on the edge of the mattress, she picked up his hand.

"Ow!" he exclaimed, pulling it back. It was then she noticed that Tom's hands were cut, bruised, and swollen; one of his pinky fingers stuck out at a weird angle and appeared to be broken.

"What'd you do to your hands?" she asked.

"A friend gave me a case of AK-47 assault rifles," he replied. "I was afraid I'd get caught, so I buried 'em along I-70."

Snider looked at his face. His eyes darted away. *Oh boy,* she thought, *here comes another Tom Luther story.*

"I borrowed a pick and shovel from your house," he said, "but I broke the shovel and had to dig with my hands."

"Yeah, right," Debrah interrupted. "Your friends don't have enough money for gas, but one of them gave you a case of rifles?" She asked what had happened to the shovel.

Relieved that she had changed the focus of her questions, Luther answered, "I threw it away." Then for sympathy he added, "My clothes and my new boots were all muddy. I took them off so I wouldn't get my car dirty and drove off with them still on top of the car. They're gone."

Tom was so contrite about the shovel and upset about the loss of his boots, she laughed. She never thought to ask what he wore home, if anything, or why he happened to have an extra set of clothes in his car.

At the moment, she was more ticked off at him for throwing away her shovel. "I could have replaced the handle, dummy." She soon relaxed as he was so lovey-dovey and obviously happy to have her back. He said he'd gone to Central City with the Eerebout boys, but wished he could have taken her instead.

Maybe the break had been good for both of them, she thought after they made love. But her joy was interrupted by a telephone call.

It was Byron. Luther listened for a minute, then exclaimed, "Shit, just my kind of luck!" He turned to look at Debrah, then let out a big sigh of relief. "She was later seen at a bingo parlor? Well, that's good."

Tom hung up. He said that Byron's girlfriend, "Shari," had disappeared. He was concerned "because I might have been the last one seen with her."

Before Snider could ask, he explained that "Shari and Byron got in a fight. I was just trying to console her and volunteered to take her to Central City to see a friend.

"But I brought her back to Byron's apartment," he added quickly and then hinted that "Shari" had a drug habit. "She's probably getting even with Byron by pretending to disappear."

Debrah had heard enough of this Tom Luther story; she got out of bed and dressed. The whole telephone call had seemed staged for her benefit. "I thought you said you went with Byron and J.D.," she said accusingly.

If Luther had been alone with a woman, sex was involved. She looked again at the injuries to his hands and wondered what the dirt under his fingernails had to do with the girl's "disappearance."

Chapter Nine

April 1, 1993—Lakewood, Colorado

The first call Scott Richardson placed on the Cher Elder case was to the Holiday Inn in nearby Golden, where she worked as a waitress. Cher picked up her paycheck that Friday, March 26, but hadn't reported for work on Sunday or since, Cher's supervisor told him.

"And that's just not like her," the man said, shaking his head. "If she wasn't going to come in, or even be just a little late, she always called."

Richardson asked the supervisor if he could speak to Carrie Schieffer, a friend and co-worker who had told Cher's father, Earl, that she saw Cher at a bingo parlor on Sunday evening, March 28.

Schieffer repeated her information. Asked by Richardson if there was anything else she could think of, the girl hesitated, then said, "Cher's friend, Karen Knott, saw her on Saturday night. She was with some older guy. Karen said that Cher had been fighting with her boyfriend."

Suddenly, the voice that had nagged him into placing the first call grew louder. So it wasn't just a missing person case anymore, it was a missing person who had been involved in a domestic dispute. Experience told him that was significant.

Still, there was no reason to assume foul play. She could have "run away" after the fight to get even with her boyfriend, Byron Eerebout. He planned to reach out to Byron soon, but first he had other bases to cover. He called the Denver business school where Elder was supposed to have begun classes on Monday, March 29. The college director checked his records: Cher Elder never attended any of her classes.

Another call to Cher's mother, Rhonda Edwards, confirmed that Cher had not checked in there either. Rhonda told him about the dream she'd had that Sunday morning. "I wrote the time down on a piece of paper," she said. "It was 3:05 A.M." She said she had lain awake all night waiting for a call. Two days later her daughter's landlady in Golden phoned to say that Cher's boss at the Holiday Inn and her school counselor were looking for her.

Rhonda said she then called her former husband, Earl, who had contacted the Lakewood police. He also began calling her friends, but Cher had disappeared without a trace.

The distraught mother told Richardson that she hadn't seen her daughter since dropping her off in January after a trip to see Van's family in Illinois during the Christmas holiday. She spoke to Cher on the telephone two weeks earlier. Her daughter had been her usual bubbly self. She hadn't mentioned any problems, or even that she had a new boyfriend. She was just excited about starting college.

Richardson thanked Rhonda and hung up. He didn't know what to think about the woman's dream or the 3:05 A.M. note. Usually, he didn't put much stock in that sort of thing, and he had to concentrate on evidence he could use in court.

He tried calling Byron Eerebout but got only a message machine. The next day, April 2, Byron returned his calls. Eerebout was in the army, and was calling from Fitzsimmons Army Medical Center in Denver. He said he had last seen Cher on Sunday morning, about 7:30.

"I was looking out my apartment window and saw her get into her car and go," he said. "We'd been arguing the day before."

"Did she come into your apartment before leaving?"

"Nope."

"Did you talk to her at all before she got in her car?"

"No, I never talked to her again."

Although only 32 years old, and a self-described "wet behind the ears puppy" compared to some of the other Lakewood detectives, Scott Richardson already had a reputation for his innovative, sometimes off-the-wall methods. Not all of his colleagues appreciated it, either; some even thought he was arrogant and pushy. But good cops recognized that what others took for arrogant and pushy was confidence and determination.

Tenacity was certainly one of Richardson's attributes as well. But where he truly excelled was in the art of interrogation. Several cases in particular had cemented his reputation for getting confessions out of his subjects.

One became known as "The Crying Tie Episode." A young Ukrainian immigrant was suspected of killing his aunt. She had not been seen by her neighbors for several days, but the police had no body and no evidence.

Richardson marched into the interrogation room and announced through an interpreter, "You got to understand. I know *everything*, but you got to tell me the truth." The young man began crying but wouldn't talk.

Richardson scooted his chair up close, reached out to touch

the suspect's arm like an understanding brother, and then removed his own tie and handed it to the young man to wipe his tears and blow his nose. Overcome by the gesture, the young man blurted out the whole story of how he had stabbed his aunt over an argument about long-distance telephone bills and then buried her.

Another case involved a double gangland stabbing in a mall parking lot that left one boy dead with sixteen wounds and another in critical condition at a local hospital with six. The chief suspect was the leader of a Latino gang who went by the nickname of Kango.

Richardson had tried every trick he knew to get the boy talking. But Kango, a tough, stocky youth, would have none of it. He just glared at the detective and stuck to his story.

Exasperated, Richardson tried a new ploy. "Ever seen the video camera on top of the building out there?" he asked.

"Yeah," Kango replied suspiciously.

Gotcha, Richardson thought. There was no video camera, but he kept his face blank as he continued. "Well, not only do we have a videotape of what happened that night, but a security guard was watching the whole thing."

Richardson stole a look at Kango, who shrugged. The detective went on. "Now in a few minutes, I'm gonna go watch that tape, and if you don't tell me the truth now, it's gonna be tough to get a jury to believe that you didn't mean for it to happen and that you're remorseful." To the detective's disappointment, Kango still did not respond.

Richardson left the room desperate. This gang-banger was one tough nut, and without a confession they weren't going to be able to make a case. Then he spotted a blank videotape that was lying on a desk outside the interrogation room. He grabbed the tape, placed a white sticker on its side, and wrote "MALL HOMICIDE" in large dark letters.

He waited a few more minutes, then he went back to the interrogation room where Kango sat impassively. Slamming the blank video down on the table, Richardson snarled, "You lied to me. I just watched that tape . . . and saw you stab those two boys."

Kango stared at the tape, shaken by the detective's sudden

personality change. Richardson could hardly keep the smile off his face as the boy blurted out his confession.

Only later did Kango learn he had been tricked by a blank tape. His defense lawyers, of course, cried to high heaven about the rights of their client. After Kango was convicted and sentenced to life in prison, his lawyers appealed but lost. *Fuss all you want,* Richardson thought at the trial, *I'll be damned if I'm going to place the rights of that asshole over those boys he stabbed.*

Getting to the truth when it came to solving the murder of another human being was everything to Richardson.

There was no denying that some cases were worse than others. Although no one deserved to be murdered, some victims seemed to be asking for it. They associated with the wrong people, were into criminal activities themselves, or hung out in dangerous places. Then there were the "true victims," especially kids, who were in the wrong place at the wrong time through no fault of their own.

The sympathy Richardson felt for true victims had escalated a hundredfold after Sabrina gave birth in 1990 to twin boys, Brent and Brandon. He knew how much he loved his family and couldn't help but put himself into the shoes of a victim's loved ones. It made solving these homicides a personal thing with him.

A couple days after he talked to Byron Eerebout, Richardson drove to the home of the elderly woman from whom Cher had rented a bedroom. The room was tidy and clean. There was nothing to indicate drug use—no marijuana butts in an ashtray, no hypodermic needles in the trash can, no mirrors smeared with cocaine residue. But what struck him was the stack of neatly arranged school books and supplies on the nightstand next to Cher's bed. It told him that this was the room of a young woman ready to embark on a new life, a life full of promise, not a runaway.

He had contacted as many of Cher's friends and family as he could locate and had yet to find one who had seen her using drugs or described her as being particularly wild. She enjoyed going to bars with her friends, but there was nothing to indicate a drinking problem, such as frequent absences from work or unpredictable behavior.

On the evening of April 12, Richardson issued a press release. He disliked involving the media and this was sure to generate a flood of red herrings and false leads. But up to now, all he had was a bunch of dead ends. The boyfriend said Cher left his apartment Sunday morning; her co-worker said she had seen her at the bingo parlor Sunday evening, but she hadn't shown up for work. There was nothing in between or since. It just didn't smell right.

The bare bones release gave Cher's physical description and that of her car. It mentioned that she had been seen at a bingo parlor on Sunday, but not since. Anyone with information was asked to call him.

The office was soon flooded with telephone calls. A woman reported seeing a girl fitting Cher's description crying in a car being driven by a fortyish man wearing a bulky coat. Another woman called to say her daughter had disappeared along with her car four years earlier and had never been heard from since; she was concerned about what Cher's family was going through and offered her assistance if needed. Yet another woman claimed to have seen someone resembling Cher being forced into a car in Grand Junction . . . except the other alleged victim was black.

The Lakewood office also received a teletype message through the National Crime Information Computer that the body of a woman matching the generic description of Cher—5'3", 130 pounds, dark brown hair—had been found floating in a Texas river. Richardson called, but the body had already been identified as a local woman.

In the meantime, on April 14, Richardson obtained the tape of the dispatch officer's telephone call to Byron Eerebout. The 23-year-old told the officer that he had been calling everywhere, including all the local hospitals in an attempt to help Cher's family locate her.

"I understand you were with her Saturday night?" the officer inquired.

"I was with her up to . . . nine o'clock," Byron replied. "Well, actually, ten o'clock on Saturday night. Before she left and she went to Central City."

"Do you know who she went up there with?"

"Uh, Tom."

"Tom?"

"Yeah. It's my brother. Basically. His real name's Jerald Edward Eerebout II. . . . And I guess she was up there with some older guy . . . so I'm not sure if my brother even went up there. I was gone."

"How did you find out she was there with an older guy?" the officer asked.

"Uh, from Lauren Councilman. I saw Cher Sunday morning when she came and picked up her car. And then one of her friends said she saw her at the bingo place, uh, Sunday night."

Richardson listened to the tape. Who was this older guy? He was immediately concerned that after her fight with Byron, Cher had gone to Central City and met this mystery man.

Central City was an old mining town crammed into a narrow granite canyon. It was famous for its old opera hall, built by miners during the gold rush to bring culture and, hopefully, women of the marrying sort to the location.

Its glory days were long past and it more closely resembled a ghost town when Colorado voters approved legislation in 1991 to legalize casino gambling in the town. Seemingly overnight, the town went from boarded-up businesses and dilapidated clapboard houses occupied by a few hardy souls to Vegas-style casinos and a main street filled with tourists and their money. Gamblers came from all over the state and country.

Richardson feared that Cher's mystery man could have flown in from some far-off city, stuck around long enough to gamble and maybe kill Cher, and then gone home. If so, the man might be impossible to trace.

The detective was sure the man had something to do with her disappearance. But the more he thought about it, the more he couldn't see Cher taking up with some stranger. And Eerebout hadn't mentioned anything about her showing up at his apartment on Sunday morning with a date.

There was something else bothering him about the taped conversation: why had Eerebout told the dispatch officer that his brother, J.D. Eerebout, went by the name "Tom"? Could it have been a slip?

No matter which way he turned this one, he kept coming back

to Eerebout. He had no place left to go with the case but back to Byron's apartment, where he and Heylin arrived on April 16.

The detectives gave each other a knowing glance when they walked in through the open apartment door and saw Eerebout painting the walls. There was no furniture in the apartment and it was evident that the rug had just been steam-cleaned.

"My lease expired, and I'm moving out," he explained. "If I want my deposit back, I have to paint and clean the carpets."

Byron was a tall young man, red-haired and blue-eyed—good-looking in a raw-boned sort of way. Richardson noticed he had cut his finger, which still had dried blood on it. The detective also noted that the bathroom's vanity mirror was broken.

"It happened a couple of weeks ago," Eerebout explained in response to the detective's questioning look. "I was pissed off about what's going on with the army.

"I was in the Gulf War, you know, and got accused of bringing back some rifles and grenades and a couple pistols. I got hurt over there. I was hit in the back of the head by a tent pole. Sometimes I don't remember things so good. Now, they're gonna discharge me for medical reasons, 'cause of that accident.'"

Eerebout volunteered that he had been arrested by Denver police on several occasions—burglaries, assault, that sort of thing. He quickly shifted the conversation away from his troubles to Cher. "You know she had this good friend, Garfus, that she could talk to, you know, as just a friend. Maybe he knows where she is?"

Richardson had already heard about Garfus from another of Elder's friends, but for the moment he had other things on his mind. "So tell me about Saturday night?"

Byron nodded as if he had been waiting for the question. "Well, I last seen her about eight o'clock—that's when I left with my friend, Adriel, to go to Whiskey Bill's. We stayed there 'til it closed.

"Cher went to Central City and came back to my place about 6:30 in the morning. She came into my bedroom and said 'bye. Then she left."

When he got up later that morning, Eerebout said, he found two "sticky notes" on the living room window. "They were from Cher. I . . . I don't remember exactly what they said, something like, 'Now you know why I haven't been with a guy in

four years,' something like that. J.D. was awake when she
showed, and he saw her leave the notes. I'll try to find 'em for
you.''

Richardson nodded. "So what do you think happened to
Cher?''

Byron shrugged. "I don't know. Maybe she went back to
Missouri?''

The detectives were getting ready to leave when Byron's
younger brothers, J.D. and Tristan, arrived. The detectives split
the boys up and took them aside to talk.

Richardson got J.D. The teenager said he first met Cher a
month or so earlier at a party that his older brother, Byron, had
also attended.

"Cher left here about seven o'clock and went to Central City
to visit her friend, Karen," J.D. said. He shook his head at the
detective's next question, "No, I didn't go with her. I went to
sleep.

"She came back early in the morning, like four o'clock. I
heard this knocking on the door and when I opened it up, there
she was. She came in, got her coat, and left."

"Did she go into Byron's room?" Richardson asked.

"No," J.D. answered, then looked up quickly, blushing as if
he'd missed something. "Or maybe she did," he stammered,
"I'm not sure."

"Was anyone with her when she came into the apartment?"

Again, the question seemed to strike a nerve. He shook his
head again. "No. No one . . . she wasn't with anybody."

Heylin's conversation with Tristan revealed nothing of importance. But Richardson left the apartment pleased. *Get their lips
moving,* he repeated to himself. He'd just caught Byron in a lie.

When he interviewed Byron that first time over the telephone,
the young man had been absolutely sure that he'd had no contact
with Cher on Sunday morning. She hadn't come into the apartment, he'd said, he'd only watched her leave from his window.
Now his story was that she'd not only come into the apartment,
but into his bedroom to say goodbye, taking the time to write
and place two notes before leaving.

Then there was J.D. He said Cher had come into the apartment,
retrieved her coat, and left. The younger brother came across as

someone desperately trying to keep a story straight, and not doing very well at it.

Richardson drove back to his office more convinced than ever that the mystery of whatever happened to Cher Elder could be solved by the Eerebout boys. It didn't bode well for her, he thought sadly. After all, why lie about a missing person case—if that's all it was?

Still, Richardson wasn't ready to put on the blinders. He placed a flag on Cher's credit cards and bank accounts; officials were to notify him immediately if there was any activity. There was nothing. He contacted the border patrol and the airlines. Again, nothing, but he hadn't expected much—her passport had been left in her room.

Nothing made sense except growing certainty that Cher was more than just missing. If anything, she was an overly responsible kid, staying in contact with mother and father, acting as a surrogate mother to Beth, her half-sister by her father's failing second marriage. She had called or visited her best friend, Karen, every day until that Sunday.

Everywhere Richardson looked—California, Colorado, Missouri—he never found anyone with anything bad to say about Cher. The deeper he dug, the cleaner she got.

Something had happened to Cher Elder between the time she left Byron's apartment, showed up in Central City with the mysterious older man, and the next morning. Why else were the Eerebout boys lying if she really had driven away from the apartment and into the blue that morning? The only item in his theory that didn't make sense was the co-worker who had seen Cher at the bingo hall on Sunday night.

On April 17, he called Carrie Schieffer and asked her again if she was sure of the date she saw Cher. "Well, let me ask my husband," Carrie replied. A minute later she came back to the telephone, chargrined. "Actually, he says it was Friday, not Sunday."

A major piece of the puzzle slammed into place. Another piece was added that afternoon when a Lakewood patrol officer called in to report finding Cher's silver Honda in the parking lot of a grocery store.

The car appeared to have been there for some time, as there was a coat of dust on it that had not been disturbed. A taillight had been broken at the scene. The car was locked, but he could see her winter coat lying on the back seat.

The discovery of the car told Richardson several things. For starters, if Elder had run away, why'd she leave her car in a grocery store parking lot? She'd either take it, or sell it, or maybe give it to a family member.

Also, the night Cher disappeared was cold and snowy. If she had picked up her coat at Byron's, as J.D. had said, she would have worn it to her car, Richardson thought to himself.

The fact the car was locked told him something else—one of those tiny, seemingly insignificant clues about the person he was seeking. If whoever brought her car to this spot was a stranger, he wouldn't have bothered to lock the doors. However, the act fit the psychological profile of "an associate murder"—the person had known Cher and locked up, probably subconsciously, much as a friend would have. Such profiles weren't 100 percent infallible, but they were right much more often than they were wrong.

The most important clue regarding the car was the grocery store's proximity to Eerebout's apartment. If Cher had met with foul play, the location of the car only four blocks from the apartment meant one of two things: Cher had driven her car there and then was abducted by a stranger in a well-lit parking lot, or someone connected with Eerebout's apartment was responsible for driving the car to the grocery store.

Added together with the locked doors, he believed the latter scenario. And that meant that whoever he was looking for was clever enough to leave the car in a busy parking lot of an all-night grocery where it wouldn't be noticed for a long time, but also a lazy son-of-a-bitch who didn't want to have to walk too far to get back to the apartment.

And that meant that whoever took Cher was probably acting alone, Richardson thought as he drove back to the office. Otherwise, he'd have an accomplice follow him in another car while he abandoned Cher's car on the other side of the state, or at least downtown Denver.

It doesn't prove anything, the little voice in his head cautioned. Maybe she was angry enough at Byron to want to make it look like she was in trouble. Then he thought of the photograph of Cher that hung on the wall of his office and considered everything he had learned about her. A devious, bitter woman, angry enough to put her family and friends through this wringer simply wasn't part of that picture.

Richardson got back to the office and filled out a roll call report to be handed out to patrol officers and detectives as they came on duty. He noted that Cher Elder's car had been found and impounded for testing. Then he hesitated before writing anymore, as if committing what he believed to be the case to paper would make it so. But there was no denying the obvious anymore. Cher was dead. He didn't have a body, there were no eyewitnesses who had come forward to say they had seen her die. But he knew.

He looked at the roll call report, sighed, and then added, "Foul play is feared." The Cher Elder case was unofficially a homicide investigation.

As far as Scott Richardson could tell, Elder's "illegal activities" consisted of using her older cousin's driver's license to get into bars and, according to her friend Karen Knott, whom he interviewed the evening after Cher's car was found, to get into Central City casinos on the night of Saturday, March 27.

Knott explained that she worked as a bartender and cocktail waitress at the Tollgate Casino. She was on duty that Saturday night when Cher walked into the casino accompanied by a man Knott did not know. She couldn't remember his name . . . only that Cher introduced him as a friend of Byron's.

"He was a white guy," she said, "forty maybe. But nice looking. Six feet or a little taller and maybe 200 pounds. He had light gray hair and kinda a square face. Oh, and he drove a nice, new blue Geo. I remember 'cause Cher talked about it."

Cher and the gray-haired man arrived about ten o'clock. After confiding that she and Byron had been fighting, Cher and the man left for another casino. Karen got off work early and joined them at the Glory Hole casino a few blocks away.

While she and Cher gossiped, Byron's friend had just hung out in the background, sipping a beer. "I talked to Byron when Cher was first missing, and he said the guy and Cher came back to his apartment Sunday morning," Knott recalled. "He said Cher left, but the guy stayed."

Richardson could almost feel the face of his suspect beginning to materialize in front of him. If what Karen Knott had said was true, Byron and his brother J.D. had been caught in yet another, much bigger, lie. Determining who the mysterious gray-haired stranger was had become even more important.

In a sense, there was a feeling of relief as Richardson drove the winding, narrow road back from Central City. At least the mystery man wasn't some untraceable stranger from out of state. He was a friend of Byron's and enough of a friend, or a threat, for both Eerebout boys to lie to protect him.

Back at the office, he received a call from Rhonda Edwards who had just learned what her daughter and Byron were fighting about. Apparently, Cher had purchased a $700 waterbed for Byron's apartment only to catch him in it with another girl.

Eerebout's painting his apartment walls and steam-cleaning the carpet were just the sort of things one might do to hide evidence of a murder. Richardson had had to wait for Byron to leave the apartment so that he wouldn't need a search warrant. He hadn't wanted to alert him or his associates.

The landlord had let Richardson into the now-vacated apartment with the crime lab crew. They had found hairs that they at first believed belonged to a dog but later confirmed were wolf hairs. They had used Luminol, a chemical which reacts with rust in blood and can be seen using a black light, and had found evidence of two types of blood.

Richardson wasn't overly excited about the blood traces they had found that day. He believed that whatever had happened to Cher Elder, happened away from the apartment. However, it would be just as important in a courtroom to prove that they had made every effort to investigate all possible suspects and crime scenes to rule out other possibilities.

Ever since he realized the case was more than a missing person, Richardson had spent every waking moment trying to make the pieces fit. Even eating dinner with his family, he was turning the facts over in his mind and hardly noticed when Sabrina or the boys demanded his attention. It wasn't like him, Sabrina thought, he was always so determined to not be like his own father when it came to his family. But the Cher Elder case was consuming him. She prayed it would all be over soon.

Her husband was hoping for the same thing, for a different reason. The longer a murder goes unsolved, the more likely it will remain that way. Trails grow cold. Witnesses move away or disappear. Suspects refine their stories. Bodies decompose, the evidence disintegrating with the flesh.

Richardson desperately wanted to find Cher's body. Nobody was going to freely admit what had happened. As far as he could tell, neither the Eerebouts nor anyone else connected to this case, had a shred of conscience. It was frustrating. Likely as not, the case rested on some tiny clue, perhaps something he had already looked at or something that would be found with Cher's remains.

For the hundredth time, he went over all the conversations, the telephone calls, the possible scenarios. He was reviewing the interview with Karen Knott when suddenly he saw the casino in his mind. It was like being hit with a lightning bolt.

Hell, there were security cameras all over those places, designed to catch cheats and robbers. With any luck, he thought, they may also have caught Cher on film with the mystery man.

But even as his hopes began to rise, so did fear. He knew that security videotapes were often recycled . . . on what timetable he didn't know. He dialed the casinos' security offices and explained what he was after.

"Well, you are in luck," said the first security chief, "those videos are scheduled to be erased tomorrow. If you—"

"Hold on to them," Richardson interrupted, "I'm on my way."

In the late afternoon of April 19, Karen Knott sat in a Lakewood Police Department interrogation room watching the videotapes Richardson had seized from the casinos. She had helped the security personnel and Richardson narrow the possibilities by recalling the areas of the casinos where Cher Elder had been.

It did not take her long now to spot her friend and the man who had accompanied her that night as they wandered through the casinos or sat at one of the gambling machines. "That's him," she said. "That's the guy."

Richardson looked closer. The tapes were grainy but the grey-haired mystery man looked like a normal, middle-aged guy—clean-cut, in shape, maybe even handsome. The mystery man now had a face.

Still, it was obvious to him that Cher and the man weren't on a "date." Cher practically ignored her companion while she gambled or talked to Knott. He just seemed to be tagging along, watching other casino patrons. Especially good-looking women, Richardson noted.

After viewing the videos, Richardson asked Knott if she could recall anything else about that night. "Just that the last time I saw Cher, she was getting into the passenger side of his car. He'd only had one beer, so he wasn't drunk, otherwise I wouldn't have let her go with him," Karen said. Then she burst into tears. "That's the last time I saw Cher."

Richardson now had a definite link between the man last seen with Cher and Byron. After his first conversation with Knott, before he had the tape, he had asked Eerebout's neighbors if they had seen a man fitting the description and his new blue Geo. Several of the neighbors recalled such a man and the car; one even recalled that the license plate frame had been from a dealership in the Fort Collins area.

With the tape in hand, Richardson asked the neighbors to come to the police station the morning after the day he met with Karen Knott. "Is that the same man you saw at Byron Eerebout's apartment?" he asked pointing to the gray-haired man following Cher around on the videotape.

"Yep, that's him," said one neighbor. "My husband got into an argument with him about a parking space. That's him, all right. What'd he do?"

Later that morning, Richardson asked Byron Eerebout to report to the Lakewood Police Department. The young man arrived and asked if the detective had any good news about Cher. *He's a cool one,* Richardson thought, full of the "outlaw" bravado that Cher had probably found romantic. He took Eerebout back to the video room and ran the tape, watching his reaction.

Pointing to the mystery man, Richardson asked, "Recognize him?"

"I've never seen that guy before," Byron replied.

Without changing his expression or tone of voice, Richardson ran the videos again and again asked the same question.

"Nope," Byron said again. "I might if I saw him in person, but that—" he pointed at the television set "—is too grainy."

Without revealing that he knew that Byron was lying, Richardson asked the young man to describe his relationship with Cher Elder and the events of the weekend that Cher disappeared.

"We were just friends," Eerebout said, correcting the detective's reference to Cher as his girlfriend. "I had sex with her but that doesn't make me her boyfriend."

Cher dropped by unexpectedly Saturday evening, he said, and then got angry when he showed up with his new girlfriend, Gina Jones. The girls shot each other "dirty looks," and then Cher began yelling when Byron announced that he was going to a bar with Gina.

"Then when I got home, there was a note, see, and there's two notes—in the bathroom on the mirrors." He and Gina had passed out but sometime in the early morning on Sunday, Cher had poked her head in the door and said, " 'Bye.' "

"Who was there when you got there with Adriel and Gina?" Richardson asked. He noticed that now the sticky notes had appeared that night rather than in the morning, as previously reported by Byron.

"J.D. and Tristan," Byron answered.

"So she says 'bye' and that's it?"

"That's all she said."

"Did you get up then?" Richardson asked recalling that Byron had originally told him about watching Cher leave from his apartment window.

"No. I just went back to sleep. It was just getting light outside."

"Did you look out to see if she was by herself or anything?"

"No," Eerebout said. He was starting to squirm in his seat, his eyes darting around as he licked his thin lips. He tried changing the subject. "This is what the note says. It says, 'Call me. We'll talk.' . . . And one says something to the effect of, 'Now you know why I haven't been with a guy for four years.' "

Eerebout decided that anger might throw the detective. Suddenly, he was blaming Karen Knott for telling the news media that he was Cher's boyfriend. "I . . . my mom and my lawyer

... they're gonna call the news and these places to get that boyfriend crap taken off, 'cause I was an acquaintance, you know. I had sex with her, but that doesn't make me her boyfriend. She came over to the house and, big deal, she left.''

Angry about the callous way the boy dismissed Cher, Richardson decided it was time to turn the screws. ''I don't know why you're making a big deal out of it. All this is, is a missing person.''

Byron nodded. ''Yeah, a missing person.'' He said he didn't even know Cher was missing until her family and friends started calling. ''I'm worried, too.''

Then why, Richardson wanted to know, was he acting so nervous?

Eerebout denied it. ''I can understand you guys comin' there, but you know, walking into the house asking questions about how the medicine cabinet got broke and stuff like that's a little—''

Richardson cut him off and pulled his chair closer. ''Well, you're acting like we're ... we're draggin' you in here ...'' he began, his voice even and reasonable.

''No, I—'' Byron protested, laughing nervously.

''... like we're accusin' you ...''

''Don't—that's not what I'm sayin'.''

''... of all these hideous crimes ...''

''No, I'm not saying that,'' Byron said, holding his hands up as if to ward off the detective. ''I'm sayin' ... ''

Richardson was relentless. ''Well, yeah, that's what you're sayin'.''

Desperately, Eerebout tried to shift the focus. He'd heard something about an unknown drug dealer that Cher had maybe mentioned to someone that she was going to visit. Richardson just stared at him, his dark eyes boring into the young man's blue ones.

''Wasn't she ... she seen at a bingo parlor?'' Byron stammered.

''Well,'' Richardson said, keeping his eyes fixed on Byron's as he leaned closer, ''we don't think that's good information.''

Byron swallowed hard. He complained that someone was spreading vicious rumors. People were starting to avoid him.

Richardson smiled. ''Man, you're sounding psychotic now.''

"No," Eerebout said, laughing nervously.

"Are you hearin' voices at night while you're sleepin', too?"

"No, it's . . . come on," Byron stuttered, "this ain't bullshit."

Just as suddenly as he had turned up the heat, Richardson backed off. He asked Byron what Cher was wearing that Saturday night.

"She has my ring," Byron volunteered. "It's her right finger she wore it on."

Richardson asked if Cher had told him that she was going to Central City. The younger man denied it. "And," Richardson said, pointing at the frozen image of the mystery man from the videotape, "you're telling me that you've never seen this guy before?"

Eerebout shook his head. "I can't recognize him from that thing."

He protested that his injury from the Gulf War made it difficult to remember things clearly. He'd suffered head injuries which, he said, led him to mess up during his Army stint—larceny, deserting, all sorts of things. He'd gotten a medical discharge.

"They said I was psycho. That I didn't know right from wrong." It was the first thing the young man said that Richardson believed.

Byron went on to talk about how easily he got angry. Just recently, he had broken the wrist and knocked out several teeth of a man who had picked a fight at a party. "And I beat the hell out of a guy with a stick last week. He had a knife and about eight other Mexicans with him . . ."

Richardson grew impatient. This punk knew more than he was saying and was trying to steer the conversation in another direction. "Did you ever tell anybody that, uh, Cher and this older guy came back from Central City, and the older guy stayed in your apartment, and Cher got her car and left?"

"No." Eerebout was shaking his head again. "Nope. See that's what I don't understand. People keep tellin' people stuff, and that ain't true."

Richardson waved his hand as if to dismiss Byron's remarks. He decided it was time to let Byron know that he'd been caught in at least one lie. "You remember when I first talked to you?"

Byron nodded so Richardson went on. "You told me she

never came into the apartment. She never talked to you and that you saw her get in her car and leave. Then I talked to you again, and you told me, 'Well, she came in, woke me up, and told me 'Bye.' ''

Eerebout sat for a moment looking like he'd been hit with a bat. Then he rubbed the back of his head and complained that he couldn't remember details.

Richardson gave him some more rope to hang himself with. ''Well, lemme put you to rest here,'' he drawled, back to his good ol' boy demeanor. ''I'm just pounding my head against the wall trying to figure out who this guy is that she's with up at the casino. Don't you find that odd?''

Byron brightened and acted like he wanted to be helpful. Maybe she stopped at a bar first and picked the guy up. ''If you ask everybody, Cher's an open person. She was always, 'Hi, who are you?' ''

Richardson stared at Byron until he began to shift uncomfortably and look at the door out of the interview room. ''You can go,'' the detective said at last. Visibly relieved, Eerebout stood up only to have the detective point once again to the videotape picture. ''You're sure you don't know this guy?''

Byron's mouth hung open, then he started to speak, but the detective didn't give him a chance to answer. ''Guess I'll have to give this to the news media,'' he shrugged instead, pulling the tape from the VCR, ''and get this guy's face plastered all over the television and newspapers . . . see if anybody knows who he is.''

The color drained from Eerebout's face. There was no way Richardson would have given such a critical piece of evidence to the media. But the younger man was apparently no poker player. Now, if everything went as planned, the gray-haired mystery man would soon get a telephone call from an obviously frightened Byron Eerebout. *Then we'll see,* Richardson thought grimly.

Two hours later, he was wishing he could be out riding on his Harley, away from people like the Eerebouts, when Donna handed him that slip of paper with a telephone number on it. ''Some guy named Tom Luther called, said he's the one you're looking for,'' she said.

Chapter Ten

April 12, 1993—Denver, Colorado

About the time that the Lakewood Police Department was issuing a press release about a missing girl for the evening newscasts, 27-year-old Heather Smith stood looking out the picture window of her living room. Large, heavy snowflakes mixed with equally large raindrops fell outside as if the weather couldn't quite decide if winter was really over and spring had truly begun. The day had been sunny and warm, and although it was now evening, the flakes melted as soon as they landed on the street turning it dark and shiny beneath the streetlight.

Heather had never even heard of Cher Elder. She knew nothing of Detective Scott Richardson. Even if she had read something, or someone had told her about the mysterious disappearance of a young woman only a thirty-minute drive from her house near downtown Denver, she wouldn't have paid much attention. It was just one of those things that happened to other people. A young woman must have made a mistake that put her into a bad situation—an error in judgment.

Smith worked as a bookkeeper at her father's company, had numerous girlfriends with whom she regularly frequented nightclubs on Friday and Saturday evenings, and was pleased to receive the admiring looks of men attracted to her green eyes, shoulder-length chestnut hair, and trim, athletic body.

All of her friends thought Heather led a charmed life. She could have almost any man she wanted. She owned a pretty little Victorian home in an older but well-kept Denver neighborhood. She always seemed so strong, so self-confident. Few knew that much of it was an act.

Most of her friends were unaware of her battle with her self-image that had resulted in bulimia, an eating disorder characterized by excessive overeating followed by self-induced vomiting. It had begun when she was 14 years old. Her swimming coach had scolded her for not doing better at a national competition. She had swum well enough to move into the higher echelons of her sport, but it wasn't good enough for him. Like many teenaged girls, she was already struggling with her self-image. With her coach's words still ringing in her ears, her esteem plummeted. That night she went to an all-you-can-eat buffet with the team, gorged herself, and then walked into the restroom where she stuck a finger down her throat to throw up.

Thirteen years later, she was still dealing with the same insecurities, although she had beat the bulimia after a half-dozen years of counseling. She managed to hide from her fears by playing the role everyone expected of her: Princess of the Ball. The outside world saw brave, strong, independent Heather.

No one guessed that behind the flashing smile and outward elan, was still a little girl afraid of monsters who lurked in the dark. She did not like sleeping in a house alone and would often start awake at the slightest sounds, trembling in the darkness and wishing that she could call for her mother, sure that she could hear someone breathing in the shadows.

There was only one problem her friends were aware of—her ex-boyfriend Jason. She and Jason had dated for four years. She had been attracted to his dark good looks, his air of mystery, and his moody artist persona (he painted but destroyed his works almost as soon as they were complete, which was so, she thought, romantic). He once told her that he had friends who "were into revenge," but he didn't elaborate. She had liked that little bit of outlaw in him. At first. But, always jealous and possessive, Jason had grown increasingly abusive.

One dark night after an argument, he ordered her out of his car in a downtown Denver alley. She had to plead in tears for him not to leave and let her back into the car. Another time when she threatened to leave him, he held a gun to his head and said, "Now you know what I have to live with every day." Frightened for him and herself, she had agreed to stay in the relationship.

Once he held her hostage in her kitchen while he systematically shredded a newspaper with a knife. Another time at a Lakewood bar he threw a dart into her leg. "To see how you'd react," he'd said laughing. That had ended it for a time, but he had begged her to take him back, turning on the charm, sending flowers and notes brimming with apologies.

The relationship was off and on more often than a light switch. In between, she dated other men, nice guys who adored her. But nice guys were boring, and she'd soon go back to Jason.

In January 1991, during one of the on-again periods, she made the mistake of borrowing $7,000 from him to help purchase her home. They talked about marriage, but the relationship ended for good a short time later.

Now, a year and a half later, he was demanding his money back. He followed her to her place of work and to bars where he would stare at her from the other side of the room through her circle of friends. He called and made threats. "I have nothing left to lose," he told her in March.

Later that same month, about the same time that Cher Elder disappeared, Heather told two friends about the threats. "If anything ever happens to me," she said, recalling the image of her ex-boyfriend holding a gun to his head, "give Jason's name to the police." She didn't know much about what he was doing these days but had heard from mutual friends that he was living over in Lakewood, hanging out in bars and pool rooms, describing her to one and all as "the bitch who used me."

In April, Heather Smith decided to sell her car, a sporty little Ford hatchback, to pay Jason. She regretted ever taking the money, but she had wanted the house. It felt solid and safe, surrounded by a nice mix of neighbors, young and old, who in the evenings often strolled the sidewalks beneath the ancient elm trees lining the street.

She ran an advertisement in the newspaper that Sunday, April 11, 1993, and then again the following day. It failed to generate a single call. She was watching the snowflakes and rain turn the street in from of her house black with moisture and contemplating whether she should drop her asking price, when the telephone rang.

"Is the car still for sale?" a man asked.

"Yes," she answered tentatively. It was eight o'clock and dark outside. She also was feeling a little under the weather and hoped he didn't want to come see it that evening.

He asked about the color of the car and the price, which she thought odd because both items were mentioned in the ad. When he asked if he could come see it, she told him she wasn't up to it and would prefer to wait until the following day. But he was insistent. "It has to be tonight," he said.

Smith gave in. This had been the only response to her ad and she had to sell the car. He wanted her address.

"What direction will you be coming from?" she asked as she gave him instructions on how to find her house.

"From downtown. I'll be about an hour."

The telephone went dead before she could ask why it would take an hour for a ten-minute drive.

Heather was a little uneasy about the man coming over. She decided she'd go talk to her next-door neighbor, Rebecca Hascall and let her know what was going on.

At Rebecca's, the two women talked for a half hour until Heather saw a man through the large picture window. He walked down the sidewalk before turning to go up the path to her house. "That must be him," she said as she went out the front door. "I'll be back in five minutes."

The man was standing on her front porch when she approached. "You here to see the car?" she asked. She had slowed as she got close. He was dressed in a green jacket and blue jeans. What she could see of his hair beneath a blue baseball cap and the half-light of her porch light appeared sandy brown, or perhaps graying, and curly.

He seemed like a normal guy, nothing dangerous. In fact, he was pretty good-looking for a middle-aged man, about six feet tall and muscular, with piercing blue eyes behind a pair of silver, square-rimmed glasses that didn't seem to quite go with his face. He had a nice smile with even white teeth.

There was, however, something peculiar about his nose, she thought. It was long and thin and his nostrils didn't flare out. She noticed things like that. She also noted that he had a little roll of fat beneath his chin on an otherwise nearly rectangular head framed by a short beard and moustache.

The man pointed to her car parked at the curb across the street and asked, "Is that it?"

Smith thought he looked more like the four-wheeler or truck type and wondered why he wanted her little sports car. "You looking for yourself or a wife or girlfriend?" she asked.

''Myself.'' It was obvious that he wasn't going to volunteer any information as he started walking toward the car.

''You can look at it,'' she said, suddenly uncomfortable. ''But I'm not going to drive anywhere tonight.''

The man ignored her. She shrugged and followed. He was an odd character, she decided. But she felt safe in her neighborhood, and Rebecca would be looking out for her if she didn't return soon.

Heather went around to the driver's side and got in. The man opened the passenger door and sat down. Deciding that she was being overly cautious, she put the key in the ignition switch and started the car. She showed him that the radio worked and the carefully kept maintenance records. She waited for him to ask questions, but he didn't. He just kept running his fingers along the dash. She noticed that he had thick fingers, like he worked with his hands.

''The only things wrong with it are a few cosmetic items,'' she said. ''A piece of plastic is missing under the hatchback.''

As though on cue, he said, ''I want to look at the back,'' and opened the door. Heather was just as happy to get out of the enclosed space with him. She turned off the ignition, walked to the rear, and opened the hatchback.

She was leaning into the car to show him where a piece of plastic had broken off when she felt a heavy blow to the back of her neck. Her first thought was that the man wanted to rape her and had struck her with a club. She shoved herself up and away from the car, reaching with her right hand for her neck. She was surprised to feel the rush of warm blood and a gap in her neck into which she pressed her fingers.

''*Rebecca! Rebecca!*'' she screamed, surprised even in her terror by the strength of her voice. Stunned, she didn't feel her assailant strike again . . . and again . . . and again . . . and again. She stumbled to her left, barely managing to catch herself as she collapsed over onto her stomach.

Time passed in a blur. She remembered the man bending over her like a vampire, a shadow, a monster. Then Rebecca was running toward her, screaming her name. The shadow drew back and was gone. ''Call 911. I'm bleeding,'' she told Rebecca who turned and ran back to her house.

The world came sharply back into focus. It was as if she was more aware than at anytime in her life. As she struggled to breathe, she could feel air passing in and out of a wound in her back and realized that her lung had been punctured.

Snow kept falling, striking the wet street and making little ripples which danced in the light from the street lamp above as she lay with her face on the ground. She noticed that the reflection from the ripples was turning pink, tinted by the blood that was spreading in a pool from her body.

Just as suddenly, she was somewhere else, talking to her mother about a school project she had done as a senior in high school. The subject was after-death experiences, and her mother was relating how, shortly after the birth of Heather's younger brother, she had gone through just such an ordeal. "I was on the operating table and had been pronounced clinically dead," her mother said. "I was floating above my body, and then I began moving toward a bright white light.

"There was a voice in the light. It asked me, 'Are you ready?' I wanted to go to the light, but then I remembered that I had three small children who needed me. So I asked to go back. I made a decision to live."

A decision to live. Her mother's voice echoed in her mind. Heather Smith also wanted to live. It wasn't fair to die so young at the hands of a stranger. She hadn't done anything wrong. I want to live, she told the pink ripples. I want to live.

Rebecca returned and began applying pressure to her wounds. The police arrived, followed a moment later by an ambulance. The paramedics assessed the situation and did what they refer to as a "scoop and go," not trying to stabilize her at the scene—there wasn't time—but throwing her into the ambulance and racing to the city's hospital, Denver General.

Heather, who had given a quick description of her attacker to the first police officer on the scene, kept talking in the ambulance as a paramedic tried to get an intravenous line into her neck. She had lost a lot of blood and needed the fluids as quickly as possible. She thought that if she just kept talking, she couldn't die. She talked about the attack. About how much she wanted to live. She told the paramedic her blood type and tried to tell him how to contact her parents. Exasperated because she kept moving as she talked, the paramedic finally ordered her to, "Just shut up!"

Heather had never had much in the way of a strong religious belief. But she found herself locked in an earnest internal conversation. *This can't be the way my life is supposed to end. I want to live. Please God, I want to live.*

Heather and the ambulance were gone. In shock, Rebecca tried her best to answer a police officer's questions. Her friend had an ex-boyfriend who had been making threats. No, she had never seen him or a picture of him. His name was Jason. Heather said it wasn't him. The man who attacked Heather wore a green jacket, blue jeans, and a blue baseball cap. But it was dark when she saw him, and she had been afraid.

Finally, the police officer let her leave to go to the hospital. She was covered with blood and looked like a victim herself. She didn't notice, she was so wracked by guilt. She had let Heather go out into the dark to meet a strange man. She hadn't known what to do as her friend lay bleeding on the street.

"I held the wrong places," she cried to emergency room personnel who rushed up to her. They looked at her quizzically.

"You may have saved her life," a nurse said. Cops and paramedics tried to console her. They didn't know how many times they had come on similar situations only to find the would-be rescuers had fainted or panicked.

Heather's family and friends were gathering in the waiting room. Her youngest brother, Trig, had been pried from his sister's side so the doctors could work. The other brother, Schyler, was already on his way to an airport in California. Hascall's boyfriend met her at the hospital. No one was saying much, or even crying. They were too stunned. Such things happened. But to Heather? Never.

Rebecca was persuaded to go home and shower. As soon as she could, she rushed back to the hospital, arriving just as a nurse came out of the intensive care unit. The news wasn't good. The doctors didn't think Heather was going to make it. She'd lost too much blood, and her injuries were too severe. "If anybody wants to say goodbye, now would be the time," the nurse said and left.

When it was her turn, Rebecca went in to where Heather lay beneath a heavy warming pad. Her friend's beautiful face was so swollen that her head seemed as big as her shoulders. Heather's eyes were open but rolled back until all that showed was white.

Rebecca grabbed her hand. "You're doing great, Heather," she said. The guilt welled up again and she felt at a loss for words. "Keep fighting," she said weakly. She tried to recall the Heather she knew, the princess of the ball, surrounded by admiring men.

"Hey," she said trying to smile. "One of the cops was pretty cute . . . just your type."

To her everlasting joy, Heather squeezed her hand. Rebecca burst into tears. Heather wasn't going to die.

Heather held her hand that night for ten minutes before she would let go. The next day, Rebecca went in to see her, and she was awake. Weak but alive.

"I'm so sorry, Heather. I should have never let you go out there by yourself."

Heather smiled and shook her head. "You saved my life," she whispered. Rebecca burst into tears again.

With his first blow to the back of her neck, Heather Smith's attacker had cut her vertebral artery, one of four that supplies blood to the brain. He had also stabbed her once in the middle of the back and then three more times, several inches apart, in a line down the right side of her back. One of those had punctured her lung, another had struck her liver, lacerating one of that organ's major veins. By the time Heather Smith arrived in the emergency room, she had lost two-thirds of her blood.

Dr. Bob Read was home sleeping when Smith was attacked. As the attending trauma surgeon at Denver General, his work tended to occur in the dead of night—car accidents, shootings, knifings, assaults. He grabbed a few hours sleep when he could get it.

The telephone call woke him up. Paramedics were bringing in a young woman with serious stab wounds. The young woman was unusual in that most stabbing victims were either dead at the scene or their wounds could be stabilized before they even got to the hospital. She was neither. This sounded like everything was going to have to go exactly right or she would die. He told the hospital to call again when she arrived and began throwing on his clothes.

The second call came as he was getting ready to head out the door. The young woman had just been brought to the emergency room. Read received the third call in his car. They were desperately pumping blood and other fluids into the girl. He met the team of resident surgeons just as they were lifting her onto the operating table.

Work in an emergency room long enough and a surgeon gets a feel for a patient's will to live. This girl was way off the scale as far as Read could tell. She had regained consciousness and was insisting that they had to save her.

He had noticed the gathering family as he arrived and saw how the cops, paramedics, and even the nurses lingered about. He hated to admit it, unsure if he was exhibiting some bias he didn't want to believe in, but this young woman was different. She didn't belong there.

Most patients brought into the inner-city hospital's ER for stabbing or gunshot wounds were right off the streets, usually intoxicated or high on something, and probably involved in some sort of criminal activity. Prostitution. Drugs. Robbery. It was no surprise to anyone in the ER when a drug dealer or a gang member came in full of holes. It was expected.

However, this young woman had been savagely stabbed and left to die outside of her own home on a quiet street not far from where many in the emergency room that night, including Read, lived. It was a nice neighborhood and she looked like a nice girl. No needle tracks. No evidence of drugs or alcohol in her blood. She was someone everyone in the ER could identify with.

"One of our own," he would later say. "It was a shock to realize as we were working to save her life that this could have happened to any one of us."

The less-experienced doctors wanted to devote the first order of business to the most obvious wound on her neck. But Read had taken a quick look and decided that whatever damage had been done there, it was not life threatening once the bleeding had been stanched. Instead, he decided to open her up, essentially splitting her from collarbone to navel.

As he suspected, the internal wounds were the real danger. Her belly was full of blood from the liver wound; a lung had also been punctured and she was drowning in blood. The only thing to do was keep pumping more blood and fluids into her—eventually enough to fill five adults—while the team of surgeons scrambled to close the holes.

After a couple of hours, they had to stop. Her body temperature had dropped to a dangerous level, and her blood had stopped clotting. Continuing might have killed her, so all they could do was pack her belly with absorbent material and try to get her warmed up. If she lived, they could finish their work later. But no one expected her to live.

Heather Smith surprised them all. She came to in the recovery room unaware that she was lying on a table still split open beneath a warming blanket. The world was fuzzy. There seemed to be something in her eyes, and it was as though she was peering through a tube. Then she became aware that her father was leaning over her. With a rush, she realized what that meant. *I'm alive. I'm alive.* Her mind rejoiced. She couldn't remember ever having been so happy, just before she passed out again.

In the morning when they removed the packing material, the surgeons discovered to their delight that Smith had stopped bleeding. They could finish their work. She wasn't out of the woods yet, but every minute she held on was a step closer toward surviving.

Heather not only lived but recovered at an amazing pace. At least physically. But the more conscious she became of her surroundings, the more the fear of her attacker replaced her joy at being alive. She recognized the fear. It was the old terror of monsters who lived under beds and in shadows, who struck in the dark when least expected and for no reason. Only now the monster had a face—blue-eyed, square-jawed, a nice smile.

While she remained in the intensive care unit, managing her fear was a little easier. There was a deputy posted to the unit because of a gang member who had been shot the same night she had been brought in. The police feared his enemies would come back to finish the job so an officer was assigned to his bedside. The deputy wasn't there for her, but his presence made her feel better.

However, she was recovering so quickly that the hospital soon moved her to another floor. There her fears grew. A Denver newspaper had run an article about the attack using her and Rebecca's names and addresses. All she could think of was that her attacker was still out there and now might come back for her because she could identify him. All she had to do was close her eyes and she could see his face clearly.

Every time the elevator opened outside her room, she held her breath and waited for the footsteps to pass her room. She expected that someday the footsteps would not pass and the man in a green jacket and blue baseball cap would be standing there in her doorway, looking at her with his blue eyes through those funny square-rimmed, silver glasses. She couldn't stand being alone. So her mother remained at her side during the day, and every night her dad or brothers would stay with her until she fell asleep and then sleep in the waiting room down the hall.

Fear was one thing. Shock at the sight of her disfigurement was another. When she was strong enough, she went into the bathroom and looked in the mirror. Instead of the princess, she saw a red-eyed, harrowed-looking woman with a throat swollen like a balloon and a hunched back. An angry red scar ran from her right shoulder and plunged between her breasts. Pulling up her gown, she traced the line of staples and stitches that marched down to her belly. She got back in bed and cried.

She thought she was hideous. That man may not have killed her, but he had taken the beauty and bravado she had hidden behind. Now she felt as though she had nothing left. Except revenge . . . she knew that the only way she could ever get back what had been taken from her was to stay alive and put him in prison.

Seven days passed from when she was brought into the hospital. She demanded to be released. The resident surgeons didn't want her to go. If she lived, their opinion was that she would be in the intensive care unit and then a recovery floor for three to four months. But she experienced none of the complications, such as infection, often associated with such wounds.

Smith continued to insist that she be allowed to leave until her attending physician at last deferred to Read. He went in to talk to her. As far as he was concerned, she was a medical miracle . . . and a testament to the teamwork that made Denver General one of the best trauma hospitals in the world.

Like everyone else, he hadn't expected her to live. Most people who had lost that much blood, who had suffered not one but several potentially fatal wounds, would have never made it past those first couple of hours.

As the days had passed and she held on, he knew that Heather owed her survival to several factors: her athlete's body and the fact that on that night everything—from Hascall applying pressure, to the paramedics' quick action, to the surgeons' skill— had gone right. But most of all Heather Smith owed her life to her will to survive.

Looking at her in her hospital room as she begged to leave the hospital, Read admired her courage. Her scars would heal, at least the outward ones; with a little plastic surgery, she would be as outwardly beautiful as she had once been.

The rest would be up to her, and those scars, the ones he couldn't see, weren't something he could deal with in a hospital. If she wanted to leave, he saw no reason to keep her. "Okay. You can go," he said, smiling as he caught her in mid-explanation.

The next day, Smith went to the Denver Police Department to give a statement to assault investigator Detective Paul Scott. The detective, a twenty-five-year veteran, was amazed to see her. After all, the file on Heather Smith had been opened as a homicide case. Then he'd been told that even if she survived, she was likely to be brain-damaged, a vegetable, because her brain had been deprived of so much oxygen-carrying blood.

Yet here she was, prepared to give a statement and help the police artist with a sketch of her attacker. Scott was already working the boyfriend angle. They had interviewed her friends and everything pointed to this guy, Jason. He even talked to the young man, but he had an alibi. Still, the detective figured that maybe he had put someone up to it. Why else would the assailant pick Heather's telephone number out of all the car advertisements in the newspaper?

Scott had another theory to add to Dr. Read's on why Smith was still alive. He believed that her attacker meant to disable her with the first blow and push her into the open hatchback of her car. But she had fallen to the ground instead and at 5'6" and 130 pounds, she would have been a handful to try to pick up, especially with Heather and her friend screaming bloody murder. The attacker simply hadn't had the time to take her someplace and finish the job at his leisure.

There was nothing much else to go on. Heather's friend, Rebecca Hascall, could only give a general description. There were no usable fingerprints from the car. And the man had simply vanished. There was nothing to link this attack to any others that had occurred in the area recently. No reason for him to have called a certain detective in the Lakewood Police Department who at almost the same moment that Heather Smith walked into Scott's office was getting his first call from Thomas Edward Luther.

After giving her statement to Scott, Heather sat down with the police sketch artist and helped him compose a picture of the man who attacked her. They worked on it for hours. Finally, the artist held up the drawing. It was the face of her monster.

"It's him," she whispered. "It's him."

Chapter Eleven

April 20, 1993—Fort Collins, Colorado

"If he raped her, the first words out of his mouth," Scott Richardson said as he stared out the passenger window of the unmarked police car that sped north to Fort Collins, "will be that they had consensual sex."

Mike Heylin didn't reply. He just kept his eyes on the road ahead, occasionally glancing at the farmlands on either side of Interstate 25 that ran north and south paralleling the front range of the Rocky Mountains in Colorado. It simply wasn't necessary to say anything, and his partner was more than likely talking to himself anyway.

Every once in awhile a dedicated cop like Richardson, the

kind of cop who went with his emotions, got so involved in a case it was all he could think about. Heylin knew that his partner had sunk his teeth into this case like a terrier grabs a rat. It worried him. He'd seen entire police departments' morales take roller-coaster rides on the outcomes of cases. Sometimes cops who got too wrapped up in their jobs lost their wives and families, even their own lives, when the stress pushed them over the edge. They drank too much, took chances, contemplated suicide.

So far, Scott was on top of his game. He was dealing with the Elder family's frustrations and fears, while juggling all the possibilities in his head without losing his perspective. But Heylin knew that Scott wasn't likely to let go of this one until he solved it or was broken by it.

The videotape was a stroke of luck, thanks to his partner's quick thinking and instincts. If Scott had delayed starting in on the case at the beginning, even by a day, the tape might have been erased. But they still didn't have a case, or a body, or even a clear idea of what happened to Cher Elder. They had no clear picture of who all was involved or how. This asshole, Luther, said he had witnesses—the Eerebout boys—who could corroborate his story about bringing Cher back to the apartment.

But Luther was an ex-convict, a violent sex offender, and to cops that pretty much meant he was a born liar. There was the sexual assault in Summit County eleven years earlier—Scott said the sheriff up there told him that Luther beat up that girl pretty bad. Lucky to be alive, he'd said. Guys like that didn't suddenly change in prison. If anything, they got worse—more angry, more dangerous.

Heylin glanced over at his partner, but Richardson was looking east at the flat farmlands that stretched beyond the horizon to Nebraska. Cotton-puff cumulus clouds floated one after the other above the ground. The land between the Denver metropolitan area, which included Lakewood, and Fort Collins was rapidly filling in with housing projects and new malls as the cities expanded toward each other. But there were still great open spaces that in the spring looked like a brown and green quilt with newly plowed fields alternating with those in which the first tips of wheat poked through.

At the moment, Richardson was wishing he was zipping down some county highway between those patchwork fields on his

Harley. Perhaps then he could, for a moment, forget Cher's face as the wind whipped past and he coaxed the bike into more speed.

Heylin had been right that he was mostly thinking outloud when he made his comment about Luther volunteering that he'd had "consensual" sex with Cher Elder. If she was dead and then her body was found, Luther would want to have a reason why his semen might be found in her. Killing someone to cover up a rape made it a capital crime and that meant the possibility of the death penalty.

Slow down, bud, Richardson cautioned himself for the hundredth time as he tore his eyes from the east to look north. His instincts told him that Luther was tied to Cher's disappearance, but they couldn't tell him how and hunches didn't mean squat in a court of law.

Maybe the guy was telling the truth. Richardson tossed the possibility up in the air. Maybe none of them were involved. Or maybe Luther was just being set up by the Eerebout boys as the fall guy. Then again, that was giving Byron and his brothers, none of them rocket scientists, a lot of credit for imagination.

The car reached the top of a hill. The detectives could see Fort Collins in the distance. Richardson took a deep breath and let it go like a prayer to calm himself. This interview might be their only shot. They wanted to keep him talking for as long as possible, let him make a mistake that the whole case might rest on a few months down the road. If they alarmed him, he'd demand a lawyer and that would be it. A lawyer would shut him up tighter than a rusted nut.

Apparently, Luther was already getting cold feet. He'd called just before the detectives left the Lakewood office to say he'd made a mistake and given them the wrong information. He said he'd accidently given them directions to his girlfriend's place. "Meet me at my place instead."

When they arrived, Luther answered their knock on the door. There was no sign of anyone else.

Entering, Richardson looked around, making mental notes that he'd later write down on a legal pad. It was a tiny apartment with few furnishings. He tried to commit even the smallest detail to memory, like the pair of silver, square-rimmed glasses that lay on the kitchen table where Luther invited them to sit.

Richardson looked at Luther. They were about the same height, 5'10" or so, but the ex-convict was thicker, as though he worked out a lot. *About all those guys in prison do is pump iron and plan crimes for when they get out,* he thought.

Luther didn't seem particularly hardcore, certainly no biker type with tattoos, long hair, and missing teeth. Except for the prison pallor that even a few months of freedom hadn't overcome, he looked like a good ol' country boy—laid-back, in a flannel shirt with a friendly smile. But his blue eyes weren't friendly, they were coldly sizing him up, too.

Luther's paranoia was already working in Richardson's favor. Often if the detective wanted to tape a conversation with a suspect, he had to hide the tape recorder, which presented a logistical problem every thirty minutes when the tape ran out and needed to be flipped. But he told Luther when he called back that he wanted to record the conversation so that the ex-con wouldn't have to worry about being misquoted. Luther, ever fearful of the police, agreed.

When Richardson set his tape recorder on the table for the interview, Luther pulled out one of his own. Amused, the detective laughed and said, "Yours will probably work and mine probably won't, and I'll say, 'Hey, Tom, I need a copy of that tape.'"

Luther grinned. He leaned forward and turned on his machine as Richardson hit his own start button. "We're gonna say it's, uh, six-forty, and today is four-twenty-ninety-three. Present is myself, Tom Luther, and also is Detectives . . ."

Despite the outward joviality, the men were immediately on guard, like fencers crossing blades for the first time, testing for weaknesses and strengths. Luther repeated his account of how he ended up in Central City with Byron's girlfriend, "Shari." They'd stayed until closing and then driven back to Byron's. There Shari, or Cher, he corrected himself, walked in on Byron and Gina. "She started cryin' and stuff, you know.

"And I think she said somethin' to the effect of—to Byron—'See you later,' or, you know, 'Kiss my ass,' or some kind of shit like that, and she went stormin' out. . . . I caught her at the bottom of the steps going out of the apartment, you know what

I mean? . . . She was cryin' and, uh, so I gave her a hug, told her, 'Just calm down a little bit.' "

Cher left to go call her friend, Gary. J.D. Eerebout saw her leave, he said, but he wasn't sure if Byron got out of bed in time. Himself, he didn't see her get in her car; he wasn't even sure what kind of car she had . . . just something small, she told him, like his.

When he went back into the apartment, the others were up. "We were all laughin,' you know, bein' a bunch of assholes. We made kind of a joke about it, you know what I mean? How she could've just jumped into bed with the two of 'em, some shit like that, that old rhetoric joke-type stuff."

Richardson let Luther do most of the talking, just tossing in a question or comment here and there to keep the pump primed. "When did you find out that Cher was missing?"

Luther appeared to give it some thought before he responded, "Um, the time before this last time that you talked to Byron."

Richardson made another mental note. Luther had slipped again, apparently without noticing: when they talked earlier that afternoon, Luther had said that Byron had just that day told him about Cher Elder being missing. He had made a big deal about the boys trying to keep him out of the investigation.

Fortunately, Richardson thought, *these guys can't keep the little things in their stories straight.* They'd set up the big alibi, like, "We all went into the convenience store," but could never remember to agree on who purchased what or what they were doing there in the first place. Interview them alone and there'd be as many stories as there were suspects.

"Why didn't you come forward?"

"What do you mean, why didn't I come forward?" Luther replied, then laughed. "Forward for what?"

"To let us know that you'd been with her that night, or somethin' . . ."

Because of his past, Luther said, the Eerebout boys wanted to protect him from "the cops harassin' me."

Richardson scowled. This was going in circles. "That don't make sense."

"It might not make sense to you," Luther said, "but it makes perfect sense to me. You don't know the kind of bullshit that I went through on this case that I was in the penitentiary on. You know, I was suspected of every murder, everything that happened in that fuckin' county up there for a year and a couple years before that.''

''Where's that?'' Richardson asked, playing dumb. Underneath he was seething; this low-life had raped a young woman with a hammer and nearly beat her to death and yet he thought that he was the victim.

''Summit County,'' Luther spat. ''Breckenridge. They hassled my girlfriend to death over the Overalster [sic] and Scheme [sic] murders. I was initially a supect.''

Richardson knew a little of this. Morales told him that Luther had been on the list of suspects in the unsolved murder of two girls before the sexual assault. If Luther wanted to volunteer something else, maybe it'd help Morales solve his cases. In any case, he wasn't going to stop Luther from blabbing. ''That don't mean nothing to me, I—''

Luther wasn't through. ''They found two girls murdered up there the month before I got arrested.''

''Up at the ski resorts?'' Richardson asked, looking puzzled. ''I'm not from Colorado, so I wouldn't know nothin' of those murders. . . . How many murders did they try to pin on you?''

''Well, those two,'' Luther said. ''I was a suspect. They didn't really try to pin me, you know, but they questioned several people, like I say, you know, they'd go down where my girlfriend at the time worked, and they would ask her questions and get her upset, and leave her there cryin'.''

Richardson asked about the sexual assault. Luther shook his head, ''Well, I'm not gonna go into all the details on that, but I picked a girl up at a bus station, you know what I mean, and, uh, you know, it ended up in an assault. It was more of an assault than it was a sexual assault, but you know how they do things.''

Luther complained that he'd been screwed by the system. He was due for mandatory parole after about six years, but ten hours before his release they changed the rules on him. ''I ended up serving ten years, ten months and three days.''

The ex-convict squirmed in his seat and mentioned that he'd have to leave for work soon. Richardson knew he needed to speed things up. In trying not to alarm Luther, he had gone slow, but if he didn't get it done now, chances were the next time, if there was a next time, it'd be with a defense attorney present.

Maybe if he could convince Luther that the investigation still centered on Byron and his brothers, he could buy a little more time. "Could you come to Lakewood tomorrow, so we can sit down and talk some more? Byron, J.D., Tristan—all these people have lied to us. Now, we gotta go back and talk to them again."

Luther grimaced like he'd eaten something rotten. "Like I told you, they know that there was no foul play on my part. They know they seen her leave there. You know, even if there is foul play, they suspect that, you know, she's lyin' up somewhere. She's a girl that had a serious drug problem in her past, you know that, right?"

Richardson struggled to keep the anger out of his eyes. "No," he said. "What kind of drug problem?"

"She hung around with a couple of dealers," Luther said. "Snorted cocaine, was, uh, you know, heavily addicted to the chemical . . ."

"Was she snorting that night?" Richardson asked.

"No. No. Not in front of me if she did," Luther said, shaking his head.

Richardson decided it was time to ask the question that had been hanging fire ever since his telephone conversation with Luther was interrupted by the presence of Debrah Snider. "What kind of sexual contact did you two have up on the hill? Honestly. I'm not gonna call your girlfriend up and say, 'Debbie, guess what?' But I want you to be honest with me."

Luther nodded. On the way back, he said, they turned off the highway and went to a little parking spot on the mountain above Golden. Richardson pictured the dry and barren hills outside of the town; one had a large "M" painted on its side for the Colorado School of Mines, a top-notch engineering college.

It was cold and windy, Luther continued. He smoked a joint. "Then we did some kissin' and some pettin' and stuff, which led to a little quick intercourse thing, you know what I mean?"

Well, they hadn't been the first words out of his mouth, Richardson thought, but just about the first chance he got. A quick little intercourse thing? Luther made it sound like an afterthought.

"In the car?" the detective asked.

"In my car."

"Front seat? Backseat?"

"Front seat. They fold back."

"Passenger side? Your side?"

"It was on her side. She was drivin.' It was just a little quick intercourse thing. She got very upset about it."

Suddenly, there was the sound of the front door opening. Luther said it would probably be his girlfriend, Debrah Snider.

Quickly, Richardson asked if he could get her to stay outside for a few minutes. He pretended it was because he didn't want Luther's girlfriend to hear about the sex with Elder, but he had another reason. Someday, he might want to question this woman, and he didn't want her trying to recall Luther's version of this conversation.

A moment later, a woman came into the kitchen. She was a slight woman with long, curly brown hair that hung nearly to her waist. She wasn't beautiful nor unattractive, just plain, sort of outdoorsy.

The woman he assumed to be Debrah Snider didn't seem particularly surprised to find her boyfriend talking to a couple of guys who introduced themselves as Lakewood cops, only that Luther hadn't left for work yet. He laughed. "It's 'cause I'm being questioned. Um, they'd like you to leave for just a few minutes. Can you go take a run around the block maybe?"

Debrah Snider stared at him for a moment, then nodded. When she left, Richardson rolled his eyes like they were prepubescent boys caught by their mothers with a *Playboy* magazine. "Geez, terrible timing for a girlfriend walking in."

Luther laughed and shrugged, then got back to his story. "Like I say, Cher got upset about it. She had these feelings for Byron, and she did it kinda out of spite. Evidently, she, you know, she made me believe that she didn't sleep around a lot, although we did a little quick thing in the front seat of a car. In fact, afterwards she threw up on my back seat."

Richardson's mental notebook was working overtime. People with head wounds or concussions often vomited. Another possibility was forced oral sex, which usually produced the same reaction.

An ex-convict like Luther knew that if the police laboratory crews ever started going over his car, they'd find the vomit and possibly be able to trace it back to Elder. He needed a good story to explain its presence.

"How come she threw up?"

"She just got sick to her stomach."

"No oral sex?"

"No oral sex. It was just straight intercourse. Neither one of us were fully unclothed ... it was just like a heat of passion thing. Real quick." She drank a few beers up in Central City, he added, and then she helped him drink a bottle of cheap red wine.

Richardson changed the subject to what happened after Luther brought Cher back to Byron's apartment. He didn't want his quarry settling in on any one part of his story.

"She left after saying something to Byron."

"Never wrote a note or nothin?" Richardson asked innocently.

"No, she didn't write no notes. She was there like about thirty seconds."

Richardson nodded. He looked at Heylin, who had remained quiet during the interview, as if to ask if he wanted to ask any questions. When Heylin shook his head, Richardson said they were about done but might need to contact him again.

"What for?" Luther asked. Now it was his turn to scowl.

Because, Richardson said, with all the new information he'd have to talk to the Eerebout boys again. He shook his head and said he couldn't quite figure out why they said some of the things they had.

"When you get a simple case," he went on, "like a missing person, I mean, this is a simple case, and you go talk to the— her boyfriend, who's the last person to see her, and they sit there and lie to ya and give you this whole story ..." Richardson threw up his hands.

Luther tried to explain. "Well, they didn't necessarily lie to ya, you know what I mean?"

It was the opening Richardson was waiting for, a good opportunity to demonstrate just how angry he was with Byron Eerebout. "Oh no," he said, "he lied like hell ..."

"He just didn't put my name into the—"

Heylin jumped in. "He denied knowing you."

Richardson quickly added, "He denied everything. He denied her comin' in. He denied the whole shootin' match. That's what I'm sayin'. He wasn't just a little lyin.' He was deceptive from day one on this thing."

The detectives figured that if they continued to heap the manure on Byron Eerebout, Luther might start worrying about what his young friend would do if the cops turned up the heat. Sow a few seeds of distrust. At the same time, they kept up the pretense of taking Luther into their confidence.

"What's relieving is to talk to somebody that's . . . that's talkin' to us, and tellin' us the truth," Richardson said, "because we been poundin' walls down tryin' to figure out what in the heck's goin' on, and why is Byron tellin' us one thing, and someone else tells us another, and nothin's addin' up . . . and then you come into the picture . . ."

Obviously, he added, it was now going to take some time to unravel all the different stories. He needed Luther to come to Lakewood after the detectives had a chance to talk to the Eerebouts again.

Luther shook his head. No, he didn't really think that'd be necessary. He'd been cooperative, but like he'd said from the beginning, he didn't trust cops . . . not since his experiences in Summit County. "This fuckin' guy bald-faced sat right there and lied that I gave him a fuckin' confession when I didn't. I mean, I've given you guys a statement. I have nothin' further to say . . ."

Uh oh, Richardson thought, *here it comes.* The door was starting to swing shut.

Heylin took one last shot. "If we developed some questions from talkin' to these other guys, we can approach you again, right? I mean, there's gonna be follow-up questions after we talk to all the other guys and . . ."

Luther invoked the magic words that cops have hated since the Miranda warnings became the accused's bill of rights. "Well, I'm gonna insist that there be an attorney present if that's the case."

Heylin shrugged; they couldn't let on that they were disappointed. "That's your . . . that's your choice."

"I've been burned," Luther continued. "And you people can't get me again like that. I think that's only reasonable that I protect myself as fully as I can. . . . I do retain full rights . . ."

Richardson looked hard at Luther. So the guy wanted an attorney? That pretty much shot any reason to keep the gloves on. In a way, he was relieved to drop the buddy-buddy act. He didn't like Luther. It went beyond the Cher Elder case, even the

Summit County rape. There was something wrong with this guy behind the cool blue eyes. He was passive as hell around other men, but dangerous as a rattlesnake when alone with women. A real Dr. Jekyll and Mr. Hyde. That much was clear.

"Well, you have all the rights in the world, and you aren't under arrest—" Richardson began.

Luther interrupted. Maybe the detectives were just barking up his tree and that of the Eerebouts' because they had no place else to turn. Cher could have met with foul play after leaving Byron's. "You people keep dead-endin' at Byron's house. That's why you keep goin' back to him."

Heylin answered for his partner. "We have zip on her gettin' molested goin' from Byron's to the grocery store where her car was found. But we've got all these lies that we've gotta sort through."

As he spoke, the men got up from the table and walked toward the door. Outside, Richardson looked over at Luther's blue Geo Metro, the car that Karen Knott had described from the last time she had seen her friend. "Do you care if we just look in your car?" he asked.

"I don't see why not," Luther shrugged.

"Well, I don't wanna make ya mad," Richardson said sarcastically as he walked toward the car, still holding his tape recorder in his hand where it could pick up the conversation. "I've never seen such a defensive group of people over a missin' person in my life."

Luther wasn't backing down. "Well, you keep shootin' them little innuendos, you know what I mean, about us bein' defensive. Well, it could be because we're not trustin' of the law. Them boys . . . their father spent years in the penitentiary. All of their father's friends spent a lot of years in the penitentiary. They seen how the guards work down there, you know, they're the most vicious bunch of fuckin' chicken farmers you ever seen in your life down there running' that spot."

"Would Byron hurt a woman?" Richardson interrupted.

"Naw. Maybe another guy. Self-defense."

"Why is a man your age hanging out with these kids?"

"When I went to the penitentiary I was a kid myself," Luther replied. He met the Eerebout boys when they were little and came to visit their father in prison. They were good kids, he said, they hadn't really lied to the detectives. They were just trying to protect a friend. Convict code, honor among thieves and all that.

Richardson waved his hand. "We do this for a livin.' You aren't the first convict we ever come across in our careers."

"But I'm sure that they didn't come to you with open arms and want to tell you everything they knew, either," Luther shot back. "Like I say, these boys were raised by a convict. They have somewhat the mentality, you know? You don't tell on nobody. You don't give the cops no information. You know what the drill is. I understand you guys gotta job to do, but I think that you guys are spinnin' your wheels in the wrong section."

Richardson looked in the driver's-side window. He could see a large stain on the backseat behind the driver's side. Immediately, he saw the implications. Luther was trying to feed them a story to explain why a crime lab would find body fluids.

Heylin looked in the window on the other side. They had a report that Byron and his brothers were suspects in a number of burglaries, including one in which some tools were taken from the garage of a man named Thomas Dunn. The detective saw a circular power saw on the backseat with the name Dunn inscribed on the handle. "Is this your saw?" he asked, pointing.

"Mmm-hmmm." Luther nodded.

"It's stolen."

Luther swallowed hard but stayed cool. "I bought it off some guy in a bar down in Lakewood, at Whiskey Bill's. I gave the guy ten bucks for it. Would you like it?"

Heylin ignored the offer and instead reached in and grabbed the saw. "We're going to take it. Byron's been named as a possible suspect in some burglaries and this guy named Dunn is missin' some saws. Now, you gotta saw with Dunn's name on it."

Further inspection revealed tools that had been reported missing from other burglaries in which Byron was a suspect. Again, Luther claimed to have purchased them from the same long-haired "biker type" at the bar.

"You guys aren't doin' no burglaries, are you?" Richardson asked.

"Hey, like I said," Luther said putting up his hands, "I just got out of the fuckin' penitentiary ... and I ain't gonna bind myself up with a bunch of fuckin' stolen shit.'' He was glaring at the detectives. He accused them of coming to Fort Collins on the pretext of looking for Cher when they just wanted to nail him for some small-time burglaries. ''This is all a fuckin' smokescreen.''

Heylin answered. ''Tom, this ain't no smokescreen and you know it. It's a legitimate missing person. I happen to glance in the car and look what's in it. I know what the fuck was taken from a burglary. Don't pin it back on us.''

But Luther was growing more agitated, pacing up and down by his car. ''Worst case scenario is happenin' right here,'' he said pointing a finger at Richardson's chest.

''I told this girl right here—'' now he indicated Debrah Snider who was sitting in her car next to the Geo Metro—''I told her the year before I got out of the penitentiary. It's the worst thing that I fear. You people are tyin' my name to any type of fuckin' shit and then riding me until my fuckin' chin falls off.''

Richardson had heard enough. In all probability, this asshole killed Cher Elder, and now he was whining like a beat dog. ''Well, I hate to burst your bubble here, but I didn't know you existed until about three hours ago,'' he spat. ''You're sittin' here sayin' that we're houndin' you, and pursuin' you, and tryin' to pin you. We didn't even know you were alive, bud, until you called my office.''

Luther looked stunned. But Richardson wasn't done with him yet. His eyes darkened beneath his black eyebrows and bored into Luther. It was his turn to point a finger at Luther's chest. ''Don't give me this crap that we've been tryin' to pin you on crimes.''

Richardson looked like he wanted to rip into Luther on the spot. To diffuse the situation, Heylin noted that it was Luther who said Elder threw up in his car. They were just checking out his story when he spotted the stolen tools.

Luther exploded. ''You wanna verify,'' he yelled, ''you wanna verify that she threw up, man, smell right there.'' He pointed his finger to the backseat. ''Smell right there! Put your nose down right there, man.''

Heylin raised his hands in mock surrender. ''That's good enough for me.''

As they drove away, Richardson looked back. Luther's girl-friend had gotten out of her car and was standing next to him, but the ex-con just stood there with his fists clenched, staring after them.

Richardson had drawn first blood, but he knew it was far from over. "This is going to get personal between me and Mr. Luther," he muttered, "real personal."

Chapter Twelve

April 20, 1993—Breckenridge, Colorado

As much as Sheriff Morales expected a call, when Detective Richardson asked what he knew about Thomas Edward Luther, it still sent a chill up his spine. "Who'd he kill?" was as much a statement as a question.

Over the past ten years, Morales had kept track of Luther. Every time that the convict appeared in court or at a parole board hearing, he was there to recount what had happened to Mary Brown. "It was a sudden, vicious, unprovoked attack," he'd say. "I believe he will always be a threat to women."

There was no question the two men hated each other. They glared at each other from across every room they shared over those ten years, Morales' soft brown eyes holding their own against the intense blue stare of Luther.

Tom Luther was 180 degrees from everything Morales believed in. He wasn't just a rapist, he was a chameleon who could appear to be the sensitive listener, any girl's friend—until she said the wrong thing or didn't go for his "ladies' man" approach. Luther was a predator and a true sociopath. His troubles were always someone else's fault, and he'd never expressed a moment's remorse for what he had done to Mary. In fact, he'd tried to have her killed so that he wouldn't have to pay for his crime.

Ten years passed. The town of Breckenridge changed and not always for the better, Morales sometimes thought. New ski trails had been opened on the mountains next to the original ski hill; million-dollar winter homes for the jet-setters were becoming more common; crime had grown along with the population.

Neighbors no longer knew their neighbors, and no one left their doors open anymore. Few in the community had lived there when Bobby Jo Oberholtzer and Annette Schnee were murdered or when Luther was arrested for the attack on Mary Brown a month later.

For Morales, 1982 was the year he and his town lost their innocence. Now he was a little heavier, although still built like the Marine tanks he once commanded. He'd earned respect in the community and they had elected him sheriff. His strong Latin features and wide smile were a hit with women, but he was always the gentleman. Their protector.

As such, he never forgot the blood-splattered interior of Luther's truck or the rusty-red imprint of Mary Brown's hand pressed desperately against the rear window. When his enemy was released in January, Morales called to warn Mary, who had since married, changed her name, and moved. The fear in her voice was palpable as she thanked him and hung up.

Then he made copies of Luther's most recent mugshot and distributed them throughout Summit County. "If you see him, call us," his officers requested as they handed out the fliers.

The receptionist at the sheriff's office taped one below the counter and facing her so that she could compare it to any man who walked through the doors requesting to see Morales. He didn't think Luther would have the balls to come gunning for him, or any man for that matter, but he wanted a warning just in case.

Shortly after the fliers were distributed, Morales got a call from Sandy, the woman who was staying with Luther and his girlfriend, Sue Potter, at the trailer on the night of his 1982 arrest. Luther had shown up at her home, she said, and after a little polite talk, he asked where Potter was now living.

Sandy knew that Potter was married and living in another state. She also knew that her friend was terrified of her former lover.

With good reason, Morales thought, recalling the reports that Luther tried to pay fellow inmates with drugs and money to have her face "blown off." And only because he couldn't get out of jail to kill "Lips" himself.

"I said I didn't know where she was," Sandy told Morales. He nodded. Potter was safe, but knew in his heart that it wouldn't be long before he heard about Luther attacking some other woman. And so it was only natural for Morales to ask Richardson when he called, "Who'd he kill?"

There was a long pause on the other end of the line. "We have a missing girl." the Lakewood detective replied.

"Was he the last one seen with her?" Morales interrupted. He knew the answer. Feared the answer. But still he had to ask.

"Yep. We got them together on a videotape from a casino up in Central City."

Morales sighed, then added, "I'm sorry. But she's toast."

After his short conversation with Richardson, Morales asked Det. Richard Eaton to come into his office to discuss the possibility of the Oberholtzer and Schnee murders being tied to Luther. He could hear as if it were yesterday, Luther's comment, "Why do I do these things?" and recalled his suspicions about Luther and the murdered women.

Like Eaton, Morales believed that the detectives working on the Oberholtzer/Schnee cases in 1982 had done their jobs. Still, Luther's name came up again from tips telephoned in after the *Unsolved Mysteries* segment aired two years earlier. He was only one of several possible suspects mentioned, but Richardson's case reinforced what Morales already knew—wherever Tom Luther went, young women were in danger.

"Maybe we ought to look at Luther again," Morales suggested and told him about the conversation with Richardson.

When his boss finished, Eaton agreed that they should reopen that area of the investigation. Despite the passage of time, he was just as determined to catch the killer of Bobby Jo and Annette and fulfill his promise to their families. Every year he received Christmas cards from Annette's family to go with the letters of encouragement and thanks; occasionally he saw Jeff Oberholtzer and could only shake his head when the young man asked if there was any news of his wife's killer.

Other cases came and went. Some went unsolved. Some were worse than others—such as the woman who gave birth, then drowned the infant in a bathtub and disposed of the tiny body by placing it in a paper bag along with an empty oil can and a half-eaten McDonald's fish sandwich. It brought tears to his eyes whenever he thought of the child who was thrown out with the trash, and he openly rejoiced in the courtroom when the jury convicted her. But there were all kinds of monsters, and the one he wanted most was still out there. The killer of Bobby Jo and Annette.

The case consumed him awake or asleep. He couldn't drive over Hoosier Pass without pulling into the parking lot at the summit to retrace Oberholtzer's flight toward the trees. If he was near Fairplay, he'd go check on the small cross he erected at the spot where Schnee died and assure the restless spirit who rustled the willows along the bank that he was still on the case.

He dreamed about the women's deaths, saw the bullets hit and their bodies fall. He could see the fear and bewilderment in Bobby Jo's eyes as she lay in the crime scene photographs, staring up at the sky. And Annette's body facedown in the stream.

But he couldn't see the face of the monster who killed them.

After the Lakewood detectives pulled out of Tom's driveway, a troubled Debrah Snider walked back into his apartment. Only a missing girl? *Like hell,* she thought. Richardson's business card was still lying on the kitchen table. It said he was a homicide detective.

A moment later, Tom came in, slamming the door behind him. "They're going to try to frame me," he snarled.

Debrah's mind was racing. In the past few weeks, he'd made a number of calls to his mother and sisters, all insisting that he was going to be a scapegoat for the disappearance of the woman he now referred to as Cher Elder. He made sure Debrah was somewhere within hearing for each telephone call—loudly protesting his innocence, saying his only saving grace was that the girl was seen at a bingo hall the day after he'd brought her back to Byron's apartment.

Then that afternoon, she came home from work to find him pacing about in her kitchen. "What's the matter, Tom?" she asked.

"Byron called. The police have a video from Central City. I'm on it with Cher," he replied. "But the boys screwed up and said they didn't know me. I called the cops, and now they want to come and talk to me.''

"I want to be there," Snider said. She had to know the truth. Luther agreed. But he wanted her to wait fifteen minutes after the police arrived and then walk in as if she didn't know anything. He left for his place.

When she arrived as planned, the two Lakewood police detectives were there. One of the detectives, the young one with the Texas drawl, said something to Tom.

"Honey, take a walk around the block would ya?" Tom responded.

She had hesitated. Taking a walk wasn't part of their agreement, and she desperately wanted to know what was going on. If she was going to lose the man she loved, she had to understand why . . . and support him if she could.

However, the conversation between Luther and the detectives was cordial enough . . . kind of like men sharing secrets they didn't want a woman to overhear. She noted Tom was recording the discussion, which seemed like a smart idea. He had repeatedly told her that the cops would try to pin something on him. He was always coming home with outlandish stories about cops pulling him over or following him just to yank his chain.

"They want to push me into doing something stupid, like maybe punching one of them out, so they can put me back behind the walls." But he was too smart for them, he'd brag; his little marijuana operation was going to set him up for life and the cops were too stupid to catch him.

The macho posturing and lying were the two main aspects of Luther's personality that Snider disliked. That and the way he thought of women.

It was as if two men lived under the same skin, struggling for control. She hoped that with her love and commitment, the "good Tom" would win over "bad Tom," as she had come to think of his different sides.

So she did her best to ignore the bragging and dismissed the tales of police harassment as more "Tom Luther stories," mixed in with a dash of prison paranoia. But who knew? The cops were here now. Maybe he wasn't just blowing smoke?

Deep inside, a voice was telling her that she was being blind, but she wouldn't listen. Couldn't. She'd thrown her lot in with this man, and their fates, good or bad, were twisted together like strands of a rope.

When Tom asked her to go take a walk, she went out and sat in her car. A few minutes later, Tom and the detectives walked outside. They seemed friendly enough. Then the detectives went over to Tom's car, and the older cop remarked about the stolen tools.

Debrah suddenly realized that the detective's comment wasn't out of the blue. She had called various police agencies telling them about packages of marijuana he was getting from Skip Eerebout in Chicago and the stolen tools, which she suspected came from burglaries with the Eerebout boys. She hoped her information would lead to Tom getting caught for something small, before it was too big and too late. These detectives were obviously aware of her telephone calls.

Suddenly, the tenor of the conversation between the men changed dramatically. Tom accused them of setting him up for a burglary fall. But everyone knew it was about the missing girl.

Richardson said he'd want to talk again. Tom replied that he'd want a lawyer present if he did.

Then Tom started yelling about vomit on the backseat of his car. She remembered that after she got back from Washington, he asked to borrow an industrial cleanser he'd seen her use on a stain in her car, blood from a package of steaks that had leaked onto her seat. She'd seen him use the cleanser on his backseat repeatedly over a period of weeks, though she couldn't remember ever smelling vomit, even before he used the cleanser.

Debrah was startled by the hatred now obvious on the faces of her lover and the younger detective. They were like a couple of the male wolves she raised, facing off all stiff-legged with their hackles up. She half expected to see their lips curl back to reveal fangs. Then the cops were gone.

An hour later, Tom was still ranting about "frame jobs." Debrah sat at the kitchen table with her head in her hands, hoping that was all there was to it.

The next morning Tom left, saying he needed to find out what really happened to Cher Elder. To do that, he had to call someone named Mortho, a Denver drug dealer who apparently knew everything that went on in the area's criminal underworld.

"I gotta go find a pay phone," Luther said. "They probably got this one tapped."

As he left, he handed her a cassette tape. "It's the interview with the cops," he said. "Mail it to Babe for me so I know it's somewhere safe."

Snider frowned but didn't say anything. She wondered if he was leaving to make his telephone call because he was worried about the cops listening in or her. And why not leave the tape with her for safekeeping?

Pam "Babe" Rivinius was the mother of the Eerebout boys and Skip Eerebout's former wife. Thin and buxom, Babe was once, years before, a Playboy bunny. Debrah couldn't help but feel jealous when Tom would go visit her, even though Babe had remarried and he promised that they were just friends.

Before the dust settled from Luther's rapid departure that morning, Snider stuck the cassette in her tape recorder. If he was going to send the tape to Babe, she felt that she at least had a right to know what the detectives were asking.

As much as she suspected that Luther had sex with Cher Elder, she wasn't ready to hear him confess to "a quick little intercourse thing" with the missing girl. When the interview ended, she angrily packaged the tape, fumbling at the wrapping through her tears, and walked it out to the mailbox.

She was still steaming when Luther got back a little while later. But before she could say anything, he blurted out, "They killed her. She was a snitch, so they cut off her lips and dumped her body along a road as a warning to other snitches."

Luther apparently didn't notice Debrah's grim expression as he continued. "Now I've got to find her and dispose of the body. With my record, they'll be coming after me."

For a moment, Snider wondered if he was telling her all the gruesome details as a warning of what could happen if she talked to the police. But she was too angry to let it trouble her for long. All her hopes and dreams were evaporating because Tom couldn't control himself around pretty young women. She told him that she listened to the tape.

"You had no right to do that," Luther yelled. "It was mine."

But Snider wasn't backing off. "You had no right to be with

that woman, Tom," she replied. "You were supposed to be in a relationship with me!"

Perhaps surprised by her vehemence, Luther backed down first. He explained that he had been drunk and that the girl, despondent over her relationship with Byron, used him for sex to get even. He was sorry. He loved only her. The thing with Cher was "a mistake" for both of them.

Debrah wanted to believe him. If she couldn't, then everything she had lived for since they'd met meant nothing. She wanted to believe that this girl, Cher Elder, was mixed up in the drug trade and paid a horrible price. That Tom was only in the wrong place at the wrong time. But he should have kept his zipper zipped.

That night they made love. When they finished, he began to cry. "I wish I never got involved with Cher," he sobbed. "I ain't going back to prison, I'd rather kill myself. I want to be buried in Vermont."

Snider noticed that he apparently felt nothing for what happened to Elder, just like she'd never heard him express any remorse for what he'd done to Mary Brown. Still, she loved him—at least that part of him who had written her hundreds of love letters, the Tom who brought her wildflowers and walked hand in hand with her and talked about an idyllic future they would create together, away from people. That man was not a killer.

So she held him until he talked and cried himself out. When he fell asleep, she turned her anger and frustration on Cher Elder. *You had no business going anywhere with my boyfriend,* she thought, struggling not to cry and wake the man who snored next to her. *If you got killed, it's your own goddamn fault!*

The next morning, she asked Tom, "What do you need?" She'd decided that if there was any hope for a future with him, she was going to have to trust that this time, he was telling the truth.

Luther smiled; she was his girl again. He said that he would need camping equipment so that he could go find and bury the body. They went to her place, a double-wide trailer parked on the dry, open bit of prairie that was her ranch, where she loaned him a red backpack.

The next two days seemed to pass as slowly as cold honey

off a spoon for Debrah. Tom didn't call or send word. She imagined the worst: that he had been arrested or hurt. Finally, his car turned into her driveway.

"Did you get it taken care of?" she asked.

"Yes, she's buried," he replied. He said he found Elder's body and took her to a spot east on Interstate 70 where he'd placed her in a shallow grave. It was near a historical marker of some sort . . . a turnoff where travelers stopped to stretch their legs and walk their dogs.

He didn't mention that before his expedition to "find" Elder's body he stopped first to see Babe and then talk to the Eerebout boys, a detour with enormous future consequences.

Over the next few days, Debrah Snider couldn't think straight. She was torn between doing what she knew was right, telling the police what she knew about a missing girl, and trying to protect Luther.

Even if he only buried Cher, he assured her that the cops would pin the murder on him. He grew more secretive. There were clandestine meetings with the Eerebout boys and repeated calls to Southy. She'd never liked Southy. He was dirty, with long, unkempt red hair, an obvious drug user, and she blamed him and the Eerebout boys for getting Tom involved with crimes. If only they'd left him alone to her.

Ten days after the blowup with the detectives, Luther quit his job working for the janitorial service and moved out of his apartment. He packed his few possessions into his car and moved onto Debrah's property, living in an old van she owned with a bed in the back.

Skip Eerebout had work for him in Chicago, he said; he needed to get out of Colorado and get a fresh start. He was more paranoid by the day. He wouldn't call from the house anymore but insisted on going to pay phones. He constantly peeking out windows whenever cars passed the long drive that led to the ranch trailer. If they went somewhere in a car, Luther drove and frequently pulled to the side of the road to watch the cars that passed. Several times he said he thought a driver looked like Detective Richardson.

Luther complained that whenever he visited one of his old

penitentiary buddies in Denver, the Lakewood detective would show up soon after he left. Most of his friends were on parole and the detective's visits would leave them rattled.

"Stay the fuck away, man," they told him. "Everytime you show up, so does that cop. And don't call. I don't want to get revoked!" She knew he was feeling isolated and cornered. He blamed and hated Richardson for it.

She had to admit that in the past few days, it seemed like the county sheriff's vehicles were using her drive a lot to turn around and go back down the highway. And on a few occasions, she noted police cars parked across the highway for a long time. But nothing happened. Richardson didn't show up with an arrest warrant. Life just went on, though uneasily.

If Tom's sudden occupation of the van and run of the house bothered her husband, Dennis, he didn't say much. He once offered to leave if Luther would promise to take responsibility for the ranch and Debrah, but Luther let the offer pass without comment. Dennis didn't even complain when she left with Tom for his van some nights. They hadn't had a sexual relationship for years, and it was almost more like Tom was the husband and Dennis the houseguest. The men had reached a unspoken truce so relaxed that the threesome would often fix popcorn and pizza and watch movies all sitting on the same couch, one big happy family.

Snider began to hope that the Cher Elder incident was going to let them alone. Tom said he thought the focus of the investigation was Byron Eerebout, not him. Maybe the cops were working that or some other more promising lead.

Then on May 6, when Luther left for some errand in Denver, two detectives from the Larimer County Sheriff's Office, Andy Josey and Rick Russell, stopped by and asked to talk to her. They said they were there to ask her about the marijuana she reported Tom receiving.

In reality, Josey and Russell were there at Richardson's request. And it wasn't long before they turned the conversation to the missing girl.

Snider said she didn't know much, just what she'd heard by listening to the tape Tom made of his conversation with the Lakewood detectives. She added that when Luther finally told her about going with Elder to Central City, he claimed Elder drove back to Byron's.

"Which was unusual because Tom normally wouldn't let anybody else drive his car, even me," she said.

As she talked, the worries of the past few weeks came out in the form of tears. She was in Washington visiting a friend the weekend that Cher Elder disappeared, she said. No, she hadn't smelled any vomit in Tom's car. Then again, she thought to herself, there was that cleanser he borrowed . . .

Had he been making any unusual telephone calls?

Well, she replied, wanting to be truthful without hurting Tom, he was calling "Southy" a lot. "He's planning to move to Chicago. He's just waiting for the deposit from his apartment and one more telephone bill."

The detectives left, saying they might want to talk to her again. She said she would be willing without saying she thought she might learn something that would help Tom.

The next night, she, Tom, Dennis, and the two boys were getting ready to watch a movie when the telephone rang. She answered. It was Detective Russell. He wanted to know if she could get away to come to the Larimer County Sheriff's Office to talk.

"It's important," he said, and she agreed.

Snider went back to where the males in her life were gathering in front of the television. "I just remembered I have to get a Mother's Day card for my mom," she said. "If I don't mail it right away, she won't get it in time. Just go ahead without me. I'll be back soon."

Tom and Dennis just nodded and sat down like old friends to watch the movie. She left feeling like she was betraying Tom. It was clear that he wasn't off the hook for the missing girl and what she knew could implicate him in Cher's death.

If he was guilty of her death, she believed that he should pay. But she wasn't convinced that he had done anything more than try to protect himself by burying her, and in that case, she didn't want to be the one to hand him over to the cops. She loved him, she wanted to be with him for the rest of her life. If he was gone, she saw no point in going on.

Snider drove to the sheriff's office where she was escorted into an interview room by Detective Russell. The conversation began with the detective asking about the marijuana shipments, but it wasn't long before the detective asked again about anything she might know regarding Elder's disappearance.

This went on for several minutes until she began to wonder what was so important that she leave her home in the evening. She couldn't tell them anything new. Then a door on the side of the room opened and the young detective she'd seen at Tom's place back in April, the one with the Texas accent, stepped into the room.

"I'm Scott Richardson," he said. "I was hopin' maybe you and I could talk."

Chapter Thirteen

Late April 1993—Lakewood, Colorado

The paranoia Tom Luther was feeling was no accident. Scott Richardson wanted Luther isolated and out of his comfort zone. The ex-con was a cocky son-of-a-bitch and seemed to think he was invulnerable when it came to Cher. So the detective had taken a number of steps to knock his confidence down a bit, including asking the Larimer County lawmen for help staking him out.

Debrah Snider's driveway was perfect for deputies to turn around on their patrols down the highway that ran past her place. They made sure they turned slowly, as if casing the property, even stopping for a moment at night to let their headlights rest on her trailer. Richardson was gratified to hear that the deputies reported a figure peeking out of the curtains just about every time they made their turns. There was also a little spot across the highway where the deputies parked and did their paperwork at the end of their evening shifts.

"It has to be driving Luther nuts," Richardson told Sabrina. Ever since they'd married, he had talked over his cases with her at the dinner table. Sometimes it was just the mention of an arrest he felt particularly good about. Other times, he ran the facts of perplexing or particularly interesting cases by her. She had practically grown up with him as a cop, and he trusted her instincts for a second opinion.

This case, however, was different. It wasn't unusual at the beginning of a homicide case for him to be gone from home for two or three days. The longer a murder investigation went, the harder it was to solve. Those initial hours, when witnesses' memories were fresh and before the killer had a chance to make up a story or get out of town, were crucial.

But after he met Luther, Richardson was gone from early in the morning until late at night, if he came home at all, instead of working right through the dawn. When he did come home, Luther was on his mind. At the dinner table, it was all he could talk about. As time passed, even the twins, as young as they were, began picking up on the added intensity in the Richardson household and knew from the meal conversations that it had something to do with a bad man named Tom Luther.

Richardson was doing what lawmen referred to as "breaking down the circle of friends." If Luther left Fort Collins, various police agencies would tail him and then hand him off as he crossed into other jurisdictions on his way south to the Denver area. Then when word came back that Luther had stopped to see one of his old prison friends, Richardson would drive over and introduce himself after Luther left.

"Aren't you on parole?" he'd ask the nervous former felons, knowing that one of the requirements of parole was to avoid contact with other ex-felons. He was sure word of his visits got back to Luther.

Richardson wanted to make this cat-and-mouse game between him and Luther personal. Richardson—he needed Luther to jump every time he heard his name. To feel hunted. A cornered animal, because a cornered animal, while more dangerous, was also desperate and apt to make mistakes. At this point, Richardson had precious little to go on except a grainy videotape taken in Central City, a series of lies and obvious cover-ups, and his instincts. There was no crime scene, no body, not even any hard evidence that Cher Elder was dead.

In spite of that, he was absolutely sure that Luther had murdered her. Nothing Richardson had learned dissuaded him from his conviction. Some pieces of the puzzle didn't quite fit, which didn't surprise him considering the number of conflicting stories he'd heard. He didn't know why or exactly where and when Cher had been killed. He also didn't know whether others, like the Eerebouts, or this Southy he'd been hearing about, were directly involved. Yet he believed that Cher and Luther left the casino and never made it back to Byron's apartment.

If Luther's old traits held, Cher had probably been beaten and strangled, but not necessarily. It is a myth, inspired by television and the movies, that a serial rapist or killer always follows the exact same pattern. For some, the only common thread is that they will rape or kill again and again until they are stopped.

Richardson believed that Luther was responsible for the two 1982 murders in Summit County. It only made sense. Two women died, then after his arrest for attacking Mary Brown, the attacks stopped.

Lightly populated mountain regions like Summit County were not immune from the unpredictable violence of serial killers. One of the most prolific sex killers in recent history, Ted Bundy, was suspected of killing a half-dozen women in and near the Colorado ski resorts of Aspen and Vail in the late 1970s.

Still, what were the chances that two murderously violent sex predators were in Summit County in January 1982? Not much.

If it was true that Luther shot Oberholtzer and Schnee, then beat Brown nearly to death, then he was an opportunistic killer who used whatever weapon was available. A gun. A hammer. His fists. As far as Richardson knew, the only thing that Luther's victims, and suspected victims, had in common was that they were all small, pretty young women, easy to overpower, and in need of a ride.

The day after he met with Luther, Richardson had talked again to Summit County Sheriff Joe Morales to learn more about the attack on Mary Brown. He also talked with Detective Eaton of Summit County and Charlie McCormick of Park County about their investigation of the Oberholtzer and Schnee murders. They shared what information they had about the two unsolved murders and what they had connecting the deaths to Luther.

It wasn't much. Eaton said he'd been reviewing the file concerning Luther and had run into an embarrassing wall of cursory police work by his own department. He had always prided himself on not getting too tunnel-visioned while working any one theory

about a case. But the detectives in 1982 had seized upon Jeff
Oberholtzer as the prime suspect and failed to check out other
leads thoroughly.

There was nothing left to do but start over, Eaton said. And
that would mean tracking down a terrified former girlfriend and
men who had spent a little time in the Summit County Jail more
than ten years earlier. He'd be lucky if they were all still alive.

Richardson commiserated. Every homicide detective worth
the gold shield knew that the longer a case went, the harder it
would be to solve or at least to get a conviction. But he had his
own problems. He was sure he had the right suspect. But where
was the body?

Maybe Luther had learned something from his time in prison;
maybe he had killed and buried Elder, rather than let her or her
body be used against him in court. It would be next to impossible
to convict him without a corpse. Richardson knew he had to
find Cher.

If this case was going to be solved, Richardson believed it
would have to be through the meticulous assembly of bits and
pieces. The Eerebouts and Luther were doing their best to blow
smoke across the trail. But sometimes he learned a lot from what
they weren't saying or when they confused their stories. He
talked to Byron's youngest brother, Tristan, just 16, who, it
turned out, went to high school with Cher's younger half-sister,
Beth Elder. Tristan said he couldn't remember who had been at
the apartment the night Cher disappeared, except for himself,
Cher, and Byron. He said he didn't remember Luther being there
or an argument between his brother and the missing girl. It was
obvious to Richardson that he was trying to remember what
story he was supposed to tell.

One of the Eerebouts' few acquaintances who seemed to be
telling the truth was Gina Jones, the girl Byron was seeing when
he had the falling out with Cher. Gina had broken off her short
relationship with Byron within a few days of Cher's disappearance and gone back to her former boyfriend.

Cher Elder, Tom Luther, Byron's brothers, and a friend were
all at the apartment that afternoon, Jones recalled. She said she
left in a huff over Cher and came back a few hours later to get

Byron. She admitted being angry when she found Elder sitting on Byron's bed. He showed her a "psycho" note Elder had written and placed on his bathroom mirror.

Jones' mention of the note interested Richardson. Byron Eerebout said he'd found two notes after he returned that night, indicating Cher had come back to the apartment from Central City and left it after finding him and Gina in bed. But Gina Jones was sure he had showed it to her before they left for the evening. They didn't return until 4 A.M., she said. "Her car was there. I got pissed because I thought she was still there. I said, 'Bullshit if I'm goin' in there with that woman!' "

"Was Thomas Luther's car there?" Richardson asked.

"No," Gina replied, "it was not."

Eerebout went into the apartment, she said, and came back out to report that only his brother J.D. was still there. Neither Cher nor Luther were present. Mollified, Gina had gone with Eerebout into the apartment where they made love before falling asleep.

About 8 A.M., Jones said she was awakened by the sound of a girl's voice. She didn't recognize the voice but said she assumed it was Cher's. "But it might have been another girl," she said. "I didn't go out in the living room. I rolled over, and Byron got out of bed and went into the living room. I heard a female voice, and I heard other voices, and then Byron came and got back into bed. He said to forget it."

Richardson, recalling that Eerebout claimed that Elder had poked her head into the bedroom and cursed him, asked if the unidentified girl's voice could have come from the doorway of the bedroom. No, Jones said, the other woman was definitely out in the living room.

Gina said she thought she heard Cher's car, which had been parked outside of Byron's window, being driven away, and when she got up that morning about eleven, it was gone. The only people around were the Eerebout boys. Several days later, Byron told her that Elder was missing.

"I asked him, 'Did Tom kill her?' And he was like, 'No.' I asked, 'Did Tom do something with her?' and he was like, 'No.' So I blew it off."

However, Byron Eerebout remained unusually agitated. That evening back at his apartment, he smashed the mirror in his bathroom and cut himself. He said it was anger over Gina not being paid by her employer. "It didn't make sense," she told the detective; it was none of Byron's business.

A day or two later, Eerebout made it a big point to tell her that he had been called by somebody who had heard from Cher. The disappearance was just a big hoax, he said, adding that he didn't know why Cher was "messing with him."

Richardson asked Jones why she thought the Eerebout boys would lie to protect Luther, who she had described as "well-groomed and nice." "I have no idea," Gina replied.

No idea, Richardson thought, but she had certainly leaped quickly to the conclusion that Luther might have killed Cher. Call it a woman's intuition.

The Lakewood Police Department and the Larimer County Sheriff's Office joined forces to assign a twenty-seven-officer task force to keep surveillance on the Eerebouts and Luther. It was generally assumed that it was a homicide case, though officially it remained a missing person.

All the pay telephones in the vicinity where Cher Elder's car was found were checked; only a few calls had been placed from those phones on the dates in question and none by Cher. Yet Luther had insisted that Cher left him to go to a telephone to call her friend.

Regarding Elder's car, two interesting facts had surfaced. One was that her coat was still in the car, but a check of the weather revealed that the night she disappeared was bitterly cold. It didn't make sense that she had gone somewhere voluntarily without it. But more importantly, a single, curly gray hair had been found on the driver's seat.

Elder's physical description was checked against every unidentified female body that resembled her in the least and had turned up on the national crime computer. Even a cynical homicide detective like Richardson was surprised at the dozens of unidentified murder victims there were on the list. But again, Cher wasn't one of them.

Richardson questioned and requestioned her family and friends hoping to turn up any odd detail that might help solve the mystery. He collected photographs of Cher to go along with the one he had hung on his office wall next to the photographs of his family. He studied them for jewelry she wore which might help identify her body when and if she was found. Among the jewelry was Byron's ring and a friendship bracelet woven of brightly colored string that her friend Karen Knott said she never took off.

He contacted the Missouri police to see if Elder had some background that might indicate she had a habit of risky behavior. But they reported no arrests, not even a driving offense. Several of the police chiefs of the small towns where she had lived remembered Cher. A nice girl, they said, no trouble at all.

A nice girl. That was Cher. No dirt. No drugs. Nothing in her past right up to the day she disappeared to place her in harm's way. Except she was perhaps too friendly and trusting.

As he focused on Luther, Richardson didn't discard the faint possibility that Elder was alive and in hiding. But people need money to survive and there was no activity on her credit cards or bank accounts, which further indicated that robbery was not the motive behind her disappearance.

Finally, he had to tell the family that he believed Elder was more than missing. It was one of the hardest things he'd ever done as a police officer. He had grown to like Cher. She hadn't deserved this. She came from a broken home, but it was clear that both sides of her family, including her stepparents, had loved her very much. Whatever troubles there had been between Rhonda and Earl, they had not made their daughter a pawn.

On a night in later April, he called the family together. Rhonda and her husband, Van, along with Cher's maternal grandmother came from Grand Junction. Earl arrived from Golden. "I may be wrong," he said. "I hope I am, but I believe that Cher's been killed. I have a suspect. He just got out of the joint from a sexual assault. He was seen with her in Central City the night she disappeared."

Rhonda and her mother burst into tears. Earl just sat in his chair blinking, stunned. Then he asked for the suspect's name and address. Maybe there was something he could do that the police could not to get information out of him.

Earl Elder was a big man who worked for the Coors beer company in Golden. In fact, if Luther had parked with Cher on Lookout Mountain as he had said, they could not have helped but notice the brightly lit Coors factory a few miles below. But apparently, Cher had not mentioned it to her "friend" Tom Luther.

Richardson remembered how when he first met Earl and then Luther, he was struck by the physical similarity between the two men. They both had blue eyes, curly graying hair, and pleasant smiles; they could have almost been brothers. It was easy to guess that a girl like Cher, heartbroken over her faithless boyfriend, had found it easy to trust a man who so resembled her father.

Looking at Cher's tormented family, Richardson thought of his own wife and twin boys and was struck by a bolt of guilt. He had been spending a lot of time on the case and sometimes didn't see the boys unless it was late at night when he came home and looked in on them as they slept.

When she bore the twins, Richardson had promised his wife that he would never be like his father. His family would come first to him.

Sabrina was sure that however much he brushed off his feelings regarding his father, Scott still felt his absence and guilt for not having been able to do something to save him. Back when they were courting, sitting outside one night on her parent's porch watching the stars wheel above Texas, he had suddenly blurted out, "You don't know how lucky you are to have parents like yours. I never really had a dad."

Sabrina looked at him. She knew he'd had it rough, but it was still unlike him to just come out and say it. She also knew something about what he had gone through because she had gone through a similar situation herself—her birth father also was an abusive alcoholic and he had killed himself when she was 6.

But there was nothing in her memory like the stories Scott told her about his father . . . like how his father made him and his older brother lug a pile of heavy flagstones from one side of the yard to the other whenever he meant to fight with his wife in the house. Afraid for themselves and their mother, the boys never questioned the purpose of moving the rocks.

One night, just before Scott's 12th birthday, the boys' mother took them to the drive-in theatre, a common place of refuge when the old man was on a tear. They returned to a quiet house and figured he had passed out. The next morning, Scott was awakened by his mother, who told him his dad had shot himself while they were gone.

It hadn't been until much later that his sons learned that their father was a bombardier during World War II and the Korean conflict, tormented into alcoholism by the ghosts from cities he helped destroy. He was a torn man. When sober, he was a counselor for troubled youths known for helping others, a man who wanted to be a good father, even if he never quite got it right.

As his sons grew, he was sober less and less often. Whatever love he might have felt for his sons, he was incapable of showing it. And then he put a gun to his head.

Unaware of what drove his father so desperately, Scott felt he was somehow responsible for his father's death. Maybe he was too demanding? Maybe he wasn't a good enough son? He should have seen that his dad was troubled and been able to help.

Scott was left with few pleasant memories of his father and no one but his hardworking mother to tell him how to be a good man. In that regard, Sabrina knew she was more fortunate. Her mother had remarried a wonderful man who had raised Sabrina and her younger siblings as his own.

"I don't remember a lot of love," Scott said that night in Texas. The only light was from the stars, but it was enough for her to see the tears running down his face.

It was one of the few times she would ever see him cry— the other would be at the birth of the twins. She had loved him from the moment she laid eyes on him; she admired his courage and thought he was the handsomest man she had ever seen. He was her knight in shining armor, fearless in the defense of others, a good man, and a dedicated cop. She had never so much as kissed another man. Now she loved him even more.

As he promised, Richardson had been the best of fathers. Constantly wrestling with the boys, bathing them, clothing them. He bought them tiny bows and arrows so that they could mimic their bow-hunting father and he talked incessantly about the day he could take them on hunting and fishing trips.

What free time he had, he spent with Sabrina and the boys, with only the occasional motorcycle ride to clear his mind. But then Luther had come into their lives, and now there was no such thing as free time.

"I'm sorry," he now said to Earl Elder. "I can't tell you how to find him." The last thing he needed was for Cher's father to go kill that son-of-a-bitch Tom Luther.

Rhonda hugged him as she left that night. "Please find her," she said. "Please find her so that we can bury her. I don't want her to be alone in some godforsaken spot."

Richardson nodded and swallowed hard. "I will," he said. "I won't give up until I do."

By late April, the Eerebouts would no longer cooperate with the investigation. Through their mother, Babe, investigators were told that if they wanted to talk to the boys, they'd have to do so in the presence of a lawyer.

Richardson had expected that door to close sooner or later. The Eerebouts were obviously in contact with Thomas Luther, and he was smart enough to tell the boys to keep their mouths shut. Then there was their father, Skip Eerebout, an ex-con who was certain to remind them of the convict code and what happens to snitches.

With the Eerebouts at least temporarily out of the picture, Richardson realized that the key to both finding Cher's body and convicting her killer might rest with Debrah Snider.

It never ceased to amaze him how basically good women fell for guys in prison. The majority of inmates would never change the traits that had landed them behind bars in the first place. If anything, prison was just a college for furthering their criminal careers. Yet there were always women who felt that they could change the leopard's spots.

Granted, these guys had a lot of time on their hands to work on the lonely hearts of these women. But he'd done some research and Debrah Snider was no dummy. After doing time for an old theft charge, she had become a regular poster child for prison rehabilitation. She had put herself through school and received degrees in nursing and psychology.

She should have known better, he thought. But she was in love, and he knew that to get Debrah to help him, he would have to drive a wedge between her and her boyfriend.

In the meantime, he might be able to use her in his quest to rattle Luther. Richardson figured she would be a "two-way street"—giving him information, but also relaying what he said back to her lover. He would have to be careful what he told her or it might come back to haunt him at trial, but if used right he might be able to push more of Luther's buttons.

In late April, he met with the Larimer County Sheriff's Narcotics Task Force headed by Sgt. Andy Josey. He asked their help in staking out Luther, and they readily agreed. Then on the afternoon of May 7, Richardson completed an affadavit for a search warrant for Luther's car and telephone records. Then he called Josey to set up an "accidental" meeting with Debrah Snider.

It was 8 P.M. when Snider arrived at the sheriff's office and was met by Detective Russell, who began the questioning while Richardson listened from an adjoining room. He wanted Russell to get her talking before he showed up.

With Russell, she would feel some control. After all, she had initiated the contact between herself and Larimer County. But he was the homicide cop she had seen arguing with her boyfriend, and he was sure he was not a popular man in the Luther household.

Richardson listened in until the interview seemed to be stalling and he sensed Debrah's impatience. It was time to introduce himself.

"I'm Scott Richardson," he said walking into the interview room. "I was hopin' maybe you and I could talk."

Debrah looked frightened.

"I'll be back soon," Snider had promised the men in her home. But the interview lasted nearly four hours.

To begin the process of "breaking the girl from the guy," Richardson repeatedly referred to Luther's admitted sexual experience with Cher Elder while Snider was out of town. After all, Richardson thought, hell hath no fury like a woman scorned.

He pointed out that Luther lied to her constantly. And he made it clear that he believed that Mary and Cher were not his first, nor would be his last, victims.

Debrah tried to be objective without giving up Luther. She

admitted that she was hurt when Tom asked her to send the tape to Babe for safekeeping. But after awhile, she said, she began to wonder if it was so that Byron and J.D. could listen to the tape "in order to get their stories straight."

Richardson wanted to know what Luther told her of his trip to Central City. She related Luther's varying stories: how he said he originally went with the Eerebout boys, and only after it was clear she would eventually hear about Elder, did he admit to going with the girl.

Snider said Luther tried to explain away the sexual incident by claiming he was drunk. They'd picked up a bottle of wine somewhere, she said. She left out the part about finding Luther in bed in the middle of the day when she got back from Washington with his sore and battered hands. The part about her missing shovel and the clothes he'd "lost" after "burying a box of rifles." She left out Mortho and drug dealers who killed young girls for talking and cut off their lips as a warning. She never mentioned Interstate 70, a stone historical marker, or an unmarked grave. She didn't know that he had done anything worse than bury Elder. She couldn't betray him just for trying to stay out of prison.

Richardson asked how Luther had been acting since his visit. He wanted to know if the pressure was having an effect.

"He's in a panic," Debrah admitted. "He's afraid you guys are going to frame him for something." She said he had been making a lot of calls to the Eerebouts and Southy that seemed to have something to do with Cher.

Richardson's reply was sarcastic. "What's he think we're going to frame him on? A missing girl?"

He moved his chair closer to Snider and brought up the rape in Summit County, how her boyfriend had lied to her about that. "And now he's out a whole three months and he's doing narcotic transactions in the mail. I mean, three months is a pretty short time, and now he goes out and has sex with another girl in a car that you bought him and then she disappears." He let the image of betrayal sink in.

Snider tried desperately to stick by her man. "I'm scared for him," she conceded. "But I don't think he's done anything to that girl. I think if he was that kind of man and as mad as I've made him over our arguments . . . then I think I would have been hurt.''

Richardson shook his head. "Do you understand that there are serial killers who are married with six kids and three grand-children that go out and kill people at night and come home and are just as charming as you always see on TV? That they're the best neighbors in the world?"

"Yeah," Debrah answered weakly. He was hitting too close to thoughts she'd had—and tried unsuccessfully to put out of her mind. "I know that that happens."

It was obvious that Snider was hurting, but Richardson wasn't about to let up. He saw a crack and meant to drive the wedge in further. He leaned closer. "There's obviously two people in Thomas; there's a Thomas you know, and a Thomas you don't. I mean, at some point the clouds have gotta break and you gotta sit there and say, 'Holy shit, this is what I'm in the middle of.' "

Debrah sat quietly blinking back her tears. Richardson decided to shift gears, remind her again of what happened on that March night. "What do you think could have made Cher vomit in the car?" he asked.

Debrah shrugged. "Maybe if he forced her to do oral sex."

Richardson nodded. And how about anal sex? he asked, recalling Luther's attack on Mary Brown. Was there any indication in Luther's past of homosexual activity?

Again Snider shrugged. He'd been in prison, she said, and he was always bragging about how he'd saved young guys from "the wolves" who wanted to rape them. But she'd noticed during visits how those young guys fawned all over him, "like they were the girlfriends, not me."

Snider looked at her watch. She had been gone much longer than it took to buy a Mother's Day card. "Do you think you're in danger now?" Detective Russell asked.

"Yeah," Debrah sighed. "I think I'm in danger of losing him." She worried, she said, that drunk, Tom might have lost control though she quickly added again that she didn't believe he would hurt the girl. "I would be really upset if there's wrong involved. If there's not wrong involved, then who am I to con-demn someone to hell?"

Suddenly, she was angry that Richardson was sitting so close.

She understood from her psychology background what he was doing—invading her space, putting her on the defensive.

In a way, she liked this man with the Texas accent and piercing eyes. He seemed honest and up front. His concern for Cher Elder was genuine and beyond what she might expect of a cop just doing his job. But at the same time, she didn't want him to think he could manipulate her so easily.

"Back off, detective," she said as he leaned near to ask his next question.

Richardson looked surprised. Then he smiled and backed away. He should have known that a psych nurse would know what he was doing. He liked this woman's grit if he didn't understand her choice in men.

"Where do you think Cher is?" he asked. He sensed that Snider knew more than she was telling and was wrestling with her conscience. If he could just ask the right question, it might all come out in a flood.

"I don't have any idea," she lied.

Richardson let it pass. *Too soon,* he thought. *She's not ready.* He decided to paint her more of a picture of the sort of man he believed Luther to be. "Has Tom ever talked to you about being accused of some other crimes before the sex assault?" he asked.

"He told me that he was a suspect in murders in some county," she nodded, "but he was cleared of that when they investigated."

"Did he tell you the nature of those murders?"

No, she replied. She just assumed that if Tom was a suspect, the victims had to be females because of what he'd done to Mary Brown.

"What would your thoughts be if I were to tell you that in 1982 in Summit County two females hitchhiking were picked up and murdered and then after Luther was arrested, the murders stopped?" Richardson said

He pointed his finger at her like a gun and said, "It was bam, bam. Then the third person, the arrest, and the homicides stopped. No more murders ever in Summit County. You're talking a county that has two women killed in a year, which quadrupled their homicide rate for the last fifteen years. And then they immediately stopped when Luther was caught on his assault."

Snider pointed out weakly that Luther let Mary Brown go. Richardson retorted that she was allowed to run from his truck only after he had hit her so hard it broke her neck and had nearly amputated a finger with the claw hammer. She was dumped, he said, semi-conscious, in sub-zero weather, in the dark. She had survived only through her own will power, not because of any last minute benevolence of Thomas Luther.

"And now you have Luther, who goes up to Central City with this girl—and I'm telling you, I've gone all the way back to where she was born and raised in the smallest fucking town you ever saw in your life—and she has disappeared.

"People disappear. And some people are prone to be homicide victims. Cher does not match any of that. She was not the kind of person who dumps her car four blocks from Byron's apartment and completely disappears, never uses a credit card, never writes a check, never calls her friends, never calls her family, and was never seen again except the last time she was with Luther. And the only way we found that out is because we threatened to put Luther's picture in the newspapers."

Now Richardson was angry. "Why all this over a missing girl? Why all these lies and deception and worry about a missing girl?"

Debrah couldn't answer. She was crying. She knew he might be right about Tom. She'd read enough about serial killers to know he fit the profile. She also knew that she fit the profile of women who fell in love with such men by denying the undeniable, even when they knew that beneath the surface lurked a monster. Such women always believed that they would be able to tame the beast . . . such women were always wrong.

"What if Luther killed Cher?" Richardson asked.

"Then he belongs in jail," she said and began to cry again.

Richardson felt sorry for her, but he had to make her understand that if she protected Luther and he killed again, it would be on her head.

"I'm going to tell you something," he said quietly as he handed Snider a tissue. "If he did the two women in Summit County and then did Cher just two months after he got out of prison, there'll be another victim, and I'm talking it ain't going to take long. I'm telling you that the next one's coming, and it's coming quick, 'cause there's no reason to quit. He got away with two, he gets caught on one, is out in three months and he kills another. I don't want another child's life on my hands."

He paused and saw the message hit home. It was time to push the boundaries back just a little bit further. "How do you think he would kill her? Do you think he'd shoot her, strangle her? Do you think he'd beat her to death?"

Snider pictured Luther when he was angry, when his eyes were those of the mad bull. "I think he would beat her to death," she mumbled, her head down.

"Can you see him strangling her?"

"That's a possibility."

"Do you think he would sexually assault her?"

Debrah recalled the constant comments about women's bodies and what he'd like to do with them. She remembered the violent, demeaning pornography—his fantasy that a raped woman would "learn to like it."

"Yeah," she told the detective.

"Do you think he'd bury the body?" Richardson asked, edging nearer to what he wanted to know.

"I know he would," she blurted out before realizing what she had said.

"You know? How do you know that?" he demanded.

She fumbled to explain. She said she only meant that it seemed the logical thing to do. But then she walked into another mistake. She'd been working in early April as a pool nurse in a town near Central City when she heard a body had been found in a local creek, she said trying to change the direction of the conversation. She said, she thought then that it might be Cher Elder.

"Wait a minute," Richardson said, "you told me earlier that the first you'd heard of Cher was the day I came to talk to Tom. April 20."

Maybe she'd mixed up the date, Snider said, panicked. The detective had caught her in a lie. But Richardson let it pass. She wasn't ready to spill the whole story, and he wasn't going to force her back to Luther's side by confronting her.

Debrah changed the subject again. "He took her to Central City but brought her back to Byron's," she said, adding hopefully, "Someone saw her at a bingo parlor."

"No one saw her at a bingo parlor after that night," the detective responded. "That wasn't true."

Richardson allowed the interview to grind to a halt. It was a good start. Debrah Snider knew more than she was saying, of that he was sure, but he could wait and let her conscience work her over. He told her that he had a search warrant for Luther's car and was going to pick it up now.

Snider looked at her watch again. It was almost 1 A.M. "I'm in trouble," she said. "I going to say you pulled me over."

Richardson nodded. "We'll back you up. We'll say we were watching the house and stopped you." He knew he had placed her in a tough, maybe dangerous, spot. "I'm sorry."

"It's not your fault," Debrah replied. "I mean I'm obviously involved in something, and it's my choice. I suspected that if this didn't get cleared up, and Cher didn't get found, that you guys would be here to talk to me."

Richardson told her that several police cars and officers would be accompanying him and the tow truck to her property. He hoped the show of force would preclude Luther from resisting.

"He's not going to cause any problems, is he?" he asked.

Debrah looked worried, but shook her head. "I don't think so."

Several officers had come into the room. "No guns, 'cause this is simple," Richardson said more to comfort her than to the men. "We're just going to tow the car."

Thomas Luther didn't resist. But he was plenty mad, especially when Richardson wouldn't let him have a small black telephone book he found in the car.

"So that's what's happened to this woman," Luther yelled, pointing to Snider. "You guys couldn't let her call home and let people know? Her husband's out lookin' for her right now. We've all been drivin' around looking on the sides of roads and shit."

"She's been with us for the last couple of hours," Sgt. Don Girson, who had accompanied Richardson from Lakewood, replied. "We stopped her on the road."

"Thomas, we're not gonna argue," Richardson interjected. "Let's just do this and get out of here, okay? If you wanna talk—"

"No," Luther said, cutting him off. "I don't wanna talk to

you fuckin' guys. Man, you're all fuckin' assholes, you know what I mean?''

Luther was pacing back and forth, his voice getting louder, and he gestured wildly. Some of the officers nervously moved their hands nearer to their guns.

"I ain't gonna jack with ya, okay?" Richardson said. "Just settle down."

But Luther kept ranting. "You ain't gonna jack with me? You're jackin' with me now. It's goddam bullshit, it's harrassment is what it is." He demanded to know when he could get his car back. "How long is it gonna take your forensic people to go through it?"

"I would say that it'll probably be done around Thursday, maybe Friday of this week," Richardson replied. "I'll call ya when we're done with it, and you can come pick it up."

The tow truck operator had gone about his business while Richardson occupied Luther and was now ready to leave. "I don't want to talk to you no more," Luther said, glaring at Richardson.

"Then don't," Richardson replied mildly. With that, he climbed in his car and the fleet of police cars and the tow truck hauling Luther's blue Geo Metro were off.

Back inside the house, Luther turned to Debrah and demanded to know what the cops had wanted with her. She told him as much about the interview as she could remember, leaving out her own thoughts and responses.

"Richardson said you're a serial killer," she said, noting to herself that it was Dennis, not Tom, who was out looking for her. She worried that Tom might burst a vein, he looked so angry.

"Do you believe him?" he asked.

Debrah looked at him, at the angry eyes and the clenched fists. "No," she said. It wasn't entirely a lie. She just wasn't ready to believe it might be true. But she was relieved to hear her husband's car pull up to the house.

Debrah Snider didn't sleep that night but lay awake going through everything that had happened since she came back from Washington. She was still thinking about it at work that afternoon

when Richardson called. He asked if she was okay, and if Luther
had caused any problems.

"No, he was fine." He hadn't asked her about the interview,
she said, but she had "volunteered some things."

Snider appreciated the detective's concern. But in the light of
day, she couldn't believe that Luther was a killer. The doubts
Richardson had planted in her mind the night before were just
shadows and ghosts.

Richardson wanted to know if Luther was planning to leave
for Chicago soon. "He's got a lot of mixed emotions about it,"
Debrah replied. "Part of him says he wants to run. Just bolt for
the mountains, and another part of him says he wants to go to
Chicago."

Snider said his paranoia was understandable considering his
background. He'd told her before he was even out of prison that
"the system" would try to hang him again. But the detective
just scoffed. "We didn't even know Luther existed before two
weeks ago."

Maybe Southy would know more, Debrah volunteered. Tom
had called him a lot, and while she hadn't been able to hear
much, it was certainly about "the missing girl."

"I don't know why Southy would do anything to her," Richardson replied, wondering who Southy was and hoping she would
say.

Snider had no comeback to that so she volunteered that Luther
had called Babe that afternoon just as she was leaving for work.
The phone seemed to have been shifted to Byron or J.D. She
heard him angrily discussing his car being taken by the police.
But at the same time, he didn't seem too concerned about the
cops finding any evidence in his car.

"He said, 'I don't have to worry about it. I already told 'em
she vomited in my car, that's all that's there. . . . That's all
they're gonna find.' He was real confident," Debrah said.

There was one other thing the detective might want to know,
she said. Luther had borrowed a shovel from work—it had been
in his car when Richardson and Heylin spotted the stolen tools,
but the shovel was gone the next day. He said he returned it to
work.

Richardson remembered the shovel. It had a funny scar on
the front of what appeared to be a brand new blade. He and

Snider hung up, both of them wondering what the other wasn't saying.

A few days later, Luther asked Debrah Snider to accompany him to the Jefferson County public defender's office in Golden. On the way, he started talking about "finding" Elder's body after Richardson's visit. "It was really stinky," he said. "It looked horrible."

It? Debrah's conscience tugged at her. "She was not an it!" she snapped. "She was a girl. She not deserve what they did to her."

Luther shrugged. What happened to Cher was not his fault. What he had done, he had done out of self-protection. Did she want him to go to prison for it?

"I don't believe that she was killed because she was an informant," Debrah said. "Did Skip pay you to kill her for Byron?"

Instead of answering her directly, Luther said, "Well, if you were in trouble and someone was going to put you away, I'd do anything to prevent it."

Angry now, he wouldn't talk to her anymore and insisted that she stay in the car when they arrived at the public defender's office. When he came back out, he said, "They told me you'd be my greatest threat. You know that I buried her." It was an accusation.

"That's not true," she said quietly. "I love you and will stand by you."

Her answer seemed to satisfy him for the moment. He knew she had already talked to the police and apparently not given him up. But that night, as she was cooking dinner, the conversation again turned to Cher.

"Cher Elder was a vindictive bitch who was going to snitch on Byron," Luther said. "She deserved what she got."

His tone made Debrah shiver. She thought about her attempts to turn him into the police for the marijuana and stolen tools.

"Tom, no one deserves to die," she said as evenly as she could. "I talked to the cops. That makes me a snitch. . . . So who's gonna kill me?"

Debrah knew she was walking on dangerous ground, but she was angry and dealing with a conscience that would not shut up. It. Vindictive bitch. Where was the man she had fallen in love with? This Tom was always making himself out to be the victim. Not Mary. Not Cher. It was always the girls' fault they got hurt.

She looked up when he didn't answer. He was staring at her with those angry blue eyes.

Chapter Fourteen

Early May 1993—Lakewood, Colorado

The technicians in the crime lab hadn't found much of anything in Luther's car, except the "vomit" stain. However, there was one important fact about the stain: it was directly behind the driver's seat. When the seat was laid back, as Luther had claimed it was during sex with Elder, there was no way the stain could have reached that spot. The seat prevented it. It made more sense that she had been laid on the backseat and then thrown up, or bled.

There was little other evidence—just some dirt, light-tan in color in the back. The dirt wouldn't be of any use unless Richardson could find the grave and compare it against the soil there. But he wasn't about to tell Luther that; he wanted him to think that the forensic lab was finding all sorts of things. And he also had no intention of returning the car right away . . . just to aggravate Luther.

In the meantime, there were a million small bits of information to run down. He called up Sgt. Josey and asked him to check with Luther's former employer about any missing shovels.

Byron Eerebout contacted Richardson's partner, Heylin, and said that Cher had called him at his old number at the army base. Heylin had checked it out; somebody claiming to be "Byron's girlfriend" had called but not left a name.

Richardson also talked to Babe and asked why the boys had lied about knowing Tom Luther. "Because they were tryin' to protect him, knowing his background and all," she replied. "Nobody feels Tom is guilty of anything, and especially not me."

A meeting had been arranged between the detective and the boys who, their mother said, would be accompanied by her and an attorney. The day of the meeting, Richardson called and canceled. "The boys had their chance to tell the truth," he told Babe. "We have their statements and if we need anything else, we'll holler." The Eerebouts knew that he knew they had lied to him; he wanted that hanging over their heads.

On May 12, Richardson contacted the FBI's Behavioral Sciences unit—the agency had specialists in serial killers and he wanted their opinion on Luther. The agents listened and looked at what he had so far and came up with a profile. The suspect's modus operandi could have changed with experience, they said. And if the attack had not been planned ahead, he might use any weapon available.

They cautioned that Luther wasn't the type to confess. However, working on his paranoia might reap rewards. The stakeouts and isolation efforts were a good start, they said. Make him think that the cops had something on him and were just working to put all their ducks in a row. It might worry him enough to go check out the grave.

The FBI evaluation reaffirmed Richardson's own game plan. He had copied the pages from the little black book in Luther's car and used the numbers in it to contact Luther's friends. Whenever he talked to Debrah Snider, Richardson casually mentioned that if Tom had buried Cher, coyotes or dogs were likely to dig up the body.

A few days after he talked to the FBI agents, Richardson received a telephone call from Gina Jones, who told him about a recent conversation she had with Byron Eerebout. During the conversation, she said, she asked her former boyfriend why he had lied to the police about Elder. "He said, 'I didn't lie. I don't know what the hell you're talkin' about.' I said, 'Well, you know, the police just came here and they questioned me and I couldn't lie . . . .' "

Jones said she could hear J.D. yelling in the background. "Then I heard Byron tell J.D., 'No, she can lie to me, but she can't fuckin' lie to the cops. She can just fuckin' only tell the truth to the cops,' " Gina said. "He told me never to call back there again."

"Do you think he had somethin' to do with her death?"
Richardson asked.

"I don't think Byron would," she replied. She didn't like
him much, but he wasn't a killer.

"Do you think Thomas killed her?" Richardson continued.

"Honestly?" she replied. "Yeah."

"Okay, I do, too."

It was just his opinion, one he couldn't prove, but a few days
later, there was an unexpected bit of information that further
reinforced his belief. It happened at a meeting of Denver-area
police agencies on sex crimes. In attendance was Dr. John Macdonald, a noted forensic psychiatrist.

Macdonald was officially retired but still went on the occasional rides with his friends with the Denver police department,
who kept his desk reserved for him out of respect and fondness.
The psychiatrist had retained a particular interest in sex crimes
and frequently attended these meetings. He was listening to
Richardson present his case when the detective mentioned a
prior crime in which his suspect had brutally raped a young
woman in Summit County with a hammer. Macdonald suddenly
recalled the young man he had interviewed many years earlier
in the Buena Vista prison.

"I believe I once talked to Mr. Luther," he told Richardson
after the meeting. "I think I have it on videotape. I'll try to find
it for you."

Macdonald found the tape and had it delivered to the Lakewood Police Department. There Richardson watched and listened
to a younger Tom Luther describe the girl he had attacked, and
imagined what happened to Cher.

"She was very friendly, saying how nice I was for driving
her," Luther said.

In his mind, Richardson heard Cher thank Luther for giving
her a shoulder to cry on. For being so nice and taking her to
see her friend Karen in Central City.

"She remind you of your mother?" a detective asked.

Luther had laughed on the video, setting Richardson's teeth
on edge. "Yeah. She did remind me of my mom . . . when she
started screamin'."

Richardson wondered about Luther's mother. Was she a key
to this case?

"I didn't get real violent with the young lady until she started screaming," Luther said on the video. "Mostly that was out of fear, I believe, just my paranoia of the cops: 'Oh my God, they're gonna catch me with coke in my pocket and pot under my seat.'"

So, Richardson thought, he'd rather kill than face arrest. His attention was brought back to the television screen when Macdonald asked Luther what had triggered the rage.

"I don't know what triggered it," Luther shrugged. "I guess it got to a point where I just didn't want to have control or didn't feel I should have control or—" Richardson recalled Snider's fears that her lover had lost control that night. "—I was completely in a rage. I should have left. But I needed to overpower the area. It was my domain. I'm the lion. This is my kingdom that you're in right now."

Richardson turned off the video seething with anger. So this asshole saw himself as a predator. He was no lion, he was a mad dog who attacked small, defenseless women who trusted him. He didn't want to get caught by the police, so he tried to silence his potential accusers—forever.

Later, Richardson called Macdonald to see if there was anything else he could tell him about Luther. The psychiatrist recalled that Luther's victim in Summit County, Mary, had physically resembled his mother, whom he claimed had abused him as a child. A pretty, petite woman with dark hair worn to her shoulders.

Richardson remembered that among the photographs he had collected of Cher Elder, there was one in which her dark hair was shoulder-length. She had it cut shortly before she disappeared, according to her friends, but after she had been introduced to Luther.

"He feels sexually inadequate," Macdonald continued. "And is very bitter toward the police. Be careful."

With the video still fresh in his mind, Richardson found it difficult to contain his feelings when Luther called Thursday, May 13, wanting his car. "Probably tomorrow," he replied. "Hopin' we'll get it done tomorrow. What stalled us is we got some body fluids and stuff like that, some forensic things, that we had to call the state lab in on. So it took a little longer than expected."

There was silence, then Luther responded, "Well, you knew that stuff was there 'cause I told you it was there."

Richardson tried to sound cocky. "Yeah, so I'll give you a call as soon as it's done. You'll be the first to know." He hung up the telephone convinced that Luther was close to the point where he would make a move.

Over the next couple of days, he made sure to mention the coyotes again to Snider and that the state crime lab was still working on the car. It was a gamble. Luther might just decide to run. But the FBI profile and his own instincts told Richardson that "the lion" would return to his kill.

On May 18, Richardson got the call from Debrah Snider that he had been hoping for: Luther was on the move. She said he'd told her that he needed to go for a hike in the mountains to clear his mind. Then he'd called J.D. Eerebout and said, "I think it's time for a road trip. Pick me up at twelve-thirty. I need you to drive me to a couple of places."

Luther threw a few things and a sleeping bag into a backpack, Debrah said. Then he'd asked to borrow her truck so that he could get money from an ATM machine. Her horse trailer was attached to the truck, but he insisted that there wasn't time to unhitch it. He got behind the wheel.

"He was driving like a madman," Snider said. He swerved across lanes of traffic, the tires squealing and the trailer tipping dangerously from side to side. He honked and shouted at other drivers, and when a woman wouldn't let him cut into her lane, it really set him off.

"You fuckin' bitch," he screamed out the window at the startled woman. "Get off the road!"

Debrah had seen him angry before, but not like this. His eyes truly resembled those of the wounded bull on her poster. Afraid that he'd turn her trailer over, she demanded that he stop and let her drive. "I said, 'You're too angry.' "

Luther slammed on the brakes in the middle of traffic and jumped out. He grabbed the backpack that was in the bed of the truck and took off without looking back.

Snider tried to find J.D. at the highway exit where Luther asked to be picked up so that J.D. would know where to look for his friend. But the boy wasn't there yet. That's when she went to a telephone booth and called Richardson.

"I think he's going to the grave," she said.

"You think he's goin' to move the body?" Richardson asked.

"At least, you know, bury it better or somethin,' " she replied.

"Okay," Richardson said, "just go ahead and tell me why you think that."

Snider realized that she had all but conceded that she knew Luther had buried Elder. The fact was, that morning he told her he wanted to place rocks on the grave to keep animals from digging up the body. But how could she explain without becoming a witness against Tom? "Well, I just do," she told Richardson. "I mean, I can't tell ya why. I don't know why, I just . . I just do."

Luther was real angry, she said. "He's tired of you jackin' him around. He says that if somebody was to take and, uh, kill your wife and family, it'd teach you a lesson."

There was a pause, then Richardson asked what sort of weapons he was carrying. Nothing that she knew of, Debrah responded, but he might stop at the Eerebouts, and they probably had guns.

"Do you feel safe?" Richardson asked.

Debrah sighed. Again, she appreciated the detective's concern. But what did it matter if Tom was gone? "I don't value my life a whole lot, Mr. Richardson," she said.

"You think he's gonna try to kill ya?"

"I don't. . . . I don't know," Snider replied. She wanted to cry. How could it have come to this, that the man she loved could conceivably want her dead? She didn't want to believe it. "I don't think I'm in that much danger, but this man's real paranoid."

"What do you think he's gonna do if a cop stops him?" Richardson asked.

"If he has somethin', he would kill 'em."

"You think he'd kill 'em?"

"Absolutely."

"Without a doubt?"

"Without a doubt. . . . 'Cause he hates cops."

"Do you think he buried her up there?" Richardson asked.

"I don't know if he buried her at all," she lied, but she was damned if she'd be a witness against Tom. "You know, I don't know if he did this. I think it's a possibility."

"Do you think he's capable of killin' her?"

She paused. In this case, the truth could not be used against Luther in court, but it might help Richardson. "Yeah, I do," she said. "I think he's capable of killin' her."

"Why is he makin' these threats against my family?" Richardson asked. "Why is he so stuck on me?"

"Well," she replied, " 'cause he sees you as tryin' to pin something on him he didn't do. . . . At least that's the excuse he tells me."

A half hour after hanging up with Snider, Richardson got another call from her. She had gone home and found Luther there with J.D. He wouldn't talk to her as he stomped around gathering a few last items for his trip. She slipped off to a back bedroom and called the detective again.

Richardson told her to hang up. He would call back and ask for Tom. Luther's threats against his family had set off alarms in his mind. He wasn't worried about himself, Luther probably didn't have the balls to take on a man—but Sabrina and the boys were another story. That was right up Luther's alley.

Richardson wanted to make this personal, and Debrah had just told him that he had succeeded. But threatening his family was taking it a step further. The stakes had increased in the last couple of weeks; Sabrina had told him she was pregnant with their third child.

Still, there was time. Luther was in Fort Collins and his family was in Lakewood, more than an hour away. He called the Larimer County Sheriff's Office and asked that an unmarked car, part of the task force, get ready to follow Luther from Snider's. Then he alerted other members of the state police and Lakewood task forces to be ready to intercept and follow Luther once he hit the interstate.

Finally, he called Luther. "Listen," he said, trying to sound smugly confident, "we just got done with your car. Can you come in tomorrow morning . . . nine o'clock?"

Luther seemed taken back by the detective's tone. "Okay,"

he said. "So are your people satisfied now that the story that I told you was true?"

Richardson kept up the bluff. "Well, we still got some questions. If you wanna talk to me, I'll talk to you tomorrow."

"Yeah, you've been bustin' my chops," Luther spat. "You fuckin' told my girl that I'm a serial killer and all kinds of crazy shit."

Richardson ignored the outburst. "You wanna come in tomorrow, nine o'clock, to pick up your car?"

"I'll be there," Luther said and slammed the phone down.

A few minutes later, Snider called back. Luther had rushed out of the house with J.D. Eerebout. Whatever Richardson had said, it had pushed him into action.

"He said you're acting too cocky," she told him. "He thinks you found the body . . . he said he has to go find out for himself." That was about all he'd say to her. He was punishing her again, but this time she hadn't just accepted it. "I told him, 'You know, you had a shot. Somebody gave you a shot, and if you have screwed your life up, that's not my fault. You can't punish me for that." But he just glared at her and jumped into J.D.'s car, a big red Mercury sedan.

"If you want a body, you guys need to find out where he's going," she said.

Richardson tried once more to get Snider to tell him everything she knew. But she wouldn't do it. "He's got so much rope, and if he gets caught and hangs himself, that's nobody's fault but his own."

The detective better watch out for his family, though, she said, Luther was on his way. And he might very well be coming to kill.

The first sign of trouble was when Larimer County lost Luther before he got out of Fort Collins. Richardson, directing the pursuit from the Lakewood headquarters, was starting to worry when the Colorado State Patrol picked him up again. Luther and Eerebout were headed south on Interstate 25 at a high rate of speed. But they were making it difficult on their pursuers by suddenly pulling over onto the shoulder of the highway to let cars pass. Then they were off again at speeds close to 100 MPH.

Twice the pursuit lost contact with Luther after being forced to continue past J.D.'s parked car. Each time, the pair were picked up again just as Richardson was about to reach for the telephone to call Sabrina.

Then Luther hit the Denver area and his pursuers lost him again. "We can't find Luther," they warned.

There was no more time. Richardson hadn't wanted to alarm Sabrina; Luther was already a source of fear in his house, but a woman-killer who had just threatened to murder his family was loose in Denver.

Richardson called the patrol desk. "Get some cars over to my house, *now!*" Then he called his wife.

"Listen," he said, "Luther's in Denver and he's been talking about how he is going to smoke our family. I want you to get your things together. There's a patrol car on the way—and stay at your brother's tonight."

It was a bright, sunny afternoon, but suddenly Sabrina felt chilled. Her husband was in a dangerous business, but he knew how to take care of himself. He'd been nearly killed in a bar brawl in Gladewater, but bloody and barely conscious he'd still managed to arrest his man. Then there was the time in a Texas jail when an inmate grabbed another officer's gun and shot Scott at point-blank range. The bullet had passed between his arm and chest, close enough to leave burn marks, but Scott had taken that man down, too.

Only once had the danger extended to her. In Texas, an informant passed on that Houston drug dealers had put a hit out on Scott. Not finding their targets at home, they blasted the hell out of Scott's truck. If it had been up to Scott, he would have stayed until he busted up the drug ring or died in the attempt. But he wouldn't take that chance with Sabrina. They'd left Texas and moved to Colorado. Sabrina had been afraid of the drug dealers. But it was nothing like the dread she now had of Luther.

The case consumed her husband. There was no escaping Luther. And that had led to arguments. Lately, she had begun to not only resent Luther, but fear him. Debrah Snider said he was angry and wanted to hurt Scott. Her husband knew what Luther was and what he had done. Anybody who'd ever met Scott realized that he saw through lies the way some men saw through binoculars. Luther had to be afraid of her husband, and fear made him dangerous.

Even the boys were terrified that Luther would someday come to get them. Too late, Sabrina and Scott realized that the twins were gleaning more from the dinner-table conversation than they had given them credit for. Once, passing a billboard with the huge, distorted photograph of a rock star—a promotion for a local radio station—they had started screaming, "That's Luther. That's the monster."

Now Scott was telling her that the police had lost Luther less than fifteen minutes from her home. It was like he was already in the house, stalking her.

Sabrina looked out the window and her heart nearly stopped at the sight of a dark figure standing on her front porch. It took a moment for her to realize that the figure was a uniformed police officer. "The patrol car's here already," she said, hanging up.

The officer repeated that she was to gather a few things as quickly as she could. No, there wasn't time to call her brother. She could call from the car. They didn't know where Luther was and they weren't taking any chances.

The twins saw the police officer and immediately picked up on their mother's fear. They cried in the patrol car all the way to their uncle's house.

Sabrina did her best to comfort them. "Daddy will protect us," she said, wishing she'd never heard of Luther. "He'll get the bad guy."

With Sabrina and the boys safe, Richardson returned his attention to trying to find Luther. The unmarked cars sitting on Babe's place reported no sign of him, although the two other Eerebout boys were seen running in and out to use local pay telephones. Another unmarked car had been stationed at Richardson's house in case Luther tried to carry out his threat, but he didn't show there either. He had disappeared at a spot where major interstates met and ran off in every direction. He could have gone anywhere.

All night, Richardson sat at his desk but there was no word. In the morning, he called Debrah Snider. "I was just checkin' on ya," he said.

"Why?"

She sounded like she had been crying, and he felt sorry for her. "Just to make sure you're all right."

Debrah seemed to appreciate the call even though they both knew that her welfare wasn't his chief worry. "Yeah, I'm okay," she said.

"Have you seen him or heard from him?" Richardson asked.

"He called this morning, but I didn't answer the phone, and it was on the recorder. All he said was, 'Bye.' "

Richardson told her that Luther hadn't been by to pick up his car. He wanted to know if all his stuff was still at her place.

"Pretty much," she said, "except what was in his backpack."

"Do you think he'll come and get it since he called?" He didn't want to admit that they'd lost Luther after she'd had the courage to alert them to his movements.

"It's hard for me to know exactly," Debrah said. "I mean, it sounded like, you know, good-bye forever. But I called Babe and she said that J.D. was gonna take him for a hike. She acted like she expected him to be back today. But I don't think this was a recreational hike that we're talking about."

Richardson thanked her and hung up. The fact that Babe thought Luther was due back that day seemed to indicate that he wasn't fleeing the state. At least not yet. With a little luck, they might find Tom Luther again.

A little luck is exactly what he got. That afternoon, one of the surveillance cars on Interstate 70 in the mountains west of Denver spotted J.D. Eerebout's car. The curious thing is that it was traveling westbound away from Denver and, though it was hard to say for sure, the pursuit team didn't think Luther was in the car.

This time, the pursuers were able to stay with Eerebout as he exited off the interstate near the little town of Empire. Just before he got to the town, he turned onto an isolated dirt road and, as the police team watched, flipped a U-turn. Suddenly, Luther leaped out from behind a large boulder and ran to where J.D. waited. He jumped in and the car sped back along the road and onto the interstate, heading east towards Denver.

Again Eerebout was hitting speeds of more than 100 MPH as he roared down the snaking six-lane interstate dodging in and out of the traffic lanes. Only once he stopped—at a gas station where Luther got out and ran into the bathroom. As soon as they were off again, detectives in one of the pursuing vehicles went into the bathroom and grabbed the trashcan and its contents for evidence. The other car stayed after J.D., trying to keep up without being spotted.

It proved too difficult. As Eerebout arrived in Denver, the pursuit lost him again.

"Dammit!" Richardson exclaimed when none of the police surveillance teams were able to re-establish contact. Where in the hell was Luther going?

The answer arrived ten minutes later when the perplexed officer at the front desk paged him. "Thomas Luther is here to get his car."

Whatever insecurity Luther had been feeling before his trip to the mountains, it had evaporated by the time Richardson met him in the lobby. The detective noted that Luther's jeans were dirty on the front; he was also wearing a dark blue work shirt and a blue baseball cap with the word "Navy" in gold on its front.

Luther was cocky; he was strutting around with his arms akimbo like a prison weightlifter, a half-smile playing on his lips. Richardson knew why. They both did. He had been to the grave and seen that it was undiscovered. Richardson didn't have the body after all, and without it he had squat.

Richardson had to bite his tongue as Luther smirked at him. Even as they talked, a massive search was beginning in Empire. He hadn't lost this hand yet. At least they had a place to start looking.

"We're concerned with Cher because there's nothin' that indicates she's alive at all," Richardson said, hoping to draw Luther out.

"Nothin' indicates she's dead though either, is there?" Luther shot back.

"Well, yeah, as a matter of fact there is," Richardson retorted. "So we're kind of steppin' up the investigation and, of course, not all of our crime lab results are back yet."

Luther shrugged it off. "You're tryin' to bust my balls. You fuckin' went up there and told Debrah that I was a fuckin' serial killer and made me a fuckin' bunch of problems at home. You know what I mean?''

"Listen," Richardson interrupted, "I'm not gonna sit here and argue with ya."

Luther nodded. "We're not even gonna talk, as a matter of fact. We ain't askin' nothin', we ain't talkin' nothin', just give me my fuckin' paperwork so I can get out of here."

The two men glared at each other as Richardson handed him the papers. Richardson didn't care if Luther knew he was *the* suspect in Cher's death. He asked him if he had someone who could verify that he was home in Fort Collins on Sunday morning after dropping Elder off at Byron's. Luther shook his head; he had no alibi.

Luther was looking at the paperwork on the search warrant for his car. He noticed that the crime lab had been done with the car for a week. He flushed red in anger.

"You sound pissed," Richardson taunted.

"Yeah, well, when she shows up in two or three months in a treatment center," Luther spat, "or some fucking thing, or out in California, you can come back and fuckin' kiss my ass, pal."

Richardson laughed, which made Luther flush more. "Well, I don't think I'll be kissin' your ass, pal," the detective said, then dismissed Luther. "You're free to go, bud. You can go anywhere you want. And if you hear from Cher, let us know."

Luther sputtered, he was so angry. "If I did hear from her, I wouldn't tell ya a goddamn thing, pal."

It was good to have Luther back on the defensive, the cornered animal. "See ya, Luther," Richardson said smiling.

Luther started to go, then turned back. His blue eyes were filled with bright red rage. "Where do you live?" he asked, then turned and walked away.

Richardson kept smiling, but his eyes were nearly black in anger. *He threatened my family,* he thought, *to my face!*

This time there was no chance he was going to lose Luther. Richardson had talked a judge into giving him permission to attach a "bird dog" monitoring device on the bottom of Luther's car. The high-tech "spy" equipment operated by sending a signal whenever the vehicle it was attached to began to move. That signal was relayed to a terminal that indicated the general direction the car was moving, which could then be translated to a map.

The bird dog was the reason Richardson wasn't surprised to hear from Snider a few hours later that Luther had arrived at her place in Fort Collins. He already knew it.

What he didn't know was that Luther had packed his possessions into his little car and was leaving, according to Debrah. Soon the bird dog verified that Luther was on the move, heading east from Fort Collins toward the Nebraska border.

Richardson had to act fast. He had been told by the Colorado Bureau of Investigation that they would need new hair and blood samples from Luther to compare to any that might be found on Cher's body and the gray, curly hair found in her car. The samples taken from him after his arrest in 1982 were no longer any good: hair color and texture changed with age. The detective had requested and received a Rule 41.1, a search warrant allowing authorities to take such samples involuntarily from Luther.

Richardson contacted the Colorado State Police and asked that they stop Luther. They had to make it quick. If he got across the state line, the Rule 41.1 was no longer valid; more importantly, a Rule 41.1 had to be served in daylight, and the sun was already low in the western sky.

There was an anxious hour before the state patrol radioed in that they had Luther in custody. They had stopped him just short of the state line.

Warned by Richardson that Luther might be armed and should be considered dangerous, they ordered him out of his car at shotgun point and made him lie facedown on the highway with his hands behind his head. Now they were heading back to Fort Collins where they would take him to a hospital to get the samples. Richardson signaled his partner, Mike Heylin, and a few minutes later they were on their way to Fort Collins again.

The Lakewood detectives arrived at the Fort Collins hospital just as the last samples were being taken from Luther. Pubic hair. When he saw Richardson, Luther's eyes bulged with anger and he began yelling.

"Fuck you, Richardson!" he screamed. "You want pubic hair? Here have as much as you want." His pants were down, and he began ripping handfuls of the hair out by the roots and offering them to the detective.

"There was more than enough in the first handful," Richardson later told his colleagues. "It had to have hurt like hell ... but I was raised to be polite and never interrupted him."

Luther stopped pulling out the hair as other police officers moved to restrain him. But he continued to curse Richardson.

"Fuck you! Fuck you, Richardson! You son-of-a-bitch, bustin' my balls. Where do you live, Richardson? *Where do you live?*"

Chapter Fifteen

May 19, 1993—Empire, Colorado

Empire was one of those tiny Colorado mining towns that were built on the hopes and fortunes of gold-seekers in the mid- to late-1800s and somehow managed to cling to existence in the high country when the gold played out. Their diggings, some hardly more than pits, others deep shafts blasted and picked far into the mountains entrails, littered the area.

In Empire's case, a nearby molydenum mine, a mineral used to strengthen and add flexibility to steel, continued as a source of jobs for residents. Otherwise the town relied on tourists in the spring and summer, passing hunters during the fall, and skiers in the winter for revenue.

The town, population 400, consisted of a single avenue of businesses lined up along the highway and maybe a hundred homes, many of them built in the old Victorian gingerbread style. It was a blink-and-you-miss-it sort of place, battered by harsh winters where snow piled up higher than a man could reach.

Empire was situated near the mouth of a narrow valley at an altitude of 8,600 feet above sea level, bordered on the downhill side by snow-fed Clear Creek, a noisy, vigorous stream that makes up in energy what it lacks in depth as it rushes eastward toward Golden. Bald-headed mountains from which some of the snow never melts, even in summer, rise on either side of the town and the highway that passes through it, paralleling the stream. The sides of the mountains are steep as a staircase; the pine-covered slopes interspersed with numerous landslides of granite rock that range in size from a man's fist to a small car.

After leaving the town, the highway runs for several miles before suddenly veering and climbing to the right, leaving the valley and the stream behind. Up it winds, through a series of U-turns until reaching Berthoud Pass, elevation 11,300 feet; then it drops down the other side to the Winter Park ski area a few miles further on.

Tom Luther and J.D. Eerebout were hardly out of Empire before a team was assembled to begin the search for Cher Elder's body. Within an hour, bloodhounds were brought in to backtrack Luther's trail from the point where he was seen jumping into Eerebout's car. The hounds led their handler and an entourage of detectives along Clear Creek, past the Empire sewage treatment plant and to a point on the highway near a small restaurant a mile beyond the town. But there, the dogs lost the trail.

Losing the scent on the road, the handler explained, was not unusual and it probably meant one of two things. One was that it could have been the spot where Luther got out of the car when J.D. first brought him to the mountains. The other was that it was where Luther crossed the road—busy highways don't hold scents well because of the passing cars.

As the dogs tried again to pick up the trail, other searchers walked along the creek looking for clothing that might have been discarded. Still others combed the hillside between the highway and the creek at the bottom, looking for any unusual disturbance of the ground that might indicate a grave.

They concentrated their efforts on the downhill side of the highway because as a general rule, most killers are too lazy to haul a body uphill for burial. Usually if a grave is found uphill, the victim was forced to walk to his, or her, execution.

The morning after his confrontation with Luther at the Fort Collins hospital, Scott Richardson was getting ready to go to Empire to help with the second day of the search when Debrah Snider called. "I just want to let you know that Tom has been here and got all his stuff . . . but I guess you already knew that,'' she said.

Richardson thought she sounded tired and hoarse, as if she'd been up all night crying. ''Yeah, we picked him up last night,'' he acknowledged. ''Where'd he say he was going? Chicago?''

''Yeah, he's goin' to that area. . . . It sounded like your encounter with him yesterday wasn't real good. He said somethin' about wantin' to whip your ass.''

The pain of betrayal was evident in her voice, and Richardson again felt sorry for her. ''He had an opportunity with you that was for a person in his position a deal of a lifetime and he just walked all over it,'' he said to make her feel better.

It only made her start crying. ''I've talked with his mom and I've basically told her the same thing, you know. And that I feel real hurt,'' she said.

The mention of Luther's mother raised an issue Richardson had been curious about since viewing Dr. Macdonald's videotape. ''He ever talk to you about her abusing him or anything like that?''

''Yeah,'' Snider responded. ''And his sister verified that she was very abusive.'' Luther had two sisters, she said, Becky, who she described as an alcoholic living in Pennsylvania, and Donna, who still resided in Vermont. It was Donna who told her that while her brother was a liar about such things as his prior military service and his two ''murdered'' children, his stories about their mother were true. Debrah said that she had met Luther's mother and thought she was nice. ''Donna says she's changed a lot, for the better.''

''What did he ever tell ya about his mom?'' Richardson asked. ''What kind of abuse?''

''That she just would go crazy and she would rant and rave and, you know, throw things and hit them,'' Snider said regaining her composure. ''And that his dad was abusive to her and that part of that abuse came from him intervening whenever she was going crazy and abusing them. You know . . . that his dad would start beating her up to stop her from abusing them.''

* * *

Arriving in Empire later that morning, Richardson got out of the car and looked around. *She's here,* he thought, *I can feel it. But where?*

Anyone of the rockslides that reached down the sides of the hills like fingers could have covered a grave. He walked over to the downhill side of the highway. It was so steep that a body thrown from the road would travel twenty yards before it stopped. Then it would be no problem to send a few rocks tumbling over the body that would look like any one of a thousand other piles of rocks in the immediate vicinity.

As he surveyed the area, Richardson was approached by a short, stocky man who identified himself as Jerry Murphy, the Empire town marshall. He'd been notified of the search and had come forward with some information of his own. He said he'd recognized Luther from photographs shown to him by the searchers. "Seen him walking east through town on the nineteenth," he said. "He was wearing blue jeans and a baseball hat with gold lettering on the front."

Richardson and Heylin began to canvas the town to see if anyone else had spotted Luther. They met John Poynter III who said he'd seen Luther as he was returning to Empire on the 19th. "He was directly across the road from the sewage plant," said Poynter, who concurred with Murphy's description except to add that when he saw him, Luther was carrying a white can.

Eventually, the Lakewood detectives ended up at the Marietta restaurant a mile west of Empire, near where the bloodhounds lost Luther's trail. Yes, said Linda and Michael Starr, the couple who owned the restaurant, on the morning of the 19th they'd seen a man matching that description walking east in front of their restaurant. He had curly gray hair under his blue baseball hat and was carrying a white can. They'd seen him again two hours later as they were leaving town.

"Down by the Dairy Queen," Michael said. "I don't know why I noticed him, guess I thought he was a little odd."

Richardson drove back to Empire the next day. He was surprised to learn that there were other searchers in the area. A team led by Detective Dave Dauenhauer of the Clear Creek

County Sheriff's Department was looking for another body east of Empire, closer to the interstate.

Richardson walked down the road to meet Dauenhauer, who told him that he was looking for the remains of Beth Ann Miller, a 14-year-old girl from the nearby town of Idaho Springs. She had disappeared while jogging ten years earlier. He now suspected that she had been abducted and killed by Edward Apodaca, an Albuquerque man. A former girlfriend of Apodaca had told people that she was with him the day he buried Beth Ann's body. But the girlfriend had since disappeared and Apodaca was slain by his wife and mother-in-law in 1990. Dauenhauer believed that the secret of Beth Ann's grave had gone with him.

Yet, Dauenhauer refused to give up. The Clear Creek detective had spent thousands of hours of his own time hoping he could give the family their daughter's body for burial.

Richardson felt for his fellow detective, but he couldn't imagine what it would be like to live with a case for ten years, or even a couple of years for that matter.

The Cher Elder case had been a real eye-opener for Richardson about the number of unsolved murder cases there were every year in the United States. He'd heard that sixty-five percent of all homicides went unsolved. But it wasn't until he began receiving the calls from police agencies all over the state and the nation, trying to determine if their cases were connected, that the statistics took on a deeper picture of the human misery involved.

Richardson and Dauenhauer agreed to stretch their resources by dividing the search area. The Clear Creek County team would concentrate its efforts from the east edge of Empire to the interstate. The Lakewood team would search the area from the town west to where the bloodhounds had followed Luther. Richardson wished Dauenhauer luck, believing that at least in Cher's case, his search would soon be over.

When Richardson went to Empire, Heylin stayed behind to chase down a few leads. That included talking to Byron Eerebout's ex-wife. She said she'd met Byron when he was AWOL from the army in 1991. He'd moved in with her and her mother shortly thereafter and soon they were married. They moved into their own apartment, the apartment where Cher Elder had been the night she disappeared, a few months later.

The marriage was a rocky one, Eerebout's ex-wife said, they fought frequently and finally split up in early February—about the time Byron started seeing Cher. Their fights had mostly consisted of screaming and slamming doors, she said, but sometimes it involved "pushing and shoving," and twice he had grabbed her by the throat and choked her. "He got really psycho," she said, but then he would end up crying and apologizing. He blamed his mood swings on a blow to the head he had suffered in Saudi Arabia during the Gulf War. "He had a lot of headaches because of it, and he can't smell or taste."

She said she had bailed Eerebout out of jail three times since she met him. Mostly petty stuff—stealing a checkbook, forging checks, traffic violations.

"He was pretty nice when you met him—flowers, dinner?" Heylin asked.

"Yeah," she sighed, "aren't all men."

Later, Heylin told Richardson about Eerebout's violent behavior. They both knew that meant they had two suspects. Two men who didn't mind slapping women around.

That afternoon Sergeant Josey of the Larimer County Sheriff's Office showed up in Empire with twenty-three nearly new shovels that he'd seized from Luther's former employer. With a dozen or so other police officers watching, Richardson placed the shovels next to each other on the ground.

"It ain't here," he said after looking them over. His fellow officers rolled their eyes and guffawed about the shovel "line-up." Josey shrugged and shook his head; the employer had purchased twenty-three shovels "and that's what I brought . . . twenty-three shovels."

It was Richardson's turn to shake his head. "I'm tellin' ya, I'd know the shovel if I saw it, and it ain't here." He asked Josey to go back and determine if the employer had been correct about the number.

The shovel "line-up" would go down in the history of Lakewood police lore, earning Richardson a lot of teasing long after the fact. But his fellow officers also had to concede that the next day, a chagrined Josey called from Fort Collins. He'd asked the employer for a bill of sale for the shovels and to both their surprise, it stated that twenty-four shovels had been purchased. "One is missing," said the Fort Collins detective.

It was Friday, May 21. Richardson was again in Empire when he took the call from Josey but there wasn't much time to lord it over his fellow officers. Yogi had arrived on the scene. Yogi was a small, rather common-looking bloodhound who worked for the Aurora Police Department south of Denver. He was fresh from his latest triumph.

Earlier in May, 5-year-old Alie Berrelez was abducted from her grandfather's yard. A massive manhunt yielded nothing until Yogi was called in. The dog led his handler for nearly ten miles from the apartment where the girl lived to the mouth of a canyon where searchers found Alie's body, stuffed in a duffel bag and thrown down a ravine by her killer. It was evident that the killer had transported her to that point in a car, yet Yogi, with one of the most sensitive noses in the animal kingdom, had been able to follow a trail that was several days old.

Now it was hoped that Yogi would pick up where the other dogs had left off on the trail of Thomas Luther. Yogi followed the same path the other dogs had and seemed to take a special interest in the area around the sanitation plant, especially a large sludge pit. There Richardson noticed a footprint in the mud at the edge of the pit, and a little further out saw that the crust that had formed above the liquid muck beneath was broken—as though something had been thrown through it. He knew then what he was going to have to do, dig out the sludge pits shovelful by slimy shovelful.

But it'd have to wait until after the weekend. In the meantime, Yogi reached the same dead end as had the other hounds near the restaurant.

On Monday, Scott Richardson got another call from Debrah Snider, who wanted to know why she hadn't seen anything in the newspapers or television about the Cher Elder case. "Why? You think we ought to put it on the news?" Richardson asked, wondering what was really eating at her.

"Well, I just wondered, you know, two months after the fact, chances of finding this girl alive are real, real, real slim but, I thought, how are you going to find her if nobody even knows she's missing?"

The detective sighed. He'd been asked the same thing by the

family. Her mother, Rhonda, in particular worried about the pace of the investigation. Now that she was coming to accept that she would never see her daughter alive again, she fretted about Cher being buried in "some cold, lonely grave." He'd spent hours trying to help her understand that slow didn't mean stopped. It was not enough to arrest somebody, he'd tell her; "I want a conviction and to do that I need to be methodical." Well, how about a press conference to develop new leads, Rhonda suggested.

Richardson didn't like talking to the press. He worried about the release of information that only the killer would know, but once released also could be used by informants looking for a deal from the police or a district attorney. Media releases also sometimes did more harm than good by drumming up "leads" that led nowhere but used valuable time and manpower to track down. He'd already discussed the advisability of a press conference with Dennis Hall, the Jefferson County deputy district attorney assigned to the case.

Hall, handsome in a boy-next-door way with light blue eyes behind round, wire-rim glasses, didn't look very tough. His quiet demeanor and appearance, however, belied his reputation for surgically dissecting defense cases while stringing together the smallest details into a complete picture for the prosecution. His ability to make complex stories simple for juries had made him the man to take on the most intricate cases.

Hall also ran the county's grand jury, which meant he was directly responsible for bringing indictments against the county's worst offenders. Richardson, who had never worked with Hall but was well aware of his reputation, knew he was going to need such a prosecutor if and when an arrest could be made in the Elder case.

They'd even talked about the possibility of prosecuting Luther for the murder of Cher Elder even if her body could not be found. "I'm not sure that's ever been done successfully," Hall said. He said he'd research the possibility, but they agreed to wait at least a while longer *and* to hold off on any press conferences.

"We've talked about releasin' somethin' to the press but so far things are workin' pretty well as is," Richardson answered Snider's question. He asked if she had seen Luther or knew where he was. It was a test. Actually, he could locate Luther just about any time he wanted because of the bird dog attached to his car.

The device had tracked Luther to Debrah's place, then south to Denver's Colfax Avenue, one of the city's oldest main thoroughfares, now notorious for its adult bookstores, pornographic movies, and sidewalk prostitutes.

In fact, Luther frequented the area so much over a few days Richardson wondered if he was on the hunt again. The truth was, Luther had nowhere to go. He avoided Snider's place, hinting, she said, that the police had it staked out, and he also stayed away from the Eerebouts. To sleep he tried to find isolated roads where he could pull over and rest in his car. But even then, Richardson allowed him no peace.

When the bird dog stopped sending its signal, indicating the car wasn't moving, a patrol car would be sent out to roust Luther. It was all handled quite innocently. The officer would act as if he had come upon Luther while making his rounds and tap on the window; "You can't sleep here." The idea was to keep Luther moving, make him tired, and increase the feeling of isolation. Richardson wanted to know where he was at all times, just in case they found Cher's body. That Sunday, they had tracked him back to the Fort Collins area.

Snider admitted that she'd seen him Sunday. He'd called her out of the blue, she said, and they'd spent the day together. When she asked him what he'd been doing, he gave her one excuse and a few minutes later another, as if he couldn't remember what he'd told her before. "He's not capable of tellin' the truth. . . . The last I heard, he's been helping J.D. fix his car, and then he's going to follow him to Chicago."

Richardson sensed that there was something upsetting Debrah, something to do with her Sunday outing with Luther. She apparently didn't want to talk about it, but at least she hadn't tried to lie about seeing him, and that was a good sign.

Richardson was aware that the bird dog had tracked Luther to the Eerebout house in Golden. The detective staking out the house had reported that Luther was currently sitting on the front porch with Babe and her sons.

Richardson got off the telephone and radioed the detective. A minute later, an unmarked police car pulled up in front of the Eerebout house next to Luther's blue Geo Metro.

As Luther gaped, the detective who'd been watching got out of his car and walked around to the curbside of the Geo Metro. Getting down on his hands and knees, the detective reached under Luther's car and pulled the bird dog from its hiding place.

If Luther was going to Chicago, the device would have been useless, and Richardson didn't want him leaving town with it. Removing it as Luther watched was just another opportunity to push his paranoia buttons.

Debrah Snider had not been able to bring herself to tell Richardson everything about the last couple of times she had seen Luther. When he arrived at her house following his confrontation with the detective at the hospital, he was so angry he wouldn't even speak to her. He had loaded a few last items in his car and reached into his pocket for his keys.

She had watched in tears. All her hopes, all the love letters, all of the moments of happiness she had found in Tom's arms now seemed like a dream. "I know I may never see you again," she said, "but I want you to know I still love you. Maybe if you can get this straightened out, you'll give me a call?"

If she was expecting an answer, she was disappointed. He remained silent. He opened the car door and was about to get in when she cried, "Can I at least get a hug goodbye?" He had looked at her and the anger in his eyes softened. He took her into his arms and in her impending loneliness, her body responded desperately to his. He picked her up and carried her into her trailer where they made love.

Afterward, Luther was talkative again. But now that he had made love, he was back to being the Tom she didn't like, the bragger and the liar. He was suddenly eager to describe the clever way he'd had J.D. drop him off, exactly where he didn't say, and then arranged to be picked up the next day. And just in case the police had managed to follow, he said, he walked ten miles out of his way before going to the grave. "I spent the whole night piling rocks on it, two feet deep."

Luther boasted that if Richardson came for him, he'd give him the slip and head for the mountains where he could run circles around the police; "They'd never catch me." The cops were so stupid, he said, they had seized all of his shoes, except the ones he had worn to the grave. As proof, he showed her a pair of black, high-topped tennis shoes.

When he left that day, Snider had supposed that he was at long last on his way to Chicago. So she was surprised when he called Sunday morning. He was at a truck stop near Fort Collins and wanted to see her but was afraid he was being followed. He asked her to meet him at Horsetooth Reservoir just west of the city.

Horsetooth was a large man-made lake set in the barren foothills overlooking Fort Collins. It had been named for a rock formation that resembled a horse's front teeth. The reservoir was a favorite hangout for the town's youth and students from Colorado State University.

Luther and Debrah didn't talk about Cher Elder, just the sorts of everyday things a couple on a picnic might—the weather, the beauty of the scenery, his upcoming trip to Chicago. When the conversation petered out, they wandered off separately to contemplate the day and enjoy the clear blue skies.

Debrah was sitting on rock staring at the cold, dark waters of the reservoir when a shadow fell on her from behind, sending a chill up her spine. Glancing over her shoulder, she saw that Luther had come up silently and now stood only a few feet away. With horror, a thought suddenly struck her. *He wants to kill me—that's why he wanted to meet me here. He knows that I know things that put him in danger.* The look on his face frightened her, yet at the same time, she found that she didn't care what happened next. If she couldn't be with him, she'd just as soon be dead. She turned back toward the water and waited.

Nothing happened. "Do you want to go to Mom's place?" she asked quietly, thinking perhaps there were too many people walking along the paths for him to carry out his plan. She also sensed that he was torn by love for her, and she wanted to put it to the test. Her mother's summer cabin was located in a remote spot in the mountains. It was a private place with few potential witnesses where he could bury her and she'd never be found. Like Cher Elder.

Debrah glanced back at Luther, who looked like a boy who'd been caught thinking bad thoughts. "Sure," he said, giving her a small, strained smile. "You bet."

They hardly spoke on the drive up to her mother's cabin.

Debrah looked out the window, trying to fathom how it was that she was on her way to quite possibly be killed by the man she loved.

All of her life she had asked God for a sign that she was deserving of love and for a dragon-slayer who would protect her. For two years she had believed her prayers had been answered with Tom. *Damn Cher Elder,* she thought, *couldn't she see how dangerous Tom was?*

They reached her mother's cabin and went inside. Luther was edgy, walking around, looking out windows. Snider wondered how long it would take for him to make up his mind. The tension in the cabin seemed to be reaching some sort of boiling point when there was a knock at the door. She and Tom both jumped.

It was a neighbor who was driving by when he saw a car that he didn't recognize and had stopped to check. Luther seemed almost more relieved by the sudden interruption than Debrah and was his friendly "good Tom" persona. When the neighbor left, so had the feeling of impending danger. "It's time to go," he said, giving her a kiss. He was anxious to start for Chicago, where there'd be no more Richardson.

"He's got nothin' on me."

"First of all, I only want to say I love ya and miss you. I got a second alone and I figured I better make good on my promise to write a little." Debrah devoured the letter from Tom eagerly. Postmarked June 8, 1993, it mostly dealt with the day-to-day business of making a living as a carpenter's helper, a job Skip had set him up with. "So until next time love ya lots and hope you can smile for me. I'll try to figure out a way to send you a hug."

A week later, there was another letter. He said he might be back to Colorado sooner than he had planned. "How would that be? It would be great for me Deb. I don't know if I'm going to be patient enough to learn all I need to."

Debrah wasn't sure how she felt about his return. On one hand, there was no denying that she still loved at least that part of him that wrote her the romantic letters. Yet, another side of her found it harder and harder to deny that he might also be a cold-blooded killer. One day she would be telling Richardson that she thought he was capable of murder, the next she would deny that he could have raped and killed Cher.

Another letter arrived assuring her of how much he loved her. The only reference to the investigation was the mention of having found his black book inside a box of letters. Otherwise, he signed off as always, "Kiss me you fox . . . on my lips, Deb!"

The day after she received his last letter, Luther called. He was in Cheyenne, Wyoming, only seventy miles north of Fort Collins, and wanted to see her. She welcomed him back and let him stay in her van while her husband and sons lived in the house. She hadn't heard from Richardson in awhile and had begun to hope that maybe the investigation had gone off on another track. Tom was back to his old sweet self and the darker possibilities receded in her mind.

Then one day, Luther got into it with her eldest son, Chance, over a tape deck he had purchased from the boy but couldn't get to work. He accused Chance of being a thief and then manipulating Debrah when she stuck up for him. "You think you can just manipulate people!" he yelled at the frightened teenager. "I wrote the book on it. You don't want to fuck with me, I've sent grown men out of prison in body bags!"

Angry with Snider for siding with her son, he left saying he had some unfinished business in Colorado Springs. She knew it had to do with drug deals and the drug dealer Mortho. She had never met him, but heard from Luther that he was grossly obese and the same man who had supposedly told him that Elder was killed because she was a snitch. Luther referred to Mortho as "the connection," and said that Mortho and Southy didn't get along. In fact, shots had been exchanged between the two over a drug deal.

Luther didn't show up or call for several days. Snider decided to call the Eerebouts to see if they had heard from him. She was surprised when he answered the telephone. He had always denied that there was anything between him and Babe, but Debrah was angry nevertheless. He ran to Babe whenever he was in trouble. *Well,* she thought, *they're perfect for each other.* They were both paranoid and constantly looking out windows whenever cars drove by.

"I'm sorry I didn't call," Tom apologized. "I just stopped

by here before you called.'' He wanted to see her again, but it couldn't be in Fort Collins. ''Meet me in Denver.''

Debrah drove to Denver. Sometimes it felt like Tom was just leading her along so he could keep her from the police, but he seemed genuinely happy to see her and they spent the night at a motel in each other's arms. She was in the bathroom that morning when she overheard a telephone conversation between Luther and Mortho. Luther said something about ''the product'' and apparently set up a meeting at another motel for the next day. When she came out, he asked her for a favor. He needed to complete a deal but was afraid he was going to be pulled over. ''I want you to follow me with this,'' he said, handing her a wad of money and a bag of white powder.

Snider objected. She didn't want to be involved in any of his drug deals and especially didn't want to carry the white powder. Luther responded angrily, ''There's nothing wrong with you sexually that a little of that wouldn't take care of.''

At last he persuaded her by promising to give up drug dealing after he had pulled off a couple of last big deals. ''If I get stopped, just keep driving,'' he said and left.

Snider was getting ready to leave when she turned and dropped the bag of white powder into the trashcan. She'd deliver the cash, but she wasn't going to ferry his drugs. As she drove down the road to the next motel, she started counting the cash he had handed her. She stopped at $800. When she arrived at the motel, Luther was again on the telephone with Mortho. A few minutes later, a young girl knocked at the door and Luther handed her the money with instructions to bring more of ''the product'' over the next morning.

Disgusted, Snider said she had to go to work. If he wanted the white powder she had given him, she said as she walked out the door, he would have to go back to the first motel and retrieve it from the trashcan. Tom looked angry, but she left before he could say anything. She drove a few blocks and pulled over at a pay telephone to call Richardson. He wasn't there, so she left a message that Tom was at a motel room and there would be a drug deal in the morning. She wanted Luther caught before he got into any more trouble.

Nothing ever came of the telephone call. Richardson, who was out of town, didn't get the message until too late.

For the next couple of weeks, there was nothing to indicate that the police were even interested in Luther. He was staying back at her place in Fort Collins, doing his little drug deals and, she believed, casing houses for burglaries with Southy and the Eerebouts. But instead of finding the silence encouraging, as she had in the past, Debrah kept waiting for the other shoe to drop.

The calm was shattered the evening of July 12 when Byron Eerebout called. "Did I see the evening news?" Tom asked, puzzled. "No." He listened for a minute, face turning bright red, then he slammed the telephone down.

"Richardson was just on the television," he shouted at Debrah. "He had my picture and even a picture of my car. He as much as said I killed her."

Chapter Sixteen

July 12, 1993—Lakewood, Colorado

Scott Richardson was frustrated. The search in Empire had yielded nothing except the feeling that Cher was so close he might have walked past her grave a dozen times.

It wasn't from a lack of trying. They had scooped out the sludge pits with a front-end loader, carefully sifting through the slop. Hazardous materials divers from Inland Marine Services had volunteered to help and gone into the sewage treatment plant's aeration tanks.

The area around Empire was littered with old, abandoned mine shafts, some several hundred feet deep. The air emanating from one in particular seemed unusually foul, as if something was decomposing in it, but it held nothing more than old garbage and a refrigerator. At considerable risk, the Gilpin County mine rescue team searched the holes but came up empty.

Even a military jet equipped with Forward-Looking Infrared Radar had been loaned for the investigation. The FLIR jet's equipment could detect differences in surface temperatures within a few square yards of soil from 30,000 feet. Soil that had been disturbed, as in a grave, gave off a different temperature than undisturbed soil right next to it. And as a body decomposes, it too gives off heat that can be detected by FLIR. This time, however, the FLIR jet detected nothing that helped locate Cher Elder's grave.

In the meantime, there were dozens of leads to chase down. A cousin of Cher's thought she had seen her missing relative briefly at an Indiana truck stop, but police there could find no one matching her description. Then there was a report of a body seen floating in Clear Creek near Central City. It turned out to be that of a 3-year-old child who had drowned.

The missing shovel from Luther's former job had turned up mysteriously, covered with dirt. Richardson asked Josey to take it to the Colorado Bureau of Investigation crime lab to have it tested for body fluids and hair.

On May 25, Detective Heylin called Pam "Babe" Rivinius to arrange a meeting with her boys and their attorney. She demanded to know why Richardson had cancelled the last meeting. He didn't want to tell her that J.D. had been followed to Empire and been seen picking Luther up, so he explained that they had been short-staffed and were checking out other leads first. "But we've come to the point where we need to talk to the boys again."

"Hopefully you people have, ah, finally come to realize that neither one of the two of these people that you have focused on here lately is involved in this situation," Babe said, referring Byron and Luther.

"I don't think your boys are in any danger of that but, ah, due to their relationship with Mr. Luther, we just wanna make sure we have all that down pat," Heylin replied.

Rivinius said she had no problem with the boys clearing up their involvement, but there was something she wanted the police to understand. "We have absolutely—the boys have absolutely—no question in their minds, and I have absolutely none in mine either, that Tom Luther is not involved in this."

"Okay," Heylin responded. "That's a fair statement on your behalf from what you understand. But we're working from a little bit different set of information and probably you don't have as much of the information as we do. But that's why we wanna talk and get it all out on the table. . . . If Tom Luther has nothing to do with this, then we'll certainly go in a different direction.''

"It's just that we will stand by him,'' Babe replied, ''because we know where he was all during that time. . . . I mean, he is . . . he is a good person. His background may not be the greatest, but Tom Luther is a good person. There's just absolutely no way that he is involved in anything to do with her disappearance.''

Heylin said he appreciated her cooperation. ''And I know this girl's parents do also,'' he added, hoping to prick her conscience.

Rivinius was quiet for a moment before responding. ''Well, the boys really cared a great deal about her,'' she said. ''They thought she was a super nice girl.''

Later, when Heylin told him about the conversation, Richardson responded angrily. If the Eerebout boys cared so much about Cher Elder why were they lying to protect Tom Luther? The Eerebouts were always looking out for number one. His opinion of them didn't change a couple days later when Gina Jones called.

Jones was frightened. She had moved out of her apartment and was staying with her mother when she heard from her boyfriend. Somebody had broken into her apartment and vandalized it, but that wasn't the worst. Whoever it was had also caught her pet cat, slit its throat, and pinned it to a wall with a knife. Then the cat-killer had spray-painted a message on the wall: ''Bitch, you'll be next.'' Gina and her boyfriend were convinced that it was a warning from Byron Eerebout or Tom Luther because she had talked to Richardson about the Cher Elder case.

An hour later, Gina's friend Tina Moore called Richardson to tell him about the cat. She had thought that Jones would be too frightened to call. The spray-painter's use of the word ''next'' to her indicated ''that there was a first, if you know what I mean.''

Moore shuddered, recalling that Byron Eerebout had once tried to set her up on a date with Luther. ''I've never met Tom, and I don't want to,'' she said. ''I'm really glad it wasn't me. I mean, not to say that I'm glad it was Cher, but I'm glad I didn't take that step.''

In the few months since he took the Elder case, Richardson had filled three four-inch thick, black, three-ring notebooks with reports and transcribed conversations. He wondered how many more he would have to fill before it was all over.

From Debrah Snider he heard about Luther's comings and goings. He worried that Luther would someday leave the state for the last time and disappear. Yet, there was nothing he could do about it. Originally, he had resisted arresting Luther for the stolen tools he and Heylin had spotted in his car. If they had taken him in then, he would have "lawyered up" and stopped any chance of getting him to talk again.

At one point, Snider had mentioned, almost in passing, that she believed that Cher Elder had been murdered because she was a police informant. He had checked with various police agencies including his own, but none had ever received any information from Cher about the Eerebouts, Luther, or anyone else for that matter.

He hadn't wanted to involve the press, but it was Cher's family who finally forced his hand. In early July, he was contacted by a television reporter who said Rhonda Edwards had called him about the investigation into the disappearance of her daughter. "I understand you have a suspect who was seen with her in Central City?" the reporter asked.

Richardson made a deal. Running the story now could jeopardize the whole case, he told the reporter, but if he'd wait, Richardson would tell him the particulars of what he knew and then when it broke, the reporter would have the complete story. The reporter agreed.

Still, it was obvious that sooner or later some other newshound would sniff out the story. If so, it would be best to use the press for his own ends. He met with Deputy District Attorney Hall and Sgt. Don Girson, his immediate supervisor.

The FBI's psychological profile of Luther suggested that he'd respond to something he viewed as a "personal thing" between himself and the detective. They'd already seen some evidence of that.

Right now, however, Luther was Mr. Macho, confident and thumbing his nose at them. Richardson was going to have to take him down a peg or two, teach him who was the hunter and who was the hunted. Remembering Luther's plea from their first meeting to not run his photograph in the newspapers or television, the detective had an idea.

Denver's television stations and newspapers were invited to attend the July 12 press conference at the Lakewood Police Department. Richardson went to the podium next to a large screen on which first Cher's, then Luther's photographs were shown, as was a photograph of Luther's car.

Richardson said that Cher Elder had been in an argument with her boyfriend, Byron Eerebout, the night she disappeared and that she had then gone to Central City with Thomas Luther. "Byron Eerebout's father was on the same cell block as Luther, who was in prison for sexual assault." Then he ran the casino videotape he had seized, pointing out where Luther was following Cher.

"She was last seen by a friend that evening, getting into Thomas Luther's vehicle at approximately 1:30 A.M. in the casino parking lot," he said. He paused for a moment to make sure his next point was understood by anyone watching. "And there is nothing to indicate that Cher is alive at this time."

"Is Luther a suspect?" a reporter shouted out.

A slight smile played on Richardson's face. Luther's face was on the screen, next to his own. The press conference was working just as he had hoped.

"Luther was the last person seen with her before she disappeared."

Scott Richardson received nearly two dozen calls generated by the press conference, most of them worthless.

James Nearen called. He said he had been Luther's defense attorney for the 1982 sexual assault case. He was living in Douglas County south of Denver and wanted extra patrol cars sent to his neighborhood. "I'm afraid he'll come after me or my family," he said. "If you find the body, and he knows he's going back to prison, he's goin' to try to settle old scores. He is not a stable individual."

Richardson shrugged. The lawyer had known what he was dealing with back in 1982, and had still done his best to get his client off, including downplaying the attack on Mary Brown and the extent of her injuries.

Nearen wanted photographs of Luther to hand out to his family and neighbors. Richardson said he couldn't help him.

Pamela Smith called to say she had worked for the Silverthorne Police Department when Luther was arrested and that she knew Sue Potter. "She's scared to death of him."

A former Summit County deputy, Bill Donahue, called to say he used to transport Luther to court hearings and doctor's appointments after the 1982 arrest. "He's violent, vindictive, and very smart. . . . He had a habit of spitting on cops," Donahue said.

The Douglas County Sheriff called from his jurisdiction southwest of Denver. They had an unidentified female corpse of about the right age. But after talking to Richardson, they ruled out that the body was Elder's.

The mother of Tiffany Crawford, Byron Eerebout's new girl-friend, called. She was afraid for her daughter's safety but couldn't talk any sense into the girl. Tiffany refused to talk to the police and after Richardson called in June, she had immediately told Byron, who in turn had gone to see his lawyer.

As Richardson believed, most of the calls generated by the press conference were of little value to the investigation. He was more interested in the press conference as a means of putting pressure on Luther. Still, three of the calls got his serious attention.

One was from Mary Brown. She wanted to meet with him. "Luther said he was going to put me in a hole where nobody would find me," she said. "He thought I was good as dead when he let me go." They arranged for her to come in the next week.

A reporter with a local television station that had aired the press conference called to say that Byron Eerebout had contacted him. "He said his life has been ruined because he is Luther's alibi," Costello said. "I called him back this morning to set up an interview, but he was crying and said his attorney told him not to say anything more."

A little later, Doug Shepard, a convict in the Canon City prison, called. He said he knew Luther from when they were on the same cell block in 1991. "He said the next time, the girl won't be around to testify."

Two days after the press conference, Richardson called Debrah Snider. Luther was asleep in a back bedroom, she said, and she could talk. He asked her response to the press conference, noting she sounded angry with him.

"Ya know, I don't know what to respond," she said. "It's like I still don't know that he did anything so how can I respond. Given that he's innocent until proven guilty, ya know, that's gonna make it really hard for him to be able to get a job or do anything. He feels that you're trying to run him out of the state."

Richardson's response was noncommittal. He was worried that she seemed to be leaning toward Luther again.

"I think he's just kind of, ya know, waiting to see if this will blow over," she went on. "He's real afraid someone's gonna shoot him now, and I know there are people that will do that. Ya know, just assume that he's guilty and save the law some money."

Richardson knew he had to bring her back to the reality of the situation. "If Cher's just missin', why the lies?" he repeated for what seemed the hundredth time. "There's very little hope that she's alive. You agree?"

"I would probably say you're correct," she conceded. "I mean, it sounds like she's not the kind of person who would have just disappeared."

Richardson jumped in, "She's not. She was a twenty-one-year-old kid that was gonna start college that Monday and was probably the most excited she'd been in the last seven years, and she was with Luther up in Central City, and she has completely disappeared." He paused to let it sink in. "And I can't come up with a single reason why Cher would come back and take her car and dump it four blocks from Byron's apartment."

Snider tried weakly to point out that maybe Cher was just trying to get even with Byron by making it look like something bad had happened to her. Richardson didn't answer, which was answer enough. Instead, he asked if she was going to tell Luther that he had called.

"I don't know," she said. "He told me not to talk to you anymore. That all you're trying to do is get me to, ya know, say something that's gonna be incriminating to him . . . which I don't know anything that's incriminating to him."

Richardson let his attitude on the telephone let her know that he didn't believe her. "People are beginning to talk," he said.

"You'd be surprised who's talkin'. Did Byron or his brothers call about the press conference."

"Yeah, Byron," she said. "He was real upset because you brought his father, Skip, into it."

Richardson decided it was time to appeal to her conscience again, as a mother. "Cher's family wants to be able to bury their daughter," he said. "I don't blame them. There's a certain sense of . . . "

Debrah finished the sentence for him. "Closure."

"Right. And if some bird called and said, 'Hey, this is where the body is. That would satisfy them. That's all they want is to be able to bury her. They don't care about prosecution or anything else." He brought up the case of Alie Berrelez. "The grandfather said, 'At least we know where she is, and that she's at peace now and with God.' That's all Cher's parents care about. They're going through total hell."

Snider was quiet, and Richardson was about to hang up on her when she spoke. "I . . . I wish you luck on this investigation. It's like, I hate to see Tom get in trouble but I mean, I don't believe in murder and hurting people and whatever happens needs to happen."

Richardson saw it as an opening to again ask if she thought Luther could have killed Cher. Someday he figured he was going to need her at trial, and he had to have her on his side.

"I can't for the life of me imagine . . ." Debrah started then stopped, before stammering again, "I've seen him with young women. I know how he's been with me. I don't believe he would have raped her."

As she said this, Debrah couldn't help but remember the other Tom, "bad Tom." Still she tried to defend him. "I think in . . . in all goodness of his heart, he went up there trying to console her, and I don't know what happened after that," she ended lamely.

"What about Summit County?" Richardson asked. "Can you imagine that? What's the difference?"

"The difference is the person, and the fact that he was, ya know, he was high on coke."

Well, Richardson said, what made her think he was drug-free now? She knew he was dealing. Did she think he wasn't using?

Marijuana, she responded, "But I don't think anything else."

Richardson changed the subject. Had she ever heard him make threats? Well, she said, there was a woman counselor when he was in prison, Gloria Greene, he didn't like. "I've heard him make a lot of threatening statements toward her . . . not that he was gonna do anything but that something should be done to her."

Snider told him that she had gone with Luther to the public defender's office in Golden. "They told him not to talk to the police," she said. "They also told him I would be the number one witness against him."

For once, Richardson was surprised. Public defender? Luther hadn't even been charged yet. And why would she be considered the "number one" witness against him?

Debrah ignored the question. Instead, she told him that Luther was angry with her again because she'd told Babe that he was involving her sons in drug deals. He wasn't talking to her as a result.

"You sound like you were sent to your room," Richardson said.

"Right."

"You hear what you're saying?"

"It's absurd . . . it's insane, I know that." Debrah sounded close to tears.

Richardson pressed the point. "I'm listening to a forty-year-old woman talking about getting 'punished' for being bad."

"Well, people do that to each other," Debrah replied. "I mean, we don't usually say that's what we're doing, but that's what is going on. I've lost a lot of faith in the last six months, nothing good ever lasts. Now, Tom's leavin'. Skip called last night and told him he needed to 'git outta Dodge.' He just doesn't have patience to let things happen and to be broke and to live life like most of us have to live it, with not enough money to meet our bills."

Snider was crying in earnest. *This is the toughest part of the job,* Richardson thought. His father had taught him hard lessons about unreciprocated love and he had not forgotten the hurt. "You're stuck on him aren't ya, Deb?"

"Fortunately, or unfortunately, yes, I am," she replied.

"What would your feelings be if I was to come out there tomorrow with a warrant for his arrest for murder?" he asked.

"I don't have any idea," she said. "At this point, I would say I'd probably stick by him. I don't ... I don't think I can survive it. I felt suicidal for a lot ... a lot of years and Tom, believe this or not, Tom's the best thing that's ever happened to me. That should tell you what kind of life I've had, and that's not to say I'm feeling sorry for myself. It's just he's the best thing that's ever happened to me, and when he's gone, I'm gone, whichever way that happens."

Snider called Richardson again the next day. There was something she hadn't told him, something that was eating at her. "The day you first met Tom, that was April 20, I believe," she said. "Well, the next day, he went to find out what happened to Cher, or so he said. He talked to this guy named Mortho, who said someone had killed her because she was an informant and cut off her lips and then dumped her body somewhere."

"How come you never told us this before?" Richardson asked.

"Well, part of it was pressure, and I didn't want to talk to you about it last night 'cause I think ... I feel real ... and I apologize for the insanity of caring about my life and then telling you I feel like committing suicide. That's just part of my pathology. I know it's crazy, I'm sorry, but anyway, I feel that if Tom—that is, you couldn't have got this information from anybody else, and if some way or another he heard, I would feel very much at risk. Not necessarily from Tom, but if it's true they would kill somebody because they think this person has been an informant ..." She let the thought hang a moment before continuing. "I mean, I'd give anything, if Cher is dead, to trade places with her. She had lots to live for and I just feel like things are dead-ended for me."

It was a couple of days after the press conference when Dennis "Southy" Healey called Snider's house looking for Tom. After taking the phone, Luther looked at her until she shrugged and walked into another room. He tried to keep his voice hushed, but she could tell he was arguing with Southy.

When he hung up and came looking for her, Luther was angry. He said he wanted to borrow her truck. His car was out in her barn to hide it from the police. "I need to meet Southy in

Longmont,'' he said, naming a small town about halfway between Denver and Fort Collins.

He was so angry, she refused to let him drive her truck. "I'll go with you and drive," she said. As they drove south, they fought, arguing about everything from his drug deals to his continued relationship with ex-convicts like Southy.

Snider pulled over onto the shoulder of the highway until they could both calm down. Luther reached over and yanked the keys from the ignition. She could tell he wanted to hit her, his fists kept clenching and unclenching as his eyes raged. Carefully, using every bit of skill she had learned as a psychiatric nurse, she began talking to him quietly, avoiding the buttons she knew would set him off. She thought she was reaching him when he punched her in the chest with the keys. It hurt, but it was not a hard punch, and he immediately turned to look out his window, saying, "Let's go. I have to meet Southy."

When they reached Longmont, Debrah pulled into a fast-food restaurant parking lot where Luther indicated he was supposed to meet his partner in crime. Snider knew something important having to do with the press conference was up. When Luther went into the restaurant to use the bathroom, she hopped out of the truck and ran across the lot to a pay phone to call Richardson. He wasn't in.

"Where'd you go?" Luther, who was waiting in the truck, asked when she got back. He was suspicious and looked behind her as if he expected the police to be following.

"I was just requesting a song on the radio," she replied. A country-western fan who often requested songs, it was a plausible explanation.

Luther went back into the restaurant and again Snider tried to call Richardson. This time when she got back, Luther was angry and was about to confront her when Healey drove up and parked next to the truck. With him was a woman and a barrel-chested man. Debrah recognized the woman as one of Healey's sisters; in fact, she had once warned her that Luther had buried Cher, but she hadn't seemed to care. She didn't know the man except that he was the other woman's boyfriend.

Ordering Snider to remain in the truck, Luther got out, as did Healey. They huddled near the back of both cars, talking quietly but animatedly. The two men returned to their respective vehicles and left the lot. Luther wouldn't talk the rest of the way to Fort Collins.

In the meantime, Southy Healey had barely pulled back onto the highway when he exclaimed that Luther was "a fuckin' asshole punk." He kept repeating the same thing until the other man, Will Fletcher, asked what he was so angry about. Fletcher had met Luther, who he knew as "Lou," only a couple of times, including once back in March or April when Luther had come to get Southy at three in the morning.

Southy would not respond to Joe's inquiry until they got home and were away from his sister. That's when he explained that Luther had "done something" to a girl.

"What do you mean?" Fletcher asked.

"She's not around anymore," Healey replied.

"Were you involved?"

"Nah. I wasn't even around when he killed her. But—" Healey hesitated. Maybe it wasn't such a good idea to say too much to his sister's boyfriend. "Anyway, he's worried that the cops are getting close to finding her body."

Fletcher nodded and let the subject drop. It didn't pay to be too nosy about killings.

Scott Richardson was struck by how frail Mary Brown seemed as they talked in the interview room. She was a pretty woman with dark, childlike eyes, but nervous and obviously still shaken by the experience more than a decade earlier.

Brown said she was afraid, more than ever now that Luther was out on the streets preying on women again. She wanted her new married identity protected so that he couldn't track her, but otherwise, she also wanted desperately to tell her story and "help anyway that I can."

The fact that the Summit County prosecutor had dropped the attempted murder charge had been beyond her comprehension. How could anyone who had seen the photographs of the blood-splattered truck have thought otherwise? Salt was rubbed in her wounds when she was told that Luther could only be charged with second-degree sexual assault because he had used a foreign object instead of his penis.

And after all that, she had been denied her day in court. So she had made it a point to attend Luther's parole hearings, recounting in horrific detail the unprovoked assault. "He meant to kill me," she always said. But even though Luther remained in prison after each hearing, it was little consolation for what she continued to suffer.

The first few months after the attack were a nightmare. She couldn't sleep without a family member in the same room. But even they were too frightened of Luther to be much assurance. Her parents sold their home and moved and had their telephone numbers unlisted. When she learned that Luther had tried to have her killed from his jail cell, she felt like sooner or later he would come after her again.

Therapy had evoked flashbacks of that night, including one in which she remembered looking back over her shoulder at the barrel of a gun pointed at her head. She could only surmise that he hadn't shot because they were in a neighborhood and someone might have heard.

At last, a friend had recommended that she read a book in which the basic premise was that a person can't control what happens, only his or her response to it. She grew determined that she would not let Thomas Luther win by ruining the rest of her life. She would watch for him and someday she hoped she would get the chance to stare him in the face and let the world know what a monster he was.

In the meantime, she took self-defense courses in basic street-fighting techniques and was so proficient that she became an instructor. But her proudest moment was when she persuaded the Colorado legislature to change the laws governing rape so that penetration with a foreign object was equal to any other sort of rape.

Months had passed into years, but still she was left with physical reminders of the attack. Nerve damage to her neck that made it impossible to relax the muscles in one shoulder. Debilitating headaches that caused her to vomit and left her too weak to stand.

Yet, the hardest obstacles to overcome were psychological. Never again could she be the naive, friendly girl who had gone to the mountains for a ski trip and accepted a ride from a nice-looking young man. Being near men, even in a group setting, caused her to panic and look for a way to escape.

It was nearly two years before she dated again, and even that caused a setback. First, her date got lost on the way to the restaurant; then he reached down under the seat to retrieve something and she began screaming. Her fear turned into embarrassment when, rather than a hammer or gun, he pulled out a dozen roses.

Little by little, Mary Brown recovered. She met her husband a year after her first date. They were taking classes together and hanging out with the same people. The courtship was slow, but fortunately he was a patient man, willing to be friends long before they were anything else. She had married him and gone on with her life, but there were few days when she was not haunted by the memory of Thomas Luther.

When Sheriff Morales called to warn her that he was out, the old fear had risen in her throat again like bile as she wondered if he would try to find her. There had been no word of Luther for months and she was hoping he had moved to another state when she picked up the July 13 newspaper; there was his photograph included in a story about a missing girl. Suddenly, she was physically ill and barely made it to the bathroom before being overcome with dizziness. When at last she could pull herself together, she had picked up the telephone and called Richardson.

"If he isn't your prime suspect, he better be," she told the detective within minutes of when they met.

Richardson had read the report about the attack on Mary Brown and seen the photographs of her taken shortly afterward in which she was wearing a neck brace, her face bruised and swollen. However, what he read did not prepare him for her graphic description of the attack. He felt sorry that she had to relive the experience, but he needed to know how the attack went down, which might give him an idea of how Cher had died.

Luther, she said, crying as she talked, attacked without provocation or warning. She felt certain he wanted to kill her and leave her body in the woods beyond the snowdrifts but had simply run out of steam after beating and raping her.

"I was definitely not his first victim," she said. "All the cursing was plural, as if he was talking to other women he had done this to."

Richardson said goodbye to Mary Brown with a better understanding of the man he hoped to bring down. Luther was what was known as a "blitz" attacker, using his superior size and strength to beat down any resistance before and during the sexual assault. He used whatever he had handy: his fists, a hammer. Mary's recollection of a gun was certainly interesting, considering the homicides over in Breckenridge. Luther took his victims to remote areas for the assault, and then apparently drove elsewhere to dump their bodies.

After Luther had worn himself out attacking her, Mary had seized on a moment of doubt or confusion on Luther's part to jump out of his truck before he reconsidered and took her "somewhere." Richardson believed that Brown was right to believe that "somewhere" meant somewhere to die. He recalled Shepard's telephone call claiming that Luther had said the next girl wouldn't live and the police would never find her body. Apparently, he learned his lesson with Mary Brown.

Luther was any woman's greatest fear. He didn't need to be provoked and even giving him what he wanted, as Mary had attempted to do to save her life, only made him angrier.

Richardson knew that his wife and kids feared Luther. Sabrina had grown up to be a tough young woman, as comfortable in the wild hunting big game as he was. But she had never quite gotten over the scare of that day when Luther had threatened to kill her and the boys. Now, in the second trimester of her pregnancy, she still carried a gun in her purse. And the twins often slept in their parents' bed or curled up on the floor next to it, afraid that Thomas Luther hid in the dark shadows of their room at night.

Richardson was still absorbing the interview with Mary when he was contacted by Bonita Freeburg, a parole officer. Luther, she said, was threatening to kill a friend and colleague of hers. Her friend's name was Gloria Greene, the woman who had run the sexual offenders program in Colorado prisons and who had kicked Luther out of class. Prison authorities, Freeburg said, had recently found letters to other inmates from Luther stating that he was going to rape and kill Greene.

Richardson called the prison counselor. Yes, Greene replied, she had been contacted by a prison investigator just two weeks earlier, who had relayed the threats made against her life by Luther.

"I'm scared to death," she said. "He hates me."

Greene's comments reiterated what Richardson had been hearing since the press conference. Whether it was prison associates, former jailers, counselors, other cops, or victims, they all thought the same thing: The animal was out of the cage, and it had only been a matter of time before he killed again.

On August 14, Debrah Snider was talking to Deputy Dan Gilliam of Larimer County about Luther's narcotic transactions and burglaries. She still hoped that if Luther was in prison, Richardson would decide that was good enough, and that maybe, someday, they could be together again. But Gilliam, who was aware of the Elder case, asked if she had anything new to add to that investigation.

"I think he may have killed her," she told the surprised deputy. She couldn't lie anymore. Luther seemed to enjoy his new title of "serial killer," at least when he was angry with her. She'd overheard him bragging to the Eerebouts and Healey that the press conference was Richardson's last shot.

"You know I have to tell Richardson," Gilliam said. She looked down and nodded, "Yeah, I know."

Richardson called Snider the next day. She admitted she had not been "one hundred percent truthful" in their previous conversations. At last, she told him that Luther had admitted burying the body after his first meeting with Richardson. "He said next to a stone historical marker on east Interstate 70."

The direction didn't make sense to Richardson. Interstate 70 was on the plains east of Denver. Empire was directly west, well up into the mountains. Then again, maybe Luther had known he was being followed and purposely led them in the wrong direction—or he had lied to Debrah.

But it was what Snider said next that really got his attention. She told him that she was gone the weekend Cher Elder disappeared, but when she returned that Monday, Luther's hands were covered with cuts and bruises. "And his little finger was broken. . . . When I called you that day and said he might be going to visit the body . . . actually he told me he was worried about animals digging up the grave and he wanted to bury her better. He said the grave was shallow, but he piled two feet of rocks on top. He spent all night doing it and walked ten miles to avoid being followed.''

The day that she and Luther had gone to the public defender's office in Golden, she said she asked him if he had killed Cher. He hadn't answered directly, saying instead, ''Well, if you were in trouble and someone was going to put you away, I'd do anything to prevent it.''

Richardson told her she needed to come to his office in Lakewood where they could sit down together and ''get this straightened out.'' She agreed to come to Lakewood.

The next day, Snider had no sooner taken a seat in an interview room than she began to weep. ''I don't know what you want from me,'' she cried.

''Well, number one, I want the truth, but I don't want parts of the truth. I need the whole truth,'' Richardson said. ''I don't have to tell ya that we're talkin' serious charges. And you don't wanna end up in the middle of it.''

Debrah looked up. ''I am in the middle of it. How can I not be in the middle of it?''

Richardson nodded. ''Start with when you got back from Washington.''

''I was surprised 'cause he was still in bed and, ya know, it's the middle of the day,'' she said. ''I can't remember everything exactly but I know his hands were real sore, they had abrasions on 'em, and his little finger on one hand was so sore he thought it was broken. And when I asked him about it, he told me that somebody had given him a whole bunch of AK-47s and that he had been afraid to drive with 'em and so he stopped and buried them along I-25. He broke my shovel ... and had to finish buryin' them by hand and that's how they got hurt.''

Richardson asked about Luther's missing boots and clothes. ''What he told me he'd done is sat them on the top of the car when he changed and forgot them and drove away.''

Debrah repeated the Mortho story, only now she added the part about going to find the body to bury her because he did not want to be connected to the murder. ''I asked him why he didn't go to the police, but he said you'd just use this to hang him and

wouldn't care about the truth. ... And also that he couldn't
snitch on his friends."

"Who do you honestly feel killed her? Richardson asked.

"I honestly don't know," Snider said. "There are times whenever I—"

Richardson interrupted; he was tired of her vacillating. Luther
had made up a nice story, he said, the misunderstood outlaw
just trying to save his friends. So her boyfriend, who thought
cops were constantly watching him, had taken this huge chance
of getting caught with a body to help someone else stay out of
prison. "It doesn't make any sense. And what about burying a
box of AK-47s the same time she disappears?"

Debrah hung her head and sighed. "It adds up to a bunch of
things that points in the direction of ... he probably hurt this
girl," she said. "He probably killed her."

Finally, Richardson thought, *a real breakthrough.* "Now I
need you to help me find the body."

"I don't know where she is," Snider complained. "I only
know he says he walked a long ways because he was suspicious.
... He got angry at me because the backpack I loaned him had
detachable pockets, and I guess one came off at the grave and
he had to go back for it."

Richardson said he could not understand why she hadn't asked
Luther more about where the body was located. "I guess curiosity
kills the cat, but I would want to know."

Debrah shook head. "You need to understand that I didn't
wanna be responsible for sending him back to prison. If I could
give you information that would help you if he has done something wrong, that wouldn't be my fault. But, I don't wanna be
responsible for sending him back to prison."

Richardson waved off her explanation. "Well, Thomas Luther
is responsible ... "

"I know, ultimately," Debrah conceded.

But Richardson wouldn't listen. "I don't care if you go out
there and show us exactly where the body is, that doesn't make
you responsible for putting Thomas Luther back in prison."

"In his mind it would."

"Well, Thomas Luther's puttin' Thomas Luther back, period.
The problem is ... this is not the kind of case where you would

want in the end to come out that the whole time you knew where the body was.''

"I don't know where it is," Snider protested.

Still, he wouldn't let up. "I mean, because then what you got is, you got Thomas Luther sinking, and he kind of reaches up and grabs Debrah Snider and pulls her right down."

Debrah reached for a tissue and wiped her eyes. "I think he's already done that, ya know, but I don't know where it is. . . . At one point when he was real anxious about the coyotes digging her up, I did contemplate going to help him. And then I changed my mind, I didn't want to know."

Luther's paranoia was getting worse, she said, and something else was troubling her. He was coming home with scratches and bruises all over his body. When she asked how he was injured, he told her he'd been hiding out in the mountains, using rough trails so that he couldn't be followed.

"He's not sleeping much at night," Snider said. "And he forgets what story he's told me. Like sometimes he goes back to the first story. That the last time he saw Cher was when he left her at Byron's apartment. He forgets he already told me that he buried her. I don't know what the truth is."

"What can we do to get him to go back to that body or take you back to the body?" Richardson asked. "The way it's sounding is, he would if you asked him."

"Sometimes I think he would," Debrah replied. "He seems to be pretty grandiose and thinks he's important and that seems to be part of what makes him important." Then she shook her head. He was too angry with her, he wasn't even talking to her, much less trusting her with his darkest secret.

"I mean beyond today," Richardson said, " 'cause you two are gonna get back together. You're gonna be together until somethin' beyond your control separates ya."

Debrah swallowed hard. The detective was telling the truth. She and Tom—their fates—were intertwined for good or bad, just like he'd told her in his letters. "You know, there is something goin' on with him," she said. "I don't know whether it's anxiety, or if in fact what you said is true . . . maybe he's showing a pattern of a serial killer."

"What are your feelings about your personal safety?" Richardson asked.

"Ah, not real good right now, especially when he's angry," she replied. It seemed like, at times, he was toying with her, trying to scare her. "Sometimes he says, 'Maybe they're just following me because they know I'm a serial killer and it's time.' "

Still, Luther was confident that the police had not found any evidence in his car. "If he killed her, I think he would've done it in such a way as it wouldn't have happened in the car. . . . I see him as being cunning enough to get her out of the car. I just think he probably learned some things, ya know, from his last situation."

Snider began to say, "If he killed her . . . " but Richardson stopped her again. There was no more room for ifs, he said. If she was still holding back, she needed to talk openly. He brought up Cher's family again. "They make you look like the happiest person in the world. They're breaking down, their kids are going through therapy. The father's broke down . . . there's a difference between breaking and broke." He got up and began pacing the little interview room.

"The mother is gone to pot. Even the kids. Cher had one brother and one sister. I think the brother's about twelve and is seeing a pyschologist. It may sound crazy, but there's a sense of comfort knowing that your daughter is not lying out under a rock pile. It's that not knowing that actually drives people to suicide."

Richardson stopped pacing and looked down on Debrah's tear-streaked face. This wasn't Interview Technique 101 anymore, this was from his heart.

"All they're doin' is they're begging me to find their daughter's body so that they can put her to rest. To the point that they will call two, three o'clock in the morning talkin' on my answering machine crying, sayin' they just had a dream and they want me to find her. They call me 'cause I'm workin' on the case and they just want a voice to talk to. That's rock bottom, Debbie. You think it's hard on you . . . think about bein' the mother of Cher Elder or the father of Cher Elder."

Debrah sobbed, her heart broken. "I'm not protecting anybody. I don't know anything else I can tell ya. If I could figure out how it happened, get him to show me where the body is, I would certainly do that. I think he's ready to leave. I think he said something about wanting to go back to Vermont.

"He's blaming me. It's all my fault."

Chapter Seventeen

September 10, 1993—Grand Junction, Colorado

Rhonda Edwards woke in a cold sweat. The room was dark, and she was afraid to move as she lay listening to the silence. The dream that awakened her had been so real—the sounds, the sensations.

In her dream she—or was it Cher? she couldn't tell—was in a car traveling down a long, dark road through the mountains. She could feel the car sway as it whipped around curves. Her head lay on a seat, her eyes looking up at the full moon rising above the black silhouettes of trees outside the window. But she couldn't move, it was as if she was being held down by some thick, invisible liquid that made it difficult to breathe and her limbs heavy.

She'd heard gravel crunching beneath the tires as the car rolled to a stop. Then she was outside in the moonlight. There was the sound of a rushing stream. Suddenly she heard an excruciatingly loud noise and felt an immense pressure against the left side of her head, behind her ear . . .

In her bed, Rhonda reached behind her head expecting to feel warm, sticky blood. There was nothing. She summoned the nerve to turn on the lamp on her nightstand. The shadows fled as she reached for her diary. Opening to a blank page, she noted the time: 3:05 A.M. and began to write what she could remember of the dream. The car ride. The moon. The sound and the pressure. "Instantly, I close my eyes as the light grows bright and there is a sudden, heavy warmth that runs through my body. I shrink into nothingness."

The dream had been more vivid than any of the others that had haunted her since Cher disappeared, but it was not the first to disturb her sleep. One of the more frequent involved driving past Victorian gingerbread-style houses of the sort common to mining towns in the mountains. Other details were usually more difficult to recall, except for the vague feeling that the dreams had something to do with her missing daughter. And when she woke from them, the clock almost always stood at 3:05 A.M., each instance dutifully noted in her diary.

Long after Detective Richardson called the family together to say that he believed Cher had been murdered and that he had a suspect, Rhonda and her second husband, Van Edwards, a long-haul trucker, refused to give up hope. Maybe Cher just got fed up and went somewhere to think things through, they told each other. They called all the friends she had in different parts of the country—California, Missouri, Illinois, Colorado. They made posters, some of which Van tacked up in truck stops during his cross-country journeys.

They'd occasionally get calls, but the leads never panned out. Van found it mysterious that at one truck stop near Chicago that summer, the poster he hung of Cher was torn down from a posterboard where dozens of other such posters, some much older than his, remained undisturbed.

As the weeks stretched into months, Rhonda would call Richardson to scream or yell or cry. She knew it wasn't his fault that the investigation seemed to crawl along, and to his credit, he always let her get it out without interrupting or getting angry. She often called just after three in the morning, following a dream. She knew he wouldn't be in. "I just wanted to hear your voice," she'd say to his message machine. "I just wanted to know you're still out there."

Rhonda was tormented by guilt. Maybe she had raised Cher to be too trusting, too independent. "Did I contribute to her death?" she asked herself in her diary. "Was I too busy at work? Did I listen enough?" She wondered if things might have worked out differently if she had allowed Cher to marry her high school boyfriend.

Lying in her bed alone, Van somewhere out on the road, Rhonda shuddered with fear recalling the apocalyptic dream and began writing again. "It felt so real . . . I wondered if He had come back to earth, and I was witnessing the end of the world.

"Or was I seeing death as Cher saw it?"

* * *

After the bars closed on the morning of September 23, 25-year-old Mark Makarov-Junev and his 21-year-old girlfriend, Patty pulled up to the drive-through at a Lakewood fast food restaurant. They just finished ordering when Mark noticed a white Pontiac Firebird pull in behind him. But he wasn't particularly alarmed when Byron Eerebout got out of the driver's side door and approached. They'd had some disagreements in the recent past but had since cleared the air. Besides, Mark could see his first cousin, Robert Makarov-Junev, was sitting on the passenger side of the white car.

The disagreement involved about $475 Mark owed Eerebout for cocaine. Byron had flattened two of his tires with an icepick a few days before. Then Makarov-Junev retaliated by locating Eerebout at an apartment and threatening to "kick your ass." Byron scurried away from Mark, a much larger young man, and ran into the kitchen where he said he was "calling Thomas Luther."

"Thomas is on the phone," he yelled at Makarov-Junev who then left, apparently the ex-convict's reputation impressed the small-time criminals and drug dealers who made up much of Eerebout's circle of associates. But just the day before, due to Pam Rivinius's intercession, the pair had shook hands and agreed to work out their differences amicably.

"What's going on?" Mark asked as Byron walked up.

"Not much," Eerebout replied as he raised a canister of Mace and sprayed Mark in the face. When Mark, blinded, raised his hands to his face, Eerebout began striking him with a wooden dowel about the thickness of a silver dollar and cursing, "You don't know who you're fucking with."

Eerebout ran back to the Firebird yelling, "I'll be back," and then sped away. Makarov-Junev and his girlfriend drove to her apartment where he ran to the bathroom to wash the Mace off. She went to check on messages left on her telephone recorder. A moment later, she yelled, "Mark, you better come hear this!"

The first message was from his cousin, Robert, wanting to know where he would be that night. However, it was the next two messages, recorded just a few minutes before they got home, that frightened Patty.

"Yo, this is Byron, guys," the first one said. "If you don't answer the phone right now and goddamn give me money, it's your ass, Mark. I'm not fuckin' scared of your ass, motherfucker. You asked me the other night who you were dealin' with. You don't know who you're dealin' with. We're on our way to her house right now dude. I ain't no fuckin' chickenshit. You can ask anybody, dude, I'll fuckin' do it. If we go rounds, dude, whoever wins, dude, that's all it takes. I'm comin' to get you, bud. You listening to this, motherfucker? Goodbye and good fuckin' riddance."

That message was followed by another from Eerebout. "You hear this, Mark," he said. A gunshot rang out. "I'm coming to get you."

The sound had hardly stop reverberating in their ears when Patty looked up and pointed out the picture window of her ground-floor apartment. A white Pontiac Firebird was cruising slowly up the street. Makarov-Junev ordered her to close the blinds, but in her panic, she pulled the whole device down. They were exposed in the car headlights.

Byron Eerebout got out of the car. They could see he was carrying a large handgun. "I'm going to kill you, you motherfucker, Mark," he screamed and raised the gun.

"Get down," Mark yelled. He and Patty fell to the floor as a bullet crashed through the picture window where they had been standing. As more shots were fired, Patty crawled to her kitchen and, reaching up, grabbed the telephone and called 911. She could hear Eerebout yelling outside, then the yelling stopped and she heard the sound of car tires screeching.

At 2 A.M., police responding to a report of "shots fired" arrived at the apartment. An officer was in the room when Eerebout called again to threaten Makarov-Junev.

After the call, the officer asked if Mark knew where they could find Eerebout, who he had identified as the attacker. Mark thought a minute, then called Mike Coovrey, who went by the nickname Garfus. He knew Garfus was out of town, but several of Byron's friends were housesitting and might know where to find him. He was surprised when Byron picked up the telephone.

A half hour later, Lakewood police officers and detectives were quietly establishing a perimeter around Coovrey's house when they saw two figures emerge from the rear of the building

and toss two large bundles over a fence. It was too dark to get
a good look at the pair, except to note that the shorter of the
two was wearing white pants.

A few minutes later, Byron Eerebout and his latest girlfriend,
Tiffany Crawford, walked out the front door where they were
met by police officers with guns drawn. The couple was forced
to lie on the sidewalk with their hands over the backs of the
necks while more officers burst into the house and arrested the
other occupants, including Robert Makarov-Junev.

Searching Eerebout's car, the police found a spent shell casing
and fifty rounds of .38-caliber ammunition. The two large bundles
on the other side of the fence contained more than twenty pounds
of marijuana.

Scott Richardson was asleep at home when Detective Mike
Powell called at 3:30. "Sorry to call so early," said Powell, "but
thought you'd want to know that we arrested Byron Eerebout an
hour ago for felony assault."

There was no danger that Richardson would be put off by the
early morning telephone call. He'd left instructions that if the
Eerebout boys turned up on *any* crime reports, he wanted to be
notified as soon as possible. The idea of honor among thieves
and convict loyalty usually lasted about as long as it took one
of these punks to get in trouble. He knew Byron wasn't the sort
to stay out of trouble long, and when he messed up, Richardson
wanted to be there to put the screws to him.

Eerebout was already on probation for forgery. And the Golden
Police Department's drug task force had been working for months
to nail him for dealing marijuana and psychedelic mushrooms.
An informant, who had sold the white Pontiac to Byron for cash
and marijuana, was close to making a buy for the police.

But this was even better, Richardson thought. Felony assault
was worth a lot of years in the joint. He was soon dressed and
on his way to the house where Byron Eerebout and his friends
were in custody. After the frustrations of the past few months,
the detective dared hope that at last he was getting a real break.

Following Debrah Snider's confession, the task force had
checked out several possible gravesites east on Interstate 70. In
particular, they had searched several suspicious areas near stone

Cher Elder, 20, shortly before she disappeared in March 1993.
(*Photo courtesy Rhonda Edwards*)

Thomas Luther, 38, after his extradition to Colorado in April 1995 to face charges of murdering Cher Elder. (*Photo courtesy Lakewood, Colorado Police Department*)

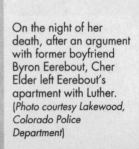

On the night of her death, after an argument with former boyfriend Byron Eerebout, Cher Elder left Eerebout's apartment with Luther. (*Photo courtesy Lakewood, Colorado Police Department*)

J.D. Eerebout, one of Byron's younger brothers, drove Luther to Empire, Colorado to check on Cher Elder's grave when Luther feared police had discovered it. *(Photo courtesy Lakewood, Colorado Police Department)*

Police correctly suspected Dennis "Southy" Healey and the Eerebouts knew more about Luther's connection to Cher Elder's death than they had originally admitted. Healey testified he drove Luther close to the gravesite so Luther could bury the body deeper. *(Photo courtesy Lakewood, Colorado Police Department)*

Nearly two weeks after she disappeared, Cher Elder's Honda Accord was discovered in a grocery store parking lot within easy walking distance of Byron Eerebout's apartment. (*Photo courtesy Lakewood, Colorado Police Department*)

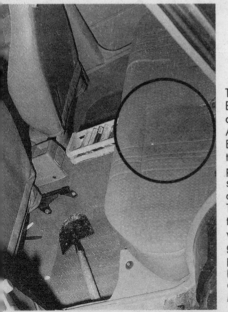

The interior of Luther's Blue Geo Metro revealed a stain on the back seat. According to Luther, Elder vomited after sex in the front seat, however police determined the stain's location was inconsistent with his story. Tests showed the dirt on the shovel was consistent with soil from Elder's grave, but could not prove it was identical. (*Photo courtesy Lakewood, Colorado Police Department*)

Aerial view of Cher Elder's gravesite near the old mining town of Empire in the mountains west of Denver. Unlike most killers, Luther carried his victim's body uphill rather than downhill, hindering the police investigation.
(*Photo courtesy Lakewood, Colorado Police Department*)

The burial site as found by Detective Scott Richardson.
(*Photo courtesy Lakewood, Colorado Police Department*)

The forensic anthropologists of NecroSearch International were called in to carefully exhume Cher Elder's remains. Detective Richardson slept next to the snowy site several nights to make sure it was not disturbed by anyone or by animals.
(*Photo courtesy Lakewood, Colorado Police Department*)

Cher Elder had been shot three times in close proximity behind her left ear, leading investigators to conclude she was either unconscious or being held down when executed.
(*Photo courtesy Lakewood, Colorado Police Department*)

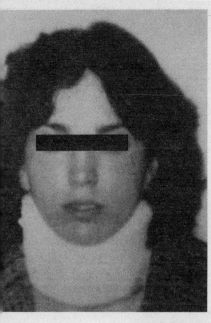

On February 12, 1982, Mary Brown was sexually assaulted and nearly beaten to death before escaping from Luther's car a few miles from Breckenridge, Colorado. Luther received a sentence of 15 years after pleading guilty to first degree assault. (*Photo courtesy Summit County, Colorado Sheriff*)

Investigators believed Luther attacked women who reminded him of his mother as she looked when he was a child. Her wedding picture shows her as petite, with shoulder-length dark hair. (*Photo courtesy Lakewood, Colorado Police Department*)

Debrah Snider and Tom Luther in the visiting room at the Colorado state penitentiary two years before his January 1993 release. Snider, a nurse, met Luther when he was hospitalized for an allergic reaction and began a correspondence with him that led to a serious relationship. (Photo courtesy Debrah Snider)

Luther (*lower right*), his mother Betty (*top center*), and his sisters and brothers. (Photo courtesy Debrah Snider)

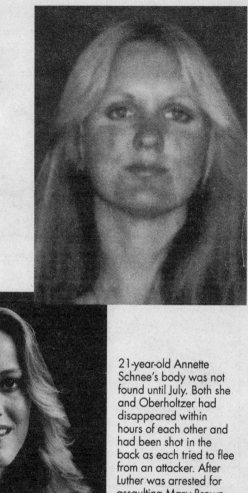

21-year-old Annette Schnee's body was not found until July. Both she and Oberholtzer had disappeared within hours of each other and had been shot in the back as each tried to flee from an attacker. After Luther was arrested for assaulting Mary Brown, he told fellow inmates about killing two other women. The timing and locale of Brown's attack and the the details of Luther's remarks, led police to suspect him in both Schnee's and Oberholtzer's murders.

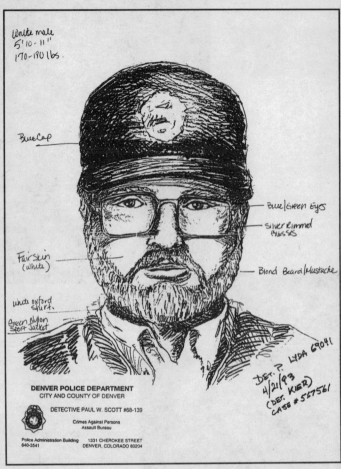

White male
5'10 - 11"
170-180 lbs.

Blue Cap

Blue/Green Eyes

Silver Rimmed Glasses

Fair Skin
(white)

Blond Beard/Mustache

White Oxford
Shirt

Green Nylon
Sport Jacket

Det. P. LYDA 69041
4/21/93
(Det. KIER)
CASE # 567561

DENVER POLICE DEPARTMENT
CITY AND COUNTY OF DENVER

DETECTIVE PAUL W. SCOTT #68-139

Crimes Against Persons
Assault Bureau

Police Administration Building
640-3541

1331 CHEROKEE STREET
DENVER, COLORADO 80204

Police composite drawing of the man who attacked Heather
Smith in April 1993, two weeks after Cher Elder disappeared.
(*Photo courtesy Denver, Colorado Police Department*)

Heather Smith was attacked and stabbed five times. She identified Luther as her attacker after seeing his photograph in a newspaper reporting his 1995 arrest for Elder's murder. (*Photo courtesy Heather Weiser*)

Luther was sentenced to 35 years for sexually assaulting and beating Bobbi Jo Jones, 32, near Delray, West Virginia in August 1994. Like many of his other victims, she bears a striking resemblance to his mother. (*Photo courtesy West Virginia State Police*)

Detective Scott Richardson of the Lakewood, Colorado Police
Department. *(Photo courtesy Scott and Sabrina Richardson)*

Cher Elder was buried in Grand Junction, Colorado in March
1995, two years after she had been murdered.
(Photo courtesy Rhonda Edwards)

historical markers. But there was nothing. More flights over Empire using the FLIR system were just as fruitless.

All the while he worried about when Luther would strike again, as he was sure he would. In early September he had been contacted by the Arapahoe County sheriff about the rape and strangulation murder of a 14-year-old girl. She had disappeared August 27 and her body was found in a rural part of the county south of Denver on September 1.

The sheriff called after seeing Richardson's bulletin stating that Luther had confessed to burying Cher Elder to his girlfriend. "Do you think there's a connection between Luther and my homicide?" he asked.

"It's a possibility," Richardson said. "He's been in the area." Whether or not Luther was the killer in this case, Richardson was sure he would attack again unless he was stopped.

Richardson arrived at Garfus's house and was briefed. He noted that Tiffany Crawford was wearing white pants. The suspects and witnesses were then transported to the Lakewood Police Department and placed in different interview rooms.

Richardson decided to save talking to Eerebout for last and began questioning the others. They all denied knowing about a shooting and the bundles of marijuana. Tiffany swore that Byron had been with her all night, never leaving her side for more than five minutes.

"Well," said Richardson, "you were either with Byron and are therefore an accomplice in an attempted murder, or you're lying to give him an alibi."

Crawford looked scared but stuck to her story. She had no idea of who threw marijuana over a fence, nor did she have any knowledge of a shooting. Yes, she said, she had talked to Byron about the disappearance of Cher Elder. "But it was confidential, and I'm not going to tell you."

Robert Makarov-Junev admitted that he had been with Byron that night, but denied any incident at the restaurant or any involvement in a shooting. "We went to a bar and then went back to the house," he said. "I was sleeping on the couch when someone said the cops are here."

At 8 A.M., Byron Eerebout was sitting alone in an interview room when in walked his worst nightmare, Det. Scott Richardson. Byron was hostile. He waived his Miranda rights but steadfastly denied any involvement in the shooting. "That's not my dope," he said of the marijuana.

"Whose was it?" Richardson asked, not that he expected an honest answer.

"Nobody's," Eerebout replied. "I've never touched it or a gun, and they didn't see me throw it, and I don't have a gun." He then demanded to see his attorneys, which brought the interview to a halt.

However, while being photographed for mugshots, Eerebout admitted that he had Maced Mark, but denied hitting him with a club. He then angrily blamed Richardson for all his recent troubles.

"Why do you keep lying for Thomas Luther about Cher Elder?" Richardson retorted.

Byron's face flushed a deep red. He nearly spit he was so angry and yelled, "I know where they went that night, and where Luther went afterwards. But it's for me to know, and you never to find out."

On a late October afternoon, two women sat in a nice older home in Denver, watching the first snowflakes of an early winter. Heather Smith and her friend Rebecca Hascall had lived with their mothers for a month after the attack before insisting they be allowed to return to their homes. They were together often these days as they tried to pick up the pieces of their lives.

Officially, the case had been declared inactive. Detective Paul Scott kept it going as long as possible, but time ran out. There were plenty of other crimes of violence that needed attention according to his sergeant.

Smith's former boyfriend had taken a lie-detector test, which had detected no lies about his involvement in the attack. (Then again, Scott mused to himself, the machine detected nothing at all. Heather's ex hadn't even responded on the graph to the control questions.)

There was little else to go on. Just the composite picture of the blue-eyed man with the workingman's hands, and the gray or light-colored curly hair beneath the blue baseball cap with gold lettering. And, of course, the strange, square, silver-rimmed glasses. But there was no suspect. Scott made a copy of the file and tucked it away in his desk while he handed the original over to be filed with other unsolved cases.

Now, as they sat in Heather's living room, Rebecca complained that the attack had turned her belief system upside down. She had been raised an anti-gun and anti-death penalty liberal. Fear had won the first round when she accepted a gun from her boyfriend.

At first, she had recoiled when he brought it over and laid it on the table. It was ugly. A cold, blue steel .38-caliber revolver.

Then her boyfriend started to cry. "I don't know what I'd do if something happened to you," he said. "I can't be there to protect you all the time." So she decided to take the gun to make him feel better and find a way to get rid of it later, when they were both stronger.

Hascall picked it up and was surprised by how comforting its weight felt in her hand. It fastened to her like a tick. She had to admit, despite her revulsion at the concept, that it made her feel safe and powerful—the ingredients that had been missing from her personality since the attack. She took the gun home and showed it to her mother who, despite being an even more dyed-in-the-wool liberal, was thrilled.

When she moved back into her own home, Hascall brought the gun with her and kept it under her pillow. Once in awhile she entertained the notion of getting rid of it, and even tried moving it to a hall closet. But it quickly made its way back to her bed following one of her frequent nightmares in which she was sure that someone was breaking into her house.

Heather Smith was another matter. Her friends were outraged when she insisted on moving back into her home. She was being reckless, they said. Her attacker was still out there. He knew where she lived and that she could identify him.

Smith read the newspapers obsessively, looking for cases of assaults and murders that might be related to hers. If she thought something seemed familiar about a suspect in another case, she called Detective Scott. But the suspects were always too short. Or they had an alibi. Or she knew they weren't the right guy, that she was reaching for straws.

She tried to pretend that she was still the strong one, always asking her friend, Rebecca, how *she* was feeling. But inside she was as timid as a mouse. He was out there somewhere, lurking in the shadows, haunting her dreams.

She wanted to talk about what had happened to her, to find a reason, but most of her friends grew tired of listening. One even told her that it had been easier to deal with Heather being hurt physically than Heather trying to heal emotionally. Among themselves they knowingly said they would never have put themselves in such a dangerous position. How could Heather have been so foolish?

Hascall heard the comments. It was as if they were blaming Heather for being attacked. Like, she sputtered, Heather had "asked for it." But the others just learned to talk behind Rebecca's back as well.

One night at her mother's house, Rebecca burst into tears over what Smith's "friends" were saying. Her mother tried explain: "They need a reason why this couldn't happen to them. They're frightened. We all are. They're trying to make sense of something that makes no sense."

Heather knew that she was making her friends uncomfortable and withdrew into her home. She was afraid to go out. Afraid to date. Only another victim could understand and so her relationship with Rebecca had grown. Their lives changed. Even the little things. Neither of them could watch snow falling in the arc of the streetlight without her chest tightening with remembrance.

Rebecca Hascall looked at her friend. The biggest outward change was that once vivacious and carefree, Smith now seemed so fragile. She had lost a lot of weight and was physically shaky, nervous. She knew that Heather was more troubled by the scars, particularly the one down her chest, than she usually let on. Once she'd caught her standing nude in front of a mirror crying. "I'm ugly," Heather had moaned as tears ran down her cheeks.

They often talked about how trapped they felt simply because they were women. Never safe to walk their dogs at night. At the mercy of whomever might break in. Men were bigger. They were violent and scary.

Winter's short days only exacerbated the feeling of being prisoners in their homes. "It's getting dark," Heather said at last as the streetlights came on, illuminating the snowflakes.

"Yes," Rebecca conceded hollowly. They both shuddered.

* * *

Byron Eerebout called Luther in a panic after his interrogation by Richardson but reached only Debrah Snider. "He's gone, Byron," she said, "and I don't know if he's comin' back."

Luther and Debrah had been fighting more and more often. She was tired of his disappearing for days at a time and suspicious of what he was doing. She also knew that he was getting the younger Eerebout boys—J.D. and Tristan—involved in his drug deals, so she called their father, Skip, and asked him to talk to his friend. "At least for the sake of your younger boys."

Skip's response was to call Luther and warn him. "She's tryin' to get you sent to prison. Get outta town."

Tom, of course, was angry with her. He had hardly spoken to her since. But he did return the day after Byron's arrest.

When she told him about the call, he nodded. "He's in jail for attempted murder." Then he was gone again, this time never to return to her home in Fort Collins.

"He's in Vermont," Snider told Richardson in early October. "He's still not talkin' to me, but his mother told me. He's going to Chicago and then heading to Pennsylvania to work with his brother-in-law. He's supposed to be in Pennsylvania on November 1."

"Do you know where?" Richardson asked. He had Eerebout on the hook for two counts of attempted murder, four counts of assault with a weapon, and another count of possessing narcotics with intent to sell. The detective wanted to know Luther's whereabouts in case the younger man cracked.

Byron's alibi had evaporated fairly quickly when Robert Makarov-Junev called and confessed, hoping to get the charges against himself dropped.

"I might as well talk or I could go to prison for motherfuckin' thirty years for not doin' a fuckin' thing," he said. "What have I got to lose, because I do my time in the joint or he kills me. . . . But I'd rather be free and let him come get me."

Robert said he only showed Eerebout where his cousin was staying with Patty because he thought the two men could talk it out after the assault at the restaurant.

"We come down the street and fuckin' there's Mark's truck and, shit, he goes, 'There the motherfucker is.' Boom. Boom.

Boom. Boom. Boom. He fuckin' threw the gun in the car and says, 'Let's get the fuck out of here.' So we took off and he said, 'You didn't see nothin', dude. You don't know what happened. Just mind your own business, dude, and everything will be all right, just stay with me.' Now, the motherfucker's gonna try to kill me when he gets out of prison.''

With Robert's help, Richardson had Eerebout right where he wanted him. But Luther was two thousand miles away.

"Let's see," Snider said as she checked her address book, "Ah, Newport . . . Newport, Pennsylvania."

Debrah volunteered that Byron's mother, Babe, had asked her to put up her property to get Byron out of jail on a $170,000 bond. The two women had been talking a lot lately.

However, Debrah told Richardson, she wasn't about to put up bail for her new friend's son. "I've been tryin' to get Byron put in jail, not the other way around."

"Anything else new?" Richardson asked.

Well, Luther, she said, had recently talked to a prison inmate named Rick Hampton about Cher Elder. And she'd just learned that he had gone to Breckenridge after his release from prison to look for his old girlfriend.

"Why is he lookin' for her?" Richardson asked.

"I don't have any idea," Snider responded. "I mean, my guess was that he was tryin' to find someone to get hooked up with different than me. Which is why he's not callin' me. I'm . . . I'm the reason that his life isn't working."

Debrah said she'd told him all she knew. There was nothing more. For her or the detective. However, she didn't call to tell him when she received a short letter from Luther a few days later.

The letter was from the nice Tom, the one who got lonely and missed her despite their differences. "It's great to be home in these little green rolly mountains of Vermont," he wrote. "I wish there were some way we could get along. I don't know what to do with you and without you. Well, this is going to be short because I'm not ready to really deal with all my feelings. But I want you to know you're in my thoughts and in my heart."

Debrah couldn't help herself. It seemed that every time she was, however unwilling, ready to accept that he was out of her life, he called or wrote. Good Tom missed her. Good Tom loved her. Good Tom wanted them to be together again someday. Caught up in the almost puppy-dog romance of his letters, it was difficult for Debrah to believe that such a man could be a killer. And so, she found herself in love all over again.

"Dear Tom," she wrote back. "I miss you so much. I know I made you angry by trying to set limits for our relationship, but maybe if you could have accepted those limits just a little better, Byron wouldn't be in jail and you wouldn't have had to leave. I don't know if we would have ever been able to work things out here, but what a waste that we didn't try harder.

"Well, love, it's hard to see you as a Walk-Away-Joe. I fought the State of Colorado for you, but you are a wimp when it came to fighting for us. I hope you one day get settled, maybe it can happen in Pennsylvania. I won't wish you luck or love with another woman, because I will always love you. . . . Maybe someday you will come home again, when you're more settled, or if that can never happen, maybe you'll call and ask me to come to you. I love you, Debrah."

Luther wrote back, "I know nothing is perfect, and I'm kinda hurt that you accept the fact that I walked away so easy. After fighting Colorado so hard to get me, you couldn't say that you would rather see me gone a couple days a month than gone forever?" Besides, how could he love her "proper" with her husband around all the time?

"I miss you, Deb. Sometimes I wish I could get you out of my system and just stay out of yours and your family's lives, but I can't seem to do that."

Indeed, Thomas Luther and Debrah Snider would, as Detective Richardson once told her, continue to get back together until something beyond her control separated them once and for all.

In November, Luther, who once told her that God put them together for a purpose, asked her to meet him "halfway" in Iowa for the Thanksgiving holiday. It was a magical four days for Debrah.

Tom was romantic, bringing her flowers, and patient with her as a lover. They hardly left the room except to eat, a fact she found only mildly disappointing because she wanted to go out dancing. The disappointment dissolved when he invited her to join him back east in February.

"I never have had, and may never have a honeymoon," she

wrote to him on December 9. "But if I never do, those few days will always be remembered as just about as good as one can get."

Two days later, the glow of the "honeymoon" was beginning to wear off. She had been unable to reach him since they parted and hadn't received any letters. She also was told by Luther's mother that because Debrah had seen him for Thanksgiving, her son would be spending Christmas with his family in Vermont.

"I don't think I'm going to make it 'til February," she wrote to him. "I put up with you because, despite the fact that you're such a pain in the ass, you're still the best thing that's ever happened to me. But I need you, and you're unavailable."

She closed her letter saying she understood about Christmas. "This is your first year out and it's appropriate that you spend it with your family. But promise me that next year, no matter where you are or what you're doing, you'll spend Christmas with me."

With renewed hope for a future with the man she loved, Debrah Snider posted the letter, forgetting Luther's own warning from prison that he had a heart half good and half bad . . . that "there's death here and pain for many."

The day after Snider wrote her letter, the nude body of an unidentified white woman, approximately 20 years old, was found on a hillside five miles from Newport, Pennsylvania. She had been raped vaginally and anally, beaten about the face, and then strangled to death.

The young woman had been pretty; petite at 5′4″ and 110 pounds. She had shoulder-length hair. Her clothes, except for a sweater, and any identification as to who she might have been, were missing.

The isolated area where the body was found was dense woods with a lot of undergrowth. The fact that she was found at all was happenstance, as two hunters stumbled upon the remains 200 feet from the nearest road or trail.

As to who the killer might be, the police had few clues, except for blood on the victim's sweater. It didn't match the young woman's, and it was assumed to be the killer's. It was blood type A one plus one.

Chapter Eighteen

January 25, 1994—Golden, Colorado

The Jefferson County Courthouse is a massive structure of glass, steel, and tan stone nicknamed the Taj Mahal, both because of what it cost to build in the mid-80s and for its domed middle segment's slight resemblance to its namesake in India. It sits on a barren hill outside of Golden within the shadow of the range of foothills that mark the eastern edge of the Rockies, including Lookout Mountain, where Luther claimed nearly a year earlier that he and Cher Elder had parked for a "quick little intercourse thing."

Just down the road from the courthouse were two lesser, but just as modern structures, the Jefferson County Jail and the building housing the district attorneys' offices. Scott Richardson could see the Taj from the room where he, Deputy District Attorney Mark Minor, who was prosecuting Byron Eerebout for the shooting case, and Byron's two lawyers were meeting.

Eerebout's lawyers had asked for the meeting. First degree attempted murder carried the possibility of forty-eight years in prison, and their client was getting nervous. The lawyers knew that even if they could get their client off on the attempted murder charges—after all, he shot up the apartment, not people—it was much less likely that he could beat the felony assault raps. With three counts of assault pending, and eight years a pop possible, that was still a lot of years for a young man.

For Richardson, the timing for the little chat could not have been better. The search around Empire had been called off because of deep snow. It was a good time to wait out Eerebout.

Minor, a large, taciturn young lawyer, told the defense attorneys that the offer was to reduce the charges against Eerebout in exchange for the location of Cher Elder's body. "What do you got?" Minor asked.

"We have a witness who saw Thomas Luther's hands bloody

and covered with mud, and a broken finger, after Cher Elder disappeared,'' one of the attorneys said. "We can also supply a witness who was standing nearby when Thomas Luther buried Cher Elder.''

That was fine and good, Richardson interjected, but he wanted more. What about the night Cher disappeared?

"Byron told us he was with Gina the night Cher Elder was killed,'' the other defense attorney said. "They went to a bar while Cher stayed behind with everyone else. About midnight, Byron and Gina returned, and at some point, he heard a woman yelling. She is someone's sister, though I can't recall the name right now. Byron also said he saw two people leave in Cher's car, but neither were Cher.''

Richardson listened intently. The scenario fit with what he knew from talking to Gina Jones. However, the allegation that two people left in Cher's car was new. But it was the lawyer's next statement that made him sit up.

"Cher was apparently killed because she did not get along with Thomas Luther and was being 'mouthy,' '' the first lawyer said.

In early February, Richardson and his new partner Stan Connally drove to Fort Collins to talk to Debrah Snider. Heylin had decided to go back to patrol where the hours were more humane. Connally was a great replacement, particularly in this case, because he had come over from the sex crimes unit.

Unknown to the detectives, Snider had visited Luther several times in Pennsylvania. The post office romance had renewed itself with a flurry of letter-writing, most of it initiated by Debrah. It was clear, even to her, that the Tom Luther she loved the most was the imprisoned romantic she had originally fallen for. "I miss the visiting room," she wrote January 6. "I miss the anticipation of seeing you. I miss your phone calls. I miss your letters. I miss you telling me that you want a simple life and that as long as we have each other, that would be enough.''

She told him about the deal that had been offered to Byron, which she had heard about from Babe. However, once the attempted murder charges were dropped, Byron planned to plead guilty to second degree assault, then tell the police "that he'd love to cooperate, but he has no information that can help them."

Snider was frightened of what an upcoming biopsy of a lump in one of her breasts might turn up. "I'm so plain anyway, I couldn't handle losing a breast. It's hard enough to accept my position with you when I see the women you're really attracted to."

Luther ignored her health concerns and wrote back that he was moving to Delray, West Virginia, where his sister Becky and her current husband had moved. It was only across the border and still an easy drive to his job in Pennsylvania.

The one subject they never wrote about was Cher Elder. Debrah almost believed that if they didn't mention it, the "trouble" as she called it, would go away. Then Richardson and his partner showed up.

Snider warned the detectives about Byron Eerebout's plans to renege once he had the worst of the charges dropped. Babe, she said, also told her that one day before the shooting incident in September Byron got drunk and began crying.

"He said he had witnessed his friend being killed, and he couldn't do anything about it," Debrah said. "Byron didn't tell her who it was he was talking about, but she believes it was Cher Elder. Babe thinks that Cher came back from Central City with Luther and that something happened to her at Byron's apartment."

Without warning, Snider began to cry herself. "I'm sorry I ever told you anything about Tom," she said.

"Why?" Richardson asked, genuinely confused by the sudden turnaround.

"Because I told Babe that Tom confessed to buryin' Cher," she said. "And now I'm afraid."

"Then why'd you tell Babe?" he asked.

"Because I was worried you'd play the tape of my confession to Byron, and I wouldn't know that Byron and Babe knew what I had done," she replied.

Snider said she thought she could trace all the misery of the past year to one thing: drugs. "He once told me, 'That's why they killed her, over drugs.' "

Now death and pain seemed to be everywhere. Byron, she said, got into a heated conversation with his girlfriend's sister and told her, "You'd better not try that shit around someone we know or you might get buried beside someone else."

Richardson asked Debrah who among Luther's acquaintances had a sister who might have been to Eerebout's former apartment. The only one she could think of was Southy Healey. He had two or three sisters, she said, one of whom he lived with.

Debrah Snider admitted that she told Luther about the deal being offered to Byron. "He said, 'Byron better not say anything because he can't do a life sentence.' "

Richardson left Snider's house feeling that he was closer than ever to cracking the case. If so, he needed to keep her on his side. He was therefore alarmed a little more than two weeks later when Debrah's son, Chance, called. The family was worried, he said. His mother had disappeared shortly after she talked to Richardson the last time.

"She didn't pack nothing or say nothing," the boy said. "We came home one day and she wasn't here. And we haven't heard from her since."

Richardson entered Debrah's name and description on a nationwide alert, stating that she might be in danger. However, the mystery was cleared up on April 2 when Snider called to say she was back home after visiting Luther in West Virginia.

Luther was still working near Newport, she said. But she decided not to tell the detective that she was in the process of looking for a job in West Virginia. However, as the date for her to move approached, Luther again seemed intent on punishing her by not writing or calling.

Richardson had sensed that Debrah was holding something back, but now that she was safe, he was preoccupied with other things. The snow was melting in the high country and soon it would be time to resume the search for Cher Elder.

Warned of Eerebout's treachery, he and Dennis Hall went back to his lawyers and said they wanted something more concrete before there would be a deal. Since then, there had been no word. However, other rumors were floating around on the prison grapevine.

Down in the penitentiary in Canon City, inmate Wesley Martin told a guard that another inmate, Rick Hampton, told him that

Luther killed and buried Cher Elder. The guard relayed the information to Richardson, who drove down to interview the two men.

Martin had nothing new to add. Hampton at first played the tough guy, shrugging when Richardson tried to appeal to his conscience by describing what Cher's family was going through. But after a few minutes, he admitted that Luther told him that he killed the girl, "but police will never find the body. He learned his lesson the last time."

Asked how he thought Luther would have killed her, Hampton said, "He would strangle her." He thought Luther probably would have buried her at a "favorite place" high in the mountains near Leadville. In their prison days, when Luther talked about killing counselor Gloria Greene, he showed Hampton a photograph of his favorite place and said that's where he'd dump Greene's body.

Richardson left the prison not knowing what to think. On one hand, Hampton could have made it all up. But they hadn't talked about any deals and, in fact, Hampton had clammed up again.

Hampton also couldn't have known that Richardson was aware of Luther's homicidal thoughts regarding Gloria Greene. And it wasn't the first time Richardson had heard about Luther's promise that the next time he would bury the body so that police couldn't find her.

Cher Elder had been missing for a year, a long time for the successful prosecution of a homicide case. In the meantime, her family suffered.

Van Edwards confided to Richardson that he was worried about his wife, Rhonda. On holidays, once a cause for large celebrations, she now hid in her room and wouldn't come out.

She had tried to keep her fears and emotions in check by playing detective, until she kept running into walls. She then threw herself into her work for the City of Grand Junction in the northwest corner of Colorado, burying herself in the troubles of her fellow citizens to ease her own horror. But it wasn't working anymore.

Van said she would come home from work and cry for hours.

"I've found her outside at night, looking up at the stars and asking, 'Where are you? Where are you?'

"Other times I wake up and she's gone. She'll be out in the kitchen, staring at a cup of coffee and smoking a cigarette. She doesn't even notice I'm there, just keeps sayin', 'I want to find my baby. I just want to find my baby.' "

Cher's father, Earl, wasn't doing any better. He'd made independent attempts to find Luther since the press conference but had been unable to locate him. Like his former wife, he was on a wild emotional ride. He'd been in the process of divorcing his second wife when Cher disappeared; Debbie, like Van, had known Cher most of the girl's life and was also devastated. But, estranged, they couldn't even lean on each other to get through the tough times.

Earl Elder suffered through days, even weeks, of severe depression when he didn't want to talk to anyone. He alternated between raging around the house and weeping in a chair. When he saw a young mother with her children, he'd recall how Cher wanted a big family and start crying.

Seeing and hearing all this, Richardson was in no mood to commiserate when he got a call on April 12 from Byron Eerebout, who whined, "Tom's friends come up to me and say they're gonna kill me and my family. They had pictures of some girl that they took care of . . . that was buried up in the mountains. It wasn't Cher. She had blond hair. They showed a picture of the grave that was dug and then they showed her in a car being lowered into it by another truck. She was a real rich girl from Summit County, her throat was slashed."

The photograph had been shown to him by a friend of Luther's who went by the nickname Mongo, Eerebout said. The message was clear: a snitch's life wasn't worth a damn in prison.

Eerebout complained that he wasn't guilty of the attempted murder in September. "It wasn't me," he said. "Everybody keeps comin' up to me, like the lawyers and stuff. And they say this is all basically being done because of the Cher Elder thing."

Richardson interrupted. He wouldn't talk to Byron about the shooting case, but if he wanted to say something about Cher . . . .

"Okay, well I told my attorney that I have the name of the person that did it. Tom was the one that got rid of it, but this other guy's the one that did it."

"We made the offer if you'd give us a location of Cher's body," Richardson said.

"See, I don't know the location, but I know who does." Byron said.

Eerebout wasn't sure if Elder had come back to his apartment, but he didn't think so because the woman he saw briefly that morning had longer hair. He thought the woman might have been Southy's sister. Southy had been at the apartment that morning wearing a torn and bloody shirt, giving the excuse that he'd been in a fight with police at a local bar. "Him and Tom were supposedly the ones that did it."

Babe Rivinius had raised the money to get her son out on bond. Now he complained to Richardson that he had recently married Tiffany and didn't want to be an old man when he got out of prison. But he wanted a new deal before he gave anymore information: no charges in the Elder case and no prison time for the shooting incident. He made an appointment to come in the next afternoon to talk.

But Eerebout never made it to Richardson's office after telling his mother and lawyers of his plan. They talked him into taking his chances in court.

In June, the jury acquitted him of the attempted murder charges but found him guilty of three counts of first degree assault, each one of which carried a maximum penalty of eight years. The terms would run consecutively. Twenty-four years in all, and he'd have to serve at least two-thirds of it.

Debrah Snider arrived in West Virginia in May determined to put Cher Elder out of her mind. There was nothing more she could do for the missing woman or her family. She had told Richardson everything she knew; he would have to do the rest if he wanted to take Tom away from her. She just wanted to make a life with the man she loved.

However, Luther didn't allow her to move into his cabin in a remote, wooded area near Delray. She should have seen it coming from a letter he wrote on April 20, exactly one year after his first confrontation with Richardson.

Luther wanted her to stop trying to manipulate him and accept him the way he was. He accused her of wanting to know where

he was and who he was with every second, to lock him up in
mind and spirit. He felt he should just cut all ties and cease
prolonging their agony. She should just stay in Colorado and
forget about him.

Snider had gone anyway and rented a space at a campground
where she lived in her van. She took a job as a nurse at Rocksbury
Correctional Institute in Hagerstown, Maryland, and saw Luther,
when he let her, on her days off. His behavior toward her swung
back and forth between "Good Tom" and "Bad Tom."

On July 4, Bad Tom had a few friends over for a cookout.
Debrah, who had complained about his other girlfriends and had
been put on restriction, was not invited. Miserable, she lay in
the weeds near his cabin and watched. At one point, he emerged
from his cabin with a rifle and a shotgun, neither of which he
was supposed to have as an ex-felon.

On July 12, the West Virginia State Patrol office in Delray
received a telephone call from a woman identifying herself as
Debrah Snider. She wanted to let them know that her soon-to-be-
ex-boyfriend, one Thomas Luther, was suspected of murdering a
missing female in Colorado. He was now living in their neck
of the woods.

She said she moved from Colorado to be with Luther and
now they were splitting up. She thought that she better warn
them that Luther recently purchased a .12-gauge shotgun and a
rifle. And he didn't like cops, particularly a Colorado detective
named Scott Richardson, who they should contact for more
information. She said she didn't care what happened next.

Yet a week later, Debrah and Tom were back together. He
was even letting her stay for longer periods of time at the cabin,
and she allowed herself to imagine that life might someday
always be so good.

In early August, they went on a small vacation to a nearby
campground for the weekend, bringing two cars because they
planned to leave from there to go their separate ways: Tom back
to Delray, Debrah to her job in Maryland.

Sunday, the day they were to leave the campground, a young
woman—athletic, slender, sculpted in her Spandex outfit—sped
by on rollerblades. Snider caught Luther watching as the girl
raced off around the corner. He had that look in his eyes he got

whenever he saw an attractive young woman and thought he wasn't being noticed. A hungry, predatory look.

As they began to leave the campground a couple of hours later, Luther, who was in the lead, suddenly pulled over and tried to wave her around. Debrah refused to pull ahead. She didn't know if she was reacting out of jealousy or a premonition, but all she could think of was the girl on rollerblades and the look in her lover's eyes.

However, he insisted that he had decided to take a nap before going home and so would stay behind. In the end, Snider, who had to get to work, left despite her fears. When she saw him a few days later, he was relaxed and said the nap had done him a lot of good.

A week later, however, Snider was at a the local post office when she noticed a new poster for a missing woman. The poster said the woman was in her 20s and had disappeared the week before.

Snider stared at the poster. She couldn't be sure, but she thought the fuzzy photograph looked like the young woman at the campground. Suddenly, she couldn't breathe. She ran out of the post office. *It couldn't be the same girl,* she told herself, *you're just imagining the worst.* But she didn't go back in to look again.

A few nights later, while working a late night shift and all alone, Debrah thought she heard a voice. She wondered who was talking before realizing that the voice was inside her own head. The voice was urging her to take Tom Luther to church.

Snider worried that the stresses of the past year had finally driven her crazy. But the voice kept insisting and she decided church might not be such a bad idea.

Although she attended irregularly, the church had given her something to cling to in the dark days when she had been in prison. Maybe the beast that sometimes raged in Tom's soul would be tamed in the presence of God.

But once again, it was too late.

Sgt. Bob Burkhart of the Bureau of Criminal Investigations, West Virginia State Police, wasted no time contacting Scott Richardson in Lakewood, Colorado. If what the Snider woman said was true, he thought he'd best find out everything he could about Luther.

Richardson responded by faxing Burkhart a five-page report on Luther's "particulars." Luther, he said, was a suspect in the disappearance and murder of Cher Elder, as well as a suspect in the January 1982 deaths of Bobby Jo Oberholtzer and Annette Schnee in Summit County. A third girl had been raped, beaten, and left for dead a month later, but lived to identify him and send him to prison.

Luther's victims tended to be petite white females, 19 to 22 years old, with shoulder-length hair, Richardson reported. Luther worked by picking up hitchhikers and watching places like bus stops for likely targets. It was thought that he would beat, strangle, and sexually assault his victims.

Burkhart agreed to find out where Luther lived and check into the information Debrah Snider provided regarding the guns. "We'll get back to you with what we find," he said.

Richardson hung up the telephone, relieved. He had lost contact with Snider, who seemed to have abandoned her ranch and family to chase after her man. Now, apparently, she was coming back around again.

The detective was satisfied with the results of Byron Eerebout's trial. He and Deputy District Attorney Minor talked it over with the judge and told him that they hoped for a stiff sentence to apply pressure to Eerebout in the hopes of solving the Elder case.

Sentencing had been set for September, after which Richardson would play a waiting game. The FBI Behavioral Sciences Unit had suggested waiting sixty days after the sentencing before approaching Eerebout again. It would give him enough time to get a taste of penitentiary life without becoming established in the convict world and deciding to do his time in silence.

A few days after they first talked, Richardson got another call from Burkhart. They had located Luther's cabin. He was driving a Ford truck and the blue Geo Metro. While he was away one afternoon, detectives got close enough to take photographs of the cabin. They'd also come across information that Luther was buying ammunition for a shotgun and a rifle. "We're trying to get enough for a search warrant," Burkhart said.

"Thanks, bud," Richardson replied. "I'll send you some

recent photographs of him. When you get a minute, you might want to get a notice out to nearby states to see if anyone has any murdered or missin' women.''

Chapter Nineteen

August 21, 1994—Delray, West Virginia

Unaware that he had already been brought to the attention of the local police, Luther was driving along a rural highway in his Geo Metro when he stopped to pick up two hitchhikers. A man and a 32-year-old woman with dark, shoulder-length hair. Her name was Bobby Jo, an irony that would not be lost on police investigators.

A few miles down the road, they met up with another woman, the man's girlfriend, who didn't appreciate that Bobby Jo Jones was there. She suspected that her boyfriend and Bobby Jo were having an affair. While the man and his girlfriend argued, Luther and Bobby Jo left—she wanted to buy some cocaine in nearby Virginia, and Luther agreed to drive.

However, Luther first took her to his cabin where he announced that he wanted to take a shower. "Care to join me?" he said slyly. Bobby Jo declined and went outside to wait. As she left the cabin, she noticed a Colorado license plate hanging on the wall.

Fifteen minutes later, Luther came out of the cabin carrying a backpack. "I might need this," he said pleasantly, but didn't elaborate.

The pair drove to Virginia and purchased cocaine from Jones' connection, most of which they promptly consumed. Bobby Jo later recalled that Luther was a good conversationalist as they drove back to West Virginia. He made no sexual advance, though she sometimes caught him looking at her strangely.

They were getting close to Delray that evening when he suddenly veered off the road into a field. As matter-of-factly as he had previously discussed the weather, he announced, "I'm going to rape you."

Jones, a single mother of two, tried to reach for the door handle when her head exploded with pain. "Bitches," he swore and hit her again. "Whores. Sluts."

As Bobby Jo tried to regain her senses, Luther got out of the car and went around to her side, where he yanked her out by her arm. She felt something pop and screamed in pain. He dragged her over to a tree where he tore her clothes off.

When he began to undress, Jones tried again to escape, but he chased her down. Spinning her around, he punched her repeatedly in the face. "You're not going anywhere."

Collapsing to the ground, Bobby Jo cried out, "Why are you doing this?

" 'Cause you're a fuckin' bitch," he snarled and punched her again.

Jones heard her jaw snap like a piece of wood. He climbed on top and began to choke her. "I'm going to kill you," he raged. She felt herself begin to lose consciousness. *God,* she prayed, *please don't let him kill me.*

Luther quit choking her. Turning her over, he attempted to rape her vaginally and anally though he could not maintain an erection. Frustrated, he flipped her over again and demanded that she perform oral sex.

When this too failed, Luther began to strangle her again but stopped just as suddenly. He stood up, panting from the exertion. He passed a hand across his eyes. Wordlessly, he picked up his clothes and began to get dressed.

"Can I put my clothes on?" Jones asked through her broken mouth. The arm Luther dragged her out of the car by hung uselessly at her side, throbbing with pain.

"Yeah," he mumbled. "Then get back in the car."

Bobby Jo gathered her torn clothing and dressed as well as she could with her one good arm. She got in the car shivering with fear and wondering what was next.

"I'm sorry," Luther said, getting in the driver's side. "I'll take you to the hospital to get help." But when they reached the intersection where Luther should have turned to take her to the hospital, he continued driving straight ahead. "Where are we going?" Jones cried.

"I've changed my mind," he said. The strange quiet that had come over him was almost more frightening than the snarling animal he had been just a few minutes earlier. "I'm taking you back to my cabin."

Jones pictured the cabin in the forest. *He's going to kill me,* she thought wildly. *He's going to bury me somewhere out there and nobody will ever know what happened.*

Luther approached another intersection. There was a stop sign, but it was clear he wasn't going to stop. However, he did slow down to check for oncoming traffic. Bobby Jo seized the moment to grab the door handle and tumbled out onto the highway.

She heard Luther slam on the brakes behind her, but even with her broken jaw and shoulder shouting with pain, she was already up and running into the woods near the road. Terrified as she crashed through the underbrush, she listened for footsteps following her. She hadn't heard Luther's car speeding off.

Bobby Jo Jones reached a clearing that led to a road across which she could see a rural grocery store. Her clothes in tatters, her face bloody and disfigured, she ran into the store screaming for help.

After Jones escaped, Luther drove in a panic to the campground where Debrah Snider lived in her van. She wasn't around. He took a set of clean clothes from his backpack. Then he removed his blood- and dirt-stained clothes and changed. He threw the soiled garments into the river that flowed near the campground.

Continuing on to his sister's house, Luther told his brother-in-law, Randy Foster, that he had beat up a woman because of a drug deal gone awry. Knowing Luther's past, Foster asked if he had also raped the woman.

"No," Luther said. "I swear I didn't. But I think I hurt her real bad." He paced around the room. "What is ailing me? I don't know what causes this to happen," he said, echoing the statement he made to Deputy Morales in Summit County more than twelve years earlier.

The next morning, Snider was asleep in her van when she was awakened by knocking on the van door. Her pleasure at seeing Tom, however, evaporated when she caught the wild, hunted look on his face. He pointed to his car, which she could see was loaded with what appeared to be all of his possessions.

"I'm heading out," he said.

"Why?"

"Richardson showed up at work. I took off," he said.

"Are you sure?" she asked. "Maybe he wasn't there to arrest you."

Luther started to say something, then stopped. His head hung. "I can't tell you that lie," he said, looking up. "I did it again. I beat someone up, a black guy and, uh, then there was a girl who jumped in and, well, I think I beat her up pretty bad."

There was a party, he explained. He'd arranged to get some drugs but the black guy ripped him off.

"Did you rape her?" Debrah asked angrily dismissing the character of the "black guy."

"I tried to get her to suck me," he responded. "I said, 'You like black dick so much, how about tryin' white. But I couldn't get it up."

It was another Tom Luther story. Snider knew it. It wasn't even a new one. Girl tries to rip him off in a drug deal, girl assaulted—it was essentially the same story he had tried to pass off for his attack on Mary Brown in 1982.

"Richardson will be coming," Luther said and turned to leave.

"Don't go," Snider implored. She was sure he had raped this girl and part of her wanted him to stay and face the consequences. Another part of her was afraid that this time if he left, she would never see him again.

Now Debrah understood how Sue Potter must have felt that night when he came back to her in Frisco after assaulting Mary Brown. All those years, Debrah had thought that Potter was weak or crazy, knowing Tom for what he was but taking him, blood and all, into her bed. She must have loved him, too, Debrah thought.

"I won't lie for you, Tom," she said grabbing his hand and pulling him into her van and into her arms. "But maybe it isn't as bad as you think."

Bobby Jo Jones was admitted to the hospital with a dislocated shoulder, a broken jaw, and a broken nose. Her face was swollen and bruised where Luther had struck her; the marks left by his fingers around her neck stood out like rope burns. But two days after the assault, she was able to lead State Police Trooper Jeff Phillips to Luther's cabin. Luther wasn't in.

On August 27, Phillips, a young enthusiastic rookie, called the cabin. Debrah Snider answered. "He's not here," she said. He'd gone to Vermont, but she expected him back in a few days.

Actually, Luther had not gone that far. He hung around the area, checking newspapers to see if the crime had been reported. It didn't make the newspapers, and he was starting to feel the danger had passed. He had returned briefly to his cabin when he got a telephone call from Jones on August 30. He was unaware that the conversation was being recorded by Phillips.

Jones played it cool, saying she had left her keys in his car and needed them. Then she mentioned that she had a lot of medical bills because of what he'd done.

"Well," he replied. "I guess I got to own up to it, part of my responsibility in this."

"I just don't know why you did it," Bobby Jo said.

Luther sighed. "Yeah, I . . . you know, I'm a fucking idiot when it comes to that."

"You beat the hell out of me," Jones continued.

There was silence. Then Luther said, "So what do you want me to do? What do you need?"

"Tom, why did you rape me?"

"I don't know."

"Do you go around raping and beating up women?"

"No, I don't. I'm sorry . . . I can't handle chemicals," he said alluding to the cocaine. "But it's no excuse."

Jones asked if Luther had any diseases she should be worried about. He assured her that he was "clean as a whistle" and besides, he had not sexually climaxed inside of her. "This wasn't a fun thing, you know," he added.

So what was it, she wanted to know, "A mistake?"

"It was more than a mistake. You can't believe how sorry I am," Luther said. He offered to help her any way he could, if she just wouldn't tell the police. "I know it isn't enough—" he started to say.

Bobby Jo interrupted. "No, it isn't. I've never been through so much pain and terror in my goddamn life.'' Then she slammed the telephone down.

The next day, Trooper Phillips staked out Luther's cabin. It was his day off, but he wanted to take this rapist down.

It so happened that about the same time, his supervisor was having breakfast with Sergeant Burkhart. ''So whatcha got going?'' Burkhart asked after a bit.

''We're sittin' on this guy's place who raped a gal and beat the holy hell out of her,'' the supervisor answered. ''My guy's on his day off, but you know rookies, all gung-ho for his first big-time collar. We're lookin' for a white guy . . . drives a blue Geo Metro.''

Burkhart nearly choked on his coffee. ''What's the suspect's name?''

''Tom Luther. Why . . . what's the—''

Burkhart quickly explained. Richardson warned him that Luther would attack again. Now they had a rookie cop trying to take down a suspected serial killer who was armed with a shotgun and hated cops.

Patrol cars were dispatched to back up Phillips. They ran into Luther first as he was driving down the road toward his cabin. He was with a woman named Pam, who they later found out had just gotten out of prison herself.

''He's been with me the whole time,'' she swore as Luther was handcuffed. ''We're friends.''

It took some time for Scott Richardson to learn of Luther's arrest. He was taking a much-needed vacation with Sabrina, hunting in Alaska.

Although Richardson had Byron Eerebout in prison and there was a chance he would talk, it was only a chance. And without Byron giving up Cher's body, he doubted he would ever make a case against Luther.

The case was taking an enormous toll on Richardson and his family. He had lost twenty pounds and missed out on the past eighteen months of the twins' life. He was pushing his marriage to the edge. So by August, he knew he needed to get as far away from the case as possible and a hunting trip to Alaska seemed like the perfect thing.

Chapter Twenty

September 15, 1994—Lakewood, Colorado

"He was taking her out to the woods when she got away."

It was his first day back from vacation, and Richardson was on the telephone talking to Sgt. Burkhart, who had called from West Virginia. Richardson wasn't surprised that Luther had attacked again, he'd expected it; he was only sorry that he hadn't been able to stop him before it happened.

"We got him on tape, confessing," Burkhart said. "I don't think he'll be walking away from this one."

"Good work," Richardson said. At least he knew where Luther would be for awhile; off the streets, no other women would be in danger.

It wasn't long before Debrah Snider called. She was worried that Luther would find out that she had told the West Virginia State Police about his guns.

"I'm feeling really bad," she said. "Including the thing with Cher, this is the second time that I've reported him for something that was minor, and shortly after I report him, he does something major. I don't know if he did anything with Cher, but he's certainly involved in it and now he's at least attempted rape and beaten a girl here."

Richardson asked if she'd talked to the West Virginia state police about her concerns. "I'm afraid to talk to them concerning this case because I do know some information about this, and I don't want to give it to them," she replied. "I think they have plenty. They recorded him, you know, talking to this girl. They don't need anything that I know."

"Yeah? What is it you know that they don't know?" Richardson asked.

"I know he told me he did it. And I don't want to have to

be a witness. They don't need me—he told his brother-in-law that he did it. He went to his Randy's house that night, you know, in a panic, because I guess he had smoked some crack and that's what preceded this event, and whenever the crack wore off and he came to his senses, then he panicked and went and told his brother-in-law.''

Richardson wanted to know what her feelings regarding the Cher Elder case were now, in light of the recent attack? ''My feelings on Cher is—you know two people that could have did it, Tom and Byron, and we know she's dead. Now, the day I got back after Cher disappeared, Tom's hands were sore, all of his body was sore. It seems awfully strange that he was in that shape the day that Cher disappeared if Byron killed her.''

Richardson didn't think Byron had killed Cher and said so. Maybe he had moved her car after the fact, maybe he was involved in some other way, but as bad as he was, he wasn't the sort to murder his girlfriend and bury her body.

''What's the rumor since we put Byron down?'' Richardson asked. ''Have you talked to his mom about Cher?''

''They don't talk about it,'' Snider said. ''Tom still doesn't talk about it. He has some concern that you guys would pressure Byron into implicating him, once he was in prison. Or that he would tell on himself, which would implicate Tom.''

Richardson noted that if Eerebout served his full sentence, he'd be fifty years old before he got out. ''Byron's got some problems. I imagine Luther's got some problems now, too?''

''Yeah, I think he does,'' Debrah conceded. ''His attorney told me that even if they could get the rape charges thrown out, he's probably lookin' at two to ten for assault.''

''Who is Mongo?'' Richardson asked. Eerebout had said this friend of Luther's had threatened him by showing a photograph of a dead girl. Sounded like bullshit to him, but he had to check it out.

''He's a guy Tom did time with. His name is Chuck, um, I don't know his last name. The time he done was over assault.''

''What does Chuck look like? Chuck's important to me right now,'' Richardson said.

''He's real stocky, but not a tall guy, probably not even as tall as Tom. About mid-thirties.''

She remembered his name would have been in Luther's little

black telephone book—good news to Richardson, who had copied the pages before handing it back to Luther.

There were two other guys he was interested in but knew only by their nicknames. Mortho, the drug dealer who supposedly told Luther that Cher had been killed because she was a snitch. And Southy, who Eerebout had claimed was involved in the murder.

"Mortho is supposedly a real heavy guy, probably an older guy," Debrah said. "I've never seen him, and I don't remember his name."

"Okay, what about Southy's real name?"

"Um, Dennis something or other?"

Richardson made the connection. "Healey?" he asked.

Snider said she thought that sounded correct.

Suddenly, Richardson felt tired. "This is dragging on and on," he said. "Luther started taking this girl to the mountains too, but she got away." Deb commiserated. "The amazing thing is that the story Tom told me is the same story he told about the girl in Summit County. That she had ripped him off for some drugs and that's why he beat her up and raped her."

"I don't understand how, knowing everything you know about Luther," Richardson asked, "how you put up with this?"

Snider paused. "I don't know either," she said at last. "I wonder if I'm crazy. It's terrible. But it's because with him is the only time I've ever felt loved in my life."

Richardson understood. In a way, she was another victim of Thomas Luther. But there were a lot of people suffering because of him. "Cher's family is going insane," he said. "I don't blame them because they know she's been killed, and there's something about burial whether you're Christian or not. It's been almost two years."

There was silence so Richardson, thinking he had touched on too raw a nerve, told Snider he would talk to the West Virginia State Police and see if they could leave out the part about her telling them of Luther's guns. "You may still have to testify about what he told you about the rape," Richardson said, "but you could always claim the police came to you for that and not the other way around."

Snider was obviously relieved. She volunteered that Luther was offering $5,000 to Bobby Jo Jones if she would disappear.

Other rumors, she said, were that if Jones didn't take the money, someone else might, to shut her up forever. "I'm just concerned, you know," she told Richardson.

"Oh hey, I hear ya," he replied. "I'd be concerned, too. I told you all along that your life's in danger. All you can do is be honest with me, Deb, and if something comes up or you need some help up there, then give me a holler."

On the afternoon of October 4, 1994, Richardson drove to the Buena Vista correctional facility where nearly ten years earlier Luther had given his "I am the lion" interview, and where Byron Eerebout was presently incarcerated. Inside, he was shown the list of people who had visited Byron. Tiffany. Babe. Byron's new attorney, Leslie Hansen. And Jerald "Skip" Eerebout.

Probably reminding him to keep his mouth shut or else, Richardson thought of the last entry. A good ol' father-to-son chat.

Before driving to Buena Vista, Richardson talked to Deputy District Attorney Dennis Hall about prosecuting a bodyless homicide. Hall had indeed found a single case where it had been done successfully, "but there's dozens where it hasn't worked."

The danger, of course, was that if they prosecuted Luther for Elder's death without her body, and he was acquitted, they wouldn't be able to try him again if her body was found later. Richardson called the family and told them about the option and its pitfalls. One drawback from the family's point of view was if they went to trial the search for her body would end; her grave might never be discovered. "Don't do it unless there's no other way," Earl Elder said and Rhonda Edwards subsequently agreed.

Richardson and Hall decided to wait at least until after the hunting season and the snows had melted. Hunters didn't always stay to the regular paths and were often the ones who stumbled upon remains left in the wilds. And they still hoped that Eerebout might talk.

Byron had no idea Richardson was coming. It had been sixty days—the FBI's magic number. A taste of prison life, the violence, the rapes, the day after day boredom, but not enough time to adjust or make new friends. There were also only a few days left of the 120-day period the judge had by law to reconsider the sentence he had handed down.

"Just pull him out of his cell and bring him here," Richardson told the guards who ushered him into a stark white interview room. "Don't tell him what for." He figured if Eerebout knew who wanted to talk to him, he'd resist coming.

A few minutes later, the door opened and Byron half-walked, half was shoved in. The door slammed shut again behind him as he pulled up short, seeing Richardson. "What the fuck are you doing here?" he spat. His blue eyes glared.

Richardson looked the young man over. It appeared prison had put a few miles on him; he looked pale and, under the hostility, nervous. "Have a seat," he said politely, gesturing to the seat across the table from the chair he was sitting in.

Eerebout just stood where he had stopped. He began to curse, but Richardson cut him off. Now his eyes were dark and his voice sharp and angry. "Sit down and shut the fuck up," he snarled. The younger man swallowed hard and complied.

Richardson leaned across the table locking his eyes on Eerebout's. "We're fixing to indict," he said. "We know what happened and who was involved, and anyone who doesn't cooperate is gonna go down."

It was a lie. He believed Luther was the killer and that Byron, and probably his brother J.D., were involved. But they didn't have a body or much else. They weren't remotely close to indicting anyone. The only thing working for him now was that Byron was under stress and Byron didn't know what he did or did not have.

"You hear about Luther?" Richardson asked.

"Yeah."

"Okay. This is what it's comin' down to. It's nut-cutting time in the Cher Elder case. Period. You got one hundred twenty days for reconsideration of your sentencing, which doesn't give you but a couple of days."

"Right." Eerebout wrinkled his brow beneath his short, red hair as if keeping up with Richardson's logic was a challenge.

"Your case is on appeal, along with about three-fourths of the inmate population in this prison."

"Yeah, I know."

"You're doing twenty-four, a lot of it mandatory before you're eligible for parole in ... "

Byron finished it for him. "2005."

So, Richardson thought, *he's got it all figured out, counting the years that he'll be staring at walls and barbed wire, watching his young wife grow old in the visiting room—if she stuck around.* "Elder is coming to a climax, big fucking time," he said. "The offer that we presented to you during the pretrial was for information on the location of the body."

Eerebout licked his lips nervously, but still tried to maintain the hardened criminal pose. Richardson didn't want to get his back up anymore. He changed his tone.

"I need your help," he said, as if asking an old friend for a favor. "Luther is pretty much burned. He picked up a female hitchhiker, raped her, broke her jaw, broke her shoulder, was taking her to the mountains when she bailed out of the car and got away. Well, you know what we've been doing in the mountains."

Eerebout nodded but didn't say anything. So Richardson continued. "I will tell you right now, the Cher Elder case is a death penalty case," he said. "That's a hell of a lot more than the year 2005. And anybody who doesn't cooperate in this investigation is going down with Tom Luther."

Eerebout mumbled something about not being involved. But Richardson interrupted and put his hand up to silence him. "I ain't askin'," he said. "I'm flat out telling you that you can live on false hopes that your appeal will go through. You can pick whatever wisp of hope there is out there and then live day to day on that. But I'm telling you that yours is one of another million in the court of appeals."

Eerebout shook his head. He complained that if he said anything, well, he'd been getting death threats from Mongo and Southy, who he'd seen before his sentencing in the Jefferson County Jail.

Richardson shrugged. "You got more problems than whatever they're sayin','" he said. "What if people, and I'm not telling you who, start implicating you in Cher's murder, guess who's going to go down? You know Cher was killed that night, there's no doubt." It was like playing poker with a weak hand, but he wanted to see if Eerebout would call his bluff.

Byron nodded. "Okay."

The bluff was working. Richardson tried to keep the excitement out of his voice. "I need the body. I need cooperation," he said. Again, he spoke like they were friends. "Me and you have always tried to get along and talk."

Eerebout brightened. Yeah, that was the way he saw it, too.

"It's always the legal system and the attorneys that block gettin' anything done," Richardson added.

"I got ya."

"In my opinion, if we were minus attorneys," Richardson continued, "you wouldn't have ended up with what you got. We offered you a hell of a deal, a simple second degree assault. If you had given me a straight fucking story the first time—but you haven't been straight with me, you've tried to fuck with me, you've tried to fuck with the system. You listened to your lawyers and others tellin' you to keep your mouth shut and look where they're tellin' you this from—the fucking inside of the walls down here in the joint."

Richardson formed a circle on the table with his hands. "What I want is the whole pie. I want to sit down and let's just clean this up right now. We may go to court without the body, and if we go to court without the body. . . . Let's use this same pie, here's Thomas Luther and here's the other people—" Richardson brought his hands together, "—the whole pie is going down."

Byron stared at the demolished "pie." "I wasn't involved—" he began to protest again, but Richardson waved it off.

"I'm tellin' you right now," he said, "somebody's talkin' and burning your ass big time. They're telling you one thing, but it's coming out a whole different side of their mouth when they're talking to us. I've got so much shit on this case, Byron, this case is eight binders." The part about the binders was true, but the rest was still a bluff.

Eerebout tried to be a tough guy and stick to his alibi. "You forget about Gina Jones? You confirmed that I was with her on that night, right? And I was there the morning that [Cher] disappeared, right? There you go. You can just drop my name out of all this bullshit and get off my back about somebody runnin' their mouth."

Richardson looked at him for a moment without saying anything. Then he exploded. "Jesus Christ!" he yelled, slamming a fist on the table. Byron jumped. "She was your girlfriend, buddy. I mean it's one thing to get rid of a girl and find another girl, but she didn't deserve to die over this shit! And you know that!''

Alarmed, Eerebout looked toward the door and shook his head. "I didn't say or do anything. I just left and that was it," he said. Then he added, as if suddenly saddened by his next thought. "I didn't know about Tom."

Finally, Richardson thought, a little remorse. Time to draw it out even more. "Let me tell you what he did," he said standing and beginning to pace. "There was a series of homicides in Summit County. The third one lived, identified him, but not before he inserted a claw hammer vaginally and anally, practically cut off her finger, strangled her, beat her, dumped her in the mountains.

"I promise ya, that's what happened to Cher. I guarantee ya she was sexually assaulted, strangled, beat to death, and buried. Then he goes up to West Virginia and, what'd I just tell ya, he fuckin' picks up another girl, strangles her, sexually assaults her and the only reason she's alive, and he's where he's at, is 'cause she got away.

"And that," Richardson, angrily pointing a finger in Eerebout's face, "is the fuck that did Cher Elder. Period."

Suddenly, the detective felt spent. He sat down, tired of all the lying punks and petty criminals who thought they were living some Jesse James fantasy. Protecting themselves and each other, like there was some bond among criminals while the body of an innocent young woman lay in an unknown grave far from her family. He sighed. "You just got wrapped up in the wrong goddam football team, bud. You don't need to go down because of Thomas Luther. Two fucking years ago I told you that you were going down for Thomas Luther. Why are you protecting him?"

Richardson didn't give Eerebout a chance to answer. He was on automatic now, trying to make sense of something that made no sense. "Did you ever meet her dad? Didn't you know her little sister? Well, her brother and sister are seeing a psychiatrist. The grandmother is eighty some years old and having a mental breakdown. The mother—she looks like shit, and I'll tell you why she looks like shit—because the whole family knows that Cher was killed, but they can't bury her. And that is driving them up a wall with the false hope that she's alive. There is no way, and you know that, and I've had to tell the family that.

"Let's get Cher back home or at least buried so that her parents and family can put this behind them. When he was in prison, Luther bragged that the next girl wasn't gonna live and the cops weren't gonna find her. That's the kind of asshole that you're protecting."

Richardson found himself out of words. He'd tried to reach this young asshole, but whatever remorse Eerebout had been feeling a minute before, it was gone. He was back to looking out for number one. He wanted a deal—out of prison and into a community corrections program.

He sneered at Richardson. "If I sit there and tell you what you need to know it makes you look good, 'Oh, Detective Richardson, he's top line, he solved the Cher Elder case, blah, blah, boom.' Detective Richardson. His name is everywhere. He's got everything. But I have to come back here. And my wife is still out there."

Eerebout looked at the white walls of the interview room. "I hate this place. It's not a place for me." If the detective wanted to know where Cher was buried, he had better figure out a way to get J.D. back from Chicago where his father was keeping him under wraps. "And guess what? We could go on a little road trip."

"Can you and J.D. take me to the body?" Richardson asked.

"Yes." But he was going to have to make a deal first or the detective might as well tell Cher's family that he was unwilling to work something out to bring her home.

"Well, at least I know what Tom Luther is," Richardson said.

"So do I," Eerebout replied, standing up. "And so does my mom."

Leaving Buena Vista, Scott Richardson drove down from the mountains to the state penitentiary in Canon City. The road wound through ancient hills, the bones of an older mountain range, dotted here and there with ranch houses and cattle grazing in high country meadows. He regretted that he wasn't on his Harley; after talking to Eerebout, he could have used the fresh air.

The day before, an attorney called to say that a client, Rick Hampton, wanted to see him again. Richardson had talked to Hampton a year earlier, when the convict had told him that Luther had killed Cher and buried her in the mountains.

It wasn't long before he found himself sitting in another prison interview room with a convict. Only this one didn't want anything in return. Hampton said he was angry about Luther's latest sexual assault case in West Virginia; he might be a criminal, but he didn't think much of a guy who went around raping women.

"I want to cooperate," he said and handed over a letter he had received from Debrah Snider in January, nearly nine months earlier.

Richardson read the letter. "I spent Christmas with him and his family," Snider had written, "but our relationship isn't doing as well as I wish it were. I know you know of the special problem I bring into our relationship, but Tom also has created his own set of problems for us.

"His involvement with that girl that disappeared was bad enough, but he chose to continue to run around with people he had been locked up with who were involved with drugs and other illegal activities. I can't condone behavior like that. If I'm asked a question by a cop regarding something illegal, I'm going to tell the cop the truth . . . that made us incompatible concerning his behavior."

That was essentially all Hampton had. However, he said he would wear a wire and go visit Luther if it would help the case. Richardson said he'd have to get back to him.

Exhausted, Richardson returned to the office. It was night and it would have been nice to go home and see the boys and Sabrina, who had entered the third trimester of her pregnancy. But there was so much to do. He had located Chuck "Mongo" Kreiner with the help of Luther's little black book and he planned to go talk to him this next morning. He was also hoping to hear from Eerebout's attorney, Leslie Hansen, so they could begin negotiations for his information.

Just then the telephone rang. It was one of the twins. "Please, Daddy, please come home. We never get to see you."

The boy sounded like he was crying and it cut Richardson to

the core. He looked at Cher's photograph on the wall. A few hours that night wasn't going to bring her back.

"You're right," he said. "I'll be right home."

The next day did not start off well. Scott Richardson arrived at the office to find a faxed message from Hansen telling him that his contact with her client had been improper and unethical. Byron Eerebout would not be talking to him again.

Richardson crumpled the fax and tossed it into the wastebasket. Unethical? Hansen was Eerebout's attorney for the shooting case, which he had been careful to avoid talking about at the prison the day before. He had every right to talk to Eerebout about any other subject.

Richardson went to the apartment Charles "Mongo" Kreiner occupied with his girlfriend. The former convict opened the door.

Being told that Mongo was "stocky" had not prepared Richardson. Mongo was huge, not fat, but the sort of guy who had muscles on top of his muscles, all of them bulging. He seemed to fill the entire doorway. *Hell, if he attacks me,* Richardson thought, *I ain't gonna shoot.* It'd only piss him off.

There was only one way to deal with a guy like Kreiner, who invited him in, and that was to get right in his face. "I'm going to be up front with you, Chuck," he said after explaining why he was there. "You're about the last person to be interviewed in this whole case. And who ain't cooperating is goin' down hard."

Kreiner nodded. He'd known Luther since 1989, when they were in the joint together. They were pretty tight, but the last time he talked to him had been March 1994. "I figured he was in Canada."

"Try prison in West Virginia," Richardson said. "Guess what he did?"

Kreiner laughed. "I have no idea."

"Just guess, Mongo, guess," Richardson pressed. But Kreiner just laughed again, only a little more nervously.

"It involves a girl, and it involves a sex assault, and it involves strangulation, broken jaw, broken shoulder, in the mountains."

Kriener listened as Richardson went through his spiel about

the trail of broken, even dead, women Luther had left in his wake. And as he listened, he grew angry.

In the joint, Luther had always talked like a big man. He said he was in for beating up a woman over a drug deal. "The story I heard was he was dealing coke. This girl owed him a lot of money and she had a Corvette. He told her the wanted the car or his money, $6,000. She wouldn't give him either one."

Kreiner said he and Luther had become friends. But now he was hearing that Luther was nothing more than a rapist and a woman killer. "You know, the way he talked in the joint was, whenever he got out, he wanted to kill some people who ran the counseling. But I always just kind of thought it was all talk." Kreiner recalled that he'd once left his girlfriend with Luther in the apartment; the thought of what might have happened made him angrier still.

Richardson saw it as a good time to check on a rumor he'd been told about a time when Luther went beserk in front of the parole board. "I heard he went into the parole board and says, 'Fuck you. Hide your women and hide your girls 'cause I'm gonna fuckin' kill them all.' "

Kreiner nodded; he was there when it happened. When Luther was taken to the auditorium where the parole board hearings were held, he said, Luther, who still thought he would have a mandatory release date assigned that day, had walked up to the chairman of the board and handed him a piece of paper. "He says, 'This is my name and number.' "

"The chairman said, 'What the hell is this for?' And Tom says, 'By the time this is over, you're gonna want to know who I am.' Right then I should have known, 'Hey, this ain't the place to be with Tom Luther.' " Then when Luther heard that the law had been changed and he wasn't getting out, it had taken Kreiner and several other inmates to drag him, raving all the way about killing the families of the parole board members, out of the auditorium.

Richardson asked if Kreiner had threatened Byron Eerebout if he talked about the case or mentioned Southy Healey or Luther. "I don't know any 'Southy,' " he said. "And I never heard of Cher Elder until we saw about it on television back in the summer of '93.

"I'm nobody's muscle man," Kreiner said, upset that Eerebout was identifying him as such. He'd only met the younger man once when he went to his apartment with Luther.

"Did Luther ever talk about getting out and what he was going to do?" Richardson asked.

"He was going to make people pay."

"Did he ever talk about what he was going to do to women or anything like that?"

"Yeah," Kreiner nodded. It wasn't in the context of a sexual assault, Luther knew his friend wouldn't like that, but "if he had to do it over again, there would be no bodies and there would be no witnesses. That's exactly what he said."

Chapter Twenty-One

October 24, 1994—Carlisle, Pennsylvania

Cpl. Les Freehling of the Pennsylvania State Patrol reread the nationwide inquiry from Colorado regarding missing or murdered women and possible connections to a Thomas Edward Luther. The report said that Luther was known to have traveled through California, Colorado, Illinois, Vermont, West Virginia, Virginia and Newport, Pennsylvania.

According to the report, Luther had been arrested in September for beating and raping a young woman near Delray, West Virginia, right across the border from the Newport area.

Freehling had something that sounded like it might be connected to Luther. In fact, he had two somethings.

They still had not been able to identify the young woman found in December 1993. But everything about what happened to her—strangulation, the beating, raped vaginally and anally— fit Luther's style as described in Richardson's report. He thought about the blood on the victim's sweater and wondered about Luther's blood type.

There was also the case of a young woman reported missing from Newport in April. Karen Denise Wells was a 20-year-old model who had been driving from her home in Oklahoma to New Jersey. She got as far as Newport where she called a friend back home, but that was the last time anyone ever heard from her.

After her family reported Wells missing, the call was traced to a Newport restaurant. Her clothes were discovered in a motel. Her car was discovered five miles as the crow flies from where the other girl's body had been found five months earlier. She had vanished into thin air or, more likely, Freehling thought, into the dense woods that covered the area.

The whole thing smacked of a single killer on the loose in his jurisdiction. He called Richardson and asked if Luther had been in Newport between December 1993 and April 1994.

"As a matter of fact," the Colorado detective responded, "I believe he was."

Richardson also believed that the Pennsylvania cases only added to what he already thought about Luther. The blood on the first victim's sweater matched Luther's, A one plus one. It wasn't an uncommon blood type, but if it looked like a duck and quacked like a duck, to Richardson, it was a duck. Or in this case, a serial killer.

The West Virginia rape case sounded solid, but nothing was certain. Debrah Snider had talked about Luther trying to have the victim paid off or killed. Juries were undependable. He might escape.

Richardson thanked Freehling for the call and said he'd be happy to send them whatever information he could. He had to stay out of their case, he warned, otherwise a defense attorney might try to claim he had a vendetta against Luther and was drumming up incidents.

He no sooner got off the telephone with Freehling than Debrah Snider called from West Virginia to tell him Luther was aware that the authorities were trying to work out a new deal with Byron Eerebout. Skip, who apparently got the information from J.D. or Babe, had told him. "Tom doesn't seem worried that you're going to find the body," she said. "But other than that, he won't talk about it."

Snider said she appreciated Richardson reaching out to the West Virginia authorities for her. Trooper Phillips assured her that they weren't going to bring up her turning Luther in for the guns or that she was talking to Richardson. In the meantime, she had been thinking a lot about Cher's family. "It haunts me," she said. "I imagine that it haunts you."

"Yep," was all he said. He didn't want to talk about the sleepless nights, or how he would stare at the photograph of Cher on his wall for hours, asking, "Where are you?" Debrah was trying hard to do the right thing, but at the same time she had withheld information that might have brought Cher back to her family a lot sooner.

The whole case had been a real eye-opener to him about the number of murders involving unidentified people across the country. In his reports, he had noted a dozen or more, but they were only those who bore some resemblance to Cher. There were dozens more—too young, too old, too big, too small— that came over the teletype that never made it into his reports. And those were just the females. He felt for all the families who wondered what had become of their daughters, wives, and mothers, sons, brothers, and fathers. They could only hope their loved ones weren't lying in some morgue or pauper's cemetery, known only as John or Jane Doe.

Meanwhile, Byron Eerebout and his attorney were playing games. Hansen now said her client was willing to work out a deal: in exchange for Cher's body and testifying against Luther in court, Byron wanted his sentence reduced and served in a community corrections facility.

Shortly after Richardson's unannounced prison visit, Eerebout had written an impassioned plea to the judge to reconsider his sentence. He was a disabled war veteran with three bronze stars, he wrote, recently married, and had been taking business classes so that he could lead "the straight life" when he got out. He had also been studying the Bible through a prison ministries program.

"I'm just sorry I did not read his word sooner," he wrote. Now, he just wanted a second chance to start a family and "lead a respectable life and teach my children the right way of life by explaining to them what happens when a person does wrong and does not abide by the law ... This is the worst place on Earth and I am very unhappy here. I know I have done wrong, but also your honor, I have done a lot of good.''

Another prison conversion, Richardson scoffed when he heard about the plea; there was nothing like the thought of spending hard time in prison to make a man find religion. But for all his new-found morals and whatever past "good" he may have been referring to, for two years Eerebout had been keeping the whereabouts of Cher Elder's body from her family.

Six days after sending the judge his letter, his request for reconsideration was denied. He was looking at least a decade in prison or spilling his guts.

Now, Hansen was saying he had chosen the latter. However, there was a major hurdle to get past and that was Byron didn't want his brother J.D. to get in trouble for whatever involvement he might have in the case. Richardson said he'd contact District Attorney Hall and get back to her. *Let 'em sweat,* he thought to himself.

By early December, everything was set. Eerebout was ready to go through with it. Luther was in prison, so he felt safer. He'd even put it in writing so that he couldn't back out or later claim he had no new information.

Richardson was waiting to hear from Hansen as to the time and place for the trip to find Cher's body, when Debrah Snider called again. Byron's mother, Babe, had taken a job in Blackhawk, she said. Blackhawk was another former mining town that had capitalized on the legalized gambling, like its nearby neighbor Central City. She had also told Luther the news and he had written her back, hinting that Babe knew something about slavery rings.

Luther was initimating that Byron and some mystery man they were "all protecting" had something to do with Cher's disappearance. "Slavery rings. It sounds like another Tom Luther story to me," Debrah said. "I wondered if Tom wasn't just telling me this, you know, to see how quickly you'd get the information, and then it would get back to him. A lot of Tom's friends have told him that I'm not safe, that I'm workin' with the cops."

Snider suddenly changed the subject. She complained that

West Virginia authorities wouldn't allow her to have contact visits with Luther. "You have to be family, or married, or have a child with his name on the birth certificate as the father."

When Debrah mentioned that she was coming back to Colorado for Christmas, Richardson had an idea. Did she think she could get Babe to talk in private about whatever secrets she claimed to know but wouldn't discuss on the telephone? "What I'm talkin' about is, uh, wiring you so we can monitor or record the conversation. It'll show your credibility, that you aren't just fabricatin' all this stuff that Babe is sayin', and I guess that's what I'm trying to say."

Richardson was taking a chance. He was asking her to betray a friend, even if it was a friend like Babe. "I'm gonna be honest with you, you're probably my best shot."

Snider wasn't sure. In fact, she was frightened of the whole idea. What if Richardson used it against her with Tom?

"Geez," he said, "I mean, if you can't trust me. Hey, have I ever lied to you?"

She sighed. There was lying and there was lying, she said at last. "Tom has never asked me directly: are you talking with the cops? So I haven't lied to him either."

"Well, lie to him, if he asks you," Richardson said and laughed. Debrah laughed, too.

Richardson decided to take another chance. "If I got you a contact visit, would you wear a wire and record it?" He grimaced as he spoke. He was no longer asking her to tape Babe, he was asking her to betray the man she still professed to love.

Snider surprised him. "I guess," she said after a moment. "Sure. If he says something, it's his own fault."

In the months following his arrest, Luther had gone back and forth in his relationship with Debrah Snider. Sometimes, he was good Tom and sometimes he was bad Tom. He wrote that he missed her and then let someone named Pam use up all his visiting time.

Every letter, it seemed, there was a different Tom. There was old "one-track Tom," focused on sex, and the Tom who had discovered Jesus and wished she would.

Most of the time, though, Luther mostly worried about himself.

The guards, he wrote, were tampering with his food and spitting in his juice. He didn't see how he could take the abuse and handle the court pressure. He advised her to save herself and let him go.

He still blamed the justice system that had "screwed" him for raping Mary Brown. He blamed his mother. "For love and closeness, I used to let a man molest me. Now she tells people things to make herself look like a saint. She's so two-faced . . . she wants me to write but not send the letters from jail so the postman doesn't see." He blamed Debrah. It was always someone else's fault. Only rarely, did he take any of the blame for himself, calling himself stupid for getting into jails and assault incidents. He wanted to know if he hated himself that much that he could be such a "fuck-up and self-destructive?"

Luther said he was what he "detested in a human being." He was sure Jones would have been more than willing to go to bed with him. It wasn't sex; it was "assault and anger, pure meanness from a subconcious level" and it scared him. "I grew up being a victim, and now I'm an offender. I think I am insane. Sometimes I do things without even thinking about what I'm doing until I'm already doing it. It's in the middle of what I've done that I come to reality and realize I've just ruined my whole life."

Debrah felt like a swimmer caught in a tide, pulled this way and that, tiring as she tried to keep her head above water. Richardson had been wrong when he thought the break was complete. Some days, she loved Luther more than ever. Other days, she despised him—such as the day he accidently enclosed a love letter from Pam in some paperwork he sent to Debrah. She decided to go confront the other woman who, she discovered, was living with another man.

Pam just laughed at her. "Sure, I fucked him," she said and let Debrah read the letters she had received from Luther to prove it. "Now get out!"

"You're just a white trash whore," Debrah yelled back.

The man living with Pam produced a gun and stuck it in Snider's face. "Maybe I should just shoot you," he said as Pam laughed behind him. "And if your boyfriend ever gets out, I'll probably just shoot him, too."

Debrah stood there, looking down the barrel. She wasn't afraid and for a moment she considered doing something to provoke the man. What did it matter anymore? But she turned and walked out of the couple's cabin, their laughter ringing in her ears.

Debrah Snider hand-delivered her letter, telling Luther she knew the truth about Pam. He read it and shrugged his shoulders. He admitted having sex with Pam. Regretted it, of course, but then again, it was the girl's fault. She had seduced him.

"I would sooner sit in the electric chair than to admit that I did what I did and that bitch knew that," he said. "She did that to break us up."

That evening, she called Richardson's office and left a message. He called back a few minutes later from his home.

"I had the opportunity to get shot the other night, but I decided to pass it up," she said and told him about the incident with Pam and her boyfriend. "Tom says it's your fault he can't commit to me, that he has this thing in Colorado hanging over his head. I asked him, 'Why don't you give them what they want?' But he said, 'I can't do that.' "

"Why?" Richardson asked.

"Well, if his only involvement was the fact that he helped dispose of Cher's body, there would be some consequences to pay, but it wouldn't be murder," Snider said. "So, I'm beginning to think that the reason that he can't possibly give you what you want is 'cause it's murder."

Luther also said he was thinking of "making up a story" about what happened in Colorado to "get it over with," she said. "I don't know that he would do that, but I don't think he'd have to make up a story, I'm sure he's got a good one."

"What do you think would happen if he heard we found the body?" Richardson asked.

"I think he'd get pretty anxious," she responded. "There were a couple of times when I was working in Colorado, and they found the body of a girl that was on the news, and he would get anxious about that."

Debrah asked Richardson if he had been able to set up the contact visit. "I'm working on it," he said. "You know how important you are to my case, I'm sure."

They had to be careful, though. Luther's request for a contact visit had been turned down because Debrah wasn't his wife. Suddenly granting his request might look suspicious if they didn't come up with a plausible excuse.

In mid-December, the jail authorities came up with one. They notified Luther that since he had been living with Debrah Snider in Colorado, she was in a sense his common-law wife. And besides, since she worked for another state's prison system, it would be a professional courtesy.

On December 17, Debrah walked into the visiting room of the jail where Thomas Luther greeted her with a hug and a chaste kiss that he tried to prolong. But conscious of the microphone taped to her skin, she pulled away.

Luther's appearance had changed a lot in the past month. He had been on a hunger strike about some petty incident at the jail since early November and lost a lot of weight. His hair was grayer and his skin back to its former prison-pallor pale.

They settled at a table in the visiting room furthest away from the guard. Richardson had told Debrah to avoid talking about his current case and concentrate on trying to get him to say something about the Cher Elder case. But Luther's mind was on his latest problem.

He thought there was a good chance he would beat the rap. Bobby Jo Jones was on probation and not supposed to use drugs or leave the state. She had done both on that day, and there was no way she could testify against him without admitting that. "Skip talked to her," he said. "He thinks she won't testify."

However, if he was convicted, he said, the judge was likely to give him as stiff a sentence as possible. "Richardson's been on it pretty good. He's using the opportunity now that I'm in jail to stir the pot and entice everybody to give up on me."

According to Luther, Richardson was everywhere. He'd seen him in Chicago when he was visiting Skip. And near the construction site where he had worked in Pennsylvania. Now he was sure the detective had been talking to the judge in this case, "filling his head with lies."

Snider saw this as a good opportunity to get back to the Cher Elder case. "I can't understand why you don't just give Richardson what the hell he wants to know," she said taking one of his hands in both of hers. "If Byron was the person involved, he's already in jail for half his life."

Luther shook his head. "You don't understand. It ain't Byron that they want. It's me they want."

He was suspicious of Babe Rivinius. "I don't want you women even talking," he said. "You get together and you talk about stupid things, and you play cop."

"It doesn't matter," Snider pleaded. "Do you know that the very worst they could give you is second degree murder. That's fifteen years. You're facing fifteen years."

Luther looked at her with scorn. "What are you talking about the worst they could give me?"

"There's no way—there's no way they could say that it was premeditated murder."

"I didn't murder nobody."

"I know."

"Why should I be involved in any of this shit? I'm tellin' ya, you don't know how it works Deb," he said, looking over at the guard. "Okay, second degree murder, do you know what second degree murder carries in the state of Colorado?"

"They can't give you more than fifteen years."

"Shit," Luther snorted. "Forty-eight years. That's for second degree murder."

"How can they do that if we can give somebody life? That's almost life."

"Life is without the possibility of parole now," Luther said. "If you get convicted for first degree murder in the State of Colorado, you're gonna die in prison.

"Beside that, Deb, if I did know something, I wouldn't cooperate with Richardson after the fucking way he did me. Fucking confiscated my car, pulled you in, tried to convince you that I'm a serial killer, gotta kill every three months, you know what I mean.

"They had a fuckin' SWAT team put me down in the middle of the road and everybody with fuckin' guns and shit pressed against my head, just so they can take me in and serve a fucking warrant on me for blood samples and shit.

"Like I say, fuck me helping that bastard. He can kiss my fucking ass."

Luther wouldn't talk anymore about the Elder case so they spent the rest of their time on small talk. "I miss you," he said quietly when she got up to leave. They kissed and hugged again briefly. The microphone felt like a hot dagger against her skin. At least he hadn't said anything incriminating.

"I miss you, too, Tom," she said as the tears welled up in her eyes. "But you know, it was better when I could be angry about it. Now I just hurt and hurt and hurt. Sometimes loving you sucks, Tom." She turned and fled down the hallway.

Snider returned to Colorado in time for Christmas. She remembered the letter she wrote to Luther the year before, asking him to promise to spend it with her. He had broken that promise, too.

The next day, Richardson showed up at her ranch in Fort Collins. "Let's take a walk," he said. "Show me your property."

Debrah was surprised. The day was bitterly cold and windy, but the detective had no hat or gloves. It was only after they had walked a bit and she saw him scanning the ground that she realized he had an ulterior motive. *He's looking for a grave,* she thought.

"I don't mind working with you, Scott. But I—" she stammered and started over. "I can't explain my insanity, but you need to understand the little bit of relationship that I have left with him is all that I have."

"I hear ya," Richardson replied though his eyes kept looking at the ground around him.

"I've talked to two different priests about this and they've told me that as long as I'm not lying to you, I'm not committing a sin," she said. "But it feels really bad for me."

"Well, I'll stay outta religion," Richardson said, apparently giving up his search and turning back toward Snider's trailer, "but you can't help but know you're doing the right thing."

"I know, religion-wise," Debrah said. "But relationship-wise, I know I'm betraying him, and I do love him."

"You're wastin' your life on that man, Deb," he said.

They walked on in silence. The frosted grass crunched beneath their feet. Now it was Debrah's eyes that focused on the ground. "You may be right," she said at last as they reached his car. "But he's the only person who ever took time to make me happy."

Richardson nodded and patted her on the shoulder. There was

a part of Debrah he was never going to be able to separate from Luther. He was just going to have accept that and hope that when it came time to choose between the truth and love, she would opt for the truth.

A few days earlier, he had received a Christmas card from Rhonda Edwards. Enclosed was a photograph of a little girl sitting in a chair, laughing at the camera. "This is Cher when she was three. She was a good kid," Rhonda wrote. "All I want for Christmas is to find her."

That's all I want, too, Richardson thought, pinning the card and photograph to his office wall below the photograph of Cher at 20 years old. But, he wondered, what Christmas will it be?

"See you this evening?" he asked Debrah. That night was her meeting with Babe Rivinius, in which she had agreed to allow them to record the conversation.

"Yeah," Debrah said. "I'll be there."

A few hours later, they met again, this time at the Lakewood Police Department. Snider thought she could get Rivinius into her van to drink a couple of beers over pizza, which might loosen her tongue. So while police technicians wired her van, she had a chance to sit down with Richardson. She wanted to tell him about an incident she had recalled that might interest him.

Shortly after the press conference in July 1993, she said, Luther got a panicky call from Southy Healey. They drove to Longmont where they met up with Southy, who was in the company of a young woman and a hispanic man, at a McDonald's. They talked only five minutes or so, and Healey had not seemed real happy when he drove off.

Richardson made a note that he needed to find Healey as soon as possible. Then the technicians came in and said the van was ready.

That evening, Debrah and Babe went out to her van to talk as planned. A few blocks away, Richardson and Sgt. Mike Rose, a specialist in covert operations, sat in a parking lot, listening in.

After a few minutes of small talk, Rivinius started in on Luther. She said she had powerful friends who would see to it that he never walked out of prison if he threatened Byron or one of her other boys.

"I would sell my soul to Satan to protect my children, and that's the only thing I would do it for," she said. "If he walks out of prison at my child's expense, I'll kill him myself. I'll pull the trigger myself. All he has to do is keep his mouth off my children, just let life go as it is."

"But he doesn't do that," Debrah said. "He said it's Byron who better keep his mouth shut 'cause Byron can't do a life sentence. Tom has maintained through this whole thing that his involvement is secondary to, you know, whatever happened. That he didn't have anything to do with what happened to Cher."

Babe snorted derisively. "Nobody believes that, Deb." But it wouldn't matter, she added; she was sure Byron was going to win his appeal and get out of prison. As long as Tom didn't talk, everything would be fine. "If he does," she added, "he's gonna dig himself a grave."

Snider said that Luther considered Byron "a loose end."

"Byron ain't doing nothing to Tom."

"Well, I know that but Tom is scared. You know, you've seen his paranoia. I mean, he looked out the kitchen window at every goddamn car that drove down the road because he thought the cops were watchin' him."

Babe Rivinius said it was all Richardson's fault. Now he was trying to pressure Byron. "He showed up at Buena Vista out of the blue," she said. "He says 'If you don't cooperate, we're gonna bust J.D. We're gonna charge him with murder.' He knew that he was putting the needles in the right place."

It wasn't fair that Byron was in prison, Babe said. It was Luther who shot at Makarov-Junev to set her son up to take the fall on Cher Elder. "If the cops thought it was Byron with the violent tendencies, it would take the heat off himself. And for that, I cannot forgive him. If Tom ever shows up here again, he's gonna be six foot under pushing daisies."

The conversation turned back to the West Virginia assault case. Luther's trial was coming up in a few weeks. Neither woman could figure out why he had taken Jones to his cabin if he planned to rape her later.

"Unless he'd wanted to kill," Snider said.

"He never intended for her to live to tell the story," Rivinius agreed.

But then why, Debrah asked, if he intended to kill Cher, why did he take her to Central City where he knew he would be seen with her? "He's not stupid."

"The person that you know took her up there, isn't the person who came back with her," Babe replied. "Something happened in his head. Something goes wrong and it's a response to something she does. Something, something, something happens in his head that changes him.

"Now, he has never threatened me. I think, telling the truth, he's scared of me. He could not look me in the eyes. And I'm telling you right now the reason he couldn't look me in the eye is a killer can't look another killer in the eye. You see yourself in their eyes and that is what frightens you."

Back in the car, Richardson thought the women sounded as if they were getting drunk. Especially Rivinius, who was becoming just plain weird. He had suggested to Snider they have a couple of beers, but now as their conversation continued, their voices had grown slurred and there were large gaps of silence—one so long that he worried that they had passed out.

Then Babe snapped out of it and told Debrah, "If you need anything, tell me, and I'll help you."

"I want this bullshit with Cher Elder settled."

Richardson and Rose sat up. This might be it.

"There's only one way we're gonna be able to do that. We have two choices," Babe slurred. "Our first choice is that we get really stupid and we say now let's go dig Richardson and tell him all these little details."

"Babe, I already told you that I did that."

But Rivinius wasn't listening. "Let's put 'em all together and let's say they possibly charge Tom and they rake things through the mud and whatever. Maybe they get lucky and they get a conviction, but I'm sure they won't. What have we accomplished? Nothing. Now, it's never really gonna go away, because you got a cop with a hard-on and they don't go away."

Thinking of Richardson sitting in a car listening, Debrah laughed. Encouraged, Babe continued, "They're crooked. They're macho. They stick together like freakin' glue, and they cover for each other all the damn time. You just can't get rid of him. So what's the next best thing? You go away someday."

Babe said that when Byron won his appeal, she planned to get her boys out of the state, then they wouldn't care about "Richardson's bullshit. I don't mean this to sound crass and crude because obviously somebody's daughter is missing or dead, but I'm not responsible for somebody else's daughter.

"Richardson is scared of me. He says, 'Yes ma'am' and 'No ma'am' when he sees me. He's a bald-headed fucking bastard, and he makes me sick. I can't stand being in the same vicinity with him. God, he gives me the willies. I just wanna rip his heart out."

"Why?" Debrah liked Richardson and while Babe's descriptions were somewhat humorous, she thought it was Babe who was afraid of the detective, not the other way around.

"Because he didn't do his job. Detective Richardson did not follow procedures. Richardson followed a vendetta."

Snider was suddenly tired of it all. Of Babe. Of Tom. Of Richardson. "I just wanna know the truth," she said. "I want the truth to come out. If that means Tom needs to take a fall, then Tom needs to take a fall. If that means your sons need to take a fall, then they need to take a fall."

Babe looked at her bleary-eyed. She leaned closer. "I'm gonna tell you the truth," she said quietly, as if she knew someone else was trying to listen. "I asked Byron if he or his brother had anything to do with Cher Elder's disappearance, and I know he was telling me the truth when he said no.

"I asked him if Tom had anything to do with Cher Elder's disappearance, and he said, 'Mom, you've got to stop asking these questions.' He never said yes or no. If it's not Tom, Tom knows who did."

The conversation lasted five hours. Little of it was any use to the investigation. Richardson went home disappointed. The next morning, he called Debrah and asked if she would try again. Maybe this time with a little less beer and more direct questions. She agreed.

Three evenings later, he and Rose were sitting in a van in another parking lot, this time listening to the women who had gone to a pizza parlor.

Rivinius was bragging again that Richardson was scared of

her. "Byron's attorney is going to kick his ass in court," she said. "Leslie Hansen told him, 'Don't ever talk to my client again or I'll slap you with a lawsuit. I called District Attorney Dave Thomas and told him he better distance himself from that rogue cop Richardson and to leave Byron alone.'"

Debrah was her friend, Babe said. And that's why she wanted to warn her that her son, J.D., was saying she better keep her mouth shut "because all they're trying to do at this point in time is a find a way to get rid of you."

Debrah nodded. She knew everyone, except maybe Richardson, would be happier if she just went away or disappeared like Cher. "I know how you feel about Tom," she said to Babe, "but more than the way I feel about Tom is the way I feel about life. I have a greater understanding of what happened with Cher than I had whenever I first got involved in this. And what happened to Cher shouldn't happen to anybody, and I want it stopped. And I think anybody that's involved with it, including Tom, needs to pay the price."

"I agree," Babe said. "I think Tom would do anything he could to cover his own ass. I think he'd sell his mother to the devil."

"He wouldn't even ask much for her," Snider said. They both laughed.

Debrah was curious about the ring. She had overheard a conversation a long time ago between Tom and Mortho Kreiner about a ring. Kreiner wanted to know where he got it from and Tom had said he got it from a girl.

Richardson almost spilled his coffee on himself with Babe's next comment. "The fact of the matter is, I know exactly what Byron saw to the letter. And Tom knows, or suspects, that Byron could implicate him. They told Byron that they cut one of her fingers off that had a ring that he gave her and that they were gonna place it in a conspicuous spot to frame him if he talked."

Snider sighed. "I don't know why I've stayed with him so long."

"You love him," Babe shrugged. "The thing is, Deb, your problem is that you love the other one and there's two of 'em. You love Tom, the Tom that you wanna believe in, the Tom you fell in love with. But you don't know the other one. You've never been maybe beat half to death. The point is he has everybody fooled.''

"Yeah, they see the charming, do-all-I-can-for-you guy.''

"I hate Richardson but not because of what he's doin' with Tom,'' Rivinius said, "but because of what he's doing to my family. Because to me that makes Richardson as bad as Tom. Not because he's trying to help Cher's family but because he's helped destroy my whole damn family in the process.''

"I think you're placing blame in the wrong place,'' Snider said.

Babe looked at her closely, but she was already onto another subject. "Has Tom threatened you? He has, hasn't he? I can see it in your face.''

Debrah nodded. "I don't know. When it's all settled, I'm still hoping that Tom will see that I just did the right thing. I told him, 'Don't put me in a position where I gonna have to choose 'cause I'm gonna do what's right.' Now I need you to help me figure out where Cher Elder is.''

"I know where she was,'' Babe said, as the detectives in the van held their breath. "I don't know if I know where she is. Byron never saw, but if he knows it's because someone told him. And that means my kids are in danger if Tom ever gets out. Skip told me that Byron better keep his mouth shut and do his time; he cares more for Tom than he does his own sons.''

Suddenly, Babe Rivinius looked old and desperate. She gripped Snider's arm. "How can I protect them from Tom?''

"Well, we know of two ways,'' Debrah said. "The first one's not a possibility 'cause, you know, we can't do that and I don't want that to happen.''

"You mean off him?''

"Well, that's one way.''

"It is a possibility,'' Babe said.

Debrah shook her head. "It's not a possibility. That ain't what I mean.''

Babe nodded. "I don't want to do that. Who am I to be judge and jury for Tom Luther? I don't think anybody needs to get by with what the hell happened to Cher. But who am I to judge? If I thought for one minute that Byron was the kind of person who could just viciously kill another human being, I would be glad that he's where he is. But I know he isn't.''

"The second way is ..." Snider stumbled looking for the right words. "If we could get J.D. to tell us where the hell he took him."

Rivinius frowned. "There was something about a restaurant, about them going into the mountains and stopping by a freakin' restaurant."

Richardson took note. The Marietta Restaurant was where the dogs had lost Luther's tracks. Was that it? But Debrah and Babe had gone on to the topic of Luther's other possible victims.

"Have you ever wondered if there are any others?" Babe asked.

"Other women? Oh yeah. Just recently there was this girl at a campground where we stayed; now there's a picture of her in the post office that says she's missing. There were times, lots of times, when he would be AWOL from home, and I wondered. And, you know, he knew all the porno places—the X-rated motels and stuff like that. And he had these cards with pick-up lines like 'I'm shy,' that he would hand to women."

Rivinius was biting her lip now as she looked at Snider, as if trying to make up her mind about something. Then she blurted out, "I'm gonna tell you point blank. I have often thought that Tom either showed J.D. something or J.D. helped with something.

"I have wondered about it at times because of how emotionally upset he was for so long and none of it made that much sense to me. Every time I would bring it up, he would get extremely angry at me and tell me not to ask questions. And when I would say anything really to him like, you know, 'If you know that Tom did something, you need to tell me.' And his answer to shit like that would be, 'Mom, you could be putting a lot of people's lives in danger.' And I often wondered if Tom didn't deliberately put J.D. in that kind of a situation on purpose.

"We don't know where it happened is the thing. All I know is that when Byron got up, he heard people out in his living room arguing. And he knows Tom was there—that he came back to the apartment. And the other unknown female was there and he thought it might have been one of Southy's sisters."

The women were quiet again. Then Debrah Snider spoke about something that had been troubling her for some time. "After he attacked that girl in Summit County, he went back to his girlfriend and they made love,'' she said. "How could you sexually assault somebody, beat them half to death, and then go crawl in bed with your girlfriend. But he did that again in West Virginia. He assaulted that girl and came to the campground that next day and got in bed with me.''

Babe shrugged. That's just how men used women. "Maybe that's what turns him on. He seems to think that no matter how violent or vicious his sex gets, it's perfectly normal.''

"Well, he thinks of women like that. He used to make me read porno magazines to 'broaden my perspective.' I can remember when we would go shopping, I would watch him watch women like he was taking their clothes off. We could hardly watch a movie together because he was always talking about how good it would be to take some actress, like Michelle Pfeiffer, to bed.

"I wanted to tell him one time, 'What do you think Michelle Pfeiffer would think if I was to tell Michelle Pfeiffer your history. You think she'd want to go to bed with you?' But I didn't have the courage to do that. I knew it would be suicide.''

The two women didn't say anything for a long time. Then Debrah spoke. "The thing that kills me is, I think it's unfair to make Cher's family suffer like this.''

Babe nodded. "I've often wanted to go over and talk to them myself,'' she said. "I wanted to tell them what Byron saw, what he knows, so that they can at least be in peace understanding that the friend that their daughter was with didn't hurt her.''

Chapter Twenty-Two

January 4, 1995—Jefferson County District Attorney's Office

For all of Babe Rivinius's bravado, Byron Eerebout's attorney, Leslie Hansen, wasn't talking about kicking anyone's ass in court. In fact, she was pleading with Dennis Hall, Mark Minor, and Scott Richardson to make a deal.

"Byron's willing, but he wants community corrections and he wants to serve it out of state," Hansen said.

"What do we get?" Hall asked.

"Byron knows the location of Cher's body," Hansen answered. "It's not firsthand knowledge but from another source who he will not disclose or testify against."

"You mean he doesn't want to testify against J.D.," Richardson said sarcastically.

Hansen nodded but she wasn't going to say it with the tape recorder running. Byron, she said, could identify the killer. "You already know who it is. And Byron can put the two of them, Cher and the killer, together. How they met, where they went, and what happened."

Eerebout could also provide the original disposal site of Elder's body, where she had been relocated to, and the identity of someone else who was involved in the homicide. "He can tell you what she was wearing, what happened to her clothes, and might even be able to find some of it," Hansen said. "The body had been disfigured in some fashion, and Luther has something from the body he's using to keep Byron quiet."

"Specifics," Richardson said. "I want more specifics."

"Byron can tell you how she was killed. What she died from," Hansen responded. "And give you a possible motive. Luther told him that he killed her."

"When will he do all this?" Richardson asked. He was close. He almost had Cher, yet he didn't feel he could let up even for a moment.

"He doesn't have the exact location of the grave yet, but he will provide it," Hansen said.

The two prosecutors and the detective looked at each other and nodded. "You get your deal," Hall said, "provided Byron had no direct involvement in the murder of Cher Elder. If he did, all bets are off. We will not be limited in what we can question him about, nor will he be able to dictate what he will testify about. And finally, he will put in all in writing."

Hansen agreed and the meeting adjourned. Richardson left muttering to himself. He didn't trust Eerebout or his mother. *I got to find Healey,* he thought, *I got to find him now.*

* * *

Scott Richardson poured all of his efforts into locating Luther's old friend. They had to have been tight. Hell, Luther had gotten Southy Healey out of prison by posing as his uncle. They were hanging together around the time of the murder, and then there was that panicked meeting following the July 1993 press conference that Debrah Snider had mentioned. If Luther had talked about the killing to anyone, it would have been Southy, and Byron was hinting that Southy was involved.

The detective called every law enforcement agency in the area, asking them to notify him if Healey was located. He was contacted by Lee Hughes, a bounty hunter who said he was also looking for Healey, who had failed to appear in court to answer burglary charges. "The last time I talked to him, on the telephone," Hughes said, "he wasn't worried about what he called any 'bogus burglary charges.' But there was some other investigation that he said, 'I don't want them to hit me with.' "

Hughes noted that Healey had come forward after his arrest for the burglary a year earlier, wanting to trade information about a homicide. But they hadn't been aware of his involvement in the Cher Elder case, and no one had believed him.

A few days later, Richardson located Healey's three sisters, one of whom said she had met Luther once but had no other information to offer. Another said she knew Mortho, Byron Eerebout, and Luther, and that she had heard of the Cher Elder case, but that was about as much information as she had.

Myra Healey, however, not only knew all the players involved, she recalled a meeting with Luther in Longmont that had particularly upset her brother. If was after the Elder case was on the television, she said. She and her boyfriend at the time, Bob Ramierez, had accompanied Healey to the meeting. When they left Longmont, Myra said, her brother was really angry with Luther.

It was music to Richardson's ears, a rift between friends. In the end, it wasn't hard to find Healey. On January 9, Richardson was called by the Adams County Sheriff's Department north of Denver. They had just arrested Dennis "Southy" Healey for brandishing a gun at a couple he claimed owed him money for drugs.

Now that he knew where Healey was, Richardson took his time going to see him. He knew that Southy was a junkie. He wanted him to be feeling the effects of withdrawal and hurting. So he waited until 4 A.M. to call the jail and asked that Healey be awakened and taken to an interview room.

Boy, am I gettin' tired of jails, Richardson thought when he arrived. Nothing but a bunch of dopers, convicts, or liars. But he was well aware of the old saying: few murders are committed in heaven with angels for witnesses. He'd take what he could get.

Healey was in the interview room when he walked in. As Richardson suspected, the young man looked badly in need of a fix. He sat hunched over in a chair and kept rubbing the back of his neck beneath his long, scraggly red hair, as if there was a pain there that wouldn't go away. His arms were covered with prison tattoos and needle tracks. His blue eyes were dull and suffering.

Richardson introduced himself and pulled a chair over next to Healey. "You have any idea why I'm here?" he asked, sitting down.

"No," Southy mumbled, his head down so that Richardson could not see his face.

"None? Well, we need to talk bad," Richardson said, leaning closer to the nervous junkie. "I'm talkin' bad. And it has nothin' to do with what you're in jail for now. Okay?"

Healey looked quickly at him out of the corner of his eye before looking away again. "Yeah."

Richardson read Healey his Miranda rights, which he waived. "We need to talk about some old stuff here, bud," Richardson began. "And we need to spend some time because the way this stuff's goin', this may be your one shot. I'm here on Thomas Luther, Byron Eerebout, and Cher Elder."

Southy's head sank lower at the mention of each name. Richardson continued, "It's two years since it happened. There's a lot of things that have changed in two years. I have waited this long to even contact you 'cause I wanted all the ducks in a row. You know where Luther is now?"

"I think he's in West Virginia," Healey said. He had a thick Boston accent.

"Yeah," Richardson nodded. "Luther's got big problems,

big problems. He grabbed a girl, took her out, raped her, and he's charged with a bunch of crimes. He's lookin' at some hard time.''

Healey nodded. He said that he had seen Byron in the Jefferson County Jail, who told him that Luther had been charged with rape and assault.

Richardson turned his head to the side to try to catch Southy's eyes. ''You're the next to the last person before everything comes to a head on this case,'' he said quietly. ''Luther knows it. Everybody knows it. In the last two years, I have done nothin' but work this case. This case is ten four-inch binders of nothin' but evidence accumulated for two years—every day, every single day. And I've been watching you—we got videotapes, taped conversations, everything.''

The detective paused to let that sink in. He could tell what Healey was thinking: Holy shit! They've been following me for two years! Which is exactly what he wanted him to believe, even if it wasn't true.

''We've been to West Virginia, Missouri, Canon City. You understand that?''

Healey nodded.

''Now it's over for everybody. People are deciding they don't want no part of it 'cause we're talkin' first degree murder. And it's one thing to be partially involved, and it's another thing to be hands on, so to speak.''

Healey slumped even farther into his chair. He looked at the floor and away from Richardson, which angered the detective. ''Do me a favor,'' he demanded. ''Sit up so we can look at each other while we talk. I want you to concentrate on me for a minute and not the floor. I'm not used to talkin' to men like that.''

Like a puppet on a string, Southy Healey jerked himself upright and looked at Richardson. Fear was in his eyes, as well as the pain of his addiction. But he was listening.

Richardson nodded and continued, ''What's happening is people are pointin' fingers and they don't wanna point fingers at themselves, period. And I'm not lying to you. Now you've got to talk to me, and we've got to be straight with each other tonight. This is your shot, period.

''I've seen your history. You've been in trouble more than you've been out of trouble. But I don't care about none of that.

I don't care about burglaries or dope or thefts. I care about one thing—I care about Cher Elder.

"You got to come clean or everybody's going down. We're talkin' first degree murder and were talkin' death penalty. I don't think you're the kind of guy that wants to go down for a first degree murder."

"What do you know about what happened?" Healey asked cautiously.

Richardson shook his head. "I'm not gonna tell you my theory. Because what I need from you is your side of what happened. And if I tell you my theory, then it's gonna alter your theory." Actually, theory was all Richardson had; if it was wrong, Southy would know and see through his bluff.

"I'll tell ya this," Richardson volunteered. "I know she was killed that night, without a doubt. Everybody knows it. And my theory is, you got sucked in like a couple other people got sucked into this. And I'll tell ya why I'm here—you're important to me. I'm not gonna deny you're important to me. But people who don't cooperate go down, period."

Healey shrugged. "Well, see I know for a fact there is nothin' you can get me for. I met Byron and J.D. maybe a couple of times at the most. They're not my people. I don't work for them, they don't work for me."

"You ever meet Cher Elder?"

Healey shook his head. "No, I don't think so."

"Were you ever over at Byron's apartment with your sister?"

"No."

"You ever take a girlfriend over there? Now think, early in the morning."

Healey shook his head more emphatically. "No."

Richardson cut to the chase. "What can you provide me, Dennis?"

A crafty look came into Healey's eyes. "I don't know. What can you provide me?"

"I can't make promises," Richardson said. "But I'm tellin' ya, you're gonna find that your information, as long as you stay honest with me, that your information on Elder is gonna be a lot more important to you than you realize. What have you been told, that's what I need to know."

Finally there was something from Healey. "Luther said she was gonna testify."

"Cher?"

"Yeah."

"But who would be scared of her?"

"I don't know," Healey said and shrugged. "Maybe Mortho. I heard that from someone else."

"Who?"

"Maybe Byron. J.D."

"Before or after she was killed?"

"I don't know that she was killed."

Richardson rolled his eyes and sat back. "I'm not gonna tell you who, but somebody is puttin' you with dumpin' Cher's car in a grocery store parking lot." It was a stretch. No one had told him that. But whether it was true or not, it might shake Healey. *Get his lips movin'*, he thought. "See, you got a lot more to gain here than you got to lose."

"It wasn't me."

"Why should I believe you?" Richardson asked leaning close again. "I ask you questions I know you have the answers to and you sit there."

"I ain't done nothin' I need to be fuckin' worried about."

"Then why are people sayin' you were in the apartment the next morning if you have nothin' to worry about?"

"They're tryin' to fuckin' protect themselves is why they're sayin' it." Healey was gettin' angry. Not defensive, just angry, which Richardson took as a sign that he really might not have anything to worry about. *Maybe this guy even has a conscience,* he thought, and that gave him an idea.

"Let me tell you this first of all, Cher Elder wasn't no snitch for anybody," Richardson said. "She was a twenty-year-old girl that got caught up in the wrong crowd. Do you have any kids?"

"Nope."

"Can you imagine what it would be like? What if something like this happened to one of your sisters?"

Healey looked like someone had just struck him in the face with a board. His brow furrowed and his hands clenched.

So the sisters are the key, Richardson thought. *He's just a big softy when it comes to family.* He decided to turn the screw a little more. "Cher's entire family is fucked up and that's bein' polite. Her dad walks like a beat child. Her little sister and brother are only about fifteen or sixteen, and they're in counseling weekly. They can't bury Cher.

"I got a picture of Cher that her mother sent me. It's from when Cher was three years old. And let me tell you, 'cause I'll never forget it, it's a picture of a little girl sittin' on a chair with a smile. Her mother wrote: 'This is Cher when she was three. She was a good kid.' "

Richardson paused. What he'd just said had hit closer to his own heart than he intended. He thought of his boys, including the infant Brian he'd hardly seen. He missed them and he missed Sabrina. Here it was five in the morning and he probably wouldn't see any of them that day, at least not when they were awake. He didn't know why he was talking about this stuff to a junkie, but he found he could not stop.

"Cherish yours while you can 'cause you never know when you'll lose 'em." He looked at Southy, who had tears in his eyes. "All I want for Christmas is for you to find her body," he said, echoing the words of Rhonda Edwards.

"Cher did not deserve to get killed. Cher Elder is one of the first victims I ever found that the deeper I dug, the cleaner she was. You know, usually a victim on a homicide starts out to be the choir girl and you find out she's runnin' dope, prostitutin', and a hundred other things. But Cher Elder was nothin' but a twenty-year-old girl gonna start college. Got hooked up with Byron Eerebout and hooked up with that group. She didn't fit, she didn't belong, and she wasn't a snitch, and there was no reason for her to be killed. None. Zero."

Richardson said he couldn't understand why the Eerebout brothers seemed to care so little about what happened to Cher. "But Luther is in a category by himself, bud. And I'll tell ya the difference between Luther and everybody else.

"He gets convicted and he ain't out two months and he does another girl. Then he leaves Colorado and does another one. Luther don't need for her to be a snitch. You know what I'm saying? He has a thing for women, and he's proven it a couple times. And that's the difference. But people are puttin' you three—Byron, Luther, and you—in the same book. You don't belong in the same book as Luther."

Richardson decided he would feed Healey a little about his

theory and see how he reacted. "Luther's the one that did Cher and buried her. Actually dumped her and went back and buried her. How's that theory sound? You're shakin' your head 'yes.' "

"I've heard that," he conceded.

"Have you ever been told the area she's buried in? What if I was to say west, would that help you remember?"

"In the mountains."

"Where?" Richardson demanded. "There's a misconception that you have to have a body to prosecute and you don't. We also have enough on this case that if we don't find the body within a couple of days, we're gonna take it to court without a body, period. But I'd like to give the Elders their daughter's body."

"I'll give you Cher."

Richardson blinked. "Don't promise what you can't deliver," he warned.

"I can take you closer than you've ever been."

"How close?"

"Say within a few hundred feet."

"Do you know how she was killed?"

"Know how?" Healey asked. "I think it was a gun."

Now that was something new. A gun? Luther liked to beat and strangle women. Then again, there were the two homicides in Summit County, both with a gun. "You just guessin' here?"

"No."

The way Healey said it, Richardson knew it was true. "What kind of gun?" The more details he could get here, the more he could rule out that Healey was "just guessing" once they found Cher's body.

"I think a .22."

Now that he had gone part way, Healey seemed willing to get it all out. "I once heard Byron tell another woman to watch out or he would 'Put Tom on you like I did that bitch.' And I heard Luther tell Mortho that he had 'taken care of business.' "

But Southy Healey had saved the best for last. He said he had been in a car with Byron and Luther "just outside a very small town in the mountains" when Eerebout had asked about Cher's grave. Luther had said it was a shallow grave and pointed at a hillside they were driving past.

"Byron said, 'Fucking right on, Tom. Fucking crazy, Tom.' "

Richardson asked if he would testify to what he knew. "I'm dead if I do and go back to prison. Tom's got some pretty serious connections inside. And Byron told me not to talk because his dad would have me taken out. But I'll think about it."

The conversation ended three hours after it began. Richardson got up to leave.

"Can I ask you a question?" Healey said.

"Sure."

"What is your opinion as to Luther's status in this case?"

"He's in trouble, big trouble."

"Byron?"

"He's in trouble."

"J.D.?"

"He's in trouble."

Healey hesitated, although they both knew what he was about to ask. "And me?"

"In the same trouble if you don't continue to cooperate."

Three days later, Scott Richardson was called by Healey's girlfriend. "He really wants to talk to you," she said. This time, he wasted no time getting over to the Adams County Jail.

Healey wanted to know if he had talked to the district attorney about getting the charges against him dropped in exchange for his information. "Not yet," Richardson said, hoping that wasn't the extent of what Southy wanted to talk about.

But the young man shrugged, as if it wasn't important any more. "I was goin' to try to use this to my advantage," he said, "but I want to help you find the body."

Healey said he had been doing some thinking, "especially what you said about the family wanting Cher's body for burial and the Christmas card from her mother. I don't care about the deal no more. I don't care if my information gets me outta anything."

Richardson could hardly believe what he was hearing. Out of all these people he'd been dealing with over the past two years, only a junkie and petty thief felt any remorse for what happened to Cher. At least enough to do something about it.

Healey said he'd been at Mortho's, who he described as a "fat drug dealer," before he ever met Eerebout, when Mortho and Luther were talking about some girl they suspected of being a police informant. That's when he first heard Luther talking about "takin' care of business." They hadn't used the girl's name and only later did he think it must have been Cher Elder they were talking about.

The trip into the mountains had been for a drug deal. But he couldn't remember the name of the little town. Only that Luther had pulled over near a restaurant. "A little town and the river goes by and on the side where the river is, is this little restaurant."

Richardson did his best to hide his excitement. Healey had just described the town of Empire, Clear Creek, and the Marietta Restaurant. "Let me ask you this, Dennis. If I came out here, picked you up, and drive you out, would you know this place?"

"Absolutely," he said. But then he was troubled by a thought. "If you took me up there, man, how would I know I'm not gonna be in any trouble?"

"How are you gonna get in trouble?"

"I don't know, showing you where the body's buried."

"Here's the deal," Richardson said. "As long as you didn't kill her, as long as you didn't bury her, as long as you didn't dump her car, I don't see how you're gonna get in trouble in this." It was a test. If Healey was guilty of any of those things, he would shut down then and there.

But he only nodded. "Well, like I said, I don't give a fuck even if it does come back on me. I want to help that family."

Richardson smiled. "I'll show ya the Christmas card when we go up there." Then he got back to questions about the trip to the little mountain town. "You sure Byron was talking about Cher?"

"Yeah," Healey answered. "And Tom said, 'Business has been taken care of.' Then Byron asked how deep he had buried her. And Tom said shallow because the ground was frozen and he didn't have much time. But he had shoved a bunch of rocks on top of the grave."

Richardson said he'd be back the next day to take him out of jail. The young man said that was okay, but he was worried what the other jail inhabitants would think if he came and went too often.

The detective had an idea. "Go back to your cell real angry and complain that you have to go back to court tomorrow," he said. "And when we come out, we'll make it look like we're transporting you to court. You're gonna have to wear shackles anyway and that'll look good."

Healey smiled. "That's cool, man," he said. "Do me one favor, man. Can you bring me a smoke?"

"Yeah," Richardson said. "I'll bring you smokes."

Scott Richardson and his partner, Stan Connally, arrived the next morning to pick up Southy Healey. "Here's your smokes," Richardson said after they had placed Healey in the right rear seat of the sedan, which he had indicated was where he was sitting on the ride with Luther and Byron Eerebout.

As anxious as the detectives were to get to the mountains, they first asked Healey to show them the apartment building where Mortho lived. Southy, who said he was high most of the time and couldn't remember numbers or street names, still took them by a building. "You go up the elevator to the fifth floor and turn right," he said.

From there, Richardson began driving in seemingly random directions although gradually working his way west. He knew Healey had been talking about Empire, but he needed him to take them there on his own if it was to stand up in court.

Innocently, he took the ramp that placed them westbound on Interstate 70. Suddenly, Healey sat up, "I think this is the right way to get there. There should be a river that comes up on the left-hand side and this road narrows."

A few miles further into the mountains, he was even more certain. "This is it," he said, looking out the window, then added, "If I see it, he's screwed."

Richardson decided to test Healey. "We think we're going to find physical evidence at the grave," he said. If he was involved with killing or transporting Cher, he had just been warned that there might be something on the body to incriminate him.

But Healey just shrugged. "I don't give a fuck," he said. "There's nothin' around her grave that's gonna connect me."

As they approached the intersection with Highway 40 that led to Empire, Healey perked up again. "Isn't there a town on the right side up here?"

Richardson didn't say anything. But when they arrived at the exit ramp, Healey told him to take it. "Man, I don't wanna see this girl," he muttered.

"Don't worry, bud," Richardson replied. "If we find her, you won't be around."

They had passed through Empire when Southy Healey spotted the Marietta Restaurant on the left-hand side of the road. He immediately began talking louder. "This is it right here. This is it. Slow down, slow down. It's right here on the right, slow down." He pointed to a horseshoe-shaped turn-off on the right side of the highway. "That's right where it is. That's where Luther showed us."

The turn-off was a fifty-foot loop on and off the highway. A man-made rock formation with a wooden pole stuck in the center stood inside the loop. Southy looked at the formation quizzically. "There used to be something hanging on it," he said, puzzled. He looked up the hillside and shook his head, "But this is where Luther was pointing when he said he had taken care of business."

Richardson got out of the car. The hillside was steep, which went against all the conventions about killers taking the bodies of their victims downhill. *No wonder we missed her,* he thought, *we were concentrating on the downhill side of the road.* He walked about fifty yards up the hill when he discovered an old, partially collapsed mine shaft. Below he could see Healey standing outside the car smoking while Connally stood guard. He walked back to the car and got on the radio to request bloodhounds.

"If he brings that dog up here right now, he'll find it," Southy said.

The bloodhounds arrived within the hour and immediately "hit" on decomposing human remains at the edge of the turn-off and again at the mine shaft entrance. Richardson crawled partway into the mine opening with a flashlight. The shaft pitched away from the entrance at a thirty-degree angle and ended in a thick, oily pool of water, next to which he could see a broken spade and a stick that appeared to have been used for digging. Recalling Debrah Snider's story about Luther having broken one of her shovels, Richardson thought, *This is it. This is where he put her.*

The mine shaft was unstable and he retreated. They would

have to call in the Gilpin County Mine Rescue team to shore it
up and pump out the water before it would be safe to proceed.
In the meantime, he decided to take Healey back to jail. It would
give him a chance to ask a few more questions.

"How do I know you weren't involved in killing her?" Richardson asked on the return trip.

Southy scowled. "I may be a doper and a petty thief, but I'm
no killer."

Richardson ignored Southy's anger. "How did Mortho get
his nickname?"

"It was in prison," Healey said. "Everytime he bought drugs
and someone asked if it was any good, he would say, 'Fine, I
need more though.' " It was such a consistent response that
everyone started calling him "More though," which became
Mortho. On the outside, Mortho dealt in a variety of drugs—
mostly cocaine, pot, and speed. He sold quite a bit to Luther,
who in turn distributed it to the Eerebouts.

Healey said he hardly knew Byron or the other brothers. "They
were introduced as the sons of a friend from the joint."

For awhile, both men were silent, looking out the window,
lost in their own thoughts. Then Healey spoke. "You know, I
was originally hoping I could get a deal for helping you out.
Now I don't want nothin.' I'm having a hard time dealing with
the fact that I didn't come forward sooner. I just want her family
to be able to bury her, I don't care what happens to me."

Richardson looked in the rearview mirror at his prisoner. He
was beginning to like Southy. He took the young man into the
Adams County Jail and handed him another pack of cigarettes
before turning him over to a guard.

As Richardson started to leave, Healey suddenly reached out
and grabbed his arm. "Tell Cher's family," he said, "that I'm
sorry I didn't say something sooner."

On the way back to Empire, Scott Richardson picked up Steve
Ireland, an archeologist with NecroSearch International.

Started in 1987 in Denver, by a group of law enforcement
investigators and scientists who were horrified with conventional
grave location methods, like backhoes and bulldozers, Necro-

Search had since established an international reputation for finding and exhuming clandestine graves.

Its members were made up of experts in a wide variety of scientific and law enforcement fields—including entomologists, geologists, biologists, anthropologists, and archeologists. They worked only for police agencies. Sometimes affectionately called "the pig people," they were known for their experiments in burying pigs to study decomposition and other variables that affect gravesites. Pig carcasses most closely resemble the human body as it decomposes.

They buried pigs with clothes on and "naked." They wrapped them in shower curtains and carpets. Then they studied the graves using ground-penetrating radar and FLIR; they looked at how plants grew at a gravesite, the presence of certain bugs, and researched how far scavengers like coyotes and birds would drag bones.

When the graves of humans were discovered, the NecroSearch teams would carefully exhume the bodies like archeologists working on ancient tombs so as not to disturb evidence. Richardson was sure their expertise would soon be needed to recover Cher's body.

Richardson and Ireland had worked together before. As always, Ireland said when climbing into the detective's car, "Another Richardson pleasure cruise?" He then pulled his cap down over his eyes and napped.

After looking at the mine entrance, the Gilpin County Mine Rescue team, Ireland, and Richardson agreed it would be better to meet again early the next day. The water would have to be pumped from the shaft and the hole reinforced.

The next morning, Richardson arrived on the scene with Ireland, who had summoned other NecroSearch members, sure that this would be the day he found Cher. However, while the others worked, there was not much for him to do. So he decided to take a walk around the area.

Following a light trail through the woods and snow, he came into a bowl-shaped clearing among the tall pines. On one side was a shelf of gray granite that hid the clearing from the highway seventy-five yards below. The wind whispered through the trees and he could plainly hear Clear Creek tumbling down the valley floor on the other side of the road.

It was a peaceful spot, almost like a chapel beneath the boughs of the trees. But what caught his attention was a pile of large rocks, perhaps two feet tall and the length of a body.

"It's a grave," he said to himself. Quickly he returned to the mine shaft and summoned the NecroSearch team members, who waited for the rescue team to finish pumping water from the shaft. They returned to the clearing and removed the rocks from the pile.

A cadaver dog, a bloodhound specially trained to detect dead bodies below the surface and even underwater, was brought to the site. But the dog detected nothing. Using a hand auger, Ireland drilled a hole the diameter of a tennis ball into the hard, cold ground. He sank the auger nineteen inches and still there was no sign of human remains.

Ireland shook his head. "The ground is really compacted," he said looking at the core removed by the auger. "It doesn't appear to have been disturbed."

The excitement Richardson had been feeling turned again to disappointment. The crew wandered back to the mine shaft. As he turned to follow them, the detective cast one more look back at the clearing. Something in him didn't want to leave. He remembered Southy Healey saying that Luther had covered the grave with rocks. But reluctantly, his boots dragging in the snow, he returned to the mine.

The mine shaft yielded nothing other than the broken spade and the fact that a mountain lion had been using it as a den. The rescue team and NecroSearch members quietly picked up their equipment and left. Richardson took the trail back to the clearing and stood for a moment looking at the cleared space on which the rocks had rested. Then he walked down around the rock shelf, got in his car and left with the pile of rocks etched in his mind.

Richardson drove to the Adams County Jail and had Healey pulled out of his cell. Angrily, he accused him of leading him on a goose chase. But Southy got right back in his face. "That was the place Luther pointed," he said. The detective left feeling that he was only getting half-truths from the young convict.

However, Healey's information about Mortho turned out to

be accurate. The apartment Healey indicated was rented to a Richard Brazell, who fit the physical description of Mortho and had an extensive criminal history dating back to a 1963 arrest for drug charges. Richardson made a note to visit the fat drug dealer soon.

On January 19, he returned a telephone call from Debrah Snider. While he was in the mountains, she had left a message saying she was frightened. "Tom's been telling his friends that I'm turning state's evidence," she said when he reached her. "I was wondering if I could be escorted to the trial to testify. I think someone might want to try and kill me."

Richardson said he would contact Trooper Phillips and make the arrangements. "What sort of threats are you getting?"

"Skip called me last week," she said. "He wanted me to go see an attorney and recant my story. Then he called Monday night. He's real icy towards me. Tom has also called his family and said that I had told the police that he was thinking of killing that girl."

Babe Rivinius was also making a lot of threats. However, these were directed at Richardson, who she said she would make "shut up."

Meanwhile, Snider said, things looked bad enough in West Virginia for Luther that he was talking about taking his chances in Colorado. "He told Skip to tell Byron to go ahead and tell the police everything about the Colorado case. He said, 'Maybe they'd drop the charges here.'

"He also told me that I've got an 'ass-kicking' coming when he gets out of jail."

Luther had smiled when he told Debrah she had an ass-kicking coming. Like it was a joke. But his blue eyes were cold and left her with a chill that wouldn't go away.

Snider had moved into a cabin in the woods where she could set up pens for her wolves and other animals, such as fallow deer and emus. But she was beginning to regret being so far from other homes. There were noises at night around the cabin, and several times she swore she heard footsteps on her front porch and wondered if Skip or some other of Tom's friends had come for her.

Luther's trial started after a delay in which the police had to find Bobby Jo Jones and bring her to court to testify. Reluctantly, she recounted what happened to her, glancing up with fear at Luther, who sat muttering under his breath and shaking his head.

Snider was scheduled to appear on the last day of the prosecution case. The night before, she received two telephone calls. One was from Tom's lawyer. He hinted that maybe she ought to just "go away for awhile," at least until the trial was over. The second was from Skip. There was no mistaking the menace in his voice when he said, "I think you should recant."

All that night, the wind howled. Branches creaked and things slammed about outside the cabin. Snider couldn't sleep. She had often considered suicide in her darkest moments, but now that death might come at the hands of violent men, she was afraid.

The morning came at last. Angry that she had been made to feel so fearful of someone she loved, Debrah dug through her papers until she found what she wanted and then went to a copying store. Arriving at the courthouse, she walked up to Luther's lawyer and handed him a sheet of paper.

"Here's Tom's resumé," she said. On the sheet were copies of three newspaper clippings. The first was dated September 8, 1983, the day following Luther's sentencing for the rape and beating of Mary Brown, also noting that he was still charged with solicitation of first degree murder. The second clipping was dated July 13, 1993, following Richardson's press conference in which Luther's photo ran directly beneath that of Cher Elder. The third was dated September 3, 1994, the article announcing his arrest for raping and beating Bobby Jo Jones.

The lawyer read the clippings and looked up, confused. "I'm leaving and won't testify," Snider said. "But if he is set free and rapes or kills someone else, understand that you share my guilt in allowing that to happen."

Debrah then turned and walked away without waiting for his reply. But she didn't leave fast enough. She hesitated in the courthouse parking lot, hoping for a glimpse of Luther when he was brought from the county jail. She wanted him to know that what she was doing she was doing for love.

However, it was Trooper Phillips who saw her first. "What are you doing?" he asked. "Shouldn't you be inside?"

Snider didn't answer and just looked at the ground.

"You know you have to testify, Deb," Phillips said softly. "Not just because you're under subpoena, but because it's the right thing to do. All you have to do is tell the truth."

When she looked up, her eyes were filled with tears. She wanted to say to him that telling the truth, especially knowing it would hurt the man she loved, wasn't as easy as he made it sound. But instead she nodded and wiped away the tears. "I know," she said. "I know."

With Trooper Phillips at her side, Debrah Snider walked back into the courthouse. That afternoon, with Tom Luther staring straight down at the defense table in front of him, Debrah testified that he had admitted attacking Bobby Jo Jones. "He said he had done it again."

When she finished and was excused, she glanced at Tom. He was looking at her and smiled. She smiled back but he turned his head. Nearly blinded by her tears, she walked quickly out of the courtroom.

In the hallway, she began to cry. Trooper Phillips came up and placed a hand on her shoulder. "Can I give you a lift home?" he asked.

Snider shook her head. "No, no thanks. I'll be okay."

The defense presented little evidence before closing. Then it took the jury less than two hours to come back with their verdict. They were unanimous: Luther was guilty of sexual assault and assault.

Luther asked to be sentenced immediately, and the judge obliged. He would serve fifteen years minimum with a thirty-five-year maximum.

Phillips drove Luther back to jail. The trooper looked into the rearview mirror and saw his prisoner staring at him with his cold blue eyes.

Luther's lip curled and his voice came out in a snarl, "You tell Richardson one thing, I'm the only one who can burst that bubble in Colorado."

Chapter
Twenty-Three

January 26, 1995—Lakewood, Colorado

Debrah Snider called Scott Richardson the day after Thomas Luther's conviction. She said she went to see him at the jail immediately following the trial and he wasn't angry with her. "He said it was the tape of him talkin' to Bobby Jo that did it," she said. "He was more resigned than anything. Said you'd be comin' for him now."

If Luther was angry with anyone, it was with Babe Rivinius. "He said something to the effect that if he could talk to her without the conversation being recorded, he would tell her exactly what Byron's involvement was in this. And that though Byron didn't kill Cher, that something he did caused these other two people to kill her."

Luther had also found God, Snider said. At first, she hoped that religion might influence him to do the right thing and reveal where he buried Cher. "But right now, all he wants is to tell lies and more lies."

Ain't that the truth, Richardson thought. But he didn't believe that any mystery men killed Cher because of something Byron Eerebout did. He still wasn't sure of the extent of the Eerebout brothers' involvement, but Luther was the killer. He was sure of that.

"Oh, by the way," Snider said, "watch out for a new Tom Luther story. He says he's going to ask Skip to have J.D. tell you that Cher's body was dumped in a Fort Collins landfill so you'll waste your time lookin' there."

"Thanks, Deb," Richardson said and hung up. There wasn't anything he could do about Luther's lies. And he had a date with a fat drug dealer he meant to keep.

Richardson arrived at Mortho's apartment to find that the drug dealer's obesity had not been exaggerated. Mortho wheezed from the exertion of answering the door, his large round face beet red and beaded with sweat. The old, long-haired biker walked only with the use of crutches, the armrests of which disappeared into the folds of his armpits; his tree-trunk-sized legs were almost useless because of diabetes.

Richard Brazell's living room was littered with drug paraphernalia. Pipes. Partially smoked marijuana cigarettes in the ashtray. Mirrors with white finger smudges from cocaine residue. "MORTHO" was etched into the surface of a mirror on the wall.

"Don't sweat the drug stuff, Mortho," Richardson said noticing the drug dealer's nervousness as he looked around the room. "I ain't here about drugs. I'm here about Thomas Luther."

Brazell played dumb. "Mortho?" he said. "Who's Mortho? And I don't know no Thomas Luther."

Richardson gave him a look and pointed to the mirror on the wall. The drug dealer shrugged and admitted to both.

"Tell me about the ring you got from Luther, Mortho," the detective said. He'd heard that Luther traded a man's ring with three diamonds in a diagonal row, Byron's ring, to Brazell for drugs. Snider said she'd overheard a conversation in which Luther was talking about "a girl's ring." And Eerebout's lawyer intimated that Luther cut Cher's finger off with a pair of bolt-cutters to get it to use as blackmail.

Richardson didn't describe the ring to Brazell.

"I don't know about no ring," Brazell said.

"Then we need to take a little ride over to Lakewood and see if that jogs your memory," Richardson said. "Anybody who doesn't cooperate is goin' down."

The trip seemed to help Brazell's memory. In the tight little interview room, he suddenly remembered that Luther once gave him a ring "with three diamonds on it."

"It was kinda small, I had to wear it on my pinky," he said, displaying fingers as big as hot dogs. "But I gave it to someone else."

Brazell also admitted talking to Luther about "taking care of" a snitch. However, he said, the snitch in question was his own daughter, Michelle, who turned on him after an arrest for drugs in Fort Collins in 1993. They'd made up since, he added.

Richardson dropped Brazell back at his apartment building. *Hope he lives long enough to get to trial,* the detective thought as Brazell hobbled and wheezed up to the front door. The ring information was important. It was one thing for a single witness to put Cher's ring with Luther; it was another thing for several different witnesses, including Luther's fat drug-dealing pal, to say the same thing.

That evening, Richardson heard from Healey's sister, Deborah. Southy, she said, asked her to tell the detective everything. She recalled that in March or April of 1993, Luther showed up at her house all nervous, constantly looking out the windows like he was being followed. "He said he had gotten into a deal that had gone bad," she said. "And that he had to get out of town because he left too many clues."

It wasn't much. But all in all, piece by piece, Richardson thought, it was a good day. He felt like he was on a train that had been heading up a long incline and just crested the hill. Slowly at first, but picking up speed, he was barreling toward a showdown with Thomas Luther.

The train increased speed in February when Byron Eerebout agreed to a deal. "Does a pile of rocks mean anything to you, Richardson?" he said looking sideways at the detective at a meeting to sign off on the details. Byron would have to serve the minimum time for his offense, but he would be allowed to do so in a community corrections program outside the state of Colorado.

In the meantime, Eerebout said he had information to add. Luther killed Cher, he said, and what he then did to her body was "grotesque. And Southy helped transport the body."

Richardson kept a straight face. Eerebout didn't know about the trip to Empire with Southy Healey or that he was cooperating. The detective didn't believe that Healey transported Cher's body. Otherwise, Healey would have had a lot more concerns about what evidence might turn up when he led them to what he believed to be the gravesite. *Just get his lips movin',* he reminded himself.

Richardson was a lot more interested in Eerebout's comment about a "pile of rocks." His mind immediately pictured the snow-covered pile he discovered on that day at the mine shaft. But he needed Byron to take him there. A witness independent of Healey would be critical in court.

Babe Rivinius was also at the meeting, having insisted. She was still outwardly hostile to the detective; however, she conceded that her sons were more involved than she originally admitted. J.D. took Luther to the grave in the mountains, she said. But what nobody seemed to understand, she complained, was that her family had been threatened by Luther. "And the boys were all just heartbroken over what happened to Cher."

"I never met her. But I have never heard them talk as highly about anyone as I have about her. And I know that it broke Byron's heart to know that something this horrendous happened to that girl.

"And I wanna tell you something, it's important for her family to realize that my family never intended them any harm and that the only reason that things have been the way they have been is because my kids had a lot to face, too. I'm talking about the fact that they had to fear for their lives. It took getting Tom put away on the other end to get it to the point to where the kids were able to deal with it a lot better."

It took all of Richardson's self-control not to react to Babe's comments. Byron Eerebout had been overheard laughing about the family wanting Cher's body back. The "kids" had done everything they could to protect a killer. Time and again, Rivinius intervened when he was trying to make a deal with Byron, stretching out the heartache for Cher's family.

Now they were so heartbroken. It made him want to gag. Somehow, he made it through the meeting without letting his feelings be known.

Even so, Babe intervened again. She thought Byron could get a better deal. Fed up, Richardson decided to hell with Eerebout and made arrangements to have him shipped back to the penitentiary. Let him explain to the guys in the joint where he'd been and who he'd been talking to, Richardson thought. He'd find Cher on his own, arrest Luther for murder and Eerebout for being an accomplice.

But when Leslie Hansen heard that her client was about to be returned to Canon City, she called Richardson in a panic. "Is the deal still good?" she asked meekly.

* \| * \| *

On February 21, Richardson drove to Empire alone. Snow had fallen the day before, blanketing everything. Richardson pulled into the turn-off and stopped next to the man-made rock cairn with the pole jutting out of it. He knew now what had confused Healey, who thought he remembered something was hanging from the post.

Every winter, the National Forest Service took down the sign that said "Welcome to Arapahoe National Forest" and hung it back in its place every March. Healey had remembered the sign.

Two days later, on the morning of February 23, Richardson received a call at home from Deputy District Attorney Dennis Hall. "They're going to take you to the grave," he said. "Now."

An hour later, Richardson, Connally, Leslie Hansen, and Byron Eerebout were on Interstate 70 heading west into the mountains. Sgt. Girson and crime lab technicians followed in a second car.

"Okay, Byron, real quick. We got a recorder goin', not gonna hide nothin' from ya. We're not gonna talk anything about the case at all," Richardson said. "All we need from you is directions on how to go."

Eerebout nodded and smiled. Even with the shackles and jail jumpsuit on, he acted like a kid on his way to a picnic. "Okeydoke," he said, then noted, "You guys are dressed pretty nice. I figured you'd be wearin' blue jeans."

Richardson told him that they had coveralls in the trunk. He didn't feel like making small talk with Byron; it would have been too difficult to disguise the contempt he felt.

Eerebout shrugged. "Take I-70 to the Berthoud Pass exit, go through the little town before we start heading up to Berthoud Pass," he said. "There's a horseshoe-shaped turn-off and there's a national park sign in the middle of it."

Richardson, of course, knew exactly where they were heading. A former pile of rocks. But it all had to come out of Byron's mouth. Southy Healey got them partway there; Eerebout had to take them those last few feet.

"When you turn in there, there'll be two trails that you gotta get out and walk on," Eerebout said. "There's one goin' to the right and there's one goin' to the left. Go up to the left and you just start walkin', and we'll run into it. I'll show you."

They drove through Empire and had just passed the Marietta Restaurant when Eerebout leaned forward and pointed up the road to the right. "It has a national forest service sign."

Richardson knew the sign was still down, but he wanted to see how Byron would react. They drove up to the turn-off and Eerebout started to point again, but then his finger dropped. He looked confused.

"I'm not sure if it's this . . . ." He looked anxiously at Richardson, who frowned. "Please don't get grumpy with me, detective," he whined. "This is hard enough as it is."

Richardson shrugged. "Oh, I'm not. I haven't said a thing." They continued driving past the turn-off but got only a little farther up the road before Eerebout told them to go back. "I was right the first time," he said. And when they returned to the turn-off, he added, "This is it. I didn't recognize it 'cause the sign's gone."

"I'll tell ya now, Byron," Richardson said, "they remove signs in the wintertime to keep 'em from weatherin.' They put 'em back up in April."

The ground was covered with another layer of fresh snow, but the sky overhead was clear and blue as a robin's egg. A lot of traffic was passing by, most of the cars topped with skis and heading for Winter Park. The police officers waited until there was a break in the traffic before jumping out of their cars and pulling on the coveralls. They didn't want to attract attention; in particular, they didn't want any media nosing around. In 1993, while searching the area with bloodhounds and dozens of people, they'd told curious onlookers that they were practicing search and rescue techiniques. Most would wander on after a few uneventful minutes.

Byron Eerebout pointed to the path that led up past the grey rock formation. "See, I told you," he said to Hansen as the detectives dressed.

"Are you sure?"

"Yes, this is it. I was standin' there," he said, sounding annoyed. "I was lookin' through the dark, okay."

"Okay, I believe you, Byron," Hansen said. "I'm not

doubting you, I just wanted to make sure. They said this is a one-shot deal." Hall had reminded her that Eerebout was to take the detectives directly to the grave, no more games, or he was getting a one-way trip back to prison.

"I know, but I will stay up here all day until I find it. Okay? You can go, I will stay up here until I find it."

Richardson came up to the car and hauled Eerebout out by his arm. "I'm gonna walk him up into the trees," he said to the other officers, "so we don't have people seein' him."

The crook and the cop immediately began heading up the trail. When they were joined by the others, Eerebout set off on the left fork. "Right here, my friends," he said as they came upon the clearing. "I believe this is it."

The tall redhead stood still for a moment, then moved off the trail and a little behind the rock formation while looking down on the clearing. He seemed to be trying to get his bearings. "I was standing over here lookin' over the rocks and watching him. It was two in the morning," he said. "My car was parked on the other side of the road. Tom's little blue Metro was parked right by the sign."

He licked his lips nervously. It was dark the last time he was there, he complained. But then he pointed to where the pile of rocks had been. "Yeah, this is it. It wasn't no further."

He looked at his lawyer. "Should I say it? I got to say it one time or another." Hansen nodded.

Eerebout took a deep breath. "He came up here to put rat poison on the body so the dogs and the wild animals wouldn't dig it up. He said it wasn't too far down, it wasn't deep enough, and he wanted to come up here to dig it deeper.

"But then he said to stay out of his fuckin' business."

Richardson and Connally took Eerebout and his attorney back to the Jefferson County Jail while Girson and the crime lab technicians stood guard in the clearing. On the way back up, the two detectives stopped to pick up Ireland and Diane France, a NecroSearch forensic anthropologist.

When he got in the car, Ireland stretched out and pulled his cap over his eyes as if to take a nap. "Another Richardson pleasure cruise?" he yawned.

Richardson smiled. "This time we got a body. I guarantee it."

Ireland looked up skeptically from under his cap. But he said nothing.

They arrived at the site to find that the technicians had already photographed the scene and established a perimeter. France began to drill into the same hole they had created in January. Three inches further down she found adipocere, a whitish, fatty substance produced in decomposing bodies exposed to moisture, such as the snows and spring runoff that pooled in the bowl-shaped clearing.

They knew they had a body. Still, they couldn't be absolutely certain it was Cher Elder, or how much of the body remained in the grave. She might have been moved. Or it could have been an unknown body that Luther used as a red-herring for the Eerebout boys. There'd been so many lies.

Under the direction of France, the tedious process of exhumation began. The forensic anthropologist was a tiny woman, but Richardson noted that long after a man would grow tired from the digging, she kept going. She and her assistants went about their business like they were unearthing the tomb of some ancient queen.

First, the gravesite was sectioned off into grids, delineated by pieces of string tied to stakes. Every bit of dirt was sifted through a screen and examined. Everything that came out of the excavation went into buckets marked for the appropriate grid space. The process of digging was made more difficult by permafrost—the first six to twelve inches of soil was frozen, which probably explained why the cadaver dog hadn't detected anything. A special torch system was brought in to warm the ground.

By the end of the first day, they had exposed one of the walls of the original grave. France was so precise, using toothbrushes to clear away dirt, that they could see the tool marks left by the gravedigger's shovel. The sun was going down behind the nearby hills when they called it a day.

After the others left, Richardson and Connally stayed behind to spend the night in their car. They couldn't take the chance that some curious local would come on the site now and call the media, or that one of Luther's associates might have seen them and try to remove the remains. Richardson wasn't worried about the local mountain lion. Cougars won't eat decayed flesh. But there were also bears in the area, and they would. Both detectives were exhausted.

"What if it ain't Cher?" Connally asked as they tried to get comfortable in the cramped vehicle.

"I don't want to think about that," Richardson said. It was a good thing, he pointed out, that they hadn't found Cher when he first stumbled on the grave in January. If they had, they wouldn't have been able to make a deal with Eerebout, who would have had no reason to come clean, and they were going to need his testimony at trial. And this way, there were two different witnesses—Southy and Byron, who by all accounts hardly knew each other and yet took them to the grave area independent of the other.

However, there remained the issue of which one was lying. Southy Healey said he came up with Byron and Luther in the daytime; Eerebout made no mention of Southy and said he spied on Luther at 2 A.M. "I don't want to think about that either," Richardson said and each detective turned to his own thoughts as he tried to get some rest.

Neither slept much and they both greeted the dawn stiff and cold. They were soon joined by the police and NecroSearch teams, who brought coffee and breakfast.

During the day, France and her assistants exposed all the walls of the original grave. NecroSearch botanist Vickey Trammell pointed out where roots from the plants above the grave had been cut by the gravedigger and other roots had since grown. "We'll be able to get a pretty good idea on how old the grave is from that," she said.

By late afternoon, they knew that most of a human body remained in the grave under the light-tan soil. About 4 P.M., France bent over and tugged at a small root in the bottom of the pit. It came up along with a small lock of dark brown hair.

The searchers were silent. Then Richardson said quietly, "It's Cher." Everyone cheered. Hands clapped him on the back. Voices said, "Congratulations, you got her." They all knew what this case meant to him and its enormous personal toll. But Richardson just wanted to get away from the celebration.

Numb, he walked off. On the other side of the clearing, he sat down on a rock outcropping that offered a view of the moun-

tain that rose above the gravesite and the chapel-like clearing
that held the remains of Cher Elder. Clear Creek sang in the valley
below, different sounding now as it appeared and disappeared
beneath an icy sheath.

It's so beautiful, he thought again. *Peaceful. A shame we have
to take her away—except that Thomas Luther put her here.*
Anger filled his mind. Luther's presence could stain even the
most heavenly place; he sullied everything he touched. Richardson hated him for it.

The detective sat for a long time trying to sort out his feelings.
I found her, his mind exalted one minute, only to be overwhelmed
by sadness the next. He was surprised to discover that even he
had held out the tiniest hope that Cher was alive somewhere.
She's dead, he told himself. *She's dead.* It sounded so final, so
unfair.

He stood up as the last light from the west bathed the snows
on the mountain above briefly in pink before leaving the world
in gray twilight. A chill wind swept down from the slopes with
the setting of the sun, and Richardson shivered. But not from
the cold.

I found her, he thought, *only now I have to tell her family.*

The sleepless night in the car, the cold, and the emotional toll
of the discovery had done in both Richardson and Connally.
They were nearly asleep on their feet when the crew called it a
day. Although they argued to remain behind, Sgt. Girson ordered
them both to go home and rest.

When he got home, Scott was pumped up. He could hardly
stop pacing. Finally, he was going to nail Tom Luther's hide to
the wall for what he'd done to Cher.

Sabrina was relieved. In part for Scott's sake; he'd put himself
under a lot of stress juggling the investigation, keeping it fresh,
while giving Cher's family a shoulder to cry on. He'd lost a lot
of weight and wasn't sleeping well—waking up in the middle
of the night to write a note to himself, then lying awake with
his mind going over next steps.

But it was also in part because she was fed up with their lives.
Luther was like a ghost in the house, always there. Scott couldn't
seem to think of anything else. If they went somewhere, the

Luther case became a topic of conversation, nothing else mattered. Scott was always tired; he had no energy for the boys. About the only time he seemed like his old self was riding with her on his Harley.

Now, she thought, *maybe we can go on with our lives.* She had no idea that the ordeal was not even close to being over.

Richardson still could not call Cher's parents. The formal identification by a coroner would have to come first. There was always the remote possibility that it might be someone else buried in the grave, and he didn't want to tell the family and then have to reverse himself.

He was still pondering how he would tell them when he got the message from a police dispatcher that Debrah Snider had called that afternoon. Wearily, he picked up the telephone and called her back.

"I'm movin' back to Fort Collins," she said sadly. "It's over between me and Tom."

There wasn't much he could say. He couldn't tell her he'd found Cher Elder's body. That had to remain a secret as long as possible. And he didn't have the heart to tell her that now that he had a body, her relationship with Thomas Luther would soon be entering a whole new phase. One that would tear her heart and challenge her conscience.

Richardson and Connally returned to the site early the next morning only to face a new problem. An avalanche had swept across the highway further up the pass, burying two people, and slowing traffic down to a crawl past the turn-off. When the occasional curious skier poked his head out the window to ask what they were up to, the detectives pointed up the road and yelled, "Avalanche."

Near panic gripped the searchers when a television news helicopter began circling overhead. It was there to record the effects of the avalanche, but had a bird's eye view of the partially exposed gravesite through the trees. Everyone breathed a sigh of relief when the road was opened and the skiers and the helicopter went away.

It wasn't until six that evening that France finished for the day. The skeletal remains of a nude woman lay exposed, looking like a mummy encased in dirt. For the most delicate work near the body, France supplemented her toothbrushes with thin bamboo sticks. Bamboo, she explained to Richardson, wouldn't scar bone as would a metal pick.

The man who buried Cher Elder had not made the grave long enough, and she was lying awkwardly on her back with her head bowed by the wall of the grave. Her left arm lay across her stomach, her right under her.

All that remained was to dig beneath Cher to gently loosen her from the ground on which she'd rested for two years. Before France left, she and Richardson gently laid a plastic tarp over the remains, folding the edges under the remains.

Stepping back, France looked up at Richardson's sad, dark eyes and reached out to touch him on the arm. He looked at the small woman at his side and smiled wistfully. "It's like we're tucking her in for the night."

France nodded. "I understand now why you took this so personally," she said. Addressing the grave, she added, "We'll be back in the morning, Cher," and walked off to her car.

Richardson and Connally again spent the night. "There's a mountain lion living around here and there's always the possibility of bears," Richardson told Sabrina when he called. But the real reason was he couldn't bring himself to leave Cher alone one more night.

They slept next to the grave in sleeping bags, one on either side. In the morning, Richardson was awakened by something wet that dripped onto his neck. He opened his eyes, puzzled that all he could see was white, and wondered for a moment if he was still dreaming of death and heaven.

It took a moment to realize that it had snowed again, so gently that it didn't wake him when several inches piled up over the small space he'd left open in his bag to breathe. He sat up to a world pure and innocent; even the horror of the grave was disguised beneath the white cover.

That night they placed the remains in a body bag and transported them to the Jefferson County coroner's office. There the dirt was carefully removed and the skull X-rayed. Comparing the X-ray to dental records, the coroner was able to make a positive identification: Cher Elder.

It was time to tell her parents.

* * *

When it looked like a deal with Byron Eerebout was imminent, Scott Richardson arranged with the Grand Junction Police Department victim's advocate to be ready to contact Rhonda Edwards. He wanted both parents told simultaneously so that one wouldn't be the first to break the news to the other.

Now Richardson, accompanied by Girson and representatives of the Jefferson County coroner and victim's advocate offices, drove to Earl Elder's home. Pulling into the driveway, he called the advocate's office in Grand Junction. "We found Cher," he said. "Tell Ronnie right now. And take her over to the police department and I'll call in an hour."

Drawing a deep breath and letting it out slowly, Richardson got out of the car and walked up to Earl's door. He'd investigated a lot of homicides in his seventeen years as a police officer and dealt with a lot of grieving families. But this was by far the hardest thing he had ever done.

Earl's car was in the drive, but there was no answer to the doorbell. "I think he's working nights," Richardson said. "So he's probably sleeping. Keep knockin' and I'll go around back."

Earl Elder was indeed asleep in his bedroom with a fan on to drown out daytime noises. He didn't hear the pounding on his doors, but was finally awakened by his dog barking.

Walking sleepily down the stairs, he looked up and saw Richardson at the back door. He knew right away why the detective was there.

Over the past two years, they had talked often. Richardson was always keeping him abreast of the investigation's progress, even when there was little to report and in the darkest days when he had to admit that he didn't know if they would ever find Cher. But he never gave up and now that he was banging on Earl's back door, it could mean only one thing.

Elder let Richardson and the others in. They sat down as he fought to keep his emotions in check. "Earl," the detective said, "I'm real sorry to have to tell you this. But we found Cher." He shook his head at the father's unasked question. "She's dead."

Earl sat quietly, struggling with the tears that sprang into his eyes. He was a private person who preferred to be alone when he got bad news so that he could absorb it in his own way. He appreciated that the others were there to try to comfort him, but he wished they would leave.

There was a searing feeling in his heart, like someone had touched it with a knife. He tried to picture Cher—always laughing, always smiling from the days she was an infant to the last time he saw her two years earlier. Even when he knew it was hopeless, he'd held on to the hope that his oldest child had simply run off on some wild, 20-year-old whim. That someday he'd hear the door open or the telephone would ring and there she'd be.

Elder escorted the others to the door. There he took Richardson's hand and shook it. "Thanks," he said, his voice barely above a whisper. "Thanks for finding her."

He closed the door and began to weep. But gradually the sadness was replaced by an anger greater than any he had ever known. That little bit of hope was now gone, snuffed out by a monster named Tom Luther. If it took the rest of his life, he would make sure that Luther paid the price.

Just six days earlier, Rhonda Edwards had reached the end of her rope. Her own mother, Cher's grandmother, was about mad with grief, sure she would die before her granddaughter was found. Neither woman could understand what was taking so long.

The previous fall, when Byron Eerebout was sent to prison, Richardson called to say he was working with an FBI psychologist to break Cher's former boyfriend down. He was sure that Byron knew where Cher's body was and what happened to her. "We might have worked out a deal already, except Byron's lawyers keep gettin' in the way," he said. "But I think we're close."

Christmas approached with no news. She sent the card with the photograph of Cher to Richardson as a way of thanking him. But Christmas Day she locked herself in her room and wouldn't come out.

The new year arrived and still there was nothing. Then February drew to a close and she faced the prospect of a second anniversary of Cher's disappearance.

How could Byron do this? she cried to her husband. Did Cher mean so little to him that he would torture her family like this?

On February 21, Rhonda Edwards picked up her diary and wrote, "How long do I have to wait?" She didn't know that on that date, Richardson had stood within a few feet of her daughter's grave, knowing he was close.

She was at work on February 27 when the victim's advocate walked into her office. She looked at the woman's face and knew what was coming before she heard the words. "They found Cher," the woman said gently. "They want you to go to the police department. Scott Richardson's going to call."

Edwards nodded and gathered her coat. Deep inside a voice began to cry, but she fought to keep it from getting out. At the police station, she called her husband Van.

"They found Cher," she said.

"Is she alive?" he asked.

Surprised by his answer, she reacted with anger. "No, Van, of course not," she snapped.

Immediately she felt ashamed. Van had known Cher since childhood and loved her like one of his own. They'd been great friends, though he was careful not to usurp Earl's role as father.

Everyone in the family hoped that Cher was somehow still alive. Van just asked what the rest of them dared not voice out loud.

"I'm sorry, Van," she said gently. "But no, Cher isn't alive."

It wasn't long after she hung up that the telephone at her side rang. It was Richardson. "I'm sorry to have to tell you this, Ronnie," he said in that soft Texas drawl she had thought was so comforting. "But we found Cher."

The day the body of Cher Elder was identified, her case was officially changed from a missing person to a homicide. The autopsy revealed that she had been shot three times in the back of the head behind her left ear with a .22 caliber at close range.

The bullet holes were so close together that the coroner at first believed she had been shot only once. It meant that Cher was either held down and unable to move, or already unconscious, when her killer pressed the gun to her head and pulled the trigger three times. She wasn't trying to flee or struggle— she'd been executed.

Decomposition of the body was too advanced to tell for sure if she'd been raped. But her skull had been fractured by a heavy blow. Contrary to Luther's claims that Cher used cocaine, there was no evidence of drugs in her body fluids or from the analysis of her hair, which retains evidence of drug use even after such use has been discontinued.

Cher was wearing the braided friendship bracelet that appeared in many of the photographs Richardson had of her. There was no ring with three diamonds. However, the forensic anthropologist who assisted the coroner found hairs on the body that he at first believed to be that of a dog but which turned out to be wolf hair.

Richardson gave a copy of the case files—now fourteen four-inch binders—to Dennis Hall to prepare for the grand jury. There would be more coming, he warned; he still needed to reinterview the Eerebout brothers and Healey. He needed to know now the whole truth about what happened to Cher and their involvement.

On March 2, Richardson went to the Jefferson County Jail to meet with Eerebout. This time, there was none of the bravado, only a docile, almost meek young man.

"When Gina and I came back to the house, Thomas Luther and Cher were gone," Byron said. "At about, I would say five or so in the morning, I heard noises out in the front room of my apartment, and I got up. Tom was there, Southy was also there.

"I have no idea what they were doing. They just came in briefly and left, so I went back to sleep. When I woke up, Tom Luther was sleeping in the living room and Cher Elder's car was not in the visitors parking lot anymore."

Eerebout said he found the angry notes from Cher when he got up in the morning, but he wasn't sure when they were written. "Cher's family kept callin', wondering where she was, but I didn't know what happened until one day when I was at Debrah Snider's place in Fort Collins." That's when, he said, he overheard Luther on the telephone talking to someone about having to move a body.

"I was nervous or whatever you'd say about doing it, but I asked Tom what he did, and Tom told me he killed her. The

reason that he gave me was that she was going to tell on me
and my brothers and some of my brothers' friends for some stuff
that we were doing."

Of course, Richardson thought, *Luther wasn't about to say,
'I got mad, so I raped, beat, and murdered your girlfriend.'*
Even a convict's kids knew where rapists were on the criminal
totem pole. He had to have a reason and it was: I protected you,
now you have to protect me. "Go on," he said.

"They went up to Central City," Tom said, and on the way
back she started yelling and screaming, saying, 'I'm going to
go to the cops. Byron fucked me over and blah, blah, blah.' "

Richardson imagined Cher angry, believing that the man who
looked so much like her father was to be trusted, a shoulder to
cry on. She couldn't have known that something much worse
than an unfaithful boyfriend sat next to her as they drove down
the dark winding road through the mountains.

Had her complaints been enough to set Luther off? According
to Mary Brown and what he'd heard of the attack in West
Virginia, Luther attacked without provocation—what criminolo-
gists like Dr. Macdonald referred to as a "blitz attack."

"He stopped on the side of the road between Golden and
Central City and shot her in the head," Eerebout said. "That's
what he told me. He stopped the car, they got out, and it happened
there. I have no idea how he transported the body, but it was
supposedly taken care of that night."

Richardson nodded. "Details," he said. "I need details. What
about the gun?"

"Let's see," Byron paused for a moment. "They got the gun,
I think it was a .22 or something like that, from a 7-Eleven store.
From a lady's purse by one of my brother's friends, and it was
given to Tom."

Eerebout said he had originally covered for his father's friend
because he didn't know for sure that Luther had done anything
to Cher and wanted to give him "the benefit of the doubt." It
was a little while after Richardson had shown him the video
taken in Central City that he'd overheard Luther and asked him
about Cher. "He threatened to kill my friends, my wife Tiffany,
and my mother, if I said anything."

At some point that April, he couldn't remember exactly when,
Luther had come by his apartment. He was nervous and said

the grave was too shallow, that he needed to go back and bury it deeper and cover it with rat poison to keep the animals away. "Myself and my brother followed Tom to that location."

After telling Eerebout about the murder and threatening his family, Luther gave him Cher's sweater and skirt. "It was sort of a threat, I guess you'd say. Letting me know that what he said was true."

"Did Luther ever say exactly where he shot her. Where on the body?" Richardson asked. He needed as many details as possible to prove that Eerebout was not making up his story. He'd told him nothing about the results of the autopsy.

"In the head," Byron answered. "A .22."

"How about where on the highway?"

"He pulled off the road before they got to Golden, on one of those little boo-bop things off the side of the road where the dirt is by the river. He said that she got out, he got out and 'boom, boom, boom.' "

Richardson noted that Eerebout made three shooting sounds, not one, not two, but three. "Do you know where the gun is now?"

"He threw it in the river between here and Central City. He shot her, he got rid of it. He's a smart person, I guess."

Richardson wanted more details about the night Byron and his brother followed Luther to the grave. Too many details and it might mean that Eerebout had a more "hands-on" involvement in the homicide than he was admitting; too few details and he might be getting all of his information from a third party. For instance, it was important that Byron wasn't looking for a pile of rocks when he pointed to Cher's grave; it indicated that he hadn't actually seen them being put in place.

Eerebout said he was working on J.D.'s car when Luther drove down from Fort Collins. "I went with him to Mortho's to pick up some crystal meth. He brought me back and left for awhile and then came back about eleven that night. He was sayin', 'I gotta go take care of the grave.' "

Luther reiterated his threats and left about twelve-thirty or one in the morning. As Luther walked off to his car, Byron said, he got the idea of following him and enlisted his brother J.D. They tracked Luther up Interstate 70 and as far as Empire when they stopped to get a soda. They then continued up the road, through the town, and a little beyond when they saw Luther's car in the turn-off.

"We went up and turned around and parked on the other side of the road. I got out and went over to Tom's car, looked inside, but nobody was there."

However, when he looked up the hill, he could see the light from a flashlight playing off the branches of the trees beyond the gray rock shelf. Quietly, he crept up the hill, sticking close to the rock formation. When he reached a point above the clearing, he looked down and saw Luther on his hands and knees, digging at the ground with a shovel he had taken from Babe's house that day. "It was one of those little, folding army trenching shovels."

"Why did you go up to the mountains?" Richardson asked. The whole story sounded strange. Following someone in the dead of night into the mountains?

"Peace of mind, I guess," Eerebout shrugged.

"Did he know you were following?"

"No," he said, shaking his head. "He came back to the house the next morning. There were bigger shovels and bolt-cutters in the back of his car. He had a sleeping bag, as if he was packed to go on vacation or a camping trip, like he knew he had to leave."

"What was the conversation between you and J.D. about Luther being up there digging a grave?"

"There really wasn't nothing. It was hush, hush. 'This is between us two. Mom's not to know, Tristan's not to know.' And that was basically it."

"Have you ever heard, prior to Cher's murder, of Cher being a snitch?"

"No."

"Of course, you already stated that after Luther confessed to killing her that she was threatening to snitch on him. Was there ever any talk that you overheard about killing Cher prior to the night this occurred?"

Again the answer was no.

"You've indicated that this was a grotesque murder. Can you explain?"

For the first time, Byron Eerebout seemed to get truly upset. "She had one of my rings. I don't know if the ring was still on her person, but he told me that he cut off her finger 'cause he couldn't get the ring off. He was going to keep the ring."

"What did he use to cut the finger off?"

"He said bolt-cutters. I think they're in the back of his car." Luther didn't say what he did with the finger he removed and Byron didn't know if he put it back in the grave.

"Did he say anything about Cher's lips being cut off?" Richardson asked. He already knew from the autopsy that no such thing occurred and neither was a finger missing. But that didn't mean Luther hadn't said such things to frighten Debrah Snider and the Eerebout boys.

Byron grimaced. No, he didn't know about that.

Luther's first story when asked about Cher's disappearance, Eerebout said, was that she must have run away. "He said he brought her back to my place and never saw her again."

"When I first called you, way back in April 1993, did you call Luther and warn him?" Richardson already knew the answer but he was again testing to see if Eerebout would tell the truth.

"Yes. He said, 'I'll take care of this, it's no problem. I'll talk to you later.' " Then later when the detective showed him the videotape, he'd called Luther again and got the same response.

"Did Luther say anything about how much he had been drinking that night?"

"Thomas Luther does not drink. He uses narcotics quite frequently, but I'm not sure if he did it before he left or while he was there, but I know he had some on him that evening."

"Did he say how much Cher had been drinking that night?"

"He said Cher was drunk."

Eerebout said he'd "heard through the grapevine" that Luther was seen by Debrah Snider after the murder with dirt underneath his fingernails and his fingers bloodied and torn up. "He told her he was buryin' AK-47s." He added that there once had been AK-47s, but they were Mongo's and long gone before Luther killed Cher.

Richardson asked if Byron had seen Luther with a backpack. Serial rapists and serial killers were known to carry what police called "rape kits," containing their tools of the trade, such as tape, rope, ski masks, and changes of clothing—particularly if they knew they might kill their victims.

Yes, Eerebout responded, Luther always kept a backpack in

his car. He often asked one of the Eerebout brothers to take him somewhere with his backpack. "He would stop and jump out of the car, or say, 'Drop me off here, I'm going hiking.' He was the kind of person who would just take off sometimes and stay out all night long doing stuff."

"Did he ever talk about what he would do if the police recovered Cher's body?"

"If it came from me, he'd get me. That's why he said he'd keep the ring. He'd blame it on me by putting it someplace where the police would find it. They'd get an anonymous tip that would lead them to me."

Luther also said he might have Gina Jones "taken care of" so she couldn't be a witness. "Do you know anything about her cat being killed or threats made to her?" Richardson asked.

"No."

"What were his plans if he was followed by the police to the grave?"

"He'll kill you. He said if anybody did anything, he'd kill them, but he really didn't think kindly of you. I'll tell you straight up, Thomas Luther hated your guts, and he wanted to kill you. It was one of those things that if you were the cop that came, he would kill you."

Richardson nodded. There were times when if the opportunity presented itself, Luther reaching for a gun maybe, he would have looked forward to beating him to the punch.

There was something still troubling him, and that was Healey's story. "Do you recall takin' a trip to the mountains with Thomas Luther and Southy, the three of you?"

Eerebout seemed genuinely puzzled. "No," he said. "Never. Southy came over to the house once before the murder and then that morning." That was all the contact they'd ever had, until he saw him at the Jefferson County Jail.

What had Skip Eerebout said about the case? Richardson asked.

"I got two letters from him and my mom called him. He just said that, 'If Byron messes with fire, he's gonna get burned.' "

"Do you have any knowledge that anybody was with Thomas Luther at the time Cher was killed?" Richardson asked. "Not later, but at the time that she was killed."

"I heard at first it was Southy and Tom, but then Tom said that it was just him."

"So Luther calls Southy after Cher was killed?"

"Yeah . . . because Southy was there in the morning."

"Thomas Luther ever talk about having sex with Cher?"

"No."

Richardson concluded the interview by asking if Luther ever discussed the best way to dispose of a body and hide the evidence.

"Yeah," Byron responded. "Just go into the mountains, dig a hole, put it in there, and get rid of the stuff in the river. He said you can't find anything in a river 'cause it always moves."

The Jefferson County grand jury was scheduled to convene on March 6 to hear the case against Thomas Luther for the murder of Cher Elder. Meanwhile, Richardson continued his investigation.

Many of the smaller pieces of his "pie" were falling into place. Pam "Babe" Rivinius was now going out of her way to be helpful. When asked, she recalled a white sweater she'd found in her basement and assumed belonged to Byron's first wife. However, she washed it and gave it to Goodwill.

The folding shovel was back in her basement, she said. Sometime after Cher Elder disappeared, a matter of weeks, Luther asked to borrow it and she told him to go ahead. The shovel was gone for several more weeks, then it mysteriously reappeared one morning in her flower bed.

Richardson went to her house and picked up the shovel. The blade still had dirt on it, but instead of the dark, rich soil of Babe's garden, it was light tan, like that from Cher's grave.

The day of the grand jury hearing arrived with Richardson troubled about several important aspects of the case. One was Eerebout's story about "following" Luther to the gravesite in the middle of the night. He thought it much more likely that Luther persuaded the brothers to come with him and stand guard down at the car. Luther probably went to the grave by himself. He had been careful about having any witnesses, such as Southy, see him with the body. However, Eerebout had crept up the hill to spy on him.

When it happened was unclear. Perhaps the day after he first met Luther in April 1993, when, according to Debrah Snider, Luther went out to "find" the body and said he buried it out east off Interstate 70. Or maybe Luther and J.D. met up with Byron on the night of May 18, 1993, and then J.D. went alone to pick Luther up in Empire the next day, when he was spotted by the police.

It didn't really matter at this point. So long as the brothers did not actively participate in the murder or burial of Cher Elder, he wasn't as concerned with Byron's story as he was with Southy's. He went back to the Adams County Jail, where he found that Southy was suddenly having reservations about testifying against his old friend.

"I wanna know, man, you're saying that the DAs aren't gonna fuck me," he said. "How do I know that?"

"You're gonna have to take me on my word," Richardson said, pushing a pack of cigarettes at the nervous convict. "If you don't, then go and play your game. I'm not gonna waste any more time."

"You seem to be the only one thinkin' it's a game," Southy retorted.

Richardson ignored the remark. "We've got grand jury starts at six-thirty tonight. I need a full breakdown of what you can testify to. Now. You're one of five people that is gonna testify. You got to tell me the truth, Dennis, because, listen to me, we know the facts of the case." Actually, the "five people" included investigators, but he wanted Healey to think that all sorts of Luther's acquaintances and friends were rolling over.

Healey swore he was telling the truth. "She was shot, right?"

Richardson shook his head. "No more guessing games, either you know or you don't," he said. "I am not gonna feed you information. You're gonna feed me. I'm the hungry dog here, bud."

Healey scowled. "I'm not gonna give you every fuckin' thing. I'm not gonna confess to you, man. You're not my priest."

Richardson put up his hands. "I'm not askin' for a Christian confession," he said.

Healey considered for a moment. Then his shoulders slumped as he gave up the tough guy act. He said he was passed out at his sister's house on the night in question when she came to wake him up. Luther was on the telephone, she said. "It was one, two, maybe three in the morning. Tom said, 'Hey bro, I need you to do me a favor.' ''

What's that, man? Southy said he replied

"I need you to drive the car for a few minutes, man, while I take care of something. I'm comin' to get ya."

He had gotten up and dressed but fell back asleep. He was awakened by Luther, who urged him out to his car. "There were a couple of shovels in it and a bunch of dirt on the back seat," which was unusual for Luther, who was fastidious about his car's upkeep.

"Where we goin'?" Southy asked when Luther told him to get in and drive.

"I gotta get rid of somethin'," Luther replied.

At the jail, Southy Healey reached for another cigarette. "He must have already put it there, man," he told Richardson. "That's where the fuckin' body is, or somewhere around there."

Healey was upset that apparently his information had not produced a body. "He wouldn't have come and got me with a body in the car because he knows right then I'd have said, 'No, no, no, no. I'm not gettin' in there.' As far as getting involved in the murder, man, he knows I'm not gonna do that. That's not my fucking game. I'm a petty thief, man. I'm fucked. I scam and I sell a little dope. I'm not a murderer. I'm not a fuckin' accomplice to murder. Although I think I may have ended up helpin' him fuckin' get rid of the body, I don't see that as complicity."

Richardson knew that he was at last hearing the truth from Southy. But he needed to keep him on edge. "The State of Colorado does," he said.

"Well, then the State of Colorado is gonna have to get me on that then," Healey said angrily. "I never saw no body. I never saw shit. He could have been up there burying a fuckin' deer, man, I don't know."

He went on with his story. They were driving up Interstate 70 when Luther blurted out, "I think I fucked up."

"What do you mean?" Healey said he asked.

"I killed her."

"Killed who?"

"A broad."

He paused to blow a cloud of blue smoke at the ceiling of

the interview room. "I knew he was in prison before for that shit. I don't know if it was murder, but I think it was for rape or some shit."

Luther directed him to drive past the little town where he'd taken the detectives that day in January. "He told me to slow down when we got to that turnoff, and that if someone came, to honk the horn. Then he jumped out of the car. I drove a little farther up the road, turned around and came back and parked."

A little while later, Luther appeared across the road and ran over to jump back in the car. Even in the dim light, Healey said, he could see that Luther's clothes were covered with dirt and sticky with what appeared to be blood. "He said the grave was shallow because the ground was too hard to dig."

He couldn't recall when he learned that Luther shot Cher. He knew that sometime after Richardson's press conference he'd overheard a conversation between Matt Marlar, a boyfriend of one of his sisters, and Luther. "Matt was demanding that Tom come get a gun he had given him. Apparently, Tom was tryin' to calm him down. He said that particular gun was not connected to nothin.' Luther showed up later, disguised in farmer's clothes, wearing a fake beard and a hat. He took the gun."

"Where'd he shoot her?" Richardson asked, trying to jog Southy's memory.

Healey thought for a moment, then nodded his head. "In the head. He must have said that 'cause I knew she got shot in the head." He stopped and looked down at the floor, frowning. "But I don't know if she got shot in the head, though."

He said he'd been doing a lot of dope in those days, and he didn't always know one day from the next, much less how he learned that Luther shot Cher. "I do remember him sayin' something about having a good time with her, that they had sex. And there was something about a ring with diamonds on it."

Richardson noted the remark about the ring. Another witness! "What did he do with her clothes?" he asked.

"I don't know." I know his went into the river."

They were driving back down the road from Empire to the interstate as Luther stripped his soiled clothes off and got into sweatclothes he had in a backpack. When they reached the place in the road that went over Clear Creek, Luther told him to slow down so that he could toss his soiled garments into the water.

"He threw his boots out, too, but one didn't make it and was lying in the road. We had to stop so he could run back and get it."

It was just beginning to get light when they got back to Denver. "Did you go to Byron's?"

Healey shook his head. "No. He dropped me off at my sister's." He was over there once before in the morning, but that wasn't during this incident.

Recalling that Byron Eerebout said that Cher's body was left at the house of one of Southy's sisters for as long as several weeks, Richardson asked, "Where was the body kept before it was buried?"

"I don't know."

Richardson nodded. He had to ask. However, a NecroSearch entomologist had studied Cher's remains and concluded her body had not been exposed for very long because she'd found only a few unhatched blow fly eggs on the remains. Blow flys are quick to lay their eggs on decomposing material. They will even lay eggs on the ground above a buried body with the larvae working their way down, so long as the distance is only a few inches.

Cher's body was far enough below the surface that larvae could not penetrate that far. A few eggs meant that her body had been exposed for a short time, probably just long enough to bury her. Left in a basement for even a week, there would have been many more eggs.

With the information he'd just learned from Healey, it was the detective's hunch that Luther killed Cher and dumped her at the spot outside of Empire in the early morning hours after they left the casino. He then returned to Byron Eerebout's apartment and moved the car. But he'd only moved it five blocks, to the first large parking lot he could find, indicating he was working alone.

Worried that someone would stumble upon the body, Luther then called his pal Southy after midnight Sunday and returned to bury Cher. After breaking Debrah's shovel, he'd injured his hands trying to dig deeper and then by moving the large granite rocks he piled on the grave. After tossing his clothes in the creek, he dropped off Healey and returned home to Fort Collins, where Debrah Snider found him in bed Monday afternoon.

Healey said he called Luther after the press conference and arranged to meet in Longmont. There a panicky Luther said, "They're on me, Southy. They're on me tough, bro."

It fit with Snider's story, but Southy couldn't have known that. Richardson decided to test him further.

"What would you say if I was to tell you that Thomas Luther said that you came up after he killed her and helped transport the body from the murder scene?" Luther, of course, had said no such thing.

"I'd say he was a liar," Southy spat out. "Simple as that, 'cause it didn't happen. The only reason he'd be sayin' somethin' like that is to cover someone else's ass. J.D. maybe. Byron. I don't know."

"What if Thomas Luther said that the body was kept in your house for a while before she's buried?"

Again, Healey reacted in anger, his eyes blazing. "I know he didn't keep the body there," he said. "There's no fuckin' way."

Well, then what about his previous story about learning of the gravesite while on a dope run with Byron and Luther? "That's how I was coverin' up the fact that I drove him up there. The trip never happened."

"How come you included Byron bein' in the car with ya?"

"Because him and Luther were close, and I figured you'd go for that."

"How do I know you're telling me the truth this time?"

He shrugged. "It doesn't matter. I told ya, pull out your polygraph, man. I guess you're just gonna have to take me for my word this time."

Then the convict softened. He'd also told that story because he didn't want the detective thinking he was involved with the murder of a girl. "I didn't want you thinkin', 'Oh, you fuckin' bastard.'"

Healey shook his head. He was sorry the grave wasn't where he thought it would be. "I thought she was fuckin' there. I wouldn'ta wasted my time or yours doin' that had I thought she'd been moved or whatnot. I thought you'd end the whole fuckin' thing right there that day. But I know if he's sayin' that I went with him to move a body, he's full of shit."

"Well, Dennis," Richardson said, not unkindly. "In a few hours, you'll get your chance in front of the grand jury to make up for whatever mistakes you made. But we're not going to subpoena you or force you to appear. If you go, it's of your own free will. I ain't makin' you no promises, or offering you nothin'.''

Southy Healey nodded. ''I ain't gonna do this for you or nobody else, except her family. I want her family to be able to say, 'At least we know what happened.' ''

The evening of March 6, 1995, the members of the Jefferson County grand jury assembled secretly in the courthouse. No media was aware of the gathering. Cher Elder's family had been asked to keep the finding of her body secret for a little while longer.

In the State of Colorado, there are two ways to bring charges against a suspect. By a direct filing of the charges, after which a hearing is held before a judge who determines if probable cause exists to bring the suspect to trial. And through a grand jury, which hears testimony from witnesses presented by the prosecution and decides whether to indict.

The grand jury in Jefferson County is used only rarely. There are about 3,000 felonies charged in the county every year through a direct filing and perhaps a dozen through the grand jury.

There are several advantages to seeking a grand jury indict- ment. For one thing, a grand jury can issue subpoenas for records and compell testimony from reluctant witnesses. For another, the prosecution can protect the identity of confidential informants—a grand jury's testimony is not public record.

A less evident advantage is that the prosecution gets to test run its case. It can then poll the jurors about holes in its theory or the believability of witnesses. In the Luther case, Dennis Hall wanted to get a feel for the community reaction to Byron Eerebout and Dennis ''Southy'' Healey. If the jurors came back and said the two simply weren't believeable, that would have been the end of the case.

Another prosecution advantage is that a grand jury hears only the prosecution side of a case and, rather than the presumption of innocence and reasonable doubt issues before a trial jury, is instructed to look at the evidence in a light most favorable for the prosecution. The statutes read that an indictment must be handed down if the evidence, taken in that most favorable light, is such that a reasonable person would believe a crime was committed and that the suspect *may* have committed the crime.

Hall would also instruct the jurors that they were only hearing a portion of the prosecution case, just enough to establish probable cause.

The danger with a grand jury is if it declines to indict, the case cannot be brought again—either before a grand jury or through a direct filing—unless significant new evidence is uncovered. However, there is no time limit to the proceedings. If a witness doesn't testify as expected, or the prosecutor believes that the jurors don't seem convinced, he can stop the proceedings for as long as needed until the evidence is better or new witnesses are found.

Dennis Hall had run the Jefferson County grand jury since the early 1990s. Some prosecutors, concerned about their win/loss records, will hand off risky or borderline cases to subordinates to take their chances. But Hall always kept the cases he filed personally, and he had filed the case against Thomas Luther. Three counts of first degree murder. A death penalty case.

District Attorney Dave Thomas had made the decision some time back that if Cher's body was found and Hall could convince the grand jury to indict him for first degree murder, they would seek the death penalty. Luther was a monster whose trail of battered and dead women left no room for pity, just as he had never shown any to his victims, nor remorse.

Still, it would be a difficult case. There were no witnesses to the murder. The witnesses who knew of the murder were mostly liars, thieves, convicts, or drug users—all of which the defense attorneys would use to impeach their credibility.

The only reasonably untainted witness who Luther admitted anything to, and then only that he buried the body, was Debrah Snider. She would be the most important witness of all; along with her own damning information, she was the link between what the other witnesses would say and Luther's actions.

But how would she come off to a jury? How could Hall explain her lapses in judgment, the length of time it took her to confess? Would the jury see her as blinded by love or an unstable, jealous woman getting even with an abusive boyfriend? And who really knew what she would do when it came time to choose between Luther and the truth?

At trial, Hall hoped to introduce Luther's other crimes against women under a provision of the law known as "similar transactions." Usually, in criminal trials, a defendant's past cannot be referred to by the prosecution in front of a jury unless the defendant takes the stand. The concept is that a defendant should be tried only for the crime with which he or she is standing trial at that moment, not their "bad character." However, on occassion prosecutors can convince a judge that former "bad acts," or similar transactions, bear so close a resemblance to the current charge and may supply a motive for the defendant's actions that they should be admissible in court. But that was for a future hearing. First, Hall needed to convince the grand jury to indict.

J.D. Eerebout was the first of the witnesses to testify. He told the jurors that Luther was a friend who he met a dozen years earlier when visiting his father in prison. The night Cher Elder and Luther left for Central City, he said, he stayed behind with his brother Tristan. The next time he saw Luther, it was dawn the next day.

He wasn't sure, but he believed that it was the day after Cher was killed that he and his brother followed Luther into the mountains. Byron got out of the car and spied on Luther digging the grave, he said.

Luther didn't tell him at the time that he killed Cher. "But we knew he had," J.D. said. "Byron seemed to have a general idea of where Tom was going."

However, J.D. denied ever going back to Empire to retrieve Luther in May 1993. The Eerebouts still had not been told that J.D. was followed by the police that day.

J.D.'s testimony took almost two hours. He was followed by Southy Healey, who essentially told the same story that he'd told to Richardson a few hours earlier. Then it was Byron Eerebout's turn to tell his story.

When they were through, Richardson was called to the stand. For several hours, he went over the details of two years worth of investigations. Cher fought with her boyfriend. She appeared in Central City with the man in the videotape, Thomas Luther. They were seen leaving at one-thirty by Karen Knott, who saw a sober Cher Elder get in the passenger-side seat. They drove to Lookout Mountain where he believed Cher was attacked, beaten—fracturing her skull—sexually assaulted, and then executed by three bullets in nearly the identical spot. The gun was thrown in Clear Creek. Cher's body was taken to Empire, where Luther returned the next night with Southy to bury it. Sometime later he confessed the murder to Byron, who with his brother followed Luther to the grave to bury it better and put rat poison on it to discourage scavengers. He talked about the torturous process of trying to wring confessions from witnesses like Byron and Southy and of Luther's prison claim that the next girl would not survive.

Then there was nothing to do but wait for the grand jury to deliberate. It didn't take long.

The Jefferson County grand jury indicted Thomas Edward Luther on three counts of first degree murder. Each count included aggravating circumstances that carried the potential of the death penalty. In count one, the aggravating circumstance was robbery—the theft of Cher's ring. In count two, the aggravating circumstance was rape, or rather that Cher was murdered to cover up the rape. In count three, the aggravating circumstance was that the murder of Cher Elder was premeditated and deliberate.

If the prosecution team could prove any one of the three, Thomas Luther would face a second phase of the trial to determine if he deserved the death penalty. Then, if there was any justice in the world, Richardson thought as he left the courthouse that night, Luther would one day be strapped to a steel table at the Colorado State Penitentiary and given a lethal injection for what he had done to Cher Elder.

The next morning, Jefferson County District Attorney Dave Thomas held a press conference announcing that the body of Cher Elder had been found and that Thomas Luther had been indicted for her murder. "We have decided to seek the death penalty and have filed the necessary papers," he added.

In closing, Thomas praised the "dogged determination" of Lakewood detective Scott Richardson. Lakewood Police Chief Charles Johnston added that "the discovery of the body was the result of the sheer determination on the part of the detective assigned to the case . . . making it possible to bring this case to a conclusion.''

Richardson stood next to the podium, the praise barely registering. Everyone was talking like the conviction of Luther was a foregone conclusion. *This ain't over,* he thought, *not by a long shot.* But he dutifully stepped to the podium when it was his turn and said, ''The family is grateful to have recovered her body and very grateful to be able to give her the Christian burial she deserves.''

The detective paused a moment. He suddenly felt weary, not just from the thirty pounds he'd lost, but emotionally drained. Cher's death had struck him like the death of one of his own. His voice cracked when he concluded, ''In a case like this, you come to know your victim very well. Cher was more like a friend. She fell in with the wrong crowd. But the more you dig into her background, the cleaner she is. She's a true victim. So there is a feeling of victory, but a sad ending.''

Richardson thanked his fellow officers and other task force members who, he said, refused to give up, and his superiors, who gave him the time and resources. But, he added, the pursuit of Thomas Luther wasn't over. ''In some ways, it's just beginning.''

Television stations covering the press conference noted that Byron Eerebout had ''been persuaded'' to lead Lakewood detectives to a wooded area north of Empire where Cher's body was discovered. Luther, they reported, met Byron's father in prison while serving time for a 1982 sexual assault. ''In prison,'' according to the indictment read on the air, ''Luther said the next girl would not live and the police would never find her body.''

When he got back to the office, Richardson called Debrah Snider in West Virginia. She still had not moved back to Colorado. She couldn't break clean from Thomas Luther.

''You sittin' down?'' Richardson asked when she answered the telephone. ''I got some news.''

At first she didn't say anything. Then, weakly, she asked, ''Bad?''

Richardson knew what she meant; it was bad news for her and Luther if for no one else. ''We found Cher's body.''

"Well, that's good," she said, sounding relieved; at least there would be time.

"Thomas Luther has been indicted by a grand jury."

Again there was silence. Finally, Debrah said, "Okay. Where was Cher at?"

"He had her buried up by Empire, along I-70." At last he could now tell her that her information had been a help. "We've been searchin' up there for about a year and a half and we finally found the grave." He asked if she was all right.

Snider said yes. In fact, she had been expecting something of the sort. Tom told her in a letter that Skip had called him and said he was going to be charged in Colorado. "He heard it from Byron's lawyer."

"He's mostly just maintaining that we're gonna, you know, send somebody to hell for somethin' he didn't do. I don't know if he's delusional or he . . ." She let her thought trail off. "I hate to have to apologize, but I still have real strong feelings for him. I'm real sorry that this had to happen. I don't know if he's crazy, but I don't think people needed to pay for it with their lives. That's why I've been willin' to work with you."

Richardson said he understood. He didn't, not really, but he felt sorry for her. Luther had ruined a lot of lives for which he would never be charged. Debrah's was one of those lives. She had offered him a real chance to make it out of prison—a place in the country, a hard-working, faithful woman as his companion—and he had thrown it all away. To hear her so devoted still made him angry, but he wanted her to feel better.

"Well, I'm gonna tell ya somthin' right now. I couldn't have done it without ya, and you should feel good about that if nothing else. The information you gave throughout the case was critical. And without your assistance, I'll tell you right now, I don't think we would have been able to give Cher's family her body back."

Debrah was sobbing, but she managed to say, "I'm glad that justice was done for Cher. I mean, she deserved that. It's too bad though, 'cause part of him is real good. It's too bad that part has to be punished with the part of him that's horrible."

Richardson tried again to thank her. "Please," she interrupted. "Don't compliment me too much. I have real mixed feelings about this."

Chapter
Twenty-Four

March 7, 1995—Delray, West Virginia

As she told Richardson, Debrah Snider wasn't surprised by his telephone call letting her know that Tom had been charged with murder. She was only surprised at the swiftness with which justice now seemed to be moving after two years at a snail's pace.

In a way, it was a relief. Her relationship with Tom since his rape conviction was like riding on a manic rollercoaster that wouldn't stop. One moment, she was the most important person in his world. The next, she was a black-hearted traitor. She suspected he was still getting visits from Pam, while keeping her on the hook, fearful of what she might say about the Cher Elder case and afraid of being left alone.

Some of his letters were written in pure anger, especially when he was getting ready to punish her for some remark. She often wondered who his words were really intended to reach.

He had stopped writing for a couple of weeks in February, and removed her from his visiting list. Then he wrote but only, he said, because he had received a letter from Debrah's mother, who'd heard about him threatening her daughter with an "ass-kicking" when he got out of prison. He reminded her that he loved her.

The letter Snider received the day before Luther's indictment was bitter. He was sure she had been talking to the cops. He was cutting her off, she'd betrayed him for the last time. It tore her heart out. She hardly heard Richardson when he called and asked if she was sitting down. There was a roaring in her ears and a veil before her eyes. She felt as if she were standing on the edge of an abyss and found herself wanting very much to fall into it.

She was happy he found Cher's body. She wanted it for the family. And she wanted it for Richardson, who she realized was the knight in shining armor she had waited for all her life. But he hadn't come to rescue her, he'd come to defeat a monster who happened to be the man she loved.

Once before, when Luther was still in the Colorado penitentiary what seemed ages ago, she had warned him that "your relationship with me will be different than with any other woman from your past." That certainly turned out to be true.

She wondered sometimes why he hadn't killed her when he had the chance. The public defender once warned him that she was the major threat to his freedom. He could have killed her at Horsetooth Reservoir, and she had sensed he wanted to. Then again, he told her once that before he hurt her, "I will shut down and go away first."

Tom had done wrong, and she had stopped him, but she felt ashamed for betraying him to his enemy.

"Please," she told Richardson. "Don't compliment me too much. I have real mixed feelings about this." She hung up the telephone, understanding vaguely that Richardson would be coming soon to West Virginia. Then the room began to spin as she fell into blackness.

The little girl forced herself to remain still in her bed. Otherwise, he, the thing that waited somewhere in the dark of her room, might pounce.

She took all the usual precautions before climbing under the covers that evening: she made doubly sure to close her closet doors and then removed any items from the backs of chairs, as well as the floor, that might later cast a shadow. Now she lay in the exact middle of her mattress, beyond the reach of any clawing hands that might come from under the bed, and curled up so that her toes would not hang over the edge.

Seven years old, Heather Smith was afraid of monsters that hid in the dark—no matter how many times her mother told her that there were no such things. Saying didn't make it so. He was there that night. She knew it. She could almost hear him breathing. The only question was whether to scream for her mother or stay quiet. There was always the possibility that if she screamed he would get her before her mother could come to the rescue. She took a chance. "Mommy! Mommy!"

As always, her mother arrived in time to turn on the lights and keep the monster at bay. "Shhhh, Heather," Mrs. Smith said softly, stroking her whimpering daughter's auburn hair. "There's no such thing as monsters."

She was wrong. Twenty-two years later, waking from the dream, Heather Smith knew it. There were monsters, and the one who hurt her was still out there somewhere.

Heather lay awake, envying her friend, Rebecca. She, at least, seemed to be moving on with her life, even though she knew it had taken what amounted to a nervous breakdown.

A little more than a year after the attack, Rebecca Hascall had been driving home late one night when she'd looked down and seen that her blouse was bright red with blood. "In my mind," she later told Heather, "I knew it wasn't real and when I looked down again, the blood was gone."

Still, she was shaken. Pulling up in front of her house, she was too terrified to get out of the car. Monsters hid in the dark shadows and bushes around her home. She sat in her car and cried for an hour before she worked up the courage to make a mad dash for her front door. Inside, she checked to make sure her gun was tucked safely beneath her pillow, and then cried herself to sleep.

"The next day, on the way to work, the same thing happened," Hascall said. "I looked down and my chest was covered with blood. I thought, 'I'm cracking up.' "

Fortunately, the two young women were attending counseling sessions at the Denver Victims Assistance Service Center. At Smith's urging, Hascall related her experiences to the counselor, who explained that she was also a victim of the violence against her friend.

"Hallucinations are all part of post-traumatic stress syndrome," the counselor said. "You may be suppressing something that needs to come out for you to heal."

The counselor persuaded Rebecca to undergo hypnosis to see if she could recall something about that night which lay hidden in her mind. Under hypnosis, Rebecca remembered the man crouching in the street, looking at her. "I was afraid," she said, "but my friend needed me." She recalled dialing 911 and then rushing back to Heather's side with a towel to place on the wounds.

Then Hascall stopped talking. Her memory had run into a wall. Gently, the counselor asked her to look behind that wall.

Only then did she remember the paramedics rolling Heather over onto her back and the sight of Heather's bloody chest. She had blocked it out.

"I was holding all the wrong places," Rebecca cried. "I thought I had killed her." She was living with the guilt that she'd almost let her friend die.

Waking Rebecca, the counselor told the young woman that the first thing she had to do was forgive herself. She had done the best she could, and it had been the right thing. "Heather survived because of you, not despite you," the counselor said.

It was a major breakthrough. Rebecca Hascall wasn't healed overnight, but from that day, she felt herself getting stronger. She even got rid of the gun; however, she replaced it with an electronic security system. Some things would never be the same.

But there were no such breakthroughs for Heather Smith. Physically, she was much better except for a nagging pain in her neck, which her doctor told her was in her imagination.

On good days, she felt emotionally strong, more like her old self. She would make an effort to see old friends or force herself to wear clothing that revealed the scar on her chest. When people asked about it, she told them her story. Talking helped.

Wanting to do something that made a statement to her attacker, whoever he was, Smith started working as a blood-drive coordinator at the Denver blood center that had supplied the eighty-seven units of blood that kept her alive. Once a week, she volunteered at the Denver Victims Assistance Service Center, talking other women through their pain and suffering.

It was a brave front and friends and family marveled at her strength. But she couldn't fool herself. No place seemed safe, even in daylight. Some days she cowered in her house, afraid to go out. But nights were worse. Her old house creaked and rattled with the slightest breeze. She particularly hated winter with its short days and long nights.

She was afraid of men she didn't know. She would cross a street to avoid passing a stranger on a sidewalk. She finally started seeing a man and began to hope for a future, but some nights she'd wake up next to him, terrified that he was about to wake and attack her.

At times, her fears reduced her to tears and hysteria and she'd curl up into a ball unable to stop sobbing. Once, her boyfriend, trying to console her, stroked her back, but when his fingers touched the scars on her side, she suddenly recalled the pain of the weapon that had pierced her. His fingers felt like knives and she screamed.

Adding insult to injury, her insurance company was fighting her medical and psychiatric counseling bills. They put her through a three-hour interrogation in which the insurance company investigator, a woman who should have known better, implied that it was Heather who had done something wrong.

Maybe she knew her attacker, the woman suggested, and didn't want to admit it. Maybe it was her old boyfriend and this was just another domestic violence case. It seemed to Smith that she was being victimized over and over again.

Listening for monsters in the dark of her room that night, she wondered if the terror would ever end. It was March 1995 and if anything, the dreams were getting worse. She fell back asleep and dreamed again.

She was at a party with her dog, Heidi. The dog began barking and wanted Heather to leave. There was a feeling of unseen danger.

Then she was outside, walking down a sidewalk next to a retaining wall. It was dark, but she could see the man who stabbed her standing behind the wall. He was wearing the green jacket, the square, silver wire-rimmed glasses, and the blue baseball cap with the gold lettering. She saw his face vividly. At first his face seemed normal, then she realized it was a just a mask hiding something evil that lurked underneath.

The man made no move. In her dream she told herself that if she could just get by him, she'd be okay. He seemed to let her pass. But as she began to believe that she was safe, she looked down. Her chest was covered with blood.

Smith woke up from the dream in terror, the memory of the man's face burning in her mind. She knew it was a face she would never forget, no matter how many years went by, no matter how he tried to disguise himself.

The day after Thomas Edward Luther was indicted for the

murder of Cher Elder, the *Denver Post* ran a front-page newspaper article under the headline: "Dogged work, nets body, key suspect.

"Nearly two years after a young Lakewood woman disappeared, her body has been unearthed from a shallow mountain grave, and the man with whom she was last seen has been indicted for her murder."

"Elder's grief-stricken mother said yesterday, 'I'm glad the search is over. Even though it may not be what you wanted to find, at least you can start dealing with something. You can't start a grieving process until you know for sure.' "

The story jumped to an inside page where there was also a photograph of Luther taken after his arrest in West Virginia. In it, he had a few days' beard growth and was wearing square-rimmed, tortoise-shell glasses.

That afternoon, Heather Smith had just walked into her psychiatrist's office when the doctor handed her the newspaper. "Did you see this?" Reading the story earlier, the psychiatrist noted the date of Cher's disappearance and wondered if there could be a connection to the attack on Heather two weeks later.

Smith sighed. People were always handing her newspaper clippings, asking her if she had seen the news about the latest violent attack on a woman. She had grown tired of such stories.

Heather Smith followed the story of Thomas Luther to the inside page of the newspaper. She knew the moment she saw the photograph that she'd found her monster. She felt blood rush to her face and for a moment was nearly overcome with dizziness. "It's him," she said quietly. "It's him."

The day the newspapers ran the story about the indictment, Scott Richardson got a call from a young woman who identified herself as Heather Smith. She told him she'd been stabbed and left for dead two weeks after Cher Elder disappeared. She thought Luther was her attacker. "As soon as I saw his picture in the paper, I said, 'That's him,' " she recalled.

Heather Smith sounded desperate. But the detective knew he couldn't afford to associate himself with another case involving Luther; defense attorneys would jump all over that. He advised her to contact the detective in her case, then he called the Denver police and told them about the call.

Richardson didn't doubt the possibility that Smith was yet another victim of Luther. He recalled Snider's statements about how Luther would leave for days at a time, and then come home looking beat-up and sleep for an entire day.

"I bet that's why he begged me not to put his picture in the paper or on television way back when I first talked to him," Richardson told Connally. "He didn't want any of his other victims identifyin' him."

Smith apparently followed his advice. The next day, Detective Paul Scott from the Denver Police Department called and told him about Heather's case and requested photographs of Luther.

Scott said that after Heather called, he'd taken a look at the photograph in the newspaper. It was almost two years since he had last seen her file, a copy of which he kept in his desk. But when he opened the file and looked at the composite drawing of her attacker, "I was shocked," he told Richardson. "It was like our artist sat down and drew the composite with Luther sitting in the room with him."

Still, Paul Scott was not satisfied and wanted to see if Heather could pick out a different picture of Luther from a photo lineup. Richardson sent a photograph of Luther in which he was clean shaven and wasn't wearing glasses.

It didn't make any difference. "The average guy on the streets wouldn't have looked at the two photographs and thought they were of the same man," Scott said. But when Heather Smith came down to the police station and looked at a photo line-up of a dozen similar-looking men, she didn't hesitate for a moment and picked Luther out from the others. "She said, 'It's him.' "

Richardson wished him luck, said he'd help anyway he could, and hung up. He was concerned about a message he got from Debrah Snider. Babe, she said, was warning her that Byron believed that she was "in grave danger."

There was a lot riding on Snider's safety. Without her binding the seams, the case would fall apart like an old book. He had discussed with Dennis Hall on more than one occasion his concerns about her safety. "I wonder why Luther didn't kill her when he had the chance."

He got off the telephone with Debrah Snider and called the

West Virginia State Police, asking them to bump up patrols around her place and be on the look out for strangers in the area. Burkhart assured him they would.

The West Virginia prison authorities were having their own problems with Luther, he said. They had just received information from an informant that Luther was planning a prison escape, when a semi- truck crashed through an outer fence while Luther was in the prison yard exercising.

Fortunately, it had rained the night before, and the truck got mired in the mud and fencing, never making it through a second perimeter fence. The inmates, including Luther, were hustled inside, and the driver, who claimed he was drunk and that the truck "got away from me," was arrested. It turned out he stole the truck, but they couldn't prove a connection to Luther.

Still, Luther was deemed a security risk and placed in maximum security. The informant's warning, as well as information provided by Debrah Snider that Luther had told her to save her money and be ready to run to Australia, made the truck accident too convenient to have been a coincidence.

Trooper Phillips told Richardson that Luther had buddied up with an inmate named Randy McBee, who was in prison for a violent crime spree that included raping an 80-year-old woman and twenty other felonies.

"McBee hasn't even been tried on all the charges and he's already got three-hundred twenty-one years," Phillips said. "He's a real bad one. When they asked him about the old lady, he just laughed and said, 'Best pussy I ever had.' Guess those two have a lot in common and nothing to lose by tryin' to escape."

Byron Eerebout was steamed. He thought the deal was that his name wouldn't be mentioned in Luther's indictment. Now he was getting threats in the jail, he said.

"I have no control over public records," Richardson shrugged. No one actually named Eerebout at the press conference, but the media had done its homework and obtained copies of the indictment.

"If you would've told me this, I would have been back up at Buena and none of this would be goin' on," Byron said.

Babe Rivinius jumped in. "We could have all been killed. There was no warning this would happen. Something should have been arranged with the grand jury to keep his name out of the indictment."

Richardson waved her off. "I'm not gonna sit here and argue this." He was tired of the Eerebouts' whining, and a lot of other things were taking his attention since the press conference. He was about to say so when Hall suddenly raised his voice, his blue eyes blazing at Byron and Babe.

"What I'd like you all to do is just be quiet," Hall said. Babe Rivinius started to protest, but his look shut her up.

Satisfied that he had everyone's attention, Hall continued. "I'm gonna tell you why it came out this way. You need to understand that I am the person in this county who knows the grand jury. Okay? I have written a lot of indictments. I have probably written more indictments than about anybody in this whole entire state system. I know how to do it.

"This case presented a very, very difficult problem because an indictment has to explain how a crime was committed. Usually all I do when I write an indictment is to explain that and say this person did this, this, this, and this. This is a crime, and then I sign it. Okay?" He looked around and everybody nodded.

"So the question comes up: what happens when somebody lies to the grand jury? That makes it almost impossible for me to write a decent indictment. And—" here he looked hard at Eerebout and his mother "—I think Byron lied. And I think J.D. lied."

Leslie Hansen began to defend her client, "Well . . ."

But Hall turned on her in a flash; the anger on his face surprised even Richardson. "Shut up," Hall spat out. "Just wait 'til I finish." Hansen slumped back into her seat, her mouth hanging open.

"How can I keep a person's name out of it when I think the person lied?" Hall asked, then explained, "Instead of saying what happened, I have to say what people testified to. You put me in an impossible position, Byron, and your brother did, too."

Hall was seething. He didn't believe the Eerebouts' story about following Luther. But that didn't matter as much as J.D. lying to the grand jury about picking Luther up in Empire.

"I am in a jam because I presented perjured testimony to the grand jury,'' he said. "I'm going to take a little time and figure out what I'm going to do about that. In the meantime, I suggest you stop complaining and start listening.'' With that, he handed the meeting back to Richardson.

The detective smiled. The outburst was out of character, but the more he got to know Hall, the more he liked him. He turned to Byron, who sat in stunned silence. *For once, I get to play good cop,* he thought, and offered a conciliatory gesture.

"Ah, it's my understanding that you were told to keep quiet, you would be all right as long as you kept quiet,'' he said. "And that if you did testify or presented the body, you would be killed. Let's get this on the table so we know who we are dealing with so we can protect you. Go back to the beginning of when Cher was killed.''

Eerebout tore his eyes from Hall and nodded. "Just like I said for the grand jury, the first was from Tom, when I confronted him after hearing him on the telephone,'' he said. "That was maybe a couple of weeks after Cher disappeared. He told me point blank right then and there. He said, 'I'll kill your girlfriend. I'll kill her mom. Don't say anything or they get hurt.' He knew where they lived; he followed them around.''

"Okay,'' Richardson said. "And when he gave you the sweater, what were the threats?''

"Just that he cut off her finger,'' Byron replied. "And he said he had that ring. He says, 'I have the stuff to make sure that you guys pay for this.' The 'pee-ons will pay' is what his exact words were. And who's the pee-ons in this? We are. He said to other people that him and Southy would make sure that the pee-ons pay.''

Eerebout said that after he was arrested for the shooting incident, he was approached by Mongo, who said that if he kept his mouth shut Mongo's father owned a lot of land in Montana, some of which would be given to Byron, along with a house, a car, and a thousand dollars a month. "Everything would be taken care of, but if I did open my mouth, I would be killed.''

Then when he was sent to prison in Buena Vista, several inmates approached him, telling him they were friends of Luther and he knew what that meant. Once an "Indian guy'' sidled up to him and said he'd overheard the other inmates talking about

Byron. "He said I better watch my back. That's when I got myself placed in protective custody."

"Skip called me last night," Rivinius interjected, "and said Byron was not in danger from Luther personally, but someone else might get to him. He said, 'He'll never make it out of there. He'll either be shanked or he'll be beaten to death. Some way or somehow, they will get to him.' And I said, 'Are you talking about Tom?' And he said, 'Byron . . . Byron has been labeled a snitch.'

"Skip told me, 'This is all you and that bitch in West Virginia's fault.' "

Eerebout stuck to his story that the gun Luther used to kill Cher Elder was stolen from a convenience store by a friend of his brother, J.D. The friend, whose name he couldn't recall, then sold it to Luther. The gun, he said, was in a woman's purse, left in a storage closet next to the bathroom. The boy didn't know a gun was in the purse when he took it. "I guess you'd call it a lucky find."

"Did J.D. ever give you a map on how to find the body?" Richardson asked.

"No, I got strip-searched every time I went back to my cell, so I couldn't have unless I stuck it up my ass, which I was not about to do."

"How about over the telephone?" Richardson asked. He didn't believe Eerebout could have been told so exactly over the telephone. There wasn't even a pile of rocks at the grave to help him identify it. But he had to ask.

"Nope," Byron replied. "We talked a little to refresh my memory, but that was it."

"Luther ever talk to you about other cases, unsolved homicides or attempted homicides?" Richardson asked. He was thinking about the Heather Smith case and so was surprised by Byron's answer.

"That isn't part of the deal," Eerebout said. "I will not discuss that with you. But I'll give you the inclination it was something that's up in Breckenridge."

As she left the meeting, Babe Rivinius told Richardson that her son, J.D., would "clear up certain issues" that afternoon.

Soon afterward, Dennis Hall was contacted by J.D.'s attorney, who wanted a meeting as soon as possible. J.D. lied about not bringing Luther back from Empire, the attorney admitted. And he had some new information about the gun.

Hall contacted Richardson and the two soon found themselves talking to a sheepish J.D. Eerebout. He began by repeating that after Luther left with Cher, he didn't see Luther again until the following morning.

"When he come in, he had this look on his face that I've never seen on anyone's face before," Eerebout said. "Kind of a real wide-eyed, like 'I been up all night on adrenaline' kind of look. He had on the same clothes he had been wearing the day before."

Some time later—now J.D. thought it might have been some time after Cher's disappearance—Luther showed up one evening and, after talking quietly to Byron, left. Byron immediately turned to him and said, "Let's go for a ride."

"I think we both knew what was going on," Eerebout said. "I assumed that Byron wanted to get somethin' on Tom. I thought it was a good idea." So they followed Luther to Empire. "That's the first time I had any clue as to where she might be. Byron got out, did his thing, and we went home."

J.D. admitted that he took Luther to Empire and dropped him off that May. On the way there, they stopped in a store off Interstate 70 and purchased a box of rat poison, he said. "I assumed this was to cover her up so dogs couldn't smell her."

"What about the gun?" Richardson asked.

Eerebout swallowed hard. The gun was stolen from a clerk's purse at a convenience store located in Evergreen, a small town in the mountains just west of Denver. "My younger brother, Tristan, went in there and took a lady's purse.

"He brought it out to the car and there was a gun in it. It was a .22, a little nine-shooter or something. We went home with the gun, and Tom was at the house, and we didn't have anything to do with the gun, so Tom just took it."

Richardson wanted to know when the theft took place. "No more than a week or so before Cher got killed," J.D. replied.

"Where's the gun now?" Richardson asked.

"I have no idea."

"Were there any bullets in it?"

"Yes. Little .22's. They weren't hollowpoints."

Richardson nodded, the bullet fragments taken from Elder's skull weren't hollowpoints either. "You ever heard of Cher Elder bein' a snitch or threatenin' to testify?"

"No." Nor did Luther give him any real information about the murder, he said.

"I don't think that I flat-out ever asked him, but I think he knew that I thought I knew. When we were goin' back up there, he said somethin' about he had to do a better job burying her and that the rat poison was to keep dogs or other animals from diggin' her up."

"There's no doubt he's talkin' about Cher Elder?" Richardson asked.

"No doubt."

"Who dumped Cher's car?"

"I assume Tom did it that morning," Eerebout said. He was sure that Southy did not come to the apartment that morning.

Which, Richardson thought, *is why Luther didn't dump the car farther from the apartment.* Noting that he had just talked to Byron and his attorney, he pretended that something was said about a map to the grave.

J.D. took the bait. "I'll tell you exactly what's goin' on with that," he said. "I did not supply him with a map. Now on the phone we went over kinda . . . You see, when all this came out we wanted to make sure we had our stories straight because he told me he was gonna plan on doin' this. So on the phone, we kind of, you know, went back and forth.

"We were reminiscing, you know what I'm sayin', trying to get it down straight. I know what you're talkin' about on that map because he mentioned something about drawin' it out, but that never happened because he took you guys up there and, I guess, you found it right away."

Richardson told Eerebout that the conversations between him and his brother had been recorded. "So you better be tellin' the truth or we'll know," he said. "Why did Byron say he needed your help to find the body?"

J.D. shrugged. "Maybe that's why he was askin' me on the phone because he didn't really remember where we went. But I can't believe he wouldn't remember 'cause we went up there specifically to find out so we'd have somethin' on Tom."

"Then why does it take you to describe exactly where the grave is to your own brother if he's been there?" Richardson asked.

Eerebout's face was the picture of concentration. "I'm tryin' to think of what you guys would have heard us say that would lead you to believe this," he said.

"Don't worry about what I know," Richardson said. "You just worry about the truth and my questions."

"Well, when we drove up there together it was the middle of the night," J.D. said. "But when I went up there again, it was daylight. So I went there three times and Byron only once."

During that second trip, Luther seemed to be going over what he needed to do. He needed to get rat poison. He got rid of the gun. "He threw it in the river or something," J.D. said. But Luther never said where he killed her, how he killed her, or why.

"I heard somethin' about that she was raped," Eerebout said. "So my instant assumption was that they went up there, got drunk, and it was a rape thing."

"Have you been threatened by your dad not to talk?" Richardson asked.

J.D. scowled. "Of course not," he said. "I'm very, very close with my dad."

In fact, he said he still had a hard time believing Luther had killed Cher. "It's kind of like, you know, let's say your friend went out and did some heinous thing. He comes back and, you know, you can't believe what's happened but what are you gonna do? You gonna have your friend go burn for it? Or are you just gonna try and stay away from it?"

Now there's a convict's kid talking, Richardson said. "Have you been threatened at all?"

"I haven't really been flat-out threatened. But I've been told many a time what happens to snitches, let's put it that way."

"By who?" asked the detective.

"By Luther."

"Since this homicide or before this homicide?"

"Before, since. A snitch is a snitch. They're the lowest on the bracket."

"Did you ever feel that he might be talkin' about you because you knew about the homicide?"

"Kind of, yeah," Eerebout said. "He never flat out threatened me. But when he'd say things, I'd catch them and he knew I would."

"Did Luther ever talk about what he was going to do if the body was found?"

"No," J.D. replied. "He knew that it was just me, Byron, and him that knew generally where it was unless he told Southy. I've heard a rumor that he called Southy to do somethin.' Maybe he called him to move the body."

"When you followed Luther up to the mountains, did Byron tell you where you were goin'?"

"He kind of directed me a little," Eerebout acknowledged. "I'm assumin' that Tom told him that he was goin' somewhere. I assumed that Byron didn't know exactly, but he knew generally.

"So I assumed Tom maybe said, 'Well, I'm goin' for a ride up to Winter Park.' Because Byron said, 'We're goin' to Winter Park.' So that's where I get my assumption. And then Tom's car was parked right on the side of the road."

"Did he ever mention Cher threatening to snitch on you?" Richardson asked.

"No," J.D. said, then thought for a moment and changed his mind. "It does seems like there was a time he was tryin' to justify what he done, when I asked him what could have possibly brought that on, and he said, 'Yeah, well she was gonna snitch you guys off.' My reaction was, 'That's a little extreme.' So I think it was just a bullshit excuse, and now I've heard that she was raped, I think it was just that."

Cher, he said, would not have willingly had sex with Luther. "She was a total flat-out sweetheart. She never did anything wrong or anything to bother me or Byron. Just that one night she was mad about Gina and took off with Tom.

"And that was a mistake right there."

Chapter
Twenty-Five

March 13, 1995—Lakewood, Colorado

In the two years he'd spent investigating the disappearance of Cher Elder, there had been days when Scott Richardson doubted he would ever be able to make enough connections to get a conviction. Then there were days like March 13, when all the pieces seemed drawn together by some invisible force, like iron shavings to a magnet.

It started in the morning. The Jefferson County Records Division called to say they had a reported theft of a .22 Baretta handgun from a convenience store in Evergreen on March 23, 1993, four days before Elder disappeared. The records clerk gave him the victim's name and the serial number of the gun.

An hour later, he was contacted by Trooper Phillips of the West Virginia State Police. Mark Dabbs, an inmate currently in the Federal Correctional Facility in Maryland but who had been housed with Luther in West Virginia, was saying that Luther was telling other inmates he killed a girl in Colorado and buried her body.

Then Richardson had no sooner hung up with Phillips when Debrah Snider called. Luther, she said, wrote her recently and that "not surprisingly" he was now blaming J.D., Byron, and Southy for Cher's murder. She read him the letter.

"I hope Skip hasn't turned on me. He tells me it's you and Babe and Southy that has brought this all on. He knows I'll go to the gas chamber with my mouth closed."

Luther was curious about the deal Byron got. He reminded Snider not to interfere with what was happening.

Luther wrote that he would now allow her to visit, Debrah said. "I went and the lies have gotten really interesting. Suppos-

edly, either Byron or Southy shot Cher and, of course, each is
blaming the other, he says. And supposedly J.D. and his friends
went up there and dug her up and played with the body and cut
that finger off to get the ring. He says he's innocent.''

"Of course, he tells you this knowing that you're going to
tell me," Richardson noted.

Debrah agreed. "Another interesting thing is that he said the
reason they took off her clothes is because that's how the police
determine when somebody got killed. People say the last time
they saw this person they were wearing this or that. Supposedly,
Byron and Southy took her clothes off so that couldn't happen.
I think those are pretty interesting statements from somebody
who's innocent. But he says he's 'educating' me.''

"What do you think?" Richardson asked.

"I don't know," Debrah hedged. "I have no doubt that there
was an execution."

The day ended with a meeting at the Lakewood Police Depart-
ment among himself and Connally, Detective Scott of the Denver
Police, and Detective Eaton of the Summit County Sheriff's
Office.

Richardson related what he could of his case against Luther
and then sat back and listened to the others. Their information
could be vital if the judge allowed Dennis Hall to introduce
similar transactions.

Back in November, Richardson let Sheriff Morales and Eaton
know that Luther was in prison in West Virginia for rape. They
all hoped that Byron Eerebout might know something about the
Summit County killings, but he had since refused to discuss
anything beyond Elder's murder. Now, with Luther in jail, Byron
might talk.

At the meeting, Eaton reported the progress he'd made tracking
down old leads. There was "Dillon" John Martin, who told
deputies in 1973 that Luther bragged about dumping bodies.
And Troy Browning, who was living under another name in a
different state because he still feared Luther after informing the
police of his trying to arrange Mary Brown's murder. Browning
claimed that Luther had also talked about other killings, one in
which he used a nylon cord to bind a girl's wrists.

Ronald Montoya, who Luther befriended in jail, recalled

Luther talking about killing two girls, Eaton said. He'd also tried to have three other people—Mary Brown, Sue Potter, and John Martin—murdered to prevent them from being witnesses against him.

"He said he picked the one girl up and tried to rape her, but he couldn't get it up, so he used the hammer," Montoya had told him. "He said he was going to kill her by shooting her when she got out of the truck, but there were houses nearby, and he was afraid the shot would be heard."

Eaton said he'd learned that the detective who showed the pharmacy clerk the dark photocopy of Sue Potter's driver's license never bothered to return with a better photograph. Now, the clerk's recollection was fuzzy. "Could be," she had said. "Maybe. It's been so long."

He also located the ballistics test on Wagner's gun. It wasn't the murder weapon used on Oberholtzer and Schnee, but several of Luther's former jailmates recalled Luther bragging about the guns he'd owned. Eaton said he still needed to find John Martin and Sue Potter.

Detective Scott went next. He recounted the attack on Heather Smith, her amazing recovery, and subsequent identification of Luther.

"Until she saw that photograph, we were at a dead end," he said. "We looked at her old boyfriend, who we suspected hired somebody to go after her. But he had an alibi and we were never able to make a connection."

Richardson perked up when Scott said the former boyfriend once lived in Fort Collins and still had connections there, and also frequented several bars in the Lakewood area known to be hangouts of the Eerebout brothers and their associates. "Maybe he and Luther got together," he suggested.

The detectives believed that so far, Luther had attacked at least seven women, four of whom were dead. There were five in Colorado—Bobby Jo Oberholtzer, Annette Schnee, Mary Brown, Cher Elder, and Heather Smith. Bobby Jo Jones in West Virginia. And the blond hitchhiker in Pennsylvania, who still had not been identified.

And those were just the ones they knew about.

* * *

The car with the dark-tinted windshield drove slowly down the Grand Junction street toward Rhonda Edwards, who sank in fear against the wall of a building. It was a bright, sunny day with many people out and about, and still she felt trapped and frightened.

She knew it was silly. Thomas Luther was in jail in West Virginia and he'd remain there, Scott Richardson had assured her, "until I go get him."

Rhonda was slowly learning the details of her daughter's death, and they were eerily similar to the nightmare she had in October 1993. Edwards shuddered, convinced that the dream had been a message from her daughter.

Finding Cher's body was an immense relief, but it brought new difficulties. Richardson had asked them to keep it secret until after Luther was indicted, which meant that for nearly two weeks they couldn't share their grief with other family members or friends. So she had busied herself planning Cher's funeral.

She knew her daughter would have liked the view of the high red cliffs of the nearby Colorado National Monument and the tall cottonwood trees that bordered the Colorado River that wound past the cemetery. She picked a bronze casket and a pink granite headstone, on which she had Van's suggestion inscribed: "Until we meet again." She sent Cher's high school gown and favorite teddy bear to the funeral home to be placed with her remains.

The funeral director called asking who would be Cher's pall-bearers. Rhonda Edwards found herself at a loss. She wasn't sure what relatives were going to be able to make it on short notice. There was Van, of course, and Van's brother, and Cher's half-brother, Jacob. But she needed four.

Suddenly, Scott Richardson's face popped into her mind. Over the past two years, he had become family. As worn out by the case as she knew he was, he always found time to talk to her, or simply listen as she poured her heart out in the bleak days before he found Cher. He had saved her when she thought she couldn't hold on any more.

Once, during one of their late-night conversations, Richardson confided that he knew Cher so well, it was like investigating the murder of one of his own children. "You know my daughter better than I do," she'd replied. "You're the brother I never had."

Now, she wondered what he'd say if she asked him to do one more thing for Cher. She called. "I know I have no right to ask this, and please don't feel obligated, it's a long ways and you've already done so much, but would you consider being one of Cher's pallbearers?"

There was silence from the other end of the line, and she feared that she'd overstepped the bounds. Then Richardson, his Texas drawl softer than any other time she'd ever heard him, said, "I was going to ask if you'd mind if I just attended the funeral."

After another long pause, his voice was hardly more than a whisper. "You just made me very, very happy."

They laid Cher Elder to rest on March 24, 1995. It was a gorgeous Colorado spring day. The sky was turquoise with only a few high, cottonball-white clouds drifting like sheep across a blue pasture. The first green buds were appearing on the branches of the cottonwoods down by the river, which was swift and swollen with melting snow.

After the ceremony, Scott Richardson went back to Rhonda's house for the wake. He was the hero, but he couldn't get past the sadness and the tears to feel much cheered by the heartfelt compliments of Cher's friends and relatives. They treated him like he walked on water, but all he could think of was what lay ahead. *If I don't convict this guy and he walks, I'll never be able to look these people in the eyes again,* he thought. *It ain't over, not by a long shot.*

Later, he drove back to Denver, slowing down when he reached the exit for Empire. He didn't turn to go to the grave, but he looked up the narrow Clear Creek valley and wondered where Cher's spirit lingered. The little clearing in the woods or the cemetery by the Colorado River. He continued on to Lakewood. He still had a job to do and that was make Luther pay for her murder.

* * *

The train of Richardson's investigation kept picking up speed. The day before the funeral, Tristan Eerebout was arrested for outstanding traffic violations and Richardson, who had been unable to find the boy, was notified.

The detective went to see the teenager at the jail. "Let me explain something," Richardson said. "I'm not going to read your rights and that's because it should give you some comfort. 'Cause if I don't read you your rights, then I can't use anything you tell me against you anyway, okay?"

"That's cool," Tristan said. "I'll answer whatever you ask me."

"I think you agree that Cher Elder did not deserve to be killed?" Richardson began.

Eerebout nodded emphatically. "Cher Elder was the coolest lady I've ever met. She was a really cool chick."

At Richardson's prodding, the boy recounted how he stole the .22 Baretta and then, "maybe a day or two later," asked Luther to take it off his hands. Other than that, he said, he tried to stay out of it.

"It was none of my business," he said. "She was a good lady, and as far as I'm concerned, whatever Tom did, he did and it's a fucking shame."

Richardson nodded. "Well, we share that."

Tristan said he had never been threatened by Luther. Nor had any member of his family told him not to talk. In fact, he said, they encouraged him to tell the truth.

"You didn't think this information about giving the gun to Luther was important when we talked to you two years ago, considering Cher was missing and presumed killed?" Richardson asked.

Eerebout shrugged. "I didn't know she was missing at the time you talked to me. I really didn't think it was important. I didn't even think about it 'cause Thomas was always such a nice man. I'm glad you found her body simply for the fact that I was good friends with her little sister. It's a fucking shame that she had to go through what she did and her parents, and I'm glad they get to put Cher to rest. As for the events of what happened, why she was killed, I never even wanted to know about it.''

"What's your feeling of Thomas Luther now?" Richardson asked.

"I still like him a lot," the teenager admitted. "It's kind of hard for me to believe that he could have did something like this. But after everything that I've read, and your coming to question me, I don't know, I guess in a way I kind of hate him. What he did, I think is disgusting.''

"What about testifying?" Richardson asked.

Eerebout laughed. "I don't want to get involved in this case.''

Richardson looked hard at the boy; these Eerebouts were something else, always looking out for themselves. "Well, that's something else we share," he said. "I didn't want to get involved in this case either. I didn't pick this case. This case picked me.

"But you're kind of like me, we are involved. You are directly involved in it because of your specific knowledge about this gun from 7-Eleven. It is our feeling, and it will ultimately be proven, that the gun you stole from 7-Eleven is the gun Luther used to kill Cher. Every case is like a pie; there's a lot of witnesses that get involved in the cases, and they all have just a little piece of the pie. They can't do the whole case by themselves. Everybody has a little itty bitty piece of it.''

Tristan nodded. "I'll give you my little itty bitty piece.''

Every day, there seemed to be some new "itty bitty piece.'' Cher's best friend, Karen Knott, remembered seeing her wearing Byron's ring the night she disappeared. Mortho Brazell was now denying again that Luther gave him a man's ring. But Southy, Byron, Debrah, and now Karen remembered it.

Southy Healey took Richardson to the highway outside of Empire where he said Luther had thrown his clothes into the creek. But nothing was recovered from the subsequent search; it had been two years and two spring runoffs. The investigators hadn't turned up any of Elder's clothes, either, or her purse and its contents. But Richardson had an idea of what had happened to at least some of her personal effects.

On a hunch, he contacted a company that pumped the outdoor toilets for the forest service. An employee there remembered that in the spring of 1993, he was pumping the toilet at the Clear Creek Campground near Empire when he saw a bra and panties in the sludge. But those items, and whatever may have been with them, had long ago gone to a landfill, he said.

Richardson located the woman who had reported her gun stolen. Ann Parson said her ex-husband had given it to her. The theft had occurred just as the Eerebout boys had described.

Having the serial number of the gun and placing it in Luther's hands was vital information. They might never recover the weapon, but John O'Neil, an agent with the Bureau of Alcohol, Tobacco and Firearms, had told Richardson that the ATF could try to find the guns made just before and after Parson's gun.

"I just testified in a case where the murder weapon couldn't be found," O'Neil said. "So we did ballistics tests on the prior gun manufactured. The ballistics between that gun and the bullet recovered from the victim were nearly identical."

Even if they never located either gun, knowing the make and model could be critical to the prosecution case. Every gun manufacturer uses a slightly, and sometimes more than slightly, different rifling—called lands and grooves—in its barrels to put a spin on the bullet. The marks on the bullet fragments taken from Cher might rule out some models and narrow it down to others.

The next day, Richardson got a panicky call from Babe Rivinius. J.D. had been arrested for burglary and was in the Jefferson County Jail with his brother, Byron. But that wasn't what was worrying her.

Rivinius said when she went to visit her sons at the jail, she noticed a group of their friends standing outside the building. As she approached the other young men, she heard a loud banging from above.

Looking up, she saw inmates hitting the windows, trying to get the attention of her boys' friends. Then one held up a sign that read, "Tristan Byron J.D. KILL!"

Two years to the day that Cher Elder disappeared, there was a memorial service in a Golden church for those who had been unable to attend her burial the week before in Grand Junction. A photograph of Cher, a copy of which hung on Richardson's office wall, leaned against the altar. The steps and floors leading to the altar were covered with dozens of white roses.

When everyone was seated, Earl Elder walked up to the altar, turned, and faced the crowd with tears streaming down his face. He expressed his gratitude to the Lakewood Police Department, "especially Scott Richardson."

"Cher was our daughter, our sister, our granddaughter, and our friend. She will always have a very special place in all of our hearts," he said.

"Cher, all of us who were part of your life, miss you so very much. We are heartsick that we will no longer be able to hug you, or kiss you, or laugh with you, or cry with you, or just spend a moment with you.

"My darling daughter, we love and miss you—a piece of all of us left with you. We pray you are at the foot of God's throne and that one day we will rejoice when we meet again."

As Earl stooped to pick up several roses to distribute to family members, Richardson walked to the altar and began to speak as the family had requested.

"It is unnatural for parents to outlive a child," he said. "You paid the ultimate price, you lived a parent's worst nightmare. For two years, you have remained silent so as not to hamper her recovery. You gave me your trust to find your daughter's body. I'm not sure if it was my own child, I could have done the same.

"The most beautiful things in the world can't be seen or touched. They must be felt in the heart. And Cher Elder is felt in our hearts today."

The next day, Richardson rode to Empire on his motorcycle, leaning into the curves as the interstate coursed around granite walls, past the remains of old mines that dotted the hillsides like the diggings of large gophers. He was still tracking down itty bitty pieces of the case when he stopped in the store where J.D. Eerebout said Luther picked up a box of rat poison. The store carried the poison in a box identical to that described by J.D. He bought one for the evidence locker.

Instead of turning back down the interstate for Golden, Richardson veered west, toward Empire. He passed through the town and pulled into the turn-off.

Climbing off the Harley, he trudged through the snow, turned slushy by the warm spring day, to the clearing. He stared down at the hole where Cher had lain for two years without knowing why he had come. There was something about that hole in the ground. Something lonely, a void that ached to be filled.

He stooped and picked up a bowling ball-sized stone and dropped it into the grave. He found another and placed it there, too. And then another, and another.

Once, as a boy, he had carried large rocks from one pile to another out of fear of his father. Now he placed rocks in a hole until it was filled, out of love for a friend.

On April 23, 1995, Detective Scott Richardson and P.C. Anderson, an investigator for the Jefferson County District Attorney's Office, flew to West Virginia. They carried with them a Governor's Blue Warrant for the extradition of Thomas Luther.

Blue warrants were the result of interstate agreements stating that when a governor of one state demanded extradition from another state, it would be immediately granted. The warrants were difficult to obtain and most often used when an incarcerated suspect was likely to fight extradition.

The pair drove to Delray where they were met by Trooper Phillips, who filled them in on the details of Luther's sexual assault case, much of which they had not yet heard. Of particular interest were comments Luther was said to have made to his brother-in-law, Randy Foster, and Debrah Snider. To the first he had asked, "What is ailing me? What causes me to do this?" And to the latter he stated, "I did it again."

Richardson also noted that Luther threw his bloody clothes into a river. Healey said he'd done the same after burying Elder. And Byron Eerebout said Luther advised him that the best way to get rid of evidence was to toss it in a river. Luther was following a familiar pattern.

That evening, Richardson called Debrah Snider and asked if she wanted to go out to dinner. She was surprised to hear they were in town but agreed to meet with him and Anderson.

Richardson had talked to Snider several times in the past couple of weeks. She called once to tell him that Luther was changing his story again; now he was saying that Byron and Southy had gone to the bingo hall where Cher's car was found that Sunday after he returned with her from Central City. They abducted and killed her that night, according to Luther.

"It's a lie," Richardson said. "It was incorrectly reported in the newspapers that Cher was seen at that bingo hall. It was actually a different bingo hall where she was seen, and it was the day before she disappeared. The true story just never appeared in the media."

The day before Richardson left for West Virginia, Snider called again to say that Luther was talking about pleading guilty to Elder's murder. "Now he says he wants the death penalty," she said.

She sounded so sad that he almost told her that he was coming the next day, but he wanted to surprise Luther. "Ya know Deb," he said instead, "you ought to get your ass back out here."

"I know," she responded. "I wanna come home. But I can't so long as Tom is here."

At dinner that night, Snider said Luther had added to his story. "Now he says Cher was killed because she got in the middle of a drug deal. Southy picked her up at the bingo parlor where you found her car and killed her."

Tom, she added, "lusts after women but hates 'bitches.' He likes sexually aggressive women, but he hates women who stand up for their rights."

When they drove her back home, Debrah handed Richardson a box of several hundred letters Luther had written to her. "He never admits to killing her," she said. "But I think there are some pretty revealing things about his character in there."

"Thanks, Deb," he said. "Well, I guess we got to be goin.' We're gonna try to talk to Randy Foster and Luther's sister, Becky, tomorrow."

"Randy might talk," Snider said. "But you won't get anything from Becky. She hates cops."

There was an awkward pause. Richardson didn't know what else to say. They'd told Debrah they were in West Virginia as part of the investigation, not to extradite Luther. He smiled and turned to go.

"Do me a favor," Debrah asked suddenly.

Richardson paused, wondering what this could be. "What's that?"

"By your own admission, you neglect your wife," she said,

her voice breaking. "I want you to send her some flowers. I think being neglected is about the worst thing in the world."

The next day, Richardson and Anderson located Randy Foster at a construction site. "Don't introduce me," Richardson said. "Just say I'm your partner." He figured Foster had probably heard plenty of bad things from Luther about the detective who pursued him. No sense antagonizing Foster.

However, Foster wouldn't talk to Anderson, a big, tough former cop. "Fuck you," Foster said and started to walk away.

Richardson stepped in front of him. "I'm Scott Richardson," he said. "Just answer a couple of questions for us."

Foster stopped and looked at the detective. "So you're the guy?" he said. However, instead of being put off, he seemed intrigued. "Well, you got about a minute before Becky gets here, and I don't want her to see me talkin' to you. The last time I talked to the police about Luther, she left me for five months."

"Did he ever say anything about this case in Colorado?" Richardson asked.

"Tom told me that he dropped that girl off at Byron's place," Foster said. "He said that Byron strangled her in his bed. He said all he done was move the girl's body and buried it under a large pile of rocks. He said you'd never find it."

Foster also conceded that after the West Virginia rape, "Tom said 'What's ailing me' " and said he ruined his life by beating that girl.

As they talked, Foster grew increasingly nervous. Becky was due any moment. "She hates cops and will do anything to protect Tom," he said. "Their mother seems to realize the truth, though."

"Did he ever tell you that Cher was killed because she was a police informant?" Richardson asked.

"No," Foster answered. "I heard Byron did it because of some dope deal. But then, there's a whole lot of lying going on about this. Tom says that he feels like writing it all out, and after he's dead, everyone would know what happened."

Foster grew more evasive. Several times he answered Richardson's more specific questions, such as, "Did he ever tell you he killed her?", with, "I can't answer that because it'll get Tom in trouble."

"Would you mind if we went to your place and looked around," Richardson asked. Specifically, he said, he was interested in a backpack Luther brought with him from Colorado, his "rape kit."

Foster shook his head. "Can't," he said. "Becky would get mad as hell. You'd need to get a warrant."

As if on cue, Becky, a skinny little woman, drove up. Anderson went up and introduced himself and asked if he could talk to her.

"Fuck off," she replied. She began to drive away as Anderson ran alongside. "We just want to talk to ya," he puffed.

But Becky just glared and started rolling up her window. "He never hurt no girl in Colorado," she yelled through the glass. She ordered her husband to get in the car and then drove off with her tires spinning in the gravel.

Richardson shrugged. He hadn't expected to get much from Becky, and it had been pretty humorous watching ol' P.C. Anderson trotting alongside the car, trying to conduct an interview. There weren't many men who'd stood up to Anderson that way. They got in their car with Richardson still laughing and drove to where Bobby Jo Jones lived.

"He was punching me like I was a man," Bobby Jo said when Richardson asked her to recount her ordeal. "Then he began choking me. I thought he was going to kill me. Then I thought he was going to take me to his cabin and kill me. Nobody would know where I was or who done it."

However, Jones said she didn't want to testify against Luther in Colorado. "I don't want to go through that again."

Late that afternoon, Richardson and Anderson finally arrived at the West Virginia State Prison. It was an imposing edifice of old stone, built during the Civil War to hold prisoners of war. Cold, dark, and brooding, it was known as "The Dungeon."

They planned to extradite Luther back to Colorado the next day, but first Richardson wanted to make one last stab at talking to him before he "lawyered up." Luther, he was warned by a prison official, had been spending a lot of time in the law library looking up statutes on the interstate transportation of prisoners. "He asked if he could get a medical excuse so he wouldn't have to fly,'' the official said. ''He wants to be transported in a vehicle. Sounds dangerous to me.''

Richardson nodded. He'd received information in Colorado from a confidential informant that Luther had been in contact with friends in Chicago. If he could arrange to be transported on the ground, they would ambush the vehicle.

Richardson asked the guards to get Luther, telling him only that he had a visitor. When Luther entered the visiting room and saw the detective, the smile disappeared off his face and hatred blazed in his eyes. ''What the fuck are you doing here?'' he snarled.

''Just wanted to talk to you, Luther,'' Richardson said, sitting down in a chair and smiling.

''You kiss my ass,'' Luther said and turned to the guard who brought him. ''Just take me back to my unit.''

''Okay,'' Richardson shrugged. ''It you don't want to talk to us . . .''

''Fuck no, I don't want to talk to you,'' Luther yelled, facing the detective again. ''You know I don't want to talk to you. I don't even know why you even fucking came here. I ain't got nothin' to say to you.''

''Well, I got something to say to you,'' Richardson replied. ''We're been working this case for two years—and it's over.''

''I know that,'' Luther sneered. ''So whadda you want me to do?''

''Everybody's coming clean,'' Richardson said, keeping his voice calm, ''and you've been indicted for the murder of Cher Elder. Now when I first talked to you up in Fort Collins, you gave me a story that wasn't true . . .''

Luther took a step toward Richardson. Anderson moved to intercept him, but Richardson just leaned further back in his chair and smiled.

''I'll have a lawyer present when I'm questioned and that's the only way that I will be questioned,'' Luther yelled. ''You ain't worked no case, the only thing you've done is everything in your fucking power to put all that bullshit on me. I'm sure you'll be able to do whatever you want. You've had two fucking years, the State of Colorado, the FBI, and everybody else fucking backing your play. All I ask is you give me a fucking attorney when I get there to fight it with, not some fucking deadbeat public defender that doesn't want to fucking do his job.''

The more Luther ranted, the wider Richardson smiled. It irritated Luther even more.

''Just like this fuckin' bullshit case here,'' Luther screamed. ''They come down on me hard because of your bullshit out in Colorado. I ain't no fuckin' serial killer. I'm an angry bastard, but I ain't no fuckin' killer. I've helped more fuckin' people out than you have ever helped out in your whole life. Well, I ain't got nothin' to say, I ain't a fuckin' rat.''

Luther turned on his heel and left the room with the guard hurrying after him. Richardson, his hands behind his head, just laughed. ''Be seein' you Luther,'' he called after the inmate's retreating back. ''Be seein' you real soon.''

After leaving Richardson, Luther called Debrah Snider and demanded to know what she had told him. Ever since the indictment in Colorado, his letters had grown more accusatory. He didn't know it for sure, but he suspected she was talking to the police.

''When I go to the gas chamber in Colorado because you think you and Babe are doing the right thing, who will you have to love you then?'' he wrote. ''You're not evil, just stupid when it comes to certain things. I'm not Tom Jekyll. I'm Tom Luther and yes I do have both good and bad in me. But only God knows how much of each.''

He even wrote to Snider's mother, telling her of her daughter's betrayal at his trial. ''The victim lied her ass off,'' he wrote. ''But the thing that hurt me most was Deb. She got mad at me and gave a statement against me to the state police, telling them that I admitted to her that I did it. Which was partly so, but she confused what I said. . . . The state had no case without Deb.

''Between her and this woman in Colorado [Babe], they'll get me in the gas chamber before they are done. Deb claims that it's a morals and principles issue with her. Lately, I've had the feeling that Deb has been working with the cops on the Colorado stuff, too.''

Luther told Debrah he wasn't even offered a deal in the rape case because of Richardson, nor could he expect one in Colorado.

In the next letter he complained that the guards were telling each other and the other inmates that he was a serial killer. He believed they were getting their information from Richardson.

"I want to go home, Tom," Debrah wrote him. "I want us to face whatever we have to face in Colorado and get on with what little we have left as a life. I want to complete my part in this Cher Elder case, face whatever I have to face with you and have it done.

"Why don't you see if you can talk Colorado into letting me die for whatever crimes you may have committed. I'm not as good or pure as Christ, but he was able to sell the world on his theory of letting one person die for the sins of a bunch . . . and my blood is as good as yours."

The day before Richardson arrived in West Virginia, Snider went to visit Luther. "I thought you said you were the only one who knew where her body was?" she asked.

Luther cocked his head, looking right through her. "Well," he said with a smirk, "I guess that wasn't true, was it?"

Now Richardson was in town, and Luther wanted to know what Debrah told him. "Nothing, Tom," she said, but he didn't seem to be listening. He was already concocting another Tom Luther story.

"Cher," he said, "had a Colombian boyfriend. He's a drug dealer. Byron set up a deal between the Colombian and Southy, but something went wrong and Cher got killed. Remember, I told you all this before?"

Snider was puzzled. The Colombian drug dealer/boyfriend was a new story, but Tom kept acting like it was old news. Then she realized what he was doing. *He thinks this is being recorded,* she thought.

"You know, Deb, the only reason Richardson's coming for me is because of you," he said. Then he sighed. "I think I'm going to plead guilty and get it over with."

Later that night, Snider called Richardson at his motel room, where he and Anderson were plowing through her letters, and told him about the Colombian boyfriend story. "That was definitely the first time I ever heard that one," she said.

Then she was crying again. "Please, please tell me when you're going to take him back to Colorado," she said. "I want one more chance to see him and say goodbye."

"It's too late, Deb," Richardson said gently. "I'm takin' him tomorrow morning."

The next morning, a Sunday, Richardson and Anderson were back at the prison. This time, they were standing in the hallway when Luther turned a corner with a dozen other inmates and saw them.

"What the fuck are you doing here?" he yelled, looking around at his comrades, putting on a big show. "I told you I didn't want to talk to you."

Richardson smiled, stepping forward. "Well, Luther," he said. "I ain't here to talk to you, either. I'm here to take you back to Colorado for the murder of Cher Elder."

The other inmates retreated and pressed their backs against the wall as they watched the confrontation. They didn't want any part of what was going down. Luther looked around, nervous without his friends. "You can't," he yelled, though he didn't sound convinced. "I'm gonna fight extradition."

"Too late," Richardson said, waving his paperwork under Luther's nose. "This here's a governor's warrant. I'm takin' you now."

With that the waiting guards pounced on Luther, who was handcuffed and his wrists shackled to a belly band. They also shackled his ankles to each other and placed his knees in braces, making it impossible for him to bend his legs or run.

He struggled and screamed profanities at Richardson. "He looks like Hannibal the Cannibal," Richardson said to Anderson, referring to the serial killer in the movie *Silence of the Lambs,* when they finished trussing his prisoner.

Luther was placed in a car between Richardson and Anderson, while a West Virginia state trooper drove toward Pennsylvania at eighty miles an hour. They were escorted by a half-dozen other state police cars with lights flashing.

At the state line, another half-dozen Pennsylvania state police cars were lined up across the road, their lights flashing, too. They took over the escort responsibilities to Pittsburgh. There the caravan was met by another six city police cruisers. At the airport, they were joined by several state police vehicles who were responsible for airport security. They sped across the airport tarmac at sixty-five miles an hour.

On the ride to the airport, Luther remained belligerent, cursing Richardson every chance he got and swearing when each new leg of the journey was met by more police escorts. Finally, Richardson got tired of it. "Luther, we've got a long day ahead of us. Why don't we just try to get along?"

It seemed to take the steam out of Luther. He looked sideways at the detective and half-smiled. "Goddam, Richardson, you lost a lot of weight," he said.

Richardson nodded. Until the day before at the prison, they hadn't seen each other since May 1993 at the Fort Collins hospital, when Luther ripped out his pubic hair as he demanded to know where Richardson lived, but they'd rarely been out of each other's thoughts in the intervening two years. The detective had lost thirty pounds; there were dark circles beneath his eyes and he often looked as tired as he felt.

"Yeah, Luther," he admitted, "thanks to you." He looked at Luther. *Well, at least I'm not the only one,* he thought. His prisoner had also lost a significant amount of weight and all of his hair had turned gray. He had wanted to make this personal between him and Luther, and he had succeeded more than he bargained.

"Jesus," the detective said, "you sure got old and gray."

"Yeah," Luther said, then laughed. "Thanks to you."

As it turned out, the first pilot wouldn't let them board. "This man isn't getting on my plane," he said, looking at the shackled prisoner.

The airline apologized and gave Richardson three $25 certificates good at airport restaurants while they waited. They soon put them to good use.

Richardson offered to buy Luther, who didn't know about the certificates, "anything you want" at the airport McDonald's if he'd promise to behave the rest of the trip.

"Yeah, the fuck you will," Luther said, eyeing him suspiciously.

"No really, even throw in french fries and a strawberry shake," the detective replied. "Deal?"

"Sure," Luther nodded. "No more trouble."

Leaving their prisoner in the airport security lockup, Richardson and Anderson then treated themselves to the biggest steaks they could find at the airport using the gift certificates. When they were finished, Richardson went to the McDonald's and got Luther a hamburger, fries, and a shake. It felt good to put one over on him.

They were finally allowed to board a flight to Chicago, though not without apprehension on the part of the flight crew and passengers. Luther's extradition took place right after the Oklahoma City bombing, and the plane was soon buzzing with the rumor that Luther was the bomber.

"Let's tell 'em he is," Anderson dead-panned. "And let the crowd have at him."

It was a joke, but they didn't forget their prisoner was dangerous. Both men noticed that every time they moved, Luther's eyes flicked over their holstered guns, as if weighing his chances. They'd already discussed that if Luther somehow managed to get a gun and had to be shot while the plane was in the air, they would aim low so that any stray bullets would go into the cargo hold, not a passenger or through the fuselage.

They were met on the taxiway at the Chicago airport by city police. "So is this the hammer man?" one officer asked as they unloaded Luther.

How the hell did they know about that, Richardson wondered. But he didn't get a chance to ask as Luther was whisked off to a holding cell at the airport to await the next plane.

Boarding the plane to Denver, they were met at the door by the pilot, who wanted to know what security measures had been taken. As he talked to the pilot, Richardson noticed that Luther was sidling away from him. He looked and saw that Luther was trying to get to a small opening between the loading ramp and the plane.

Knee braces, shackles and all, Luther was thinking about jumping the twelve feet to the ground and running for it. Richardson put an arm on his prisoner and guided him back to his seat.

After they were seated, a late-arriving woman passenger came down the aisle and started to take a seat in the aisle across from them. Seeing the three men, she smiled and asked if they were going to Denver on business.

"Yeah," Luther said.

"What for?" she asked.

"Court," Luther responded.

"Oh," she said, addressing Richardson. "Are you lawyers?"

"No, ma'am," Richardson replied. "Police."

She looked at Luther. "You're all police officers?"

"No, ma'am," Luther replied and smiled wide. "I'm a convict."

The woman suddenly noticed the handcuffs and shackles. She screamed and ran down the aisle. A couple of minutes later, she returned. "I'm so embarrassed," she apologized. "I can't believe I did that."

Luther leaned over toward Richardson and whispered, "Wait 'til she sees who I am on the five o'clock news."

Luther was talkative on the remainder of the flight. "Did you ever talk to the Colombian?" he asked.

"So now you're blaming Cher's death on a drug cartel?" Richardson asked.

Luther just smiled and looked out the window. A few minutes later, he turned back to Richardson and said, "I feel like writing it all out. I know I'm going to be convicted." He sighed. "I can't believe Byron and J.D. talked."

He looked out the window again for several minutes before speaking anymore. Then he said he regretted never having made it to Mexico. "If I ever get a chance to escape," he said, "that's where I'm goin'."

"Hold on," Richardson said, "let me get a map so you can put an 'X' at the place where I can find you."

They arrived in Denver without further incident. Richardson took Luther to the jail to have him photographed and locked up.

As Luther was being led away by deputies, he looked back at Richardson. "You know, I'm kinda glad it's over," he said. "I don't want to spend the rest of my life lookin' over my shoulder for you."

The next day, Denver's two daily newspapers ran Cher Elder's obituary. There was no mention of how she died, only the date: March 28, 1993.

Next to obituaries of people who'd had the chance to live long full lives, the few lines dedicated to Cher noted that she was "a 20-year-old waitress at a Holiday Inn, a graduate of Purdy High School in Missouri, who enjoyed cross-stitch, reading, art, photography and writing poetry." The obituary closed with the notation that her parents, grandparents, and siblings grieved for her.

At home in Lakewood, Colorado, after putting his boys to bed, so did a detective.

Chapter Twenty-Six

July 12, 1995—New Jersey State Penitentiary

John Martin didn't look so good. His skin, pulled taut over the bones of his face, looked waxy; his hands shook as he took a proffered cigarette and put it to his lips. "Got cancer," he explained to Det. Richard Eaton, and lit the cigarette. "They tell me it's terminal. It's a good thing you found me, I probably won't be around much longer."

Martin nodded when Eaton asked if he remembered Thomas Luther. "So somebody finally wants to talk about that son of a bitch," the 55-year-old convict said. "What took you so long?"

It was Eaton's turn to nod. It had taken a long time to work his way back to what was essentially the beginning.

In May, Eaton, with the help of the Colorado Bureau of Investigations, found Luther's old girlfriend, Sue Potter. She was living a thousand miles away in another state with her husband. And she was still afraid of Tom Luther.

"I don't want to talk about him," she said when he reached her on the phone. "Even if he is facing charges, I know how the system works and he could get out." Potter said she hadn't talked to Luther since his conviction in 1983.

A few days later, Eaton talked to the detective, since retired, who had submitted Potter's service revolver for testing. "Sure, I knew the test was negative," the retired cop said. "Guess we must have lost the results."

Eaton was curious why the detectives at the time had dropped

Luther as a suspect in the murders of Barbara "Bobby Jo" Oberholtzer and Annette Schnee. "Because," the retired detective shrugged, "we couldn't determine he was around here at the time of the murders."

It was nonsense. Luther had a 1978 arrest record for a simple assault in Summit County. And he'd told investigators that he had been living with Potter in Frisco since 1981. Eaton found Luther's work record with the taxi cab company which showed he didn't work the day of the murders or the day after. His predecessors simply hadn't done a thorough enough job.

They apparently hadn't paid any attention to claims of other Summit County Jail inmates like Martin, who Eaton had finally tracked to the New Jersey prison where he was serving time for embezzlement.

Luther picked him out his first day in jail, Martin told Eaton, "because I was wearing a Colorado penitentiary uniform. I was already in the joint. But they brought me to Summit County on another charge. Luther must have thought I'd make a good ally 'cause I told him I was in for assaulting a cop."

Trying to impress the older inmate, Luther liked to brag. The second night, he told Martin that he had "beat and fucked" a girl with a hammer and now she was afraid for her life and wouldn't testify. "He was confident he wouldn't be convicted."

"He said he got off on hurting women—that it was better than drugs or booze. 'Fuck them and then kill them,' that's what he said. He said he had assaulted a lot of women and killed a few. He thought he was a real ladies' man. Said he could always talk to them and make them feel safe. He said, 'They drop their defenses and I have them at my mercy.' "

Martin claimed that Luther boasted about killing a woman he met in a Breckenridge bar after she declined his advances. "Buried her in the woods by a stream. Thirty, forty miles over a mountain away from Breckenridge."

Except for the part about meeting her in a bar, Eaton wondered, recalling the image of Annette lying facedown in a stream, if Luther was talking about the Schnee homicide.

Luther, Martin continued, talked often about killing two Summit County women. "A 'sweet young thing' named Ann or Anna and a second older one who put up a hell of a fight. The second woman's name was . . . Babs . . . or Jackie O." Martin scrunched his face trying to remember, then he brightened. The second woman's name was similar to a female judge who had once sentenced him in Pennsylvania, Barbara Obelinas.

Martin said Luther claimed to have killed the younger woman first, then drove the older woman around for awhile before killing her, too. Luther, he said, also claimed to have killed a woman at a Vermont ski area.

"He doesn't think of himself as a bad person," Martin said. "He was usually doing drugs or drinkin' when the violent urges came over him."

Martin said that in May 1982, he took his information to a Summit County deputy at the jail but was told there were no unsolved murders or missing women that fit his description. He offered to wear a wire, Martin said, but nothing came of it.

Eaton was thinking. He had a note written by a former deputy at the jail regarding Martin's information. But consistent with the sloppiness that defined the whole investigation at that time, the note was not dated. And that was significant because Annette Schnee's body wasn't found until that July.

In September 1982, Martin said, he was back at the Summit County Jail for another hearing when he ran into Luther again. This time, Luther wasn't friendly—word was out that Martin was a snitch.

When Luther saw him, he walked over and grabbed Martin. "He said, 'I'm going to kill you just like those girls,' " Martin told Eaton. "I yelled for help and was rescued by a deputy."

When he was returned to the penitentiary, Martin said, he was locked up in maximum security. "They said there was a contract out on my life." He was later released from prison for his testimony against another inmate in a Pueblo murder trial.

Eaton left the New Jersey prison excited, but cautious, about Martin's recollections. Inmates were always trying to strike a deal in exchange for information, he reminded himself. They were born liars, and the Oberholtzer and Schnee cases had gotten a lot of publicity. But the part about Luther attacking Martin in September had been documented, as was his being placed in protective custody because of an alleged hit planned by Luther.

Why would Luther have wanted to kill Martin unless something he'd told the older inmate could hurt him? From what he had been able to ascertain, Martin and Montoya had never met.

Yet their stories were amazingly similar. As were the recollections of Troy Browning, who had proved that Luther thought nothing of killing witnesses to protect himself.

Luther supposedly told all three that he had killed other women and dumped their bodies in the woods, which was also what Dillon John Curtis had said in his interview. Martin and Montoya also claimed that Luther considered shooting Mary Brown before deciding against it because he thought a shot might be heard.

Before leaving for Colorado, Eaton contacted Special Agent Bruce Kammerman of the FBI in New York, whom Martin claimed to have helped with several cases. "How reliable is Martin?" Eaton asked the agent.

"Outstanding," Kammerman said. "Unbelievable."

Apparently, Martin had a real knack for winning the confidence of his fellow inmates and getting them to brag about their crimes. He'd helped the feds solve a series of bank and armored car robberies in New Jersey. "And he just put a killer away for the state."

"Heck," Kammerman said and laughed, "for all the help he's been to us, I'd let him marry my daughter."

Southy Healey told Richardson that he wasn't concerned that Luther was trying to pin the murder on him. "Luther's the one that fucked her, he is the one that killed her, he is the one that buried her, and your physical evidence will prove all of that," he said.

The ballistics report on the .22-caliber Healey was carrying following his arrest came back from the CBI. It was not the gun used to killed Cher Elder.

The crime lab had also narrowed the possible murder weapon down to just three models from the markings on the largest bullet fragment from Elder's skull. One of the three was a .22 Baretta, the same weapon stolen from the Evergreen 7-Eleven.

In the meantime, Richardson began contacting people Luther knew in Vermont. If Luther was convicted of first degree murder and faced the death penalty phase of the trial, these people might be called upon by either side to testify for or against his character. He had to know what they would say.

One of the first he reached was Rick Gutzman, a former boyfriend of Luther's mother.

"She was always defending her kids. They could do no wrong," Gutzman said. "I didn't know Tom very well, he was in prison most of the time I was with his mother."

Gutzman was unaware of the West Virginia conviction and the murder charges in Colorado. "I'm not surprised," he said. "I don't know why they ever let him out. He always had a big chip on his shoulder. He was a big-partier, into drugs, and a real 'sweet-talker.' "

Sometime in the fall of 1993, Luther arrived in Vermont with a girl, Gutzman recalled. "No, it wasn't Deb Snider," he said in answer to the detective's next question. "But I don't remember her name."

Richardson also talked to Luther's brother, William, who was reluctant to say anything. They'd had a good family life, he said, but all the kids had gone their separate ways as adults. He knew Tom had been arrested in West Virginia, "but I never heard the outcome, and he never said nothin' about a missin' girl in Colorado."

After a minute, William decided he wasn't going to answer anymore questions. But just as he was beginning to hang up, he blurted out, "If he done what you say he has, he should pay for it."

It took several attempts for Richardson to reach Luther's mother, Betty. When he did, she also didn't want to talk. "I love him and don't believe that he did these things," she said. "Thomas told me you are a very smart man and an intelligent investigator. I'm only hoping and praying that you turn up something in his favor."

Tommy had visited her several times after his release from prison, she said, but never mentioned he was a suspect in a Colorado case until after his arrest. "I don't want to talk about him," she repeated. "He was always a nice boy. His troubles began when he got involved with drugs. But I love him very much."

Richardson then talked to Police Chief Leslie Dimick of the Hardwick, Vermont, police department. Dimick said he grew up with Tom Luther and knew most of the family.

"He was a pretty normal kid," Dimick said. "I do remember

his brother, William, shot a woman with a shotgun and his sister, Becky had some trouble over the years. She was married to a guy up here, had a couple of children, left him, then she married some other guy, and had another kid.

"Anything else?" Richardson asked.

Well, Dimick said, there was some talk about Tom Luther being involved in an unsolved homicide over in Stowe, Vermont, a ski resort town. Way back in the 1970s, a girl came up missing and then what was left of her body was found in the woods. They knew Luther had worked at Stowe about the same period of time. He'd gone on to Southern California after that, but that was as far as it went.

A female friend of Luther's from Vermont, called Richardson, having heard that he was asking questions about Tom's past relationships. She remembered when Luther was much younger, before he'd left Vermont, he had a girlfriend who called her several times complaining that he had "gotten rough with her. She'd say stuff like, 'Tom's acting crazy and abusive.' "

Richardson's attention was soon directed to another part of the country when Detective Eaton called and gave him Sue Potter's telephone number. She, too, was reluctant to talk but answered a few questions.

No, she said, she didn't have any "flex" cuffs of the sort found on Bobby Jo Oberholtzer. Yes, Tom had a strong sex drive, "but nothing weird."

"He was always gone a lot," she said. "He came and went pretty much as he pleased. I knew the good side of Thomas, not the other side."

Then she clammed up. "I don't need that guy or his twisted mind," she said. "He don't need to be out to get me hurt. All he has to do on the inside is contact someone on the outside."

In late July, Luther appeared in Jefferson County District Court before Judge Christopher Munch. With him was defense attorney Lauren Cleaver. Formally apprised of the charges, he stood and entered his plea: "Not guilty."

Afterward, Richardson met with Debrah Snider outside the courtroom. She had recently moved back to Colorado, although she wasn't sure she was going to stay until the trial, which was scheduled for late fall.

Tom, she said, planned to stick to his story that Cher was killed during a drug deal set up by Byron and Southy. "He still can't figure out how Byron knew how to find the grave," she said. "He says he only told him the general area where she was buried."

Snider was angry. She'd talked to Deputy District Attorney Dennis Hall who told her she wouldn't be allowed in the courtroom during the trial. And on the other side, some of Tom's friends were trying to persuade her to stay out of it all together.

"I'm sick and tired of tryin' to do the right thing," she said. "You know I got nothing to gain by testifying against Tom, except keeping the only thing I ever kept in my life, and that's the truth. But I could sure end all my problems and keep the man I love, if I testified that I lied to you."

"You know we recorded all of our conversations," Richardson reminded her.

"Yeah, I know," she replied. "Don't worry, I'll tell the truth."

Debrah felt like a piece of cloth being ripped in two directions. She was either going to have to betray Tom or the truth. And this time, if she chose the latter, it could cost him his life.

Luther seemed just as torn in his letters to her. Even when the defense team received some of the investigation reports from the prosecution and he learned exactly what Debrah's role had been, he still signed his letters, "Love, Tom."

Until the last one, the one he sent just after he pleaded not guilty. "I hope you're as lonely and hurt and full of pain as me. . . . Why couldn't you believe I loved you?"

When Debrah Snider returned to Colorado she drove Luther's blue Geo Metro, which she turned over to Richardson for further testing.

"Thomas told me that he did not want my name on the title in case he got caught doing something illegal in the car," she said. "You know, we only bought the car ten days before Cher was killed."

After he pleaded not guilty, and before the last letter, he'd called. "He's not happy with me," she said sarcastically. "He says that every time we had a fight, I gave you information and that his lawyers are going to use that to attack me in court. They're goin' to say that I'm just a vindictive bitch."

Luther had even called her mother. "Tell Debrah she got what she wanted," he'd said. "I'm going to just lie down and go to sleep."

Snider said Luther was trying to convince her that he injured his hands the week after Elder disappeared. "But I know when it was," she said. "I got back from my trip and he was in bed."

Babe Rivinius called her after she got back to Colorado to tell her J.D. had fled with Skip and wouldn't be comin' back to Colorado to testify. Rivinius also said that if anything happened to her family, she planned to kill Richardson.

After a few moments of awkward silence, Richardson got the feeling that Debrah wanted to ask him something but was having a hard time getting it out. "What is it, Deb?" he probed gently.

She hesitated, started to say something, then stopped. But finally she asked, "I was wondering if you thought it would be okay for me to visit Cher's grave? I'm havin' a hard time dealing with the fact that it took me so long to tell you the whole truth. I won't bother her folks, but I just thought I'd like to tell her that I'm sorry."

Richardson gave her instructions on how to find the grave in Grand Junction, and she drove there the next day. She didn't know why exactly. She hoped to find an answer, or at least some peace. She wanted to see if she could feel whether Cher was finally at rest.

However, all she felt as she stood next to the pink granite gravestone was self-loathing. She remembered how she had blamed Cher for going with Tom, for not being able to see how dangerous he was. She remembered how long it had taken her to tell Richardson the whole truth.

She stared at the fresh flowers recently left on the grave, testament to the family's still raw grief. "I'm sorry, Cher," she said as her tears fell on the new grass growing on the grave. "It should have been me."

* * *

In August, Scott Richardson received a letter from Wesley Cheung, an inmate at the Jefferson County Jail, who he had once arrested for some minor incident. Cheung said he'd heard Richardson's name come up while talking to another inmate, Thomas Luther.

"I decided to pass on this information because my conscience calls and because someone else might get the chair for no reason."

A few days later, Richardson paid Cheung a visit. The inmate said he'd been housed next to Luther in the jail and the two had talked quite a bit. Luther never told him anything directly related to the murder, but several things he said led Cheung to believe he could be a killer.

For instance, one day while watching a television cop show that depicted a homicide victim who had been found lying on the ground, Luther said, "He should have buried her." More interesting, Cheung said, was Luther seemed to know a lot of details about another Denver homicide.

The woman, Luther reportedly told Cheung, had been picked up and taken to her apartment. There she had been choked and stabbed, her body left lying under an American flag.

"Check it out," Cheung said. "If what I say is true, come back, I have more information. In exchange, I want out of here and into a drug treatment program."

Richardson told Cheung that Luther was probably just setting him up to see if he was a snitch. But he called the Denver Police Department anyway. "You guys got a homicide with a female victim, choked, stabbed, and found under an American flag?" he asked a detective.

"As a matter of fact, I think we do," the other detective responded. It took him a few minutes to find the report, but it matched Cheung's description.

In June 1994, the victim, one Anne Marie Baldauf, was found dead in her apartment. The apartment was in a secured building, and there was no sign of forced entry—she apparently invited her killer in.

Baldauf was nude except for a bra and a t-shirt, both of which had been pulled up over her breasts but not removed. She was discovered lying on her stomach, stabbed in the back of the neck and three times in her left breast. There were bruises on her neck, indicating she had been choked. And, yes, her body had been covered with an American flag.

Richardson went back to talk to Cheung, who said he wasn't going to say anymore until he was out of the Jefferson County Jail. "I'm afraid of Luther," he admitted.

"How do we know you didn't kill her?" Richardson asked.

"That's easy," Cheung said. "I was in jail."

At the Denver detective's request, Richardson asked that some of the blood and hair taken from Luther at the Fort Collins hospital be handed over to compare to a single, curly gray hair found at the crime scene.

The hair, it turned out, was microscopically "in the same class" as Luther's. But was Luther back in Colorado in June 1994? No one knew. But like he had in other instances, such as Heather Smith's, Richardson stayed out of this case. It would be up to the Denver police to work out a deal with Cheung for his information.

A few days later, Richardson received a call from Detective Scott in Denver. They had filed first degree attempted murder and first degree assault charges against Luther in the Heather Smith case. However, Scott said he'd just received a telephone call from a woman in Vermont that seemed more related to Richardson's case. "Something about Luther telling her about waking up next to a dead woman." The caller's name was Helen Conyers.

Richardson called and asked Conyers to repeat her information. She said she was a former friend of Luther's who had stayed in touch with him while he was in prison in Colorado. "He never told me what for," she said. "Anyway, he showed up that fall after he got out. I was with a couple of friends when he drove up in this little blue car."

Luther, she said, was good looking and personable, "but he made us nervous. We were sitting at my kitchen table, drinking wine, when he started talking about how he had been partying with this woman and they had gone to bed together. When he woke up the next morning, she was dead."

"Did he say how she died?" Richardson asked.

"No. He didn't elaborate. He was just strange and weird."

Conyers gave Richardson the name of one of the other women who was present during the discussion. That woman repeated the story of Luther waking up next to a dead woman. "But I don't think he ever told us how she died."

In September, one of Healey's sisters called Richardson to tell him that she'd been contacted by defense investigators. "They asked if I had information, and I told 'em the only information I got is incriminatin' against Luther," she said. "They said that Dennis was involved in the murder, but I told 'em that he might be a thief and a liar, but he is not a murderer."

She did recall one thing that might help Richardson, though. Late one night in the spring of 1993, she said, Luther called for her brother who was sleeping on the couch at her house. "Luther showed up, all anxious to get going," she said. "That's when I heard him say, 'A deal went bad, I fucked up, I left too many clues.' He saw me listening and started whispering to Dennis."

Luther and her brother left together. Her brother returned early the next morning, "just when it was starting to get light." It was only later, Healey's sister said, that she realized the incident was about the same time Cher Elder disappeared.

Richardson asked if she recalled going to Longmont with her brother to meet Luther in July 1993. No, she said, but that might have been one of her sisters.

The detective called the sister. Yes, she said, they made the trip to Longmont, although she didn't know why. Only that her brother was angry about whatever had been said on the drive home. "My old boyfriend, Bob Ramierez, might remember more," she added.

One evening in October, a knock on her front door startled Rebecca Hascall. The arrest of Thomas Luther and the subsequent identification of him by Heather Smith as her attacker had thrown them both for a loop.

Hascall had come to view the process of healing from violent crime as something akin to piecing together a broken china vase. From a distance, it might look the same, but up close the cracks still showed, and it would never be as strong again. She saw herself, and Heather even more so, as broken vases—appearing whole, but fragile. The arrest of Thomas Luther exposed the cracks.

Answering the knock by looking out a peephole, Hascall saw a woman standing on her front porch. In the old days before the attack, she would have opened the door, invited the woman in. Now she left her standing there in the yellow porch light. "What do you want?" she asked.

"I have a book I need to give to Heather," the woman said. "Does she still live next door?"

"Heather doesn't live around here anymore," Rebecca answered, the hair on the back of her neck standing on end. Heather had moved several blocks away to a different house. "You can leave the book, and when I run into her, I'll give it to her."

The woman seemed to think for a moment, then asked, "Well, could I use your telephone?"

"No," Hascall answered. She felt bad, but she was afraid. The man in the green coat had done that to her.

"Do you have a portable telephone you could hand me?" the woman asked, sounding exasperated.

"Just leave the book," Rebecca repeated. "What is it, anyway?"

"Well," the woman said. "It's not really a book. It's an Avon catalogue Heather ordered."

Finally, the woman walked off into the night, without leaving anything. As her fear dissipated, Rebecca rebuked herself for being paranoid. She called Heather.

"Did you order an Avon catalogue?" she asked.

"No. Why?"

Hascall explained what had just occurred. "Some poor Avon lady now thinks I'm crazy as a loon," she said and they both laughed. But the laughter was followed by an uncomfortable silence. They both knew that Luther had sent girlfriends on his errands before.

Just a week earlier, Heather Smith and Mary Brown talked for the first time through a mutual friend who knew both women's stories and their connection to Luther. They met at a restaurant. There, Smith heard first hand from Brown about being approached in the Summit County courthouse by Luther's girl-friend at the time, Sue Potter. And about how he had tried to have Brown killed so she couldn't testify.

Smith was surprised at how strong the other woman seemed. She herself had moved from the little home she loved. There were too many dark memories there, and it no longer felt safe.

She'd recently had another setback, this one physical. The pain in her neck had grown, until she had difficulties holding her head up. Then it was discovered that her doctor had missed a fracture of the C7 vertebra, the same vertebra she later learned Luther had fractured in Brown's neck. It had required a risky operation that might have left her paralyzed, but once again she had pulled through.

Ever since, she had worked hard to get herself physically and emotionally fit for the trial, which was tentatively scheduled for after Luther's murder trial. She trained to enter road races to regain her athlete's confidence. At home, she read murder mysteries to test the limits of her fears. And she dreamed of revenge. Luther tried to kill her, and she wished she could return the favor—stab him five times and see if he had the courage and strength she had shown.

Heather Smith was sure she had the right man—his face had never left her memory—but she was afraid that something would go wrong. That someone would come along with an alibi for Luther. And she did not look forward to being interrogated by Luther's attorney Lauren Cleaver, who at several hearings had intimated that Heather was lying or psychologically impaired. Cleaver even told a newspaper reporter, after Luther pleaded not guilty to charges, that Smith's accusation was "a bogus case. That's not what's exciting in Mr. Luther's life."

Detective Scott had come to her defense, telling the reporter, "I have the best evidence there is. My victim is still alive. There's a whole lot of credibility when a victim can get up on the witness stand, point to the defendant and say, 'That's the man.' And Heather will be a great witness."

At the restaurant, Mary Brown admitted that she feared Luther even when he was in prison, afraid that someday he would decide to get even. Fear had almost overwhelmed her when she saw the press conference about Cher Elder, though it had subsided somewhat when Richardson arrested Luther for the murder.

Brown was still living with the physical and emotional scars of the attack. The beating cost her some of her hearing and she was tormented by migraine headaches. "But I didn't let him ruin my life," she told Heather. "I made a choice to live, just like the choice you made. I met someone, fell in love, and got married. I made a decision to be happy and you can, too. I've even learned not to be afraid of the night again."

Mary Brown said she'd been told that if Luther was convicted of first degree murder in the death of Cher Elder, she might be called to testify about what he had done to her. After all these years, she might at last get her day in court and face Thomas Luther, the monster. Maybe.

"In a way," she told Heather Smith, "I envy you."

Hardwick, Vermont, lay in a remote, wooded part of the state known for its hunting. It was the sort of place where strangers stood out.

Ever since Richardson and prosecution investigator John Newhouse arrived on November 11, heads swiveled to follow their every move. Even pumping gas, the locals in their plaid wool shirts stopped whatever they were doing to watch.

Richardson drove to the police station where he asked Chief Dimick to direct them to Betty Luther's home. "Take you there myself," Dimick volunteered. "She knows me and might be more willin' to talk."

"That'd be great," Richardson said. "Only don't introduce me, just Newhouse here."

Betty Luther's home, a small, yellow clapboard affair, lay on the outskirts of Hardwick. She opened the door and, seeing Dimick, invited them in and offered coffee.

They were surprised to be so warmly received. Then they found out why. Lauren Cleaver and her investigator were in town and had called. Betty thought they were with the defense team!

Betty Luther's mood quickly changed when Dimick introduced Newhouse as being with the prosecution. She stiffened and turned to the detective. "Are you Mr. Richardson?" she asked.

"Yes, ma'am," he answered. Again to their surprise, Betty

Luther didn't ask them to leave, though she remained hostile and kept throwing Richardson hard looks.

She also didn't add much to what they already knew. She said she married at 17 and bore Tom a year later. Her husband had worked a lot, but it was not an abusive household, "just the sort of discipline that was common for the time."

"If I can ask, what was the color of your hair when your son was young?" Newhouse asked.

"I'm a brunette, if that's what you mean," she said. "But I started turning gray at an early age." She pointed to a recent photograph of her family on the wall. She used to wear her hair like her daughter, Donna, in that picture, she said, dark and shoulder-length.

Richardson didn't say anything. They had agreed beforehand that Newhouse would conduct this interview so as not to antagonize her. But he couldn't help but note the similarity between the photograph of Donna and those he had of Cher Elder, Mary Brown, and Bobby Jo Jones. *Could have been sisters,* he thought.

"Do you have any evidence to help prove that your son did not commit this crime?" Newhouse asked.

"No," she replied. "But I know he's innocent."

The investigators left Betty Luther's home and drove to the home of Gary Powers, whose sons were said to be good friends of Thomas Luther. "Hey," he said, "you're my second visitors. A coupla' gals from the defense were just here."

Powers said he didn't know Luther well. "Just met him two years ago," he said. "He showed up in a blue Geo with a woman named Kathy. She was about, I'd say, thirty-five, dirty blond hair. Said they were on their way to West Virginia. My son might know more if you want to check back."

Next, they went to talk to Luther's sister, Donna, who also mistook them for the defense team. "I know you guys are trying to build a defense that Tom was abused," she said. "But it's not true."

When they explained who they were, she shrugged. She had nothing to hide. At Richardson's request, she showed them a photograph of her mother taken on her wedding day. In it, Betty Luther had dark shoulder-length hair. She gave them the photograph when Richardson promised to return it.

Donna, too, remembered Luther bringing a woman named

Kathy with him when he visited in the fall of 1993. He never said anything about a missing girl in Colorado, however. Then again, they weren't very close.

Donna's husband, Ted, came home and was introduced to the investigators. He clearly did not like his brother-in-law, who he described as ''a blowhard with a chip on his shoulder. He was with some girl named Kathy and bragging that he had a lot of land and was raising wolves.''

From Donna's house, the detectives went to see George Luther, the youngest brother. Tom had moved out, he said, when he was still very young and they weren't close.

''He was always hot-tempered,'' George said.

''How would he show that?'' Newhouse asked.

''Well, he's a strong guy, you know,'' Luther replied. His sister, Becky, had told him some things about the murder case. ''It had something to do with drug deals, and the girl was a heavy user,'' he said. ''Tom took her out and brought her back, then she was killed.''

William Luther was waiting for them when Richardson and Newhouse arrived. George had called to warn him.

Tom left home at an early age, William said, and he never knew him to have serious relationships with a woman. ''He was used to getting his way one way or another, though,'' he said.

''Any idea why Tom might commit this offense?'' Newhouse asked.

William Luther eyed them suspiciously. ''Well, what kind of stories have you guys heard? You aren't going to help him are you?''

Newhouse ignored the questions and asked his own. ''Think it had anything to do with your mother?''

Luther paused, then said slowly, ''I don't think so. He never said why he attacked women, like that girl he went to prison for.

''I heard this Cher was working undercover drugs and her boyfriend had shot her,'' he said, but wouldn't reveal who he heard it from. ''But if he did what they say he did, he deserves to be punished.''

The next interview was with Jennie Ross, who surprised Richardson by asking ''Do you and Lauren Cleaver have a personal or business relationship?''

Richardson responded that he only knew Cleaver because of the case. "I never met her before. Why?"

Well, Ross said, Cleaver had already been by, and she wasn't exactly kind in her description of the detective. "She said this is an ego trip for you, another notch in your belt. She used really offensive language about you, really harsh, and to tell you the truth, I was offended. I thought maybe you two had lived together or something and had a falling out."

Richardson nodded. The defense team had already shown they meant to play hard ball. Twice a defense investigator had come by his office and dropped off what the investigator called "evidence"—two .22-caliber shell casings and a leather jacket—but without saying where the evidence was found or how it related to the case. Cleaver also refused to say anything about the so-called evidence.

Cleaver had called Debrah Snider and said she knew who killed Cher Elder because Luther told her. The defense lawyer claimed that they had the clothes Luther wore that night, which Southy Healey said had been thrown in the creek. And they were going to portray Snider as "a vindictive bitch" at the trial.

"She told me that Luther was abused by his family," Ross said. "I never heard that until she said it. I've known him since he was seventeen and thought he was a pretty good kid."

Two years ago, she said, in the fall, Luther showed up with a hitchhiker who looked about 25. "The next morning she was gone, and nobody's seen her since."

The investigators returned to the Powers' home and found Gary's son, Nelson, who said he'd visited his friend in jail after his arrest in Summit County. "He said he wished the girl was gone and out of his life," Nelson recalled. "I think he wanted me to do something to her. I told him not to talk like that or I wouldn't be back to visit."

As the sun began to set in Hardwick, Richardson and Newhouse located one last person they hoped could shed some light on Luther. Becky's former husband, Carl.

Carl said he started living with Becky, who he described as having an drinking problem and cocaine habit, after she abandoned her first husband and child. "I remember Tom as being pretty good with his fists," he said. "Becky told me once that

Tom killed a man over a $50,000 dope deal back in the 'eighties, before his first arrest out there in Colorado.''

After Luther showed up with the hitchhiker, the two of them had stayed in an isolated hunting cabin owned by his mother. ''The girl just disappeared one day,'' Carl said. ''When I asked him about it, he said he gave her some money to go on to West Virginia, which I always thought was kind of funny 'cause he left for there the next day.

''We been kind of worried, figurin' a body's goin' to turn up somewhere around that cabin.''

After Vermont, Richardson and Newhouse flew to West Virginia. The first person they stopped to see was Debrah Snider, who had moved back when Luther stopped writing or allowing her to visit that past summer.

The visit to Snider's was mostly a social call. She did say Cleaver's investigator called and asked if she had ever known Luther to wear a green jacket, a blue baseball cap, or facial hair.

''I remembered he had a green nylon windbreaker and a blue cap with the word 'Navy' on it,'' she said. ''He never really kept a beard, but he'd go for days without shaving when he would go on his little excursions, and he has pretty heavy facial hair.''

Richardson recognized the defense investigator's questions as pertaining to the Heather Smith case. They couldn't have been too happy with Deb's answers, he thought to himself. Too bad. He recalled that one of Southy's sisters and her boyfriend, Matt Marlar, said that Luther showed up to get his gun wearing a beard and farmer's clothes as a disguise.

Leaving Snider's, they drove to see Randy Foster. He was angry with Richardson. Cleaver was saying that Foster told Richardson that Luther had confessed to killing and burying Cher Elder. ''I never told you that. I said Luther told me Byron strangled Cher,'' Foster said. ''Now it's caused all sorts of problems between me and Becky.''

More lawyers' tricks, Richardson thought. ''That's not in any of my reports,'' he told Foster. ''I never said you told me he confessed. She's makin' that up.''

Didn't matter, Foster said, he wasn't going to come back to

Colorado and testify against his brother-in-law. "You can arrest me and put me in jail," he said. "But I won't help you."

"Well, you got any evidence to prove Luther's innocence?" Richardson responded.

Foster laughed. "If I had anything like that, I would have given it to everybody a long time ago. All I can say is there's a lot of lying going on around here."

On November 14, Richardson and Newhouse made their last stop. This time in Purdy, Missouri. Richardson was sure the defense would try to attack Cher Elder's character, accuse her of being into drugs and sexually promiscuous to explain her "quick little intercourse thing" with Luther.

However, like he once told Southy Healey, the more Richardson dug into Elder's background, the cleaner she got. Friends described her as boisterous, especially for a small southern town not used to teenagers speaking out. But no one knew her to ever do anything to harm someone else.

Neither were there any indications that she used drugs or drank much, according to friends and the local police. She was described as a hard worker, who paid her own bills while attending high school, where she was a straight-A student.

No one knew her to be sexually active. In fact, she had turned in a high school coach who was having an affair with a friend of hers. The coach and a member of the school board who supported him had been forced to resign.

No one could think of a single bad thing to say about Cher Elder. She was a bubbly, outspoken teenager who loved to talk and was well-liked.

Richardson was proud of her.

After granting a continuance to the defense, the trial of Thomas Luther for the murder of Cher Elder was rescheduled by Judge Munch to begin January 16. It would be a death penalty case— if Luther was convicted he would go through a second trial to determine if he should be put to death by lethal injection.

Deputy District Attorney Dennis Hall filed the required paperwork indicating that he intended to introduce as evidence "similar transactions"—the attacks on Mary Brown and Bobby Jo Jones. In general, evidence of other crimes or actions is not admissible to prove the character of a suspect. However, in Colorado, the limitations are relaxed in certain cases, especially felony-murder involving first a sexual assault, and the prosecution, Hall wrote, "may introduce evidence of other similar acts or transactions of the defendant for the purpose of showing a common plan, scheme, design, identity, modus operandi, motive, guilty knowledge, or intent."

Hall said he needed the similar transactions evidence for two reasons. One was identity—that there were significantly distinctive features to the three crimes as to identify Luther as the offender. Those features were: each victim was a young woman of similar height and weight with collar-length dark hair; each victim voluntarily entered Luther's car, and spent some time in the car with him; after a period of ordinary conversation in the car, and without warning or provocation, Luther announced his attention to sexually assault his victims; Luther then physically and sexually assaulted the victims.

The second reason was motive—that Luther felt anger and hostility towards women because, as several psychiatrists had noted through the years, of the abuse he perceived he suffered at the hands of his mother. "Defendant expanded upon the similarities between Mary Brown and his mother in an interview with Dr. John Macdonald and several Denver detectives in 1985. In this interview, defendant described similarities between Ms. Brown's hair and defendant's mother's hair when defendant's mother was young, and stated that Ms. Brown 'reminded him' of his mother, 'especially when she began screaming.' "

Hall noted that in both the assault on Mary Brown and then eleven years later on Bobby Jo Jones, Luther made statements reflecting his subconscious motivation. "Why do I do these things?" to the Summit County deputies. And then "What is ailing me? I don't know what causes this to happen," to his brother-in-law.

The prosecutor included the photographs of Brown, Jones, Elder, and Betty Luther. "It is the People's theory that defendant's motive for assaulting and murdering Ms. Elder is that Ms. Elder, like Ms. Brown and Ms. Jones, physically resembles defendant's mother; and that, after spending some period of time in close physical proximity with persons like defendant's mother, defendant without warning or provocation physically and sexually assaults them.''

Dennis Hall knew that the case might very well hang on whether the judge allowed the evidence of similar transactions. Otherwise, there was very little evidence against Luther, except the testimony of admittedly poor witnesses and a single, curly gray hair found in Elder's car that was "in the same class" as Luther's, though the science could not say for certain it was his. Everything else—the vomit on the back seat, the "quick, little intercourse thing"—Luther had explained away in his first meeting with Richardson.

The similar transactions hearing was heated. Cleaver, who had been joined at the defense table by the more experienced attorney Mike Enwall, a former judge, opposed their introduction saying, "The lack of similarity between Cher Elder's death and the two sexual assaults in Summit County and West Virginia are striking.''

For one thing, Elder was shot, the other girls beaten and strangled. And, most importantly, they lived. "It would be improper to use prior bad acts to convict him of another.''

"If you allow the prosecution to use this," she warned the judge, "you'll be signing his death warrant.''

Cleaver contended that her client's rights to due process had been violated by law enforcement personnel, "particularly Detective Richardson," who she said was out to "get Tom Luther at any cost.''

Judge Munch took the arguments under consideration. Office personnel later said they had never seen him so torn over a decision. On one hand, he believed that he might very well allow a serial killer get away with murder if he ruled against allowing the prior similars. On the other, he feared jurors, told about the terrors of the two rapes Luther was convicted of, would be unable to look at this case solely on its merits.

Several days passed. Hall had a sinking feeling that things were not going his way. Judges were often like the general television-watching public in that they were indoctrinated to believe that serial killers always committed their crimes in exactly the same fashion. They didn't take into account the opportunistic killer who struck when and how the mood took him.

In his book, Dr. Macdonald described men like Luther as anger-retaliatory rapists, "a moody, argumentative man with a violent temper."

"He uses a blitz attack. The attack occurs on the spur of the moment, perhaps someone he knows or just met in a bar. The attack is violent, and he will use any weapon at hand. He will strike her with his fists or a club, and he may kick her before ripping off her clothing. There is much profanity, and he may continue to beat her during the sexual assault. Anal sex precedes oral sex. If there is sexual dysfunction, it will be retarded ejaculation."

The way Richardson and Hall saw it, Luther didn't set out on the morning of March 27, 1993, to sexually assault and murder Cher Elder, though he probably had his "rape kit" along just in case the mood took him. He also had the gun the Eerebout boys had given him several days earlier stuffed under the front seat.

Then later, in the car with Cher, she angered him and he attacked without warning. Beating her senseless, he raped her and then, to cover up that crime, he killed her with the weapon he had available. A .22 Baretta.

And the murder was premeditated. The public thinks of "premeditated" as a carefully planned-out crime. But all premeditated really means in the legal sense is that the perpetrator gave the act some thought—in Cher's case, Luther knew he would be sent back to prison for rape and assault and decided to kill her to cover up the crime. He executed her while she was helpless with not one shot, but three. It wasn't accidental, it wasn't in the act of her fleeing or struggling, it was an execution.

But judges in Jefferson County were said to grant prior similars motions only for "fingerprint" crimes. That is, crimes in which the perpetrator did everything exactly the same from crime to crime. Same time. Same way. Same weapon. Same words.

It was late Friday when the decision was delivered to the district attorney's office. Munch had sided with Cleaver on the prior similars.

While the three women—Mary, Bobby Jo, and Cher—"bear a striking resemblance to each other," Munch wrote in his opinion, the prosecution had not persuaded him that there was enough evidence outside of Luther's "bad character" to make a case that he sexually assaulted, beat, and choked Elder. Nor had the prosecution demonstrated that it could prove Luther attacked women "because they reminded him of his mother."

Munch, however, did not entirely side with defense motions. Cleaver wanted the court to exclude statements "allegedly made by Luther" to other inmates and to Debrah Snider. But Munch said he wouldn't necessarily preclude the prosecution from entering some such evidence, including Luther's remarks that he would kill the next woman he raped and bury her body, so long as the prosecution could work around the issue of his prior convictions.

The similar transactions ruling was a serious blow to the prosecution. So serious that Hall believed the pendulum had swung clearly to the side of the defense. He even explained to Cher Elder's parents, who attended every hearing, that the case was now in grave jeopardy.

Unable to refer to Luther's history with women, Hall wouldn't be able to show why a nice-looking, 37-year-old man would attack a young woman out of the blue. Luther would look like a Boy Scout. Meanwhile, the prosecution witnesses, other than Debrah Snider and law enforcement personnel, were criminals or liars whom the defense would have a field day impeaching— even accusing Byron Eerebout, who had argued with Elder the day of her disappearance, or Healey of the murder.

It became clear in the weeks that followed that the defense team knew they had crippled the prosecution case. They didn't even bother to approach the prosecution about a deal, highly unusual in a death penalty case.

However, Hall wasn't about to back down. While some prosecutors worry about win/loss records, and wouldn't even prosecute "iffy" cases, he believed that his responsibility was to place the evidence before a jury and let the chips fall where they might. If they won a first degree conviction, all of Luther's past would be fair game, and the death penalty would be a slam dunk.

"If he walks," he told Richardson, whom he called with Munch's decision, "at least it won't be because we didn't try."

Chapter
Twenty-Seven

January 1996—Jefferson County, Colorado

Like a long-distance runner drawing on his last reserves of energy to finish strong, Scott Richardson didn't let the approach of the trial slow his investigation. Indeed, the defense attorneys, who at one time complained to Judge Munch that they weren't receiving the prosecution's evidence fast enough, now complained that they kept getting so much new information from the investigation team that they couldn't keep up.

Much of the latest buzz had to do with Dennis "Southy" Healey, who told Richardson about a curious visit from Cleaver and her female defense investigator. He said that during an interview, the defense investigator shoved a letter across the table to Healey.

It was from Luther. "It said, 'You know, bro, that Byron is the one who killed her,' " Healey told the detective.

The letter was an obvious appeal from his former friend to switch sides and implicate Byron Eerebout for Elder's murder. Cleaver acted like that she had never seen the letter before and was as surprised at its sudden appearance as Healey. But she also snatched it up before leaving.

The other information involving Southy Healey came from a James Greenlow, who had once done time in prison with Luther. Now he claimed that while in the Jefferson County Jail, Healey told him that Luther wasn't involved in the murder. "It was Southy and Byron Eerebout," Greenlow told Richardson.

Richardson didn't believe him, but Greenlow said he'd be willing to take a lie-detector test to back up his allegations. He said he just didn't want to see an innocent man face the death penalty for something he didn't do.

The results of lie-detector, or polygraph, tests aren't admissible in Colorado courts. However, Greenlow passing such a test would certainly have cast a cloud over Healey's story. Richardson arranged for the test, but Greenlow didn't show. His wife said she didn't know where he was.

Angry, Richardson warned Greenlow's wife that he would personally see to it that anyone who perjured themselves in the case would be prosecuted. When the detective finally caught up to Greenlow again, the ex-con had decided against taking the test.

Just a week before the trial was set to start, Richardson got an unexpected boost for the prosecution when he heard from Bob Ramierez, the former boyfriend of Myra Healey. He'd been trying to find Fletcher without success to that point.

Ramierez said he wasn't sure what help he could be, and judging from his comments, he didn't seem to know that Elder's body had been found. However, he recalled a trip he made with Southy and Myra to Longmont in July 1993, where they met up with a man he knew as "Lou," one of Luther's nicknames.

Southy, he said, got out of the car and talked privately to Lou. When Southy Healey got back in the car, "He kept calling Lou a 'fuckin' asshole punk.' I asked him why he was so pissed off, but he wouldn't say anymore while Myra was around."

Later, however, Healey told him that Lou "did something to a girl." When Ramierez asked what he meant, he replied, "She's not around anymore."

Ramierez kept pressing, and Southy Healey finally told him that Lou had "killed a broad and was afraid that the cops had found the body. I don't remember if he said Lou shot her or knifed her, but shooting sticks out more in my mind."

"What about Healey? What's his involvement?" Richardson asked.

"He said he wasn't involved," replied Ramierez, who had since split up with Myra Healey. "He wasn't even around when Lou killed her."

There wasn't much else he could think of, Ramierez said. Except that Lou once came over to Myra's house earlier that spring at 3 A.M. to get her brother, "and that seemed strange."

Then, just days before jury selection was set to begin, Richardson got another call, this one from a Jefferson County Jail inmate named Robert Cooper. He said Luther had told him about killing a girl and he wanted to come forward.

Richardson told Cooper he'd be out to see him. Then he got an idea. If Luther was bragging, maybe other inmates would have something to say. If not, it was another chance to put the fire to Luther's toes.

The next day, Richardson, several other Lakewood detectives, and district attorney investigators assembled in the parking lot outside the Jefferson County Jail. There was a detective for every inmate in Luther's section, or "pod," at the jail.

"We're pulling them all out at once," Richardson said as he gave last-minute instructions to his colleagues. "Everyone 'cept Luther. He'll be in there all alone, wondering what's goin' on and who's sayin' what.

"Even if your guy don't say nothin', keep him at least forty-five minutes before you let him go back."

Pulling them out at the same time served a couple of purposes. One, it wouldn't expose any real informants, like Cooper, and it would make Luther nervous and even more paranoid.

Richardson could visualize the scene on the pod when the first inmate returned.

"What were you talkin' to the cops about?" he imagined Luther saying.

"Nothin'," would be the reply, whether it was the truth or not.

"Nothing? Forty-five minutes and you said nothing?"

Then the next guy would return and the process would start all over. Again and again.

The detectives went in. Richardson met with Cooper, who said he had known Luther since August. Neither man was much for playing basketball or watching television, so they had naturally started talking to pass the time. It was quickly evident to Cooper that Luther didn't much like women.

"Whenever we're watching television and he sees a good-lookin' girl," Cooper said, "he calls them 'tramps' and 'sluts' and 'whores.' "

Nor did Luther have a soft spot for the law. "He refers to you as an asshole and a prick," Cooper said. "But I got two daughters of my own, and just thought I should say somethin'."

"You ain't lookin' for a deal?" Richardson asked skeptically.

Cooper shook his head. "I've already pleaded guilty to the charge against me, and I don't want nothin'."

Luther told him in December that he had "killed a girl and buried her up a dirt road. He said they had gone to a bar and gotten into a fight. He said 'I slapped her around' before he killed her."

A few minutes later, Cooper said, he was walking past Luther, who was talking to another inmate, when he heard Luther say "about five shots to the head." He assumed Luther was still talking about the girl he murdered.

Luther also told him that if he was convicted, he hoped the state would "just do it to him and get it over with. He said if he beat this one, the police would just pin another one on him."

Apparently, Luther was already preparing for the death penalty phase of his trial if what Cooper said was the truth. "I heard him talkin' to his sister on the telephone," Cooper recalled. "He said, 'You know how our family life was. We were abused and mistreated. Don't lie, tell them that we were abused and mistreated.' Then he got really angry and slammed the telephone down."

Richardson kept Cooper for forty-five minutes before sending him back to the pod. The other inmates were just filtering back then, too.

Back out in the parking lot, talking to the other detectives, Richardson was rewarded by a pounding on the windows on the second floor of the jail. He looked and saw Luther, his face a mask of rage and hate, beating his fists against the glass.

Richardson couldn't make out what Luther was screaming, although he was sure it wasn't pleasant. The deputy sitting at the intake desk inside the building walked out. Pointing up to where Luther was still pounding on the glass, he smiled and said, "Hey, I think you made a friend up there."

The trial of Thomas Edward Luther began January 16, 1996, with the jury selection process. And even that was unusual.

The disappearance and subsequent unearthing of Cher Elder, followed by the arrest of Luther, had generated a storm of press coverage. Luther even contributed when he wrote a letter to a Denver newspaper saying he was being framed.

Luther's lawyers asked for a change of venue due to the publicity. Judge Munch denied their request; however, he ordered that a particularly large jury pool be assembled from which to choose. More than 400 notices were sent out, of which 250 people showed up at the Taj Mahal causing a traffic snarl and parking fiasco that eased only after the prospective jurors were assigned dates to return to the courthouse to be questioned about what they knew of the case and their feelings about the death penalty.

A death penalty jury is different in several respects from a standard jury. A standard jury only decides if the prosecution has proved a defendant's guilt beyond a reasonable doubt. A death penalty case, however, may contain two parts for the jury. The first to determine if the defendant is guilty or not, and, if found guilty, a second phase to determine if the defendant should be put to death.

The verdict must be unanimous to go on to the second phase, at which the prosecution and defense do their best to portray the defendant in the worst and best lights possible. In the Luther case, the prosecution team knew their case was weak but were confident that the death penalty phase, if they got that far, would be a given. At that point, all of Luther's past crimes would be fair game.

As would strike home in the Luther case, there are often misconceptions by the public about who may be excluded from a death penalty jury. Mere opposition to the death penalty is not enough to be automatically excluded, if the prospective juror promises that under the right legal conditions they can follow the law and sentence someone to death.

There are two schools of thought about which side is favored by having a jury sworn to be willing to carry out the death penalty. Anti-death penalty activists and, of course, defense attorneys contend that such a jury is more conservative and law-enforcement oriented.

On the other hand, prosecutors and police say that the enormity of what's at stake—a man's life—makes such jurors more likely to err on the side of caution than risk sentencing a potentially innocent man to death. The general school of thought among prosecutors is that if the case is shaky, it is better to seek life without parole than put a jury in the position of making life and death decisions.

Eighteen prospective jurors at a time, who first made it through the initial phase of answering questionnaires without being thrown off for cause (such as claiming that under no circumstances could they invoke the death penalty), were brought into the Jefferson County courtroom to answer questions from the attorneys and judge. It was there that those who would eventually make up the jury got their first glimpse of the contrasts of the two sides.

On the defense side were Enwall and Cleaver. Silver-haired and silver-tongued, well-dressed in expensive, tailored suits, Enwall would take the lead for the defense. Cleaver, fortyish and a former public defender, made it a point in front of the jurors to sit close to Luther, leaning close to converse and share inside jokes, as if to prove he was no danger to women.

Some jurors would later say that it took them awhile to realize that Luther was the defendant. He appeared a good-looking, middle-aged, blue-eyed cowboy in his boots and new blue jeans. He smiled a lot and seemed much more relaxed than the prosecution team.

On the other side of the aisle sat Hall, Richardson, and Mark Minor, the deputy district attorney who had prosecuted Byron Eerebout for the shooting incident and would now assist at the murder trial. Slight and boyish, Hall was his usual mild-mannered self, with a habit of placing one hand on his cheek while cupping his elbow with the other hand, even while standing. Minor was his physical opposite, heavy-set with a neck that bulged over the collar of his shirts and a football player-sized body stuffed into ill-fitting suits. He rarely smiled and gave the impression that he would rather be almost anywhere else but in the courtroom.

Then there was Richardson. He favored dark suits, the pants legs of which he pulled down over his cowboy boots. His dark, intense eyes seemed to follow every move made in the courtroom and, with his fu manchu moustache, some jurors would later say, he seemed at first glance somewhat intimidating. Some even believed in the beginning that he was the defendant.

Judge Munch, a round, owl-faced man, had decided to seat fifteen jurors, including three alternates who would not take part in the final deliberations unless another juror fell ill or had to be replaced. For all the so-called jury experts who are sometimes paid to help pick the right jurors, it's an inexact science. Each side had its own theory on how to winnow the obvious threats, but after that it was a guessing game.

The prosecution team assigned numbers to how individuals answered each question, adding the numbers together to indicate those they felt were weak or strong. They were satisfied with the first fourteen jurors to be seated, even though several had indicated reluctance to impose the death penalty. But for the final spot, it came down to choosing the lesser of several evils.

For instance, the prosecution team didn't want a 65-year-old housewife, a Catholic who said she did not support the death penalty and seemed to be stuck on a concept of guilt "beyond the shadow of a doubt," rather than "reasonable doubt." But, under questioning by Munch, she agreed that if convinced beyond a shadow of a doubt that Luther was guilty of first degree murder, she could follow instructions that might lead to Luther being sentenced to death.

It was the prosecution team's bad luck that the next two jurors in line behind the woman had ranked even lower in their scoring. And with only two preemptory challenges to have prospective jurors removed without having to show cause, they allowed the woman to be seated as the fifteenth juror.

It had taken a week, but at last there was a jury of six men and nine women. No one was told who would be the alternates so that the three would listen just as attentively as the other twelve, in case they were called upon.

Munch announced that opening statements would be heard the next day, January 23, beginning at 9 A.M. The wait was over.

January 23, 1996

The morning of the trial arrived with deceptively blue and sunny skies. Outside, the temperature was bitterly cold, made more so by a stiff wind.

It was going to be a long trial, but then it had been a long time in the making. Scott Richardson had talked to more than 1,000 people over the course of his investigation—from crime lab technicians to family members to the assortment of drug dealers, thieves, liars, and convicts who were former friends, associates, and enemies of Thomas Luther and the Eerebout brothers. Many of those conversations were recorded on more than 150 audio cassettes, some fifty videotapes, and eighteen four-inch volumes of typed notes and transcripts. He'd followed up on dozens of reports of unidentified bodies found throughout the United States. And he'd logged more than 1,000 paid hours, maybe twice that much unpaid, working on the case alone since April 1, 1993.

In the next couple of weeks, he'd know whether any of it had meant a damn thing. The only thing he knew for sure now was that he never wanted to go through another case like this again. It had sapped him emotionally and physically, like the wind carrying away the small clouds of condensed breath of the people hurrying into the building. He took a deep breath. It was time.

The courtroom was small. Three rows of long benches on either side of the aisle made up the spectator gallery, separated from the rest of the room by a wooden banister.

On the other side of the banister, the prosecution table, where Dennis Hall and Mark Minor already sat, was on the right, in front of the jury box. On the left was the defense table, where Enwall and Cleaver busied themselves at laptop computers, closest to the witness stand and judge's podium.

There were no windows in the wood-paneled walls, just doors. One led to the judge's chambers, the other to an elevator in which the prisoner would be brought up from a holding cell in the bowels of the building.

The courtroom was already packed. Cher's family sat in the rows behind the prosecution table. Earl Elder and his wife, Claudette. His former wife, Debbie. Rhonda Edwards and her husband, Van. Cher's half sister, Beth, and half brother, Jacob. Her grandparents. The media was out in force, occupying seats on both sides of the aisle. And there were the usual assortment of court watchers who followed crime stories like some people follow soap operas.

In the first row on the prosecution side, against the wall next to Elder's maternal grandmother, sat a pretty, blond woman. It was Sabrina. Richardson saw her immediately but didn't acknowledge her. She'd only been to one other trial, the murder case against a boy who had been found guilty in a heartbeat.

Richardson worried that someone might hunt her to get even with him.

Sabrina had wanted to come to this to support Scott. But also because she wanted to look at the face of the monster who had haunted her family for so long. She wanted to see fear in his eyes when he realized that her husband was going to put him away for a long, long time, maybe even forever.

The defense side of the spectator gallery had filled only when there was no room left on the prosecution side. The jury might be kept in the dark about Luther's past, but onlookers were well aware and gave their opinion about his guilt or innocence by where they sat.

It was 9 A.M., but the jurors were still in the jury room, waiting to be summoned by the judge. Already there was a delay.

As with most trials, Luther's defense attorneys had successfully petitioned the court to have their client appear in civilian clothes rather than his jail jumpsuit. He was also to be led into the courtroom before the jury so that they wouldn't see his guards remove the shackles from his ankles or the handcuffs from his wrists. It would be as though he had walked in off the streets on his own volition. However, Luther had decided he didn't want to come to court. He was refusing to leave the holding cell.

"I don't care how you do it," a perturbed Judge Munch growled to the sheriff's deputies who handled court security, "but get him in here *now!*"

A few minutes later, down in the basement, a large German Shepherd dog was brought muzzle-to-face with Luther, who quickly decided he'd rather appear in court. From that point on, dogs were posted in the hallways outside the courtroom. Every once in awhile throughout the trial, their handlers would get the dogs to bark once or twice just to remind Luther, who flinched at the sound, that they were there. Five large deputies also were present in the courtroom at all times, one standing close to the defense table, the others guarding the doors.

Brought into the courtroom, Luther looked quickly back at the gallery while the deputies removed his handcuffs. Seeing no friendly faces, he turned his attention to his attorneys and smiled. Munch warned Luther and his attorneys that if he acted up in the courtroom, he'd be bound and gagged. And if that didn't work, he'd have to watch his trial on television from another room.

By the time the jurors were escorted into the courtroom, Luther was acting like he'd been there all along, anxious to get started. He joked quietly with Cleaver and smiled at a number of pretty, young female law students the defense had seated immediately behind its table. He was casually dressed in a green, short-sleeved shirt with new jeans.

Finally, an hour later than planned, Dennis Hall stood to make his opening statements. He knew he faced a daunting task, had known it since Munch ruled against allowing Luther's past into evidence. Despite what's shown in the movies and television, it's not necessary to prove motive to obtain a murder conviction. However, as Hall knew full well, it's only human to want to know why a man would kill an innocent young girl in cold blood.

Luther's motive, Hall believed, was as simple as he was a serial killer, who raped and murdered women who reminded him of his mother when they made him angry. But with Luther's prior history off limits, the prosecution had only weak, hypothetical explanations to feed the jury—that Luther killed because she was a police informant or got into an argument with Luther for some unexplained reason on their drive back from Central City.

At a prior hearing, Munch had already thrown out one of the murder indictments—the one that contended Luther killed Cher Elder in the commission of a robbery, the theft of her ring. He said there was not enough evidence. And now it was going to be damn difficult to prove the second count—that Luther killed Elder to cover up having raped her. That would leave only the third count—that he premeditated her murder.

Hall knew he couldn't hide the truth about Southy Healey's and Byron Eerebout's pasts. Luther would look like a choir boy to the jury, and he would have to find a way to dance around his criminal activities. But in the meantime, the defense lawyers were certain to rip into the questionable backgrounds of Luther's accusers like sharks into a bloody carcass. So he might as well steal their thunder, and use it to show the jury that the prosecution wasn't trying to hide anything.

Debrah Snider was an unknown. They still didn't know how

she would testify or come off to a jury. What he had going for him was Richardson, as dedicated a detective as he'd ever met, and a lot of little pieces that fit together. And he had a portrait of Cher Elder, a nice girl who wasn't the sort to have casual sex with a man almost twice her age.

Hall stood and faced the jury. "Once again, good morning everyone. You've all heard some bits and pieces of this case over the last week or so, and I assume you're all wondering when you're going to hear what it's all about.

"I thought it would help to understand what this case is about if I begin by sort of setting out the cast of characters, and as I told you in the jury selection, it's a pretty interesting cast.

"The victim in this case was a young woman named Cher Elder. Cher was about twenty years old at the time of her death. She had plans to go on to college. She was not married. She had no children. And she had a sometime boyfriend named Byron Eerebout.

"It was through Byron that Cher met Thomas Luther, who is the defendant in this case. Thomas Luther in March 1993 was working for a janitorial service in Fort Collins. Luther was a very close friend of Byron Eerebout's father. Luther frequently came to Denver to visit Byron and his brothers, and frequently stayed over at Byron's apartment in Lakewood.

"Dennis Healey is one of the more colorful people you'll meet in this case. Healey is a convicted felon and a drug addict who is currently in a rehabilitation center. He was a close friend of Tom Luther's. Healey had met Byron once or twice, didn't know him very well, and isn't sure whether he ever met Cher.

"The last person I want to introduce to you before I start with what happened in this case is a woman named Debrah Snider. Of all the witnesses you'll meet in this case, Deborah Snider is probably the most puzzling. Debrah Snider, who back in 1993 was Luther's girlfriend, lived with her husband outside of Fort Collins. Deb Snider observed many of Luther's actions during the spring and summer of 1993, and she had a number of conversations with him about Cher Elder and about what happened to Cher."

On the evening of March 27, a Saturday, Hall continued, Cher had argued with Byron over his newest girlfriend, Gina Jones. So she decided to go to Central City to visit her friend Karen

Knott. "So that's what she did as a way of getting her boyfriend off her mind. That was probably a pretty good idea, but she made a mistake. She went up there with Tom Luther."

Two years later, he said, her body was found in a shallow grave a mile or so north of the town of Empire. She'd been killed by three shots fired at point-blank range in close proximity to each other.

"It took a long, long time to find her because for quite a while many of the people who knew what happened wouldn't tell us the truth. One of the people who didn't tell the truth was Tom Luther.

"It's taken us almost three years now to put all these pieces together and it's going to take us a week or maybe up to two weeks to show you how they all fit. You'll hear from the experts and pathologists and a couple of doctors who will tell you how Cher died. You'll hear from some crime scene analysts who will tell you that a hair matching the hair from Tom Luther's head was found in Cher Elder's car, the car that Luther said he'd never seen and never been inside, and you will hear from Luther's friends—from Healey, from Eerebout, from Deb Snider—who were told by Luther what he'd done and why he'd done it.

"At the very end of the case you will hear Tom Luther's final statements to the police. He told Detective Richardson he knows he'll be convicted. When you've heard all the evidence, you will see that Tom Luther was right."

Hall took his seat as Enwall rose. Little half-moon glasses were perched partway down the former judge's nose, giving him the appearance of a distinguished professor about to lecture students. He shook his head slowly, as if he couldn't believe the case had made it this far, and then he began.

"This case is a senseless chapter in a relationship between Cher Elder and Byron Eerebout. Cher Elder was a good decent human being getting her life on course, excited about her future.

"Cher Elder thought that Byron Eerebout was her boyfriend. She thought it was a real relationship. She even bought him a $700 waterbed. But Byron thought that this was just a casual sexual relationship.

"Byron had another girlfriend and Cher was a problem to them. This new girlfriend, Gina Jones, wasn't at all happy that

Cher kept coming around. Byron assured Gina that Cher was just crazy and didn't get it, but that he would take care of it.''

Yes, Enwall said, Cher Elder was angry that night and went to Central City with Tom Luther, where they stayed until 2 A.M. "And as you've heard, they had sex on a mountainside, probably Lookout Mountain. She was retaliating against Byron and made that clear to Tom. And she felt badly afterward. She felt that she wasn't the kind of girl who slept around and had been angry and done something that she regretted.''

However, Cher and Tom returned to Byron's apartment, only to find him in bed with Gina. Tom tried to console her and she left to call a friend, but she never made that call. "It was the last anyone will admit to having seen Cher Elder alive.''

But in September, Enwall said, Byron found himself in trouble. He'd beaten a man with a baseball bat and emptied a .357 magnum at him. "He wanted a deal to get out of trouble. First, he said Southy killed Cher and Tom buried the body.'' But when it became clear that Richardson thought either Byron or Luther had killed Cher, he decided to pin it on Luther.

"After all, there was no question Tom was the last one seen with her. And because of a bizarre and misguided sense of loyalty, Tom had buried the body. Pointing the finger at Tom would take the focus away from Byron and make Detective Richardson happy.''

However, Enwall said, in order for Luther to be the killer and not just the person who buried the body, Eerebout had to reconstruct his story. "He had to have Cher disappear the night Tom took her to Central City. And, after repeatedly saying that Cher came back to his apartment, he decided that she had not. That he just heard a voice and thought it was her or somebody else. It was the only way his story made sense.''

However, Enwall told the jury, Byron had to have a reason why he knew where Cher's body was. So he made up a story about following Luther to the gravesite.

"Somewhere along the line, Dennis Healey gets involved. It's not clear whether it's before or after Cher Elder was killed.

"The evidence will be,'' Enwall said, raising his voice, that Dennis Healey and Byron Eerebout, "a violent man with an explosive temper, are compulsive liars.

"They have an enormous amount to gain by seeing Tom

Luther convicted in this case. Neither one of them is sitting over here," he said, placing a hand on Luther's shoulder, "but they both should be."

Hall was a little bit surprised by Enwall's opening. He expected the attack on Healey and Eerebout as liars, but not the outright accusation that they were the killers.

Enwall's rather fuzzy motive was apparently that Eerebout killed Elder to please his new girlfriend. But when? He was with Gina Jones all of Saturday night and Sunday. And there didn't seem to be a motive for Healey's involvement.

Some of what Enwall said would be easy to refute. Eerebout's first story wasn't that Healey killed Elder and Luther buried the body. Eerebout's first statement after his arrest in the shooting incident, when Richardson asked him why he was protecting Luther, was that he knew where Cher and Luther went and where Luther went afterward. Healey wasn't mentioned until later.

Luther was the one who first told Debrah Snider that Elder was killed because she was an informant, not Eerebout, as Enwall claimed. And Healey didn't tell Richardson that Luther had never talked to him about the case, he just said that his information was secondhand.

It was risky to make claims that wouldn't hold up in the course of a trial. Jurors weren't stupid. But in the meantime, Hall had a case to prosecute and couldn't worry about the defense tactics. He called his first witness, Karen Knott.

A thin, dishwater blonde, Knott looked frightened but determined as she made her way to the stand. Cher, she said, arrived in Central City with an older man she introduced as a friend of Byron's. They were definitely not on a date and the man mostly hung back by himself while the girls chatted.

Cher was upset with Byron, Knott said, but otherwise her usual happy-go-lucky self. She had no more than two drinks and the man with her sipped one or two beers.

"They weren't drunk or I would never have let her drive back with him," she insisted.

Karen Knott disputed Luther's claim that he and Cher Elder bought a bottle of wine in Central City that they later shared, causing Cher to vomit. There are no liquor stores in the gambling towns as a matter of law, she said.

"Did you ever know Cher to use cocaine?" Hall asked.

"No. And she could have if she wanted, because I sometimes used it. But she wouldn't."

"Based on your opinion, would she willingly have had sex with the older man?"

"No way," Karen Knott scoffed. In his seat, Luther's face turned red.

Knott said she saw Cher Elder get into the passenger side of the man's car, not the driver's side as Luther claimed. "It was the last time I saw her," she added, her voice cracking.

Cher, she said, was her best friend. They saw each other or called every day. Until that Sunday.

Enwall's cross-examination was brief. "You were her best friend but she saw other people," he noted.

"I got six days," Knott retorted. "They got one. I saw her every Sunday and Monday night."

Knott was excused. She'd held up well and established that Elder likely died after leaving Central City, never having called her best friend on Sunday. Karen made it as far as the hallway outside the courtroom before bursting into tears.

Richardson was called to the stand next, but only to guide the jurors through the casino videotape. He pointed to Elder and the man following her, as the jurors looked back and forth from the tape to Luther.

After the tape finished, Richardson described how he had shown the tape to Byron Eerebout on April 20, 1993. And how Eerebout denied knowing the man, only to receive a call from Luther an hour later. The testimony was a lead-in to Richardson's taped interview with Luther, which the jury then heard, omitting, of course, Luther's comments about his prior conviction for sexual assault.

Gina Jones was the next witness. Her distaste for Byron Eerebout was soon evident. Their relationship, she said, had lasted a matter of days. Hardly the sort of love to kill for.

She recounted how she had asked Eerebout if Luther had anything to do with Elder's disappearance. He'd said no, but later threatened her to "be careful or you'll wind up in a shallow grave."

After Jones left the room, Hall turned to Munch and said, "We'll call Dennis Healey to the stand."

Healey walked quickly to the witness stand where he was sworn in. The 28-year-old had changed a lot since his first meeting with Richardson. Instead of long and scraggly, his red hair was cut short and combed back; he wore a coat and tie and looked like a young stockbroker.

It's not unusual for defense attorneys to clean up their clients for trial. In this case, however, it wasn't the prosecution team who had changed Healey's image. It had been required by a get-tough drug rehabilitation center where he was currently living.

In fact, it was Hall who took apart the new image. "During the time you've been here in Colorado, what kinds of jobs have you held?" he asked.

"Not many," Healey said in his thick Boston accent. "Just, I don't know, three or four. Laborer, painter, never one for very long."

"How did you make money?"

"Mostly dealing drugs or burglaries, whatever, theft."

"Are you serving a sentence now, Mr. Healey?"

"Yes, I am. Eighteen months for attempted burglary."

"Do you recall how many other felony convictions you have?"

"Three. Right now I'm in a drug rehabilitation program."

Before getting into the program, Healey said, he was released to a halfway house.

"Did you want to be released?"

"No."

"Why?"

"I told the Department of Corrections I didn't want to be released out onto the streets on parole because I had a drug problem and knew I wouldn't get the treatment I needed."

Healey said he only lasted seven days at the halfway house before running away and getting back on drugs. Then he did something he'd never done before: "I turned myself in." He was arrested and put back in jail, until being placed in the rehabilitation program just two weeks earlier.

"How long would you have if you went back to jail and did your time?"

"Eight months."

"And how long before you can get out of rehab?

"Fourteen to sixteen months," Southy replied.

"You think you're going to finish this program?" Hall asked.

"I hope so. It's hard. But I'm not looking six months down the line. I'm not looking a month down the line. I'm looking to, like, tomorrow."

Hall didn't dare look at the jury to see how they were responding. They hadn't rehearsed this testimony, purposely, because he wanted Healey to come off just as he was—a drug addict who stole and sold drugs to support his habit. A young man who had lost his way and now was trying to make it one day at a time. He thought they'd succeeded; it was time to go on.

"In the spring of 1993, how would you have described your relationship with Tom Luther?" Hall asked. "Good friend? Casual friend?"

"At that time," Healey said, glancing at Luther, who sat staring at the defense table, "he was probably my best friend."

Hall led him through the events of late March 1993. The late-night telephone call. "Hey, bro, I need some help." The car with the dirt in the back. "I fucked up. Killed this broad." Standing lookout. The dirt and something wet and shiny on Luther's clothes. A grave too shallow.

"He said he took her out. They were having a good time, doing their little thing, and then he killed her," Healey said. "I was mad. I said, 'Hey bud, you fucked up. I don't want to be in this. This ain't me.' Yeah, I'm a drug addict. Yeah, I'm a thief. I'm a conniver, whatever you want to call me, but I ain't no murderer, you know what I mean. That's just not me."

Hall took a seat as Enwall rose to cross-examine. "Good afternoon, Mr. Healey."

"How you doing?" Healey responded, his thick accent and cheerful greeting bringing smiles to jurors and spectators alike.

"Have you turned over a new leaf here?" Enwall asked.

"I'm trying."

"But this clean-cut look is not the real you, is it?" Enwall asked. "You're more used to kind of shoulder-length hair and biker clothes?"

"Biker clothes?" Healey looked puzzled. "If jeans and a t-shirt is biker clothes, I guess so."

"But this appearance that you've got here today is pretty astonishingly different from what you looked like last time you were in court, wouldn't you say?"

Healey smiled and tugged on his tie. "Oh yeah. I'd say for the better, you know. How about you?" Again there were smiles and even a few titters from the jurors.

Enwall frowned. "I don't know, Mr. Healey. We'll see, I guess."

The defense attorney dove into Healey's past. But since he'd already admitted it, the questioning devolved into nit-picking about the exact number of convictions.

"But you do have a habit of lying to police?" Enwall said.

"I'd have to disagree with that," Healey replied. When he got caught for a crime, he admitted, he'd try to work out a plea bargain. "So I wouldn't say it was a habit, but I surely have relied upon it on occasion. But I've never been convicted, all my time was done on voluntary pleas."

Enwall was getting nowhere. Healey was an obviously personable young man who didn't have the usual criminal's habit of trying to place the blame for his actions on others.

The defense attorney tried to establish a link between Healey and Byron Eerebout. But Healey said he'd only met him a couple of times, both with Luther. And while both sold drugs, they weren't in business together.

Healey recalled speaking to Eerebout once in jail back in the winter of 1995. "He told me Tom's in jail."

Munch realized that Healey had crossed into dangerous territory by mentioning Luther being in jail. At that point, the jury didn't know that it was for the West Virginia sexual assault and not for the present crime. Still, he told Enwall, "This is going nowhere. Move on."

Enwall asked if Healey recalled showing up at Byron Eerebout's house in torn, bloody clothes. He was referring to Eerebout's statement to Richardson that Healey once came over, claiming to have been in a fight at a bar with police officers.

"I don't think so," Healey said, furrowing his brow, confused. "I do believe I'd remember that."

"I would think so, and you don't?" Enwall asked sarcastically.

"I don't because it didn't happen," Healey shot back. "There's no memory lapse. That just never happened. If I'd been in a fight with Lakewood cops, I don't think I'd be at Byron's talking about it. I'd probably have been under arrest, sitting in a jail."

Enwall returned to Healey and Eerebout talking in the jail. "For instance, didn't you say something about Cher's dad wanting the body to be found?"

"Yeah, that was said." Healey scowled.

"What was his reaction to that?"

"Basically, 'Tough Shit.' " Back in the spectator gallery, Rhonda Edwards stifled a sob, while Earl Elder's head dropped to his chest.

"Was there ever a time when Cher's body was stored in your sister's basement?"

"No."

"You heard that one before?"

"Yes, I did."

"There's not even a little bit of truth to it?"

"No." Now it was his turn to reply sarcastically. "I think we'd have seen it."

At the prosecution table, Richardson smiled quickly before catching himself. Healey was no dummy when off drugs and was holding his own against Enwall.

Apparently, the defense attorney thought so as well. He told the judge he had reached a good stopping point for the day.

Munch agreed. He admonished the jury to avoid reading or watching anything to do with the trial. "Avoid anyone who wants to talk about it. Don't go investigate anything on your own. Don't drive by places you hear mentioned.

"And keep a free and open mind. See you tomorrow morning."

January 24, 1996

Before the jury was brought into the courtroom on the second day of the trial, Hall announced that the prosecution was releasing Luther's brother-in-law, Randy Foster, who had been subpoenaed. "He's a hostile witness," Hall said, "and has indicated that he won't answer our questions." Luther smiled.

With the jurors summoned back to their seats, Dennis Healey

was again called to the stand. Now Enwall tried to show that Healey's story had evolved as he talked to Richardson.

"Did your sister ever tell you that there was a time when Tom made a statement like he had to get out of state because he left too many clues?" Enwall asked.

"She told me that she recalled a conversation between me and Tom in the kitchen of her house when she heard that, yeah."

"Did you tell her to call the police and tell them?"

"During the investigation?" Healey asked. Enwall nodded. "Yeah, I told her not to hide anything. 'Just tell the truth.' "

"Did you first tell Richardson that Tom Luther never talked to you at all about what happened to Cher Elder?"

"I don't believe Tom had specifically named anyone at that point. It all kind of came together for me when it was broadcast over the news that she had disappeared and Tom was a suspect."

"Did Richardson tell you that others were pointing the finger at you, and that his theory was that without a doubt, Cher was killed Saturday night?"

"I don't remember his words exactly," Healey said. "I think he told me it was his job to find who killed her. But I don't remember him saying that Tom killed Cher. He did tell me that the case was broke and anyone that didn't cooperate, they were going to go after them."

"And that he had enough to take them down?" Enwall asked.

"I don't remember," Healey shrugged. "It wasn't a big concern."

"Why wasn't it a big concern?" Enwall asked.

"I had nothing to hide."

"But you wanted a deal. No charges and no prison time," Enwall said accusingly.

"I didn't want to take a fall for nobody else," Healey explained. "Deals happen all the time."

"But you lied to Detective Richardson about how you knew where the grave was. You said you went up there with Byron and Tom," Enwall said.

Healey nodded. "I was trying to cover my own back. I didn't want to make it look like me and Tom had been there alone to take care of—"

Enwall interrupted. "So it was okay to lie about it?"

"I'm not saying it was okay, but I did it."

"Do you believe you have immunity from prosecution in this case?"

"As long as I was not directly involved in the murder of Cher Elder, yes, sir."

"So it's imporant for you to not be found to have any involvement with her death?" Enwall asked and looked at the jurors.

"Well . . ." Healey began to answer but Enwall angrily cut him off.

"Mr. Healey could you please answer the question, if you wouldn't mind," he said. "It's important for you to be found not to have any involvement in her death, correct?"

"Well, yeah."

"And Tom Luther did not tell you specifically that he shot Cher Elder in the head?"

"No. He said, 'I fucked up and killed a broad.' "

"What did you mean when you told Detective Richardson that you weren't going to confess to him on that day, Mr. Healey? That, and I quote, 'You're not my priest.' "

Healey frowned. "That I'm not going to confess to something I didn't do."

Enwall turned his back on the witness and faced the jury. "What you meant was you weren't going to confess to him your involvement with Byron Eerebout or somebody else in the killing of Cher Elder?"

Healey shook his head. "No. What I wasn't going to confess to him was something I didn't do."

Enwall frowned. He'd lost that round. "No further questions."

Hall rose for a follow-up question. "Mr. Healy, what's your understanding of what it is we've given you in return for your truthful testimony here?"

"I guess it is the accomplice or accessory to murder or whatnot for the things that I did to help Tom after he'd already killed her," Healey said. "But I believe I wasn't going to be charged in the first place because I didn't have anything to do with the actual murder."

"Was there anything else promised?"

"No," Healey answered, looking at the jury. Excused, he stood and walked out of the courtroom without looking at Luther.

"Your next witness please," Munch said.

"We'll call Bob Ramierez," Hall responded.

A barrel-chested man walked slowly up the aisle and through the swinging gates to the witness stand. "How long have you known Dennis Healey?" Hall began.

Ramierez looked up for a moment, then said, "A couple of years. In the spring and summer of '93 he was living with me and his sister off and on."

"Do you recall a trip to Longmont?" Hall asked.

Ramierez nodded. "Yeah, we met Lou," he said pointing to Luther, who sat staring at the witness with his mouth open, "at a McDonald's."

"Do you remember when . . . what time of year?"

"Summer," Ramierez said. "I remember it was a real hot day."

"What do you recall from that meeting?"

"We was driving back and Dennis said Lou had done a number on a broad."

"Was that all?"

"Some time later, he said Lou did away with some girl and now he had to get out of town."

Hall sat. This time Cleaver rose to question the witness. "Did Dennis say that Mr. Luther had killed a woman?"

Ramierez shook his head. "He didn't say killed. But I was high a lot of the time back then, and I wasn't paying much attention."

Cleaver nodded. "In fact, that was typical for you. You were high a lot?"

"Yes, sir," Ramierez replied before catching himself. "I mean, ma'am."

Richardson put a hand to his mouth to cover a smile. He didn't like Cleaver and enjoyed her embarrassment.

Cleaver went on. "Dennis never said what was done to the woman?"

Ramierez shook his head. "No. I don't know. I think I remember she was shot."

The rest of the morning and into the afternoon was taken up by expert witnesses who testified about efforts to locate forensic evidence.

A crime lab technician testified that a single, curly gray hair was found on the driver's seat of Cher's car. Compared to Luther's hair sample, she said it was in the same class, which meant it had matched seventeen different characteristics of Luther's hair. Not enough without a bit of blood attached to it, as it might have had if it had been pulled out, to be sure. But very close.

A ballistics expert testified. They had not been able to locate the guns made just before and after the gun stolen by Tristan Eerebout for that comparison. However, the expert said, the bullet fragments taken from Cher Elder's skull could only have come from a few select handguns. One of them was a .22 Baretta.

Another expert testified about efforts made to look for blood both in Luther's car and Byron Eerebout's apartment. Among other techniques, the crime lab had sprayed a chemical called Luminol, which reacts with iron in blood. There was a slight reaction with the stain on the back seat of Luther's car; however, Luminol will react with other rust, such as that left by tools, and other tests could not determine if the stain contained blood.

Luminol had reacted strongly in Eerebout's apartment. However, tests proved that the blood causing those reactions had come from a dog and from Eerebout. The expert testified that technicians had even dismantled sink traps to see if blood had been washed down them.

An expert also testified about the samples taken from Luther in May 1993 at the Fort Collins hospital. "Mr. Luther pulled pubic hairs on his own," the expert, who had been there, deadpanned as Richardson smiled. Luther's blood type, he said, was "A one plus one."

Aerial photographs of the gravesite and the town of Empire were introduced into evidence, as was a scale model of the gravesite, including the turn-off. Michael Starr, the owner of the Marietta Restaurant, was called to the stand to describe the day in May 1993 when he saw the defendant walking past his restaurant, wearing a blue shirt, blue jeans, and a blue baseball cap with gold lettering on the front.

Late in the afternoon, after the jury returned from a break, Hall called Scott Richardson. He took the stand, his eyes going from juror to juror before returning to Hall.

Hall took him back to April 20, 1993, and asked what he'd done to verify some of the things Luther had told him about in the taped interview.

"I went to check to see if there was a pay phone where he

said Cher went to make a call,'' he said. "Then I got the records of all calls made from that telephone after 1:45 A.M. and ran them down. Not one of them knew Cher or any of the other people involved.''

After seizing Luther's car, did he make arrangements to have the car picked up on May 19 at 9 A.M.? Hall asked.

"Yes."

"Did he show up on time?"

"No. He showed up late that afternoon," Richardson responded.

"And what was he wearing?"

"Blue jeans, a blue shirt, and a blue baseball cap with gold lettering that said 'Navy' on the front.''

Hall asked about the incident in which Byron Eerebout was arrested for shooting at Mark Makarov-Junev and his girlfriend Patty, and the comment that Eerebout knew what had happened to Cher Elder after she left with Luther. "I had asked him why he continued to lie regarding Cher Elder, and he was very angry at me. He was eventually convicted and sentenced to twenty-four years."

"I want to direct your attention between May 1993, when you seized Luther's car, and Byron Eerebout's sentencing in July 1994," Hall said. "During all of that time were you still investigating the Cher Elder case?"

"Yes, the whole time," Richardson said.

"Can you give the jury an idea of how much of your workday would be devoted to Cher Elder?"

"The majority," he said, and described the scope of the investigation.

"Did a lot of those things turn out to be false leads?"

"Yes," Richardson replied. He described all the effort. The unidentified bodies. The scuba divers sent into the Empire sewage plant. The mine shaft excavations. The FLIR jets and bloodhounds.

Richardson knew that Hall was establishing that the investigation had not just haphazardly picked Luther as a suspect and then concentrated only on him.

"At the time of Eerebout's sentencing in July 1994, did it appear to you that you were any closer to finding Cher's body than you had been a year and a half before?" Hall asked.

"No. We were concentrating that search up in Empire. I felt that she was probably up in that area, but no."

Richardson explained why he waited to talk to Byron Eerebout after his sentencing. "I wanted Byron to sit in prison long enough to realize that this is going to be the next twenty-four years and get a good taste of what prison life was really going to be like. But I didn't want him sitting down there long enough to develop friends and get comfortable."

At the meeting in Buena Vista, "I told him, just be quiet and listen to me. I just explained the facts—twenty-four years in prison and that I felt he had information about the disappearance of Cher Elder. Eventually he said he would cooperate."

And eventually, Richardson testified, a deal was struck. Eerebout would be granted a sentence reduction and allowed to serve his time in a minimum security facility. He would be required to testify "truthfully" at Luther's trial. But first, he said, Eerebout had to prove he knew exactly where the grave was.

With his eyes on the jurors, who sat rapt in their seats, Richardson recounted first the trip with Healey and how he discovered the pile of rocks while other searchers worked to make a mine shaft safe.

Then he recalled for the jurors the trip back to the grave with Eerebout, and the resulting discovery of Elder's body.

"Did you maintain security up there when people weren't working on the grave?"

"Slept by it," Richardson said. For the first time in his testimony, his voice wavered. But the jurors seemed to understand and several nodded their heads.

Hall produced photographs of the excavation. One by one, Richardson described the contents of the photographs and handed them to the grim-faced jurors. As he got to the photographs showing Elder's remains, Richardson hesitated. He looked back to where Earl Elder and Rhonda Edwards sat. He didn't want them to hear this. They seemed to get the idea and the family stood and rushed from the courtroom. The detective finished his descriptions.

Under Hall's questioning, Richardson described how he had searched every turn-off between Golden and Central City. "How long did it take you to drive from those turn-offs to the grave?" Hall asked.

"Driving the speed limit, occasionally slowed by traffic, the trip is about thirty-five minutes," Richardson answered. "And if you go straight from Central City, twenty-five minutes. And about forty-five minutes from Byron Eerebout's former apartment."

"And how long from the grave to where Dennis Healey was staying?"

"About an hour."

Hall shifted gears. Now, he wanted to know about comments Luther made after his arrest in West Virginia, carefully skirting the fact that it was an extradition from prison.

Richardson described the drive to the airport with the police escorts. "It wasn't pleasant in any way whatsoever—angry, hostile, yelling."

In his seat, Luther stared at Richardson, who acted as if his enemy wasn't even present. "He was yelling at me about things that I didn't do in the case," the detective recalled. "Yelling at me about a Colombian. He says, 'How come you didn't follow up on the Colombian.' I wasn't paying much attention to him. I was trying to avoid a confrontation because I knew this was going to be a long day.

"Finally, I responded, 'What are you telling me? That the Colombians killed Cher Elder? You're blaming it on the cartel?' And he kind of looked at me and smiled, and that was about it with the Colombian."

Several times on the plane rides back to Colorado, Richardson said, Luther told him he knew he was going to be convicted. "He said he felt like writing down what happened and getting it over with. And he made a comment that he couldn't believe Byron and J.D. told on him."

Richardson also recounted the humorous moments, like when he asked Luther to mark the spot on a map of Mexico, where he'd be in case he escaped. "He said I had lost a lot of weight and that I looked like crap. And I said, 'Yeah, because of you.' I looked at his hair and said, 'Jesus, you got a lot of gray hairs,' and he kind of laughed and said, 'Yeah, because of you.' "

Richardson smiled. Luther chuckled. And the jurors smiled for the first time since they'd seen the photographs.

"And at the end of bringing him back to Denver, he made the comment, 'You know, I'm kind of glad this is over because

I don't have to spend the rest of my life looking behind my back for you.' ''

Hall turned the questioning over to Enwall, who immediately attacked Richardson for destroying the notes he'd made of Luther's comments on the trip back.

Richardson shrugged. That was his practice after his secretary transcribed notes and he'd proofread them. There was a tape-recording of the conversations, a copy of which had been given to the defense, Richardson said. But he acknowledged that due to background noise it was all but inaudible. ''You can hear a lot of yelling and something about Colombians.''

Enwall accused Richardson of telling Healey and Eerebout his theory so that they could tailor their own stories to fit. ''In general, isn't it a good idea not to give witnesses too much information?''

''Depends on the interview,'' Richardson shrugged. ''There's some interviews where you would do it to show that you know what you're talking about, you know what happened, and you may feed information to them, but there's certain details that you don't tell.

''That way when they feed information back to you, if it works, if they think you know what's going on, then you can tell what is accurate information or are they really just kind of going with what you're doing, or are they giving you real information. That's a common procedure.''

But, Enwall said, the detective told Southy Healey that it was his theory that Tom Luther killed Cher Elder that Saturday night. ''Which was certainly true at that point, that that was your theory.''

''Yes, sir.''

Enwall went back and forth on essentially the same question when Judge Munch interrupted. ''It's been a long day, and I believe it's time to quit.''

Again he admonished the jury, and sent them on their way.

When the jurors were gone, Munch listened to the attorneys discuss whether other statements Luther had made the day before his extradition should be allowed.

Enwall wanted certain parts removed that he said would preju-dice the jury, including all of the comment, ''Just like this fucking bullshit case I've got here, and all that fucking come down on me hard because of your bullshit out in Colorado.''

Hall said he already figured that because it mentioned Luther's West Virginia case it was off limits.

Enwall wanted to select lines from the next comment, some of which he wanted out and some of which he wanted left in. He wanted the line, "I ain't no fucking serial killer," out because it implied Luther had killed before. But he wanted to keep, "I'm not a fucking rat," because it reinforced the defense argument that Luther was on trial because he refused to identify the real killers. Enwall also wanted to keep, "I'm an angry bastard, but I ain't no killer."

Hall argued that they were all part of the same statement. It was Luther, not some other witness or even in response to a question, who contended he wasn't a serial killer.

The judge said he'd think about it overnight and let them know his decision in the morning.

January 25, 1996

The courtroom filled quickly every morning of the trial. Many of the spectators, even those who weren't part of Cher Elder's family or the press, remained the same, such as two women who brought their children every day for a civics lesson as part of their home schooling. But there were always new faces. This morning, Detectives Richard Eaton and Charlie McCormick were in the rows behind the prosecution, as were Heather Smith's father and brother.

It angered Cher's family and others like Heather's father that Luther got to sit there, looking like an overgrown Boy Scout, while the integrity of the prosecution witnesses, including Richardson, was attacked.

Everyone else in the courtroom knew Luther's real story. Waiting for the jury to be brought in that morning, Luther suddenly draped his arm around the back of defense lawyer Cleaver's chair. When the defense attorney made no move to separate herself from her client, a female spectator gasped loud enough to be heard throughout the gallery, "How can she stand to sit so close?''

Luther looked back and smiled, but kept his arm in place. Otherwise, he had rarely glanced at the spectators during the trial. He usually looked at the witness on the stand ten feet straight ahead or scribbled notes on a pad on the table in front of him. The defense lawyers and the young law students, who Richardson noted didn't seem to do anything but provide female companionship for Luther, frequently engaged him in conversations, especially when the jury was present.

In contrast, the prosecutors often looked tired, even though the trial had gone well to this point. Healey was a star, and Enwall was making no headway against Richardson, but Minor, who mostly handled questioning the expert witnesses, looked tense. Hall often sat in his chair with his head in his hands.

Before the jurors were brought in or Richardson called back to the stand, Munch ruled on the statements from the day before. The statement that included a reference to his West Virginia case was out. But he was going to allow the other statement in its entirety, in part because it might even help the defendant. "The statement could be interpreted that he made the statement about being convicted not because he thought he was guilty but because he felt he was being 'railroaded' by Richardson and others."

With that out of the way, Richardson retook the stand. Enwall produced a transcript of the statements Munch had just ruled on. He handed Richardson a copy to read. "Ironically, I would like to play you and have you play Mr. Luther."

"The transcript," Enwall said, "starts with you saying, 'Like what?'"

"Yeah, you kiss my ass, that's what you do. Just take me back to my unit," Richardson read. He disliked playing the part of Luther, it made him feel dirty. Meanwhile, Luther was smiling, apparently enjoying the little play.

"Okay. Don't want to talk to us?" Enwall said, playing Richardson.

"Fuck, no, I don't want to talk to you," Richardson read. "You know I don't want to talk to you. I don't even know why you even fucking come here. I ain't got nothing to say to you."

Enwall read the statment about Richardson having worked the case for two years. "And now it's over."

"You ain't worked no case," Richardson read. "I ain't no

fucking serial killer. I'm an angry bastard, but I ain't no fucking killer, ya know. I ain't a fucking rat."

Enwall concluded his cross-examination by again questioning Richardson's tactics. Why did he believe Healey? Why had he dropped Byron Eerebout as a suspect? Maybe he'd put blinders on and now wouldn't admit that he was after the wrong man?

Throughout the attack, Richardson remained calm and polite. He answered each question with as little emotion as possible, while Enwall grew more sarcastic and accusatory. And at last, Enwall called it quits.

Hall rose to ask a few questions raised by the defense attorney.

"There was a lot of testimony with Mr. Enwall about the 'deal' Dennis Healey got," Hall said. "Could you summarize that deal for us?"

"He was told we were only interested in the person who actually murdered Cher Elder," Richardson replied. "If he did not perjure himself or lie in his testimony, we would not pursue any accessory after the fact murder charges on Dennis Healey for watching out during the night of the burial."

"Did we give him anything else in return for his truthful testimony?"

"Nope," Richardson replied, then he paused and smiled. "I bought him a pack of cigarettes one day on this trip because he didn't have any."

"You explained to Mr. Enwall that Healey originally gave you a story about going to the grave with Byron and Tom Luther, and later he said he lied."

"That's correct," Richardson said.

"Did he explain why he lied?" Hall asked.

"Yes," Richardson nodded. "He was scared and he didn't want me to know he was actually watching for the cops while Luther went to the grave. And he wanted the Elder family to have the body."

With Richardson off the stand, the prosecution case had reached its most critical juncture—the Eerebout brothers.

J.D. Eerebout was missing. They'd heard that he was with his father, Skip, but the two had disappeared so that he couldn't testify. There was a nationwide warrant put out for his arrest, but they'd not been heard from.

Hall called Tristan Eerebout, 16 years old, to the stand. His testimony, his "itty bitty piece," was that he stole a .22 Baretta which he then gave to Luther.

Then, 25-year-old Byron Eerebout was called to the stand. Tall and lean, with his red hair cut close to his head and a smirk on his face, Byron swaggered to the witness stand while both Luther and Earl Elder glared at him.

Hall took a deep breath as he looked over his notes one more time. On his own, he knew that Eerebout's testimony would have been laughed out of court. He was exactly what the jury was going to see, a smirking, not terribly bright, petty criminal. But together with the other testimony, what he had to say fit the prosecution puzzle and was crucial.

Hall's biggest concern was that Eerebout would slip and say something about Luther having been in prison. He'd warned him against it dozens of times and tried to prepare his questions in such a way to minimize the possibility. But he still needed to establish that Luther was a friend of the family, someone who had given and received Byron's trust. And there was the danger.

It was late afternoon when Eerebout took the stand. It was snowing outside and the roads were getting slick. Before allowing Hall to proceed, Munch told the jurors that he would let them go a little early because of the weather conditions.

Hall began by leading Eerebout through a series of questions about his background, including his stint in the Army and stationing in Saudi Arabia during the Gulf War. While there, Eerebout said, a storm came up, there was a fire outside the large tent in which he was living, and then he felt a heavy blow to the back of his head from a collapsing tent pole. "Now I can't taste or smell and I have a problem with short-term memory loss. I forget things but sometimes a key word will make things come back to me."

"Do you have any felony convictions?" Hall asked.

Yes, Eerebout replied. A forgery. A theft. And the three assault accounts against him for the incident in September 1993.

In March 1993, he recalled, he was living in an apartment with his brother, J.D. "Tom Luther stayed with me occasionally," he said. "Cher never stayed the night, but she was there."

Eerebout said he met Cher at a party. "We saw each other off and on. It was a casual relationship until we had sex."

"And at some point in your relationship, did she end up with your ring?" Hall asked.

"Yes, she did." She'd found it in the bathroom and began wearing it. "I believe it was on her wedding finger," he answered. But it was not a serious relationship. "I didn't consider us boyfriend or girlfriend."

Hall moved into more dangerous waters. "You also know Thomas Luther?"

"Yes, sir."

Hall nodded to remind Eerebout to take it slow. "How long?"

"Since I was a kid."

Good. He'd stayed away from visiting Luther and his father in prison. "Would it be fair to say that Tom Luther is a pretty good friend of your family?"

"He was a good friend of my father, yes, Jerry Eerebout. He had a good relationship with me and my brothers. With Mom it was off and on."

Hall began to relax; they had moved past the most dangerous area, while establishing that Luther was a friend of the family. "Now, did there come a time in the spring of 1993 when Tom Luther began to socialize with you and your brothers down here in the Lakewood/Golden area?"

"Yes, my father was released from prison before Tom was, I believe. I'm—"

A hush had fallen over the courtroom. Eerebout turned red as Hall visibly blanched on his feet. Everyone knew something was wrong, even if they didn't know what.

The silence lasted only a moment. Then Enwall leaped to his feet. "Your honor, may we approach the bench, please?"

Munch sighed. "Sure."

Luther smirked and smiled as he leaned over to whisper to Cleaver, who nodded.

After a brief conference, the attorneys returned to their places. Hall tried to salvage the day. "Byron, do you mean that your dad was released from prison before you began to socialize with Tom Luther back in the spring of '93?"

Eerebout, whose face remained crimson, nodded. "Yes."

Munch frowned. "Counsel, I take it you're going to be moving on to another area."

Hall, who seemed to still not have recovered, blinked. "Yes, judge."

Then Munch thought better of it. He turned to the jury. "We're going to go ahead and and break for the evening. Remember what I've told you. Don't discuss the case. Avoid the media. Keep a free and open mind."

After the jurors were escorted out, an angry judge turned on Byron. "Mr. Eerebout, would you step down and go into the witness waiting room." He then turned to the attorneys and asked for their responses.

Enwall demanded that Munch declare a mistrial. Eerebout's statement, he said, had caused "irreparable prejudice" to Luther's defense. "I'm sure he was repeatedly instructed not to do what he just did. Why he did it, we don't know, but it was just clear as a bell, and I'm sure it rang a bell for the jury. There's no unringing that bell."

Munch turned to Hall, whose color had still not returned to his face. The prosecutor held his hands up. "I specifically told him to avoid that a number of times. I don't think he did it on purpose."

Still shaken, Hall retreated to the prosecution table where he buried his face in his hands. Everything to that point had gone perfectly. The defense had made no ground on the witnesses, but he could never expect to do so well again. A mistrial would be a disaster.

Munch said he would take the matter under advisement and hear arguments in the morning before rendering a decision on Enwall's demand.

Out in the hallway, Cher's family was in tears. Earl Elder looked dazed, like someone had clubbed him in his sleep. Richardson tried to console them. "If there's a mistrial, we'll come back in a few months with even a stronger case," he said.

Rhonda Edwards blinked back her tears and looked at him hopefully. He prayed she couldn't see the despair in his eyes. "Hey," he said putting an arm around her shoulders. "You've trusted me this long. We'll do it, we'll get him."

To himself he said, *We're fucked.*

January 26, 1996

The next morning, with the jurors still out, Hall offered to do what he could to mitigate the damage. He, Minor, and Richardson had stayed up the entire night, digging up case law that might apply to unwitting slips by witnesses. Perhaps by asking leading questions that would turn the jurors' attention away from the previous day, he suggested.

Otherwise, he argued, the slip was unintentional and made after every effort had been taken to see that it didn't happen. Case law, he pointed out, held that if a witness misstepped but it wasn't the prosecution's fault, it would be unfair to hold the prosecution accountable.

Enwall argued that the damage was done. The defense team had worked long and hard to keep Luther's criminal background out of the trial, and the judge had ruled in their favor.

However, Munch agreed with Hall. It wasn't the prosecution's fault. There had been no mention of what sort of crime Luther was in prison for. "We'll go forward from here."

First, though, he had Byron Eerebout called to the stand and warned him not to slip up again or face the consequences. The young man swallowed hard and nodded.

Then, rather than pretending the slip had not occurred, Munch brought the jury in and told them to ignore the remark. "It's only human nature to assume that because a person committed one crime that they will commit another. But that's simply not true and you can't rely on that. You're to consider only the evidence relating to this crime. Is that understood?"

The jurors nodded. "Fine," Munch said, and nodded for Hall to resume questioning Byron Eerebout. Which he did by asking about the events of March 1993.

Eerebout said he explained to Gina that he and Cher were not boyfriend/girlfriend. She was upset, he added, but it was no big deal.

Early Sunday morning, while it was still dark out, he said he was awakened by a woman yelling in his apartment. "I thought it sounded like Cher. But I just laid there. Then I heard what sounded like my front door and I got up."

Looking out, Eerebout testified, he saw Tom Luther and Dennis Healey just leaving the apartment. When he got up the next morning, Tom was asleep in the apartment.

He first learned Cher was missing when her family and friends started calling. He wasn't exactly sure when he first heard from Richardson, but he admitted that he lied about not knowing the man with Cher when the detective showed him the videotape. "I drove straight back to the house, contacted Tom to let him know that they had a picture of him up in Central City with Cher. Tom said, 'Thanks, I'll take care of it.' That was it."

"When did you first suspect that Tom Luther was involved in her disappearance?" Hall asked.

Eerebout said he overheard a telephone conversation while visiting Luther at Debrah Snider's ranch. He presumed Luther was talking to Southy when he heard him refer to a body that was stinking and needed to be taken care of.

Then, he wasn't sure how much later, he said he asked Luther "if he did what they said he did. I just asked him if he killed her." Luther, he said, responded by making threats and admitting, "I shot her in the head."

"He said she was yelling. He took her to Central City to calm her down but on the way back she was saying, 'I'm going to go to the cops and tell them everything about Byron and his brothers.' And he told me that he pulled off to the side of the road. She got out of the car. He got out of the car. And he shot her in the back of the head, bam, bam, bam."

"Did he say what he did with her?" Hall asked.

"He said he put her by a monument."

"What did he do with the gun?"

"He threw it in the river."

Hall skipped ahead to Eerebout's arrest in September, when Richardson asked about Cher Elder.

"I said a lot of stuff that night that I shouldn't have said," Eerebout recalled. "I told Detective Richardson that I knew what happened to Cher, that I knew who she left with and basically where they went and where Tom went that night. I told him that it was 'for me to know and you to never find out.' "

He said he didn't take the original deal because he was afraid of Luther. "He made threats to me and my family." Those threats included giving him Cher's clothes, as if to prove that what he had said was true. "Later, he told me that he cut off her finger to get the ring off and that he cut off her lips to make an example to snitches. He also said he needed to go back and dig deeper and put rat poison on it so the animals wouldn't get it and to put rocks on it so it looked like a rock pile."

Sometime afterward, Luther arrived at Eerebout's mother's home and said he was heading to the grave that evening. "He picked up a little folding army shovel. Then later that night, around midnight, he came over to my apartment and said he was 'going to take care of this thing.'" Eerebout said he and J.D. then decided to follow Luther into the mountains.

"Why did you want to do that?" Hall asked.

"This may sound stupid," Eerebout said, looking at the jury, "but it was so we would know where it was, because me and J.D., we were going to slide a note under Cher's family's door of the location so they could have their daughter back."

In the gallery, Cher's family gasped. Richardson scowled. This note under the door bit was new. And no one believed it. For two years, the Eerebouts had plenty of time to personally or anonymously give Cher's body to her family. For two years, they'd done nothing.

Creeping up the hill outside of Empire, Eerebout said he peered through the trees and saw Luther on his hands and knees, digging with the little shovel. "I only watched for a few seconds, then split."

On cross-examination, Enwall asked why no one in the army, including at Eerebout's court martial, seemed to have any record of his head injury.

Eerebout shrugged. His friend had reported it, otherwise he didn't know. However, he noted, he was given an honorable discharge from the army for medical reasons.

But, Enwall said, wasn't he diagnosed in the army as having an antisocial personality, that he didn't know right from wrong?

Eerebout retorted that he was only antisocial to people who were rude to him.

Enwall went on to question him about his relationship with Cher Elder. "So it was a just a casual sexual relationship?"

"We had sex once," Eerebout replied. "In my view we were good friends."

"But Gina wanted this business with Cher to stop?" Enwall asked.

"She never gave me an order stop seeing Cher," Eerebout said. "But she was upset about it, yes."

"You told her that you would take care of the problem?"

"I told Gina that I would talk to Cher and take care of the situation, yes. Not that I would take care of the problem."

"Did Cher do drugs?"

"No, she did not."

"Well, you told Richardson that she was going to see a drug dealer in Central City?"

"She had a friend over there who was a drug dealer and that's how she referred to him. But the guy told Karen that he didn't see her that night."

At that point, Munch called a lunch break so that he could rule on an issue in which Enwall wanted to refer to a statement Byron Eerebout had made to Richardson and others about fights he'd been in.

"I want to show that he's a violent man," Enwall said when the jurors were gone. "He's prone to acts of spontaneous violence."

But the same rule that Munch applied to keep Luther's past out of the trial applied equally to Eerebout's, the judge ruled. Enwall could refer to any violence directly related to this case, such as the shooting incident, but nothing else.

With the jurors back, Enwall returned to the night Cher Elder went with Luther to Central City. "Didn't you say she stuck her head in your door and told you to fuck off?"

"I thought it was her," Eerebout shrugged.

"But isn't it a fact that you didn't tell Richardson that she didn't come back to the apartment until April 1994, a year later?" Enwall asked.

Eerebout shrugged again. He'd lied about a lot of things.

"Do you know anything about Gina's cat's throat being slit and it being stuck to the side of Gina's trailer?"

"No, I do not."

"Do you remember telling Gina that she might find herself in a shallow grave?"

"I remember the comment and that it was a warning to her, as in: don't go to the cops against Tom or you'll find yourself in a shallow grave."

"I see," Enwall replied, rolling his eyes. "So you were just protecting Tom?"

Eerebout nodded. "That's right."

As the day wore on, Enwall grew more exasperated. Eerebout, blaming his head injury, couldn't seem to remember dates or when certain events happened.

Enwall questioned how he and his brother could have followed Luther in the dead of night to Empire. It was easy, came the reply, they had a fast car and there's only one road leading up into the mountains and then one road in and out of Empire.

"Mr. Eerebout, do you have a quick temper?"

"Yes, I do. It just depends on what it is and who's saying it."

"Mr. Eerebout, your habit when the police questioned you about something was to lie."

"No. I just don't like police officers."

"One of the conditions of your deal is that you're not involved in the killing of Cher Elder isn't it?"

"Yes, it is."

"So if we could prove to the satisfaction of the district attorney and the police that you killed Cher Elder, you think that you wouldn't go back to prison on the twenty-four years?"

"Well, I'd go back to prison on the twenty-four years, but I sure wouldn't go back to prison for killing Cher Elder because I didn't kill Cher Elder. Tom Luther killed Cher Elder."

"We know that's what you say, Mr. Eerebout. And it's important to you that Tom Luther be convicted for killing Cher Elder?"

"It's not important to me," Eerebout retorted. "It's what's right. You should be punished for your crimes. Just like I was, he should be."

"You have no interest in protecting yourself, Mr. Eerebout?"

"If I did something, then I guess I would have to protect myself, yeah."

"Like if you had killed Cher Elder, one would think you might do a lot of things like tell a lot of different lies to the police, mightn't you?"

"No. I might have or might not have. I can't tell you what's in the future or what could have been or would have been."

"Are you telling us that if you killed her that you would come into this courtroom and fess up to it?"

"I can't tell you that."

"Can you tell us if you killed her, you'd lie about it?"

"I can't tell you that either?"

Hall stood to ask Byron Eerebout more questions. He thought it was a mistake for Enwall to have gone so hard after Eerebout as the killer of Cher Elder. Eerebout had an alibi for Saturday and Sunday. Gina Jones, who had already voiced her dislike for her former boyfriend. And Karen Knott, who said she and Cher always got together on Sunday and Monday nights, had pretty much established that Cher disappeared sometime between leaving Central City and Sunday morning.

It seemed that Southy Healey would have made a better target. However, Healey had no motive or even the opportunity, unless Luther had stopped on the way back from Central City to get him so that they could both kill her.

But then for all the reasons Eerebout and Healey didn't fit, Luther did.

"In all your conversations with Detective Richardson did you tell him the whole truth?" Hall asked Eerebout.

"No."

"Could you keep straight what you told him from one time to another?"

"No."

"When do you think it was that you finally came clean with all of this?"

"Not until the grand jury and, I'd say, today." Eerebout replied. "Today is a big part. It's all getting out finally."

At last, Byron Eerebout was told he could step down. His swagger had returned as he passed the defense table. He glanced quickly at Luther with a slight smile on his face. Then he left the courtroom, where he seemed to appreciate being mobbed by the television camera crews.

A few minutes later, out in the hallway during a break, Earl Elder could only respond to the testimony of his daughter's former boyfriend with, "Byron gives me a headache."

During the break, the attorneys approached Munch with a new concern. The prosecution's next witness, Hall said, "is distraught." It was an understatement.

There had been a major slip-up on the part of the prosecution team and police. A slip-up potentially worse than Byron Eerebout's comment about Tom Luther and prison. Lost in the concern about the potential mistrial, someone had forgotten to pick up Debrah Snider from her motel that morning.

Snider was left with no way to get to the courthouse. It had already been a rough night worrying about her testimony the next day and seeing Tom for the first time in nearly nine months.

But that wasn't the worst of it. She was angry. Here she was, having made the decision to testify against the man she still loved, because she felt the truth was more important, and she was being told that she wouldn't be allowed to tell the truth. At least, not the whole truth.

The district attorney had instructed her that she couldn't mention Tom's other crimes. She couldn't say anything about how he viewed women, the comments he made, the pornographic movies where women were raped "and learned to like it." She wouldn't be allowed to explain why she was testifying against him. She wanted the truth to come out and, to her, she was being asked to lie.

Now, she had also been forgotten. She waited with her bags packed for hours before catching a bus to the courthouse. But her troubles didn't end there. Inside the Taj Mahal, she had purchased a cup of coffee to settle her nerves, but the security officers at the metal detectors, who had no idea who she was, wouldn't let her through with the drink.

That's when it all boiled over. She cursed the guards and made such a fuss that she was physically escorted from the building. It was only when Richardson went looking for her that he discovered the prosecution's key witness had been tossed out onto the streets.

Richardson put out a bulletin to all cab drivers and bus drivers to be on the lookout for her. The airport was called and told not to let her board. Finally, while Eerebout was testifying, a bus driver reported that he had taken a woman matching Snider's description to a mall.

Police officers were dispatched to find her, which they did, wandering in tears, clutching her plane ticket back to West Virginia. She was within minutes of leaving for the airport and forgetting the whole Cher Elder affair.

Now she was waiting in the witness room, an emotional wreck. The actions of the security officers had convinced her that what Tom had once told her about his attorneys preparing to portray her as a vindictive bitch was about to come true. They would all be laughing at the crazy woman who loved a man she knew was a killer.

Cleaver broke in. "Mr. Hall has indicated that the next witness is . . . distraught," she said with a dramatic pause. "I happen to believe that the next witness is somewhat bizarre, and we're very worried that we've gotten through one difficult witness and we may get another one.

"I hope if we get to any point where we think the woman is not going to follow directions she's received, such as not revealing Mr. Luther's criminal history, that we stop. I think it might be helpful if you would tell her that she cannot bring up a variety of things. I'm concerned that she is going to do whatever it is she wants."

Munch said he'd be happy to warn Snider not to mention Luther's history or pending charges. He asked that she be brought into the courtroom

Debrah marched in, her face red from crying. She swept past the defense table to stand before the judge without looking at Luther, who stared at her.

"Ms. Snider, I'm Judge Munch, and all that I wanted to chat with you about is just one or two things," he said. "Court is generally a very stressful place for everybody and most witnesses, and it may well end up being that way for you, too. And very frankly, sometimes when people are being asked questions by lawyers, it's hard to understand exactly what they mean and exactly what they're asking."

Munch didn't get a chance to finish. Angrily, Snider cut him off. "Sir, I don't have a single thing wrong with understanding what people ask me, but if I feel I'm not being respected, I have a problem with my temper."

The outburst surprised Munch. "Well, Ms. Snider, then you and I have to talk about something. Okay?"

But Debrah wasn't backing down. "And I don't mind going to jail if that's what you're going to warn me about."

Munch was puzzled. "What are you talking about?"

"I'm talking about if this court doesn't see that I am respected, and you want to put me in jail for contempt of court, let's go," she shouted. "I expect to be respected here by everybody. And I know that that is sometimes a problem."

It was Munch's turn to blush red. He looked at the lawyers. Hall held up his hands in surrender and Cleaver smirked an I-told-you-so. "Counsel, do you have any idea why this woman is going off?" Munch asked.

It was Snider who answered. "Yes, because I've already had a pretty bad day."

Munch held up a hand. "Just be quiet. Counsel, either of you have any idea what's behind this?"

Hall replied, "Judge, I think this whole matter is a very stressful situation for Ms. Snider."

Cleaver added, "I was told that she was escorted out of the courthouse earlier today by security. I don't know what the details are of that. I also think that Mr. Richardson has told her that we are going to cross-examine her and frame her as a 'vindictive bitch.' So I don't know what she's expecting."

Richardson, who sat grimacing through Snider's outburst, now looked at the defense attorney angrily. What in the hell was Cleaver talking about? It was Luther, who was now sitting in his seat shaking his head, who had told Debrah about his attorneys' plans.

Munch turned to Hall. "Mr. Hall, I've really never had a witness who I was just trying to explain the rules tell me to go ahead and put them in jail for contempt. I am not particularly inclined to have her testify today. That's an unusual reaction from a person.

"How much of a problem does it create for you if I direct that this witness be called Monday rather than today so that she has a chance to gather her thoughts?"

"That is no inconvenience to us," Hall said, breathing a sigh of relief. "I'm not sure what Ms. Snider's schedule is. She lives in the state of West Virginia and has flown out here to testify at this trial."

Judge turned to Debrah. "Ms. Snider, it seems to me, very candidly, you're quite upset."

Debrah nodded. "Absolutely."

"I'm not sure it's the world's best idea for you to testify in this frame of mind. I'm inclined to have you stay here over the weekend and come back and testify on Monday."

"That's fine."

"I also don't think it makes a lot of sense for us to have this chat right now because I think you're angry, and I'm not sure why. So we'll talk about it on Monday morning instead.''

Again, Debrah nodded. ''Fine.''

Munch left the court muttering and shaking his head.

Later that evening, Richardson took Snider out to dinner. He knew the trial hung on her keeping it together in front of the jury. It was going to be hard enough to explain Debrah's motivations over the past three years. If she acted unstable, angry and, quite frankly, vindictive, she'd lose all credibility with the jurors.

Richardson knew what was bothering her. She had at long last chosen the truth over love, and now she was being told she couldn't tell the whole truth. In a way, he didn't blame her.

''We've worked together for three years and all along you've told me you wanted to do the right thing,'' he said looking into her eyes as they filled with tears. ''Now, I'm tired. If you want Thomas Luther to walk away a free man—and honestly, you're going to have to reach down into your heart and make the decision yourself—then don't show up for court Monday.''

It was a huge gamble. He'd given her the keys to the car and told her that as far as he was concerned, she was free to leave. He had driven the wedge between her and Luther as deep as he could, now it was up to her to determine whether she would pull it out or leave it in.

January 29, 1996

Scott Richardson didn't hear from Debrah Snider again that weekend. He couldn't sleep or think straight. To clear his head, he climbed on his motorcycle and roared into the mountains toward Empire, the cold wind slapping his face.

He didn't know whether he had won or lost the gamble until he arrived at the courthouse on Monday morning. Snider was there with her bags, waiting to get in.

He smiled and she smiled back. ''Didn't think I'd leave you in the lurch, did ya?'' she laughed.

''Nope,'' he lied.

Actually, once she calmed down Friday evening, Debrah had known she wouldn't leave. But she appreciated Richardson's show of faith by leaving it up to her. And really, there had been

no decision to make. She owed her testimony to everybody—
to Cher's family for taking so long, to Richardson, the dragon-
slayer who cared so much about someone he had never even
known. And in a way, she owed it to Tom, at least the good
side of him who had once told her that if he was doing wrong,
she should stop him.

But most of all, she owed it to herself. To the one thing whose
value she never doubted, the truth.

She loved Tom, and knew that she always would. But like
her wolves, he was not safe to run loose. The man she loved
was only safe to others so long as he was behind prison walls.

So that morning, she tied a white feather into her long gray
and brown hair and pulled on a buckskin dress with fringes and
a large, silver belt buckle. It was the dress her husband once
told her looked like a bathrobe, but Tom had said made her look
like an Indian princess . . . and him the warrior who wanted to
make love to her on the spot. She wore it now to let Tom know
that she still cared for him, and to remind him of what he had
thrown away.

After the jurors were seated that morning, Debrah Snider
walked into the courtroom with her head high. She'd had a short
conversation with Judge Munch, who'd told her that he was
sorry and hadn't meant to have her feel threatened the Friday
before. He just wanted to let her know the rules, but otherwise,
he assured her he wouldn't let anyone harass her.

Hall gently began questioning her about her background. She
said she was a psychiatric nurse who now worked in a hospital
in West Virginia. In the spring of 1993, she was not living with
Tom Luther, "but I spent as much time with him as I could."

On the afternoon of March 29, just after she had returned
from a trip to visit friends in Washington state, she had gone
over to Tom's apartment and found him in bed. His hands were
covered with scrapes and bruises, a finger was broken. He told
her a story about burying a box of AK-47 rifles. "It sounded
so absurd. I mean, who is going to give Tom Luther AK-47s?"

Snider remained calm and to the point as she testified. Piece
by piece, she linked her own recollections of life with Tom
Luther into the stories the jurors had heard from Healey, Eerebout, Ramierez, and Richardson. It was like listening to the

cylinders in a bank vault click into place as the door was prepared to open.

As she spoke, Snider didn't try to hide her own role in the tragedy. "I'm kind of ashamed to admit it, but I participated in suggestions, you know, helping him plan the day he was going to go bury the body."

Neither did she try to cover up for Luther. She gave him the cleanser to clean the stain where he said Cher vomited. But, she told Hall, she had been in his car the day she got back and never smelled anything like vomit.

The decision to tell the truth, she admitted, came slowly. Speaking about the drive with Luther to the public defender's office in Golden, she had felt little for what had happened to Cher Elder. "Prior to this, Cher was somebody I didn't know and I didn't care. I was angry with her for having been with Tom. She had no business with my boyfriend and so I didn't care about her."

But when Tom referred to Cher as 'it,' "it made me angry because she was not an it. I said, 'She was never an it. She was a person.' It just made him more angry."

And later that night, when she told Luther that she didn't believe a mysterious "they" had killed Cher, she asked him who was going to kill her for talking to the police.

"What did he say?" Hall asked.

"He ignored the question."

When Hall finished his questions, Snider reached for a cup of water and took a drink, as Cleaver stood. So far, Cleaver had done very little of the questioning, except for the expert witnesses.

It was clear the defense attorney saw this as her chance to strike a blow. She began by attacking Debrah's description of herself as a truthful person.

Wasn't it true, Cleaver asked, that Debrah took months to tell Richardson about Tom burying the body?

"Yes."

"And in fact, what you tell us is that you actually helped plan to bury a woman's body, correct?"

"I suppose that's correct."

And wasn't it true, Cleaver asked, that she only called Richardson after fights with Tom?

"There were a lot of fights, so it could have been."

"At one point in time, Tom said that Cher Elder was killed because she was a snitch."

"Correct."

"But you didn't tell that to Richardson until April or May. And you tell us that in your mind it made sense that you would actually be angry at Cher Elder because she shouldn't have been having sex with your boyfriend, right?"

Snider nodded. "She had no business with him regardless of what she did with him."

And wasn't it true she had a husband and two sons in Fort Collins while she carried on an affair with Luther?

"Yes."

"And throughout your life, you've had quite a lot of problems, is that fair to say?"

"Absolutely."

"And since you were fairly young, you've attempted to kill yourself a variey of different times, right?"

Hall jumped to his feet. "I object to that, judge. That isn't relevant to anything."

"Sustained," the judge replied.

Cleaver asked to approach the bench. There she argued that the jurors deserved to know that Debrah Snider was a troubled woman and had been for some time. But Munch ruled that only suicide attempts made in relation to the case could be delved into.

"During the time you were living with Tom Luther, or he was your boyfriend," Cleaver said sarcastically, "you tried to kill yourself a couple times, is that right?"

"Wrong. I tried once."

"And you have a felony conviction, is that right?"

"Correct."

"And through the two years you were with Luther, the only thing he ever admitted to was burying Cher, isn't that true?" Cleaver said.

"Right."

"And throughout all of this investigation, Tom always told you that he did not kill Cher?"

"Right."

"He was real clear on that, wasn't he?"

"He was very clear on that."

"And he told you that he didn't want to be a snitch, correct?"

"Right."

"He told you that he was going to go to hell for something he didn't do, correct?"

"He said he was going to pay for something he is not responsible for."

"Told you that Byron better keep his mouth shut because he could not do a life sentence."

"Yes, he said that."

"And when you asked him to step forward with who killed Cher Elder, he said no, correct?"

"Correct."

Finally, Cleaver had no more questions. Debrah Snider had not cracked under the pressure. She'd told the truth, no more, no less.

But Hall had just one more thing to ask her. "There is a question about whether you told Scott Richardson everything you knew about this. Why hadn't you?"

For the first time that day, Debrah's eyes filled with tears and her voice cracked as she answered. "Because it was something that had happened that nobody could undo, and I wanted to preserve my relationship with Tom Luther."

She stole a glance at Tom. But he was looking down.

The prosecution case was drawing to a close. There were just two witnesses left.

The first was Robert Cooper, the Jefferson County inmate who had come forward just before the trial. "He said he shot a lady in the head and carried her up a road and buried her," Cooper testified. "Before he killed her, he said he slapped her around."

The last was Charles "Mongo" Kreiner. But first the jurors were excused for a break, while Cleaver first objected to Kreiner testifying and then insisted the judge make sure he understood that he couldn't mention where Luther made his comments or anything that would give the impression that Luther had previously commited a sexual assault.

Munch finally told Cleaver to sit down and be quiet. Turning to Kreiner he asked, "Do you have any question as to what it is that you are to say and you're not to say?"

"No sir," Kreiner said. "I'm smarter than I look."

The jurors were brought back into the courtroom, and Kreiner was called, squeezing his muscular body into the cramped confines of the witness stand.

He said he knew Luther simply as a friend.

"Did he ever say anything about if he committed a crime, what he would do?" Hall asked.

"He said that if he were to commit an act of crime, there would be no witnesses—no one to testify."

And on that note, the prosecution rested its case.

January 30, 1996

After the prosecution rested its case, Judge Munch threw out the first degree murder charge based on the indictment count that Luther killed Cher Elder to cover up the evidence of a rape. The body had been too decomposed to ascertain if she had been raped. And except for Southy Healey's statement that Luther said he was having a good time with Cher Elder when he "fucked up and killed her," and Luther's own admission of consensual sex, there was no evidence to support the charge.

It left the prosecution with only a single count of premeditated first degree murder after deliberation.

At the start of the defense case, Luther stood and announced that he would not be testifying on his own behalf. "I choose to remain silent as I have through this whole case," he said.

Enwall then recalled Byron Eerebout to the stand, mostly to repeat questions about whether or not he saw Cher Elder return to the apartment as he originally told police. "And why you decided to change your mind."

"We'd like to call Lauren Councilman," Cleaver announced when Byron left.

Councilman was a friend of Cher Elder's who obviously didn't want to be there as a witness for the man she believed killed Cher. But the defense wanted to know about two telephone calls she received from Cher on the fateful weekend.

The first time she spoke to Cher Elder personally on that Saturday evening. Elder was upset with Byron, she conceded, but before the conversation got much farther, Cher announced she had to go and hung up.

Lauren Councilman said she went out that night and didn't get back until late. She also got up late on Sunday and when she checked her messages, there was another from Elder, apologizing for hanging up on her and said she'd try again later. The defense intimated that meant that Cher was alive on Sunday afternoon when she called the second time.

However, on cross-examination, Hall was able to get Councilman to point out that she didn't know what time the second call came in. It could have come shortly after she left Saturday night, or even from Central City.

James Greenlow was called next. As he took the stand, he glanced at Richardson, who pulled out a pen and prepared to write, a reminder of what would happen if Greenlow committed perjury.

Suddenly, Greenlow couldn't remember much. He said he heard Southy Healey talking about a murder in the jail, but that was about it. Luther scowled as Cleaver tried to get him to recall the statement that Southy told him that he and Byron were responsible for Cher's death.

Hall easily disposed of Greenlow on cross-examination. "Did Southy ever say the name Cher Elder?"

"No," the ex-con shrugged.

"Did he say who had killed someone?"

"No," Greenlow said again as the defense team fumed in their seats.

The biggest surprise in the defense case was when they called Mark Makarov-Junev to the stand. Richardson sat stunned and angry as he listened to Makarov-Junev claim that he had rejoined Byron Eerebout's circle of friends in the summer of 1993 because he was personally investigating the disappearance of Cher Elder.

Makarov-Junev said Byron Eerebout tried to kill him after he repeatedly accused Eerebout of being Cher's killer. "He thought I was going to go to the police," Makarov-Junev testified. "I told him I would." And, oh yeah, he added, he owed Eerebout $400 for drugs.

Richardson was livid. At no point in the investigation of the shooting, including interviews with Mark and his cousin, was

there any mention of Makarov-Junev investigating Elder's death.
It was all about money and drugs.

Makarov-Junev hadn't even bothered to show up for the trial
against Eerebout, and he was the victim. They'd convicted Eerebout anyway. Lately Richardson had heard that Makarov-Junev
was angry that Byron got a deal. But he hadn't expected this
low blow.

But once again Hall dealt with the problem. He asked why
Makarov-Junev hadn't mentioned this rather important motive
during the year it took to bring Eerebout to court. Makarov-
Junev shrugged. It was an independent investigation and he
didn't think the cops would believe him.

The defense then rested their case after less than a day of
testimony. Apparently, they believed that they had cast enough
doubt on the prosecution witnesses that there was no need to go
any farther.

Munch announced that closing arguments would begin first
thing in the morning. "Talk to no one about the case. Avoid
the media. Keep a free and open mind," he told the jurors and
sent them on their way.

January 31, 1996

In the American justice system, the prosecution gets two shots
at the jury during closing arguments under the premise that the
state has the greater burden. It must prove a defendant's guilt
beyond a reasonable doubt; until then he is presumed innocent.
As opposed to opening statements, which generally outline a
case and give jurors an idea of what to expect from either side,
closing arguments are just that—arguments over the merits of
the evidence. The prosecution goes first, followed by the defense,
after which the prosecution follows with any rebuttal arguments.

Hall gathered his thoughts as he waited that morning for the
jury to be brought to the courtroom. All the work of the past
three years, all the heartache, would be boiled down in what he
said over the next twenty minutes.

He couldn't have been happier with how the trial had gone,
even with Eerebout's slip. Healey had more than held his own
and, Hall believed, come off as believeable. Debrah Snider dealt

with her demons and came back to court to tell her story hero-ically, even poignantly. Eerebout had scored a point or two when he matter-of-factly insisted that he didn't kill Cher Elder, "Tom Luther killed Cher Elder." And Richardson was the perfect police witness—direct, polite, sure of himself, a defender of right, emotionally involved in the case without having lost his objectivity. He'd slept by Cher's grave to protect it, for God's sake.

They'd lost a couple along the way. Mortho had retracted what he'd said about the ring, so they didn't call him. The West Virginia inmate, Mark Dabbs, who said Luther had told him about the murder, refused to testify unless he was moved to another prison. They'd dropped him, too.

Rick Hampton, who never was offered a deal for his testimony about Luther saying he'd kill his next victim and bury the body, also refused at the last minute to testify. But Cooper, who'd had nothing at all to gain by testifying, and Ramierez, another piece glued into place by Debrah Snider, had made up for the losses.

Hall looked around. Luther sat staring at the floor, chewing his lower lip. Every once in awhile, he said something to Cleaver, but she seemed off in another world and would only nod. Enwall studied his notes, making notations here and there. Minor sat, Buddah-like, waiting, just waiting. Richardson seemed tense and at the same time relieved that it was almost over. Cher Elder's family smiled at him, but looked frightened.

At last the jury arrived. They too seemed ready to get it over with. With a nod from Munch, Hall stood and cleared his throat.

"Once again, good morning. In my opening statement, I told you that we spent almost two years putting the pieces of this case together. But I didn't tell you how all the pieces fit.

"Today I'm going to tell you how it all fits together and I'm going to tell you why the evidence you've heard proves to you, beyond a reasonable doubt, that Thomas Luther killed Cher Elder."

There were two or three main things they needed to keep in mind as they began their deliberations. "The first one is the presumption of innocence, which can only be overcome by the second one—proof beyond a reasonable doubt based on reason and common sense. It is not some vague, speculative, or imaginary doubt, but doubt that would cause a reasonable person to hesitate to act in matters of importance to themselves.

"The third major issue concerns the way crimes are defined in our country. The law defines crimes by lists of things that are called elements. Make your decision by reading each element of this crime and asking yourself whether we have proved that element beyond reasonable doubt. If we have proved them all, you must find Thomas Luther guilty; if we failed, you must find him not guilty.

"I think what you will see is that all of the elements in this case are not in dispute. There is no dispute, for example, that Cher Elder was murdered on or about the date and place we've indicated. There is no credible dispute that whoever killed Cher Elder did so with the intent to kill her, causing her death after deliberation—there is simply no other explanation for three point-blank shots to the back of her head. The question, element number one, is who did it?"

Hall paused as he stuck his hands in his pockets. If Enwall was the college professor, Hall was the earnest young teacher with a message for his students. "I know you heard from some pretty unsavory characters in this case. I assume you didn't like those people very much, and I know that you probably wouldn't want them moving onto your street. I'm not going to make excuses for those folks. All I can tell you is that we don't choose witnesses, but Thomas Luther chose his friends, and the people you heard from were his friends."

Hall paused again to let the message sink in. Murders are not committed in heaven with angels for witnesses. "No one of Thomas Luther's former friends knows the whole story, or in fact, no one person knows the whole story. And the recollections of all the people you're heard from over the past week have been colored by the passage of time, and they have inconsistences, and they've been tainted by the lies that Thomas Luther told all of them. But regardless of all of that, what they told you fits together, and it explains to you what happened to Cher Elder on the evening of March 27th, 28th, 1993, and this is how it fits together.

"Cher and Tom Luther left the casino. Luther drove. Karen said neither was drunk. The plan was to go back to Byron's. That's where Cher's car was.

"But something happened. It wasn't a bottle of wine. It wasn't casual sex in the front seat of a Geo Metro. We know that story isn't true. But something went wrong, and both Robert Cooper and Byron told you, there was an argument between Cher Elder and Thomas Luther. What about, we don't know.'' *Or,* Hall thought, *we can't tell you.*

"Where did it take place? We don't know exactly. It could have happened in the car on way back. Or it could have happened at Byron's. But whatever it was about and wherever it took place, it happened after they left the parking lot.

"As a result of the argument, Tom Luther told Robert Cooper, Byron Eerebout and Dennis Healey he shot Cher in the head.''

There is a flip side to the elements, he said. "We are not required and don't need to prove things that are not element. We don't need to prove exactly where the argument took place, and we don't need to prove exactly where Cher was shot. Nor do we need to prove the exact moment in time at which Tom Luther shot her. What we have to prove, though, is who pulled the trigger.''

Hall poured himself a glass of water and took a drink. Placing the cup down, he continued, "Let's get back to our story. In the hours after Tom Luther shoots Cher, he does two things. First, he gets Cher's car keys and moves her car about five blocks. We know that happened because we know from the testimony of crime scene people that the car wasn't broken into and the ignition not forced. That means whoever moved it had the keys. And we know from Karen that Cher left her coat and keys at Byron's.

"And we know that there was a hair on the front seat of that car. It was Tom Luther's hair, and Tom Luther told Scott Richardson that he had never been in that car.''

"Tom Luther did something else in those hours. He did something with Cher's body. What?'' Hall shrugged, his hands in his pockets, and took a couple of steps toward the jurors.

"Well, we don't know. He hid it somewhere. We do know a couple of things. We know that a few weeks later, Tom Luther talked to Deb Snider about cleaning his car. Deb had spilt some blood, blood from a steak, on the upholstery of her car, and she'd used some kind of cleaner to get it out. Tom Luther asked to borrow that cleaner and used it on his car.

"We also know that by the next night, Sunday the 28th and

Monday the 29th, there's no body in the car, but there's dirt in the back of it.'' Hall reminded the jurors of the midnight call to Healey.

''Deb Snider was out of town on Saturday and Sunday. When she got to Tom's apartment, Luther was still in bed. There were fresh scratches on his hands and a finger was broken. He gave her a story about AK-47s, but like Debrah Snider told you, 'Who's going to give Tom Luther a box of machine guns?' There were no guns. Tom Luther spent Sunday night burying Cher's body.

''But the ground was too hard. He couldn't dig it deep enough. Instead of spending a long time and digging it deep, which is why he needed Healey as a lookout, he dug a shallow grave and carried rocks over it. It was carrying rocks that hurt his hands and finger.

''Weeks later, Luther, as Deb told you, becomes anxious and paranoid. He tells her a number of stories about Cher being a snitch and that her body was mutilated in some way. He talks about a mysterious 'other' killing Cher and dumping her body as a message to other people. But you know Cher was not an informant and her body was not mutilated.

''The only thing he told the truth about is that Cher's body is buried. Buried too shallowly. He had to wait until later in spring when the ground warmed up.''

Hall described the case as a giant jigsaw puzzle in which the box is missing. ''You know it's supposed to be a building or a landscape, but you don't have a picture to go by. So you use your reason and common sense. You turn the pieces this way and that and see how they fit. The pieces in this case show a cold-blooded murderer of a young woman.

''This case is all about common sense and reason. Keep in mind what it is we need to know: who pulled the trigger? Compare the testimony.

''For example, compare the testimony of Healey to the testimony of Eerebout on this point. Healey tells you that Tom Luther told him, 'I fucked up and killed a broad.' Then he took Healey to a place where he buried her. Byron told you that Tom Luther said, 'I killed her, I shot her in the head.' And Byron followed him to where he buried the body.

''There's no evidence these two men ever talked to each other.

They met only a couple of times. Yet both of them took us to the same place.

"Go through and compare. You'll come to one conclusion: the pieces fit in a single way, and that the man who pulled the trigger on the gun that killed Cher Elder that night is the man seated right over there." Hall whirled and pointed a finger at the defense table. "Thomas Luther."

Turning back to the jury, as he walked to his seat, Hall added, "Now I'm going to sit and let the defense attorneys show how reason and common sense tell you something else."

Hall took his time getting back in his seat. Enwall pretended not to notice as he stood and studied his notes one more time, his glasses slipped near the end of his nose, one hand in a pants pocket. After Hall took his seat, Enwall continued to stand looking at his notes as his free hand moved thoughtfully to cup his chin.

As if only just aware of the jurors, he looked up, pursed his lips and addressed his audience like an actor on a stage. "Tom Luther has come here to tell you that he's not guilty of murder."

Now he wagged a finger at the jurors. "Not that he hasn't done anything wrong, not that he's not up to his ears in covering up this murder, not that he's not guilty of a very serious crime. But that, in his words, he's not a killer.

"You've been asked to believe that if you move some pieces around, the most accomplished liars on the planet have come clean and decided as good citizens to come into this courtroom, and tell you the truth. The problem is, their new stories don't make any more sense than their old stories."

Enwall smiled and shook his head. "And they're as transparent as clear glass. Byron and Dennis lied systematically. They lied about big things and lied about small things. That's how they operate in life, they lie."

Looking back at Luther, Enwall said, "The words Tom said to Richardson in West Virginia tell the whole story of why he's here: 'I'm an angry son of a bitch, but I ain't a killer. I ain't a rat, and I ain't going to be one.' "

Enwall raised his hands, palm up and shrugged. "I'm sorry you're stuck with that, but we all are. He obviously thinks that's a normal trait. I'm sure you don't. It's macho. It's stupid. In this case, it's self-destructive to Tom Luther. If he didn't have this attitude, he wouldn't have buried a body and covered up a murder in the first place.''

"Tom Luther has served time in prison," Enwall said, knowing he had to do some damage control. "But as the judge told you, that has nothing to do with the facts in this case.''

When police discovered that Tom Luther was in Central City with Cher, he voluntarily went to them and said that they had consensual sex, Enwall said. "And that Cher was getting back at Byron.''

"Now," Enwall said, jerking his head over his shoulder at Hall, Minor, and Richardson, "the prosecution has given up. They concede she came back. Just moving the pieces around.''

Enwall called Debrah Snider "the most credible witness in the whole trial. Now there are an enormous number of ways to get abrasions on your hands, it can happen at work.'' He held up his well-manicured hands as if examining them for cuts, then looked back at the jurors. "But the prosecution wants you to believe he got them burying a body. You'll remember Debrah telling you about Tom crying. He'd got involved in something he shouldn't have. That he wishes he hadn't. Helping somebody cover up one of the most heinous crimes you can imagine.''

The defense attorney looked sideways at Richardson. He planned to attack the detective, but he had to be subtle. He began by saying Richardson made Luther a scapegoat just because he had done prison time. Of course, it was from the noblest intentions—he had an important and unusual mission, "finding Cher Elder's body for this family," he said, his hand sweeping back toward the gallery. "And I don't think any of us are prepared to say that that objective isn't worth taking some chances.

"The problem is that mission blinded Detective Richardson from looking in more than one direction.''

Several jurors looked at the detective, but he just sat impassively waiting for the defense attorney to move on. He expected the attack. He hoped the jury would see it as a weakness in the defense case.

Southy may have been the real killer. Byron and Jimmy Greenlow had said so. "Tom wasn't there, Southy was. But Richardson had blinders on and so he believed that Dennis Healey had come to Jesus. 'You ain't my priest.' But,'' Enwall looked from juror to juror, "maybe Jimmy is the priest.

"Southy tells Richardson that Tom 'fucked up and killed a broad.' But he doesn't give a motive, there's certainly no deliberation—just fucked up and killed her."

The three men at the prosecution kept their faces impassive, but anger rose as Enwall asked where was Luther's motive. The same defense attorney had argued against Luther's motive being introduced. He was a monster, plain and simple. Hall also recognized that Enwall was hedging his bets for a second degree murder conviction, by subtly contending that Luther had not deliberated before killing Cher.

Enwall mocked the theory that with "a superhuman effort" Luther killed Cher, hauled her body up a hill, went back and got Southy, and then returned to Denver before dawn.

"Healey got a deal," Enwall said. "He was facing a serious charge and gets rehab."

Eerebout was just a liar. "First he tells Richardson that she came back, said fuck you, and left. He said he heard her car start. But then Byron is very concerned that no one think they're boyfriend/girlfriend, it's just sex. But there was a serious difference with how Cher perceived the relationship."

Then there was Mark Makarov-Junev, Enwall noted to the jury. "He's looking into Cher's disappearance and Byron comes at him with a bat and then unloads a .357 at him, or maybe it had to do with $400. But why kill for $400? To kill somebody you're afraid may know something about a case in which you're a murderer—that might be worth taking a few shots at somebody."

Enwall paused as though to let the juror ponder his last statement. Then quietly, as if instructing recalcitrant children, he said, "Tom Luther had a very strong, close relationship—a strange relationship, I agree—but a strong relationship with Debrah Snider. He tells Deb over and over, 'I buried a body, but I didn't kill her.'"

Then Enwall flipped back to the "unbelieveable" night Byron and his brother J.D. supposedly followed Luther into the mountains, and found him after stopping for a soda, "in the dead of night. And why did they supposedly go up there?"

Enwall stopped and shook his head sadly. "That was maybe the most shameful thing that happened in this trial. Byron Eerebout tells you that they're going up there so they can find the location of the grave so that they can put an anonymous note under the Elders' door to let them know where their daughter was. That's the same guy who, according to Southy, laughs when he talks about Cher Elder's dad wanting her body. Leaving the note under the Elders' door was, I guess, something they just didn't get to or it slipped their minds."

The trip never happened, Enwall contended. It was cooked up to justify how the Eerebouts knew where the body was. "And how come Byron knows where the body is, if he had nothing to do with killing Cher Elder?"

Enwall reminded the jurors that the hair found in Cher's car was only similar to Luther's. "It could have been someone else's." And there was no real evidence of blood in the back of Luther's car, "or at least, that's their implication, that Tom was cleaning up blood not vomit. But this woman is supposedly bleeding all over the place and not a drop shows up on the seat."

Lauren Councilman had proved that Cher was alive on Sunday. "There's no reason to believe she wasn't."

Enwall returned several more times to reasons why the jury should believe that Cher Elder returned to Byron's and drove away. The last time, he said, Tom Luther saw her. And he repeated over and over statements that proved Byron Eerebout and Southey Healey were liars. He backtracked so often that those watching noticed that he was losing the jurors, some of whom were yawning or looking into the gallery, studying the faces rather than looking at Enwall.

The defense attorney apparently noticed the growing antipathy as well and worked his way to the end of his arguments, already more than three times as long as Hall's.

"Tom Luther is in this courtroom today because he won't tell police, the judge, or you who killed Cher Elder. That may be and I would submit to you it is despicable behavior, but it's not murder. He's here because he buried a body to avoid her murder being detected. That again, no question about it, is despicable behavior and it's a very serious crime. It's accessory to murder, but it's not murder.

"This trial hasn't shown conclusively who killed Cher Elder or when or why. It hasn't even established whether it's first degree murder or second degree murder. But it's pointing some pretty strong fingers. The prosecution tells you that those fingers point at Tom Luther."

Enwall pointed to his client, but then his finger drifted over toward the prosecution table. "It's up to you to tell Detective Richardson, 'You were wrong about the assumptions you made.' And tell Mr. Hall, 'You're wrong about the assumptions you made.'

"If you convict Tom Luther, you're convicting the wrong man. If you convict him, you'll be closing down the investigation in this case, and I submit to you the investigation of who killed Cher Elder ain't done. It's produced a result, but it's the wrong result.

"This isn't a case about reasonable doubt. This is a case of massive unmitigated doubt. This is obviously a supremely important day in Tom Luther's life. If you convict him of first degree murder, his very existence is at stake. But it's also an enormously important day for somebody else. It's enormously important to the person who put three bullets in Cher Elder's head because if you convict Tom Luther, that person goes free.

"We are not asking you to let a murderer go free in this case. We're not asking you to let Tom Luther go free. We're asking you to convict Tom Luther for the crime that he committed, accessory to murder, burying the body."

It was a smart move, the defense lawyer asking the jury to convict his own client for accessory. He couldn't be both an accessory and a killer. Any juror who had qualms about convicting Luther of murder but didn't want to take a chance that their mistake would let him back on the streets, could still vote to put him in prison.

Hall knew the strategy was sound. However, he also believed that the defense had committed a cardinal sin. Instead of trying to poke holes in the prosecution case and leaving the identity of the killer up to the imagination of the jurors, they had tried to label Southy and Byron as the killers, but without ever really saying which one. Or was it both? But then how and when? The prosecution had at least given them a realistic storyline.

And did Enwall really expect the jury to believe that Luther would rather face the death penalty than "rat" on two guys who were ratting on him? It wasn't like he hadn't already told Debrah Snider, who told Richardson, the same thing. He had tried to rat. It just hadn't worked because it wasn't the truth. The irony of that logic caused Hall to make a last-minute revision to his rebuttal argument which he stood to deliver.

Hall had seen the wavering attention of the jury and told the jurors that he would keep his remarks brief. He also said he wouldn't try to refute every wrong statement the defense attorney had made, he'd let them do that. "You know this case as well as I do now. My recollection of the facts isn't the same as his. But it's not our recollection that matters, it's yours."

He touched briefly on Lauren Councilman's testimony that the second call could have come anytime Saturday night. He asked when Dennis Healey and Byron Eerebout supposedly talked in jail, Enwall having alluded to them making up their story at that time. "I don't recall any testimony about that."

"You heard a lot about us changing our theory and conceding things," Hall said, strolling over toward the jury with a hand on his cheek, which he dropped and placed in a pocket. "But we haven't done that. Our theory has always been the same. Cher was killed sometime between after she left the casino parking lot and dawn. We don't know when or exactly where."

Hall was now only a few feet directly in front of the jurors, who were all looking up at him, and some had begun to nod. "The defense theory is that Byron is not a nice guy and Dennis Healey is not a nice guy, and there's a whole bunch of lies in this case."

Hall shrugged and made a face. "Well, I agree with that. But Mr. Enwall also told you that Tom Luther knows who killed Cher Elder, and he would rather face the death penalty than tell you the truth about it, so I guess the theory is that either Dennis Healey or Byron Eerebout killed Cher Elder.

"We did check Byron out as a suspect. We searched his apartment and found blood, not because we needed the practice, and there is not any evidence to say he is the person who killed Cher.

"We thought about Dennis as a suspect. We found a gun under his car seat and checked it out. It was not the gun that killed Cher."

Hall asked the jury to again remember to consider only the elements of crime. "You may have reasonable doubt about whose voice Byron heard that morning. But that's not an element here.

"You may have reasonable doubt about the date that Byron

and J.D. went up to the mountains to see Tom Luther burying Cher's body. You probably do, but that isn't an element either

"Mr. Enwall says that some of the pieces of this jigsaw puzzle don't fit. That may be. But it doesn't matter. This puzzle is a very big picture, it's like a panorama. It has a lot of people in it, a lot of scenes. But all of those things don't matter because they are not elements of this crime.

"The part that matters, the piece we need to know is the piece that shows the face of the person who pulled the trigger. And reason and common sense tells me that face isn't the face of Byron Eerebout. It's not the face of Dennis Healey.

"It's the face," Hall whirled and pointed at Luther who scowled and looked down, "of the man sitting right there. It's the face of Thomas Luther."

Chapter Twenty-Eight

February 1, 1996—Jefferson County Courthouse

It didn't take long for the jury to make a request to review some of the evidence. They wanted to see the video from the Central City casino in which Luther followed Cher Elder around. Several jurors needed a reminder that the relationship that evening between Luther and Elder was anything but a date.

When they first went back into the jury deliberation room, the jurors selected a foreman and took a quick poll. Half were ready to convict Luther of murder, either first or second degree; the other half weren't sure or leaned toward accessory.

However, after just five or ten minutes of going over the major points of the testimony, they were all convinced that Luther killed Cher Elder. They split on the degree of his guilt—seven were for manslaughter, four for second degree, and one for first.

Through the trial, the jurors had gotten along with each other very well. They weren't supposed to discuss the proceedings, so they spent time between court appearances talking about families, and work, and hobbies. Of the fifteen, only the 65-year-old woman who had been selected last kept herself apart from the others, though she would speak if spoken to.

After closing arguments, Judge Munch had dismissed the three alternates, two men and a woman. Some thought the 65-year-old woman might ask to be excused. Her ankle was in a cast and her husband, who had been driving her back and forth to the courthouse, had just been hospitalized. But she insisted it was no problem. She'd remain.

Over the course of the trial, the jurors had formed opinions about the personalities making up the two sides. Enwall, they all agreed, was the most polished. However, they'd also found him overly dramatic, especially during the closing arguments, when he kept going on and on as if he didn't quite believe what he was saying. Cleaver had turned them off with her overly solicitous routine with Luther, which they saw through as a charade for their benefit, and the hostile manner in which she treated prosecution witnesses and referred to Detective Richardson.

Hall's habit of placing a hand on his cheek as he talked had bothered some, and at first the jurors had pegged him as meek and unsure of what he was doing. That gradually changed, however, when they saw how meticulously he pieced together the complex evidence into a convincing, as he called it, jigsaw puzzle. Minor had been direct, if not wildly entertaining.

Richardson, however, was the key. They all agreed he could be trusted, and had kept his cool while the defense hammered at him. No one bought the argument that he had focused on Luther to the exclusion of other possibilities; he'd checked it out and still arrived back at Luther. They had also seen how emotionally involved he was in the case, how he'd cared for Cher Elder's family. His sleeping by Cher's grave had left a lasting impression of his dedication and humanity.

One of the first things the jurors did when sent to deliberate was discuss how they felt about the testimony of the witnesses. On the prosecution side, they believed Southy Healey when he said, "I'm a thief and a conniver, but I ain't a killer." And there was simply no evidence that he was, or that he'd done anything more than stand guard while Luther buried Elder's body. It didn't make him a good guy, but the prosecution hadn't tried to say he was.

Taken on his own, they might have dismissed Eerebout as a pathological liar. He was a smirking criminal without a lot going on upstairs. However, his obvious slip had not surprised them about Luther.

"It was like 'Whoops,' " said one juror, "we weren't supposed to hear that. But it was obvious Luther had been in prison, look who his friends were. I just didn't know what it was for. It could have been shoplifting or murder. It didn't matter."

And in the end, even his critics conceded, Eerebout had acquitted himself well. "Enwall just kept pushing and pushing," a juror noted, "but Byron just sat there and said, 'I didn't kill Cher Elder. Tom Luther killed Cher Elder.' I believed him."

Another juror said she didn't understand why Enwall was going so hard after Eerebout when he had an alibi. "He was in bed with Gina."

Robert Cooper and Chuck "Mongo" Kreiner were also convincing. And for once, neither witness had anything to gain by testifying against a former friend.

Of all the prosecution witnesses, at least those who weren't there in an official capacity, Debrah Snider was the most convincing and did the most to sew up the loose ends and tie it all together. It helped that she was obviously, however strangely, still in love with Luther, so much so that it had looked like it physically hurt her to tell the truth. She hadn't tried to elaborate on what she knew; she never said that Luther confessed to her, and yet she had damned him just the same.

The defense case was confusing in its paucity. "It was like they thought no one would believe any of the prosecution case," said a juror. "Cleaver looked like the cat who swallowed the canary, as if she knew so much more than we did."

Greenlow was a joke. He was obviously just trying to help his old friend Luther and even at that hadn't said anything terribly damaging, just that he'd heard Healey talking about a murder. And neither did the jurors believe that Makarov-Junev had been "investigating" Elder's disappearance when Eerebout attacked him. As Hall had pointed out, why hadn't he said something during the investigation of the shooting when he knew Richardson would have jumped at whatever information he had.

But the most damaging statement to Luther had come from his own defense attorney, Enwall, when instead of saying Luther didn't want to rat on some anonymous friend, he said Luther wouldn't rat on two guys who were ratting on him.

Hall had summed it up nicely for the jurors when he asked: would Thomas Luther rather face the death penalty than rat on Byron and Southy? "I mean Enwall was standing there accusing Byron and Southy of killing Cher. Who wasn't ratting?" said a juror. "That pretty much put the nail in the coffin for me."

Still, the jurors felt they owed it to everyone involved to carefully, step by step, go over the evidence and testimony to see, as Hall said, if the pieces fit. Or if there was another interpretation.

The jurors went home the first day after deliberating for four hours. More than half were now convinced that Luther was guilty of first degree murder, the others were standing on second degree and wanted to talk more about the concept of whether Luther deliberated before killing Elder. The jurors were convinced that they'd reach the required unanimous decision by the next day.

Thursday morning, they met again and began reviewing the evidence. At one point they asked that the testimony of the ballistics expert be read back to them, just to answer some confusion about whether he said the gun stolen by Tristan Eerebout could have been the murder weapon. The testimony quickly cleared that up—the stolen gun was one of only three types that could have been used out of dozens of .22-caliber handguns on the market.

By noon, only seven hours into deliberations, eleven jurors were in favor of convicting Luther of first degree murder. They had decided the issue of premeditation not so much on what the witnesses had said as on the forensic evidence. All three bullets had entered Cher Elder's skull in close proximity, indicating that she was unconscious or unable to move when she was killed. "She wasn't trying to get away or struggling," said a juror. "One shot could have been an accident or in the heat of the moment. But three? She was executed."

The jurors had even come up with their own scenario of what they thought could have happened. Coming back to Byron's apartment with Luther, only to find her "boyfriend" in bed with

Gina, Cher had caused a scene. Luther took her outside, where they struggled and he knocked her unconscious, causing the fracture to her skull. He then put her into his car, where she vomited on the backseat due to the blow to her head.

Some felt he probably raped her—there was something about the sex between Luther and Cher they believed they were not told about—before or after he took her to Empire. There he dragged her into the woods and pumped three bullets into her head. They felt he planned to kill her during the forty-five-minute drive to Empire.

However, one woman, the 65-year-old housewife, did not agree. But her arguments made no sense, logically or legally. She kept insisting that while she thought Luther was guilty of second degree murder, the prosecution had not proved "beyond a shadow of a doubt" the first degree charge. She said she thought Luther acted "knowingly" but not "deliberately," the required threshold for first degree murder.

How, the other jurors asked her, could Luther shoot a helpless woman three times without deliberately intending to murder her? "It's not supposed to be 'beyond a shadow of a doubt,' " a juror argued. "The judge explained that we can't ever be one hundred percent sure of anything. It's 'beyond a reasonable doubt.' What a reasonable person might conclude looking at the evidence." They tried to get her to explain her reasoning, but suddenly she stopped talking to them completely.

The other jurors grew angry. "You're not using your common sense or life experiences like the judge told us," said one.

"And you're also breaking the law by refusing to deliberate or explain yourself," said another when the holdout juror remained mum.

Frustrated, the jurors went home Thursday afternoon. They'd have to try again Friday.

It didn't go any better the next day. In fact, it got worse and turned ugly. The eleven jurors took turns getting in the woman's face. What was wrong with her, they asked. Was she stupid? "Tell us your scenario," one yelled. "At least if you could tell me why you think it's only second degree, I could respect that!"

"I don't have to. I don't have to tell you anything," she replied and turned her back.

Resignedly, the eleven jurors went step by step over all the evidence again, hoping that the holdout juror would see where their logic had taken them. But she still refused to even discuss it.

During breaks in the deliberations, the eleven jurors stood in the cold outside air, wondering what it would take to convince the woman. The bitterness of the deliberations had reduced some to tears. Others reported being unable to sleep at night.

Those watching the trial saw the jurors in their groups during breaks and wondered at the obvious anger and frustration on their faces. The strain was tearing Cher Elder's family apart all over again. Rhonda and Beth were in tears. Earl paced the hallways, angry and worried.

Richardson and Hall tried to assure them that the delay was not all that uncommon. "It just means the jurors are being careful and reviewing all the evidence," Hall said. But privately, the prosecution team worried that the jurors were split between the murder charge and accessory, which might have meant a hung jury and a mistrial. Also, jurors had been known to settle for a lesser charge rather than let someone go free.

Back in the deliberation room, the eleven jurors kept at the woman. Some tried to reason calmly with her. Others just yelled and then stomped off. Finally, she spoke again, "If you don't leave me alone, I'm going for accessory."

The room was silent. The other jurors were stunned. How could she be ready to vote for second degree murder one minute and then say she would vote for accessory the next? Except out of spite. Her statement brought the other jurors, including the men, to tears. But she turned her back again and wouldn't speak.

At the end of the day, the other jurors voted to go home for the weekend and return on Monday. Perhaps, if the holdout had some time to herself to think, she'd review the evidence and come to her senses. Or at least be willing to deliberate. "Maybe you'll be able to persuade us," someone suggested. She nodded.

On Monday, the eleven returned with renewed hope. It soon changed to despair when the holdout juror walked into the deliberation room carrying a large, new romance novel. She took a seat with her back to them and began to read.

The eleven jurors discussed whether they should say something to Judge Munch, but decided it was their duty to continue trying to reach a verdict. But at 9:45 A.M., the holdout put her book down and scribbled a note which she gave to the bailiff to hand to the judge. It read, "Judge, we can't reach an agreement."

The other jurors then decided to send a note of their own. "We are at an impasse. One of us has not kept an open mind. She has not used her logic, common sense, or life experience in making a decision. We are wondering if it is possible to call in an alternate?"

Munch responded that it was not possible. Alternates are generally only called in if someone was ill or had clearly violated the rules—such as reading newspaper accounts. He urged them to continue their deliberations.

In the courtroom, where the family and spectators had gathered when Munch received the notes, little was said. The family was bewildered by what it all meant. However, it was some relief to the prosecution team as it became clear eleven jurors were pulling for a murder conviction. Hall did not want to retry the case. It had gone better than he could have hoped, and the defense, he believed, had made several key errors.

At 10:50 A.M., the holdout juror sent the judge another note, saying the jury was "hopelessly deadlocked." The other eleven responded with a note of their own. "The reason we are deadlocked is we have one juror that will not discuss reasons for her decision. At this time, the person has refused to listen to everyone else or give us her opinion."

Munch renewed his instructions that it was their duty to deliberate with one another. But at 2:10 P.M,, there was one last note from the eleven jurors. "The jury cannot come to a unanimous decision—with our apologies."

Then Munch asked the prosecution and defense attorneys if he should give the jury what are known as the "Lewis instructions." Lewis was the name of a Denver case in which a jury had deadlocked not over the defendant's guilt or innocence, but the degree of the crime. The instructions given by the judge in that case were that if they could not reach a unanimous decision for the greater count, they must find the defendant guilty of the lesser charge.

Enwall and Cleaver readily agreed that the Lewis instructions be given. After it had become clear that the jury had decided on murder, they simply hoped to avoid first degree and a death penalty phase.

Hall contacted his boss, District Attorney Dave Thomas, who said not to agree to the Lewis instructions. Better a hung jury and a mistrial than letting Luther off on the lesser offense, Thomas said. But Hall thought about it and knew that retrying the case meant a very real possibility of losing the murder conviction the next time around. Reluctantly, he agreed that Munch should give the instructions.

The eleven jurors were shocked by Munch's order. Several argued they'd rather a mistrial and let another jury find Luther guilty of first degree murder. But now the judge was telling them it was the law, they *had* to find Luther guilty of second degree murder. Twenty minutes after receiving the instructions, they sent a note announcing they had reached a verdict.

The three alternates were called at their homes to come back to court, as Munch had promised they would be. Each to themselves, the three had reviewed the evidence at home and decided they would have voted for first degree murder. So they were surprised to arrive at the deliberation room and see their colleagues in tears.

They were bustled onto the elevator for the ride to the fourth floor. The alternates noticed that no one would stand near the 65-year-old woman, who stood scowling in the corner.

"What happened?" an alternate whispered over the sniffles and muttered curses of the others.

"Second degree," someone said.

Cher Elder's family, the press, and other spectators were already assembled in the courtroom. They were alarmed when the jury entered and they saw that some were crying.

Papers were passed to Munch, who read the verdict. "Guilty of second degree murder."

The assembly gasped as several jurors sobbed loudly. The prosecution team sat in their seats, grim-faced. As much as they knew what was coming, it was hard to stomach after getting so close. A single vote.

Luther and his attorneys were all smiles. He hugged Cleaver and then shook hands with Enwall. Looking over at Richardson, he stretched and said, "Now I can start lifting weights again and get my body back in shape."

The jurors were led from the room and back to the elevator. Cher Elder's stunned family was ushered through the hallway to another elevator as television and newspaper cameras caught their tears and frustration.

The press had to wait outside the district attorney's offices on the bottom floor while the jurors and the family gathered themselves. The holdout juror was the first to leave, although no one in the media knew her role at that point as she limped quickly past, angrily refusing to comment.

Back beyond the offices, the other eleven jurors were leaving the deliberation room when they saw Richardson standing with Cher Elder's family. Several women broke into a run toward them, tears streaming down their faces. "We're so sorry," they cried, explaining what had happened.

Richardson had never seen anything like it. Even some of the men were crying, others just shook his hand and walked out, saying they were too angry to talk about it right then. Other jurors stayed to talk to the family, apologizing over and over "for letting you down."

Earl and Beth Elder went out to the hallway to meet with the assembled media. "That is what is screwed up about our system," Cher's furious father said. "The holdout juror was a coward who shirked her duty."

A television reporter asked if it wasn't enough that Luther would now be off the streets for possibly the rest of his life.

"Was it enough for my daughter?" Earl Elder shot back. "She's dead. He's not. He's still living and breathing. That's not right. We give too many rights to criminals and don't think enough about the victims."

"We'd have rather had a mistrial," said 18-year-old Beth, her eyes red from crying. "Another jury would have convicted him for first degree murder."

The jurors also began filtering out, some stopping to talk to the press.

"There were three shots to the back of her head," said one. "The first could have been a mistake, but the other two were deliberate. And four times he went back to her grave to make sure she wouldn't be found."

"I felt an incredible sadness," said another woman juror as tears fell from her cheeks. "I don't think it is fair. It was the law, but it is not a law I care for."

"We're obviously upset that one juror wouldn't agree to convict him of first degree murder,'' said another tearful woman. ''We're very sorry.''

Hall was also surprised by the jury response. He told the media that he was concerned that the Lewis instructions had ''forced a number of jurors to compromise their beliefs. Our system has flaws. And this may be one of those flaws where the views of one are allowed to outweigh the views of eleven others.''

Considering the type of evidence, Richardson was actually relieved that the jury had come back with a murder conviction. Still, he too was angry that a single holdout had saved Luther from the death penalty.

''Thomas Luther is guilty of first degree murder. He knows it. I know it. And eleven jurors know it.''

The pen moved across the page as if guided by some other hand than hers, leaving behind fragmented thoughts and raw emotions. Sometimes it seemed that writing in her diary was the only thing that kept Rhonda Edwards sane.

Just a few hours earlier, Thomas Edward Luther had been found guilty of second degree murder. Rhonda knew that she should have been happy he was convicted, or at least felt some sense of relief. She'd been told Luther would probably now receive a forty-eight-year sentence to go with a fifteen-to-thirty-five-year sentence he got in 1995 for the rape of a woman in West Virginia.

Nailing him for Cher's death had been no sure thing. When it was apparent the jury was deadlocked, she had feared the worst—that man, that smirking, laughing monster who sat at the defense table might not have been held accountable for her death at all.

Instead, she wrote as she sat in a friend's living room in Golden waiting for the evening news to come on the television, ''I feel anger, rage, and resentment. I have lost a piece of myself . . .''

''. . . I know I will never be the same as I was before her death, some sorrows leave deeper scars than others. A mother's loss of her child is a deep scar . . .''

Justice seemed hollow, as empty as the hole into which they'd lowered Cher's casket. "There is a vacuum that can never be filled . . . a terrible emptiness . . ."

". . . Cher didn't get a fair trial . . ." all because one juror, a 65-year-old woman, held out for second degree murder when her eleven colleagues believed he was guilty of murder in the first degree. She wouldn't even explain her reasoning.

Now there would be no death penalty phase. No public hearing to expose the real truth about Luther instead of the white-washed version that appeared in court. Worst of all, there would be no equal payment for what he had done to Cher, no retribution for what he had put her family through.

Rhonda Edwards had held together after the verdict just long enough to get out of the courtroom before she burst into tears. She hadn't wanted him to see her cry as he smiled and hugged his attorneys like he'd won. She couldn't believe how he had callously talked about getting back in shape in the prison weight room.

And what did she have? Memories. Guilt. Frustration. "Our justice system can be twisted, because of one person who cannot see that execution by three bullets to the back of the head is deliberate murder. I hope crime never hits her family so she doesn't feel the wrath and anger that comes with the system.

"To be able to talk to your child you have to go to a cemetery and visit a cold stone, it is the most heartbreak a mother can have."

For several days following the verdict, radio talk shows, television newscasts, and newspaper columns were swamped by the outrage of a community that wondered how a single person could have held eleven others hostage.

Cleaver no longer sounded quite so sure when she was quoted saying, "All along our client told us he didn't do it, and maybe he didn't. We're just happy we're not proceeding to the penalty phase."

Mary Brown was interviewed. She said she had hoped to testify against Luther in the death penalty phase, only to be once again frustrated and in tears because of the system.

"I wanted to be there for all victims to say, 'You can go on. You don't have to let men like this ruin your lives,' " she said.

"I wanted to look him in the face and let him know that he didn't win." Several other states, she noted, didn't require unanimous verdicts.

The jurors went on the air to say they felt coerced by the judge's instructions. If the jurors were upset after the verdict, they were absolutely outraged when they finally got to read and hear about Luther's past. They said they believed that if they'd been allowed to hear about Luther's track record of attacking other women and unsanitized statements he made—"Why do I do these things?" and "The next girl won't live"—even the holdout juror would have come around.

Traumatized, the jurors called each other to cry and lend support. They'd done their best, but felt like failures.

Kate Stone, one of the alternate jurors, recognized that there needed to be some sort of closure. She called the others and invited them to a get-together at her house, telling them to bring their spouses so they could hear what the jurors were going through as a group. Nine jurors and their spouses showed up— one could not be reached and another had to work and, of course, no one invited the twelfth.

At the get-together, the jurors decided they wanted to do something to express their displeasure. They wondered if the judge would let them speak at Luther's sentencing, scheduled for April 5.

A week later, they got together again. This time, they invited Richardson. He was surprised at how torn they remained. "You got nothin' to be sorry for," he assured them. He told them about an anonymous call he'd received in the days following the verdict. The caller said he knew the holdout juror and that she had gone to her priest during the trial and the priest had instructed her to do nothing that would expose Luther to the death penalty.

It meant the woman had violated the judge's admonition to not discuss the case with anyone. Richardson knew that some of the other jurors had moral qualms about the death penalty— he had his own reservations about it, except in this case—and that was fine with him. But if the holdout juror had looked into her heart and decided she could not follow the law regarding the death penalty, she should have told the judge and asked to be excused. Now, he wondered if she had known all along that she wouldn't agree to first degree murder and had lied to get on the jury to thwart the law.

As far as the jurors speaking at the sentencing, he'd never heard of such a thing. It wouldn't hurt to ask the judge, he told them, but personally, he still had to stay out of it. Luther's lawyers had already said they would be appealing the conviction.

Kate Stone contacted Munch, who said the jurors could read a statement. So together they drafted what they wanted to say.

April 5 arrived. Cher Elder's family and friends arrived at the courthouse to find it packed with not just the press, but well-wishers, the jurors, and Mary Brown. The tension made the courtroom air feel hot and dense, and there was a collective gasp when Luther was led into the courtroom, the chains that bound his handcuffed wrists to a belly band and shackled his ankles clinking as he shuffled to the defense table. Instead of the nice clothes his lawyers had dressed him in for the trial, he wore the more familiar bright orange jail jumpsuit over a white t-shirt. He smiled when he saw his attorneys but, looking back at the gallery, appeared stunned that the courtroom was so full of unfriendly faces. He turned quickly away.

Munch called for the first witness to approach the podium that had been set up between the prosecution and defense tables. A slight, pretty woman with dark hair in a floral dress stood and walked to the microphone.

Looking at Munch and ignoring Luther, who glanced once at her and turned his head away, Mary Brown began to speak. "Death is inevitable. It comes to all living things. Although it is said that we all die alone, that is not exactly true. Each of us hopes to die surrounded by people that we love, to be able to say goodbye, to let them know how much we loved life and loved them. While many events may keep this from happening, most that I can think of are accidental.

"Cher Elder never got to say goodbye. She saw her death approaching on the face of a stranger—the same stranger who I thought would end my life. And reflected in that face was rage, hate, and the intent of inflicting extraordinary pain and terror on her and ultimately to end her life.

"As I now recall the sound of my own neck bones and skull crunching in my ears, beyond the pain and terror, I thought of my family, my friends, and how very much I loved them. I did not want to be some faceless, nameless body rotting in the snow, my loved ones never knowing what had become of their friend, their daughter, sister, co-worker.''

As she spoke, Mary Brown's voice grew stronger. She kept her head high, her small frame straight, looking down occasionally to check the typed notes of her speech. Soon there were few dry eyes in the gallery. Cleaver and Enwall slumped in their chairs, while Luther's face turned crimson.

''The pain of an anonymous death is almost indescribable, except to one who nearly experienced it,'' Brown continued. ''During my attack, Thomas Luther systematically shredded my dignity and dehumanized me. He violated my body, my mind, my soul. I was stripped of my innocent belief in the goodness of mankind.

''I could not undersand why. What had I ever done? Didn't he know I was a kind, good person? I'm sure that Cher wondered as well.

''During my first imaginings of confronting Luther after my assault, I did not see myself trying to hurt him or to get even. I just saw myself in a room telling him, telling everyone, my life story. I guess I believed that if he knew how good I was, this would not have happened. I had lost so much. It was incomprehensible that anyone that looked like a human being could treat another human being in such a way. My entire person, my whole world view had been destroyed. I did not know who I was anymore.''

Mary Brown paused as if remembering the ordeal she'd been through. Cher Elder's family and strangers alike could be heard crying in the gallery.

''The road to recovery has been a very long and painful one. I have had to draw on inner resources I did not know that I had. I feel extraordinarily lucky to have a second chance at life—to enjoy friendships, to create a family, and to accomplish worthy goals.

''While I feel that it is only the grace of God that sustained me, I carry with me a deep feeling of guilt for survival itself when I know other equally deserving women have died. Sadness is part of my life, and my heart feels the loss of Cher and all those who are still nameless.

''The world has lost their potential. Their families have suf-

fered the deepest loss imaginable. I hope and pray that Thomas
Luther is never given the opportunity to make a decision like
that again—a decision as to the life and death of another human
being.''

Mary Brown finally looked at Luther, but he did not return
her gaze, though he must surely have been aware of it. It was
Mary's triumph, her day in court at long last, where she could
expose the monster for what he was. She turned back to the
judge, and left no doubt that she in part blamed the courts.

"As you consider Thomas Luther's sentence, I would ask you
to keep these facts in mind. Fourteen years ago, Luther, a man
charged with attempted murder, rape, and kidnapping pleaded
not guilty by reason of insanity. He was found sane, and then
changed his plea to not guilty. His defense lawyer prevented me
from telling my story, to avoid 'undue emotional influence on
a jury,' and then trivialized both the events and their effects in
a court of law.

"The district attorney and a defense lawyer, in the guise of
protecting me, plea-bargained the case without ever asking my
opinion. Luther served eleven years for his crime.

"After his release, he was convicted of violently assaulting
another woman, and he killed Cher Elder. But Thomas Luther
was presented to this jury looking as clean as a Boy Scout, with
no mention of his prior record.

"There are other Thomas Luthers out there. A system of
justice that protects the accused at the expense of present and
future victims, that hides the truth to avoid emotion, that plea-
bargains and paroles to clear the prisons, must share the responsibility for Cher Elder's death."

Munch sat with his face turning red, blinking behind his round
glasses as Mary Brown spoke. When she finished, he cleared
his throat and asked who was next.

With Kate Stone leading them, nine jurors and two alternates
walked to the podium. They had decided it would be better,
more objective, for Stone to read their message, but they were
all together to support her.

Luther slid further into his seat as Kate Stone began to speak.
Cleaver stared straight ahead, while Enwall turned to listen.

"After careful and thoughtful deliberation, in a very short
amount of time, it was quite apparent to eleven of us that Thomas

Luther was and is guilty of murder in the first degree," Stone began.

"Your Honor, we feel a profound sense of failure. Logically, we know that we need not feel this way. We followed the law and instructions given to us. We know that all of this was caused first of all by the actions of Thomas Luther in killing Cher, and then by the actions of one juror. We are sincerely disappointed that one of our fellow jurors held out for second degree murder. We know that this is a legal verdict, but it is not a just verdict.

"While we could not convict on first degree, we are absolutely adamant that this heinous individual should serve the maximum sentence of the lesser charge of second degree murder. We also ask that the sentence that you give Thomas Luther be served consecutively with any other sentence pending. Your Honor, we feel that Thomas Luther should pay for what he did to Cher all by itself. Cher deserves at least this.

"We were appalled to learn about the other crimes that Thomas Luther has been convicted of, in addition to the charges that are currently pending against him. All of these crimes have strengthened our resolve to see that this man serves the maximum penalty.

"It is obvious to us that Thomas Luther should not be allowed to be part of a free society to prey on anyone in the future, as he has in the past. Cher and her family definitely have the right to expect that justice be served. Society has the right to expect protection from this sort of violence.

"We are *all* so strongly united as a jury in this opinion that we are now in direct contact with our senators and legislators, who are also concerned, to change the existing laws to allow for a conviction based on a majority vote.

"Your Honor, please help the public see justice done."

It was then time for Cher Elder's family to speak. Her grandfather, Edward Simpson, described how he had looked forward to the day Cher married and brought a great-grandchild into the world. "That juror violated her oath."

Cher's grandmother, Mary Ellen Elbert, who had feared that she would die before Cher was found, spoke next. "She was an easy child to love . . . beautiful and talented," she said.

Then Beth Elder, a beautiful young woman despite the tears that streamed down her face, stepped up. "I have never seen a person touch as many lives as Cher did,'' she said quietly. "Not until I met Tom Luther.

"When he touches anything, it shatters. He's made victims of us all, taking away what can never be replaced.

"Cher was the most unique person I have ever met. She was a little piece of everyone who loved her and when she was brutally executed, she took more than a little piece of me with her.''

Beth Elder's last words came out as a cry. She paused and took a breath before continuing. "Her death stripped me of my trust, my happiness, my innocence, and my only sister. It took away my friend, my surrogate mother, and my guardian angel. There are no words that can express how I feel about Cher and the words that express how I feel about Tom Luther aren't for human ears.

"To me he isn't fit to be a member of society. He needs to be locked up for as long as the law allows, not just for retribution but to protect society from him. Everywhere this man goes, he leaves victims in his wake. It's time he was stopped. I'm asking you to please sentence him to the forty-eight-year maximum to be served consecutively to the West Virginia sentence.''

Beth Elder took her seat next to her father who put his arm around her and pulled his only daughter to him. From the row in front of him, Rhonda Edwards stood up. She looked much as her daughter would have. Those who knew them both often said that Rhonda and Cher had shared the same outgoing, trusting personality. But Cher's death had changed her mother so that it seemed a great sadness followed her like a shadow.

Back in February, just days after the verdict, Rhonda went to visit Cher's grave for the first time since the trial began. Winter still had a hold on the high country; the cottonwoods down by the river had not yet begun to blossom.

Rhonda had brought flowers with her, including purple roses from friends, Cher's favorite color. "I took them to the grave and talked awhile,'' she wrote that afternoon in her diary. "Told her I was sorry about the trial not giving us what we thought she would want. My daughter wasn't given a choice. Why should her killer have one?

"We would have rather had a mistrial. We could have tried

again to give this monster what he deserves. I see his face and I see Satan.''

Since then Rhonda and Earl had talked about starting a campaign through the Colorado legislature to change the laws. Several lawmakers had offered to help. But who knew if they would be successful? All she could do now was let Judge Munch know how badly she was hurt.

"There are no words to accurately describe the impact that Cher's death has had on me and others,'' she said. "It's like someone tore my heart out and I'm left to figure out how to put it back.

"We'll never see Cher get married and have children. She was my only child. I can't hold her, talk to her, feel with her what comes with life. Her beautiful smile is gone, and now just a memory in my heart.

"In the past, I could call her or go see her. Now I go to a lonely cemetery to talk to a cold gravestone which says, 'Until we meet again.'

"I'll never be the same as time doesn't heal the pain, it only masks it so you can appear normal to others. The sorrow leaves a scar that will never heal. Cher's spirit is here today asking for the maximum sentence. I believe my daughter deserves to hear justice being done today.''

Rhonda Edwards paused to catch herself. She was not going to cry in front of Tom Luther. She continued on. "In this era of 'I've got a right,' 'I'm entitled,' 'You owe me,' 'I've been discriminated against,' it's time for us to hear, 'I'm responsible for what I did. I'm responsible for my actions.'

"Cher had many dreams, as did all his victims. It's time to stop the cycle of repeat offenders. It's time for you, as a representative of our justice system to say, 'Stop!' It's time to quit coddling animals like Luther and make them pay for the crimes they commit.''

Rhonda Edwards turned and walked back to where her husband, Van, took her in his arms as she sobbed. Patting her on the shoulder, Earl walked past and up to the podium.

There was so much he wanted to say about what Cher's murder had done to him and his family. Beth Elder had been cheated out of her childhood. At a time when, ideally, the worst thing she should have had to worry about was who was going to take her to the prom, she was wondering if her half sister would ever be found. Yet Beth was strong; there had been a lot of tears, but she'd shown her spirit would not be broken forever by speaking there that day. He was more worried about the long-term affect on Cher's half brother, Jacob; to that day he had refused to discuss what had happened to Cher.

Earl Elder looked at Luther, sitting like a big, dumb animal, his mouth hanging open as he stared straight ahead. *Well,* Earl thought, *you killed my daughter and tried to destroy this family, but we're still here and will be all those years you'll be staring at prison walls and fences.*

"Your Honor," Elder said, turning back to Judge Munch. "I would remind the court that Cher was shot three times in the back of the head. She was executed.

"And Cher was not the first woman that Thomas Luther brutalized, just the first that he has been convicted of murdering. My feeling is and always will be that Thomas Luther should reside on death row. But because of the verdict of guilty of second degree murder, Thomas Luther does not have to face the death penalty or even life in prison, but we, Cher's family are faced with a lifetime of grieving, sorrow, and heartache. We have been give a life sentence because Thomas Luther decided to execute Cher.

"We suffered for nearly two years before Cher's body was found and she could be laid to rest. Suffering the anguish and uncertainty of what had happened to Cher. Hoping beyond hope that she would make it back to us alive and well.

"Thomas Luther made certain that we would never see Cher alive again. He even tried to be sure that we would not be able to say goodbye to her in death, by burying her body in a hidden, shallow grave.

"When Thomas Luther heard the verdict of guilty of second degree murder, he smiled and told his lawyers he couldn't wait to get on with his life in prison and start lifting weights to build up his body.

"For what?" Earl Elder shouted, now turning to address Luther. "So it will be easier to carry the next body up to a shallow grave?" He paused as if expecting an answer, but Luther just bowed his head and stared at his hands.

Elder shook his head and turned back to the judge. "Thomas

Luther has proven that he will rape, brutalize, and murder young women with no regard for the fear and pain that he inflicts on them or their families.

"If the sentence for Cher's execution is not served consecutively with any other sentence he is serving, it will be as if this murderer will not have been punished at all for her death.

"The sooner Thomas Luther is able to leave prison, the sooner some other young woman will pay the price of any leniency the court shows him today."

After Elder sat down, Judge Munch asked if Luther had anything to say for himself. "Yes, sir," he said, standing up as he tried to hold onto some notes with his wrists handcuffed.

"First I want to thank God and my attorneys for their hard work to give me a fightin' chance," he said, as Cleaver looked up and smiled. Then her jaw dropped as he announced he was going to tell the real truth about what had happened, "not even my attorneys have been told the whole truth."

The courtroom was suddenly silent. Richardson sat up and looked hopefully at Luther. *At last,* he thought, *maybe we get the details of where he killed her and what led up to her murder and then burial.* But within a few minutes, he slumped back in his seat; Luther was doing what Luther did best, besides attacking women. He lied.

The thing was, they weren't even very well thought-out lies. In a rambling twenty-five-minute speech, Luther talked about how after Central City, he and Cher had both cried about their relationships—she over Byron, and he over Debrah Snider. They'd hugged and that had led to sex.

They'd returned to Byron's, he said. Cher left after finding Byron in bed with Gina. And he had gone to sleep in the apartment. A little later, Cher returned and got into fight with Byron. She fell in the bathroom and was knocked unconscious. Byron and J.D. then wrapped her in a rug and placed her in J.D.'s car.

Luther said he was the one who then followed J.D. into the mountains, communicating over walkie-talkies. J.D. took Cher to the woods, where he rolled her out of the rug and removed her clothes. "Then J.D. shot her twice in the back of the head, turned her over, and shot her once in the eye."

Richardson scowled and looked away as Luther rambled on. The story didn't make sense. It didn't even fit the forensic evidence that Cher Elder was shot three times, *all* in the back of the head. Wasn't Luther even listening when the forensic evidence was introduced? Then again, he'd always had trouble keeping his stories straight.

It was J.D. who moved the car, Luther claimed. All he did was help bury her.

Luther said he and the two Eerebout brothers then concocted the story that Cher had died as a result of a drug deal gone bad. But he was betrayed by the brothers after Byron got in trouble.

Denying that he ever told Southy he killed anyone, Luther said, "I told him I was mixed up in some crap. He just figured I did it. His loyalty and friendship should have been unquestioned."

Of course, Luther didn't explain why his own loyalty to Healey hadn't prevented him from trying to pin the murder on Eerebout and Healey months before his own arrest. Or why he let his lawyers portray Healey as the killer.

While his other two assaults were "plenty bad," Luther said, they're weren't as bad as they were made out to be. "I never tried to kill them. I let them go. I get mad, blow up, and hurt girls, but when I stop, I feel bad."

Luther tried to claim that he hadn't raped Mary Brown or Bobby Jo Jones because he couldn't get an erection when he attacked them. "I'm a no-good son-of-a-bitch," he offered. "And for what I did in 1982, that woman has the right to say anything she wants about me. But she can't imagine how truly sorry I am, and there'll never be enough punishment for what I did." He had apparently forgotten his complaints that the system had screwed him by making him serve eleven out of fifteen years.

"But being a son-of-a-bitch, don't make me a killer." He looked back at Cher Elder's family. "I hope to see you all in heaven."

"God doesn't let people like you in heaven," Beth Elder responded. "That's why there's a hell."

Luther began to sit but before he had even settled into his chair, Munch sentenced him to forty-eight years in prison, the most he could, to be served after he finished his West Virginia sentence. "Realizing that in all practicality, this is a life sentence," Munch added.

Munch said he took into account Luther's past, calling the attacks on Mary Brown and Bobby Jo Jones, "violent, sadistic, brutal, and dehumanizing."

"I see no realistic possibility of rehabilitation," Munch said, excluding the possibility of Luther having time knocked off for good behavior under the habitual criminal sentencing provisions of Colorado law.

"This man will be an extreme danger to women his entire life," Munch added and remanded Luther to Denver authorities to await his trial for the attempted murder of Heather Smith.

The blow to the back of Heather Smith's neck woke her from a deep sleep. Her shoulder and right side seared with pain where her attacker stabbed her.

Oh God, he found me, she thought as she lay on her stomach in the darkness of her bedroom. She could feel her blood flowing out of the wounds but didn't dare move.

She listened and waited for him to come back to finish her off. Where was Heidi? she wondered. Why hadn't the dog barked to warn her? And where was he?

Smith stared at the darkest of the shadows in front of her eyes. Was he there in the blackness, playing with her? Was he creeping around the bottom of her bed, getting ready to jump up?

If her mother had been living in the house, Heather would have called out, hoping she would arrive on time to turn on the light and chase away the monster. But Smith was alone, lying in bed as her blood seeped into the sheets.

She stayed frozen in place for what seemed like hours and still he didn't return. Cautiously she moved her hand to her side. No blood. She shifted her hand to the gaping wound in the back of her neck. Again no blood.

Heather began to cry. It had been a dream, or more like a flashback. She could still feel the first blow and realized just how hard Luther had hit her three years earlier to break her neck. Her side ached and she felt the path of the knife deep inside her chest. It was just a dream and still she was too frightened to move, until the dawn arrived gray, filled with the songs of birds, and the shadows fled.

It was April 12, exactly three years since the attack, a week after Luther's sentencing for Cher Elder's murder, and just three weeks to go before her trial.

Until the dream, she'd been feeling pretty good about finally getting to face Thomas Luther in court. Denver Deputy District Attorney Doug Jackson had coached her on what to expect. He took her into the courtroom and showed her the witness stand and where Luther would be sitting a few feet away. "Just keep your eyes on me," Jackson said, "and I'll get you through it."

They knew from preliminary hearings that Luther's attorney, Lauren Cleaver, planned to attack her credibility and portray her as a desperate woman willing to have anyone convicted for attacking her. Tom Luther was just handy.

Jackson and Heather Smith were stunned when Luther waived his right to a jury trial and placed the outcome in the hands of Denver District Court Judge Richard Spriggs. Cleaver advised the move because of extensive publicity on the Cher Elder case and the unpredictablility of jurors. She was still stunned by the jurors' remarks at the sentencing.

A few days before the trial, Luther offered to plead guilty to attempted murder if the judge would let him serve the sentence concurrently with his other sentences. His pleading guilty would have essentially eliminated the chance of the case being overturned on appeal, and Smith wouldn't have had to face Cleaver. But when Jackson left it up to her, Heather Smith said she wanted her day in court, no matter how ugly it might get.

Getting out of bed, rubbing the back of her neck where she could still feel the ghost of the blow three years earlier, Smith wondered if she'd made the right decision. Thomas Luther was in jail, but he also haunted the shadows of her memories.

The trial of Thomas Luther for the attempted murder and assault of Heather Smith lasted only three days.

Detective Paul Scott testified about the attack and the subsequent investigation, which had run into a dead end until Heather Smith's call. Doctors testified about the gravity of her wounds, and their surprise that she had not died. And for the third time in as many trials, Debrah Snider drove a stake into Thomas Luther.

Snider had arrived back in West Virginia after her testimony in the Cher Elder trial to find her cabin ransacked. Lamps and photographs had been knocked from a table in the living room. In the kitchen, a radio and toaster had been thrown on the floor.

Retribution, she thought, *for what I did in Colorado.* But by whom? Luther's family was in denial about his guilt, and his sister, Becky, and brother-in-law, Randy, still lived in the area. Or could it have been one of Luther's friends? And if so, were they still around? Perhaps watching the cabin at that moment?

Then she heard a noise. Frightened, she looked behind her, then laughed. The vandal was a squirrel who had found a way in past the kitchen screen.

Debrah Snider arrived back in Colorado, subpoenaed by Deputy District Attorney Jackson, clutching a small brown package. She was glad Tom didn't get the death penalty. "That would have been too hard," she told a reporter. "Remember, Jesus took the murderer with him to heaven, not the thief, because the murderer asked for forgiveness. I hope Tom will someday ask for forgiveness. I'm still angry at him for what he did to those girls. But I'm sorry, I still love him."

Called to the stand, Snider told Spriggs that Luther used to disappear for several days at a time, coming back with sore muscles and bruises "like he'd been in a fight," and several days' growth of a heavy beard. And yes, she replied to Jackson's questions, he owned a green nylon windbreaker and a blue baseball cap with gold lettering.

Debrah Snider unsealed the brown packet at Jackson's request and produced a pair of silver, square-rimmed glasses that she said she'd loaned to Luther in 1993. Jackson took the glasses and entered them into the evidence.

At the beginning of the second day of the trial, there was angry muttering in the spectator gallery, where Heather Smith's family and a large contingent of friends sat, when Cleaver entered the courtroom. In the papers that morning there had been a photograph of Luther with his arm draped around a grinning Lauren Cleaver as they had walked down the hallway on the first day. He'd actually caught her by surprise. Even if Cleaver didn't believe he was guilty of Cher Elder's murder, she knew he'd committed the sexual assaults, but she acted like they were best friends.

Heather Smith was waiting to be called that morning in the witness room when an older gentleman walked in. "I'm Cher's grandfather," he said. "And I just wanted you to know that we're here to support you."

Smith smiled and said thanks. Between the old man and the family and friends she knew were lined up in rows behind Luther, she was no longer afraid of Cleaver.

Finally, she was called and entered the courtroom, keeping her eyes first on Jackson and then the witness stand. Even then, as she walked past the defense table, she could feel Luther's presence like an angry, black cloud.

Under Jackson's guidance, Heather recounted in vivid detail the events of April 12, 1993, and the man who attacked her, including what he was wearing and his workingman's hands. She said she had seen those hands again in a police photograph in which Luther was holding up a name plaque.

Jackson asked that Luther hold up his hands. Cleaver objected but was overruled by Judge Spriggs. Luther held up his hands with a smirk on his face.

"Are those the hands of the man who attacked you?" Jackson asked.

Smith had not yet looked at Luther and still didn't make eye contact when she looked at his hands. "Yes," she said.

"And is that the man who attacked you?" Jackson asked.

Heather Smith raised her gaze and looked into Luther's cold, blue eyes. His smile seemed to be mocking her. "Yes," she said, raising her hand and pointing. "I'm certain it's him."

As Jackson continued to ask her follow-up questions, Heather could hear Luther cursing her under his breath. "Bitch. Fuckin' whore." Two rows away, Heather's mother could even hear him. But if Judge Spriggs noticed, he did not give any indication.

Then Cleaver went on the attack. Wasn't it true she had misidentified other potential suspects? Wasn't it true the man she said attacked her had blond hair and a full beard? Isn't it true she was so desperate to find the man who attacked her, she picked Cleaver's client out of a newspaper story?

But Smith stuck to her guns. The other men were just possibilities she had wanted Scott to check out. She'd said the man had light hair and it was mostly covered by a baseball cap. And she'd described him as having a well-groomed or new beard;

the composite sketch gave the impression of a fuller beard. And no, since the day she had seen Luther's photograph in the newspaper, she knew she'd found her attacker.

Cleaver returned to the same questions so often without getting anywhere that Spriggs directed her to move on. And in the end, Heather was the one holding her head up while Cleaver plopped back in her chair angry and frustrated as the prosecution rested its case.

The third day of the trial started poorly for the defense. Cleaver had subpoenaed Richardson. She believed she could get him to testify that he had never known Luther to have a beard or silver glasses.

What she didn't know was that Richardson had been told by Matt Marlar about Luther showing up in a disguise that included a beard. And he'd noted the silver, square-rimmed glasses on Luther's kitchen table when they first met.

Cleaver tried to interview him before the trial, but he said he would only respond to the subpoena. The morning of the third day, she caught him on his way to the courtroom.

"Can I ask you a few questions before you go in?" Cleaver said.

"Swear me in on the witness stand and you can ask all you want," he replied.

Cleaver looked at him angrily. "You can get out of here," she said. "We won't be calling you."

The defense lawyer did call Smith's old boyfriend Jason to testify that Heather was prone to exaggeration, including her account about the incident in which he held a gun to his head. The defense attorney's tone was mocking, with a lot of eye-rolling thrown in.

On cross-examination, Jackson asked Jason about the time when he threw a dart into Heather's leg. "I suppose that was exaggerated?" Jackson asked.

Jason blushed. "It was an accident."

"An accident? How could it have been an accident when the dartboard was the other direction?" To that, Jason had no explanation.

Cleaver called a man who had been Luther's co-worker at the janitorial service in April 1993. He said they always worked as a team and there was never a day when he went to work that

Luther wasn't also there, including the night of April 12. Cleaver introduced a time card that showed Luther had punched in.

But the card never showed him punching back out. And Jackson was able to show that several days the week before the attack, Luther had not shown up for work. In fact, there was no supervisor who could say that Luther stayed at work the night Heather Smith was attacked.

The closing arguments were short and sweet. Jackson noted that Heather had plenty of time to study her attacker under normal conditions and had made a positive identification. Luther's alibi, he said, didn't wash.

Cleaver again went back to portraying Smith as a desperate woman, tormented by the violence done to her, seeking closure by convicting Tom Luther after being shown a photograph in the newspaper ''by her psychiatrist.'' She stressed the last three words.

Judge Spriggs then left the bench to go over the evidence in the quiet of his chambers. He said he expected to render a verdict after noon. With nothing else to do, Heather and her mother went to lunch and arrived back at the courthouse just as it was announced that the judge had reached a decision.

Smith took a seat with her family three rows behind and to the side of Luther so that she could just see his profile. The judge entered and sat down, shuffling through his papers for what seemed like an eternity.

When he began to speak, it immediately didn't sound good, and Smith felt her heart sink. ''Initially, I want to point out that this court is acutely aware that sometimes persons are unjustly convicted as a result of good-faith, but mistaken, eyewitness identification,'' the judge said. ''In fact, it's the one single factor most likely to lead to unjust conviction in a given case.''

Oh no, Heather thought, *he's trying to make me feel better, but he believes Cleaver.* Her mother seemed to sense Heather's fears, or was perhaps thinking the same way, and squeezed her daughter's hand.

''I have, in the past,'' the judge continued, ''had some personal experience with situations like this one many years ago, when a person was in prison for some period of time as a result of erroneous eyewitness identification by a deputy sheriff.

''More recently, a few years ago I recall a case where the

young lady was stabbed to death after getting off a bus. A young suspect was arrested who fit the description of the eyewitness and who was a resident of a nearby halfway house, and who gave a statement to the police admitting that he was on the bus and he got off at that stop, but denied any participation in the killing. The man was identified by two eyewitnesses at a preliminary hearing, bound over for trial, and fortunately, most fortunately for him, the actual perpetrator subsequently confessed to a roommate, who was kind enough to call the police and tell them the situation, thereby exonerating the person who had been improperly identified and ultimately leading to the conviction of the true perpetrators.

"So I'm anything but blind to the possibility of inaccurate, or mistaken, eyewitness identification testimony."

Luther and Cleaver looked at each other and smiled. Heather saw it and tears sprang to her eyes. But then the judge's tone began to change.

"Having listened carefully to the testimony of the witnesses in this case and having had occasion to judge and assess their credibility, the court makes the following findings of fact," the judge said.

"The court has spent some time comparing the sketch of attacker with the photograph of the defendant. I have seen a fair number of these police sketches over the years, and frankly, in my experience at least, this is about as good as it gets."

Spriggs noted that the glasses brought by Debrah Snider matched those described by Heather Smith. He also noted that Snider had described the green jacket "as a nylon windbreaker," exactly as had Smith.

"In assessing the credibility of this testimony, and the court notes first of all, Ms. Smith is an exceptionally detailed historian, unlike many crime victims called upon to give a description of someone, or make an eyewitness identification."

Again, tears welled up in Heather's eyes, but this time they were tears of happiness. For the rest of her life, she would remember the judge's description of her as an exceptional historian. *He believes me!* she rejoiced. *He believes me!*

Cleaver's smile had turned to a frown. Luther glared briefly at her.

Spriggs noted that Heather had a long time to observe her

attacker. And that from what he could see for himself, Luther matched her description of the attacker. Same size. Same build. The eyes, nose, chin, and particularly his hands.

The discrepancy about the beard, he said, could be explained several ways. One being that Luther had a heavy beard; even shaved it stood out against his pale skin. The other lay in Debrah Snider's testimony about how he would go several days without shaving when out on his forays.

Luther's evidence of an alibi—his co-worker—"is wholly unpersuasive," Spriggs said. "The court concludes beyond a reasonable doubt that Mr. Luther is, in fact, the perpetrator of these offenses."

Heather Smith began crying as Spriggs announced that Luther was "guilty as charged." After all the years, she was vindicated.

Stunned, Cleaver spoke briefly with Luther then asked that her client be sentenced immediately.

"All right," Spriggs nodded. "Mr. Luther come up here to the podium with your counsel, please." When the two were standing before him, the judge asked, "Mr. Luther, is there any statement you would like to make to the court on behalf of mitigation of your defense?"

Luther nodded. "Yes, sir. I hope that Ms. Smith is happy she has gotten someone convicted of this crime she suffered. I'm sorry for her and I'm sorry for her family that suffered through all of her pains, but I will say this, I'm not the man that attacked this woman. I'm not the guy that did it."

It didn't matter to Heather. Luther had said the same thing every time he got caught. *I'm not the guy who did it.* Or it was blown out of proportion. But Luther no longer mattered to her.

The judge then turned to the prosecutor. "Mr. Jackson, what is the People's position?"

Jackson replied, "The People ask the court to give Mr. Luther the maximum sentence."

"All right," the judge said. "In light of the nature of this crime, which is almost inexplicable, it appears to be without motive, other than plain old vexation. I don't know what triggered this, what would cause someone to answer an ad in the paper, look up a total stranger, converse with them for ten or fifteen minutes, and then for absolutely no reason whatsoever, try to hack them to death with a knife. But that's certainly more of a problem for psychiatrists than for judges. I certainly don't pretend to understand this, and I strongly suspect the perpetrator doesn't understand it either.

"In any event, it's clear to this court, Mr. Luther, for whatever reasons, you're a serious menace to the public, and I don't think I have really any choice in this matter but to give you every day the law allows.

"So it will be the judgment of the court that the defendant is remanded with all convenient speed to the custody of the Department of Corrections, to be confined in an institution for a period of fifty years on count one and fifty years on count two."

Even those in the courtroom hoping to see Luther get his just desserts hadn't expected this. Fifty years! Using the habitual offender provisions, Spriggs had given Luther more than he got for murdering Cher Elder. He remanded Luther to the Colorado Department of Corrections.

Cleaver glumly noted that Luther had to return to West Virginia to serve his sentence there first.

"I understand that," Spriggs said. "And I understand that he has a substantial sentence out of Jefferson County."

"Actually, less time than you gave him here, judge," Cleaver said, not quite managing to keep the sarcasm out of her voice.

The judge arched his eyebrow and replied dryly, "I know that, too. The judge out there gave him every day the law allows, and I gave him every day the law allowed. And I did so, and don't mind saying it, because it's my intention this man never be released, and that he remain in prison until the day he dies."

Luther was immediately surrounded by deputies. Turning back to where Heather Smith's family and friends were congratulating her, he dropped the polite act he'd played during his trial. With the mask off, his face screwed up in hate as he snarled, "At least I get to go back to where I don't have to be nice anymore."

Epilogue

July 1998—Denver, Colorado

In the spring of 1998, Thomas Edward Luther's conviction for the murder of Cher Elder was upheld by the Colorado Court of Appeals. He claimed he didn't get a fair trial. The court said otherwise.

Luther once complained to Debrah Snider that he always gets blamed for more than he does. But if he is not a serial killer, and merely a self-professed "angry motherfucker" with a heart "half good, half bad," and a twice-convicted brutal sexual predator, as well as your run-of-the-mill murderer, then he is certainly dogged by the horrible coincidence that wherever he goes, young women are sexually assaulted in the same manner, disappear, and die. Their bodies are left to rot faceless and nameless in remote wooded areas.

Following Luther's trail, one comes upon a number of police agencies, even friends, who wonder if he is the killer of some young woman in their jurisdiction. Sometimes, it has been too long, the trail too cold to ever know the truth, unless somewhere down the line there is a confession.

In Vermont, police officials can only speculate about the young woman from Stowe who disappeared and died in the woods two decades ago, at a time when Luther was reported to have lived in the ski resort town. And even his former friends in Hardwick still worry about the blond hitchhiker he showed up with in the fall of 1993 after leaving Colorado. He said she left for West Virginia the day before he did; they wonder if she ever left at all.

In Pennsylvania, Les Freehling of the state patrol believes that Luther is his prime suspect for the attacks on two women in his area. The woman whose body was discovered Dec. 10, 1993—beaten, strangled, raped vaginally and anally—has still not been identified. She, like thousands of others across the country, remains a Jane Doe. However, Freehling says, his investigation has revealed that she was a transient often seen hitchhiking near the construction site where Luther and his brother-in-law, Randy Foster, worked during that time.

Neither has the body of Karen Denise Wells, who disappeared from Newport, Pennsylvania, in April 1994, ever been found. Just her car, five miles from where the other girl's body was discovered, and her clothes in a motel. Luther was still working in the area and commuting to nearby Delray.

Another unhappy coincidence? Freehling notes that the coincidences stopped after Luther was arrested in September.

And then there was Debrah Snider's recollection of the girl from the West Virginia campground, whose likeness appeared in the "missing" flyer on the post office wall. But with Luther in prison, apparently for the rest of his life, there has been no urgency to pursue the cases, though Freehling keeps them open and at hand. The task of comparing Luther's blood DNA to the blood on the first victim's sweater remains undone.

In Denver, homicide detectives are stymied in the case of the woman found sexually assaulted and stabbed in her apartment, and left under an American flag in June 1994. They have only a single, gray curly hair discovered on the body, and the word of a former Jefferson County inmate who claims Luther told him details about the murder only the killer should have known.

In Summit County, Colorado, the DNA test done on the blood found on Bobby Jo Oberholtzer's mitten came back negative for Luther and his girlfriend, Sue Potter, although her blood type initially matched. Was Luther accompanied by someone else

that night? Or was he not involved at all in the murders of Bobby
Jo and Annette Schnee?

Detectives Richard Eaton and Charlie McCormick keep Luther
on the short list of suspects and follow each lead as it appears.
They have tried to trace a report that an airline stewardess in
California, who sold Luther the truck he was driving in 1982
when he assaulted Mary Brown, was later found beaten to death.
But so far, it remains a rumor.

In the meantime, Eaton is looking more closely at another
convicted killer from Idaho, who was known for shooting his
victims in the back. However, there is no evidence that other
killer was ever in the state of Colorado.

Initially, Eaton was troubled that Bobby Jo and Annette were
executed with a gun, while Luther attacked his other known
victims, Mary Brown and Bobby Jo Jones, with a hammer and
his hands. But then Luther was convicted of shooting Cher Elder.

Breckenridge is no longer a stranger to murders and other
violent crime. It keeps Eaton too busy to devote much time to
the murders of Bobby Jo and Annette. But he still pulls over
whenever he reaches the summit of Hoosier Pass and also pauses
by the small white cross beside the stream if other matters take
him to Alma. "No one stops being a suspect until I got the guy
who did it," he says.

Although they're not his cases and he keeps a discreet distance,
Richardson remains convinced that Oberholtzer and Schnee are
Luther's work. He, like Freehling in Pennsylvania, points out
that the murders, rare for the area back then, stopped when
Luther was arrested.

"Luther is an opportunistic killer," he says. "It's only in
television and the movies that a serial killer always kills the
exact same way. Luther'd take a trashcan and shove it down
your throat if that's what he had. On the night Cher died, he
just happened to have a gun in the car because numb-nuts, the
Eerebout brothers, had given it to him a couple days before."

There are other factors that continue to point the finger at
Luther for the murders. He wasn't working the day of or after
the murders, though he told investigators that he was. He drove
a truck similar to the truck the hitchhiking Breckenridge couple
insisted having seen Bobby Jo in. And by his own accounts, he
had access to several guns.

Sue Potter's photograph was similar enough to the composite sketch of the dark-haired woman seen with Annette Schnee the night she disappeared that a judge in the state where she currently lives believed there was grounds to have her forced to give blood samples at a hospital. The blood on Bobby Jo's mitten didn't match. But does that exclude Sue Potter from having been with Luther and Annette at some point during that late afternoon?

Then there are Luther's comments, which still haunt Sheriff Joe Morales. "Why do I do these things?" *What things? How many? When?* Morales wonders. "It won't be over for me until he's dead," says the sheriff.

Mary Brown insists, as she has for several years, that she recalls Luther pointing a gun at her back during the assault. Her imagination? Or is it only a coincidence that several of Luther's former jailmates, who Mary had no contact with, claim he said he intended to shoot her but feared waking the neighbors?

Unfortunately, after the passage of time and leads not pursued by the original investigators, there are more possibilities than proof. Did John Martin tell the deputy of Luther bragging about leaving a woman he had raped face down in a creek in May, before the body of Annette Schnee was found, or not until September?

If not until September, why did Luther assault him for being a snitch? And for that matter, why did Luther then try to arrange the murders of Martin and Sue Potter? Revenge, anger—or because he feared what they might say?

Tantalizing questions, but will there ever be answers? The last Eaton heard, Martin, who told him that he had terminal cancer, was released in 1996 from the New Jersey prison and living with his family. But he hasn't been heard from since.

If a case can ever be made against Luther in Summit County, the prosecutor there may find it easier to get a judge to allow evidence of similar transactions. One of Cleaver's arguments that swayed Judge Munch was that Luther didn't use a gun on Mary Brown and Bobby Jo Jones and that he let them live. After Cher Elder, that argument no longers washes.

Extraordinary coincidences, if they are coincidences. But only the passage of time will determine if the fates of more young women can be tied to the brutal nature of Thomas Luther.

And what is the nature of Luther? Was he just the scorpion

riding on the frog's back? And can it be linked to his own recollections of having been molested by a male relative as a boy? The victim becoming the perpetrator, as Luther once wrote to Debrah Snider.

At various times in his "career," Luther has been diagnosed as having personality disorders. The general public tends to think of personality disorders as some lesser, not so dangerous, and distant cousin of the diagnosis "insane." An eccentric as opposed to a blood-crazed loony.

However, the person with the personality disorder may be more dangerous. For one thing, insanity is an illness that often can be mitigated or even cured through drugs or psychotherapy. Someone may even have a psychotic episode over a given period of time and then recover, never to experience it again.

It's another story entirely with personality disorders, according to forensic psychiatrist John Macdonald. "Everyone has personality traits. It's what makes people individuals. For instance, some people are outgoing, others are introverts. There is nothing wrong or dangerous about either, unless taken to extremes. Personality traits become disorders when they interfere with a person's ability to function normally and legally within society.

"A man who obsessively cleans his desk for a few minutes before leaving from work each day may draw no attention from his colleagues, except perhaps being teased for being a 'neatnik.'

"However, the man who spends hours after work going through various rituals so that his desk is spotless, and then explodes in rage if a single paperclip is found out of order, has a disabling personality disorder that is easily recognizable and may cost him his job."

Unfortunately, personality disorders are as much a part of someone's interior makeup as blue eyes and blond hair are part of their physical exterior. They can be covered up for a time the way contact lenses or hair dye create temporary outward changes, but a personality disorder does not go away, says Macdonald.

"People who are insane most often suffer from delusions and hallucinations. They may tell acquaintances for months that some mysterious 'they' are invading his brain with radio waves. They this person may kill to stop his 'persecutors,' who in reality may just be his unfortunate neighbor.

"Sometimes people do things that normal people think of as 'crazy,' such as killing someone for no apparent reason. However, the legal test for insanity in most states is whether the person knew at the time of the murder the difference between right and wrong, and whether the accused can assist their lawyer in their defense.

"People with personality disorders know the difference between right and wrong. They just don't care, or they believe they're right and society is wrong. They can assist with their defense. In fact, they tend to be above average in intelligence, which is why they can appear 'normal' when they want to, why these guys always seem to have wives and girlfriends who don't have a clue who they're living with. Ted Bundy was like that.

"These disorders generally become apparent by adolescence and remain for life, though the most extremes of the behavior tend to tone down with age."

The Federal Bureau of Investigation defines a serial killer as someone who has killed three times in different incidents separated by time and distance. A mass murderer simply goes on a spree. Macdonald says it's not the number that matters but the fact that once started, the serial killer will murder over and over until he is stopped.

Luther has been labeled at various times with different varieties of personality disorders. And several of them seem to fit him like a surgeon's glove, such as narcissistic personality disorder, described by the handbook of forensic psychiatrists, *The Diagnostic and Statistical Manual of Mental Disorders IV,* as "having a grandiose sense of self-importance or uniqueness; preoccupation with fantasies of unlimited success; exhibitionistic need for constant attention and admiration; and characteristic disturbances in interpersonal relationships, such as feelings of entitlement, interpersonal exploitiveness, relationships that alternate between extremes of over-idealization and devaluation, and lack of empathy.

"Fantasies involve achieving unlimited ability, power, wealth, brilliance, beauty, or ideal love. In response to criticism, defeat, or disappointment, there is either a cool indifference or marked feelings of rage, inferiority, shame, humiliation, or emptiness."

But the term usually applied to Luther has been sociopath, the most dangerous of the lot, because while the sociopath knows killing is wrong, and doesn't care, it also is what makes him feel good or powerful. "And getting away with it only increases its pull," says Macdonald. "Most serial killers are sexually motivated and sadistic. They get sexual pleasure out of causing pain, humiliation, and death."

Three percent of American males and one percent of American females are believed to be sociopaths. According to the *DSM IV,* those with an antisocial personality disorder have a "history of continuous and chronic antisocial behavior in which the rights of others are violated." They have an "inability to maintain enduring attachment to a sexual partner ... irritability and aggressiveness as indicated by repeated fights or assault ... impulsivity ... and a disregard for the truth."

Sociopaths mimic real people, says Macdonald, and conform their behavior to get what they want. Serial killers—along with the childhood behavioral triad of firesetting, cruelty to animals, and bedwetting—were usually sexually abused as children and witnessed violence in the home.

"As abused children, they learned to disassociate themselves from their bodies. As adults, they disassociate themselves from their actions."

J.D. Eerebout returned to Colorado after the trial and was arrested and sentenced to prison. He whined to Dennis Hall that his father wouldn't let him return to Colorado for the trial. Byron Eerebout is serving the remainder of his sentence out of state in a community corrections program.

Dennis "Southy" Healey called Richardson a year after the trial. "I don't want anything," he said. "I just wanted you to know that I'm clean and I got a job." Chuck "Mongo" Kreiner has also stayed out of trouble and is gainfully employed in a management position.

Richard "Mortho" Brazell died in 1997. Informed of the death, Richardson told the coroner to look for signs of a cocaine overdose. Mortho died, however, of natural causes.

Thomas Luther continues to haunt many more people than he ever physically hurt. The jurors in the Cher Elder trial still have not fully recovered and keep in touch, even if that has grown more sporadic over the intervening two years. Some no longer will talk about the case, but will chat again about family, work, and hobbies. Other still have nightmares and talk about the case obsessively.

"He preys on my mind, it's an unclosed wound," says Kate Stone, "and it will be until he dies in prison. Life will never again be so innocent. Colorado will never feel as safe as I once thought when I read stories about Los Angeles or New York."

Heather Smith no longer dreams about Luther. But he continues to infect her life, and he wasn't alone. Until late 1997, she struggled with the continued victimization this society imparts to people like her. Lawyers, insurance companies, doctors, and the hospital all fought over who was responsible for her medical bills, including the surgery for the undiagnosed broken neck. Her credit was ruined and her life put on hold while it all finally got sorted out in the fall of 1997.

"Sometimes it seems like I've been in a coma for four years," she says. "I lost that part of my life, even after the trial, and I can never get it back again." But the cracks in the vase are harder to see these days. She isn't so self-conscious about the scar on her chest, and when she talks about Luther, it's with disdain, not fear. He's in prison and she helped put him there.

"I still get afraid, especially at night," she says. "And I still don't trust people, especially men, like I used to. But I can feel myself getting stronger all the time."

Strong enough that she's dating again and hoping to meet Prince Charming. However, she no longer feels she has to be the Princess of the Ball. That girl was short-sighted, self-absorbed. The woman is wiser, more interested in those things that last through all travails—love, friendship, family. She's getting closer to being Heather again. "Only now, I'm the queen of the ball," she laughs. Rebecca Hascall, married her boyfriend and has a child.

It was nearly a year before Deputy District Attorney Dennis Hall could bring himself to take on another murder case. Until then, he just didn't think he could deal with another victim's family.

Some things about the Tom Luther case he has blocked out.

Such as what he was going to say to the jury to convince them to put Luther to death.

For a recent serial arsonist case, he needed the legal terminology for asking a judge to allow similar transactions. He pulled the paperwork he filed in the Luther case for the first time in two years. He read it and when he finished he was still convinced that the statutes were written for a case like Luther's. Behind the paperwork were the photographs of Mary Brown, Bobby Jo Jones, Betty Luther, and Cher Elder; it looked like a family reunion. How could the judge not have seen?

Cher's family and friends continue to mourn her death. "Christmas and birthdays are still the hardest," Rhonda Edwards says. "That's when I cry. Or when I go through her things and think about all the plans she had for the future and realize there is no future."

A mile or so along the highway beyond Empire, up a hill from a turn-off, a path turns to the left and a few yards farther breaks through the trees and into a chapel-like clearing. An oblong hole there has been filled with large, gray granite stones. A short distance away, a memorial plaque has been attached to a steel post and anchored a foot above the ground by Van Edwards. It reads simply, "Cher Elder, 1973-1993." It is surrounded by a small altar of stones on which flowers, real and plastic, are frequently laid, along with items such as a teddy bear and Christmas ornaments. Her family and friends visit frequently. And a week or two before Christmas, Earl Elder takes a tree to the chapel and decorates it for his first daughter.

After the sentencing, Earl joined a support group for parents of murdered children. He doesn't go as much anymore. The others there still have festering wounds and he'd rather remember his daughter in peace. "We were lucky," he says. "We had Scott Richardson. I was struck by how many people in the group had bad experiences with, and even blame, the cops and the system."

The movement to change the unanimous verdict law lost momentum when it made no headway in the 1997 legislative session. But Earl Elder says he'll keep trying.

"Other than that," he says, "I'm determined that I will live at least long enough to make sure that Thomas Luther never leaves prison again, except in a box."

Det. Scott Richardson is one of those who stops frequently at the place where Luther buried Cher. He brings flowers. He's grateful that he could find her and the peace that gave him and her family. It could have been otherwise.

Det. Dave Dauenhauer of the Clear Creek County Sheriff's Department has since moved on to the Colorado Bureau of Investigation, but he has not forgotten Beth Ann Miller. He hopes that the latest "break" in the case will pan out to be a real one.

In December 1997, a former resident of Idaho Springs was arrested in Ohio on child pornography charges; in his possession were newspaper clippings of Beth Ann's disappearance and a topographical map of the area on which he had drawn three Xs. So far, he has refused to talk to Clear Creek detectives.

"Betcha after the snow melts that I'll be up there with Necro-Search," says Richardson, who was inducted into the elite group and given a hat on which the nickname "Bulldog" had been embroidered.

The photographs of other victims have come and gone from the walls of Richardson's office. But Cher Elder's photographs, including her as a 3-year-old, remain next to those of his family. He bought Sabrina a Harley of her own for their wedding anniversary.

A photograph of Luther causes his eyes to grow dark with anger. He points a finger and makes a shooting motion. However, when Luther's appeals are through and the killer has nothing more to lose, Richardson plans to visit his old arch-enemy in the West Virginia prison. He hopes that then Luther will finally tell the whole truth.

A year ago, on the anniversary of Luther's conviction for murdering Cher Elder, Debrah Snider wrote Richardson a letter. "I used to think that Tom was my dragon-slayer," she said. "Now I realize that he was the monster and that you were the dragon-slayer."

"I would go to trial against the devil with Dennis Hall," Richardson says. He pauses, then laughs. "I guess I already did."

Debrah Snider lives in West Virginia with her wolves. She knows she did the right thing—three times, as a matter of fact—

but it cost her the love of her life. She tried to write to Tom, but was told by his lawyer to quit.

"There is not much I am afraid of at night, because I know how to take care of myself and avoid most areas where monsters hide," she wrote instead to this author.

"The monsters who scare me most wear the diguise of ordinary people, so having to deal with 'good honest people' during the daylight hours frightens me a lot. At night, for some reason, people seem to be more of their real selves, so it's easier for me to assess them correctly.

"I know Tom Luther better than he knows himself. I knew when he was lying. I learned to tell when he had the urge to prowl. I'm still torn between wishing Tom could hold me and protect me from my monsters and hating him for the pain he has caused other people."

There is one dream Debrah still looks forward to in her weaker moments, when the wind is howling outside and she is cold and lonely. Tom, old, mellow, is let out of prison. She stands at the prison gate, waiting for him. The hair on both of their heads has turned white.

"I missed you," he says. And they leave for a little place in the country with no people around, only animals.

She'd take that as the sign from God that she has waited for all her life. That the little girl who ran away from home, hoping someone would notice she was gone, at last had someone to go home with.

"As good of a world as we are supposed to be living in," she concluded her letter, "it's a hard world for Tom Luther and me.

"I don't understand God's purpose for either of us."

ACKNOWLEDGMENTS

The author would like to thank Detective Scott Richardson, a true dragon-slayer, and the Lakewood Police Department, Dennis Hall and the Jefferson County District Attorney's office, Sheriff Joe Morales and Detective Richard Eaton of Summit County, Heather Smith, Deborah Snider, and of course, Rhonda Edwards and Earl Elder, who survived what no parent should have to with dignity and courage. I would also like to thank the editors who've helped me along the way—Bill Florence, Jon Franklin, Patty Calhoun—and my agent Mike Hamilburg and his *consigliore*, Joanie Socola, for taking a chance, and Paul Dinas and Karen Haas at Kensington for the opportunity. And, as always, I want to thank my wife, Carla, for her love, faith, and support.

REAL HORROR STORIES!
PINNACLE TRUE CRIME

SAVAGE VENGEANCE   (0-7860-0251-4, $5.99)
By Gary C. King and Don Lasseter
On a sunny day in December, 1974, Charles Campbell attacked
Renae Ahlers Wicklund, brutally raping her in her own home in
front of her 16-month-old daughter. After Campbell was released
from prison after only 8 years, he sought revenge. When Campbell
was through, he left behind the most gruesome crime scene local
investigators had ever encountered.

NO REMORSE   (0-7860-0231-X, $5.99)
By Bob Stewart
Kenneth Allen McDuff was a career criminal by the time he was
a teenager. Then, in Fort Worth, Texas in 1966, he upped the ante.
Arrested for three brutal murders, McDuff was sentenced to death.
In 1972, his sentence was commuted to life imprisonment. He
was paroled after only 23 years behind bars. In 1991 McDuff
struck again, carving a bloody rampage of torture and murder
across Texas.

BROKEN SILENCE   (0-7860-0343-X, $5.99)
The Truth About Lee Harvey Oswald, LBJ,
and the Assassination of JFK
By Ray "Tex" Brown with Don Lasseter
In 1963, two men approached Texas bounty hunter Ray "Tex"
Brown. They needed someone to teach them how to shoot at a
moving target—and they needed it fast. One of the men was Jack
Ruby. The other was Lee Harvey Oswald. . . . Weeks later, after
the assassination of JFK, Ray Brown was offered $5,000 to leave
Ft. Worth and keep silent the rest of his life. The deal was ar-
ranged by none other than America's new president: Lyndon
Baines Johnson.

*Available wherever paperbacks are sold, or order direct from the
Publisher. Send cover price plus 50¢ per copy for mailing and
handling to Kensington Publishing Corp., Consumer Orders,
or call (toll free) 888-345-BOOK, to place your order using
Mastercard or Visa. Residents of New York and Tennessee
must include sales tax. DO NOT SEND CASH.*